ENGLAND'S GREATEST SPY
Éamon de Valera

ENGLAND'S GREATEST SPY
Éamon de Valera

A Biography by
John J. Turi

England's Greatest Spy
Éamon de Valera

Published by
Stacey International
128 Kensington Church Street
London W8 4BH
Tel: +44 (0)20 7221 7166 Fax: +44 (0)20 7792 9288
E-mail: info@stacey-international.co.uk
www.stacey-international.co.uk

© John Turi 2009

Photographs © Getty Images

ISBN: 978-1-906768-09-6

British Library Catalogue in Publication Data:
A catalogue record for this book is available from
the British Library.

Printed and bound in the UK by CPI William Clowes Beccles NR34 7TL

Contents

There is a photographic plate section located between pages 234 and 235

Dedicated to the memory of

MICHAEL COLLINS
ARTHUR GRIFFITH
AND
JOHN DEVOY

the three greatest Irishmen who ever lived.
They loved Ireland more than life itself.

Foreword

Throughout its long history, Ireland has suffered at the hands of England, aided and abetted by a succession of spies, traitors and informers in its suppression of the Irish people. Many of these agents have been identified and are objects of scorn and hatred in the Emerald Isle.

In this work, *England's Greatest Spy – Eamon de Valera*, John J. Turi presents startling new evidence to prove that the man who led Ireland throughout most of the 20th century, and whose dominance was such that he was identified with Ireland long after his death, was not a sainted national leader of high purpose and moral principle. Instead, he was an agent for England subverting Irish aspirations while working diligently to promote English interests in Ireland and America. Rather than lionize deValera, as a succession of Irish writers have done for more than half a century, Turi puts him in the dock and exposes the ways and means by which every major decision of the Irish President worked to the benefit of England with disastrous results for Ireland.

In doing so, Turi turns Irish history on its head. He calls for a re-examination of almost the entire pantheon of 20th century Irish heroes and villains, saints and sinners. His work questions almost every article of faith in the Irish historical canon and answers questions that heretofore have gone unanswered. He challenges beliefs that have gone unchallenged. He poses daunting issues for traditionalist and revisionist alike.

England's Greatest Spy – Eamon de Valera is fascinating reading not only for Irish scholars but also for history and mystery buffs everywhere.

Professor Donald J. McNamara,
Kutztown University, PA

Preface

Winston Churchill, in William Manchester's book, *The Last Lion*, heaped glowing praise on Michael Collins. Manchester wrote of these two friendly adversaries: "Collins and Churchill were alike in many ways: fearless, charismatic, fiercely patriotic, ready to sacrifice everything for principle. Both had cherubic features but bulldog expressions...Winston would take his recent enemy home and sit up late, talking, arguing, drinking, and even singing."[1] When Collins complained about the British putting a price of £5,000 ($25,000) on his head, Churchill said he should have been proud of such a high sum since the Boers had only offered £25 ($125) for his. The Lloyd George Government had initially placed the £5,000 reward with no takers – the ante was upped to £10,000, a fortune in those days, with similar results. No one was going to betray Collins.

"When Churchill slyly produced a thumbnail appraisal of himself which Collins had written: 'Will sacrifice all for political gain. Inclined to be bombastic. Full of ex-officer jingo or similar outlook. Don't actually trust him.' There was a moment of silence; then both men burst into laughter."[2]

Collins, whom I had never heard of before, piqued my interest and after quizzing a few Irish friends, I found, to my surprise, that they, too, pleaded ignorance of this great Irishman. After reading Rex Taylor's *Michael Collins*, I was hooked on his marvelous exploits, gentleness of heart, intelligence and love of Ireland that contrasted so sharply with his uncompromising and sometimes brutal warfare against English occupation of his beloved country.

I originally intended this book to be a Michael Collins biography, but as I devoured one Collins book after another, time and again, as Ireland appeared on the cusp of greatness and success, Éamon de Valera cast his long black shadow on events and Ireland's hopes and aspirations were shattered. Various Irish authors, many contemporaries of de Valera and his times, acknowledged his catastrophic blunders, but were unable to face the reality – that the leader of Ireland was yet another British agent in a long line of Irish traitors. They attributed his unremitting blunders to a dysfunctional childhood and to his later power struggles with John Devoy and Judge Daniel Cohalan in America and Michael Collins and Arthur Griffith in Ireland.

In their eagerness to lionize de Valera, many authors were not forthright or honest in their portrayals of the Irish President. The most noteworthy mythmakers included Longford and O'Neill's distortions in *Éamon de Valera*; Desmond Ryan's initial canonizing of Éamon de Valera in the *Unique Dictator*; John Whelan's exaltation of the man in his *De Valera*; Dorothy Macardle's paean to her idol in *The Irish Republic*; Patrick McCartan's obsequious fabrications in *With de Valera in America*, and T. Ryle Dwyer's mythical *De Valera, The Man & the Myths*.

In contrast, Pieras Beaslai's *Michael Collins and the Making of a New Ireland*, and Patrick S. O'Hegarty's *The Victory of Sinn Féin* presented a more candid depiction of Éamon de Valera and Michael Collins.

Lord Longford and Thomas P. O'Neill's official biography, *Éamon de Valera*, a propagandist puff piece, reportedly an autobiographical account by the Irish President, is riddled with half-truths and outright lies. Tim Pat Coogan, in his meticulously researched *Éamon de Valera, the Man Who Was Ireland*, also questioned the veracity of Longford and O'Neill. Coogan, however, attempted to be all things to all people by trying to appease those who venerated de Valera as well as those who hated him, and his book suffered as a result. He often approached the precipice of de Valera's treason, acknowledged a conspiracy, but he, too, failed to recognize the conspirator and the traitor.

The more I read of Michael Collins, the more suspicious I became that there was more to de Valera's unbroken string of disastrous actions than merely the result of a dysfunctional childhood or inferiority complex as his literary apologists contended. From the pens of Irish writers themselves, as well as extensive research, I set forth the evidence of de Valera's foul deeds. There came to be no doubt in my mind that de Valera was a British agent. From the moment of his surrender after his participation in the 1916 Easter Rising in Dublin, and the failure of the English to execute the Commandant credited with inflicting half of all British casualties during that calamitous week, every single major decision of his more than fifty-year political career benefited England to the detriment of Ireland.

His trail of treason became obvious, the evidence overwhelming. Again and again de Valera rejected advancement of the Irish cause resulting in colossal English triumphs.

Forsaken by father, mother, uncle, aunt and every other parental figure, including the Catholic Church when his application for the priesthood was rejected due to the illegitimacy of his birth, de Valera grew up lonely and bitter, hating the Irish and Ireland. What emerged from his joyless youth spent enduring pitiless gossip as to the circumstances of his birth, was a man less than human. His dysfunctional childhood matured into a dysfunctional adult liar with an overpowering desire to be the man in charge, the man who gave the orders. From the day he was born till the day he died, de Valera's life was a mountain of lies, half-truths, innuendoes, abandonment, rejection, deceit, betrayal, treachery and even murder.

This sordid side of de Valera's character, so long clouded by obsequious writers and revisionist henchmen cannot but shock those ignorant of the facts surrounding the Great Pretender. The legacy of de Valera and his counterfeit Republican heirs is the enormous historical loss to the Irish people and especially to the Irish youth of today. The three greatest Irishmen who ever lived have been relegated to the depths of anonymity and virtual elimination from Gaelic history books by de Valera and his posturing heirs in Fianna Fáil, the Irish President's surviving political party. Over the course of my research in Dublin, I was dismayed by the lack of historical perspective as to the heroic roles played by Michael Collins, Arthur Griffith and John Devoy.

I developed a deep admiration for Michael Collins and Arthur Griffith as amazing patriots who not only spent a lifetime successfully ousting the British after more than seven centuries of utmost horror but literally sacrificed their lives for their indomitable belief in a free Ireland. John Devoy also committed a lifetime of labor working on behalf of Ireland and the Irish people. To these men and their memory, I dedicate my feeble effort in the hope it may shed light on their enormous contribution to Irish freedom and de Valera's treachery.

Official records concerning England's master spy lay buried deep in the vaults of British archives, and may never see the light of day. The facts relating to nearly every aspect of de Valera's life remain almost equally obscure. Accounts by contemporaries and by his biographers, official and unofficial, Irish or not, contain a multitude of contradictions.

The final verdict is up to you, the reader, and jury, to weigh the evidence I present in the following pages and render a decision to my charge of treason against Mr. de Valera.

Of course, you must be a citizen of a country in order to be charged with treason and Mr. de Valera, as his wife, Sinead contended, was an American citizen who never officially became an Irish citizen.

J.J.T.

Notes
1   Manchester, William, *The Last Lion*, *Winston Spenser Churchill*, Little, Brown
    & Co, Boston, Toronto, 1983, p. 723
2   *ibid*

INTRODUCTION
An Historical Perspective

"... Going back as far as the rebellion of 1798 and earlier, the Government always had 'friends' in the rebel camp ..."[1]

Augustine Birrell, Chief Secretary in Ireland

For centuries, in darkened smoke-filled hovels and alehouses, later in dingy hotel rooms or lonely out of the way thatched cottages, grim men schemed and plotted. In their hidden enclaves immersed in their intrigues, alternately whispering and shouting, reasonable and irrational, heroes and cowards, attempting the impossible, they accomplished nothing but imprisonment and death.

All too often it happened: suddenly a door would be hammered open and in would rush a swarm of screaming demons, sometimes in uniform, sometimes not, bludgeoning or shooting indiscriminately. Those conspirators, who were not killed, were beaten senseless. Another informer, another traitor had dealt another death-blow to another failed Irish insurrection. Every protest, every undertaking to rise up against their English oppressors inevitably produced the same result – disaster.

Irish rebel conspirators spent years languishing in dank prisons, forbidden to speak, forbidden to be spoken to, inexorably driven mad. The English oppressors transported approximately 75,000 Irish "convicts" to the prototype Devil's Island, Van Dieman's Land (later Tasmania) and another 112,500 dispatched to the Australian penal colonies. The last penal settlement closed in 1877. Forgotten, forlorn and forsaken, most were fated never to see home again; they lived lives of persecution, hard labor and hopelessness. They died lonely deaths, buried in unmarked graves – unmourned and unremembered. The pitiful few who eventually made their way back to Ireland decades later were broken in mind and body.

Ireland's history has been one not only of internal strife but also of spoliation, confiscation and utmost cruelty, from the invasions of the Norsemen in the eighth century through the English occupation in 1166 until 1922 when Michael Collins forced the British to abandon Ireland.

The English, however, retained six of the nine counties of Ulster in Northern Ireland as a Unionist enclave.

Intermittently, for more than seven centuries, the English mercilessly and systematically attempted to eradicate the native Irish. The *modus operandi* was always the same, as the Irish chafed at their bonds; the English turned the screws of repression to precipitate another rebellion. The Irish defiantly rose up to meet the challenge and were slaughtered by the thousands. The struggle for freedom was ineffectual for the country was made up of dozens of miniature Kingdoms, each Irish "King" jealous of his neighbors and continually involved in raiding for land, cattle and women, many fighting alongside the English against their neighbors.

In the twelfth century, Pope Adrian IV, Nicholas Breakspear, the only English Pope, made Henry II an offer he couldn't refuse: sovereignty over Ireland in return for paying the Vatican one penny per Irish household and the privilege of converting the savage Irish to the Roman version of Catholicism.

In 1166 Diarmuid MacMurrough, King of Leinster, was overthrown and fled to England, where he enlisted the aid of the English barons. He promised Richard de Clare, Earl of Pembroke, known as "Strongbow," the hand of his daughter and succession to his throne. With the consent of Henry II, Pembroke and a host of Norman warrior barons including the de Prendergasts, Fitzgeralds, de Barris and others, landed in Ireland under the aegis of Pope Adrian and were welcomed by every Bishop and initially by every petty Irish monarch except Broderick, "The Bashful." But even he eventually got over his shyness and threw in his lot with the English power brokers.

As time went by, native opposition to the Anglo-Norman oppression fuelled in England a hatred of the Irish and especially of those Anglo-Normans (and there were many) who adopted the ways and habits of the native Irish. The Anglo-Normans had little trouble conquering the feuding Irish but the natives steadfastly retained their customs: only Ulster was able to continue for the most part in the hands of the Irish under the formidable opposition of the O'Neills and O'Donnells.

In 1315, the Irish sought to overthrow the occupation by offering the crown of Ireland to Edward Bruce, King of Scotland. Bruce accepted but was defeated in 1318, resulting in another wave of land confiscations of the native Irish. The Anglo-Normans, harassed by the natives, set up the "Pale," a fortified ditch that defended parts of Dublin, Meath, Kildare and Louth counties against the marauding Irish.

In the 1530s after breaking from the Catholic Church, Henry VIII assumed the position as supreme head of the Church in England, dissolved the monasteries and confiscated their land and monies. He took the title of King of Ireland and ordered all those under the control of England to accept his religious reforms, a policy pressed further by his son, Edward VI (1547-53) despite fierce opposition from the native Irish. Queen Mary (1553-58) restored the Catholic Church in both England and Ireland, but introduced the policy of "Plantation" – confiscation of the land of those Irish chieftains who opposed the English, then "planting" those lands with English settlers loyal to the Crown.

Elizabeth continued the Reformation, and enforced a strict policy in religious and civil affairs. The persecution of Catholic bishops and priests was vigorously pursued. When the dispossessed Chiefs and their followers – sometimes native Irish, sometimes the old Anglo-Norman families such as the Geraldines and Fitzgeralds – resisted, the English committed terrible atrocities to maintain obedience to the Crown. A typical example was the 1577 Massacre of Mullaghmast, in which the English, under the mask of a peace conference, invited many of the chiefs to a conference. They were then murdered as they sat down to discuss "peace" proposals.

In 1580 a small contingent of Spanish soldiers landed at Smerwick on the Dingle Peninsula. Regarded as representatives of the Pope – at a time when Catholics were generally seen as a threat – they were defeated at Cashel by the Queen's envoy, Lord Grey, who then laid waste to the country, slaying and starving the native Irish by the thousands.

The Plantation of the country resulted in the distribution to English settlers of nearly 600,000 acres of Irish land. In 1594 Hugh O'Neill rebelled, and for nine years contested this seizure. English forces under Lord Mountjoy, Lord Deputy of Ireland under Queen Elizabeth I and later as Lord Lieutenant under King James I, ranged throughout the country laying waste to the land, murdering the inhabitants, burning their homes and slaughtering their cattle.

In 1601 Spain again sent a contingent of soldiers to aid the hard-pressed Irish. They landed at Kinsale and the subsequent battle ended in the overwhelming defeat of the Spanish and Irish by Mountjoy. O'Neill yielded two years later, the last major rebel to surrender.

Under James I (1566-1625), the only child of Mary, Queen of Scots and her second husband, Henry Stuart, more than half a million acres in the counties of Tyrone, Armagh, Derry, Donegal, Fermanagh and Cavan were declared forfeit and the Plantation extended on a grand scale, with many Protestant English and Presbyterian Scottish settlers pouring into Ireland.

An "insurrection" in 1641 gave the English a pretext to impose even harsher reprisals and laws. As justification for another massacre of the native Irish Catholics, the British claimed 500,000 Protestants had been murdered in a frenzy of revenge by the Irish; several thousand might have been nearer the truth, for there were not half a million Protestants in all of Ireland at the time.

Charles I, always urgently in need of money, promised a relaxation of the oppressive laws against Irish Catholics in return for a lump sum. Charles got his money, but Wentworth, his Deputy in Ireland, refused to carry out the terms of the bargain, and instead increased the terror.

In 1649 there came to Irish shores that plague of all plagues, Oliver Cromwell, flushed with success against Charles I and determined to settle the Irish question once and for all. He massacred his way through Ireland and Plantation was extended on an even larger scale. Catholic landowners were subject to confiscation of their lands unless they could prove their active participation on the side of Cromwell's Parliamentarians. More than eleven million acres, half of all Ireland, were seized and the inhabitants offered the choice of "Hell or Connaught," death or exile to the barren lands of West Ireland. The confiscated lands were divided among "investors" who advanced money to finance Cromwell and the soldiers who fought with him. Before Cromwell, the native Irish and "Old English" Catholics held approximately half the land; after him they were in possession of less than one eighth of the country while making up more than eighty per cent of the population.

In 1685 the Catholic James II became King and attempted to end the conflict, placing his Catholic and Protestant subjects in Ireland on an equal footing, but his policy was so clumsily implemented that the Protestants, fearing for their safety, rebelled. In 1688 James II fled to France and William of Orange, his nephew and husband of James' elder daughter Mary, was invited by the English Parliament to assume the Crown. The Irish were defeated at the Battle of the Boyne in July 1690, and William eventually controlled all of Ireland except Limerick. On October 13, 1691 this last Jacobite outpost surrendered and the Articles of Limerick were signed. Peace should once again have returned to Ireland, for the Articles granted Catholics the right to practice their religion freely, and returned all civil rights to them. The Irish Protestants in Parliament, however, ignored the Limerick Compact and instituted a new campaign of terror. Opinion in England supported the repression, resulting in the introduction of the Penal Laws of 1697-1727. Catholics were deprived of the right to vote. Native Irish men could not marry Protestant women, and while Catholic women could marry Protestants, any children had to be raised as Protestants. Irish children were denied education and refused university admittance. Catholics could not hold public office and were excluded from the professions. They were prevented from purchasing land, nor could they own a horse worth more than five pounds. All priests had to be registered, and bishops were exiled or executed.

The Church of England was declared the State religion. With few parishioners, its clergy held vast estates supported by Irish Catholics who were required to pay tithes to the Anglican Church amounting to ten per cent of their income.

And so it went on. Between rebellion and repression were sullen intervals that could not be called peace because there was no peace, only a pause in land confiscations, crushing taxation, evictions, and tithes paid to a foreign church. Edmund Burke, British statesman and political writer in the late eighteenth century, noted the depravity of his fellow countrymen inflicted upon the Irish: "They [Penal Laws] were a machine of wise and elaborate contrivance as well fitted for the oppression, impoverishment and degradation of a people and the debasement in them of human nature itself as ever proceeded from the perverted ingenuity of man."[2]

Not only were the Penal Laws pressed home against Catholics: English merchants encouraged the Parliament at Westminster to enact restrictions on Irish trade that had a crippling economic effect on their fellow Protestants who were now the owners of the ruined industries in Ireland confiscated from the native Irish.

The political situation in Ireland was marked by corruption and discrimination. Rotten Boroughs – parliamentary constituencies that retained the right to elect members despite having a very reduced population – were common in Ireland. A single representative might own more than twenty seats. These seats – each one a vote in the Irish Parliament – were sold to the highest bidder.

The American Revolution drew English troops across the Atlantic, and the Protestant Irish were able to bring pressure against the Government and, in 1780 the trade restrictions were repealed. In 1782 the subordination of the Irish Parliament to the Privy Council in Westminster was declared at an end: Ireland now had legislative independence, and was united to England only by allegiance to the Crown.

In 1791 the Protestant Theobold Wolfe Tone founded the United Irishmen, an organization comprising both Protestants and Catholics, and an appeal in 1796 to France for aid in a planned insurrection to establish an Irish Republic resulted in the failed Rising of 1798. The English authorities in Ireland – the Viceroy, Lord Cornwallis, fresh from his defeat in America, and the Chief Secretary, Lord Castlereagh –

offered pensions, peerages and positions to the Protestant Irish legislators in return for votes for a permanent Union with England. On January 1, 1801 the Irish Parliament legislated itself out of existence. Promises made to Catholics were ignored and the persecutions continued unabated.

Catholics continued to appeal for justice, and in 1823 Daniel O'Connell founded the Catholic Association, a pacifist organization seeking Catholic Emancipation, and repeal of the Act of Union of 1801. Eventually, in 1829, the repressive political laws against Catholics were repealed. O'Connell, however, fell foul of the law and was imprisoned in 1843. He was released in 1844 but his movement was shattered and he died three years later.

In the mid nineteenth century it seemed that Nature itself was determined to take a turn in punishing the Irish when a fungus destroyed the potato crop, the staple food of the Irish farm laborers. There never was a Famine nor an actual shortage of food in Ireland at the time as meat and grain were shipped to England by the shipload rather than being diverted to feed the starving Irish rural poor. W. G. Fitzgerald wrote: "Troops convoyed out of the city the grain that would have saved millions of our people during the Great Famine."[3] More than a million starved to death, and the population plummeted from more than eight million to four million in less than half a century as survivors fled the blighted land.

Frustrated by discriminatory laws, rack-rents, tenant evictions, a starvation policy and emigration, men turned to force as the only means to oust the British. James Stephens, a disciple of Wolfe Tone, the leader of the 1798 insurrection, devoted his life to realizing Tone's republican principles. He organized the Irish Republican Brotherhood in Ireland modeled after the Fenian Brotherhood (later Clan na Gael) in America. Yet every attempt to drive out the English was betrayed by spies, traitors or informers. Imprisonment, hangings and prison hulk ships were commonplace in nineteenth-century Ireland.

Charles Stewart Parnell, a Protestant landowner who entered the House of Commons in 1875, provided the most serious challenge to the English over the *status quo* in Ireland. Parnell lent his considerable influence to land reform organizations such as the Land League established by Michael Davitt in 1878 and supported by John Devoy, leader of the Clan na Gael in America. The land Acts of the late nineteenth and early twentieth centuries initiated the return of the land to the tillers of the soil. Parnell was ousted following a nasty divorce scandal that aroused the opposition of Catholic Bishops in Ireland, and he died in 1891 at the age of 45.

The Liberal Prime Minister William Gladstone introduced the first Home Rule bill for Ireland (a semblance of self-government Act) but it was defeated by Conservatives in June 1886.

Abject poverty was a feature of life in Ireland in general and the cities in particular even into the twentieth century. In the filth and wretchedness of the Dublin slums, "home" for tens of thousands of families was no more than one room overlooking an open sewer of an alleyway. The sewage-laden river Liffey pulsed through the heart of Dublin. The classic grandeur of public buildings such as the Four Courts judicial complex and the Customs House were faded but not dimmed by the decay of more than a century of economic oppression and political neglect. Stately Georgian mansions, now decrepit, hinted of another more prosperous era. They were Ireland's "Potemkin Village", but hardly masked the worst putrescent slums not only of Europe but of the world.

One commentator wrote, "One third of the people of Dublin are underfed, half the children attending Irish primary schools are ill-nourished...There is no use in visiting schools in Ireland after one or two in the afternoon as the children are too weak and drowsy with hunger to be capable of answering intelligently..."[4]

With the Liberals back in power at Westminster, a semblance of Irish self-government was encompassed in the Home Rule Bill of 1912. Protestants' threats of revolution, and instances of sectarian violence, aided and abetted by the Conservative Party in England, raged throughout Ulster. Edward Carson, leader of the Ulster Protestants, faced down Prime Minister Henry Asquith's government. The Orangemen of Northern Ireland prepared a clandestine petition to Kaiser Wilhelm of Germany, in which they considered redirecting their allegiance should Home Rule – which they called "Rome Rule" – become the law of the land.

According to author Tim Pat Coogan: "There is evidence that the threat of Civil War posed by the Unionists, the Kaiser's Ulster friends and their Conservative allies, made such an impact that experienced foreign observers in Berlin and Vienna certainly believed that the Central Powers calculated upon England's being unable to take any active part if war should come. Carson had been received by the Kaiser in Hamburg in 1913 and Von Kuhlman, the respected Counselor of the German Embassy in London, was reported by John Dillon, the Irish Parliamentary Party leader, to have been visiting leading Unionists in Belfast as close to the outbreak of war as July 12, 1914. According to Dillon, the embassy's report made the Emperor 'determined to go on with the war.'"[5]

James W. Gerard, American Ambassador to Germany, noted: "... German spies reported as a real and serious revolutionary movement [by

Ulster Unionism], and, of course it was believed by the Germans that Ireland would rise in rebellion the moment that war was declared."[6] As late as July 29, 1914, in a dispatch from Baron Heyens, Belgian Minister at Berlin, he noted that the Germans believed, "England...is paralyzed by internal dissensions and her Irish quarrels."[7]

An editorial in *The Irish Churchman*, of November 14, 1913 stated: "Should our King sign the Home Rule Bill, the Protestants of Ireland will welcome this continental deliverer [Kaiser Wilhelm] as their forefathers, under similar circumstances [William of Orange] did once before."[8] John Horgan noted: "It is not often that political chickens come home to roost as quickly as those which were hatched in Northeast Ulster during the years 1912-14. Rebellion was openly preached, men were drilled, arms were landed, the assistance of the Kaiser was invoked, the forces of the Crown were defied and their commanders seduced from their allegiance...No wonder that German statesmen, ignorant of the cant, insincerity and humbug of English politics, believed that England was so divided and rent with domestic discord that the time had come to make a bold bid for the dominion of the world."[9]

Max Caulfield wrote: "In Berlin [April 1914] Kaiser Wilhelm II and his advisers watched the unfolding drama with keenest interest. Deep in the mire of irresolvable Irish politics, irregular armies stumping about all over the place threatening civil war or revolution, the regular armed forces mutinous and disobedient, the two great political parties ready to fling themselves at each others' throats; what had they [the Germans] to fear from England? In August, therefore, the Kaiser struck – a month after a conference of all parties, called by King George at Buckingham Palace had broken down in immutable intransigence."[10]

According to F. X. Martin: "Paradoxically, the Orangemen were also relying on the German threat to England as an argument to strengthen their case. James Craig and Belfast Mayor Frederick Hugh Crawford had made clear that Orangemen were prepared to swear allegiance to the German Emperor rather than submit to a parliament in Dublin."[11]

And so the Kaiser went to war convinced that the British were too preoccupied with threats of revolt in Ireland and at home over the contentious matter of Home Rule to intervene militarily in Europe. The Germans were stunned when England entered the War on the side of France.

As the First World War – The Great War – exploded on the Continent, Home Rule was finally adopted on September 18, 1914, but with a suspensory clause postponing its implementation until the conclusion of the conflict. Once again native Irish hopes for a semblance of self-government were dashed on the shoals of political expediency.

If the Orangemen's call to revolution had not turned Ireland into an armed camp threatening civil war in Northern Ireland and England itself, the Kaiser's hand may have been stayed. The killing fields of Flanders and France were the final resting-place of one million English youths, an entire generation.

As the War raged on, the very survival of Britain hung in the balance. Anxious to guard against any invasion through their backdoor of Ireland, the English sought to crush any threat from disaffected Nationalists and Catholics. But they hesitated to move against the National Irish Volunteers, inaugurated in 1913 in defence of Home Rule, well aware that any action against them would result in an Irish-American political backlash. With the outcome of the War still in doubt, the British were counting on America entering the War on the side of the Allies. The Irish-American voting bloc had become a major player in US politics and John Devoy and Judge Daniel Cohalan, leaders of a united and politically powerful Irish-American organization, were only too ready to campaign vociferously against British interests and, if they could, prevent the United States from entering the War on the side of England.

American public opinion was crucial to England's survival. Only if the British were perceived to be moving against a traitorous fifth-column revolt when the country was engaged in a war in which its very survival was at stake, would Americans rally to England's cause. Americans were duly disgusted by the Easter Rising of 1916; and there is overwhelming evidence that the British Government knew of and abetted the Rising.

The English had for long operated the greatest espionage system in history. They had not come to rule half the world from an insignificant island by military power alone. The system was implemented by bribery, intimidation, and murder or transportation to penal colonies in Australia and the West Indies.

The English "mole" or "sleeper", planted – often for decades – in rival political circles, was part of this tradition of espionage, and a host of spies, traitors and informers, known and unknown, are responsible for the suffering of countless Irish men, women and children through the centuries.

The narrative that follows concerns one of a long line of infamous and mostly anonymous Irishmen who betrayed country and conscience, many for gold, others for power – and a few, like the man considered here, to save his own skin, in the outcome achieving both power and position for decades.

Notes

1. Martin F.X., *Leaders & Men of the Easter Rising Dublin 1916*, Cornell U. Press, Ithaca, NY, 1967, p. 11
2. Fitzgerald, W.G.(ed.), *The Voice of Ireland, A survey of the Race & Nation from all Angles*, Virtue Ltd., Dublin/London, p. 28
3. *ibid*, p. 43
4. Coffey, Thomas M. *Agony at Easter*, Macmillan NY, 1969, p. 57
5. Coogan, Tim P, *De Valera: The man who was Ireland*, Harper, 1996, p. 61
6. Horgan, John J. *The Complete Grammar of Anarchy*, Maunsel, London, 1918, p. 38
7. *ibid*, p. 39
8. *ibid*, p. 27
9. *ibid*, p. v
10. Caulfield, Max: *The Easter Rebellion*, Frederick Muller, London, 1963, p. 33
11. Martin, F.X. & Byrne, F. J. (eds): *The Scholar Revolutionary, Eoin MacNeill 1867–1945 & the Making of a New Ireland*, Irish U. Press 1973, p. 114

CHAPTER I
The Metamorphosis of Éamon de Valera

É amon de Valera had seen visions of freedom and dreamed dreams of glory; now he plummeted to the depths of disillusionment, completely disenchanted with the idea of an Irish Republic. After his surrender during the 1916 Easter Rising, dismay, shock and bitterness burned deep as he marched to his doom with the people's taunts, curses and virulent condemnation of the rebels' sacrifice for Irish freedom resounding through his tortured brain.

De Valera was marched aboard the last shipload of insurgents captured during the April 1916 Easter Rising. Crammed amid the filth of foul-smelling pens of a cattle boat as it heaved and rolled through a choppy Irish Sea, they hunkered down to a bleak future in dank and dreaded English prisons. Consternation and sadness were their sailing companions at the inexplicable rejection by the people of their attempt to free Ireland from centuries of British domination.

Prime Minister Henry Asquith's Government had fallen in December 1916 and his successor, Lloyd George, promptly announced his intention to release most of the untried Irish prisoners by Christmas, a necessary gesture towards neutralizing the powerful anti-Administration Irish-American influence. It was a time when England's very survival was in doubt unless the Americans could be persuaded to enter the war. In a further effort to pull the teeth of the Irish-American opposition to President Woodrow Wilson's pro-British administration, Lloyd George announced a Convention to "settle the Irish question" once and for all. The Irish Nationalist party, Sinn Féin (Ourselves alone), refused to attend, rightly claiming that it was bound to be rigged.

The British were well aware of the political clout of the Irish-Americans, whom John Devoy and Judge Daniel Cohalan had organized into a cohesive and effective group. "The prisoner releases were a public relations gesture aimed at stemming the growing power of Irish-American criticism of Britain's Irish policies...Lloyd George...was only too keenly aware of the necessity for American men and munitions if Germany was to be defeated."[1]

On April 6, 1917, America declared war on Germany and American men and materiel were on their way to relieve Britain and her beleaguered allies. In June 1917, at the behest of President Wilson, Lloyd George undermined the powerful Irish-American political juggernaut by releasing the last of the Irish rebels imprisoned for their part in the Easter Rebellion.

In an amazing transformation, upon the prisoners return to Ireland, thousands of Dubliners, crowded together at waterfront piers and lined the streets. There were cheers for a tall, thin, pale and a bit hesitatant Éamon de Valera as he led the last of the recently released rebels down the gangplank of the Liverpool to Dublin ferry. Éamon de Valera, the inept Commandant of Boland's Bakery, had metamorphosed into the "Hero of the 1916 Rising." A wildly exultant throng now recognized the "last" commandant to surrender as the accepted leader of Sinn Féin, the nationalistic organization that had emerged from the embers of the charred Dublin buildings of O'Connell Street.

What had changed? Intermittent and inconsistent extreme penalties meted out to fourteen rebels over a period of more than a week after the 1916 rebellion had been crushed, transformed the perception of the rebels from a gang of crackpot Sinn Feiners into folk heroes – brave young men willing to sacrifice their lives to free Ireland from centuries of cruel repression. Another contributing factor to this change of loyalties was the indiscriminate arrest and imprisonment of thousands of innocent, mostly pro-English, Irishmen resulting in their conversion into rabid pro-Sinn Féin supporters.

But, who was Éamon de Valera?

The greatest mystery arising out of the Easter Rebellion was not the execution of fourteen men but the failure to execute one man, Éamon de Valera. Men, some mere boys, who had inflicted nary a pinprick on the British military were executed but not de Valera. He was the only Commandant, and as Brigade Adjutant, the second highest ranking military officer, who was credited, albeit wrongly, with having inflicted half of all the British casualties during that week of bedlam. Yet, he was never even brought to trial. Initially, his "miraculous" escape from General John Maxwell's firing squad raised more than a few eyebrows. Thanks to the complicity of prison authorities, his subsequent incitement to riots, destruction, disobedience, and intimidation of prison wardens during his thirteen month incarceration became the stuff of legend and suspicions were muted.

The legend of de Valera's "heroism" during the Easter rebellion was fabricated out of a trumped-up court-martial, non-existent death sentence, alleged last-minute reprieve and subsequent exploits in English prisons. The British were aided and abetted by Irish writers in perpetuating a monumental hoax.

Bizarrely enough, the only court-martial de Valera ever faced was one held by his fellow prisoners at Richmond Barracks the night before he was taken to Kilmainham Jail. According to Tim Pat Coogan, his own men, in droll capriciousness, found him guilty, sentenced him to death, and dispatched him with staccato hand-claps simulating a firing-squad. The macabre performance sent him into such convulsive tears that he had to be restrained. De Valera was left in a near catatonic stupor. Curiously, this fake court martial and death sentence held more terror for de Valera than the threat of an actual trial and sentence twenty-four hours later.

The next day was decisive for on that May 8 morning, Edward Kent, Michael Mallin, Con Colbert, and Sean Heuston were executed. Their deaths did not have the effect of plunging de Valera into deeper gloom. In an incredible shift of emotions, the depressed and disillusioned psychological wreck of the previous night metamorphosed into the cheerleader of born-again Republicanism. Immediately after his alleged court-martial, de Valera was a completely changed man. From his cell in Kilmainham Gaol, he became positively jovial, writing droll letters to acquaintances informing them in a jocular manner that he was to be shot the following morning, May 9, and that he would not be able to play cards with his buddies again.

He wrote to Sister Gonzaga, head of Carysfort College: "I have just been told that I am to be shot for my part in the rebellion. Just a parting line to thank you and all the sisters (especially Mother Attracta) for your unvarying kindness to me in the past and to ask you to pray for my soul and for my poor wife and little children whom I leave unprovided for behind. Ask the girls to remember me in their prayers. Goodbye, I hope I'll be in heaven to meet you."[2]

In a letter to Frank Hughes, an old friend: "Just a line to say a last goodbye. I am to be shot for my part in the Rebellion. If you can give any advice to Sinead and the little ones I know you'll try. Remember me to your wife, Mother, Aunt Stan etc. Pray for my soul. DeV."[3]

To Mick Ryan, a former rugby teammate: "Just a line to say I played my last match last week and lost. I am to be shot, an old sport who unselfishly played the game. Remember me to Pat, Jack, Nora, Margaret and the Mrs. Tell Colgan we will never have another game of nap together or beat Rice's bog or the Wood. Farewell old friend, you are in my thoughts. DeV."[4]

The simple explanation for his psychological turnaround is, of course, that there had been no British court-martial or sentence of death and, therefore, no last-minute reprieve: de Valera was not about to face a firing-squad. His claim that he was to be shot the following morning was a lie.

Yet while de Valera highlighted the plight of his wife and children in his letter to others, no letter was written to those supposedly most dear to him. It was a manifestation of his dysfunctional family life. Years later, he attempted to explain his failure to write to his wife and children by claiming that it was because his execution had not been finally determined. If that was the case, why portray himself to others as bravely facing death?

De Valera was already adept at manipulating the truth and he lied in anticipation of all the questions that should have been raised as to the circumstances surrounding his miraculous avoidance of the death penalty. It might have been more convincing if the British had staged a court-martial, but even supposing he had been tried, the failure of the British to execute him would have raised just as many questions. Why were General John Maxwell's criteria for execution of any rebel responsible for the death of a British soldier or policeman applicable to everyone but de Valera, the man "responsible for half of all British casualties" during the Rising?

From his cell at Kilmainham, de Valera was moved to various prisons where he threw caution to the wind, defying wardens, violating prison regulations and initiating riots and strikes. According to his own uncorroborated word, his punishment did not exceed mild admonishment or brief periods on short rations. He also stepped up his new image-making campaign using the prison system's limited letter-writing privileges – still not to his own wife and children, but to the wives of influential rebels such as John MacNeill chirping encouragement to the men outside: "Tell the boys we are all well and to keep the old flag up."[5]

De Valera's instigation of prison revolts and his outrageous displays of defiance towards prison wardens – none of which ever resulted in disciplinary action of any substance – were all part of a deliberate ploy designed to thrust him into a position of leadership among the Irish Nationalists. His campaign of self-aggrandizement began immediately after his transfer to Dartmoor Prison.[6] His authorized biographers Longford and O'Neill claim de Valera admitted that what followed was a planned response designed to curry favor with John MacNeill, the Commander-in-Chief of the Irish Volunteers, and to impress the other prisoners, many of whom blamed MacNeill's countermanding order for the failure of the Easter Week Rising.

Having set in motion a campaign: "to acquire control over his comrades through winning their admiration by confrontation with the prison officials. He managed to get to the top of the line and at the moment MacNeill appeared, he sprang from his place and shouted: 'shun' to the twenty others and then 'eyes right.'"[7] After the incident, "[t]he warden ordered him to his cell and followed him there. 'Why did you do that?' he asked. 'To salute my Commander-in-Chief in the proper manner,' de Valera answered. [The warden replied] 'Do you know that any such action is mutiny, the most serious crime a prisoner can commit and that flogging is the punishment?'...De Valera got mild punishment."[8]

Engaging in military behavior was a punishable offense for Irish Volunteers inside a British prison.[9] Yet in response to his act of mutiny, the warden simply "admonished" de Valera. The salute to MacNeill became an act of "heroism" in the retelling, and thus was the myth of de Valera launched by the British with the cooperation of prison authorities. His jailers went to extraordinary lengths to make it appear that he was causing maximum trouble within the prison system, thereby raising his stature to that of a valiant hero defying his captors.

"Amazed at the chivalry of the salute [to MacNeill] the men obeyed. It was the first act of revolt inside jail."[10]

No officially recorded instance of physical punishment meted out to de Valera throughout his years of incarceration has ever been uncovered. Despite the most severe provocations, not a hair on his head was ever harmed. On the contrary, it was de Valera who allegedly intimidated one prison warden after another, and made them cower before him time and again. Minor infractions by other inmates, however, led to beatings or solitary confinement, manacled for days lying in their own excrement and hosed down in cold water. De Valera rampaged through one prison after another for thirteen months, untouched and unpunished.

When he wasn't creating mayhem, de Valera was being given whatever writing materials, books, newspapers and food he requested. He even wrote a letter to *The Manchester Guardian*, complimenting the British newspaper on its impartial reporting. He spent his time playing chess, participating in athletic contests, boning up on his quaternion theories, and perfecting his Gaelic.

Parcere subjectis et debellare superbos – "spare the submissive and wear down the proud," – Virgil's watchword of Roman imperialism is inscribed above the gateway to Dartmoor Prison. De Valera was the darling of Dartmoor. The prison was noted for the strictness of its rules and regulations, yet it was at Dartmoor that de Valera's reputation for facing down wardens and guards led to his leadership of the prisoners.

A June 23, 1916 prison memo to the Prison Commissioner notes a request from de Valera for fountain pen and writing paper, to enable him to "continue certain researches in higher applied mathematics." Remarkably, the petition form notes that de Valera's conduct had received the highest grade – good – and, that...he had received no "Marks for remission forfeited or not earned..."[11]

On July 28, 1916, the warden of Dartmoor sought official instructions regarding de Valera's request: "to receive the following educational books: Machanique Rationelle...Geometry of Three Dimensions, Vols. 1-3."[12] By contrast, MacNeill's request for the English publication, *Ancient Laws of Ireland*, was denied by the warden without reference to higher authorities.

A note dated October 19, 1916 from Home Office to the Warden of Dartmoor Prison refers to: "...the case of Edward de Valera who excused himself for throwing a loaf of bread to another prisoner by saying that the other inmate had applied for more food and had failed to get it..."[13] It is curious that the Home Office in London should take note of such a minor incident, the outcome of which was that de Valera was not disciplined in any manner but his action resulted in a punishment of three days on bread and water of the other prisoner. This was treatment so blatantly partial that de Valera obviously felt it might arouse suspicion: "...He decided to retaliate by going on a hunger strike for so long as McArdle remained on bread and water...He managed to maintain the fast for three or four days until 'at last the Warden gave in' and he was transferred to the prison infirmary."[14]

He emerged from his self-imposed fast none the worse for wear, and the incident had its desired effect: the prisoners were duly impressed, as it was intended they should be. De Valera emerged as an heroic figure defying English authority.

It was extraordinary how prison wardens catered to all his demands. When he complained about the food, the British authorities ensured that he had enough to eat. According to Coogan: "de Valera decided that the supply of calories was insufficient and organized petitions for an increase. These resulted in the prisoners being given kippers three days a week."[15]

"Even in prison, de Valera did what lay within his power to influence the course of events in Ireland, by intervening in the issue of whether or not by-elections should be contested."[16] As a first step in assuming control over the Sinn Féin movement, de Valera ordered that no Sinn Féin candidate should stand for election. Michael Collins ignored de Valera and ran a prisoner named Joseph McGuinness on the slogan: "Put him in, to get him out!" during a by-election contest in County Longford on May 4, 1917.

De Valera refused to back the McGuinness candidacy, claiming a defeat would irreparably harm the Sinn Féin movement. It was the first but by no means the last time he declined to support an initiative that might have been unfavorable to the English.

Despite his misgivings, McGuinness won, and de Valera had no choice but to take another tack. While his ability to control events "inside" was unquestioned, something more was needed before he could demand obedience outside.

After his self-imposed hunger strike in support of McArdle, de Valera "was taken in chains to Maidstone Prison in Kent, where the warden had the reputation of being a great hand at breaking stubborn men..."[17] His biographer, John Whelan, recounted how de Valera, confronted this warden, as he had at Dartmoor. "When taken to the warden's office, de Valera refused either to stand to attention or button his jacket. The warden ordered the guards to take him outside and button him up before continuing the interview, but on re-entering the room, de Valera tore his jacket open again, 'sending the buttons flying'. He got three days 'bread and water' for this but when the warden visited his cell during his rounds, de Valera continued his defiance by refusing to stand up. The guards stood him up forcibly and he told the Warden that he was a 'miserable little coxcomb'. He said, 'I have more contempt for you standing up than I had lying down.'

"The following day, he again refused to stand for the Warden and was once again forcibly stood up; but on this occasion, he used his great physical strength to shake the guards off him. The warden, thinking that he was about to be attacked, immediately got behind his men.

"De Valera seized this opportunity for a telling insult. Knowing the man was of military age and there was talk in the prison about his not joining up, he said to the Warden, 'Aye, you are running behind your guards now as you ran behind other men when it came to joining the Army...' The Warden never entered de Valera's cell again."[18]

It is straining credulity to believe that any prison warden, especially one noted for "breaking stubborn men", and surrounded by his own guards, would put up with such conduct on the part of a prisoner, especially an Irish prisoner. For him to tolerate being humiliated before his own men would have been to destroy all prison discipline, and a loss of respect of the warden.

Yet the warden at Dartmoor had felt it necessary to consult "higher authorities" when it came to dealing with de Valera, so it is possible that, in the interest of myth-making, the "breaker of men at Maidstone" steeled himself to overlook insolence from this particular prisoner.

The incident was recorded by Whelan as it had been told to him by de Valera, and it certainly had the desired effect. A typical Irish response was that of Frank Gallagher, who commented. "For a man with the certainty of 15 years before him, this stand of the Chief's was magnificent."[19] It was in Lewes Prison "...that he became known to his fellow inmates as the 'Chief,'"[20] having been elected leader of the prisoners. He never hesitated to play to the gallery. When a minor incident occurred and a man was put on bread and water, "de Valera ordered a general strike and again the warden came to terms."[21] On May 28, 1917: "within 19 days of McGuinness' by-election victory, de Valera demanded 'prisoner of war' status for all Irish prisoners; if his ultimatum was not met, they would do no prison work. Harry Boland, unconnected to Boland's Bakery, wrote to his mother that initially several windows in each cell were broken, then the plot escalated into a riot and the prison was wrecked. The letter made it clear that the protest had been carefully organized and orchestrated by the prisoners' committee, headed by de Valera..."[22]

Early in June 1917, in an apparent effort to restore a semblance of order, the prison authorities transferred de Valera, the 'ringleader' of the Lewes Prison revolt, back to Maidstone Prison. The way the British shifted de Valera from one prison to another showcased his confrontational antics before the largest audience of prisoners.

De Valera had injured his back during a wrestling match at Lewes Prison so after his transfer to Maidstone, he "had to lie on the flag-stoned floor with his feet raised, resting against the wall. Looking up, he noticed his cell window was made of glass and therefore breakable. Pain or no pain, he got up and broke the glass. It was the last protest he was called upon to make in Maidstone, for, as he had calculated, the Government announced the freeing of all 1916 prisoners shortly afterwards on June 15, 1917."[23]

The chaos de Valera provoked while in prison generated enormous publicity and catapulted him to the leadership of the National movement. Writing in 1936, Desmond Ryan could not find enough words of praise for his hero: "From his release onwards, the de Valera legend grew and survived...He had, apart from the respect and affection of the Irish people that he never lost, apart from the Easter magic and miracle, apart from his leadership in the prisons, apart from his sincerity and ability, other allies to perpetuate this legend..."[24] Ryan was assuredly one such ally and, on the British side, Neville Chamberlain, David Lloyd George and Winston Churchill were three more who for years were complicit in advancing de Valera's political fortunes.

A Sinn Féin convention was called for in October 1917 following the general release of prisoners in June. In the intervening months, many were arrested, charged with "making speeches designed to cause disaffection", or for illegal drilling and military display, such as wearing their Volunteer uniform in public. De Valera was not among those arrested – though he was roaming the length and breadth of Ireland, preaching "cold-blooded incitements to rebellion" in his Volunteer uniform.

In his book, *De Valera, the Man and the Myths*, T. Ryle Dwyer alternately credits de Valera's political genius whenever he tweaked the British lion's tail, and when his actions were beneficial to England and disastrous for Ireland attributed it to naivety. The East Clare election of July 1917 marked de Valera's first foray into the political arena. "Adopting the tactics of a seasoned politician, de Valera remained as vague as possible during the campaign...He relied most heavily on an emotional appeal associating himself with the ideals of the executed leaders of the Easter Rebellion." With MacNeill beside him on the election platform, he declared: "To assert in arms, were there a fair chance of military success, I would consider a sacred duty."[25] This was a clear echo of MacNeill's policy before the Rising, of favoring an insurrection only when it stood a reasonable chance of success.

It was during the East Clare political campaign that de Valera made a statement that was to be thrown back repeatedly at him in the course of his political career: "'We want an Irish republic,' he explained, 'because if Ireland had her freedom, it is, I believe, the most likely form of government.' Nevertheless, he emphasized, he was not a doctrinaire republican. He was not firmly committed to any form of government: 'So long as it was an Irish government, I would not put a word against it.'"[26]

De Valera's controversial election speeches in County Clare resulted in such strong anti-British sentiment that martial law was introduced on February 27, 1918. But British rules had no effect upon de Valera's campaigning. Traveling by public transport, he barnstormed through the county preaching his seditious sermons without the slightest interference. Longford and O'Neill noted: "Despite a British military order de Valera always wore his Volunteer uniform."[27]

Coogan claimed that de Valera's political objective throughout his campaign was to cause the greatest possible degree of disaffection to England and the Crown: "...to make English rule absolutely impossible in Ireland."[28]

The absurdity of Coogan's conclusion was obvious since the British could have removed this Irish thorn in their side at any time, had they wanted to do so. His many violations of various edicts provided them with every excuse for arrest or even assassination. Furthermore, they could have destroyed the myth of his having been court-martialled. This weapon of exposure could have been used against him at any time throughout his decades in office – yet it was not.

Notes

1. Coogan, Tim Pat, *De Valera, The Man who was Ireland*, Harper, 1996, p. 81
2. Longford, Earl of & O'Neill, Thomas P., *Éamon de Valera*, Hutchinson, London, 1970, p. 48
3. Coogan, Tim Pat, *De Valera, The Man who was Ireland*, Harper, 1996, p. 77
4. Farragher, Sean P. CSSP, *Dev and his Alma Mater*, Paraclete Press, Dublin & London, 1984, p. 113
5. HO 144/10309, 50833
6. Coogan, Tim Pat, *De Valera, The Man who was Ireland*, Harper, 1996, p. 80
7. *ibid*, P. 79
8. *ibid*, p. 80
9. *ibid*
10. Whelan, John (Seán O'Faoláin), *De Valera*, Penguin Books, England 1939, p. 42
11. PRO HO (Public Record Office, Home Office) 144/10309, 315, 944/2
12. PRO HO 144/10309, 50833
13. PRO HO 144/10309, 50833/12
14. Coogan, Tim Pat, *De Valera, The Man who was Ireland*, Harper, 1996, p. 81
15. *ibid*, p. 82
16. *ibid*
17. *ibid*, p. 81
18. *ibid*, p. 86
19. *ibid*, p. 87
20. Brasier, A. & Kelly, J., *Harry Boland A Man Divided*, New Century Publications, Dublin 2000, p. 46
21. Whelan, John (Seán O'Faoláin), *De Valera*, Penguin Books, England 1939, p. 43
22. Brasier, A. & Kelly, J., *Harry Boland A Man Divided*, New Century Publications, Dublin 2000, p.46
23. Coogan, Tim Pat, *De Valera, The Man who was Ireland*, Harper, 1996, p. 87
24. Ryan, Desmond, *Unique Dictator*, Arthur. Barker, London, 1936, p. 68
25. Dwyer, T. Ryle, De Valera, *The Man & the Myths*, Poolbeg, Dublin, 1991, p. 20
26. *ibid*, p. 21
27. Longford, Earl of & O'Neill, Thomas P., *Éamon de Valera*, Hutchinson, London, 1970, p. 66
28. Coogan, Tim Pat, *De Valera, The Man who was Ireland*, Harper, 1996, p. 104

CHAPTER II
From Birth to 1916

"Three bad harvests in the past four years had reduced the rack-rented tenant farmers to a state of misery not equaled since Black Forty-seven...Unless the present system of landlordism ends, and ends soon, Ireland is doomed."

M. J. MacManus

In 1859, in the midst of a never-ending flood of Irish calamities, Patrick Coll, a farm laborer, and his wife, Elizabeth, delivered their first child, a girl named Catherine who grew up known as Kate, the eldest child of two brothers, Patrick and Ned (Edward) and a sister Hannah (Hannie). The Colls lived in Knockmore, a hamlet a mile north of the village of Bruree, fifteen miles south of the county capitol Limerick in the Province of Munster.

Kate had little education, and from the age of fifteen worked as a housemaid for neighboring landowners. There was no future for her in Ireland, and one Autumn day in 1879, aged twenty, she left for America disembarking from yet another ship bearing refugees from the famine aftermath and stepped ashore at the New York immigration center at Castle Gardens in Lower Manhattan. She carried a letter of introduction to an aunt who lived in Brooklyn. Castle Garden was America's initial immigration center. Today it comprises the 23-acre Battery Park fronting on the Hudson River and is also known as Castle Clinton National Monument named after Governor DeWitt Clinton of New York. Under the Immigration Act of 1882, the Federal Government assumed control of all immigrant stations in the US which had formally been the sole responsibility of individual states. The Government's Ellis Island in New York harbor opened in 1892 with over 12 million immigrants passing through its portals until it closed in 1954.

The slight, dark-haired young girl dressed in her rustic best, found herself alone in an alien world of huge buildings and bustling crowds. Gingerly side-stepping mounds of horse droppings that littered every street, her nostrils burning from the stench of sewer-laden alleyways disposing their effluent curbside overpowering the aroma of peddlers' carts roasting ethnic foods. Sidewalk venders hawked their goods amid hustlers attempting to steal whatever meager savings immigrants possessed accosted her at every turn. Undaunted, she made her way past the squalor of lower Manhattan with its overcrowded rat-invested tenements where people suffered the ravages of typhus, smallpox and a host of other diseases festering among the urban poor.

It was a frightening and wondrous experience of sight, sound and smell for the wisp of a girl from rural Ireland.

She lived with her aunt in Brooklyn until she was able to find work, once again as a domestic. In the 1880s, only menial opportunities were open to immigrants, especially those from Ireland. Reportedly, she found employment in the household of a family named Bennett who lived on Park Avenue in Brooklyn, subsequently leaving for a position with a family named Giraud (Gerow) on Myrtle Avenue, also in Brooklyn. She was so well thought of by the Girauds that when they moved to Gold Street, they invited her to continue with them as a live-in maid.[1] There is scant evidence concerning the Girauds and no trace of them in the genealogy records of the time.

It is allegedly at the Girauds' that Kate first met Vivion de Valera, supposedly a guest in their home. De Valera apologists variously described Vivion as a Spaniard, a Portuguese, a Cuban, and an Argentinian; he was a sculptor, professor, artist, music teacher, actor, and singer, a doctor, accountant, or intellectual. He was reputed to be a linguist capable of speaking fluent English, Spanish, German, and French, the son of a sugar magnate – and a man of royal blood.

Lack of evidence as to the existence of the man known as Vivion de Valera has never inhibited writers from fabricating intimate descriptions of him. He was "bright and vivacious and very highly educated.... [N]ot content with the study of Irish music...soon after his marriage he devoted some of his spare moments to the study of the Irish language becoming proficient in a matter of months."[2]

In another version, Vivion suffered from tuberculosis. Funded by his father, he apparently deserted wife and infant son and headed west, for Colorado, where he allegedly died in Denver in 1884. The Colorado State Archives do not contain a record of the death of any de Valera between the years 1865 and 1900. In any case, why would a talented man from a wealthy family desert wife and newborn child?

Vivion's parentage was grist for speculation. It was claimed that Juan de Valera "held high military rank in the Spanish army. He was a typical Spaniard and, on the maternal side, descended from one of the noble houses of Spain."[3] de Valera's parentage was further clouded as his father's name was alleged to be Juan Vivion de Valera, that he came from either the Basque region in Spain, or South America or Cuba where he was supposedly a sugar planter; others claimed he was Portuguese and attributed Jewish blood to him.[4]

Those who favour the story of a marriage between Kate Coll and a Spanish de Valera with a wealthy father suggest that after his son's death, Juan de Valera, the wealthy grandfather who apparently would not pay for his dying son's wife and child to accompany him to Colorado, suddenly developed such an attachment to the boy that he traveled to New York to claim his grandson. However, "Fate was already at work, for the liner had hardly sailed when Vivion de Valera's father arrived in New York from Cuba with the intention of taking charge of his grandson. He saw his daughter-in-law, but the decision had been made and he returned home disappointed."[5] He then abandoned any further claim and, leaving his daughter-in-law to fend for herself, disappeared whence he came and conveniently died without a trace. The supposedly wealthy grandfather apparently left neither inheritance nor recognition to his grandson.

Another version has it that the de Valera name belonged to a "Mexican waiter who died of galloping consumption [tuberculosis] at the age of 22." In this scenario, Kate told people that he was her husband, and gave the child his last name.[6] Other writers suggest: "There was probably no '[Éamon] de Valera' father. No record of him has been found. He, like so much of Éamon de Valera, was imagined."[7]

The most plausible theory is that Vivion de Valera, if a man of his name existed, was actually a part-time waiter/dishwasher at a diner frequented by the down-and-out, and that it was there he and Kate met. The short-lived illicit romance that purportedly followed resulted in the birth on October 14, 1882, of an illegitimate son, named George.

There is further evidence of a haste in George (Edward then Eamon) de Valera's birth certificate in which Kate misspelled her alleged husband's name, listing her son as George deValero and his alleged father as Vivion deValero. In June 1916, following the Easter Rising, Kate legally amended the name on her son's birth certificate to Edward. But she began calling him Eddie as an infant after her brother Edward (Ned). While de Valera was in prison in June 1916 for his part in the Easter uprising, his mother presented evidence of his American citizenship in order to ameliorate his alleged prison sentence. Her plea came too late, more than a month after his alleged court martial and sentence of death, when his penalty had already been downgraded to penal servitude for life.

Given the stigma attached to illegitimacy, it is a reasonable assumption that Kate fabricated a story about a marriage to a husband who conveniently met an untimely death. Yet some writers have taken Kate's version unquestioningly. As Kate told it, she opted for a change of scene from the Girauds and left Brooklyn for a position in New Jersey: "Vivion followed and the couple was reportedly married on September 19, 1881 in the Church of St. Patrick, Greenville, in what is now Jersey City."[8]

According to the law of the time, all religious marriages were not only recorded in church ledgers but also noted in the local government register. There is no evidence of any such marriage in the meticulous records of Saint Patrick's Church. An inspection of the local municipal records, which were later transferred to the state archives in Trenton, the state capital, also fail to evince any reference to a de Valera-Coll marriage. There are no missing pages or gaps in the neatly kept records of either the church or state for years before and after the alleged nuptials took place.

Even those who accept that Kate lied about having married a man named Vivion de Valera seem ready to accept her claim that this man was the father of her son. But why would Kate, so appreciated by the Girauds, suddenly opt to move across the Hudson River to Greenville, New Jersey? As there is no record there of a marriage between her and the Latin hidalgo, it is possible that Vivion de Valera was no more the father of her child than he was her husband. If he was not the father, who was?

Kate Coll was no naive innocent when she arrived in New York. Edward Atkinson, one of her Irish employers, was a lecher who attempted to bed any woman he met, especially those within his employ. Some writers claimed Kate was pregnant by him with young Éamon and that he sponsored her move to America. There is no evidence of a pregnancy upon Kate's arrival in America and Éamon was born more than three years afterwards.

However, it is within the realm of possibility that the father of her child was a member of the household of her American employers, the Girauds, and not a man named de Valera after all. In such circumstances it was not unusual for the disgraced servant to be offered a gratuity in exchange for agreeing to name no names and to sever all contact with the family. Kate left Brooklyn and moved, most likely to a friend's home in the Irish enclave of Greenville, to await the arrival of her baby. When it was time to deliver, she travelled to New York City to the Nursery and Child's Hospital on Lexington Avenue in Manhattan, which provided free maternity service. It was there that the myth of Vivion de Valera was hatched.

But none of these suppositions has ever been verified. As long ago as 1939, one biographer of Éamon de Valera noted: "The total of our knowledge about de Valera's origins is small and he himself has consistently refused to help biographers."⁹

Whatever the circumstances, Kate found herself with a child she did not want. She did not abandon the baby but did what many other mothers of illegitimate children did at the time and sent him to live with distant relatives. She seized the opportunity when Ned, her younger brother, who had followed her to America, decided to return to Ireland. Ned had contracted malaria and was returning to Ireland to recuperate. After a short stay in Ireland, he returned to America.

It would be hard to question her son's legitimacy 3,000 miles away. While readily admitting that the child was not theirs, the baby's relatives could cover up the details of his birth. So it was that Kate reportedly bought little Eddie a new velvet suit, bundled him up, and waved him good-bye as an Ireland-bound ocean liner removed an unwanted burden from her life. On April 20, 1885, Ned and Eddie, less than thirty months old, arrived in Bruree, in the home of his brother Patrick, sister Hannah (Hannie) and mother.

Bruree was and is a depressing hamlet located not far from the Shannon River in a dreary countryside surrounded by farmlands and patches of woods. The scene is "enlivened only by a little puffing train that appears and disappears among the trees on its way from Cork to Limerick or Dublin. The main road into Limerick has long, straight stretches that follow the course of the River Maigue."¹⁰

In 1880, the year after Kate left Bruree for America, General Charles G. Gordon, the British soldier and administrator, had written to Prime Minister William Gladstone: "I must say from all accounts and from my own observations, that the state of our fellow countrymen, in the parts of Ireland I have named, is worse than that of any people in the world, let alone Europe. They are patient beyond belief, but at the same time, broken-spirited and desperate, living on the verge of starvation, in places in which we would not keep our cattle."¹¹

Barely five years later, Kate Coll dispatched her unwanted son to that same godforsaken land. She sent her only child to a country so poor it could not sustain an ever-decreasing population to live with his maternal relations in the mud-walled hovel from which she had fled. The claim that "de Valera's first Irish home was a one-room, dirt-floored thatched cottage – the Irish equivalent of the American log cabin,"¹² is somewhat at variance with the truth, though convenient enough for de Valera's political purpose in later years. The fact is that the British, stung by worldwide condemnation of the squalid living conditions of the Irish, had initiated a housing program for farm workers. Éamon's Uncle Patrick, a political hanger-on, had recently been awarded a newly constructed three-room cottage. The Colls' new home had a low ceiling, stone floor and no running water; the fireplace in the kitchen was the only means for both cooking and heating, and there were only two other rooms.[13] Not a palace but better than the one-room, mud-floored hovel in which Éamon spent all of one night. The Colls had not yet moved into their new home, and the morning after little Eddie's arrival, the entire family went off to inspect it, quite forgetting about the boy asleep in the loft. When he awoke, Éamon, confused and frightened, found himself abandoned once more, this time by an entire family of strangers.

At first the child was the particular responsibility of Kate's fifteen-year-old sister Hannah. If she didn't exactly love little Eddie, she gave what care she could to the boy. Conditions were so stark and opportunities so limited in Ireland that Kate, now comfortably established in America, sent not for her son but for her sister. His surrogate mother abandoned him also. Little Eddie, clasping his grandmother's hand, waved a tearful goodbye to Aunt "Hannie" as the puffing train tootled into the distance, taking away the only mother figure he knew.

The care of little Eddie now fell to his aged grandmother. When she became deathly ill, Hannah returned briefly to tend to her needs. Kate remained in America as her mother lay dying. After her death, Hannah returned to the United States, leaving little Eddie worse off than before, this time in the care of his Uncle Pat. As hard-hearted as his sister Kate, Uncle Pat reportedly added housework to the boy's long list of daily chores.

On May 7, 1888, aged five and a half, little Eddie began his first day at the National School in Bruree, and for the next eight years he walked the mile or so to and from Uncle Patrick's house.

In such a closed society suspicions as to little Eddie's birth surfaced and were gossiped over. When he was old enough to understand the gibes of other children and the whispers of neighbors, bitterness etched itself indelibly into his very marrow. Lying became part of de Valera's life, his escape from reality, a flight from taunting children and the cruel speculation of grownups. Obfuscation became a shield against hurt when parents warned their children to stay away from the "devil's kin" and "devout" Catholics hastily made the sign of the cross whenever the young boy crossed their path.

Not only was there gossip about his birth; the boy also looked different from other boys. "There was nothing Irish about the face of de Valera," his biographer John Whelan noted. "One must presume that his Spanish [French, Giraud?] father gave him that something which can

16

only be called a foreign look; the width of the mouth, the tawny color of the skin, the deep dark-brown eyes…"[14]

To escape the sniggering taunts of other children, de Valera attempted to be Eddie Coll for a time; he wanted to be Irish like all the other boys. His tall, gangly stature, doubtful birth, and Spanish-sounding name condemned him to merciless teasing: "He fought many a battle by the pump at the Bruree crossroads,"[15] ashamed to be called "de Valera, the Spaniard." He usually walked to and from school alone because he had few friends, spending his idle time in the fields and hills surrounding Bruree hunting by himself, long solitary hours in the countryside with nothing but his lonely bitterness to keep him company. He was an alien in a hostile land. The pain of rejection had stabbed deep into his heart and seared his consciousness.

To add to his loneliness, Uncle Pat heaped chores upon him. "Sent early in the morning to the creamery, he would read as he waited, his feet dangling over the side of the cart, his head in a book, until it was his turn to unload the big cans of milk. The other boys would congregate round the warmth of the boiler in the creamery to pitch pennies, but Eddie did not join in, only raising his eyes from his page to see who might be winning."[16] He also had to graze the cows, clean the sheds and tend the garden as well as prepare the meals.

An Irish mother is a jealous mother and an unfortunate daughter-in-law is viewed not as a new daughter but as a competitor for her son's affections. As a consequence, many men in Ireland marry late in life. When de Valera's grandmother died, Uncle Pat promptly wed his girlfriend of many years, and little Eddie once again found himself odd man out. It was indeed a forlorn and friendless world for him, living in a home with a strange woman as head of the household. What little attention Uncle Pat had paid him in the past was now transferred to his new wife, who never showed the boy even the meager affection displayed by his Aunt Hannie. Uncle Pat and his wife had three children of their own, and Eddie was nothing more than a tolerated irritant.

When de Valera was five, Kate returned home to Bruree for a visit to the "oulde sod," not to bond with her son but to renew her Irishness. He begged his mother to take him back to America with her. He cried that he could not stand living in Bruree: he hated Ireland. But Kate was engaged to be married and left her tormented child in tears as she boarded the train that would take her to a life that did not include her son. Already de Valera had been abandoned and rejected by every person who had come into his short life. He never had a chance to bond with a mother or father figure. "As even one historian not unsympathetic to de Valera inscribed on a copy of his biography: 'If behind the cold, impersonal countenance of the subject of this biography there seems to be no real humanity, possibly it's because there was none.'"[17]

Kate returned to a life in Rochester, New York, with her "second" husband, Charles Wheelwright, an easy-going English Protestant who enjoyed a pint or two and was employed as a groom for a wealthy family. Wheelwright and Kate had two children, Thomas and Annie. The girl died when she was ten, and Thomas went on to become a Redemptorist priest. Had Kate really wanted to, she "possessed the determination and force necessary to get her second husband to accept her child [Eamon]...She did, after all, persuade the Protestant Wheelwright to bear the expense of making his own son a Catholic priest."[18] Wheelwright died in 1929 and Kate followed him in 1932.

In the Ireland of the 1880s, illegitimacy conferred a stigma hard to imagine today. A child born out of wedlock was regarded as a fearful curse, an evil omen, a demon in the making unworthy of God's grace – an impure spirit to be ostracized and condemned. Such prejudice was encouraged by the Catholic Church which endorsed the notion that illegitimacy marked a child with an unpardonable moral stain that prevented him from becoming a member of the Church. Doubts as to his birth were to blight de Valera's religious, educational, and professional aspirations.

Patrick Coll was cheap to the point of miserliness and unwilling to spend his hard-earned money educating someone else's child so, at thirteen, when his national schooling ended, young de Valera found himself at a crossroads. If he did not continue his schooling, he was destined to spend a lifetime as a farm laborer. De Valera got to Charleville secondary school by making his mother an offer she could not refuse: he insisted that she either send the tuition fees to Charleville or his passage money for America. Kate evidently shrank from bringing her first born to the United States: Charleville it was. But the price of this Pyrrhic victory was another rejection by his mother.

De Valera was fourteen years old when he enrolled at the Christian Brothers' secondary school at Charleville. Mythologizing accounts of de Valera's early life claim that come rain, shine, or snow, the boy walked seven miles to and from school every day. In fact the train ran close behind de Valera's home and he had but a short walk to the station. Some days, rather than wait two or three hours after school for the next train back to Bruree, de Valera would saunter along the dirt roads, often hitching a ride on the back of a farmer's cart. But his day did not end when he got home as Uncle Pat always had farm or house chores for him to do.

De Valera set his sights on further education but upon graduation, despite his excellent grades, he was rejected by two prestigious Jesuit colleges. Fortunately for Eddie, his parish priest had met the president of Blackrock College in Dublin on a train ride and told him of his promising parishioner; de Valera was accepted midyear.[19] In 1898, when he was sixteen, de Valera had been awarded a scholarship with a £20 stipend per year. This did not cover his room, board, and tuition, but the college accepted the £20 award in lieu of the standard £40 admission fee. Uncle Pat betrayed his miserliness to the school authorities when he asked "the college authorities for five pounds out of the scholarship for himself. The request was indignantly ignored."[20]

On his first night at Blackrock, de Valera was astounded to find that one of his new classmates actually missed family, friends, and home. The boy finally cried himself to sleep. De Valera, on the other hand, was overjoyed to be rid of Uncle Pat and his cousins. A stable home life and a loving family were foreign to him. He was a loner throughout his college days, apparently needing neither friend nor family. Rather than go home, he usually spent his holidays at Blackrock. On the occasions when he did return, it was not to renew old acquaintances. Just as in his younger days, his hours were spent hunting alone amid the forests, hills, and lowlands around Bruree.

By this time de Valera was a thin, tall, dark-complexioned youth with sparkling brown eyes whose infrequent smile seemed to transform his somber personality, giving him an almost friendly expression. Like his schooldays in Bruree, his time at Blackrock College was spent as an alien in a world of cliques. His foreign appearance and those old rumors about his birth were enough to ensure that he was rather tolerated than accepted by his peers. Through sheer willpower, he achieved good but not outstanding marks for his work. He joined the athletic teams, where he did not excel.

When he graduated from Blackrock College, de Valera applied for a scholarship to the Protestant Trinity College in Dublin but faced another rejection. Shifting gears, he applied to the Catholic National University to study for a master's degree in quaternion calculus and was accepted. Scholastically, he had done well "in the semi-cloistered atmosphere of Blackrock College, but unrestricted city life and its distractions saw his grades spiral downward. He worked for another ten years toward a master's degree, but in the end, he was awarded only a diploma in education."[21] He had neither "the motivation nor the aptitude to voluntarily ascend to higher academic peaks."[22]

His merely passable academic achievements ruled out the university career de Valera thought he deserved, but a friendly priest helped him find a low-paying teaching job at Carysfort Training College for Women, where he taught for ten years, supplementing his salary with part-time tutoring.

De Valera was not the great intellectual claimed by later myth-makers; rather he was a better-than-average student who achieved respectable results by serious study and hard work in a controlled academic environment. Much later in life, he was able to compensate for his academic mediocrity when, as prime minister, he fulfilled his aspirations and appointed himself to the top of the educational hierarchy – Chancellor of the National University.

Not that de Valera had always sought an academic career. In a letter to his mother while he was still at Blackrock College, he first expressed an interest in joining the priesthood. It was a time when many a rural Irish parish priest was mired in superstition and barely literate. On the face of it, someone of de Valera's educational attainments would have been an asset to the Catholic Church. The Church's rejection of his first and three subsequent attempts to enter the priesthood must presumably be attributed to his illegitimacy.

The Holy Ghost Fathers of Blackrock College, his alma mater, not only refused to acknowledge any priestly vocation in the boy, but they also rejected his application for a teacher's position. While accepting that rumors of de Valera's illegitimacy influenced these rejections, biographer Tim Pat Coogan also asks: "Was there a sense that, despite his obvious potential for giving valuable service to the Church, perhaps at a high level, de Valera might create problems for authority?"[23]

Ever conscious of his "foreign" birth, de Valera attempted on more than one occasion to become "more Irish than the Irish." In 1893 the Protestant Douglas Hyde had founded the Gaelic League for the purpose of resurrecting the Irish language and culture. De Valera, in 1908, believing that a fluency in Irish would further his teaching career and his acceptance in Irish society, joined Ard-Chraobh, the central branch of the Gaelic League in Dublin. His Irish language studies began a new chapter in his life, which he marked by changing his name from Edward to the Irish spelling, Eamon. De Valera reportedly was unpronounceable in Gaelic.

It was through his Irish language studies at Leinster College that he met his future wife, Jane Flanagan (1878-1975). Born in Balbriggan, County Dublin, she was a primary school teacher four years his senior, who also taught Irish at the Gaelic League in Dublin. One of her pupils was Éamon de Valera and she, too, changed her name to the Gaelic equivalent Sinéad. She was an amateur actress of sorts and had considered a life in the theater, but after a discouraging critical review opted for marriage to de Valera.

Gaelic was the bond that brought them together – they were passionate fans of anything Irish, participating in Gaelic-speaking social, educational, and political meetings. Like Arthur Griffith, who founded Sinn Féin, they bought only Irish goods and clothing and spent their summers learning Gaelic in the Irish-speaking western counties. They became engaged and spent the summer of 1909 at the Irish College in Tourmekeady, "an Irish-speaking district set amidst the wild beauty of the Partry-Lough Mask area of the Galway-Mayo border, not far from Maamstrasna. The couple visited the west coast city of Galway, the capital of what was left of Gaelic Ireland."[24]

After an engagement of nearly seven months, they were married on January 8, 1910, in Saint Paul's Church in Dublin. Sinéad was deeply religious and bore five sons and two daughters: Vivion born in 1911, Máirín 1912, Éamon 1913, Brian 1915, Ruairi 1916, Emer 1918, and Terrence 1922. Brian died in a 1936 auto accident. Though highly political, Sinéad shied away from public appearances and was prim and proper outside her home. With de Valera away for such extended periods, she maintained strict discipline and a no-nonsense environment within.

Upon graduation from the Catholic University, de Valera continued his teaching career, securing a teaching diploma at Leinster College and gaining a diploma in Irish from the Royal University. In 1911 he was appointed director of an Irish summer school in Tawin, one of the bridge-linked western islands. That same year, he stood for election to the Gaelic League's governing body, but Seán O'Muirthile, a member of the Irish Republican Brotherhood (IRB), had rigged the election in favour of his man. De Valera believed it was Sinn Féin that had conspired to deprive him of what he saw as his rightful seat on the Gaelic League's governing board and, irony of fate, vowed never to join the party he was destined to lead.

Notes

1. Coogan, Tim P., *De Valera, The Man Who Was Ireland*, Harper 1996, p. 6
2. McCarthy, Tony, "Éamon de Valera's Paternity, *Irish Roots*, No. 1, 1990, p. 29
3. *ibid*
4. Bromage, Mary C., *De Valera and the March of a Nation*, Hutchinson, London, 1956, p. 14
5. MacManus, M.J., *Éamon de Valera*, Ziff-Davis 1946, p. 6
6. Coogan, Tim P., *De Valera, The Man Who Was Ireland*, Harper 1996, p. 5
7. McCarthy, Tony, "Éamon de Valera's Paternity", *Irish Roots*, No. 1, 1990, p. 28

8. Coogan, Tim P., *De Valera, The Man Who Was Ireland*, Harper 1996, p. 6
9. Whelan, John (Seán O'Faoláin), *De Valera*, Penguin Books, England.1939, p. 5
10. *ibid*, p. 7
11. Lyons, F.S.L., *Ireland since the Famine*, Charles Scribner's Sons, NY, 1971, p. 161
12. Dwyer, T. Ryle, *Éamon de Valera*, Gill & Macmillan, 1980, p. 1
13. Bromage, Mary C., *De Valera and the March of a Nation*, Hutchinson, London, 1956, p. 17
14. Whelan, John (Seán O'Faoláin), *De Valera*, Penguin Books, England.1939, p. 6
15. Longford, Earl of & O'Neill, Thomas P., *Éamon de Valera*, Hutchinson, London 1970, p. 3
16. Bromage, Mary C., *De Valera and the March of a Nation*, Hutchinson, London, 1956, p. 20
17. Coogan, Tim P., *De Valera, The Man who was Ireland*, Harper, 1996, p. 10
18. *ibid*, p. 14
19. *ibid*, p. 22
20. Dwyer, T. Ryle, *De Valera, The Man & the Myths*, Poolbeg, Dublin 1991, p. 3
21. *ibid*, p. 10
22. Coogan, Tim P., *De Valera, The Man who was Ireland*, Harper, 1996, p. 35
23. *ibid*, p. 23
24. *ibid*, p. 40

CHAPTER III

The 1916 Easter Rising

"Those princes who have done great things have held good faith of little account. They knew how to circumvent the intellect of men by craft and in the end have overcome those who have relied on their word."

Niccolò Machiavelli[1]

In a centuries-long unbroken procession of failed rebellions and repressive laws, Ireland was plunged into national apathy and hopelessness. It was not until the turn of the twentieth century that young men came to the fore once again to shoulder the banner of opposition to English rule. The Irish Republican Brotherhood (IRB) evolved in the nineteenth century and was forged on the anvil of continuous unsuccessful attempts by the Irish to win control of their destiny by physical force.

Thomas Clarke, arrested during a dynamite foray in London, served fifteen years in British prisons. He had been sentenced to penal servitude for life in 1883 and slowly watched his comrades go insane over the brutal treatment they received. After his release, he emigrated to America and found a benefactor in the aging Fenian John Devoy. Clarke became a naturalized American citizen and worked at the *Gaelic American* newspaper under Devoy. Returning to Ireland, Clarke opened a tobacconist's shop in Dublin that became a mecca for nationalists the likes of P. S. O'Hegarty, Bulmer Hobson, Denis McCullough, and Seán McDermott. Under their leadership, the IRB infiltrated every Irish organization that hinted of future service to the men determined to oust the English by physical force. The IRB proclaimed itself a government in exile, stating in its constitution:

> The Supreme Council of the Irish Republican Brotherhood is hereby declared in fact, as well as by right, the sole Government of the Irish Republic. Its enactments shall be the laws of the Irish Republic until Ireland secures absolute National Independence and a permanent Republican Government is established.

The President of the Irish Republican Brotherhood is in fact as well as by right President of the Irish Republic. He shall direct the working of the Irish Republican Brotherhood subject to the control of the Supreme Council.[2]

On November 25, 1913, at a packed public meeting at the Rotunda Rink in Dublin, John MacNeill, member of the faculty and professor of early Irish history at University College, Dublin, launched the organization known as the Irish Volunteers. MacNeill introduced the concept of the Volunteers in an article written for the Gaelic League newspaper *An Claideamh Soluis*. He wrote that, in forming the Ulster Volunteers in opposition to Home Rule (limited Irish self-government), Northern Ireland Unionists under the leadership of Edward Carson, had shown the Southern Irish the way to form their own militia. There was heavy irony in the fact that after centuries of supporting government from Westminster, "loyal" Ulstermen were in 1912, prepared to take up arms against a properly enacted statute while the "rebels" of the south were – on the face of it – just as determined to defend the will of the Parliament they had opposed for the same period.

MacNeill's suggestion was greeted by Irish Catholics and Nationalists with overwhelming enthusiasm. The IRB leapt at the opportunity and proposed MacNeill to head the organization while they themselves secretly infiltrated every major position. Among those who sat enthralled that day was Éamon de Valera. He was one of more than 4,000 men who signed up that night. Within months, 150,000 Irish Volunteers were on the rolls.

MacNeill claimed that the purpose and object of the Irish Volunteers was "to secure and maintain the rights and liberties common to all the people of Ireland; to train, discipline, arm and equip a body of Irish Volunteers for the above purpose; to unite for this purpose, Irishmen of every creed and of every party and class."[3] Their duties, he said, "will be defensive and protective, and they will not contemplate either aggression or domination." He saw the Irish Volunteers as a defensive force capable of safeguarding Home Rule against the Conservatives and the Ulster Unionists.

The leaders of the Irish Republican Brotherhood – Thomas Clarke, Patrick Pearse, and Seán MacDermott – recognized the tactical advantage of such an organization having as its figurehead a moderate scholarly advocate like MacNeill. Had it been organized under the auspices of the IRB, moderate Irish opinion would have been alienated, and the government would have moved quickly to suppress it. MacNeill made the perfect straw man. Initially the IRB remained a shadowy force behind the Volunteer movement; convinced that Home Rule would never be delivered, they held every position of importance and responsibility.

Companies of Volunteers sprang up everywhere, and drilling proceeded initially with the assistance of former Irish soldiers of the British army. Manual training went very well, but the Volunteers lacked arms and ammunition as well as the money with which to acquire them. Lack of funds was perceived to be an even greater obstacle than the government proclamation announced soon after prohibiting the import of arms.

De Valera took to the military ethos enthusiastically. He attended drill sessions regularly and his diligence earned him election as captain of the newly formed Donnybrook Company. Membership in the Irish Volunteers brought de Valera some of the power his soul craved. The Irish respected education and the Volunteers, many of them unschooled, usually voted for the most educated as their leaders; a man's military qualifications were rarely considered. De Valera was finally "somebody": he was the officer-in-charge. He commanded men, and they obeyed. But it was an expensive business: Volunteers had to provide their own weapons, uniforms, and associated paraphernalia. De Valera outfitted himself with a £5 Mauser carbine and accoutrements that drained sorely needed funds from his family. "Uniforms, which had to be made by private tailors, cost 35 shillings at the lowest."[4] In time, a sidecar motorcycle was added to his military equipment. De Valera's salary as a teacher was modest, and his family was growing – in the autumn of 1913 his third child was born – yet self-centered as he was, he spared no expense in fitting himself out. Lacking any sense of family, he seemed indifferent to the dire financial straits in which this left them. The pleas of Mrs. De Valera went unheeded in his quest for recognition.

In April 1914 the Ulster Volunteers successfully landed an illicit cargo of thirty-five thousand guns and five million rounds of ammunition under the nose of the not uncooperative local government officials. In so doing, they served notice to London of their defiance and opposition to Home Rule.

The government bowed to the Unionists' threats. On September 18, the bill received the royal assent but with the caveat of a suspensory clause postponing implementation until after the war and not before further debate.

Sir Roger Casement and other Anglo-Irish sympathizers raised the necessary funds to equip the Volunteers. Erskine Childers – author, former British intelligence officer, clerk of the House of Commons, and a convinced Home Ruler – bought one thousand antiquated rifles and approximately thirty thousand rounds of ammunition in Germany; half the arms were landed at Howth outside Dublin from his yacht the *Asgard* on July 26. Waiting at Howth to unload the cargo and march away with the coveted arms and ammunition were men of the Irish Volunteers, among them Éamon de Valera.

The local authorities were not blind to the landing of arms and while marching to Dublin, the Volunteers found their way blocked by a contingent of the British Army, the King's Own Scottish Borderers, led by W. V. Harrell of the Dublin Metropolitan Police (DMP). As their leaders distracted the authorities in discussion, men and arms began to slip away unnoticed. De Valera commanded every third man to collect the rifles of his comrades, the remaining two to disperse. Throughout the afternoon he ferried the men with the guns away in his motorcycle sidecar. De Valera was praised for his leadership by the Volunteer Executive.

Returning to Dublin after the standoff, the British soldiers were confronted by an angry mob hurling stones and abuse; the Kings Own Scottish Borderers fired on the crowd leaving three people dead and over thirty wounded. That the anger and resentment caused by the Dublin skirmish did not escalate was probably due in part to the distraction of the Volunteer leadership and the joy at having acquired arms.

De Valera's enthusiasm and determination succeeded in gaining the attention of Patrick Pearse and the other leaders. He was able to recruit enough new blood to fill out his company; and for his efforts he was named commandant of the Third Battalion in March 1915. In his new position, de Valera discovered that plans had been set for an uprising. His attention to detail earned him a further promotion, adjutant to the brigade commander, Thomas MacDonagh, which resulted in his formally joining the Irish Republican Brotherhood.

Irish Volunteer membership had grown to more than 150,000; John Redmond, head of the Irish Parliamentary Party (IPP), was fearful that a badly organized political challenge might jeopardize Home Rule so he set about taking over leadership of the Volunteers. On June 9, 1914, he demanded that twenty-five men appointed by the IPP be added to the Provisional Committee, the governing body managing the Irish Volunteers. Since he was supported by a moderate majority in Ireland, this amounted to a not-so-veiled threat: if his nominees were not approved, he had the power to split the Irish Volunteers. Lack of unity had in the past always spelled doom for Irish nationalist hopes. It was a bitter compromise, but eventually Volunteer leaders bowed to Redmond's demands. A violently opposed minority claimed that division was inevitable and now only postponed. Not that it was postponed for long.

The intransigence of Carson's Ulstermen had stalled the passage of the Home Rule Bill, and an Amendment Bill to deal with it was being negotiated when shots rang out in Sarajevo, and war erupted in Europe. There was a risk that the government would simply abandon the bill, and this Redmond was determined to prevent. On August 3, 1916, Redmond pledged Ireland's support of England in the event of war, urging the government to entrust the defense of Irish shores to the Volunteers of north and south. The *quid pro quo* he hoped for was the passage of the Home Rule Bill, but Sinn Féin's Arthur Griffith was skeptical: "The [British] confidence trick has been too often played upon us to deceive us again. If the Irish Volunteers are to defend Ireland, they must defend it for Ireland, under Ireland's flag and under Irish officers. Otherwise they will only help to perpetuate the enslavement of their country."[5]

On September 20, Redmond dealt the death blow to unity among the Irish Volunteers. In a speech at Woodenbridge in County Wicklow, he urged the Irish Volunteers to fight beyond the shores of Ireland: "Go on drilling and make yourselves efficient for the work, and then account yourselves as men, not only in Ireland itself, but wherever the firing line extends in defense of right, of freedom and religion in this war."[6]

After seven centuries of British might over right, the denial of basic freedoms and monstrous religious persecution, Redmond's call to arms in defense of right, freedom, and religion rang hollow to the ardent nationalists of the IRB. After Woodenbridge, they deemed cooperation with Redmond impossible. Redmond's nominees on the original committee were ousted and more than 11,000 Irish Volunteers, including de Valera, continued under MacNeill while the majority, perhaps 140,000, formed the National Volunteers under Redmond. Again, Irish leadership had been found wanting.

As 1916 dawned, the leaders of the Irish Republican Brotherhood prepared for their generation's rising against English rule. Fittingly, Easter Sunday, April 23, was designated as Ireland's resurrection as an independent nation.

Orders signed by P. H. Pearse, Commander-in-Chief of the Military Council of the Irish Republican Brotherhood, were dispatched to Irish Volunteers throughout the country to hold maneuvers during the Easter holidays. Similar route march and field operation exercises had been held off and on during the past year without rousing British authorities to any action.

The Irish Volunteers were still short of arms and the odds against the success of their plans were overwhelming, but this mattered little to Pearse and his IRB colleagues. They were convinced that their martyrdom would inspire all Ireland to finally free herself from English oppression. Pearse's overriding obsession was clear from the motto he chose for Saint Enda's, the bilingual school founded by him in 1908. The words were ascribed to the mythological hero Cu Chulainn*: "I care not though I were to live but one day and one night, If only my fame and my deeds live after me."

MacNeill was ignorant of Pearse's plans. His contention was that any insurrection must wait until the war was over, when it could be bolstered by the return of the approximately 150,000 Irish veterans then serving in the British armed forces. This did not suit Pearse and the other IRB leaders: quite apart from their enthusiasm for martyrdom and their perception that a catalyst for a revival of Irish nationalist fervour needed to be revived, there was always the possibility of their amateur leadership being shouldered aside by more capable and experienced men.

On February 5, 1916, Tommy O'Connor, a courier dispatched by the IRB Executive in Dublin, strode into the New York City office of John Devoy, dedicated Fenian, head of the IRB-affiliated Clan na Gael and editor of the Irish-American newspaper, *The Gaelic American*. Devoy was informed that an insurrection was planned for Easter Sunday and the IRB requested Clan na Gael to "send a shipload of arms to Limerick Quay between April 20–23."[7]

Devoy was born in County Kildare in 1842 and at nineteen, joined the French Foreign Legion to learn the art of war to better fight the English. Upon his return, he obtained commitments from tens of thousands of Irishmen serving in the British Army in Ireland to take part in a planned uprising in 1866. The British got wind of the plot and the Irish regiments were quickly transferred out of the country – another informer, another failed insurrection. Devoy was arrested and jailed. Five years later, he and four other prisoners were released but exiled to America where he found employment as a reporter with the *New York Herald*. In 1916, at age 74, he was practically deaf, a severe handicap, but his allegiance to the men in Ireland was unconditional: "The Supreme Council of the IRB had not asked our advice. They simply announced a decision already taken. As we had already recognized the right of the Home Organization to make the supreme decision, our plain duty was to accept it and give them all the help we could."[8]

---

*Cu Chulainn killed Culann's fierce guard dog in self-defense. He offered to take the dog's place until another replacement could be found. Single-handedly at the age of 17, he defended Ulster against Queen Medb of Connacht's armies. His great deeds gave him everlasting fame but in return, his life would be short.

Devoy single-handedly kept the embers of Irish nationalism alive in America. The Irish tendency to argue among themselves would have tried the patience of a saint. The iron-willed Devoy, tireless, implacable, and unwavering in the cause of Irish freedom, yielded to neither despair nor any man.

In 1875, he organized the rescue of six Fenians serving long sentences in Fremantle Prison in Western Australia by financing the refitting and manning of the *Catalpa*, a former whaling vessel. He was involved in monumental issues facing Ireland during his lifetime. He molded the Clan na Gael into a political juggernaut and was instrumental in aligning it with the Irish Republican Brotherhood in 1877. He established the *Gaelic American*, the most influential Irish-American newspaper in America. He may have been churlish, stubborn, and vitriolic towards anyone who threatened Irish interests but his fertile mind recognized people and projects beneficial to Ireland. Devoy never hesitated to change gear and he supported Michael Davitt and the "New Departure," a movement in Ireland to return the land to the native Irish tillers of the soil. He backed Charles Stewart Parnell and financed the 1916 Easter Rising. Padraig Pearse received funds to keep his Saint Enda's school functioning and along with Judge Daniel Cohalan, Devoy initiated the Friends of Irish Freedom, a powerful political proponent of the Irish cause in America.

His eyes sparkled with anticipation when he financed John Philip Holland's submarine and contemplated sinking the entire British Navy. Holland was born in County Clare in 1840 and emigrated to America in 1873. His first successful submarine was purchased by the US Navy in 1900 and commissioned the *USS Holland* in 1901. Unfortunately, by this time, Holland and the Fenians had a falling out and Devoy's dream of scuttling the British fleet was lost.

Devoy persevered against all odds and was successful in uniting the disputatious Irish into the most formidable political organization of its time. He devoted his life to Ireland, even above his youthful love, Eliza Kenny. On a visit to Ireland in 1924, when he met the woman who had been his sweetheart some sixty years before, Eliza Kenny said she had waited a dozen years for a letter from him. In turn he lamented that he had waited all his life for her. Devoy died in 1928, at the age of eighty-six and is buried in Glasnevin Cemetery in his beloved Ireland.

The prospect of the coming 1916 Easter Rising revitalized the ageing Fenian who sprang into action and immediately contacted the German Embassy to negotiate a shipment of arms. As the United States was a declared neutral at this time, the Irish-American was violating no U.S. law.

At a meeting with the German Ambassador, Count von Bernstorff, at the German Legation offices in New York City, Devoy negotiated a shipment of arms to be dispatched to Ireland on April 21, 1916. Devoy insisted, however, that it was German arms and men the Irish wanted not German gold: "If we take their money, they will expect us to take their orders, but we must retain our independence of action. If we are not willing to finance our own fight for freedom, we don't deserve freedom."[9]

Berlin replied on March 5, 1916, that two or three trawlers would arrive off Fenit Pier in Tralee Bay on Thursday, April 20-21 with twenty thousand rifles, ten machine guns, and one million rounds of ammunition. The trawlers were later changed to one larger vessel, the *Aud*, carrying the same amount of arms. Detailed arrangements for a rendezvous were immediately communicated to Ireland: a reply was necessary only if the offer was not acceptable or if there was a change of plan. Clan na Gael also sent $25,000 to Dublin to pay for whatever arms were available in Ireland.

Devoy was flabbergasted when on Friday, April 14, less than seven days before the scheduled arms landing, another Military Council courier of the IRB, Philomena Plunkett, arrived with a request for the rendezvous with the arms ship to be postponed to April 23. He immediately contacted the Germans, who informed him that the *Aud* had already left port with the arms and did not have a radio aboard: the shipment could not be rescheduled. Devoy immediately notified Dublin.

By means of lies and deceit, the leaders of the rebellion managed to keep their Easter Sunday insurrection plot a secret from the Irish Volunteer commander-in-chief, John MacNeill. It was not until Maundy Thursday – April 20 – that MacNeill learned of the scheme; he immediately took steps to counter the conspiracy. He was furious – not because he was against fighting the British, but because in his estimation the plot had not the slightest chance of success, and he could see no sense in sacrificing the lives of practically defenseless men.

That night, MacNeill roused Pearse, who admitted that a rising was indeed planned for the coming Sunday. He confessed to MacNeill: "Yes, you were deceived, but it was necessary." MacNeill swore to do everything within his power to stop the insurrection, short of notifying government authorities.

The following morning, Good Friday, April 21, the IRB leaders Pearse, Seán MacDermott, and Thomas MacDonagh called on MacNeill, who agreed to see MacDermott but refused to talk to Pearse, whom he felt had betrayed him. Then, as MacNeill later recorded:

"MacDermott disclosed to me for the first time that a ship with arms from Germany carrying 20,000 rifles, machine guns, grenades and millions of rounds of ammunition was expected at that very time...It was, of course, evident to me that in the circumstances a landing of arms from Germany meant an immediate challenge to the English Government and I said to MacDermott: 'Very well, if that is the state of the case, I'm in it with you.'"[10] MacDermott's phrase, "expected at that very time" – that is, Friday, April 21 – confirmed that Devoy's relayed message from the Germans that the arms schedule could not be altered had reached the IRB leaders in time.

MacNeill's standing orders for the Irish Volunteers were to resist by all means possible any British attempt to disarm them. The landing of arms from Germany would precipitate just such an attempt by the authorities, and the required resistance on the part of the Irish Volunteers would escalate into a general fight. It was clear to MacNeill that there was no way he could prevent the IRB's insurrection. "'Well, if we have to fight or be suppressed, then I suppose I'm ready to fight...' When he entered the drawing room, he at once approached Pearse and shook hands. Then to show that full amity had been restored, he invited them all to stay for breakfast."[11]

In his own memorandum of the events of those days, MacNeill related that after MacDermott's visit "I made my own preparations to join the Dublin Volunteers...It is untrue that I changed my mind several times. For a few hours, I was convinced that all was over with our movement and nothing left for us except to sell our lives as dearly as possible."[12]

With MacNeill having agreed to join the insurrection, the Military Council of the IRB could surely count on a full complement of men turning out for the Rising – tens of thousands throughout Ireland was a conservative estimate. On the face of it, men armed with those twenty thousand German rifles marching on Dublin would initially outmatch the forces available to the British. The British could muster some six thousand troops stationed in Ireland plus a considerable number of recovering war wounded, in addition to nine thousand armed members of the Royal Irish Constabulary and about one thousand unarmed Dublin Metropolitan Police.

If Pearse and his fellow conspirators had taken him into their confidence, he would have agreed to the arrangements made with the Germans to arm the Volunteers, especially since the Unionists in the North had successfully landed so many arms themselves. The IRB's passion for secrecy, combined with its belief in the regenerative virtues of martyrdom, led it into entirely unnecessary and self-defeating deception.

Prior to the Rising there were many who sensed that the English were engaged in their all-too-familiar *modus operandi*: incite the Irish to rebellion and then slaughter them, thereby ensuring another generation of sullen peace. In a February 1916 memo, MacNeill forecast how the British government would aid and abet a rising and subsequently crush the Irish Volunteers. He predicted with uncanny accuracy the effect it would have on the international community, especially the United States, where there would be widespread shock at the perceived treachery of the Irish stabbing the mother country in the back when she was engaged in a mortal struggle for survival: "England...has more than ample power to crush us [the Irish Volunteer Organization] in the military sense...Why then has it not been crushed? Why has it been allowed to grow stronger and stronger? Why has the Government's hostility...been mainly in tentative acts of provocation...? The answer is that the occasion which the Government wants for more drastic action is open revolt. If the Government knew that a revolt was about to take place, it would allow the revolt [to break out]...The Government might even pretend to allow a revolt to make headway for some days, taking only such military measures as would prevent the revolt getting the upper hand...The Government would then intervene with the double or treble justification of asserting the supremacy of the state – in which it would have the sympathy of all states (especially the United States) not actively hostile to it – and of preventing the Irish people from killing each other. In short, the Irish Volunteers would have committed the ghastly crime of enabling the English government to put itself in the right and the entire population of Ireland in the wrong."[13]

The stench of conspiracy was apparently so pungent that even Dublin's leading pacifist, Francis Sheehy-Skeffington, was able to detect it. Like MacNeill, he too, was ignored. In a letter to *The New Statesman* on April 7, three weeks before the Easter Rising, Sheehy-Skeffington wrote: "The conduct of British officers was becoming intolerable and it looked very much as if they wanted to drive the people into revolt...'If Major General Friend [Commander of Crown Forces in Ireland] and his subordinate militarists proceed either to disarm the Volunteers or to raid the Labor Press, it can only be because they want bloodshed – because they want to provoke another [1798 revolt] and to get an excuse for a machine-gun massacre.'[14] 'When the explosion, which they have provoked, occurs, they will endeavor to delude the British Public as to where the responsibility lies.'"[15]

After the Rising, *The New York Times* reported on April 26, "[t]he bulk of informed comment in London, in regard to the outbreak in Dublin, was expressed in terms of astonishment. In view of the information which must have been in the possession of the authorities, as to the preparation for a rebellion, which was known to be in the making, no precautionary measures adequate to crush the movement in its inception were taken. *The Times* of London, about 10 days ago, gave a half-column report from its Dublin correspondent of the seditious movement there."[16]

Sir Alfred Ewing, director of naval education, was the man responsible for assembling the group of expert cryptographers who, under the acronym Room 40 O.B., monitored German naval codes during the First World War. A historian of the times recorded Ewing as saying: "Besides intercepting naval signals, the cryptographers dealt successfully with many coded messages to Germany's agents...One group of deciphered messages threw useful light in advance on the Easter Rebellion...Captain Reginald Hall, in charge of the cryptologists, was able to follow every move of the plotters during the week before Easter Sunday."[17]

Indeed, as early as September 1914 the French had presented the British with the key to the German military code, and in October the Russians sent them a copy of the German naval signal codes recovered from the German cruiser *Magdeburg* after it ran aground on the island of Odenholm in the Baltic. The British therefore had access to all military correspondence between Berlin, Devoy and the German authorities in America; they also had the cooperation of the American Secret Service and a mole in the German Embassy in Washington. On top of this, the Royal Irish Constabulary (RIC) and the Dublin Metropolitan Police ran their own network of spies in Ireland.

Devoy had conveyed a letter outlining the plans for an insurrection to Captain Franz von Papen, a member of the German delegation in America, on February 7, 1916, and it was immediately wirelessed to Berlin. Captain Hall's department was so efficient that it had read the letter before it reached the German capital.

Acting on another British tip, US Secret Service agents, on April 18, raided the New York offices of Wolf von Igel, a German Embassy staffer. They confiscated a note from Devoy outlining his request to change the landing date. The confiscated documents were immediately dispatched to the British Embassy in Washington and transmitted to London that afternoon. Devoy's message had been sent to Berlin on April 17, and the very next day the British Admiral at Queenstown was notifying the men under his command of the contents.

According to one account, the news of a rising was so widespread that "Admiral Sir Lewis Bayly at Queenstown told General Stafford, commanding officer of the South, who told General Friend, the

Commander-in-Chief, Ireland, who told Sir Matthew Nathan, the Under Secretary, who told Lord Wimborne, the Viceroy, that the British Admiralty had told him that a German vessel, the *Aud*, was on its way to Ireland with arms for an intended Rising ..."[18] Even this was not the full extent of Dublin Castle's intelligence regarding trouble ahead. On March 22, Major-General G. M. W. MacDonagh [no relation to the Irish Volunteer Brigade Commander Thomas MacDonagh] notified Field Marshall Lord Lieutenant French: "Irish extremists were in communication with Germany with a view to obtaining German assistance, and...Germany [agreed] to supply arms and ammunition to Limerick."[19]

On April 14, Admiral Bayly notified the Galway Naval District that Germans: "were about to dispatch two submarines for special service on the West Coast of Ireland...This landing is expected to be connected with a Rising which some say will take place about Easter."[20] On April 16, British intelligence notified Admiral Bayly and Brigadier-General Stafford with accurate information that a German ship was to land arms and ammunition on the southwest coast of Ireland on April 21 and a rising was to begin the following Saturday. That same day, General Friend "received a notification from the British Admiralty that a disguised German ship was due to arrive off the coast of Ireland on April 21 or 22 and that a Rising was timed for Easter Eve."[21] The April issue of the Volunteers' publication, *The Irish Volunteer*, gave instructions for a route march and maneuvers over the Easter weekend while British intelligence had reported that the Irish Volunteers' training and numbers had increased dramatically in recent months.

The Easter Rising obviously came as no surprise to anyone except MacNeill.

In his account of the Rising, historian Desmond Ryan, a former pupil of Pearse's at Saint Enda's School, confirms MacNeill's contention that there was a plot to lure the Irish into a rebellion: "[A]ll the evidence points to an incredible carelessness on the part of the British military and civilian authorities or a *sinister complacency* on the part of some, at least, in allowing the insurrection to mature and break out in the hope that both Sinn Féin and any prospect of Irish autonomy could be defeated."[22] Indeed, Dublin Castle officials calmly went off to enjoy the Easter holidays. Their failure to take even the most minimal precautions despite multiple warnings that an insurrection was imminent had to be purposeful and suspicious.

On April 9, 1916, the German arms shipment destined for Ireland set sail from Lubeck on board the *Libau* under the command of Captain Karl

Spindler. Once past Travemünde, Germany, the *Libau* changed its name to *Aud* and its colors to those of a Norwegian tramp steamer; its manifest detailed a shipment of household goods destined for the Iberian Peninsula. The *Aud* is said to have sailed as far north as the Arctic Circle in order to slip down to Ireland behind the British naval blockade. Spindler reported encountering British ships on several occasions; though scrutinized, he was never stopped. "The *Aud* commander asked himself again and again during his voyage whether the British naval patrols which hovered round his ship and then let her pass unchallenged were silly or subtle."[23] Some of the worst storms in years hammered the little arms ship as she made her roundabout way to her rendezvous on the Kerry coast.

What neither MacNeill nor the IRB leaders knew as they breakfasted on Good Friday morning, April 21, was that the shipload of arms, the imminent arrival of which had persuaded MacNeill to reluctantly support the Rising, was already circling Tralee Bay. Spindler, in a feat of masterful sailing, had arrived in the late afternoon of Thursday, April 20, 1916, in accordance with the original schedule, except that instead of the landing party he expected at Fenit Pier, he found only a lone British sentry. Incredibly, Austin Stack, in charge of the landing party had failed to post a single lookout for the arms ship.

Spindler spent many hours attempting to locate someone to unload his precious cargo; as night fell he flashed the prearranged signal but no response was forthcoming; finally dropping anchor after 1 a.m. on Friday morning.

The coming of the dawn produced no better results. The skipper of an armed trawler, *Setter II*, spotted the *Aud* and went aboard, ordering Spindler to open his cargo hatch. But the German's good fortune held: having surveyed the pots and pans apparently bound for Portugal that concealed the arms, the British skipper explained to Spindler that he was looking for a German arms ship that was expected at any time. "He even promised me a reward if, in the event of my sighting the German boat, I would report her to the next signaling station."[24]

A subsequent message from the Smirwick Station that a foreign vessel was "heaving things overboard" led to the dispatch of another armed vessel, the *Lord Heneage*, which scurried to Tralee Bay. Spotting the fast-approaching British warship, Spindler quickly got underway and outraced his pursuer. Two more British warships, the *Zinnia* and the *Bluebell*, caught sight of the *Aud* and were ordered by Bayly to bring the suspicious ship into Queenstown.

The Captain of *Bluebell* duly ordered Spindler to follow him into port; Spindler hesitated, until a shot across his bow convinced him that the jig was up. The following morning, Saturday, April 22, as the *Aud* and her escorts were approaching Queenstown, Spindler ordered his men into their naval uniforms, and the boats to be lowered. As they pulled away from the *Aud*, an explosion ripped her hull apart and sent her spinning to the bottom of the sea. With her went any hope of success for another Irish rebellion. Spindler and his crew spent the duration of the war in various British prisons.

One curious feature of the *Aud's* adventure: she was allowed to remain in Tralee Bay unchallenged for twenty-four hours. The message about "heaving things overboard" suggests that the British expected and indeed hoped her contraband cargo would be unloaded in that time.

Sir Roger Casement was an Anglo-Irishman who retired from the British Foreign Service in 1913 and was involved in fund-raising for arms procurement. To aid those planning the Rising, John Devoy sent Casement to Germany to secure support for a declaration of Irish independence, to recruit an Irish brigade from among German-held Irish prisoners of war to fight in Ireland, and to arrange for the shipment of any purchased arms. The recruitment in particular was a dismal failure, and Casement became generally disillusioned, doubting that the Germans would keep their promise of arms for the Irish rebels. He left Wilhelmshaven, Germany, on April 12 on board a submarine. With his assistant, Captain Robert Monteith and Sergeant Daniel Bailey, one of his few recruits, Casement arrived off Banna Strand on the west coast of Ireland at 3 a.m. on Good Friday, April 21, 1916.

The rubber raft in which they disembarked from the submarine capsized in the surf, and they struggled ashore. Casement, too exhausted to go on, sought refuge in an abandoned fort while the other two went in search of Austin Stack, the man in charge of the Volunteer party assigned to meet the *Aud* and unload the arms. Casement was later found and arrested by the local constabulary.

At 8 a.m. Monteith and Bailey arrived at Spicer's Café in Tralee and urgently requested to see Stack. He was notified of their arrival but refused to interrupt his leisurely breakfast, eventually strolling into the café at ten. Monteith told Stack that Casement feared the Rising was doomed and informed him "of the presence of the *Aud* in the Bay, the details of the arms, machine guns and munitions on the ship – that field crews and German officers were not coming." When Monteith inquired about the pilot boat that was to have met the submarine, Stack told him he thought it was supposed to arrive on Sunday.[25] As a result, Stack had not assigned a single scout to look out for the arms ship.

An excellent soccer player, Austin Stack had joined the Irish Volunteers on December 10, 1913, and was elected an officer in the Kerry Volunteers because of his prowess on the ball field rather than on the battlefield. He was taken into the confidence of the IRB leaders in Dublin and especially by Pearse, whose shortcomings as a military tactician were exceeded only by his inability to recognize poor leadership. He appointed Stack commandant of the Irish Volunteers in Tralee.

MacNeill has been widely blamed for the fiasco of the Easter insurrection by countermanding orders for a Rising after the sinking of the arms ship. But it was Stack, however, the man in charge of the landing operation, who was unquestionably at fault in neglecting to assign a lookout for the ship. He was certainly well aware that the vagaries of the North Sea weather combined with the British naval presence made precision timing of the rendezvous with the arms ship all but impossible.

In a meeting with Pearse nearly two months prior to the scheduled arrival of the arms ship, "Stack had [specifically]...raised questions as to the difficulties of running the British blockade, the risks of delay by storm or fog and the uncertainty of the ship arriving at Tralee to a strict timetable."[26] Incredibly, once Monteith had told Stack at 10 a.m. that the arms ship was in Tralee Bay, Stack neither sent a scout to confirm Monteith's statement nor alerted the landing party, though the *Aud* remained in Tralee Bay until at least 1:30 p.m., so that there were still three and a half hours in which to land the arms. Instead, Stack ignored his primary responsibility and went off in search of Casement.

Stack's behavior was bizarre. His orders had been to avoid arrest and not to provoke any incident likely to result in a shootout until the arrival of the arms ship. While he was on his way to find Casement the police stopped his car. Asked if the occupants were carrying firearms, Stack brandished his automatic: "Yes, I have this, but will not give it up to anybody."[27] Those were trying years in Ireland, and many men voluntarily turned themselves in to the authorities in order to sit out danger in the relative safety of prison. Stack was deliberately attempting to have himself arrested so as to distance himself from the Rising, perhaps convinced by Casement's gloomy prediction that it was destined to fail.

The general consensus among historians is that the failure to land the German arms shipment doomed the insurrection.[28] T. M. Coffey comes closest to laying the responsibility for the Rising's failure at Stack's feet: "All those precious guns, the only hope the uprising ever had, sitting on the bottom of the Atlantic, simply because there had been no men on hand to unload them at Tralee Thursday night...Without the German guns and ammunition, it was suicide to face the power of the British military."[29]

Liam Mellowes led a failed rising of Volunteers in Galway. "The capture of the arms ship had dealt the greatest blow to the insurrection in the west where 3,000 rifles were to have been distributed." Mellowes said that if the gun-running had been successful: "The entire country would have been in our hands by Easter Monday."[30] Mellowes's men were said to have had 60 rifles, 350 shotguns, and 12 revolvers for nearly 1,000 men.

Details of Stack's doings in the days preceding the Rising are also curious and suggestive. On Wednesday, April 19, he sent a message to M. J. O'Connell, a member of the landing party, asking how many horses and carts the members of the company could supply for the Rising.[31] Some of the information about these and other similar arrangements found their way to the authorities, including Admiral Bayly, whose knowledge of the number of carts to be assembled on Fenit Pier in Tralee Bay was sent on to Queenstown.[32]

It is stretching credulity too far to assume that there was no connection between Stack's cart inquiry, his visit to the local police station resulting in his arrest two days later on April 21, and Admiral Bayly's memorandum to the authorities, written sometime between the 19th and 21st. The admiral's knowledge of the number of "carts" to be assembled on Fenit Pier cannot have come from any intercepted German correspondence; the likely conclusion – the British had an informer close to Stack, perhaps even Stack himself.

Admiral Bayly's behavior was as odd in its own way as Stack's. Despite knowing that the arrival of an arms ship was imminent, he never sent a single ship, soldier, or policeman to investigate why so many "car[t]s should gather at Fenit Pier." Such indifference suggests that Bayly deliberately allowed enough time for the arms ship to unload its cargo before he acted, further evidence that the British allowed the insurrection to begin.

Returning to Tralee after a futile search for Casement, Stack attended a Volunteer staff meeting that afternoon at the local Rink, where his officers were awaiting orders to unload and distribute the arms which Stack continued to insist were due on Sunday. Without checking to see if the arms ship had indeed arrived, Stack continued to claim the arms ship was not due for two days. He dispatched two men to Dublin to notify the leaders of Casement's arrest and inform them that "the arrival of the arms ship at Fenit was imminent."[33] While Stack acknowledged that the arrival of the *Aud* was anticipated, he still did not order a scout to Fenit

Pier. Though he had been rushing about all day, flourishing his automatic pistol, Stack reiterated to his men the standing orders to do nothing to provoke an incident or call attention to themselves.

During the meeting at the Rink, Michael Flynn, a member of the Kerry Volunteers, arrived to report that Con Collins (no relation to Michael Collins), an officer of the Kerry contingent, had been arrested, and had requested Stack come to the police station, where another prisoner whose name he didn't know (it was Casement) was also being held. The note was obviously a ploy by the police to lure the leader of the rebels to the station. Flynn suspected a plot and warned Stack he would most likely be arrested if he set foot in the police station.

Before the assembled men at the Rink, Stack made an ostentatious display of checking his pockets, and handed over his revolver and declared to Cahill for all to hear that "none of the papers, which he carried, were incriminating and went to the police barracks to see Con Collins. He was immediately arrested."[34]

While interrogated by police, he was found to be carrying important information regarding the Volunteers, and in particular about MacNeill. Anthony J. Gaughan, Stack's biographer, finds his performance "puzzling." The papers couldn't have been more incriminating, and included maps with roads and telegraph lines marked, the oath of the Irish Volunteers, meeting notes, a letter from the American Committee of the Irish Volunteers in New York signed by Patrick Griffin, and other letters inciting insurrection signed by his compatriots.[35] In the subsequent court-martial of MacNeill, he was found guilty primarily on the grounds of documents relevant to the Rising. It would be instructive to know whether the material found on Stack supplied the prosecution case against MacNeill.

Stack's biographer struggled to find a plausible reason for Stack's ready surrender: Stack claimed, "He wished to ensure that the British forces would not be placed on the alert." But even Gaughan admits that few people would find this very convincing.[36]

The IRB board of inquiry that followed the failure of the Rising went looking for scapegoats in all the wrong places, and Stack, unlike MacNeill, never appeared at an official hearing before either the British or the IRB. The leaders of the Cork Brigade, however, had to defend themselves for not having carried out their assignment to which they responded, "The loss of the arms ship left them with no assignment to carry out."

The most logical explanation for Stack's behavior is that he had been spooked by Casement's dire prediction regarding the Rising and believed he was less likely to be executed if he was safely locked up in jail by the time the Rising broke out. Who could then charge him with having supplied the arms that resulted in British casualties? Self-preservation was more important to him than carrying a supply of arms to a doomed insurrection. This was not the only time Stack's cowardice came to the fore. In 1923, during the Civil War, after exhorting his men to fight to the last against the pro-Treaty forces, he was discovered cowering in a ditch after throwing away his loaded gun.

On April 21, 1916, Stack was arrested by the Tralee Royal Irish Constabulary as he entered the police station and spent the next fourteen months in various jails across England; escaping execution because there was no evidence he had been complicit in any British casualties. He was released on June 17, 1917, along with de Valera and other survivors of the 1916 Rising.

MacNeill, informed on Saturday, April 22, that the *Aud* along with the arms she carried had been scuttled outside Queenstown Harbor, knew that all hope of a successful Rising had gone down with her. In an effort to prevent needless slaughter, he decided to call off the insurrection. As he later wrote, the news of the sinking of the arms ship and arrest of Casement: "helped to persuade me that the situation was beyond remedy – though I was then ready to take part in the rising, I did not see the least prospect of success for it. I had consented [to fight] because I held that we were entitled to protect ourselves [and arms] in the most effective way and to the utmost in our power."[37]

MacNeill notified MacDermott and MacDonagh on Saturday, April 22, that he would wait until midnight for a response from Pearse before making any move of his own to call off the Rising. He waited as late as he dared and then, having received no indication that Pearse and the others had changed their minds, hurried to the *Sunday Independent* and released the following announcement signed in his own name as chief of staff, "Owing to the very critical position, all orders given to Irish Volunteers for tomorrow, Easter Sunday, are hereby rescinded and no parades, marches or other movements of Irish Volunteers will take place. Each individual Volunteer will obey this order strictly in every particular."

The outbreak was not due to begin until late on April 23. That morning, MacNeill sent out orders to the various commandants based in and around Dublin, among them de Valera, adjutant of the Dublin Brigade and commandant of the Third Battalion: "As Comm't MacDonagh is not accessible, I have to give you this order direct. Comm't. MacDonagh left me last night with the understanding that he would return or send me a message. He has done neither. (Signed) John MacNeill."[38]

But at an emergency meeting that same Sunday morning, it was decided to counter MacNeill's cancellation of the "manoeveres" and to call the Volunteers out on Monday instead. MacDonagh, as brigade commander, ordered all Volunteers to remain in Dublin and instructed the commandants of the four battle zones to prepare for action. Pearse issued orders for the Volunteers to report to their stations by 10 a.m. on Monday, April 24. De Valera duly took up his command post at Boland's Bakery at the specified time.

Unfortunately for the soon-to-be martyrs, many of the Volunteers heeded MacNeill's orders and resorted to holiday plans or were traveling to their homes, and did not receive MacDonagh's countermanding instructions. Fewer than 1,000 men reported to their stations in Dublin, and that no more than 1,200 – less than half the "paper" Volunteers in Dublin – eventually took part in the Dublin action. The manning of vital defensive positions was severely compromised.

At noon on Monday, April 24, the first shots of the Easter Rising were fired at the gates of Dublin Castle, the ancient symbol of English military and political power in Ireland. At the entrance gate, one of the two police officers on duty called on the attackers to halt and was shot dead as the attack was pressed home. The Volunteers did not know, with the majority of the garrison on leave, they might well have taken the Castle and won a propaganda coup. "The remaining sentry, dodging another bullet, rushed for reinforcements and before the insurgents could get through, the gates were closed...The small company of Volunteers then withdrew,"[39] occupying Liberty Hall and other nearby buildings commanding the main castle entrance.

Other key points seized by the Volunteers that day were the Four Courts Judicial complex, the South Dublin Union railway station, the Mendicity Institute, Jacob's Biscuit Factory, Boland's Bakery, Saint Stephen's Green and the General Post Office. Once the Volunteers had secured the General Post Office (GPO) – Pearse, commandant general of the Rising and presumptive president of the Irish Republic – issued the following proclamation before a mocking crowd of disinterested onlookers: "We hereby proclaim the Irish Republic as a Sovereign Independent State, and we pledge our lives and the lives of our comrades in arms to the cause of its freedom, of its welfare and of its exaltation among the nations.

"The Republic guarantees religious and civil liberty, equal rights and equal opportunities to all its citizens, and declares its resolve to pursue the happiness and prosperity of the whole nation and of all its parts, cherishing all the children of the nation equally and oblivious of the differences carefully fostered by an alien Government, which have divided a minority from the majority in the past.

"Until our arms have brought the opportune moment for the establishment of a permanent National Government, representative of the whole people of Ireland and elected by the suffrages of all her men and women, the Provisional Government, hereby constituted, will administer the civil and military affairs of the Republic in trust for the people."

The Proclamation was signed by Thomas J. Clarke, Seán McDermott, P. H. Pearse, James Connolly, Thomas MacDonagh, Edmund Kent [Eamonn Ceannt], and Joseph Plunkett.

According to reports, there were no more than two thousand British officers and men in Dublin when the first shots of the insurrection rang out. The following day, Tuesday, April 25, troops began to pour into Dublin from all parts of Ireland and England. Within two days of the insurrection, the British had more than twenty thousand men assigned to trouble spots throughout Ireland.

Brigadier General W. H. M. Lowe was initially in charge of Crown forces in the Dublin area. By the time General Sir John Maxwell arrived to take overall command on Friday, April 28, the rebellion was all but over. Pearse officially surrendered the next day at 3:45 p.m. Rebel communications were nonexistent, however, and on Sunday, April 30, several of the commandants were still unaware that Pearse had surrendered the day before.

The insurrection, with the exception of Michael Malone's ambush at Mount Street Bridge, was merely a series of skirmishes that lasted but a couple of days; the rest of the time was spent mopping up snipers. Boland's Bakery, de Valera's Third Battalion command post, MacDonagh's Second Battalion stronghold at Jacobs Biscuit Factory, and Edmund Kent's Fourth Battalion at South Dublin Union were so tactically insignificant that they were mostly ignored by British forces throughout the entire weeklong insurgency.

The rebels were not only numerically weak, they were also tactically naive. At Stephen's Green, for example, they dug themselves into foxholes, overlooking the fact that they were surrounded by tall buildings and thus exposing themselves to withering sniper fire from nearby rooftops. They eventually took over the College of Surgeons, but would have done better seizing the taller buildings such as the Shelbourne Hotel.

Following the Volunteers' seizure of key points and Pearse's proclamation, the rest of Monday was spent shoring up defensive emplacements. British reaction was slow but steady; men were dispatched from the Curragh Military Command Post, and troops mobilized in England were boarding transports to cross the Irish Sea.

It was a trying time for the Volunteers. Throughout Monday night, it was pouring rain as the men huddled under blankets, although the temperature never dipped below 50 degrees – warm for Dublin.[40]

On Tuesday, many of the rebels, sleepless, soaked, and shivering, found themselves coming under pressure from increasing numbers of British forces. Artillery was being brought in, and by evening shelling of the Volunteers' barricades had begun. Incendiary bombs were used, and by the windy dawn of Wednesday, April 26, fire was sweeping Lower Abbey and O'Connell streets. At about eight o'clock in the morning an English gunboat, the *Helga*, sailed up the Liffey and lobbed shells at Liberty Hall, which was empty but suffered extensive damage.

The only significant opposition was at Mount Street Bridge, on the direct route from Kingstown into the city, where Michael Malone and a handful of Volunteers – less than a dozen in all – repeatedly repulsed several British companies of Sherwood Foresters, inflicting, it was later said, half of all the British casualties suffered during the Easter Rising.

On Thursday the British stepped up their firepower and field-guns systematically reduced to rubble the buildings within which the rebels defended themselves, as the wind furiously fanned the flames. Field artillery opened up on the GPO. James Connolly, socialist labour leader, had claimed that property was so sacred to the Imperial capitalists that they would never resort to its destruction. But that evening, the GPO gleamed brightly as flames enveloped the bombed-out building.

Looters took advantage of the disruption and destruction, and the Volunteers were helpless to stop them. Threats and warning shots had no effect; appeals to their patriotism were ignored. Nothing would deter the maddened crowds who fought among themselves over the booty.

On Friday the 28th, Pearse, apparently enthralled by the thought of his approaching martyrdom, issued another manifesto, addressed to no one in particular lauding the rebels' valiant fight: "For four days they have fought and toiled, almost without cessation, without sleep, and in the intervals of fighting, they have sung songs of the freedom of Ireland. No man has complained; no man has asked 'Why?'...If they do not win the fight, they will at least deserve to win it. But win it they will, although they may win it in death. Already they have won a great thing. They have redeemed Dublin from the many shames and made her name splendid among the names of cities."[41]

A British doctor, captured in the initial fighting, tended James Connolly, whose lower leg had been shattered by a ricocheting bullet. He was lying in a bed set up at the GPO, reading, when his aide, Harry Walpole reported. Connolly looked up and with a grin said, "A book like this, plenty of rest and an insurrection – at the same time – this is revolution deluxe."[42]

The GPO was clearly doomed and the men there worked feverishly through the night, breaking through the walls of adjoining houses in order to escape the bombardment. With the roof of the post office falling in on them, they made their escape and moved their headquarters to No. 16 Moore Street.

As Saturday noon approached Pearse, Clarke, Connolly, and MacDermott decided there had been enough sacrifice and their planned martyrdom was assured. Elizabeth O'Farrell, one of the few women who had remained with the contingent of leaders at the GPO, carried a message to the British seeking terms for a cease-fire. At 12:45 p.m. on Saturday April 29, O'Farrell, waving a white flag, marched along Moore Street North to the British positions. Taken before General Lowe, she notified him that the Volunteers were ready to surrender.

At 2:30 p.m. Pearse parlayed with General Lowe and two of his aides at the corner of Moore and Parnell streets. Lowe demanded unconditional surrender, his only concession being permission for O'Farrell to notify the other commandants of Pearse's surrender order. It was after 4 p.m. before she set off with those orders, which read: "In order to prevent the further slaughter of Dublin citizens and, in the hope of saving the lives of our followers now surrounded and hopelessly outnumbered, the members of the Provisional Government present at Headquarters have agreed to an unconditional surrender and the Commandants of the various districts in the City and Country will order their commands to lay down arms."

Connolly added a postscript: "I agree to these conditions for the men only under my own command in the Moore Street District and for the men in the Stephen's Green Command."[43]

It was 9 p.m. before the men who had served in the Post Office marched through the desolation of O'Connell Street and laid down their arms under the O'Connell monument. Upon surrendering Pearse said, "I am satisfied that we have saved Ireland's honor...We should have accomplished the task of enthroning, as well as proclaiming, the Irish Republic as a Sovereign State had our arrangements for a simultaneous Rising of the whole country, with a combined plan as sound as the Dublin plan has proved to be, been allowed to go through on Easter Sunday."[44]

Pearse was in effect blaming MacNeill's countermanding of the IRB mobilization orders for the failure of the Rising. But it was Stack's dereliction that led to the failure to rendezvous with the *Aud* that doomed the Rising as was generally recognized when the full story came out. "In America, John Devoy refused to defend the deception of MacNeill. '[T]he Military Council were fanatically bent on having their way and this blinded them to the slickness of the methods employed to involve their colleagues and to any moral issue at stake in their resort to what can most mildly be described as equivocation.'"[45]

In his own account, Devoy wrote: "Had the rifles from Germany been landed and distributed in 1916, the Insurrection, instead of being practically confined to Dublin, would have extended all over Ireland... The 'Easter Week' insurrection was foredoomed to military failure with the sinking of the *Aud*."[46] He exonerated MacNeill, pointing out the consequences of Stack's horrific blunder and treachery, and what it would have meant to Ireland if he had carried out his duty: "With these arms in the hands of the Irish, the chaotic conditions which resulted from the sinking of the *Aud*...would never have arisen. MacNeill's final countermanding order would doubtless never have been issued."[47]

Michael Collins, another of the Headquarters party in the GPO, who was destined to lead a successful guerilla campaign against the English, also noted Stack's failure to meet the arms ship as the primary cause of the failure of the Rising. MacNeill's biographer, Michael Tierney, wrote, "Collins did not believe in blood sacrifices being made in order to ensure continuity with the Fenian tradition, irrespective of any hope of success ...With the German arms at the bottom of Queenstown harbor, it must have seemed an act of madness."[48]

The truth was that those directly responsible for the fiasco were Stack, and ultimately the IRB leaders themselves. They were most adroit, however, in casting a cloud over John MacNeill. As he awaited trial in Richmond Barracks, Seán MacDermott said in response to criticism of MacNeill: "He has done what he believed to be good and Ireland will have need of him like the best of her men." Among his last recorded sentences was a plea that "no dishonor should rest on MacNeill's name."[49] The day before his surrender, Pearse said that "[b]oth John MacNeill and we have acted in the best interests of Ireland."[50] Neither Pearse nor MacDermott was averse to lying directly or by implication in order to bring about the ends they sought. In claiming that MacNeill had done what he thought was right, they cleverly insinuated it was in reality MacNeill who had been responsible for the failure of the Rising. Tierney saw through them: "This piece of self-contradictory rhetoric cannot hide the fact that the purpose of the statement was to put on MacNeill the blame for having by his 'fatal countermanding order' prevented 'our arrangements for a simultaneous rising of the whole country.'"[51]

It is not surprising that Pearse and MacDermott would attribute the failure of the Rising to MacNeill rather than admit that their plans were seriously flawed. Incredibly, not one accusatory word was directed at Stack.

The Germans have often been criticized for failing to support the Rising. Though that support was not as extensive as some of the insurgents might have wished, it was what the Germans had agreed to, and they carried out their end of the bargain to the letter. They sent the stated number of guns and delivered them at the time specified; they also launched an airship attack on London on Monday, April 24, and early on that same morning six German airships were sighted north of Cromer on the Norfolk coast, heading toward London. Several hours later a fleet of battle cruisers, light cruisers and destroyers attacked Lowestoft on the Suffolk coast.

British casualties in the Rising numbered 108 killed and 334 more or less seriously wounded. Overall casualties, including civilians, rebels, and military personnel, came to 1,351 killed and at least 2,000 injured. Over two hundred buildings were either damaged or destroyed and more than 100,000 Dubliners required public assistance. The IRB leaders – Pearse, Clarke, Connolly, MacDermott, and Joseph Plunkett – who had established their headquarters at the General Post Office on O'Connell Street – were subsequently tried and executed thereby achieving their planned martyrdom.

Major Ivor Price, chief intelligence officer in Ireland, reported to the investigating Commission on the Rebellion in May 1916 that he had had discussions with government officials prior to the planned insurgency. "I likened myself to John the Baptist preaching in the Wilderness as to taking steps on the subject. The civil authorities did not think it desirable to take steps."[52]

Why didn't they?

Notes
1. Machiavelli, Niccolò, *The Prince* (Translated by W.K. Marriott), J&M Dent & Sons, London 1908, p. 97
2. Coogan, Tim Pat, *De Valera, The Man who was Ireland*, Harper, 1996, p. 43
3. Beaslai, Pieras, *Michael Collins and the Making of a New Ireland*, Vol. I, Harper Bros. NY 1926, Vol., p. 34

4. Bromage, Mary C., *De Valera and the March of a Nation*, Hutchinson, London, 1956, p. 35
5. Longford and O'Neill, *Éamon de Valera*, Arrow Books, London 1974, p. 43
6. Devoy, John, *Recollections of an Irish Rebel*, Irish University Press, Shannon, 1969, p. 414
7. *ibid*, p. 458
8. *ibid*, p. 459
9. Coogan, Tim Pat, *De Valera, The Man who was Ireland*, Harper, 1996, p. 62
10. Tierney, Michael (Ed. F. X. Martin), *Eoin MacNeill: Scholar & Man of Action 1867-1945*, Clarendon Press, Oxford 1980, p. 199
11. Caulfield, Max, *The Easter Rebellion*, Frederick Muller, London, 1963, p. 61
12. Tierney, Michael (Ed. F. X. Martin): Eoin MacNeill, *Scholar & Man of Action 1867-1945*, Clarendon Press, Oxford 1980, p. 202
13. Martin, F.X., "Eoin MacNeill on the 1916 Rising," *Irish Historical Studies*, Vol XII 1961, p. 237
14. Joy, Maurice (Ed.), *The Irish Rebellion of 1916 & Its Martyrs: Erin's Tragic Easter*, Devin-Adair, NY 1916, p. 73
15. *ibid*, p. 74
16. *The New York Times*, April 26,1916
17. Gaughan, J. Anthony, *Austin Stack, Portrait of a Separatist*, Kingdom books, Dublin, 1977, p. 278-9
18. Whelan, John (Seán O'Faoláin), *De Valera*, Penguin Books, England.1939, p. 27
19. Gaughan, J. Anthony, *Austin Stack, Portrait of a Separatist*, Kingdom books, Dublin, 1977, p. 280
20. *ibid*, p. 281
21. Beaslai, Pieras, *Michael Collins and the Making of a New Ireland*, Vol. I, Harper Bros. NY 1926, p. 84
22. Ryan, Desmond, *The Rising*, Golden Eagle Books, Dublin, 1949, p. 69
23. *ibid*
24. Fitzgerald, W.G., *The voice of Ireland, A Survey of the Race & Nation from All Angles*, Virtue Ltd, Dublin/London, p. 123.
25. Ryan, Desmond, *The Rising*, Golden Eagle Books, Dublin, 1949, p. 237
26. *ibid*, p. 80
27. *ibid*, p. 239
28. *ibid*, p. 14
29. Coffey, Thomas M., *Agony at Easter*, Macmillian, NY, 1969, p. 89
30. Ryan, Desmond, *The Rising*, Golden Eagle Books, Dublin, 1949, p. 244
31. Gaughan, J. Anthony, *Austin Stack, Portrait of a Separatist*, Kingdom books, Dublin, 1977, p. 49
32. *ibid*, p. 50
33. *ibid*, p. 61
34. *ibid*

35. *ibid*
36. *ibid*, p. 62
37. Tierney, Michael (Ed. F. X. Martin), *Eoin MacNeill: Scholar & Man of Action 1867-1945*, Clarendon Press, Oxford 1980, p. 203
38. MacManus, M.J., *Éamon de Valera*, Ziff – Davis, 1946, p. 24
39. Joy, Maurice (Ed.), *The Irish Rebellion of 1916 & it's Martyrs*: Devin-Adair, NY 1916, p. 138
40. Coffey, Thomas M., *Agony at Easter*, Macmillian, NY, 1969, p. 80
41. Joy, Maurice (Ed.), *The Irish Rebellion of 1916 & Its Martyrs: Erin's Tragic Easter*, Devin-Adair, NY 1916, p. 120
42. Caulfield, Max, *The Easter Rebellion*, Frederick Muller, London, 1963, p. 311
43. Coffey, Thomas M., *Agony at Easter*, Macmillian, NY, 1969, p. 252
44. Joy, Maurice (Ed.), *The Irish Rebellion of 1916 & it's Martyrs: Erin's Tragic Easter*, Devin-Adair, NY 1916, p. 121
45. Ryan, Desmond, *The Rising*, Golden Eagle Books, Dublin, 1949, p. 84
46. Devoy, John, *Recollections of an Irish Rebel*, Irish University Press, Shannon, 1969, p. 481
47. *ibid, p. 481*
48. Tierney, Michael (Ed. F. X. Martin), *Eoin MacNeill, Scholar & Man of Action 1867-1945*, Clarendon Press, Oxford 1980, p. 257
49. Martin, F.X., "Eoin MacNeill on the 1916 Rising," *Irish Historical Studies*, Vol. XII 1961, p. 263
50. Ryan, Desmond, *The Rising*, Golden Eagle Books, Dublin, 1949, p. 145
51. Tierney, Michael (Ed. F. X. Martin), *Eoin MacNeill: Scholar & Man of Action 1867-1945*, Clarendon Press, Oxford 1980, p. 183
52. Joy, Maurice (Ed.), *The Irish Rebellion of 1916 & it's Martyrs: Erin's Tragic Easter*, Devin-Adair, NY 1916, p. 196

CHAPTER IV
De Valera in Command

"Michael Malone dispatched a courier to de Valera with a request for men, food and ammunition. De Valera responded with a fruit cake and ten bullets."[1]

Apart from the Headquarters post at the General Post Office, the insurgents involved in the Easter Rising were divided into four battalions covering four key areas of the city.

Edmund Daly, with Pieras Beaslai as his vice commandant, commanded the First Battalion holding the Four Courts, a beautiful eighteenth-century building housing barristers' chambers and the High Court. Also under his command were the Mendicity Institute, held by nineteen-year-old Sean Heuston, and Stephen's Green under Michael Mallin and Countess Markiewicz. Daly surrendered on Saturday afternoon, shortly after Pearse's capitulation. Daly, Mallin, and Heuston were tried and executed while Markiewicz was tried and sentenced to death, later amended to penal servitude.

In Leon O'Broin's biography of the prosecutor, *W.E. Wylie and the Irish Revolution 1916-1921*, Wylie states: "...Countess Markiewicz, whom they quite expected would make a scene and throw things at the judge and counsel, in fact, I saw the general getting out his revolver and putting it on the table beside him. But he needn't have troubled, for she curled up completely. She cried, 'I am only a woman, and you cannot shoot a woman. You must not shoot a woman.' She never stopped moaning the whole time she was in the courtroom.

"She had been in command of a contingent of the Irish Citizen Army in the Stephen's Green area and, according to reports, 'had been full of fight, but she crumpled up at the court martial. I think we all felt slightly disgusted. She had been preaching a lot of silly boys death and glory, die for your country, etc and yet she was literally crawling. I won't say any more, it revolts me still.' She was sentenced to death, but was reprieved and died many years later..."[2]

Elsie Mahaffy, daughter of the Provost of Trinity College had this to say about the Countess at her court martial: "All her 'dash' and 'go' left her – she utterly broke down; cried and sobbed and tried to incite pity in General Blackadder, it was a terrible scene – the gaunt wreck of a once lovely lady."[3]

Five years later, during the Free State Treaty debate, Markiewicz engaged in a vitriolic slander against Michael Collins, in which she ridiculed him and boasted of her willingness to die for her Republican principles: "I am opposed to this Treaty...because I stand on my principles as a Republican, as one pledged to the death for the freedom of Ireland..."[4]

Pearse had appointed Éamon de Valera commandant of the Third Battalion, with headquarters at Boland's Bakery and, in addition, as adjutant to the Dublin Brigade Commander, Thomas MacDonagh. De Valera played no part in the actual planning and implementation of the Easter Rising. Without a word, he deserted his men at noon, officially surrendering at 1 p.m. on Sunday, April 30; he was never tried, nor sentenced to death nor reprieved.

De Valera was the only battalion commandant of the Easter Rising to escape trial and execution. Over time, he was cloaked by an Irish mist of fabricated glory. He was portrayed as having personally fought off khaki-clad hordes of English troops attacking his position and lionized as the last commandant to surrender. The saga of his brave vigil after a trial, at which he was allegedly sentenced to death and miraculously reprieved at the last moment was the stuff of legend.

However, it was all a long-running hoax played on the Irish people. The national fervour for martyrdom had left the Irish with no living heroes, so they did not hesitate to invent one. A heroic myth was spun around de Valera, the man who exhibited the worst leadership, poorest judgment, and least faith in the men who risked their lives under his command. An incompetent and neurotic military bungler amid a host of bunglers who participated in the Rising was hailed as a Napoleonic genius.

The perception of de Valera before the Rising was somewhat different than the much loved and respected hero painted by Irish writers. Solemn, long-nosed, gangly, bespectacled: a six-foot-three-inch giant elf clad in a green uniform wearing red socks and topped by a leather aviator's cap with dangling earflaps; he arrived at clandestine Volunteer training camps on his bicycle eliciting snickers of derision and ridicule from the men under his command.

Irish respect for education had ensured his election to the command of a newly formed company, but did not blind the men to his faults. His men lacked respect for de Valera, found him humorless and grim, and made fun of him behind his back. He was equally contemptuous of his subordinates, considering them socially and intellectually inferior. When drilling his men, he even ordered them about in Irish, even though none of them knew the language.[5] As for his later fabled Napoleonic military "genius," the truth is revealed by his prior decision to outfit his men with pikes – those ten-foot spears that had been so ineffective when employed by the Gaels against British longbows centuries earlier. "The blistering curses of those who carried them and the hilarious jibes of Dublin wits soon hustled pole and pike head back to the scrap heap."[6]

John MacNeill's countermand and the hastily announced revised plans for an uprising on Monday, April 24, instead of Sunday, the day before, presumably meant that de Valera, like many others, had little sleep over the weekend as frantic preparations were made for events that were spinning out of control.

On Monday morning, he pedalled directly to his designated headquarters at Boland's Bakery on Grand Canal Street, where 120 men awaited his orders. His area of command ran from Sandymount to Westland Row Train Station, including the Ringsend area and a number of mills, shops, and warehouses. The bakery itself was 150 yards east of Lieutenant Michael Malone's outposts encompassing 24 Northumberland Road, Saint Stephen's Hall, and Clanwilliam House overlooking the Mount Street Bridge.

Little versed in military tactics, de Valera overestimated the importance of his position and struck fear into his nervous and inexperienced troops by claiming they were in imminent danger of a bayonet charge. He ordered the men to maintain battle readiness from sunset to dawn, awaiting an attack that never came. With daybreak he was finally persuaded to allow the men to leave their battle stations to eat and rest. Still convinced that his position was in grave danger of attack by British forces, de Valera ordered the men back to their stations to prepare for a daylight raid. Those who were supposed to be on guard duty were found fast asleep. The men were so exhausted that the officers had a difficult time waking them. At that point "[i]t would have taken little to demoralize them completely...[and] the sight of de Valera's strained and anxious figure did nothing to relieve the jitters which had been so bad during the night that a few men were shot by their own comrades...De Valera...narrowly missed death when he gave the wrong password."[7]

Several of de Valera's biographers confirm his unease. According to Max Caulfield: "Commandant de Valera, already strained and haggard-looking from lack of sleep for the past two nights, roamed about ceaselessly, shotgun in hand, a restless, continually dissatisfied, strangely-odd exotic figure."[8] Tim Pat Coogan quotes the testimony of officers and men who served under de Valera: "Eyewitnesses recalled seeing a tall, gangling figure in green Volunteer uniform and red socks running around day and night without sleep getting trenches dug, giving contradictory orders."[9] Anxiety and lack of sleep did not improve de Valera's leadership abilities, and he appeared to be on the brink of a nervous collapse.

On Thursday at 2 p.m., de Valera ordered Michael Cullen and three men to occupy a water tower several hundred yards from Boland's Bakery and allegedly called for an Irish flag to be hoisted atop the tower. British artillery promptly opened fire and two shells landed within the Bakery confines, one of which did no damage while the other crashed through a wall and destroyed a delivery truck; neither caused any casualties.

Another errant shell whistled over the tower and landed in the Liffey, narrowly missing the British gunship *Helga*. Believing himself to be under attack from the insurgents, *Helga*'s captain responded with a bombardment of his own, and an exchange of salvos arched over the water tower. As the British gunship exchanged crossfire with British artillery, de Valera hop-scotched up and down the railway, laughing hysterically and cheering at the display of English friendly fire falling. The men were less amused, more concerned with what would happen to the tower when the British resumed their bombardment with the men de Valera had ordered still in there.[10] The "Battle of Boland's Bakery" had lasted all of several minutes and consumed less than a dozen shells.

Against later assertions that de Valera's order to fly the flag from the tower was a clever tactical ploy to divert shelling from Boland's Bakery or Liberty Hall must be set the fact that as shells rained down upon the tower, he neglected to withdraw his men. British gunners found its range, but de Valera was dancing while Cullen and his three comrades were left to stagger from the shell-pocked tower as it disintegrated and Liberty Hall demolished. Writing in 1963, Max Caulfield found that the myth lingered on: "The majority...give him the credit for a brilliant stratagem...It was the most critical moment of the week for de Valera. Upon his behavior now was to rest much of his later reputation as a soldier and a leader."[11]

This shelling was the only attack suffered by the Bakery position throughout the entire week. The major hazard at Boland's Bakery, other than British long-range snipers, was the anxiety of waiting for an attack that never came and the tensions generated by de Valera's contradictory commands on his men.[12]

It was different at Mount Street Bridge, 150 yards away, technically within de Valera's area of command but held by Lieutenant Michael Malone and, initially, 13 men, including his four unit commanders – George Reynolds, James Grace, Denis O'Donoghue, and Patrick Doyle.

On Tuesday morning Doyle returned from an inspection of the outlying posts and reported to Malone that the three men assigned to a nearby school had been recalled to Boland's Bakery, seriously weakening their position. Malone dispatched a courier to de Valera with a request for men, food, and ammunition; de Valera responded with a fruitcake and ten rounds of .303 ammunition. The messenger was immediately sent back with an urgent reiteration of his request; Ireland's Napoleon refused to send any men or arms.

Malone deployed his meager resources as best he could. Reynolds, who was suffering from blood poisoning in his left hand from an accident the week before, occupied Clanwilliam House with four men. It was an ideal ambush site, overlooking the Canal and providing an excellent line of fire against anyone attempting to cross the Mount Street Bridge. Doyle and three men occupied Saint Stephen's Parochial Hall, while Malone, with James Grace, occupied 25 Northumberland Road: allowing for the three men who had retreated to the Bakery and Malone having sent two boys home, the Mount Street contingent ultimately consisted of eight men. On Wednesday, April 26, Malone and his little band ambushed a relief column of Sherwood Foresters, recently disembarked from England. The Foresters, nearly two thousand strong, split into two groups, a little over a half taking a circular route into the city while eight hundred men proceeded across the Lower Mount Street Bridge. As if on parade they marched four abreast into the waiting fire of Malone, Grace, Reynolds, and their men. Faced with one-hundred-to-one odds, Malone and the seven men under his command nevertheless took a fearful toll of the Foresters, inflicting half the total number of British casualties sustained during the entire week of fighting.

While the battle raged at Malone's position, the Boland's Bakery garrison sat on its heels and, as evening fell, watched the flames consuming Clanwilliam House. Designated a "keep," its garrison was to maintain its post to the bitter end. It would have been a simple matter for de Valera to deploy some of his men to attack the Sherwood Foresters from the rear; his refusal to do so cast a pall of gloom over the men at the Bakery. They could hear the shouts and curses of Malone and his men as they fought off wave upon wave of British troops; when Mount Street Bridge fell silent and the flames engulfed Clanwilliam House, they knew that that gallant band had perished.

53

Author Desmond Ryan was one of the headquarters party at the General Post Office during the Rising and initially one of the myth makers. In his book *Unique Dictator*, published twenty years after the Rising, he thought it strange that the heroic stand of Malone and his men at Mount Street Bridge had never been told in detail. Stranger still was that de Valera's own actions during that defense had been obscured in rhetorical generalities and a vague halo. Ryan wrote: "From his headquarters and outposts, de Valera directed one of the most important achievements of the Five Days, inflicting serious losses on the attackers, holding up reinforcements sent from England to suppress the outbreak and making his name as one of the most astute and determined of the Irish Volunteer Commandants."[13]

But de Valera had nothing to do with inflicting serious losses on anyone, certainly not on British soldiers. By the time his next book, *The Rising*, was published in 1949, Ryan's position had shifted and he contradicted his earlier claim that de Valera was in the thick of the battle. "De Valera's headquarters was passed in silence. He and his men sat through the long hours listening to the firing at distant commands while they were left to themselves...It was in this area, Mount Street Bridge, that the outstanding action of the week was fought, that more than half the British casualties were incurred and that de Valera first gripped the imagination of Ireland."[14]

Ryan stated that de Valera was nowhere near the action at Mount Street Bridge and that he did nothing to aid the doomed garrison. Acknowledging Malone's outpost received neither men, food nor ammunition from de Valera: Ryan wrote: "No message, no aid reached them from Boland's Bakery...equally, the only news that reached [de Valera's] Third Battalion Headquarters of the greatest fight of Easter Week were the flames roaring high above Clanwilliam House."[15]

In 1936, the same year that Desmond Ryan published his first, lionizing of de Valera's contribution to the Rising, another mytholizer, the American, John Gunther, wrote in *Strand Magazine* that de Valera "had a handful of men in occupation of a place outside Dublin called Boland's Mills. This was a key spot, because the British had to pass it to reach Dublin from the sea. From Boland's Mills a murderous fire raked the British troops. De Valera's men were the best trained, the best led in the Irish Army".[16] The British did not pass Boland's Bakery, nor was there ever a murderous fire raked upon British troops from de Valera's command as his position was out of sight of Mount Street Bridge. When all was said and done, de Valera's men were the worst trained and poorest led of all the insurgent battalions.

De Valera's leadership was questionable from the very first day. Not only were his men at battle stations round the clock but after digging foxholes and setting up defensive positions, they were jarred awake at midnight by shouts of "the enemy is coming." They fired at shadows with an [occasional] answering flash and [the subsequent] quiet left jangled nerves.[17]

Gunther asserted that de Valera's men were the best trained and the best led, but the facts tell a contradictory tale. No other command reported a crazed Volunteer murdering one of his fellow comrades. De Valera's men inflicted more casualties on themselves than were incurred by the English, and when they were not shooting one another, they were clubbing some hapless comrade to prevent his going mad. There were no other instances of a commandant constantly issuing orders and then countermanding them; the sole account during the entire week of men ignoring their commandant was under de Valera's command. He was the only commandant who did not consult his men before surrendering, the only leader who deserted his troops in order to arrange surrender for himself, the only commandant who did not trust his men.

Sam Irwin, a member of de Valera's Third Battalion at Boland's Bakery, accurately summed up the events of that week: "That wasn't much of a fight, but it wasn't the fault of the men. They weren't put into the position to fight. Any trained corporal in today's army would have disposed the troops of Boland's garrison to better effect than de Valera."[18] This was the real de Valera, the "hero" of Boland's Bakery.

A typical example of de Valera's countermanded orders came at midnight on Monday after he instructed Simon Donnelly and a squad of men to scout the area leading from Kingstown for the approach of British reinforcements. Donnelly and his men were loaded down with full equipment, rations, water and rifles and as an added precaution to keep his jittery troops from losing each other in the dark made the men rub flour on the back of the man in front of him. As they were about to move out, de Valera initiated his week-long practice of ordering and canceling brilliant strategies: he changed his mind and rescinded the order and the men returned grumbling.[19]

In contrast to de Valera, with "his fluctuating orders which were to so distinguish his tense, constantly anxious leadership throughout the insurrection...Donnelly...inspired a confidence which 'The Spaniard' in his tense exhausted state was quite unable to arouse."[20]

On Tuesday de Valera was still without sleep, still issuing orders and then almost immediately countermanding them. He did so again in an incident involving orders to relieve the men at Saint Stephens Green. His indecision only underscored the plight of the men under his command. They were anxious to fight; and his on-again-off-again orders pushed them to the brink of physical and mental fatigue.

Late on Friday night de Valera decided to evacuate the Bakery. Donnelly led the men up onto the railway line, from where they had an excellent view of the central positions in O'Connell Street, now ablaze. But "an order came soon after from de Valera to re-occupy the bakery which was held till the surrender,"[21] despite the fact that "the British could have entered it during the Volunteers' absence...De Valera, however, was too far gone in anxiety and exhaustion to evaluate such possibilities by that stage in the fighting."[22]

It was not just his tactics that his men questioned; they questioned his sanity as well. Despite his officers' pleadings, de Valera had not slept in days because he distrusted his men, fearing if he slept they would desert their posts. Lieutenant Joseph Fitzgerald tried to convince de Valera to get some sleep. "I can't trust the men – they'll leave their posts or fall asleep if I don't watch them,"[23] was his response. Seeing their leader walking about in a hallucinatory state hardly instilled confidence in him by his men. Finally de Valera allowed himself to rest; he instantly fell asleep, and almost at once "began to toss restlessly, disturbed by some nightmare. Suddenly, his face beaded with sweat, his eyes wild, he sat bolt upright and in an awful voice, bawled, 'Set fire to the railway! Set fire to the railway!'"[24]

"Believing that he was having a nervous breakdown, de Valera's officers attempted to calm the agitated commandant...but he adamantly demanded that Westland Row Station be torched. Lieutenant John Quinn...questioned de Valera's sanity but obeyed the order nonetheless. Bundles of paper soaked in whisky were tossed into booking offices, waiting rooms and empty trains – and a good blaze had been started."[25] Eventually, Captain John McMahon persuaded de Valera to listen to reason, and the men were ordered into the station to put out the fire, hardly the type of leadership designed to instill faith and confidence in such a man.

His biographer John Whalen recorded that a dazed de Valera: "...took his place at loopholes [openings between the bags of a flour barricade], emptying and re-emptying the magazine of his rifle until, when he did rest, the record shows that the barrel was 'red-hot'"[26] – this was at a time when, according to Joseph O'Connor, one of his officers, "our supplies of ammunition were very limited and we had to restrain our firing until we actually saw the enemy."[27]

According to Desmond Ryan, after running amok with his gun wasting precious ammunition, de Valera sent a frantic message to

MacDonagh, brigade commander and commandant of the Second Battalion at Jacob's Biscuit Factory, that "the situation at Boland's Bakery was somewhat critical. Food was plentiful but ammunition was running low and an attack by the British was expected."[28] Rather than sit on his heels as de Valera had when Malone requested food and reinforcements and when Saint Stephen's Green was pinned down, MacDonagh moved his men out to counter the alleged threat. When they found, after having risked their lives, that there was no substance to de Valera's fears, they returned to the Biscuit Factory muttering over the false alarm.

On Thursday, Donnelly had to restrain a fellow officer, Captain Cullen, who had a nervous breakdown and in his delirium, fired on a colleague. Donnelly knocked him unconscious with a blow to the head with his rifle butt. "The fires [at Clanwilliam House and O'Connell Street], combined with the knowledge that the outpost at Mount Street Bridge had fallen the previous day, had a profoundly depressing effect on everyone, with the man whom Donnelly restrained becoming 'completely shattered.'"[29]

In his early book *Unique Dictator*, Desmond Ryan records a bizarre and somewhat fanciful account of de Valera's conduct and activities during that week: "Despite it all, only 12 men were killed and some twenty wounded," he observed, "...and in this inferno of a Boland's Bakery, fell the gentle Peadar Macken.'"[30] In his later account of the Rising, Ryan contradicts his earlier assessment, asserting that "[o]ne Volunteer grew more and more strange... [W]hen advised to rest he refused and talked louder and louder...Macken several times appealed to the Volunteer with the strangely bright eyes and loud rambling tongue...The man suddenly ran amok and shot Macken through the heart and attacked a sentry who shot him dead."[31] The only "inferno" in which de Valera and his men were involved was of their own making: the whiskey torching of Westland Row train station. Those at Clanwilliam House and Saint Stephen's Parochial Hall, however, knew what an inferno was really like.

There were several other casualties at Boland's Bakery. Tom Scully was shot in the leg by one of his own men when a rifle accidentally went off as they occupied Westland Row Station, while Leo Casey and Charlie Murphy were allegedly shot by sniper fire – whether from friend or foe was never corroborated.

Throughout the entire week, there was but one reported British casualty inflicted by the Boland's Bakery contingent, and it occurred as the men began their occupation of the building on Monday. Tom Walshe was unloading supplies when a British soldier approached and demanded to know what they were doing. Another Irish Volunteer told the soldier to clear out or be shot: the soldier began berating them, and was killed.

Max Caulfield credits the Boland's Bakery contingent with inflicting three more unconfirmed British casualties at Beggars Bush Barracks by means of long-range sniping.[32] Malone had dispatched Grace and two men to the corners of Northumberland and Haddington to cover that Army barracks. At this point, the barracks was in their direct line of fire, and the sniping could just as well have been the work of Malone's men.

Writing about de Valera in 1991, T. Ryle Dwyer asserted: "When the fighting was over, it became apparent that de Valera's men had inflicted the heaviest casualties on the British."[33] If it is accepted that the Mount Street Bridge area was technically part of de Valera's command, this claim is correct, though somewhat disingenuous.

Desmond Ryan, initially an admirer of de Valera and his military prowess, wrote: "...at Boland's, de Valera moved from point to point in the thickest and most dangerous scenes of the conflict, along the railway line, from barricade to barricade, from bullet-swept positions, a tall, tense, inspiring, silent man, except when some curt order or terse expression of indifference to the repeated warnings addressed to him by his affectionate and anxious followers escaped his tightened lips: 'You are our leader, Dev,' urged one officer. 'We don't want to lose you.'"[34]

The picture painted by Caulfield is somewhat different: "Reserved and aloof, even with his officers, everyone respected him for his intellectual powers. However, the rank and file found his manner a little too quick and nervously perceptive for their liking. His tendency to suggest a scheme and then suddenly cancel it failed to enhance their confidence in him as a military leader, although they continued to admire him..."[35]

In his later book *The Rising*, Ryan painted a more accurate picture: "[T]he strain on the small and scattered garrison hourly increased. Nightly they *could see* the glare of the huge fires in the city and *hear the noise* of the distant fighting, the snipers' battles over the O'Connell rooftops, the rattling machine guns, the crash of buildings falling afar off and the shells bursting."[36] The men under de Valera's command could see and hear the danger, but did not have to face it. Far from being raked with fire, Boland's Bakery did not receive a single confirmed British bullet. Coogan noted circumspectly that as late as Saturday, the day Pearse capitulated: "Isolated and, as yet, unchallenged pockets of resistances such as de Valera's command must assuredly soon be attacked."[37] But no attack ever materialized.

Coogan acknowledged the historical loss resulting from de Valera's refusal to record his activities during the Easter week rising: "... It would have been both instructive and valuable to have had from de Valera himself a record of that week which cast him in a more human role than the consistently high-heroic public figure that emerges from his authorized biography."[38] De Valera encouraged the portrayal of himself as the hero of the Rising, but he consistently refused to document his "heroics," doubtless because there were still too many alive who knew the truth: "Probably the most telling comment on de Valera's behavior during 1916 is his own silence...[H]is was a career, which in large measure observed the dictum: 'When the truth becomes legend, print the legend.'"[39] When it suited his purposes, de Valera ignored the truth and condoned the lies.

When word of the surrender arrived, de Valera abandoned his men and slipped out of Boland's Bakery at noon on Sunday April 30, taking with him a British prisoner, Cadet Mackay, and giving himself up to the first British officer he could find. Dwyer noted that "de Valera did not actually surrender with his men..."[40] and in order to save himself, he "...decided that he would have some hope of surviving if he surrendered in the company of Cadet Mackay, living proof that the Irish did not shoot prisoners. Accordingly, he marched out from his men accompanied only by Mackay."[41]

John Whelan, an assiduous de Valera apologist, put his own spin on the incident: "With difficulty, de Valera induced his men to obey the surrender order."[42] In fact, he was the only commandant who did not discuss the surrender and its implications with the men under his command. They were furious when they learned that he had abandoned them and surrendered without a word. After spending a week as spectators, they wanted either to fight or to break out and make for the hills to continue the struggle. "[H]is men heard the news [of the surrender and de Valera's desertion] with incredulity, and had to be convinced that the order came from headquarters before they agreed to surrender."[43]

Coogan saw the position a little more clearly: "[T]here was little bonding in the relationship between de Valera and the handful of working class men who passed that week in hell with him. Clearly, he felt it necessary to withhold, rather than to share his decision to surrender from what were, after all, fellow Volunteers...In the circumstances, the men's anger was understandable."[44] According to Caulfield, "In the end, on the plea that only by surrendering immediately were they likely to save de Valera's life, they gave in..."[45] It seems far-fetched to infer that men deserted by their commandant would surrender to spare his life.

In his early mythologizing book, Desmond Ryan paints de Valera's surrender in even more heroic colours than most Irish writers: "...de Valera and his men held out long after the other strongholds had surrendered...Splashing their medley of rifles, worn, antique and new, into the sweeping angry khaki waves, once in anger, charging down upon a storming party with their crude bayonets and sending the attackers in a panic rout..."[46] This never happened; it is pure fiction. Yet it was this centerpiece – his "gallant," solitary stand against hordes of English soldiers hammering at the gates of Boland's Bakery and as the last commandant to surrender during the 1916 Rising – around which de Valera's subsequent political career was built. De Valera the cowardly, incompetent, mentally unstable officer who deserted his troops was repackaged as de Valera the lonely hero fighting valiantly against overwhelming odds, enabling him throughout his political career to masquerade as the Beowulf of Boland's Bakery.

It is alleged that when Pearse's personal envoy Elizabeth O'Farrell presented the rebel commander's surrender order to de Valera before noon on Sunday April 30, de Valera refused to acknowledge the surrender as authentic without the counter-signature of MacDonagh, the brigade commander. According to Joseph O'Connor, "She took the order back, but she returned very soon and satisfied the Commandant that it was his duty to surrender."[47] She may have returned, but she certainly did not bring with her a surrender order countersigned by MacDonagh for he had refused to accept Pearse's order to surrender, claiming it had been made under duress while Pearse was a prisoner and was thereby invalid. With Pearse's surrender, MacDonagh, as Brigade Adjutant, assumed he was now in charge of the rebellion.

Having slipped away from his men, and with Cadet Mackay as his insurance against being shot before he could surrender, de Valera made his way out of the bakery at noon on Sunday, April 30. On Grand Canal Street, directly opposite Boland's Bakery, he encountered Dr. Myles Keogh, on his way to the hospital there; he told the doctor his name, rank, and his desire to surrender.

De Valera kept his own note of his surrender and what ensued:

Sunday, April 30: Surrender order received and executed 1 p.m.
April 30, 1916: 2 p.m. (Sunday, April 30) to Tuesday, May 2, 1916 [at] Ballsbridge Showgrounds.
Tuesday, May 2 to May 5 [Friday morning]: Richmond Barracks detention Cells;
Friday, May 5 (morning) to Saturday May 6, 1916 (afternoon) Gymnasium, Richmond Barracks;

Saturday May 6, 1916 to Monday May 8, Room 4 (L. Block),
 Richmond Barracks;
Monday, May 8, 9:45 a.m. Trial with Ashe, two Lawlesses, Dr
 Hayes, and a couple of others.
Monday, May 8, 1916; Kilmainham, Cell 59.

Prisoners were generally tried separately after the Rising. Not one of the
men allegedly tried with de Valera ever confirmed that such a trial took
place, and there is no trace in the British Public Record Office at Kew of
any trial, sentence, or commutation of sentence involving de Valera.

As to the assertion that de Valera was the last commandant to
surrender, the truth was again quite different. Thomas MacDonagh
conferred with Brig. General W. H. M. Lowe on Sunday afternoon after
which the General placed his staff car at MacDonagh's disposal to drive
to Eamonn Kent's command post at South Dublin Union to discuss
surrender. "...Finally around 7 p.m. [seven hours after de Valera deserted
his men and surrendered] [MacDonagh], Kent and William Cosgrave
walked over to the South Dublin Union together with General Lowe to
confirm the surrender arrangements."[48]

Thomas MacDonagh was brigade commander and also commandant of
the Second Battalion at Jacob's Factory, where the tall twin towers
provided excellent sniper positions from which to pick off soldiers as
they entered and left Portobello and Richmond barracks. He did not
surrender until after 7:00 p.m. on Sunday, April 30; he was subsequently
tried and executed.

The Fourth Battalion under Edmund Kent occupied the South Dublin
Union, a huge sprawling complex of buildings comprising 52 acres. His
position was never seriously attacked by the British forces; however, his
vice commandant, Charles Burgess, was seriously wounded in a
skirmish. On Sunday afternoon, at 7:30 p.m. six and half-hours after de
Valera, Kent surrendered. He was tried and executed. Burgess was
unable to stand trial because of the seriousness of his wounds.

Writing in 1989, Leon O'Broin refuted Ryan's claims about the
surrender timing: "On Sunday – by which time all the other positions
held by the rebels had capitulated – Lt Evelyn Wylie was directed by
General Carlton to guide two battalions he was sending to force the
surrender of the rebels in Jacob's Factory [MacDonagh's headquarters]
At about 3:30 p.m. [Sunday, 30 April] it was announced that the rebels
[at Jacob's Biscuit Factory] had surrendered. Then, the [Jacobs Biscuit]
bakery garrison, about 120 in all, came down the street where Wylie was
positioned with MacDonagh and John MacBride at their head. ...They

stood in front of their men talking and laughing until another contingent of rebels marched in under Edmund Kent [after 7:30 p.m.]..."[49]

Notes

1. Caulfield, Max, *The Easter Rebellion*, Frederick Muller, London, 1964, p. 177
2. Coffey, Thomas M, *Agony at Easter*, Macmillian, NY, 1969, p. 260
3. Townshend, Charles, *Easter 1916*, Penguin Books, London 2006, p. 286
4. *New York Times*, 1/4/1922, 3:2
5. Coogan, Tim Pat, *De Valera, The Man who was Ireland*, Harper, 1996, p. 54
6. Ryan, Desmond, *Unique Dictator*, Arthur. Barker, London, 1936, p. 35
7. Caulfield, Max, *The Easter Rebellion*, Frederick Muller, London, 1963, p. 277
8. *ibid*, p. 255
9. Coogan, Tim Pat, *De Valera, The Man who was Ireland*, Harper, 1996, p. 69
10. Caulfield, Max, *The Easter Rebellion*, Frederick Muller, London, 1963, p. 281
11. *ibid*, p. 280
12. Coogan, Tim Pat, *De Valera, The Man who was Ireland*, Harper, 1996, p. 67
13. Ryan, Desmond, *Unique Dictator*, Arthur. Barker, London, 1936, p. 44
14. Ryan, Desmond, *The Rising*, Golden Eagle Books, Dublin, 1949, p. 187
15. *ibid*, p. 199
16. Gunther, John, "The Truth About de Valera", *Strand Magazine*, June/July 1936, p. 265
17. Caulfield, Max, *The Easter Rebellion*, Frederick Muller, London, 1963, p. 161
18. Tierney, Michael (Ed. By F.X. Martin), *Eoin MacNeill: Scholar & Man of Action 1867-1945*, Clarendon Press, Oxford 1980
19. Caulfield, Max, *The Easter Rebellion*, Frederick Muller, London, 1963, p. 194
20. *ibid*, p. 277
21. Ryan, Desmond, *The Rising*, Golden Eagle Books, Dublin, 1949, p. 192
22. Coogan, Tim Pat, *De Valera, The Man who was Ireland*, Harper, 1996, p. 71
23. Caulfield, Max, *The Easter Rebellion*, Frederick Muller, London, 1963, p. 318
24. *ibid*, p. 319
25. *ibid*
26. Whelan, John (Seán O'Faoláin), *De Valera*, Penguin Books, England 1939, p. 32
27. O'Connor, Joseph, 'Boland's Mills Area,' *Capuchin Manuel 1966*, p. 248
28. Ryan, Desmond, *The Rising*, Golden Eagle Books, Dublin, 1949, p. 170
29. Coogan, Tim Pat, *De Valera, The Man who was Ireland*, Harper, 1996, p. 71
30. Ryan, Desmond, *Unique Dictator*, Arthur. Barker, London, 1936, p. 53
31. Ryan, Desmond, *The Rising*, Golden Eagle Books, Dublin, 1949, p. 191
32. Caulfield, Max, *The Easter Rebellion*, Frederick Muller, London, 1963, p. 280
33. Dwyer, T. Ryle, *Éamon de Valera*, Gill & Macmillan, 1980, p. 7
34. Ryan, Desmond, *Unique Dictator*, Arthur. Barker, London, 1936, p. 51

35. Caulfield, Max, *The Easter Rebellion*, Frederick Muller, London, 1963, p. 195
36. Ryan, Desmond, *The Rising*, Golden Eagle Books, Dublin, 1949, p. 191
37. Coogan, Tim Pat, *De Valera, The Man who was Ireland*, Harper, 1996, p. 73
38. *ibid*, p. 67
39. *ibid*, p. 72
40. Dwyer, T. Ryle, *De Valera, The Man & the Myths*, Poolbeg, Dublin, 1991, p. 16
41. Coogan, Tim Pat, *De Valera, The Man who was Ireland*, Harper, 1996, p. 73
42. Whelan, John (Seán O'Faoláin), *De Valera*, Penguin Books, England 1939, p. 37
43. Coogan, Tim Pat, *De Valera, The Man who was Ireland*, Harper, 1996, p. 73
44. *ibid*, p. 74
45. Caulfield, Max, *The Easter Rebellion*, Frederick Muller, London, 1963, p. 355
46. Ryan, Desmond, *Unique Dictator*, Arthur. Barker, London, 1936, p. 53
47. O'Connor, Joseph, "Boland's Mills Area," *Capuchin Manuel*, 1966, p. 251
48. Townshend, Charles, *The Irish Rebellion*, Penguin Books, London, 2006, p. 250
49. O'Broin, L., *W.E. Wylie and the Irish Revolution*, Macmillan, 1989. p19

CHAPTER V

Death or a Deal

The most intriguing question arising out of the 1916 Rising was raised not by an execution, but by the failure to carry one out.

The prison-bound rebels were bombarded with barrages of rotten fruit and rocks hurled over the heads of their military escorts by black-shrouded women shrilling obscenities while trying to break through the ranks of the military. It was only British bayonets that prevented them from physically attacking the "bloody Shinners."

The men were astonished, saddened, and angry at the virulent reaction of the people. Depressed and on the verge of a nervous breakdown, de Valera considered the "cause" of Irish freedom dead and his attempt to rid the country of the English oppressor had been all in vain.[1] The rebels' farcical proclamations and their claim to represent the provisional government of an independent Irish republic were met with derision. Political and press reactions were hostile in the extreme.

One of the most effective means of persuading men to give evidence against their comrades was employed by Major Ivor Price, the British intelligence officer at Dublin Castle reporting directly to General John Maxwell. He paraded prisoners in front of a mock firing squad. By threats and intimidation, he aimed to turn as many Irish rebels as he could, from John MacNeill, chief of staff of the Irish Volunteers, to mere boys. According to a *New York Times* account, the nationalist John Dillon informed the House of Commons in Westminster, "…Men had been threatened with death unless they gave evidence against comrades. In one case, a 15-year-old boy was ordered to give evidence. He said, 'I won't,' and the officer said, 'You will be shot.' The boy replied, 'Shoot away.' The boy was then blindfolded and taken away and was asked again to inform, but replied 'No.' He was then made to hear the click of rifles. Afterward the bandages were taken from his eyes and he was sent home."[2]

MacNeill related how Price had walked him in front of a firing squad, an obvious hint of what awaited him. Upon his return to his cell, Price told MacNeill that he could guarantee he would not be executed if he became an informer. For his freedom, MacNeill was to implicate John Dillon and Joseph Devlin, also a Member of Parliament, with complicity in the Rising. MacNeill wrote, "... [T]hey intended to make a clean sweep... I learned that the trench that was dug to receive the bodies of those who were to be executed was capable of holding about 300."[3]

Price himself admitted to "...having endeavored to secure statements from a prisoner under threat of execution."[4] If Major Price was brazen enough to attempt to turn MacNeill and callous enough to place a fifteen-year-old boy as well as others before a firing squad, it is not unreasonable to assume he would not have hesitated to do the same with de Valera. Price could grimly point out the bullet-pitted wall where in previous days eight of de Valera's comrades-in-arms had been dispatched into the lime pits of General John Maxwell's Arbour Hill prison cemetery. In his already stressed condition, and the morning after his jailhouse court martial, de Valera must have trembled at the thought of his present fate and his impending launch into eternity.

Imprisoned for over a week for his part in the Easter Rising, de Valera had more than ample time to reflect on his past, to contemplate what might have been, to ponder his imminent doom. Abandoned by father, mother, aunt, and uncle, ridiculed by children because of his "foreign" looks, and spurned for his illegitimacy, he recalled the anguish of his lonely youth.

Four times he sought solace within the fraternity of the priesthood, only to be dismissed by the hierarchy because of his illegitimacy. The teaching profession had often denied him grades and positions to which the superior qualifications he deluded himself he possessed entitled him. He was rejected for educational posts by a bigoted Irish society perceiving him to be Jewish.

Reflecting upon the failed insurrection, he cursed the Irish people for their acrimonious repudiation of the rebels' bid to overthrow English rule. "If only the people had come out with hay forks," he had cried upon surrendering. The sacrifice of the men who took part in the rebellion had been squandered on a people undeserving of freedom. They sided with the British oppressors, they scoffed at the "cause" and scorned the Irish Republic. The dream and faith of the men of Easter Week died before the firing squads in Stonebreakers Yard; the "cause" no longer existed.

The only solace de Valera had found during his short life was not in the gospels of Matthew, Mark, Luke, or John but in *The Prince*, Machiavelli's bible of political revelations, a blueprint that revealed the true path to success and power in a cruel and heartless world ruled by wicked men. His looming death; the trauma of martyrdom; the reality of the firing squad; the thought of bullets tearing through his body for a rejected cause, made his sacrifice meaningless. The fight for freedom was a lost cause; his comrades-in-arms had surrendered, and all the leaders had been executed.

Fear and despair alone are not sufficient to account for the closeness which seems to have developed between de Valera and Major Price. Doubtless, Price was skilled at manipulating weakness. Perhaps, he also fulfilled the paternal role which was so painfully absent from de Valera's life. He was already a mature man of 34 with four small children but he seems always to have been detached from his family. Fatherhood may even have revealed to him his difficulty connecting with others and his corresponding desire to belong to someone. De Valera's schooldays with the Christian Brothers at Charleville would have groomed him to obey a powerful yet remote father-figure like Price who pushed all the right buttons.

Did Price make de Valera an offer he could not refuse? Or, did de Valera, the political realist and student of Machiavelli's *The Prince*, decide that he was not prepared to die for the Irish who had done nothing but ridicule and reject him all his life and offer Price his services in exchange for his life?

It was most likely in Stonebreakers Yard while facing a mock firing squad that Éamon de Valera, forsaking martyrdom, made his Faustian bargain with the devil, Major Ivor Price, and chose a lifetime of treachery? In any event, he was not tried; he was not executed. He was alive; he had survived. Machiavelli was right!

On the evening of Monday May 1, Lieutenant William E. Wylie was ordered to begin prosecuting the prisoners at military courts martial the following day. Having had scant time to prepare, he duly reported to General C. G. Blackadder, president of the court, at Richmond Barracks on Tuesday morning.

The standard court martial procedure rendered no formal sentence during the trial. Prisoners were not permitted lawyers, nor allowed to submit any evidence in their defence.

In the course of proceedings, Wylie made use of the reports and witness accounts submitted by the "G" Division, the political department of the Dublin Metropolitan Police dealing with subversive activities, by the Royal Irish Constabulary, and by Price's military intelligence.[5] Relying on these records, he prosecuted a startling twenty-two cases that first day. Clarke, Pearse, and MacDonagh were convicted and sentenced to die by firing-squad. They were notified of their sentences that evening in their cells at Kilmainham Gaol, and executed the following morning.

All courts martial were tried at Richmond Barracks; men sentenced to death were subsequently transferred to Kilmainham Gaol, where executions took place the following dawn in Stonebreakers' Yard. Fourteen men were executed there between May 3 and 12.

The New York Times took a close interest in the procedures involved, reporting on May 7: "... The judgment [of the Court] is laid before General Sir John Maxwell for confirmation...He never has failed to peruse the evidence himself before putting the final seal on a sentence...The confirmed judgment is promulgated by an Army officer and the following morning the condemned prisoner is shot ..."[6]

Maxwell familiarized himself with the conduct of each and every one of the men sentenced to death. If de Valera had been one of these, Maxwell would presumably have scrutinized his record as he had all the others, and discovered his involvement in the British debacle at Mount Street Bridge. He certainly would have been familiar with de Valera's name and activities when he dined with Wylie on May 8, the evening of de Valera's alleged court martial and sentence of death. Yet Maxwell told Wylie that evening that he had never heard of de Valera, and Wylie later confirmed that de Valera had never faced a court martial or sentence of death.

If what he claimed was true, by May 8, Maxwell must have been the only man in Dublin unaware of the fact that de Valera had – technically, at least – been in charge of the area in which the English military had suffered half of all casualties reported that week. De Valera was falsely credited with Michael Malone's exploits at Mount Street Bridge against the Sherwood Foresters, and his name was being bandied about in newspaper headlines. It is too great a stretch of the imagination to believe that Maxwell, as commanding officer, failed to insist on a report as to who was responsible for the bloodbath at Mount Street Bridge. Every intelligence department in Ireland must have been keen to expose the leader of the men who had apparently inflicted such horrendous casualties on British troops. Two of the officers sitting on the court martial panel were Sherwood Foresters. It is not hard to imagine what sentence they would have recommended for the commandant of the men at Mount Street Bridge if he had appeared before them.

Yet, while the commandants of the First, Second and Fourth Battalions were tried and executed, the commandant of the Third Battalion was not. Why didn't the authorities insist that he appear at a court martial?

It is a popular fallacy that de Valera escaped court-martial and execution because he was relatively unknown. At the time of de Valera's screening on May 5 at the Richmond Barracks Gymnasium, the Dublin Police, the Royal Irish Constabulary, and Major Price's military intelligence were all well aware of his seditious activities prior to the Rising, his position in the Volunteers and his area of responsibility during the Rising. In his early book about de Valera, Desmond Ryan gave the lie to any claim that his subject was not well known: "As the insurrection drew near, de Valera was one of the best known Volunteer Commandants in Dublin and, as Adjutant to Thomas MacDonagh, one of the most important. He was so important that in the absence of Pearse or MacDonagh, it was to de Valera that MacNeill, as Chief of Staff, at a critical stage had to send his orders to call off any movements in Dublin."[7]

Had de Valera actually faced a court martial, his activities would have fallen within Maxwell's criteria for execution – the shooting of His Majesty's troops. The Dublin Metropolitan Police (DMP) and the Royal Irish Constabulary (RIC) maintained detailed daily records of all training exercises carried out by the Volunteers, and de Valera was one of the more active and recognized leaders, drilling locally and in the outlying districts of Dublin. "Granite" and "Chalk" were pseudonyms of two spies specifically assigned to de Valera. They made frequent reports on his activities, his membership in seditious organizations, involvement in drill instructions and in arms manufacture and distribution.

"Early in February 1916, the police were able to identify nine Volunteers who led 200 men with rifles from Blackhall Place to Phoenix Park on a skirmish, lasting, according to police reports, from evening till two in the morning. Among the nine listed was the name of "Edward de Valera."[8]

If there was a court martial, the documents should be available in the Public Record Office at Kew, as they are for James Connolly and others. Connolly's records read: "At Dublin this 8th day of May 1916... I hereby convene a Field General Court Martial to try the said persons [Connolly and MacDermott]... Signèd: Sir John Maxwell, General, Commanding the Forces in Ireland.

The accompanying report, dated May 9, 1916, states: Offenses Charged:

Alternative 1: ...to wit [Connolly] did take part in an armed rebellion and in the waging of war against His Majesty The King, such act being of such a nature as to be calculated to be prejudicial to the Defense of the Realm and being done with the intention and for the purpose of assisting the enemy.

Alternative 2: Did attempt to cause disaffection among the civilian population of His Majesty.

A later note reads: "Sentences of death passed on James Connolly and John MacDermott were carried out this morning [May 12, 1916]. As previously reported, these men were tried on May 9 and sentence was confirmed by me (Maxwell) on that date."[9]

The report of Connolly's court martial contains no surprising or unusual information, nothing that could be held to threaten national security. The reason for delaying his execution was that Connolly had been seriously wounded: he had to be transported in an ambulance to Kilmainham Gaol and propped up in a chair before being shot along with MacDermott. All others executed had been notified the evening of their trial and shot the following morning.

The charges against Connolly and MacDermott applied still more strongly to de Valera, yet no charges were ever brought against him.

On May 8 (the date de Valera was allegedly court martialed and sentenced to death) W. Evelyn Wylie, the court prosecutor, was invited to dine with General Maxwell at the Royal Hospital: "After dinner, Wylie could see that Maxwell was in a bit of a splutter. 'Read this,' the General said, handing me [Wylie] a telegram. It was from Asquith, the Prime Minister, and said that the executions must stop at once."[10] O'Broin went on to admit he exaggerated: "The telegram was probably not quite so emphatic, but expressed Asquith's hope that the executions would soon be completed unless in some quite exceptional case."[11] Obviously, de Valera was not such a case.

One of few Irish writers to question why de Valera had not faced a firing squad, Leon O'Broin noted: "Commandants of other areas had been executed...and none of them had inflicted such heavy losses on the state forces as de Valera's volunteers had done in the Mount Street district ..."[12]

Extensive research among the Asquith Papers at the Bodleian Library in Oxford revealed no trace of the copy Asquith must surely have kept of any such telegram ordering Maxwell to halt the executions. But They do contain a suggestive memo. It is not a copy of a telegram (though it is perhaps a note of one to be sent), it is addressed to no one in particular, and is undated. Yet, it would not be unreasonable to assume it was meant for General Maxwell and that it was sent on May 8, a day on which four men were executed and on the day of which de Valera had allegedly been tried.

The note runs: "From: 10 Downing Street, Whitehall SW: Four men shot this morning feel that it is my duty to represent grave danger of general and bitter resentment. Vengeance on for comparatively little. Reassuring statement needed without delay."[13] The executions were not halted, but continued even while Asquith visited Dublin on May 12.

After showing Wylie Asquith's "telegram," Maxwell asked Wylie who was next on his list for court martial, no doubt wondering whether there was anyone likely to be executed. Wylie named de Valera but Maxwell claimed he never heard of him. Wylie explained that he was in Command of Boland's Bakery in the Ringsend area but failed to mention that Mount Street Bridge, the scene of the ambush that had killed and wounded so many British soldiers, was in the area under de Valera's command. Maxwell asked if he would be the source of any further trouble in the future. Wylie responded, "I wouldn't think so, sir. I don't think he is important enough. From all I can hear, he is not one of the leaders."

"All right then," said the commander-in-chief. "Stop now except for the public trials..."[14] Maxwell did not order the secret courts martial to stop. They continued beyond May 24; a total of 171 were tried, with 161 convictions.

It is a reasonable deduction that a recommendation made by Price, with the consent of General Maxwell but without the knowledge of the prosecutor, Wylie, spared de Valera. What did the English expect – and what did they receive – from de Valera? Speculation as to why de Valera had not been executed simmered throughout his political career, yet the most logical explanation – that he had made a deal with Price and became an English spy was never mooted. Irish writers propounded a multitude of theories as to why he escaped the firing squad: because he was an American; because he was initially interned at Ballsbridge Showgrounds instead of Richmond Barracks; because public opinion halted the executions before his sentence could be carried out; because he was only a schoolmaster; because he was not an active member of the IRB; because he was not a signatory of the Proclamation; because he was unknown to the authorities; or because of American intervention on his behalf. Every assertion proved false.

The simple truth is that de Valera was never court martialed; with no court-martial there could be no death sentence; with no death sentence, there could be no reprieve. Yet he was moved to Kilmainham Gaol ostensibly to await his execution: clearly the British wished to create the impression that de Valera had been tried and sentenced. If de Valera had not entered into a compact with the English, why the elaborate charade? It would have been a simple matter for the English to have put him through a sham trial, but de Valera was probably too emotionally fragile to face a court martial. The most intriguing question arising out of the 1916 Rising was raised not by an execution, but by the failure to carry one out.

General Sir John Maxwell, commander, English forces in Ireland, proclaimed martial law throughout Ireland. Immediately upon the cessation of hostilities, courts martial were initiated for the rebels. It was later charged that General Maxwell had been merciless in his enforcement of martial law. However, out of approximately fifteen hundred men who ultimately participated in the Dublin Rising, only fourteen (less than 1 percent) were executed by firing squad. The executions were agonizingly spread out over a ten-day period, during which time public opinion slowly turned in favour of the rebels.

According to correspondence with Prime Minister Henry Asquith, General Maxwell's criterion for inflicting the "extreme penalty" on any rebel was whether he was a "leader of the movement or a commander of rebels who were engaged in the shooting down of His Majesty's troops and subjects." Yet, Éamon de Valera, commandant of the Third Battalion and second in command to the overall commander of the Dublin Brigade, credited with having inflicted half of all the casualties suffered by the British forces during the Easter Rising, was never tried, never sentenced to death, and never reprieved. This alone presents ample justification for speculation as to a conspiracy.

After the Rising, nearly two thousand suspects were either imprisoned, tried, or executed. The English were not overly concerned by any reactions in Ireland; it was to the United States she looked for salvation at a time when the outcome of the war with Germany was very much in doubt. In America there was widespread approval of the executions, as just deserts for rebels who would stab their mother country in the back as the Germans were grinding a generation of English youth into the mud of Flanders. The number of executions was not regarded as unduly excessive.

A *New York Times* editorial dated May 4, reflected the prevailing public opinion regarding the Irish insurrection: "War is a stern business and the subject who sets himself against the Government when the nation is straining every resource to overcome enemies in the field, can hardly expect mercy...The ally at home of the enemy abroad confesses himself a traitor.... Great Britain is engaged in a terrible war, of which the end is not yet in view. It can hardly be doubted that in like circumstances, any other Government would, in like manner, have enforced the law in its full rigor."

Britain's very existence hung in the balance. The Irish failed to understand that the British, in allowing the insurrection to take place, were after bigger game – American public opinion and to counter John Devoy and the Irish-Americans who were engaged in orchestrating a cacophony of protests designed to rupture Anglo-American relations. The American people had to be persuaded to enter the war on the side of England and the Allies.

As Maxwell and Wylie were dining, de Valera was supposedly languishing in Kilmainham Gaol awaiting General Maxwell's decision on a death sentence reportedly handed down at his court martial that very morning. Wylie could hardly have informed Maxwell that de Valera was next in line for court martial if he had already been prosecuted that very day. De Valera's biographers accepted de Valera's contention that he had been tried, sentenced to death and reprieved at the last moment, and all, with the exception of O'Broin, ignored or discounted prosecutor Wylie's attestation confirming the lack of a court martial for de Valera. There is no evidence that Maxwell ever reviewed a death sentence passed upon de Valera. Wylie's papers might have thrown further light on the matter, but Public Record Office officials claim that in 1941 Wylie allegedly destroyed his papers relating to those times. However, two important letters from Wylie were discovered in the Public Record Office at Kew and are described below.

Another suggestive item in the Asquith papers is a note from General Maxwell dated May 9, apparently in reply to something from the prime minister. It reads in part: "I have confirmed no death sentence unless I have been convinced by the evidence that the *convict was either a leader of the movement or a commander of rebels who were engaged in shooting down His Majesty's troops and subjects* [emphasis added]. Today, May 9, there still remain to be tried, Connolly and McEgmott [obviously MacDermott]. If convicted, they must suffer the extreme penalty. This will be the last to suffer capital punishment as far as I can now state. Any cases of proved murder of soldiers or police in the execution of their duty, which have or may occur, are, of course, excepted by me."[15] De Valera was allegedly tried prior to Connolly and MacDermott.

In the House of Commons on May 11, 1916 the Prime Minister specifically endorsed Maxwell's right to use his own judgment as to who should – or should not – be executed. Asquith never countermanded a single Maxwell execution order. The Prime Minister was quoted in the *Manchester Guardian* the next day: "There is not the least intention on the part of the Government...to interfere with or in any way control...Sir John Maxwell's discretion...I am personally perfectly satisfied with the manner in which General Maxwell has discharged his duties."[16] It was further reported that Asquith actually favoured the death penalty for certain men and "was unable to reconcile it with his conscience or his judgment that differential or preferential treatment should be accorded in the case of men of equal guilt."[17] His conscience obviously didn't bother him over the differential and preferential treatment of de Valera.

At a Cabinet session on May 6, Asquith iterated his support for Maxwell's criteria: "Death was only to be inflicted on ringleaders and proved murderers and...it was understood that Maxwell must have discretion in individual cases ..."[18] On May 9, it was reported that "... General Maxwell's instructions, which conformed to his [Asquith's] own judgment, were to sanction the inflicting of the extreme penalty as sparingly as possible and only in the case of responsible persons guilty in the first degree."[19] De Valera reportedly had been tried the day before and was credited with being responsible for half of all British casualties.

On May 12, it was reported that the Prime Minister divided those to be executed into three categories: "The first was composed of those who signed the proclamation of the provisional government and were the leaders of the actual rebellion in Dublin. Of these, five out of seven had suffered the extreme penalty. [Connolly and MacDermott were executed after this report was written.]

"The second class consisted of those who were in command of the rebels actually shooting down troops and police. Of these, there were four commandants. The third class comprised men like Thomas Kent who had been guilty of murder in a separate incident in the city of Cork."[20]

These criteria were not consistently adhered to: Patrick Pearse's 19-year-old brother Willie was executed, as was Sir Roger Casement, yet neither was a leader nor were they responsible for deaths or casualties of British troops. De Valera was technically responsible for the deaths of many Sherwood Foresters at Mount Street Bridge – yet de Valera never faced a court martial.

Another popular explanation for de Valera's otherwise incomprehensible escape from execution is that he was initially held at Ballsbridge Show Grounds, a convenient holding pen close to Boland's Bakery area, until he and his men could be marched directly to the prison at Richmond Barracks. De Valera was segregated from his men and confined to a separate room during his stay at the fair grounds. His biographer Tim Pat Coogan puts it thus: "The time lapse involved before he was transferred to Richmond Barracks for court-martial meant that it was May 8, 1916 before his case was dealt with. By then, the pendulum of public opinion was swinging against the policy of executions and in his favour."[21]

Coogan assumed de Valera had faced a court martial and had been sentenced to death. Not one Irish writer questioned why the "pendulum of public opinion" did not swing similarly for those executed on and after May 8. De Valera arrived at Richmond Barracks on May 2. The initial courts martial of Pearse, MacDonagh, and Clarke and nineteen others took place that very day. The following day, Price interrogated MacNeill there. There is no record of him having interrogated the Third Battalion commandant.

Papers relating to the 1916 courts martial are embargoed until the year 2016. At the same time, Public Records officials maintain that no records exist of a de Valera court martial. What can be so sensitive about the Easter Rising that it must be kept from public inspection for more than a century?

Roger Nixon, a professional researcher working at Kew and familiar with the Public Record Office stated: "What I still cannot understand is why there are so many military and civilian courts martial but none showing de Valera...in an Irish State Paper of October 1916, listing the Field General Courts Martial for Complicity in the Irish Revolt 1916...and 'List of Persons sentenced by Court Martial'...Despite a thorough trawl through everything relevant, I have been unable to find a court martial report for Éamon de Valera. Nobody on the PRO staff can explain its absence ..."[22] Its absence can be attributed to the fact that de Valera was never court martialed.

William Evelyn Wylie, King's Counselor, and prosecutor of the Irish rebels in 1916, emphatically declared on at least two occasions that de Valera was never court martialed. In a letter of Wylie's which survived his alleged destruction of his official papers, a copy of which is in the Public Record Office,[23] he vehemently rebuts the account of a de Valera court martial set forth in an article by Mary Bromage, in "The de Valera Story," which appeared in the *Sunday Independent* on December 2, 1956.[24] She quotes de Valera describing his court martial in explicit and minute detail. Wylie hotly refuted both her facts and her conclusions. Bromage claimed that Wylie was a Captain born in Northern Ireland and educated at Trinity College and noted his fairness despite his Northern Ireland origins.[25] She conjured up a court martial scene in which a British officer, Captain Hitzen testified against de Valera. No cross-questioning was permitted and within minutes the court martial was concluded as "the prisoner [de Valera], with unbowed head and steady stare, watched the proceedings in which he was punished. Like the rest, he was sentenced to death."

Wylie's response was succinct: "I was not born in the North. I was never a Captain [He was a Lieutenant at the time of the court martial].

I did not prosecute de Valera! I record this [that de Valera was never tried] because apparently it is again being raised that de Valera was prosecuted and got away on some such plea as that he was an American citizen. That is quite untrue. Many years ago I wrote why there was no prosecution against him."[25] According to his biographer Leon O'Broin, Wylie was emphatic on this last point: "de Valera's American connections were not mentioned, as was so often said later."[26]

Eight years after the appearance of Mary Bromage's article, in a letter dated April 30, 1964, Wylie was even more adamant that de Valera had never been court martialed: "I think I should record an incident that happened yesterday. In the ante-room before the Punchestown Lunch, [a horse breeders' and racing association] the President [Mr. De Valera] spoke to me and said; "You prosecuted (me) in 1916 and a man is inquiring from me at present what I said and how I defended myself at that time. I cannot recollect anything about it or who was there or what was said. Do you remember? "I very bluntly said, 'You were not prosecuted at that time and there is nothing to remember!'"[27] Ten years later, Lord Longford and Thomas O'Neill, de Valera's official biographers, stated that de Valera recalled his court martial in great detail; it is perhaps significant that his account, as related by his biographers, mirrored Mary Bromage's fantasy.[28]

If de Valera was never tried, he could not have been sentenced to death; if he was not sentenced to death, he could not have been reprieved. Yet Irish writers and the Irish President have continued to perpetuate the hoax of de Valera's "valiant and lonely vigil" awaiting a death sentence that never was. John Whelan wrote: "… since it [the story of the court martial, etc] is sponsored by Mr. De Valera himself, we may presume it to be accurate."[29]

Even Tim Pat Coogan was apparently taken in by Bromage's false allegations. He wrote: "The [de Valera] court-martial itself was a brief affair. Evidence was given that he was in charge of his post, that he had been born in New York and that Cadet Mackay had been treated properly whilst a prisoner. He was then taken to Cell No. 59 in Kilmainham Gaol to await the verdict; his comrades had been executed in the jail yard…."[30]

No evidence documenting a de Valera court martial has ever been produced: nor has anyone allegedly tried with him ever confirmed any of his claims, a point conceded by John Whelan: "We gather very little about de Valera from the records of those who were jailed with him."[31]

Wylie did not prosecute de Valera, but he was relentless in his prosecution of John MacNeill. Summing up, he presented a case history of MacNeill's involvement in the Volunteer Movement: MacNeill was "the President of the Irish Volunteers, the editor of their newspaper, the maker of their speeches and obviously the brain of the enterprise... he was the forefront, the 'essential man' in the organization."[32] MacNeill avoided the death penalty because the prosecution was unable to produce evidence of collusion between MacNeill and the Germans, or of his direct responsibility for the death of a single British soldier; he was convicted on a lesser charge based on his orders as Volunteer Commander-in-Chief. MacNeill was only charged with "inciting to rebellion" and convicted on the basis of documents signed over his signature: John MacNeill, Chief of Staff of the Irish Volunteers[33] – could these have been the documents found on Stack after he was arrested?

MacNeill's dispatch to de Valera calling for a halt to any movements leading to the rebellion clearly implicated de Valera as a major player. Given his zeal in prosecuting MacNeill, why did Wylie ignore de Valera? Evidently, it had been decided not to try him. If so, why and by whom?

John Gunther, in his article "The Truth about de Valera," published in 1936, claimed: "de Valera was saved from execution after the Easter Rebellion in 1916 purely because the British Military Tribunal had no wish to alienate American opinion by shooting an American citizen."[34] Gunther ignored the fact that one of the first men shot in consequence of the Rising was a fifty-nine-year-old naturalized-American citizen named Thomas Clarke. The United States Government considered the Easter Rebellion an internal English matter and refused to become involved at that time.

On July 7, 1916, more than two months after the Rising, President Woodrow Wilson responded to an increasingly vocal Senate appeal on behalf of *Americans of Irish birth* being held by the British in Ireland. In a direct reply to Democratic Senator James D. Phelan of California, Wilson said: "*American citizens of Irish birth* [emphasis added] have been arrested and held without trial and there are reports that one such citizen has been condemned by court-martial to capital punishment... Where the fate of an American citizen was involved, I have secured favorable action..."[35]

Wilson cannot have been referring to de Valera, who was an *Irish citizen of American birth*, and had supposedly been tried two months earlier; nor to Thomas Clarke, who was indeed an *American citizen of Irish birth* but who had been executed on May 2. He can only have been referring to Diarmuid Lynch, a naturalized American held by the British and known to be under threat of execution.

There remains an interesting point to note in connection with de Valera's American citizenship. In a letter of July 11, 1916, to Frank

Hughes, de Valera's wife Sinead wrote: "... He [de Valera] could have shared the death sentence with the others only I got the American Consul to intervene on his behalf. I had his baptismal certificate showing that he had been born in America and that he had never taken out naturalization papers here [Ireland]. So he was an American citizen ..."[36] Sinead seems to have been following a script. In fact, at the time of de Valera's alleged trial and sentence of death early in May, over two months before Sinead's letter to Hughes, his American birth certificate listed him as "George" de Valera. In June 1916, his mother Kate had the name on the birth certificate changed from "George" to "Edward" in an effort to convince the authorities it was really de Valera's birth certificate. Furthermore, any citizen taking part in a foreign war as an officer was automatically deprived of his American citizenship.

It has been suggested that Major Ivor Price was instrumental in brokering the deal that resulted in the British failure to try, sentence, and execute de Valera. The Public Record Office claims to have no record for Major Ivor Price, despite admitting his number was on file. Like his activities in Ireland, his subsequent service in Palestine had also allegedly been expunged. A search of territorial and temporary officer indexes has revealed no folder in his name. Price is recorded as having joined the Army on August 5, 1914 and to have retired with the rank of Lieutenant Colonel. His life and work remain otherwise obscure.

In the aftermath of the Rising, more than 3,400 men and nearly 80 women were arrested throughout Ireland; of these, 1,400 men and 70 women were released; approximately 1,800 men and 5 women were imprisoned without benefit of trial. A total of 160 men and one woman were tried, convicted, and sentenced to terms ranging from six months in prison to death.

Not one was Éamon de Valera.

Notes

1. Coffey, Thomas M., *Agony at Easter*, Macmillian, NY, 1969, p. 260
2. *New York Times*, 5/12/1916m 3:1
3. Tierney, Michael, (Ed. By F.X. Martin), *Eoin MacNeill Scholar & Man of Action 1867-1945*, Clarendon Press, Oxford 1980, p. 224
4. *ibid,* p. 267
5. Ryan, Desmond, *The Rising*, Golden Eagle Books, Dublin, 1949, p. 259
6. *New York Times*, 5/7/1916, 19:2
7. Ryan, Desmond, *Unique Dictator*, Arthur. Barker, London, 1936, p. 35

8. Bromage Mary C., *De Valera and the March of a Nation*, Hutchinson, London, 1956, p. 47
9. WO 35/69
10. O'Broin, Leon, *W. E. Wylie and the Irish Revolution*, Macmillan, 1989, p. 30
11. *ibid*
12. *ibid*, p. 32
13. Asquith Papers
14. O'Broin, Leon, *W. E. Wylie and the Irish Revolution*, Macmillan, 1989, p. 32
15. Asquith Papers
16. *New York Times*, 5/11/1916, 1:3
17. *ibid*, 3:1
18. O'Broin, Leon, Wylie, *W. E. and the Irish Revolution*, Macmillan, 1989, p. 31
19. *NY Times & Manchester Guardian* 5/12/1916
20. *ibid*
21. Coogan, Tim Pat, *De Valera, The Man who was Ireland*, Harper, 1996, p. 75
22. Author's Personal Files
23. PRO 30/89/10
24. PRO 30/89/10/18 & 30/89/10/7467
25. *ibid*
26. O'Broin, Leon, *W. E. Wylie and the Irish Revolution*, Macmillan, 1989, p. 32
27. PRO 30/89/10
28. Longford, Earl of & O'Neill, Thomas P., *Éamon de Valera*, Hutchinson, London, 1970, p. 48
29. Whelan, John (Seán O'Faoláin), *De Valera*, Penguin Books, England 1939, p. 34
30. Coogan, Tim Pat, *De Valera, The Man who was Ireland*, Harper, 1996, p. 76
31. Whelan, John (Seán O'Faoláin), *De Valera*, Penguin Books, England 1939, p. 41
32. Tierney, Michael, *Eoin MacNeill, Scholar & man of Action 1867-1945*, Clarendon Press, Oxford 1983, p. 231
33. *ibid*, p. 232
34. Gunther, John, "The Truth about de Valera", *Strand Magazine*, 6/6/1936, p. 260
35. Tansill, Charles C., *America and the Fight for Irish Freedom 1866-1922*, Devin-Adair, NY 1957, p. 218-219
36. Farragher, Sean P. CSSP, *Dev and his Alma Mater*, Paraclete Press, Dublin & London, 1984, p. 113

CHAPTER VI

"Assignment Sinn Féin"

"Generally going back as far as the Rebellion of 1798 and earlier, the Government always had "friends" in the rebel camp."[1]
Augustine Burrell, British Chief Secretary for Ireland

Alarmed by the growing strength of the anti-British Irish-Americans under John Devoy and Judge Daniel Cohalan, President Woodrow Wilson wrote to US Ambassador Page in London on April 10, 1917, four days after America declared war on Germany: "Please convey to the Prime Minister [Lloyd George], in the most confidential manner, the information that the only circumstance which seems now to stand in the way of an absolutely cordial cooperation with Great Britain by practically all Americans who are not influenced by ties of blood directly associating them with Germany is the failure so far to find a satisfactory method of self-government for Ireland... Successful action now would absolutely divorce our citizens of Irish birth and sympathy from the German sympathizer."[2]

Lloyd George responded within a month of Wilson's plea, calling for a Convention, ostensibly to settle the Irish Question. The conference met between July 1917 and the spring of 1918. It was boycotted by Sinn Féin and organized labor, and the Ulster Unionists remained unyielding in their opposition to Home Rule in any form. Nothing was achieved but that the British went through the motions of making an attempt to steer the Irish towards self-government.

De Valera's biographer Tim Pat Coogan argued that the sincerity of Lloyd George's intentions was open to doubt from the beginning: "...The reality of British policy was revealed...by the British Government spokesman, Lord Birkenhead [F.E. Smith], in an interview with the *Boston Pilot* on January 14, 1918. He said that it [the Convention] was only a talking shop aimed at impressing American public opinion as Wilson persuaded his countrymen to go to war. He was quoted as saying that Lloyd George had hired some members of the convention at a guinea a day to keep them talking."[3]

Most of the Irish imprisoned following the Easter Rising had been released in December 1916. In a further attempt to damp down the opposition of the Irish-Americans, and to make Wilson's task easier, Lloyd George ordered the release of all the remaining prisoners, including de Valera, in June 1917.

De Valera had initially been regarded with suspicion by a number of survivors of the 1916 Rising, because of his "miraculous" escape from the firing-squad, but as tales of his jailhouse heroics spread, he emerged as the accepted leader of the men of the Easter Rising.

Sinn Féin scheduled their own Ard Fheis or Convention for October 25-26, 1917 and the days leading up to the Convention saw the British reverting to their centuries-old modus operandi for dealing with Ireland – divide and rule. The British were well aware the Irish would rally round anyone who appeared to be standing up to the English. The knee-jerk Irish impulse to any anti-British action was treated as heroic and would instantly turn its object into an Irish hero.

Two days before the Sinn Féin convention, in a not so subtle attempt to bolster de Valera in the eyes of the Irish, the British Prime Minister, Lloyd George, engaged in a bitter attack on de Valera in the House of Commons while at the same time building up his Irish credentials. In extolling and condemning de Valera, his tirade had the desired effect in Irish eyes. "De Valera's speeches were not excited and, so far as language is concerned, they are not violent. They are plain, deliberate and, I might also say, cold-blooded incitements to rebellion...This is not a case of violent, abusive and excitable language. It is the case of a man of great ability, of considerable influence, deliberately going down to the districts...to stir people up to rebellion against the authorities."[4]

De Valera's travels and speeches were under constant surveillance and it would have been a simple matter for him to be arrested, imprisoned or even deported to his country of origin, America. But no attempt was made to restrict his movements or speeches designed to cause disaffection to the Crown.

Lloyd George's plot crystallized when the authorities allowed the Ard Fheis Convention to take place despite its potential to foment civil strife. The intention that lay behind this unprecedented move by the British was apparently confirmed by de Valera himself. His official biographers Lord Longford and Thomas O'Neill noting: "... It was thought that the British Government only permitted the meeting because it could precipitate a split in the organization."

Tim Pat Coogan took the same position and recognized the British plot: "The Dublin Castle authorities...had only refrained from banning the Convention because their intelligence had assured them that if it were allowed to go ahead, it would inevitably result in a split."[5]

Obviously there was a mole inside Sinn Féin, and there was only one man capable of initiating a "split" – de Valera himself. The candidates vying for the leadership of Sinn Féin, besides de Valera, were Count Plunkett, a nonentity who stood not the slightest chance and Arthur Griffith, who was the frontrunner and prohibitive favourite.

De Valera immediately set in motion "Assignment Sinn Féin" by challenging Arthur Griffith for the presidency of the fledgling organization. "... de Valera told Griffith he wanted him to stand down as President of Sinn Féin and to nominate him (de Valera) instead. If Griffith insisted on having a contest, he told Griffith he would stand against him and was certain to win. In fact, this was far from certain...almost certainly, the majority...would have voted for Griffith. However, although Griffith now stood on the threshold of seeing his ideas triumph after a lifetime spent in penury in the cause of independence, for the sake of unity he readily stood down ..."[6]

Coogan recognized the conspiracy but not the conspirator. Had de Valera engaged in a contest with Griffith and lost, it can scarcely be doubted that he would have engineered a break within Sinn Féin, thereby bringing about the anticipated "split" and another round of the traditional Irish "dance of death." de Valera's attempt to "split" Sinn Féin was foiled by Arthur Griffith's decision to put his love of Ireland above personal ambition. Griffith feared nothing and no one, but shrank at the thought of a split in Irish ranks. He was well aware of the long history of divisive leadership which had crushed every Irish movement. Rather than be the cause of a division himself, he stepped aside and nominated de Valera.

Writing in 1926, Pieras Beaslai observed of Griffith: "His unselfish patriotism on this occasion has never received proper acknowledgment...He surrendered the leadership to a new, almost unknown, man in order to avoid any cleavage in the national ranks."[7] In his study of Sinn Féin, P S. O'Hegarty, wrote in 1924: "It was a misfortune that, when Sinn Féin was reconstructed in 1917, the direction of it was taken out of Griffith's hands. It could not have been done had he chosen to fight against it...So that the Dáil came to be manned almost wholly by people who, when their great test came, proved to have neither moral courage nor political intelligence."[8]

Before the Ard Fheis Convention, a committee set about drafting a new constitution for Sinn Féin, to be presented to the full convention. It was allegedly de Valera who, at the last moment, came up with the following: "Sinn Féin aims at securing the international recognition of

Ireland as an independent Irish republic. Having achieved that state, the Irish people may by referendum freely choose their own form of government."

Temporarily at least, this seemed to satisfy most parties. In his acceptance speech following his election to the Sinn Féin presidency, de Valera stated: "...the party was not irrevocably committed to a republic...We do not wish to bind the people to any form of government...We are not doctrinaire Republicans."[9] He then contradicted himself by announcing that it was "necessary to be united now under the flag for which we are going to fight for our freedom, the flag of the Irish Republic. We have nailed that flag to the mast; we shall never lower it."[10] He declared the Irish would "...draw the naked sword to make England bare her own naked sword, to drag the hypocritical mask off her face and to show her to the world for what she is, the accursed oppressor of nations."[11]

In the view of the Irish writer T. Ryle Dwyer, "Nobody could have been sure exactly where de Valera stood, with the result that he was hailed as a born leader. Everybody was supposedly following him, even though none of them could have been sure of exactly where he was going."[12]

De Valera addressed his Ard Fheis audience as a schoolteacher instructing children, repeating and explaining each motion and the comments of each speaker, droning on to the dismay of his listeners: "...de Valera was a slow-moving, painfully uncouth, massive speaker, with a disarming habit of pouring forth as new discoveries, things which had been for 20 years the commonplace of separatist thoughts."[13] John Whelan commented: "... it is not to be denied that [de Valera] was – and is – a poor orator – one of the very poorest in Irish history. He is long winded...has a habit of explaining things too much..."[14]

At a secret meeting the day after the Sinn Féin Convention, de Valera was also elected president of the Irish Volunteers. This was a startling development as President of Sinn Féin and the Volunteers, he was now the undisputed leader of the Irish separatist movement. From that time to the end of his long career, every major decision made by de Valera was to prove beneficial to England and detrimental to Ireland.

English luck held when it came to the Irish. The projected "split" never materialized but their man emerged triumphant.

De Valera's resurrection was complete: the phoenix was soaring.

Notes
1. Martin, F.X., *Leaders & Men of the Easter Rising,* Dublin 1916, Cornell U. Press, Ithaca, NY 1967, p. 11
2. Tansill, Charles C., *America and the Fight for Irish Freedom 1866 – 1922,* Devin-Adair NY 1957, p. 230
3. Coogan, Tim Pat, *De Valera, The Man who was Ireland,* Harper, 1996, p. 104
4. *ibid,* p. 99
5. *ibid,* p. 96
6. *ibid,* p. 96
7. Beaslai, Pieras, *Michael Collins and the Making of a New Ireland,* Vol I, Harper Bros. NY 1926, p. 172
8. O'Hegarty, P.S., *The Victory of Sinn Féin & How It Used It,* Talbot Press, Dublin 1924, p. 134
9. Dwyer, T. Ryle, *De Valera, The Man & the Myths,* Poolbeg, Dublin, 1991, p. 21
10. *ibid,* p. 21
11. *ibid,* p. 22
12. *ibid,* p. 22
13. O'Hegarty, P.S., *The Victory of Sinn Féin & How It Used It,* Talbot Press, Dublin 1924, p. 21
14. Whelan, John(Seán O'Faoláin), *De Valera,* Penguin Books, England 1939, p. 52

CHAPTER VII

The Great Lincoln Jail "Escape"

"The Irish are the most easily humbugged people on earth."

James O'Mara

The First World War saw Britain bury one million of her young men in the mud of France. The German offensive of March 1918 found the British Army dangerously short of men. General Henry Wilson, Chief of the British Imperial General Staff, was calling for a minimum of 20,000 "wastage" per month to counter the horrendous losses. Although well aware of the furore it would cause, the Lloyd George government allegedly contemplated the conscription of Ireland's untapped source of available men.

On April 10, 1918, the Prime Minister introduced a military service bill which did not impose direct and automatic conscription in Ireland, but which enabled the government to do so should the need arise. It was linked with a promise to introduce a measure for Home Rule before any such military service began but the Irish were inevitably dubious of Lloyd George's assurances.

The Lord Mayor of Dublin called a conference of Irish representatives of all political stripes on April 18. A pledge drafted by de Valera was agreed which denied the British Government's right to impose conscription in Ireland. The following Sunday, April 21, this pledge was taken at church doors throughout Ireland by tens of thousands of Irishmen.

The British were facing staggering losses each month and without the influx of American men and materiel, the outcome of the war was very much in doubt. President Wilson promised 100,000 American troops per month. The proposal for conscription in Ireland was merely a smokescreen for a British public relations campaign in America to place on record, the pro-German Irish bias. Once American troops began pouring into France, the defeat of Germany was all but assured. Anticipating Irish-American post-war maneuvers, the British used Irish rejection of conscription to paint them as traitors, this time not only to the mother country but also to America. The plan worked to perfection.

In anticipation of trouble in the event of conscription being enforced, the civilian Lord-Lieutenant Lord Wimborne was replaced by Field Marshal Lord French, who was given broad powers to suppress any disorder. On the night of May 17, 1918 almost the entire leadership of Sinn Féin and the Volunteers (with the exception of Michael Collins) was arrested, and the newspapers the following day carried details of Sinn Féin's involvement in an alleged German plot. Evidence of "treasonable conspiracy" was never produced, and few people in Ireland believed it at the time. John Devoy and the Irish-Americans were accused of resuming contacts with the Germans after the Rising, and it was rumoured that U-boats had been in contact with Irish agents off the coast of Ireland. This was the pretext for the arrests and the means of weakening what the British saw as the malign influence of the Irish-American lobby on Anglo-American cooperation.

Forewarned by Michael Collins, the Sinn Féin leaders supposedly allowed themselves to be arrested counting on a favorable public opinion response in Ireland and especially in America.

A general election throughout England and Ireland was called in the wake of the Armistice of November 1918. The fact that many of the Sinn Féin candidates were in prison did not put a dent in their popularity. John Redmond's call for the Irish to fight alongside the English in World War I and his failure to bring about Home Rule doomed his Irish Parliamentary Party (IPP) and catapulted Sinn Féin into the leading party in Ireland, all but wiping out the IPP. The number of Sinn Féin seats in Parliament at Westminster rose from seven to seventy-three, with the Unionists holding twenty-six and Redmond's Irish Parliamentary Party (IPP) reduced to six. Sinn Féin refused to take their seats at Westminster.

Redmond, an Irish nationalist politician, barrister, and Member of Parliament succeeded Charles Stewart Parnell as leader of the IPP from 1900 until his death in 1918. He tried unsuccessfully for years to convince the British to enact Home Rule and was successful to the extent that the only applicable legislation, the Government Act of 1912, reduced the House of Lords veto power to two years. The Home Rule legislation, which was passed in 1914 included a suspensory clause for the duration of the war. The 1916 Easter rebellion and Sinn Féin election effectively ruled out any meaningful Irish self-government until Collins' guerilla campaign forced the English to the negotiating table in 1921.

In New York City on December 10, 1918, four days before Britain's general election, that old firebrand John Devoy organized what was probably the greatest anti-English demonstration in American history.

With the war over, the Irish-Americans under Devoy and Judge Daniel Cohalan resumed their anti-English agenda with a call for the United States to support self-determination for Ireland. Tens of thousands crowded into Madison Square Garden and overflowed into the surrounding streets and meeting halls. The British government had long been aware of the threat to Anglo-American relations posed by Devoy and the Irish-Americans. With this latest flexing of political muscle, the English were astonished at the political juggernaut Devoy and Judge Cohalan had created. The Irish-Americans were a political force to be reckoned with and had the potential to influence the Presidential elections in 1920.

Ahead lay the problem for the English of dealing with its forty-billion dollar war debt to America. Clearly, this hurdle would be much easier to overcome if the presidential election of 1920 were won by a pro-British candidate. What the English needed was a credible Irish figure to travel to America to sow dissension among the Irish-Americans. Who better for this task than the president of Sinn Féin and the Volunteers, Éamon de Valera, then languishing in Lincoln Jail? If he were to escape, the publicity could only add to his mystique and elevate him to mythic stature, not only in Ireland but throughout the Irish Diaspora.

What followed was little less than high comedy, a farce in several acts calling for a greater suspension of belief than most theatrical productions.

As the curtain rose on the opening act, de Valera was leading fellow prisoners Sean McGarry and Sean Milroy on one of their daily strolls around the exercise yard of the Lincoln City prison on a damp and cold December day in 1918. De Valera paused and, staring at a door in the thirty-foot high stone prison wall, wondered aloud whether it might be a way out of the prison. They became "convinced" that it did indeed lead out onto a grassy enclosure ringed by barbed-wire fronting onto Wragby Road. It was the gateway to freedom "if, they could open their cell doors…the doors in the corridors, the jail gates and, finally, this door in the exercise grounds. Assuming…their colleagues outside could organize a party to spirit them away – they could escape."[1]

While serving at Mass, de Valera noticed that the prison chaplain habitually left his keys in the sacristy. With melted wax from the chapel candles he could make impressions of any number of keys and detailed dimensions could be passed on to Michael Collins, who remained free having narrowly avoided arrest with the other republican luminaries.

So began one of the most nonsensical and laughable prison escapes in history, and with it, Devoy and Judge Daniel Cohalan's fate was sealed.

Fellow prisoner, Sean Milroy, an excellent artist, sketched a humorous Christmas card depicting a tipsy Sean McGarry trying to stuff a miniature key into the lock of his front door of his home with the caption: "Xmas 1917, I can't get in." On the inside of the card, McGarry was seen in a jail cell attempting to fit a huge key into the lock of his cell with the comment "Xmas 1918; I can't get out." As author Florence O'Donoghue remarked in his book about IRA jail escapes: "No doubt, the jail censor (upon seeing the card) had smiled in appreciation of the grim humor of a prisoner. What he did not realize was that the huge key in the sketch was one of the jail keys, exact in every detail. And so, the card was allowed through to Mrs. McGarry, who did not understand its significance (and did not pass it on to Michael Collins)."[2]

Enclosed in the envelope along with the card was a note from John O'Mahony, another prisoner: "'My dear Tommy, The best wishes I can send are those de Valera wrote in my autograph book. Field will translate,' (Field was Collins' pseudonym). There followed in de Valera's handwriting an explanation in Irish that the key in the picture was an exact drawing of the prison key and that the keyhole showed a cross-section of it. This key would open the inner doors and the back gate on the north side of the prison. He asked that a key, made to these dimensions, and some files be sent in a cake and that arrangements be made to meet him outside the prison."[3]

No response was received and de Valera panicked. On December 24, O'Mahony and Sam Flaherty wrote a second letter, this time in Latin, to Father Kavanagh, a curate in Leeds known for his nationalist sympathies. "The message was veiled as if it were a quotation from the ancient classics...It was replete with details of the prison and its surroundings, laying particular stress on the possible escape route. He even mentioned how the prisoners at a high window could give and receive a signal."[4] This missive contained an obvious reference to the famous escape from Dublin Castle on Christmas Eve in 1591 of the legendary Hugh Roe O'Donnell and two companions, no doubt in some measure a not-so-subtle attempt on de Valera's part to thrust himself into the pantheon of Irish immortals. The O'Donnells were an ancient and powerful Irish clan, which together with the O'Neills fought the English to a standstill for years before finally being defeated at the battle of Kinsale in 1601.

"The kindly guard who posted the letter was allegedly unaware of the implication of the apparently innocuous missive. Enclosed with this letter of O'Mahony's was a note from McGarry to his wife in Irish asking if she had received the Christmas card at all? This was also composed by de Valera. The instructions about sending the key [in a cake] were given and he arranged that, if it fitted, he would mention in his next letter: 'Your last cake was a treat'".[5]

This second letter also failed to elicit any response – perhaps Father Kavanagh understood neither Gaelic nor Latin. Eventually, on January 10, 1919, O'Mahony wrote a third letter. This time: "... a little piece of Latin in the middle of his letter was in de Valera's handwriting."[6] The Latin, of course, described the escape plans. The letter was dutifully passed by the bemused censor and finally to have found its way to someone in Ireland who could read Gaelic and Latin.

Not long after the third letter was sent, the Lincoln Jail warden was visited by an articulate and smartly dressed individual claiming to be a friend of a prisoner. This man, Fintan Murphy, was a member of the Irish Republican Brotherhood who had fought in the 1916 Easter Rising and a friend of Michael Collins. Murphy convinced the warden to allow him to leave some miscellaneous items for his friend, and these were presented for inspection. One of the parcels held a delicious-looking iced cake, the like of which the surly guard conducting the inspection had not seen since before the war. Rationing during the previous four years had deprived the English of sweets of any kind. The English jailers played the good censor/bad inspector routine with the good censor passing the messages while the bad inspector ranted and raged at the special treatment for Irish traitors.

Murphy graciously turned the cake over to the glaring guard who, producing a large knife proceeded to cut and stab at the cake. Whether his knife hit one of the keys, he never let on, but kept muttering about the inedible war bread loyal Englishmen had to endure while iced cakes were provided for a pack of treacherous pro-German scoundrels. The more the guard stabbed the cake the more infuriated he became, cursing with every thrust of the knife.[7]

Is it not odd that a guard who by all accounts resented so strongly the cake going to pro-German Irish traitors would not have found a way of impounding a slice or two of that cake – for "inspection purposes," that subsequently found its way to his family's table?

In any event, the key in this first cake was found to be too small. Milroy inscribed another card with the Gaelic words "Ecoir na Saoirse" (Key to Freedom) along with another drawing of a key, and this duly found its way into the hands of one of Michael Collins's operatives.

Following this fourth communiqué, on January 24, 1919 – the date originally set for the escape – the cooperative warden allowed Frank Kelly to deliver a second cake. The gloomy guard repeated his slashing act, but once again the key in the cake passed undetected. But Irish bad luck held: the chaplain's key was not a master key, it opened some doors but not others.

It was now decided that Paddy de Loughrey, another prisoner and a locksmith, would dismantle one of the corridor door locks from which a master key could be made that would also open the cell doors. Two further letters in Gaelic were dispatched, requesting blank keys and files. On January 27, Harry Boland appeared with a third cake; the blank it contained once again escaped detection under the customary onslaught of the infuriated prison guard, "But the blank was of the wrong design."[8]

So, a seventh Gaelic missive passed the compliant censor and, on January 29, an Irish teacher named Kathleen Talty delivered a fourth cake containing blanks, files and cutting tools with which the prisoners would be able to make their own keys. Desmond Ryan notes: "The most unreasonably adventurous and daring cake ever smuggled into any jail was packed with blank keys, files and key-cutting tools...It was heavy, but the "gloomy guard" was now resigned to cakes for the cut-throats and bore it, heavy though it was, with scarcely a prod or an expletive to the pampered traitors."[9]

This procession of cakes of ever-increasing weight should have aroused suspicion, but no doubt, there were those in authority who were in on the deception, among them perhaps the gloomy guard in charge of inspecting incoming goods and the kindly bemused censor in charge of outgoing mails.

On January 31 an eighth letter notified Michael Collins that there was now a key to fit every door in Lincoln Jail. Longford and O'Neill noted: "On de Valera's instructions McGarry wrote, in Irish, '... they would be ready on the evening arranged.' The long delays and various mishaps which had taken six weeks or more to overcome were at an end."[10]

The "escape" was to take place between Saturday, February 1 and Monday February 3, so that all preparations had to be completed by Friday January 31 at the latest. Since the fourth cake containing all those essential key-making tools was not delivered until January 29, this left the prisoners – in particular the locksmith Paddy de Loughrey – a mere two days in which to make sure that all the necessary keys were ready.

After initial delays, events moved more swiftly, and a mere five days passed between the delivery of the second cake on January 24 and the fourth. Tim Pat Coogan concluded: "... On a memorable day in Lincoln Jail, de Valera got word out to Collins complimenting him on the quality of the ingredients of a cake he had just received. In a real sense, the cake contained a recipe for de Valera's success."[11] Coogan had his own views as to de Valera's success: what seems clear, however, is that the "escape" paved the way for the series of British triumphs and corresponding Irish disasters which marked the course of de Valera's career.

A damp and overcast February day passed drearily into a typical bone-chillingly wet moonless winter evening as Michael Collins, Harry Boland, and Frank Kelly arrived in Lincoln, a city nearly equidistant from London and Liverpool, and not far from the North Sea coast. The massive walls of Lincoln Jail loomed forbiddingly in the mist beyond a barbed-wired grass enclosure that surrounded the prison. On Wragby Road, a heavy rusted wrought-iron gate opened out of the prison enclave and fronted onto a military hospital. The gate was a favorite trysting spot for recuperating servicemen and their sweethearts. The whispering wistful lovers were apparently oblivious to the sharp sounds of the wire-cutters Collins and Boland used to snip through the barbed-wire barrier. As the three men wormed their way through the tall, damp grass, Kelly lost his bearings and was separated from the others.

Collins and Boland, their ears alert to the muffled murmuring of lovers, kept their eyes riveted on the tower windows of the prison. Time passed excruciatingly slowly but finally, at the appointed time of 6:40, Boland gave the pre-arranged signal – a quick flash from his flashlight. The switch jammed, and the lamp kept flashing until the panic-stricken Boland doused it by stuffing it into his pocket. Only a blind man could have failed to see it: de Valera, McGarry and Milroy grimaced with consternation, breathing a sigh of relief when the gleaming signal was finally extinguished. As they waited anxiously for an answering signal, Collins and Boland were taken aback when a brilliant flash lit up one of the tower windows, illuminating three men peering out from behind prison bars. In attempting to light several matches, McGarry had set off the entire box in a dazzling burst of flame that must have been visible to anyone within sight of the prison.

There was more slapstick in store. "One of Milroy's soles came loose from its upper and flapped noisily in Chaplinesque fashion as the trio tried to steal silently through the jail."[12] The flapping shoe sole echoed along the flagstone corridors as the three flip-flopped noisily to their rendezvous with destiny. Each door and gate opened easily and noiselessly. To cover their tracks, de Valera quietly locked each one behind him.

Thus far, the men's antics might have been featured on a vaudeville playbill: *Kelly's Disappearing Act, Boland's Magic Lantern that Wouldn't Go Out, McGarry's Exploding Matchbox Shtick* and *Milroy's Flapping Shoe Dance.*

"At last the trio reached the back wall gate. Again it opened easily, but they found themselves faced by yet another door. There was a double gate through the wall."[13] Collins had a duplicate key. How he got it was never disclosed, but presumably (though the time constraints involved are remarkable) it had been smuggled out of the jail. When he and Boland heard the prisoners' noisy approach, Collins thrust his duplicate into the keyhole and it promptly broke off, just as de Valera, McGarry and Milroy swung open the interior gate. Once again disaster loomed but de Valera, holding his breath, inserted his own key and gently pushed the broken one out. The lock turned smoothly but the outside gate was so old and rusted that it needed all five men pulling and pushing to open it wide enough for the prisoners to squeeze through. All the while, the screeching of metal reverberated throughout the prison yard and outside the prison enclosure. "The rusted gate swung open with a grating sound that should have brought guards running..."[14] But no guards materialized.

It is remarkable that the hinges of this long-disused gate were so badly rusted while the lock – like all the hinges and locks inside the prison – opened smoothly. No one questioned why the prison guards were so conspicuous by their absence; not one of them heard three men trundling noisily along flagstone corridors even though, according to another account, Collins and Boland, outside 30-foot prison walls: "... heard the approaching footsteps of the three prisoners."[15]

Abandoning Kelly, who was still wandering about the prison enclosure slipping and sloshing through the tall wet grass, Collins, Boland, de Valera, Milroy and McGarry made their way towards Wragby Road and that rusted wrought-iron gate with its trysting couples. As Longford and O'Neill had the story related to them by de Valera: "...Boland put his heavy fur-lined coat on de Valera and donned his own light raincoat. Arm-in-arm, like a fond couple, they ran the gauntlet, Harry, the supposed lady, adding to the pretense with an occasional 'Good night, chums' to soldiers who were too engrossed to take any notice."[16]

It is hardly credible, that loitering soldiers and their lovers raised nary a suspicious eyebrow as five apparitions suddenly materialized through a creaking gate exiting the prison enclosure wishing them a hearty Irish-accented "Goodnight Chums." More than likely the rapt lovers were actually security officers, stationed there to ensure that no alert recuperating soldier, less than deeply engrossed with his lady friend, should challenge four men and a woman emerging from a prison compound known to house a contingent of pro-German Irishmen.

The comedy was not yet over. "They all got through [the hospital gate] safely, only to find the car which was waiting to take the prisoners away could not be found."[17] Paddy O'Donoghue, the wheelman, cold and damp, had sought out a nearby pub for a pint or two, leaving the President of Sinn Féin and the head of the Irish Republican Brotherhood frantically searching for their getaway car. "At last, the car was located outside the Adam and Eve Inn."[18]

Florence O'Donoghue wrote: "The British press raged and sought to track down de Valera...Never before was there such a hue and cry; never such a hunt for an escaped prisoner...Of the many dramatic escapes from British jails by Irish political prisoners, there has been nothing quite comparable with the escape of de Valera from Lincoln."[19] In the days following the escape: "The [Irish] people were delirious with joy. De Valera was not only a leader; he was a wizard who could outsmart the British anytime he wished. Among the British authorities, there was consternation and continuous speculation ..."[20] Headlines reported sightings of de Valera in Paris, Ireland and Holland.

Desmond Ryan came closer to the truth when he suggested that the howling and the cries of anguish on the British side were solely for public consumption: "A Dublin Castle official took aside special correspondents and whispered the search was all eye-wash; it was a subtle move; the extremists had grown restive; de Valera would be a restraining influence; so a paternal eye had relaxed its vigilance. The door had been not unlocked so much as the hinges [and locks] oiled and the Irish left alone to plot and what else could you expect but that the wild Irish and their milder leader would leg it. He would return to Ireland and give admirable advice to his hotheads. 'Take it from me,' said the official blandly, 'that we let him escape. This is, of course, in confidence.'"[21]

De Valera's comic opera "escape" from Lincoln Jail on February 3, 1919 ensured that his "... transformation into herodom had been completed ..."[22]

He had always insisted that he must escape from Lincoln Jail before the British Government got around to declaring a general amnesty precisely in order to generate the sort of publicity that did indeed ensue. The Irish leaders in Dublin set in motion plans for a massive civic reception to take full advantage of all the publicity for the "wizard" who had outfoxed the English.

But de Valera had a surprise in store. He confounded his companions by declaring within minutes of his breakout, while speeding away from Lincoln, with the announcement that he would not be returning to

Ireland to reap the publicity bonanza after all. He was "... determined upon a secret visit to America."[23] He explained to Collins, "A twofold purpose would be served [by his going to America]; first, obtaining American recognition for the *de facto* Irish Republic and second, raising funds to support the Republican government..."[24]

De Valera apparently had no plans to visit his family before scurrying off to America. At great personal risk, Collins took it upon himself to visit Sinead weekly and play with the children while de Valera was absent. He provided her with news of her husband and money to cover her expenses. By this time, Sinead had resigned herself to de Valera's extended absences and was content to run the family alone.

The Irish president was so anxious to get away and so unconcerned about the risk of recapture that he even attempted to make his own travel arrangements rather than wait for Collins to use his undercover contacts on the steamship lines. Whether by accident or design, however, British security failed once again to spot him. "The hazards to which Dev exposed himself by one abortive attempt to leave for America left Collins aghast."[25]

The Volunteers were disappointed and outraged when they learned from Collins of de Valera's decision not to return to Ireland. Pieras Beaslai, a member of the executive at that meeting, wrote: "The statement of his going to America was received by all of us with dismay. We felt de Valera's departure would be a fatal mistake, that the country would misunderstand his motives and regard it as selfish or even cowardly desertion...The meeting took the view that the place for an Irish leader was in Ireland where the strength of the fight put up would determine the support in America. It was decided to send Burgess to England to urge de Valera either not to go at all, or, failing that, to show himself first in Ireland so that the publicity of his escape should not be dissipated."[26]

Burgess arrived in Manchester the weekend of February 7-9, and informed de Valera that the leaders demanded his return to Ireland. Burgess's stern argument apparently convinced de Valera to put in an obligatory appearance at home. But he was still, technically, a wanted man and could not go back to Ireland at once. He lay (fairly) low in England and was in Liverpool completing the arrangements for his visit to the United States when he was notified that the rest of the "German Plot" prisoners had been released on March 8, 1919. It has been suggested that the British, in facilitating de Valera's "escape," held up the release of the rest of the prisoners in order to add drama and excitement to de Valera's escape. Whatever the reason, as Desmond Ryan noted, the remaining Sinn Féin prisoners were suddenly liberated and Castle officials shrugged their shoulders and asked; "What did we say? It's nothing to us. We want no more playacting."[27]

Notes

1. O'Donoghue, Florence, *Sworn to be Free, The Complete Book of IRA Jailbreaks 1918-1921*, Anvil Books, Tralee, Ireland 1971, p. 38
2. *ibid,* p. 39
3. Longford, Earl of & O'Neill, Thomas P., *Éamon de Valera*, Hutchinson, London, 1970, p. 82
4. *ibid,* p. 83
5. *ibid*
6. *ibid*
7. Ryan, Desmond, *Unique Dictator*, Arthur. Barker, London, 1936, p. 90
8. Coogan, Tim Pat, *De Valera, The Man who was Ireland*, Harper, 1996, p. 125
9. Ryan, Desmond, *Unique Dictator,* Arthur. Barker, London, 1936, p. 92
10. Longford, Earl of & O'Neill, Thomas P., *Éamon de Valera*, Hutchinson, London, 1970, p. 84
11. Coogan, Tim Pat, *De Valera, The Man who was Ireland*, Harper, 1996, p. 122
12. *ibid,* p. 126
13. Longford, Earl of & O'Neill, Thomas P., *Éamon de Valera*, Hutchinson, London, 1970, p. 85
14. Coogan, Tim Pat, *De Valera, The Man who was Ireland*, Harper, 1996, p. 126
15. O'Donoghue, Florence, *Sworn to be Free, The Complete Book of IRA Jailbreaks 1918-1921*, Anvil Books, Tralee, Ireland 1971, p. 42
16. Longford, Earl of & O'Neill, Thomas P., *Éamon de Valera*, Hutchinson, London, 1970, p. 86
17. *ibid*
18. *ibid*
19. O'Donoghue, Florence, *Sworn to be Free, The Complete Book of IRA Jailbreaks 1918-1921*, Anvil Books, Tralee,Ireland 1971, p. 44
20. Longford, Earl of & O'Neill, Thomas P., *Éamon de Valera*, Hutchinson, London, 1970, p. 86
21. Ryan, Desmond, *Unique Dictator,* Arthur. Barker, London, 1936, p. 95
22. Bromage Mary C., *De Valera and the March of a Nation*, Hutchinson, London, 1956, p. 85
23. Tansill, Charles C., *America and the Fight for Irish Freedom 1866 – 1922*, Devin-Adair NY 1957, p. 340
24. Bromage Mary C., *De Valera and the March of a Nation*, Hutchinson, London, 1956, p. 84
25. *ibid,* p. 85

26. Beaslai, Pieras, *Michael Collins, and the Making of a New Ireland*, Vol I, Harper Bros. NY 1926, p. 269
27. Ryan, Desmond, *Unique Dictator*, Arthur. Barker, London, 1936, p. 95

CHAPTER VIII

Dublin: Lost Opportunity

"Men are so simple and, so subject to present necessities, that he who seeks to deceive, will always find someone who will allow himself to be deceived."[1]

During the period between the General Election in December 1918 and de Valera's "heroic escape" from Lincoln Jail in February 1919, Sinn Féin had triumphed. But most of its leaders and many of the newly elected Members of Parliament (MPs) were languishing in (or plotting to escape from) jails in Ireland and England. One thing was certain: not even those Sinn Féin MPs who retained their freedom had any intention of actually taking their seats at Westminster. Instead, they laid plans for the formation of a separate, independent Irish Parliament. To this end, an invitation was extended to all MPs, of whatever stripe, elected throughout Ireland in December, to attend the first meeting of the new Dáil Éireann, or Assembly of Ireland, to be held on January 21, 1919. The invitation was ignored by the Ulster Unionists and by the rump of the six remaining members of Redmond's Irish Parliamentary Party, and with the majority of Sinn Féin MPs in prison only twenty-seven members were present. Naturally the Ulster Unionists would have nothing to do with any Irish nationalists and Redmond's party was still smarting over the trouncing Sinn Féin had given them the month before.

A declaration of independence was read reaffirming the Irish Republic declared on Easter Monday, 1916. Three delegates were appointed, one of them Éamon de Valera, to attend the peace conference being held in Paris, to seek the recognition and support of the civilized world for Irish independence. The Dáil was to meet next on April 1, 1919.

On Saturday March 22, 1919, the following announcement from Sinn Féin headquarters was published in the Dublin newspapers: "President de Valera will arrive in Ireland on Wednesday evening next, the 26th instant and the Executive of Dáil Éireann will offer him a national welcome. It is expected that the homecoming of de Valera will be an occasion of national rejoicing and full arrangements will be made for marshalling the procession. The Lord Mayor of Dublin will receive him at the gate of the city and will escort him to the Mansion House where he will deliver a message to the Irish people. All organizations and bands wishing to participate in the demonstration should apply to 6 Harcourt Street on Monday the 24th instant up to 6 p.m."[2]

The reception was to include the presentation to de Valera on Mount Street Bridge by the Lord Mayor, Laurence O'Neill, of the keys to the city of Dublin. "De Valera (initially) liked the idea and returned from Liverpool prepared to deliver a suitably fiery speech at the scene of Captain Michael Malone's heroism."[3].

De Valera was looking forward to the reception, and "[I]n preparation for the day, he drafted a speech in uncompromising terms in which he paid tribute to Mick Malone and the men who fell defending that bridge three years before."[4] Mount Street Bridge was the site where the British military had suffered the greatest number of casualties during the 1916 Easter Rising at the hands of Malone and his heroic little band. De Valera and most of his men were sitting on their heels 150 yards away at Boland's Bakery listening to the firing that culminated in Malone's death, but since it occurred within an area technically under his command, de Valera never missed a chance to take credit for Malone's heroism. As often as de Valera linked his name to that of the valiant Malone, it is interesting to note that the Irish President allowed the greatest hero of the Easter Rising to be buried in Glasnevin Cemetery under a fifty cent curbstone.

Michael Collins was well aware of the golden opportunity such a reception presented. He knew the British would find it difficult to cope with a massive rally in the streets of Dublin without incident, and that they could easily be provoked into using force to quell any trouble. Collins would make sure the world's press were there to report it. A British over-reaction would swing the pendulum of international public opinion – especially in the United States – in Ireland's favor. It would demonstrate to the world that England ruled Ireland solely by brute force and lead to international recognition of the nation's acceptance of Sinn Féin. "... Collins made it clear to the Party Executive that he was looking for a confrontation with the British. Ireland was likely to get more out of a state of general disorder than from a continuance of the situation as it then stood. The proper people to take decisions of that kind were ready to face the British military, and were resolved to force the issue. And they were not to be deterred by weaklings and cowards."[5]

De Valera presumably thought at first that the proposed reception fitted in with British plans to promote his leadership. The British, however, like Collins, were alert to the potential for a public relations disaster inherent in such a mass demonstration, and the reception was promptly banned by the government. The authorities did not want their Irish hero to be used as a figurehead fomenting civil unrest and violence; they wanted de Valera in America, and they wanted him there as soon as possible.

De Valera's initial purpose in planning an escape was the enormous political bonanza it would provide to the morale of the Irish people. He had said prior to his "escape": "Such a coup would be of immense publicity value to the Irish cause and would be a serious setback to the British Government ..."[6]

Irish writers have generally failed to draw any particular conclusions from de Valera's initial enthusiasm for Collins's plans and his sudden turnaround and adamant withdrawal from the civic reception. Tim Pat Coogan, for example, commented: "Collins was prepared to go to war if need be, but de Valera was more disposed to go to America."[7]

Once made aware that the British were opposed to the reception, de Valera immediately backpedalled: "The occasion was not one on which he could call the people to incur any danger ..."[8] He skulked silently into Dublin under cover of darkness, unobserved, and under wraps. After all, he was only following Machiavelli's edict: "It is necessary for a prince to have a mind ready to turn itself accordingly as the winds and variations of fortune force it."

The Sinn Féin executive placed another announcement in the Dublin papers on March 25, 1919 canceling the event, and de Valera explained in a letter to the Executive why he now favored this move. Calling off the Dublin Demonstration was de Valera's initial international disaster for Ireland. In an attempt to justify his rejection of the demonstration, he cited the stark contrast between the advantages to Ireland and the enormous detriment to England that such a reception in the Irish capital presented. In a letter to the Sinn Féin Executive calling off the Demonstration, he said:

> "It is obvious that our English Government could not allow foreign correspondents and others to get such a clear insight into the real position of Ireland which your proposed demonstration would give.
>
> "The contrast between how the people would receive government by their own and government by the foreigner would be too sharp. The world would see how the people were in favor of Sinn Féin and anti-British.

"It would never do that the peoples of other countries should be forced to ask themselves how is it that men whom the de facto government of Ireland branded as criminals and put away as dangerous, should be received with such evident marks of approbation.

"Think of what a shock it would give to those who believed English ministers when they echoed America's cry, "Government with the consent of the governed, and an end to military despotism everywhere."

"Besides, the present moment would never suit at all. Think of Egypt and India and even British Labor itself. No oligarchs could stand it.

"British justice, too, and the very great Magna Carta – why, to use the famous word, it would be "unthinkable ..."[9]

De Valera concluded: "I think you must all agree with me that the present occasion is scarcely one on which we would be justified in risking the lives of citizens. I am certain it would not...We who have waited know how to wait. Many a heavy fish is caught even with a fine line if the angler is patient."[10] On the face of it, de Valera was explaining why the British authorities looked upon such a demonstration as a disaster in the making, not only in Ireland and the Empire but internationally as well. De Valera's upside-down logic: since the English would prevent the demonstration by force if necessary to prevent an international public relations disaster, it was therefore in Ireland's interests to cancel the event. Irish writers never blinked at this ambiguity.

De Valera was playing England's hand in refusing to let foreign correspondents discover the real situation in Ireland. By calling off the demonstration, de Valera made sure the world was denied the opportunity of seeing that the Irish people accepted Sinn Féin, that the British held Ireland solely by force of arms, and that the men England branded as criminals were actually hailed as patriots. Not only America but the Commonwealth nations would be outraged at any heavy-handed British suppression of a massive outpouring of support for self-government. The truth was that de Valera supported cancellation of the reception not because it might have risked the lives of citizens, but because it would have devastated English interests.

De Valera had not always been so reluctant to shed Irish blood. His selective conscience and alleged humanitarianism were called into play only when British interests were concerned. In a publicity stunt less than a year previously, on March 16, 1918, de Valera had risked the lives of thousands of Irish Nationalists in Belfast, right smack in the middle of the den of Unionist goons. He had crossed over the Mourne Mountains in the middle of the night on his way to a rally in Belfast, earning himself the sobriquet of "Professor Moonlight." In Bessborough he charged: "The Unionists are a rock in the road…We must, if necessary, blast it out of our path."[11]

Thousands of Republican Nationalists greeted him in Belfast and, with torches and hurley sticks they marched to a previously hired hall, only to find it padlocked by the police. Undeterred, "Professor Moonlight" led the rally to a nearby athletic field. "Out of the darkness, Belfast police officers appeared, but the crowd, emboldened by the bravado of Professor Moonlight, refused to disperse. Clubs flailed out in the red light of the torches. Rioting ran wild – a crowd of 2,500 clubbed each other, hurled stones, and even fired off revolvers from midnight until four a.m., sending many people, including some policemen, to the hospital."[12] But by the next morning de Valera was back on home territory, free and unharmed.[13]

Having so recklessly risked the lives of nationalists within the Unionist bastion of Belfast the year before; he was now reluctant to hazard a demonstration in the confines of the nationalist city of Dublin with the opportunity to parade the heavy hand of British repression before the eyes of the world. Prior to the English ban on any public rally, he and Collins were prepared to shed Irish blood to exploit the publicity bonanza generated by the return of Sinn Féin's president to Irish soil. But when de Valera discovered the British were opposed to any demonstration, he had a change of heart.

When the Dáil Éireann met on April 1, 1919, the fifty-two Sinn Féin MPs present elected Éamon de Valera prime minister or, as he was more usually known, President of the Dáil. The next day, the ministers who would effectively be in charge while he was absent in America were nominated; they included Arthur Griffith as acting President and Michael Collins as finance minister.

On June 6, 1919 de Valera left for America. His avowed aims were to unite Irish-Americans, to persuade the American political parties to support self-determination for Ireland, to secure government recognition of an Irish Republic, and to raise money to support the military struggle against Britain.

Newly minted as the "greatest living Irishman," de Valera proceeded to the United States as the saviour of the Irish Republic endowed with the authority to dictate Irish policy in America. The Irish-Americans, and

Devoy and Cohalan in particular, welcomed a British spy in the guise of an Irish hero.

They discovered their folly too late.

Notes

1. Machiavelli, Niccolo, *The Prince (Translated by W.K. Marriott)*, J&M Dent & Sons, London 1908, p. 98
2. O'Donoghue, Florence, *Sworn to be Free, The Complete Book of IRA Jailbreaks 1918-1921*, Anvil Books, Tralee, Ireland 1971, p. 46
3. Coogan, Tim Pat, *De Valera, The Man who was Ireland*, Harper, 1996, p. 131
4. Longford, Earl of & O'Neill, Thomas P., *Éamon de Valera*, Hutchinson, London, 1970, p. 90
5. Dwyer, T. Ryle, *De Valera, The Man & the Myths*, Poolbeg, Dublin, 1991, p. 28
6. Coogan, Tim Pat, *De Valera, The Man who was Ireland*, Harper, 1996, p. 131
7. O'Donoghue, Florence, *Sworn to be Free, The Complete Book of IRA Jailbreaks 1918-1921*, Anvil Books, Tralee, Ireland 1971, p. 46
8. Beaslai, Pieras, *Michael Collins and the Making of a New Ireland*, Vol I, Harper Bros. NY 1926, p. 282
9. Beaslai, Pieras, *Michael Collins and the Making of a New Ireland*, Vol I, Harper Bros. NY 1926, p. 284
10. Bromage Mary C., *De Valera and the March of a Nation*, Hutchinson, London, 1956, p. 73
11. *New York Times*, 3/18/1918, 1:2, NYT, 3/18/1916, 7:2
12. Bromage Mary C., *De Valera and the March of a Nation*, Hutchinson, London, 1956, p. 73

CHAPTER IX
"Assignment America"

"Now came to the shores of America Éamon de Valera...and after him, the deluge...No envoy that ever arrived here from Ireland was hailed with greater enthusiasm or was so unanimously associated with greater hope for the future of Ireland's freedom than he...That he found on his arrival here a splendid unity among the friends of Ireland is an historical fact; that he left chaos and dissension behind him is undeniable ..."[1]

John J. Splain, Friends of Irish Freedom

At 10 p.m. on the night of June 11, 1919 de Valera stepped ashore from the SS *Lapland* in the city of his birth. He was met by his secretary and fanatical follower, Harry Boland* and Joseph McGarrity. That very same night they left New York for Philadelphia. It might have been expected that de Valera's first move in New York would be to make himself known to Devoy and Cohalan, celebrated in Ireland as defenders of the nationalist cause in America. His failure to do so was tantamount to a deliberate affront and marked the first discordant note of his mission.

"Assignment America" was Éamon de Valera's initial international covert mission on behalf of England. The British wanted de Valera in America to counter the overwhelmingly Democratic and anti-English Irish-American political organization under the leadership of John Devoy and Judge Daniel Cohalan. They posed a serious threat to Anglo-American relations. It was imperative to England's interest that no pro-Irish president be nominated in the coming 1920 elections. In order to accomplish this, de Valera's "assignment" was to split the Irish-Americans and discredit its leaders. Following the English *modus operandi,* de Valera had the Irish-Americans finance their own destruction.

---

* A former tailor, and unconnected with Boland's Mill (Bakery) which served as deValera's headquarters during the 1916 Easter Rising.

England was in debt to the United States to the tune of $40 billion for war materiel supplied to the Allies in World War I. The repayment of even the interest on this debt represented an enormous financial burden. In the event the influence of the Irish Americans led to the election of a president sympathetic to the Irish cause; he could apply political and economic pressure on the English to not only resolve the Irish question but to demand payment on its First World War debt.

Among the cast of characters involved on one side or the other were John Devoy, Judge Daniel F. Cohalan, and the gadflies Joseph McGarrity, and Dr. Patrick McCartan.

Devoy had plotted all his life to rid Ireland of the English. At the age of 19, he enlisted in the French Foreign Legion as the best way to gain the military experience he wanted to fight Ireland's oppressor. After a year, he deserted, returned to Ireland, and became involved in persuading Irishmen serving in the British Army to join the Irish Republican Brotherhood (IRB). He was remarkably successful, and over the winter of 1865–66 thousands pledged to take up arms in a projected Rising. Once again, informers, indecision and inaction on the part of Irish leaders failed the people, and the anticipated insurrection withered into yet another exercise in futility. Devoy himself was seized in February 1866, tried for treason and sentenced to fifteen years penal servitude. Irish troops were hastily transferred out of Ireland and replaced by British regiments. Devoy was released in January 1871 and exiled to the United States. His arrival in America did not dampen his anti-English resolve and he joined the Clan na Gael, founded in 1867 as the American prototype for the Irish Republican Brotherhood (IRB) established in 1877. He rose quickly in its ranks and was prepared to support any initiative that might rid Ireland of the English. In 1879, Devoy convinced the Clan na Gael to support Charles Stewart Parnell and Michael Davitt in a "New Departure." This eventually led to the enactment of a series of land laws which financed the buy-out of absentee landowners' estates and returned the land to the native Irish farmers in return for sixty-year mortgages.

Irascible and short-tempered, Devoy was loyal to a fault, generous and quick to change direction when he believed it benefited Ireland. He often said that Irish-Americans never interfered with the men in Ireland but were always ready and willing to aid them in whatever decision they made. When he heard of the plans for the 1916 Rising he arranged the procurement from Germany of the arms that were so essential to any chance of success. He was bitterly disappointed when the incompetence of Austin Stack led to the arms ship being scuttled in Queenstown Harbor.

103

England's Greatest Spy

Devoy was editor of the weekly *Gaelic American*, the voice of Clan na Gael from 1903 until his death in 1928; he never married, but devoted his life to his only love – Ireland. He never made more than a pittance for his labors on behalf of Irish independence. Patrick Pearse, leader of the 1916 Easter Rising, called him the "greatest Fenian." Devoy was a tenacious crusader laboring for more than half a century over a thankless and at times excruciatingly vexing task. Like Michael Collins, Devoy had more trouble with the genetically disputatious Irish than with the enemies of Irish freedom. Desmond Ryan had this to say about Devoy: "Of all the men of the Fenian movement, Devoy was the greatest...No situation was too great for his pertinacity; when he failed, he began again...He made the Irish cause a power in the United States. He left his mark on Irish history when he joined forces with Michael Davitt in the Land League...His work among the Irish soldiers made him the most formidable conspirator of them all."[2] Devoy was plagued later in life by deafness causing him serious grief during public and private meetings.

In his keynote speech, at the Irish Race Convention in Philadelphia in 1919, Cardinal William O'Connell of Boston stated: "When Ireland ultimately gains her freedom, to one American of Irish blood, more than any other man, will her victory be due – Judge Daniel Cohalan of New York, whose great intellect and wonderful organizing skill has contributed so much towards solidifying the Race in America."[3]

Cohalan, the son of Irish immigrant parents, became a successful attorney and was appointed to the New York State Supreme Court in 1910. Through his political activities he attended the National Democratic conventions in 1904 and 1908 but later had a falling-out with the Democrats over the nomination of Woodrow Wilson for President. Having failed to prevent Wilson's nomination, he bolted from the party and worked for the Republican nominee, thus earning Wilson's lifelong enmity. Wilson had a long memory, he never forgave or forgot. "In 1916, Wilson had stooped very low in his drive against Sinn Féin leaders and against some important Irish-Americans like Judge Cohalan...The Department of State had forged evidence against Cohalan and in 1918, Secret Service agents fabricated confessions that were vehemently repudiated by Liam Mellowes and Patrick McCartan."[4]

With Theodore Roosevelt and William Howard Taft dividing the Republican vote, Wilson was elected in 1912 with 42 percent of the vote compared to Roosevelt's 27 percent and Taft's 23 percent. In 1916, Wilson narrowly defeated Charles Evans Hughes.

104

Irish-Americans in general were eager to praise Cohalan for his dedication and his achievements on Ireland's behalf. Desmond Ryan, no fan of the judge, said: "... Cohalan, in spite of his remarkable record, at best was a brilliant politician and in the last resort an American patriot first and last. Cohalan, however, had a case against de Valera who combined the roles of dictator, politician, and statesman in his usual, bewildering manner."[5]

Cohalan waged an unrelenting political campaign against Anglo-American interests, for which he never received a salary; his only recompense was occasional expenses for travel throughout the country to make appearances and speeches, and present his arguments before Congress.

De Valera possessed a Machiavellian ability to exploit human weakness and inspire a cadre of sycophants. One such lackey was Dr Patrick McCartan, active in the Supreme Council of the IRB between 1908 and 1914. He was dispatched to America in 1917 as envoy of the Irish Republic. In addition to his duties as the IRB's envoy he was editor of Joseph McGarrity's *Irish Press* in Philadelphia.

McGarrity arrived in America at the age of sixteen and proceeded to make and lose fortunes in real estate and liquor. Even before de Valera's arrival, these two had banded together in opposition to Devoy and Cohalan. "They were critical of the Friends of Irish Freedom [FOIF, founded by Devoy and Cohalan in 1916 as an offshoot of Clan na Gael] for allegedly devoting more attention to American politics than to Irish affairs."[6] Devoy and Cohalan recognized that America was the key to Irish freedom and their main efforts were directed toward influencing Congress to that end.

On March 4, 1919, three months before de Valera's arrival in America, Devoy and Cohalan had finally convinced Congress to pass a resolution: "That it is the earnest hope of the Congress of the United States of America that the Paris Peace Conference...will favorably consider the claims of Ireland to self-determination." Here was recognition of the Irish people's right to choose their own form of government.

Upon his arrival in New York City in June 1919, de Valera lost no time initiating his campaign to discredit Devoy and Cohalan. He swiftly recognized McGarrity's value as a lever to split the Irish-American movement and on June 17, 1919, less than a week after arriving in America, he dispatched his secretary, Harry Boland, along with McGarrity, to a convention of the American Federation of Labor (AF of L) in Atlantic City. McGarrity and McCartan had long been opposed to

Devoy and Cohalan's efforts to persuade the U.S. government to recognize Ireland's right to self-determination; they demanded immediate, unqualified American recognition of an Irish Republic.

In Atlantic City Thomas Rock, Devoy's emissary to the convention, had a Friends of Irish Freedom (FOIF) resolution calling for Irish self-determination wrenched out of his hands and torn up by McGarrity, who managed to persuade him and other influential delegates that he, McGarrity, was carrying a substitute resolution approved by the Irish-American leadership: "Resolved…that the Congress of the United States recognize the present Irish Republic," was the version adopted.

The critical difference between recognition of an Irish Republic and calling for the right of the Irish people to choose their own form of government was: in the former, the United States would be directly interfering in the internal affairs of England while in the latter, claims to self-determination was a reiteration of American policy that all people should be free to decide their own form of government. The United States was not about to interfere in the internal affairs of a wartime ally on behalf of the pro-German Irish.

The pattern had been set, and from this time forward de Valera never passed up an opportunity to insult or humiliate Devoy and Cohalan. In following the English *modus operandi* of making it appear that the Irish attacked first de Valera's strategy was to goad Devoy and Cohalan into criticizing the Irish President publicly so that he, in turn, could then charge them with initiating an attack against him. In order not to be perceived as himself antagonizing the Irish-Americans, de Valera publicly espoused self-determination until the 1920 presidential conventions.

On June 23, 1919 at the Waldorf-Astoria, less than a week after he had condoned Boland and McGarrity's caper in Atlantic City, de Valera reversed course and stated: "I am in America as the official head of the Irish Republic established by the will of the Irish people in accordance with the principle of self-determination…"[7]

Less than three months later, de Valera's henchmen went to work again, this time striking at Devoy and Cohalan in their own bailiwick, New York City. On September 14 the British Government had finally moved to officially suppress the Sinn Féin Parliament. McGarrity and McCartan were in New York when the news reached them, and it was decided to call a mass meeting of protest. Nothing wrong with that, of course, except that de Valera sanctioned the holding of the meeting at the Lexington Avenue Theater in New York City right under the noses of Devoy and Cohalan without informing them. His contempt and arrogance were made even more obvious when it became clear that Devoy and Cohalan had not even been invited to speak at the rally. Two weeks later, McGarrity added insult to injury by sending a bill for $1,500 to cover the expenses of the affair to the Friends of Irish Freedom. Even de Valera's official biographers admit, "Such occurrences were looked upon as evidence of de Valera's ill-will..."[8]

Devoy refused to be drawn into an open confrontation, and the bill was paid. But he sent Judge Cohalan his own account of the Lexington Avenue event, which he described as: "'The latest development in the effort to sidetrack us.' He telephoned the Waldorf Astoria where Harry Boland and the others were staying, and got through to McCartan, to whom he said, 'If there is a repetition of last night's work, I'll wash my hands of the whole business.'"[9]

One of the stated reasons for Britain's declaration of war against Germany in 1914 had been to uphold the rights of small nations, specifically Belgium. The Irish considered themselves in a similar context and this prompted many Irishmen to willingly join the British forces. Of approximately 180,000 Irish volunteers, one third never came home and tens of thousands were left crippled in mind and body.

After the Armistice of 1918, President Wilson, descendant of English transplanted Protestants in Northern Ireland and a lifelong Anglophile, prodded England and France into agreeing to a League of Nations, "to make the world safe for democracy." He steadfastly refused, however, to consider the problem of Ireland as anything more than an internal affair of Great Britain, the same position he had taken in 1916 in the aftermath of the Rising. The Irish took Wilson's call for making the world safe for democracy as nothing more than self-serving hot air. Even Robert Lansing, Wilson's Secretary of State, derided the President: "There are certain phrases in the President's 'Fourteen Points' which I am sure will cause trouble in the future because their meaning and application have not been thought out...The President is a phrase-maker par excellence. He admires trite sayings and revels in formulating them. But when it comes to their practical application he is so vague that their worth may well be doubted...In fact he does not seem to care just so that his words sound well."[10]

At Versailles, Wilson was an ardent champion of Armenia, Czechoslovakia, Poland and Yugoslavia but had no words for Ireland. The Peace Conference at Versailles served to set up the conditions for the Second World War. The victorious English and French propped up their colonial assets while stripping Germany of hers; in the process stacking the deck in their favor in controlling the proposed League of Nations.

The Irish-Americans under Devoy and Cohalan were scathing in their opposition to Wilson's approach. In the *Gaelic American* of February 22,

1919, Devoy commented on a draft of the League of Nations Covenant, "A precious document it is. Reading it critically, one seems to hear the clanging of the machinery forging the chains that are to bind the masses of humanity." In March, the *Irish World* reported: "It would be an insult to the intelligence and to the patriotism of the American people to doubt for a moment what course they will adopt when the national degradation involved in the acceptance of the British-made constitution of the League of Nations becomes known to them in all its repulsive hideousness."

Republican Senator William E. Borah of Idaho wrote to Cohalan through the Friends of Irish Freedom on March 29, 1919: "If America ever wants to do anything for little Ireland...she had better do so before this League of Nations is clapped down upon the world and fastened upon it by military power ..."[11]

The Irish-Americans represented a cohesive bloc of votes and with a presidential election looming the following year, President Wilson sought to temper their opposition. On a tour of the Western states in September 1919 to promote the League of Nations, Wilson attempted to convince Irish-Americans that Article X of the Covenant of the League of Nations would lead to Ireland's case being heard before that body. The President interpreted Article X as stating: "...We [League of Nations] will respect and preserve against external aggression the territorial integrity and existing political independence of other nations...and 'I stand for it absolutely.'"[12]

Wilson was being somewhat disingenuous. What Article X actually stated was: "The High Contracting Powers [effectively England and France] undertake to respect and *preserve against external aggression the territorial integrity and existing political independence of all States members of the League* [emphasis added]. In case of any such aggression or in case of any threat of danger of such aggression, the Executive Council shall advise upon the means by which this obligation shall be fulfilled."[13] Ireland was not an independent member of the League, but a part of Great Britain and therefore Article X actually preserved the "territorial integrity" of England to the detriment of Ireland.

As a League of Nations member, the United States would be acting illegally in sending financial aid to those who strove for an independent Ireland, and was bound to intervene militarily in England's defence in the event of any external aggressors seeking to support the Irish claim to freedom.

Not being an "independent small nation," Ireland could not bring her plight before the League of Nations. There was minimal hope in Article XI of the Covenant, which stated: "Members of the League...shall take any action that may be deemed wise...to safeguard the peace of a nation...It is also declared to be the friendly right of each Member to bring to the attention of the Assembly...any circumstance whatever affecting international relations, which threatens to disturb international peace."

Wilson's forebears were products of the Scottish Plantation of Ireland; he was a staunch Ulster Presbyterian and an Anglophile with little sympathy for Irish pleas for independence. He tried to convince the Irish-Americans: "...Once the treaty was ratified...the United States would be able to take up Ireland's cause at the League of Nations because Article XI of the Covenant provided that 'every matter that is likely to affect the peace of the world is everybody's business.'" But Wilson's claim that Ireland's plight could be considered by the League of Nations after the US was admitted as a member also rang hollow in the ears of Irish-Americans. After all, Britain and her former colonies with their six seats could easily outvote the one seat the United States held in the League.

De Valera, in following the English line, saw things differently from the Irish-Americans. Almost immediately upon his arrival in America in June 1919, and without consulting Devoy and Cohalan, he pledged Irish-American support for the League. This was a red flag to Devoy: de Valera had no right to speak for Irish-Americans, especially when his view conflicted with the FOIF's campaign to reject the League of Nations. At a meeting of prominent Irish-Americans, de Valera refused to discuss the League of Nations issue with Judge Cohalan. Jeremiah Lynch, national secretary of the Friends of Irish Freedom, was baffled by de Valera's insulting behaviour. He wrote: "The situation thus created was passed over in silence out of deference to the office held by de Valera. This silence was a great mistake. Men present on that occasion had a right to demand a full explanation of this unwarrantable attitude. Had they grappled with the situation then and there, the machinations of the few disturbing elements would in all probability have been exposed and the whole position clarified at the outset of President de Valera's campaign in America."[14]

De Valera should properly have discussed the position to be taken on the League of Nations with Devoy and Cohalan at the beginning of his visit. But his aim was to run them out of the Irish-American movement while promoting an English agenda. In a letter to the Dáil Cabinet he admitted: "The fight for the League of Nations was purely an American affair attacked from a purely American angle." On July 9, 1919, in a letter to Arthur Griffith, acting President of the Dáil during his absence in America, de Valera said: "The political situation here is obscure for the moment. I am trying to let Wilson know that if he goes for his fourteen points and a true League of Nations, men and women of Irish blood will be behind him ..."[15]

De Valera embarked on a Clan na Gael-sponsored cross-country tour during which he continued his pro-League of Nations campaign: "In his first week of speech-making, he generated a storm of booing and hissing even from enthusiasts at Madison Square Garden simply by mentioning President Wilson's name. He had to trim his sails a few days later at Wrigley Field in Chicago where, prior to his speaking, a resolution was adopted declaring that the meeting was "unalterably opposed" to the Covenant. He got out of allying himself with this position by stating that it was based on "purely American grounds" and that he felt "as a stranger and a guest here, he could not presume to interfere."[16]

Here was a typical de Valera tactic, one he would use again and again, yet it seemingly never caused a ripple of suspicion in Irish circles. Confronted with a united or overwhelming opposition, he temporarily either ceased to oppose or appeared to side with that majority consensus until he was in a position to reverse it. The genius of de Valera lay in his ability to recognize when it was best to cut his losses and move on. When it came to a vote in the Senate on November 11, 1919, support for the Treaty failed to secure the necessary two-thirds majority – a resounding victory for Republicans and also for Devoy and Cohalan personally. A major point of contention by Republicans was their claim that Great Britain would command six votes through its hold over the Commonwealth nations, whereas the US, would only have one vote. Others feared the League of Nations would mean American entanglement in Europe's constant wars.

Daniel T. O'Connell, director of the Irish Bureau of Information in Washington, D.C., an adjunct of the Friends of Irish Freedom, confirmed de Valera's pro-League of Nations stance, his attempt to dictate FOIF anti-League policy, and his denial of both when forced to explain his actions. "I was visited at the Bureau in Washington, D.C. by Dr McCartan, who, with some agitation, gave me a message from de Valera ordering me not to speak further against the League. I resented this.

"Later in the day, November 7, 1919 McCartan left a written message for O'Connell: "The President asked me to tell you to be careful about your statements on such things as Senator Walsh's resolution, as he might be forced to repudiate you and that would do harm to the whole movement! I told him politely to mind his own business."[17]

O'Connell continued: "At the Park Avenue Hotel Conference in New York City in March 1920, de Valera denied that any such message had been given by McCartan [to O'Connell]. When confronted with the document, he first said it was false and then repudiated McCartan, saying he had no authority to write such a message. This latter assertion deceived no one."[18]

In a November 1919 editorial in the *Gaelic American*, Devoy recognized the British scheme, and by implication de Valera, to destroy Irish-American influence. In an eerie forecast of things to come, he wrote: "The most dangerous English propaganda that ever menaced the Irish Cause is now being carried on here in America under the pretense of zeal for the Irish Republic. Its object is to sow dissension in the Irish movement at a time when unity is absolutely necessary and to destroy confidence in the leadership when that leadership is achieving results most beneficial to Ireland and injurious to England. If it should succeed, the Irish movement in America would be destroyed or rendered powerless and Ireland, when she most needs American help, would be deprived of it."[19]

Through de Valera, the British accomplished exactly what Devoy predicted, yet hardly a whisper was heard questioning de Valera's motives or conduct. In a bizarre defense of de Valera, Desmond Ryan wrote: "de Valera's most spectacular triumph was the defeat of the League of Nations in the American Senate. 'Sign that Treaty as it stands and you enslave Ireland!' was his constant cry...No searcher of his American speeches of this time will ever be able to resurrect a line or word likely to embarrass de Valera today."[20]

Once he returned to Ireland, any memory of de Valera's early support for the League of Nations was obliterated. "Indeed, when he addressed the Dáil in January 1921, he actually listed the defeat of the League of Nations as the first of his objectives in going to the United States ..."[21]

With the Republican and Democratic conventions fast approaching, de Valera shifted "Assignment America" into fast forward. In a February 1920 interview with the British newspaper, *Westminster Gazette*, he knocked the props out from under the Irish claim for independence and downgraded Ireland's demand for recognition of an Irish Republic to that of a satellite of Britain. He cited the treaty between America and Cuba, arrived at under the aegis of the Monroe Doctrine. Included in the terms of that treaty, the Government of Cuba: "shall never enter into any treaty or other compact with any foreign Power or Powers which will impair or tend to impair the independence of Cuba, nor in any manner authorize or permit any foreign Power or Powers to obtain by colonization or for military or naval purposes or otherwise, lodgment in or control over any portion of said island."

Without having previously consulted anyone, de Valera now made an odd proposal: "Why doesn't Britain make a stipulation like this to safeguard herself against foreign attack as the United States did with Cuba? Why doesn't Britain declare a Monroe Doctrine for the two neighboring islands? The people of Ireland, so far from objecting, would cooperate with their whole soul."[22] The *Westminster Gazette* interview appeared the next day in the *New York Globe*.

Devoy had so far shown himself a model of forbearance in the face of the provocations of de Valera, but this was too much. In an editorial in the *Gaelic American* on February 14, 1920, he set forth his point of view: "de Valera's proposal opens the way for the discussion of compromise, or a change in objective, while England has her hands on Ireland's throat. It will be hailed in England as an offer of surrender...it amounts to a proposal for a self-governing Ireland under an English Protectorate, or some kind of an international guarantee ...

"The Irish Cause has nothing to fear from a free and fair discussion or from frank statements of the truth. But there is no race more easily influenced by slander and falsehood than the Irish. Slander and falsehood are the weak and venomous Irishman's deadliest weapons when he is bent on mischief."[23] Was de Valera the "weak and venomous Irishman" Devoy had in mind?

McCartan, normally a de Valera lackey, was aghast at the ramifications of de Valera's proposal, claiming it: "... introduces a new principle. It is a withdrawal by the official head of the Irish Republic [de Valera] of the demand Ireland be set free to decide her own international relations."[24] Writing in 1932 McCartan admitted that de Valera betrayed his office. He described the Cuba interview as a "clear-intimation that the President of the Republic of Ireland was prepared to accept much less than complete sovereignty for Ireland...The choice of the *Westminster Gazette* (an English newspaper) seemed appropriate to inform Lloyd George that Ireland's President was willing to downgrade her claim to the level of a domestic issue of England ..."[25] On still another occasion, McCartan charged that the Irish leader "...had usurped the right to speak and act for Ireland and the situation left us without the power to challenge him."[26]

McCartan admitted: "...The whole movement towards recognition was shattered by de Valera's Cuban interview of February 5, 1920."[27] De Valera was out of control, neither seeking nor accepting advice from anyone. One moment, he would drop his demands for recognition of an Irish Republic, as in his *Westminster Gazette* interview in February; the next, as at the Republican and Democratic conventions in June, demand immediate recognition of an Irish Republic by the United States.

Incredibly, his contradictory positions never seemed to raise a suspicion as to his motives.

As for the Dáil Cabinet in Dublin, de Valera's *Westminster Gazette* interview had placed its members on the horns of a dilemma: either they publicly repudiate the leader of the Irish movement or enter a vote of confidence in him. McCartan, after charging the Irish President with shattering the whole movement towards recognition, in an obsequious comment stated: "... de Valera...wrote to the Cabinet at home, that if they doubted him, they should let him know. But they knew well that he would say nothing in America which he would not be willing to say at home."[28] They also knew that to repudiate him would cause an internationally embarrassing split in Irish ranks both at home and in America. Neither Collins nor Griffith were about to revive the historical Irish tendency to split the country at every critical moment; nor would their loyalty to de Valera permit them to embarrass him publicly.

McCartan records the following message of continued support sent by the Dáil Cabinet to de Valera: "The Dáil Éireann, assembled in full session at Dublin today, unanimously reaffirms the allegiance of the citizens of Ireland to your policy, expresses complete satisfaction with the work you have performed and relies with confidence upon the great American nation to accord recognition to the Republic of Ireland, now in fact and law established."[29]

This message was in part the result of personal reports to the Dáil by McCartan and Boland who were dispatched by de Valera to Dublin in order to place Devoy and Cohalan in a bad light while praising the Irish President's position. "McCartan did not agree with what de Valera had done and as a highly respected IRB man could easily have swayed opinion against him had he chosen to [tell the truth]..."[30] In an incredible admission of having misled the Cabinet, MacCartan noted in his book, *With de Valera in America*: "...The impression grew on me that I had wrongfully helped to fix the eyes of the Cabinet on our fight for their Chief Executive, de Valera, and not on the fight for recognition... I had forgotten to mention Cohalan's stand for recognition... It might have cheered the Cabinet to know that our American leader [Cohalan] had publicly testified for the Republic on the eve of its public denial by our Irish leader [de Valera]."[31]

In a further admission of wrongdoing, McCartan wrote: "I gave de Valera's explanation of the *Westminster Gazette* interview, which was substantially...that only his enemies, and Devoy and Cohalan, had put a hostile construction on the interview, in pursuance of the campaign they had started against him when he arrived in the United States, and which overtly and covertly, they had since continued. I did not say a word about the merits or demerits of the Cuban proposal."[32]

With the pieces of his "Assignment America" now in place, de Valera moved inexorably against Devoy and Cohalan. The *Westminster Gazette* interview was the straw as far as Devoy was concerned, catapulting both he and Cohalan into public criticism of the President of the Irish Republic, just as de Valera had planned. Despite their superhuman patience, the Irish Machiavelli was about to engineer the public split he had come to America to accomplish.

In his February 14 editorial in the *Gaelic American*, Devoy presented an analysis of de Valera's *Westminster Gazette* interview. McCartan attacked Devoy's assessment of the interview, but the old Fenian was quick to defend himself: "de Valera's interview with the *Westminster Gazette's* correspondent was discussed on its merits without one disrespectful word to the President – de Valera was not misrepresented, misquoted or misinterpreted...On the contrary, I quoted his exact words and I reprinted his fuller article in which he repeated the statements to which I respectfully took exception...The Irish people in America...have given President de Valera magnificent support on the faith of Dáil Éireann's Declaration of Independence and Proclamation of the Irish Republic ..."[33] He declared, "... No man, not even the President of the Irish Republic, has the authority to change it ..."[34]

De Valera fueled the controversy by refusing to meet Devoy. In 1916 the British had insisted that the Irish must fire the first shot of any insurrection so that the English would not appear to have initiated the conflict. De Valera now used the same strategy in goading Devoy into firing the first public salvo, then charging that it was the old Fenian who had initiated the "split." He allowed McGarrity, Boland, and McCartan to attack Devoy while he personally challenged Cohalan demanding that the Judge disassociate himself from Devoy's editorial policy. He also called on Cohalan to acknowledge him [de Valera] as the leader of all things Irish in America. "De Valera was not only ready to inflict the savage bite upon the hand of Cohalan; he was also ready to inspire a drive against the Judge that he hoped would eliminate him as an outstanding leader of the Irish-American element in America."[35]

He dispatched Boland to Cohalan with a letter accusing him of being the puppeteer and Devoy a puppet in his hands: "After mature consideration, I have decided that to continue to ignore the articles in the *Gaelic American* would result in injury to the cause I have been sent here to promote. The articles themselves are, of course, the least matter. It is the evident purpose behind them and the general attitude of mind they reveal that is the menace."

Cohalan rebutted the charges; "I respectfully suggest...that you would be well-advised if you hesitate before you jeopardize or imperil that solidarity of opinion and unity of action among millions of American citizens, which you found here among us when you came, which have been the despair of England's friends and have already accomplished so much for America and Ireland ..."[36]

Cohalan failed to recognize that de Valera's purpose in coming to America was to "jeopardize and imperil that solidarity of opinion and unity of action." Rather than question de Valera's motives, T. Ryle Dwyer charged de Valera's letter to Cohalan as: "An extremely naïve piece of insensitive arrogance."[37] The opposite hypothesis – that de Valera exhibited political sophistication in luring Devoy and Cohalan into a public controversy – was never considered.

De Valera did not reply to Cohalan but sent Griffith and Collins a copy of Cohalan's letter with a long outline of his grief against the Irish-Americans and Cohalan in particular. He declared Cohalan's letter to be "A willful misrepresentation of my whole attitude: The production of a tricky police court lawyer." He explained that he had not replied to the letter "because the only reply I could make would be a broadside of a kind which would make it absolutely impossible to work with the Judge in any way. This letter shows what distance petty, personal rivalries will drive men ..."[38]

On March 6, 1920, he wrote to Griffith, "I labour under no misapprehension as to the relations between us. They are, unfortunately, only too well defined by the Judge's attitude from the beginning. So clear were they from the first that I was actually considering the question of whether it would not be better for our cause that I should return or go elsewhere...I realized early that, nevertheless, and big as the country is, it was not big enough to hold the Judge and myself."[39]

He further informed Griffith that he suspected an ulterior motive: "He was to be a rubber stamp for somebody...The position I have held (I was rapidly driven to assert it or surrender) is the following: 'No American has the right to dictate policy of the Irish people. We are here with a definite objective. Americans banded under the trade name "Friends of Irish Freedom" (FOIF) ought to help us to obtain the objective, if they are truly what the name implies.'"[40]

De Valera trivialized the rift; "'... The trouble is purely one of personalities. I cannot feel confidence enough in a certain man [Cohalan] to let him have implicit control of tactics here, without consultation and agreement with me...on the ways and means they have to be consulted,' he admitted, but he stipulated that he reserved 'the right to use my judgment as to whether any means suggested is or is not in conformity with our purpose.'"[41]

Irish writers of the period have been consistent only in the way they have contradicted one another in assessing de Valera's purpose at this time. Official biographers, Longford and O'Neill, writing in 1970, defended the Irish President's abandonment of the Irish Republic in his *Westminster Gazette* interview. According to them, de Valera admitted: "He did not weigh every word and every sentence of a speech and of an interview as if it was a legal document..."[42] Elsewhere, they claimed: "de Valera could be and was, subtle in argument and... ultra-careful of every word he spoke ..."[43]

According to Irish writers, de Valera's inexplicable and inexcusable actions were the result of his either weighing or not weighing every word. He drove everyone to distraction with his habit of poring over every written detail, every nuance of every word of every speech and public release that went out under his name.

Writing in 1936, John Gunther noted: "de Valera is very particular about newspaper interviews...Everything must be written and okayed by him."[44] Dwyer noted: "de Valera [had] also irritated Collins by agonizing over the wording of the Irish submission to the Paris Peace Conference. 'The damned Peace Conference will be over before he's satisfied,' Collins had grumbled in frustration."[45]

Despite their differences, Cohalan continued his efforts to promote the Irish President and Ireland. Devoy had arranged a huge Fifth Avenue parade for Saint Patrick's Day 1920, and Cohalan graciously relinquished his place of honour to de Valera. At a Friendly Sons of St. Patrick dinner that evening he introduced de Valera in glowing terms: "A man who is a soldier, who is a scholar, who is a patriot and who is the elected head of the Republic of Ireland – Éamon de Valera." During the festivities, in a further attempt at unity, he proposed a meeting of leading Irish-Americans. "The Judge suggested a conference of about 100 important men identified with the Irish movement. The conference would meet in New York City on March 19."[46] Cohalan's proposal was met with overwhelming approval, and he and Devoy duly made the arrangements.

On the face of it, this was a straightforward proposal. Yet there are as many subtle and not-so-subtle shaded accounts of that daylong meeting and the events surrounding it as there are biographers and historians who have written about them. McCartan, who was not in attendance, alleged that it was a kangaroo court rather than a conference, convened with the aim of discrediting the absent de Valera, who was allegedly to be decoyed to Chicago to attend a spurious engagement there. Longford and O'Neill make no reference to this fake Chicago engagement. It was elsewhere said that de Valera had to force his way into the meeting, and a good deal of confusion was apparently caused by Devoy's deafness.

Much was made of a letter in which de Valera and McGarrity claimed Devoy had written: "de Valera must be sent back to Ireland defeated and discredited." Devoy, in the letter, referred to a rumor that de Valera was plotting to discredit him. The letter actually stated that if de Valera attempted such a thing "He would go back to Ireland defeated and discredited" – not quite the same thing at all.

Despite the fact that neither de Valera, McCartan nor McGarrity ever produced any such letter written by Devoy, Irish writers summarily dismissed Devoy's account. In an editorial in the *Gaelic American* of June 26, 1920 Devoy not only denied the charge that he had threatened to send de Valera back to Ireland "defeated and discredited," but presented a number of prominent Irish-Americans to confirm his version of the letter. At the same time, the statements of impartial men of unimpeachable credentials such as John P. Grace, John A. Murphy, Richard F. Dalton, Laurance Rice and a host of other prominent Irish-Americans who attested to the contents of Devoy's letter were all but ignored. De Valera's refusal to produce the letter substantiated Devoy's contention.

The meeting presented de Valera in a sorry light. One man who was present wrote to a friend: "I confess before Heaven that President de Valera was that day revealed to me as either laboring under some psychopathic condition or that the evil spirit himself had taken hold of the Irish movement...whatever President de Valera's qualities might be, his leadership was an accident. He had clearly fallen into the hands of men moved by selfish, and some by sinister motives. For ten hours that day about one hundred of us...were tortured by such an exhibition of intolerance and ingratitude as I have never witnessed before...I beg to repeat that, not having seen him before, as for those ten hours, he unfolded himself, I thought the man was crazy."[47]

When the dust had settled, it was finally agreed that Devoy and Cohalan would steer clear of purely Irish affairs, while in return de Valera agreed not to interfere in purely American matters. The value of de Valera's promise was made plain in a letter to Arthur Griffith of March 23, only four days after the conference, seeking authorization from Griffith and the Dáil to spend $500,000 on the upcoming Presidential election and an additional $1 million on obtaining American recognition of an Irish Republic. He asked the matter be kept secret so as not to interfere with the Clan na Gael and the FOIF fundraising efforts under Devoy, which between them raised ninety per cent of the money earmarked for the benefit of Ireland. As Dwyer wrote in 1991: "All this was clearly a violation of [de Valera's] agreement to stay out of American affairs...another clash with the Cohalan-Devoy faction was inevitable..."[48]

"It was thought all misunderstandings had now been composed but alas, within 48 hours de Valera had renewed his tactics...and his friends were again slandering Cohalan and Devoy."[49] McCartan also admitted that de Valera had no intention of keeping his word: "The de Valera-Cohalan war was resumed shortly after their prayers for peace...The first aggressive move was taken by de Valera..."[50]

The meeting marked the moment of de Valera's triumph in America. When the conference turned from a discussion of the danger he posed to the Irish-American cause to one of toleration of his actions, the destruction of the Irish-American influence in the United States accelerated and the discrediting of Devoy and Cohalan was under way.

In December 1919, Judge Cohalan had set forth before a Congressional Committee a brilliant exposition of the arguments in favour of the recognition by the United States of an Irish Republic. On December 12, 1919 Republican Congressman William E. Mason of Illinois introduced what became known as the Mason Bill, which called for the appropriation of $14,000 to provide salaries for American consular and diplomatic envoys to Ireland. If Congress were to approve the bill, it would in effect be recognizing the Irish Republic.

Cohalan had presented Ireland's case with such consummate legal and political brilliance that even his critics were impressed. Boland embraced him enthusiastically while McCartan claimed that the judge's performance had assured Ireland's ultimate goal of recognition as an independent Republic. Recalling Cohalan's summation, McCartan later wrote: "I rushed to shake his hand and my enthusiasm he visibly appreciated. With Frank P. Walsh, and Cohalan to champion us, there would be nothing to stop us in achieving final victory. It might be delayed – but no longer than similar action in other cases had been delayed – but the ultimate result was beyond doubt."[51]

Walsh was a prominent lawyer and appointee to the American Commission for Irish Independence, a fact-finding group attempting to present Ireland's case before the victorious powers at the Paris Peace talks. Lloyd George refused to grant them an audience and President Wilson voiced no objection to the British Prime Minister's refusal.

Boland, McGarrity and McCartan surprisingly credited Cohalan with a significant accomplishment on behalf of recognition of an Irish

Republic. McCartan wrote: "To secure recognition of the Republic of Ireland by the American Government was the sole remaining task of President de Valera."[52]

During the early months of 1920, the Mason Bill became bogged down in Committee, and on May 22 a conference was held in Washington, DC attended by de Valera, Cohalan, Congressman Mason and three other Congressmen. As a result of those deliberations, the following resolution was released to the floor of the House of Representatives for a vote: "In the interest of world peace and international good will, be it Resolved by the House of Representatives (the Senate concurring) that the Congress of the United States views with concern and solicitude these conditions [in Ireland] and expresses its sympathy with the aspirations of the Irish people for a government of their own choice."[53]

The Irish-American community greeted this watered-down Resolution with outrage, and McCartan and McGarrity fingered Judge Cohalan as the culprit responsible. It was not long, however, before whispers began to circulate that de Valera was the author. This has been mostly denied by Irish writers favourable to de Valera, and in his account of events, McCartan wrote: "It was rumoured that de Valera, himself, had drafted this resolution, but to me de Valera explicitly and emphatically denied this rumor."[54]

At a Council meeting of the FOIF on June 18 1920, McCartan again accused Cohalan of being the author of the Congressional resolution. McCartan charged: "There was but one strong alternative resolution; one submitted by de Valera, when it was seen the Mason Bill was doomed...[he] had de Valera's word on it."[55] Cohalan, however, produced a copy of the Resolution that was drafted on May 22, in which he claimed: "It was written by de Valera and witnessed by Mason and three other Congressmen. Cohalan supported his assertion by pointing out interdelineations which several councilors recognized as being in de Valera's handwriting."[56]

According to McCartan: "Cohalan had confounded me by drawing from his pocket a manuscript of the resolution – the first part of which – and the only part I looked at – was beyond doubt in de Valera's handwriting. I went straight to de Valera. He explained to me he had tried to draft a suitable resolution and having failed, threw the paper on the table and that evidently Cohalan had finished it."[57]

Here surely was a golden opportunity for de Valera and McCartan to present evidence of Cohalan's alleged mischief; had he publicly challenged Cohalan to produce the entire document, he could have proven that he had only written the first part, as he claimed, and

119

Cohalan the rest. Such a revelation would have ruined Cohalan politically and personally. Yet neither de Valera nor McCartan demanded that Cohalan produce the entire document nor did they question the witnesses to its writing.

Characteristically, de Valera sidestepped the issue. He had bigger fish to fry, and was not about to get into a public spitting contest with Cohalan over the Mason Resolution that he could not win. His eye was on the Republican Convention in Chicago two weeks later on June 6.

A bold plan to create a "Commission on British Atrocities in Ireland" to try England before the court of American public opinion was presented by Dr. W. J. Maloney, a close friend of McCartan, whom Devoy accused of being an English spy. During the February 1919 Philadelphia Irish Race Convention, Maloney was so disruptive as a member of the Committee on Resolutions, that Michael J. Ryan, enraged at his antics, charged: "If the British had a man on the resolutions committee he would be doing exactly what Maloney was doing."[58]

McCartan set up a meeting between de Valera and Maloney to discuss the holding of the "Commission on British Atrocities" scheme. According to Maloney, "The primary purpose of the Commission on British Atrocities in Ireland was to enlist the moral forces of the world to the end that the murder of Irish citizens may cease and public opinion may compel Britain to evacuate Ireland."[59]

McCartan recognized the public relations possibilities of the plan; at a meeting at the Waldorf Astoria attended by de Valera, Dudley Field Malone, McGarrity and McCartan: "We were all enthusiastic except de Valera."[60] The Irish President discouraged anti-British activities, and fell back on the sort of argument he had put forward against the Dublin Proclamation. He claimed that in a public trial an American court would favor the United Kingdom: "... The Imperial resources of England would overwhelm the presentation of our case; English witnesses would far outnumber and outweigh ours and the result of the investigation would be our condemnation."[61]

Just as de Valera sought to temper actions against the British, so McCartan sought to justify de Valera's negative attitude: "These objections sounded as if de Valera was hostile to the plan but he, being fearful for Ireland, was prudently seeking reassurance and when Maloney met his objections and de Valera could think of no more, he [allegedly] agreed to go ahead."[62]

The newspaper *The Nation* offered to back Maloney's plan if an impressive committee could be put together. "De Valera promised to send out telegrams asking our influential supporters to urge those they knew among the invited by *The Nation* to accept the invitations to join the Committee." The response was most disappointing, and it was eventually discovered that the promised telegrams had not been sent out. When they finally were, the response was enthusiastic. De Valera blamed one of his minions for the omission. This was the usual course of events: de Valera was reluctant to endorse any anti-English activities in America but when initiated, he actively did what he could to derail such undertakings. When found out, his standard response was to deny involvement or blame someone else.

De Valera was not about to be deterred in his attempt to sabotage the Commission and adamantly refused to loosen the purse strings on the $3 million sitting idle in American banks in order to fund the project. Without funds, the enterprise was doomed. Finally, through the intercession of Boland, de Valera relented. He would commit himself to an anti-British plan only when his objections were overwhelmingly opposed and he feared his refusal would rouse suspicion as to his motives.

The "Committee on British Atrocities in Ireland" did excellent work; America was held spellbound as witness after witness confirmed instances of terror and murder by the English in Ireland. The British people themselves were disgusted with the behavior of their men in Ireland. On March 31, 1920 the *Manchester Guardian*, in an editorial on the proceedings of the Commission, reported: "In the main, the facts, unhappily, are only too far past dispute, like those of the German reign of terror in Belgium in 1914. One can only read the report with a kind of helpless rage...resentment [of an outsider judging the English] quickly passes into a stronger and more bitter one against those whose unfaithfulness has laid us open to an impeachment so galling because it is so unanswerable...To dispute the few details, to point out a few excesses in this detestable American report, would only advertise its crushing remainder of truth."[63] Despite de Valera's efforts to block it, the Committee garnered worldwide sympathy for the Irish cause coupled with international revulsion against British repression in Ireland.

Raising funds for the relief of the families of prisoners and IRA members on the run had supposedly been one of de Valera's primary objectives in deserting the fight in Ireland and his hasty flight to America. A relief ship carrying food and medical supplies – such as had been sent to Belgium in the Great War – cost nearly a quarter of a million dollars. De Valera refused to touch the $3 million lying idle in American banks for this purpose, but through the efforts of prominent Irish-Americans $313,095 was raised; Michael Collins never failed to meet a challenge, raising $313,215, topping the American donations by $120.

De Valera's passive-aggressive policy was again manifest in his approval and subsequent stonewalling a proposal from Arthur Griffith in late July. Griffith suggested that an American committee be organized to promote the adoption of devastated Irish towns by American cities and raise funds for the reconstruction of those communities destroyed by the Black and Tans, English enlisted men sent to Ireland to supplement the Royal Irish Constabulary, which had been rendered impotent by Collins campaign of intimidation and assassination. They were disillusioned unemployed Army veterans looking for excitement and an income: with pay at ten shillings a day, there was no shortage of recruits. There were not enough dark green Royal Irish Constabulary uniforms for them and, outfitted partly in khaki with black constabulary belts, they were immediately dubbed "Black and Tans" after a famous pack of Irish hounds. Having survived the brutal trench warfare in France, they had little patience with Collins' guerillas. Their brutality turned many pro-British supporters into Sinn Féin supporters.

Griffith was one man de Valera could not ignore, and he reluctantly passed on Griffith's reconstruction proposal to Bishop Gallagher, President of the FOIF. The Bishop set matters in train and preparations were well in hand when Boland sent word that the President of Ireland had other plans. He hoped to interest the Knights of Columbus in the fund and said that the Friends of Irish Freedom should not proceed in the matter. "Months have now elapsed and practically little has been done to give any appreciable relief to the actual sufferers in Ireland."[64]

Another Machiavellian stroke of de Valera's was his version of the "German Plot." His apologists put it down to political naivety, but de Valera hardly endeared himself and his cause to the American people when he publicly espoused the line that "The Irish people wished and hoped that Germany might win the war."[65] With the war hardly over and thousands of homeward-bound American soldiers still marking time in Europe, such comments could only distance the Irish-American community from mainstream America. McCartan acknowledged the fact that; "...The mass of American people were inclined more to their ally England than to us, whom they still regarded as having a German flavor..."[66] de Valera was criticized in the newspapers for his ill-timed and tactless pro-German speeches: "American Legionnaires demanded that he be deported. To those Americans who had only recently laid down their arms against the Kaiser, his views verged on the traitorous."[67]

Notes

1. Fitzgerald, W.G., *The voice of Ireland, A Survey of the Race & Nation from all Angles*, Virtue Ltd. Dublin/London, p. 235

2. Ryan, Desmond, *The Phoenix Flame*, Arthur Baker, London 1937, p. 318

3. Fitzgerald, W.G., *The voice of Ireland, A Survey of the Race & Nation from all Angles*, Virtue Ltd. Dublin/London, p. 229

4. Tansill, Charles, *America and the Fight for Irish Freedom 1866-1922*, Devin-Adair, NY 1957, p. 265

5. Ryan, Desmond, *Unique Dictator*, Arthur Barker, London, 1936, p. 109

6. Dwyer, T. Ryle, *De Valera's Darkest Hour 1919-1932*, Mercier Press, Dublin/Cork, 1982, p. 33

7. Coogan, Tim Pat, *De Valera, The Man who was Ireland*, Harper, 1996, p. 143

8. Longford, Earl of & O'Neill, Thomas P., *Éamon de Valera*, Hutchinson, London, 1970, p. 106

9. Devoy to Cohalan, 9/16/1919

10. Tansill, Charles C., *America and the Fight for Irish Freedom, 1866-1922*, Devin-Adair, NY 1957, 282, and Lansing MSS, Library of Congress, p. 282

11. Maxwell, Kenneth, "Irish Americans and the Fight for Treaty Ratification", *Public Opinion Quarterly*, U. of Chicago Press, Vol. 31, Winter 1967 – 1968, p. 627

12. Tansill, Charles C., *America and the Fight for Irish Freedom, 1866-1922*, Devin-Adair NY 1957, p. 334

13. Macardle, Dorothy, *The Irish Republic*, V. Gollancz, Irish Press, London, 1951, p. 281, p. 281

14. Tansill, Charles C., *America and the Fight for Irish Freedom 1866-1922*, Devin-Adair NY 1957, p. 341

15. Longford, Earl of & O'Neill, Thomas P., *Éamon de Valera*, Hutchinson, London, 1970, p. 99

16. Coogan, Tim Pat, *De Valera, The Man who was Ireland*, Harper, 1996, p. 149

17. Tansill, Charles C., *America and the Fight for Irish Freedom 1866-1922*, Devin-Adair NY 1957, p. 342

18. Fitzgerald, W.G., *The voice of Ireland, A Survey of the Race & Nation from all Angles*, Virtue Ltd. Dublin/London, p. 238

19. Tansill, Charles C., *America and the Fight for Irish Freedom 1866-1922*, Devin-Adair NY 1957, p. 349

20. Ryan, Desmond, *Unique Dictator*, Arthur Barker, London, 1936, p. 128

21. Dwyer, T. Ryle, *De Valera, The Man & the Myths*, Poolbe Dublin, 1991, p. 173

22. McCartan, Patrick, *With de Valera in America*, Brentano/NY 1932, p. 150

23. *Gaelic American*, 2/14/1920

24. McCartan, Patrick, *With de Valera in America*, Brentano/NY 1932, p. 151

25. *ibid,* p. 151

26. *ibid,* p. 155

27. *ibid,* p. 218
28. Longford, Earl of & O'Neill, Thomas P., *Éamon de Valera,* Hutchinson, London, 1970, p. 106
29. *New York Times,* 7/2/1920, 1:6, 3:3
30. Coogan, Tim Pat, *De Valera, The Man who was Ireland,* Harper, 1996, p. 167
31. McCartan, Patrick, *With de Valera in America,* Brentano/NY 1932, p. 155
32. *ibid,* p. 153
33. *Gaelic American,* 3/13/1920, p. 1
34. *ibid,* 2/21/1920, p. 1
35. Tansill, Charles C., *America and the Fight for Irish Freedom 1866-1922,* Devin-Adair NY 1957, p. 339
36. Coogan, Tim Pat, *De Valera, The Man who was Ireland,* Harper, 1996, p. 164
37. Dwyer, T. Ryle, *De Valera, The Man & the Myths,* Poolbeg, Dublin, 1991, p. 38
38. Beaslai, Pieras, *Michael Collins and the Making of a New Ireland,* Vol II, Harper Bros. NY 1926, p. 14
39. *ibid,* p. 4
40. Coogan, Tim Pat, *De Valera, The Man who was Ireland,* Harper, 1996, p. 166
41. *ibid,* p. 107
42. Longford, Earl of & O'Neill, Thomas P., *Éamon de Valera,* Hutchinson, London, 1970, p. 107
43. *ibid,* p. 344
44. Gunther, John, "The Truth about de Valera", *Strand Magazine,* 6/6/1936, p. 324
45. Tansill, Charles C., *America and the Fight for Irish Freedom 1866-1922,* Devin-Adair NY 1957, p. 365
46. *ibid,* p. 368
47. Dwyer, T. Ryle, *De Valera, The Man & the Myths,* Poolbeg, Dublin, p. 41
48. Fitzgerald, W.G., *The voice of Ireland, A Survey of the Race & Nation from all Angles,* Virtue Ltd. Dublin/London, p. 247
49. McCartan, Patrick, *With de Valera in America,* Brentano/NY 1932, p. 182
50. *ibid,* p. 149
51. *ibid*
52. *Gaelic American,* 6/5/1920
53. McCartan, Patrick, *With de Valera in America,* Brentano/NY 1932, p. 187
54. Fitzgerald, W.G., *The voice of Ireland, A Survey of the Race & Nation from all Angles,* Virtue Ltd. Dublin/London, p. 245
55. *ibid,* p. 245
56. McCartan, Patrick, *With de Valera in America,* Brentano/NY 1932, p. 188
57. Tansill, Charles C., *America and the fight for Irish Freedom 1866-1922,* Derin – Adair, NY. 1757, p. 139
58. McCartan, Patrick, *With de Valera in America,* Brentano/NY 1932, Appendix IV, p. 259
59. *ibid,* p. 300

60. *ibid,* p. 210
61. *ibid,* p. 210
62. *ibid,* p. 211
63. *ibid,* p. 239
64. *ibid,* p. 208 fn
65. Bromage, Mary C., *De Valera and the March of a Nation*, Hutchinson, London, 1956, p. 93
66. McCartan, Patrick, *With de Valera in America*, Brentano/NY 1932, p. 121
67. Bromage, Mary C., *De Valera and the March of a Nation*, Hutchinson, London, 1956, p. 94

CHAPTER X
Bond Certificate Drive

"De Valera rejected all advice, snubbed several of the most consistent workers for the Race and insisted upon a Loan in such form as would constitute recognition of the existing Irish Republic... It was his first exhibition of the temperamental outbreaks that revealed his incapacity for leadership and the beginning of the impolitic actions that resulted in splitting the Irish ranks in America wide open."[1]   John J. Splain, Vice President Friends of Irish Freedom

Dáil Éireann, the Irish Parliament, elected Éamon de Valera Prime Minister on Fool's Day, April 1, 1919. At the opening session, de Valera proposed a national loan of £250,000 ($1.25 million) and an international loan in the U.S. for a similar amount.

De Valera justified his dash to America on the grounds that Ireland desperately needed funds to operate the various departments of the Republican Government, to provide for the starving families of men on the run or serving time and to purchase arms. Only one in every eight men serving in the Irish Republican Brotherhood (IRB), later designated the Irish Republican Army (IRA), possessed weapons. Most importantly, he contended that he was going to America to seek recognition of an Irish Republic and lend his efforts to uniting the Irish-Americans.

In every one of his alleged reasons for traveling to America, de Valera failed Ireland, but his efforts once again successfully crowned British interests. His American Bond Certificate fund-raising campaign was another major coup for the English. Throughout seven long centuries, the English had not only confiscated Irish land, tortured, murdered, and transported an endless line of Irish to the Gulags of Australia, West Indies, and Connaught, but made the Irish pay for the privilege.

De Valera's triumphant public appearance on June 23, 1919 culminated in a huge motor caravan inching its way through New York City streets. Tens of thousands of Irish-Americans pushed and shoved to get a glimpse of the 1916 Easter Rising Commandant who had cheated

General Maxwell's firing squad; the "Wizard" who "escaped" from Lincoln Jail. "Up de Valera" echoed through skyscraper canyons as he stepped out of his car in front of the Waldorf-Astoria Hotel to be greeted by John Devoy and Judge Daniel Cohalan, the organizers of the huge reception.

The Irish President, rather than unite Irish-Americans, succeeded in alienating them within two weeks of his arrival. "He rejected all advice, snubbed several of the most consistent workers for the Race and insisted upon a Loan in such form as would constitute [United States] recognition of the existing Irish Republic...It was his first exhibition of the temperamental outbreaks that revealed his incapacity for leadership and the beginning of the impolitic actions that later resulted in splitting the Irish ranks in America wide open."[2]

Contrary to de Valera's charge that Cohalan was uncooperative "from the first," Judge Cohalan convened a conference of twenty-five prominent Irish-American lawyers, bankers, and businessmen to assist de Valera. The Irish President did not ask the Irish-Americans for their advice but dictated to them his plan to establish a Republic of Ireland Bond Drive to raise $10 million. He declared that the Irish Republic Bonds would be underwritten and sold over the counter by American banks.

De Valera ignored the objections raised by Judge Cohalan, Michael J. Ryan, Judge John W. Goff, and other leading Irish-American lawyers and bankers' contention that a Republic of Ireland Bond Drive was a violation of American "Blue Sky" laws – state laws enacted to prevent the promotion of fraudulent securities. He provoked a quarrel charging Cohalan's opposition to his plan was spiteful and petty and insisted that the sale of Republic of Ireland Bonds was legal.

John J. Splain, National Vice President of the Friends of Irish Freedom, noted: "Judge Cohalan contended that the proposed sale of Republic of Ireland Bonds would be illegal unless the United States recognized the Irish Republic first. As a trained lawyer on the bench of the New York Supreme Court, he knew what he was talking about."[3]

The critical issue was that an internationally recognized Irish Republic was a legal prerequisite for de Valera's Republic of Ireland Bonds. In contrast, the bond certificates proposed by the Irish-Americans were considered a "loan" to subscribers and repayable one month after international recognition of an Irish Republic thereby complying with American law.

Cohalan and the other Irish-American leaders, despite the hostile, confrontational attitude of de Valera, offered to deliver whatever amount of money de Valera requested.

127

On the advice of Joseph McGarrity, de Valera submitted the Republic of Ireland Bonds issue to Martin Conboy, an Irish-American lawyer in New York City, for his legal opinion. De Valera claimed Conboy contradicted the Irish-American leaders and declared the sale of "Republic of Ireland Bonds" legal. Conboy had actually recommended a second opinion, and the issue was submitted to Franklin Delano Roosevelt, at that time a partner in the New York law firm of Emmet, Marvin, and Martin. De Valera's official biographers, Longford and O'Neill, falsely asserted: "Roosevelt met de Valera, and pronounced his formula safe."[4]

This was a deliberate deception by the Irish President; neither Conboy nor Roosevelt approved the sale of "Republic of Ireland Bonds." de Valera fabricated the myth that the funds raised were sold as Republic of Ireland Bonds. He actually confirmed that his "formula" was never declared legal by Conboy or Roosevelt by personally approving the sale of "Bond Certificates" over his signature, validating the course advocated by Cohalan and other leading Irish-Americans.

De Valera demanded that the Bond Certificates be non-interest bearing until one year after recognition of an Irish Republic. Considering the fact that he never did declare an Irish Republic, under his proposal, an investor would have had to wait 30 years, until 1949, a year after the John Costello Government formally declared an Irish Republic, to begin earning a penny on his investment.

He chided Michael Collins, who had stipulated that interest on the Irish Internal Loan should be calculated from the day the Certificates were paid in full. De Valera told Collins: "It should be, of course, from the date of the recognition (of the Irish Republic) and evacuation (of the British troops). I hope you have not made that mistake in your proposed issue in Ireland."[5] Collins insisted that the Bond Certificates bear interest from the date of purchase. The American Bond Certificates were amended accordingly.

In a revealing letter to Arthur Griffith, de Valera set the stage for a split. "Our first clash came about the bonds. Cohalan pooh-poohed the idea of bonds in any shape...then I wanted to be let into the political steps, which he was going to take...He didn't want me to go near the political end at all – anyhow, the rift was developing. I did my best to stop it."[6]

On July 1, 1919, in another snub to Devoy and Cohalan, de Valera made sure he controlled the funds by naming Bishop Michael Fogarty, James O'Mara, and himself trustees of the Bond Certificate funds. Though the Irish-Americans were expected to raise the entire amount of the Bond Certificate Drive, only native Irish were appointed as Trustees.

Within three weeks of his arrival, de Valera had managed to insult the Irish-Americans at least once a week.

Patrick McCartan cited a typical example of de Valera's goading of Cohalan. In a four-hour discussion over de Valera's insistence that a circular advertising the Bond Certificates must include the words "peasant" and "steers," Cohalan, "contended that the term 'peasant' was associated in the American mind with 'peon,' conveying an inferior type of humanity; and that the word 'steer' was also objectionable to Americans. President de Valera maintained that 'peasant' had a poetic flavor and 'steer' was expressive, and as he met me, he voiced his satisfaction that he had held out and not given in to Judge Cohalan."[7]

Before approving any document, de Valera was irritating to the point of frustration in his meticulous, thorough, and elaborate quibbling over the wording of any release over his name. Yet, whenever a controversial document such as the Mason Resolution or *Westminster Gazette* interview was revealed as his handiwork, he and his army of sycophants charged that the controversy was merely due to oversight.

Longford and O'Neill fabricated the notion that: "Cohalan...set himself to oppose de Valera at every point. They claimed that the success of the Irish Bond Drive [Certificates] proved that Cohalan was not infallible on the American position. It made de Valera more steadfast in following the dictates of his own judgment."[8] The implementation of the Bond Certificate Drive, actually proved the wisdom of the Irish-American leaders rather than de Valera. His charge of obstruction by Judge Cohalan was baseless as the Clan na Gael and Friends of Irish Freedom accounted for nine out of ten dollars raised by the Bond Certificate, not Republican Bond, drive.

De Valera's biographers painted an aura of legitimacy over de Valera's Republic of Ireland Bond proposal by deliberately distorting the facts: "Delays persisted, but de Valera pushed ahead impatiently during July and August (1919). He had little help from Irish-Americans..."[9] The reality was quite different. It was the Irish President, himself, who impeded the launching of the Bond Certificate Drive. He delayed the September 1 kickoff by nitpicking the application form by repeatedly finding fault and by the time he got through with his quibbling, J. E. C. Donnelly & Co. had to reprint literally thousands of Bond Certificate applications. Finally, on December 2, 1919, a public announcement was made that a Bond Certificate, and not a Republic of Ireland Bond, fundraising campaign was to be launched in mid-January. De Valera's procrastination delayed the anticipated September inauguration of the fundraising drive by nearly five months.

In a letter dated September 20, 1919, to the Trustees of the FOIF, de

Valera estimated that the expenses of the Bond Certificate Drive would be $1 million (ten percent) of the $10 million goal. He hoped that the expenses would not exceed six percent ($600,000) of the total.

De Valera's initial attempt to wrest control of the FOIF occurred on November 7, 1919, six months after his arrival in America. He dispatched McGarrity to a National Council meeting at which McGarrity demanded the FOIF absorb the estimated $1 million expenses of the $10 million Bond Certificate drive. Such expenditure would have bankrupted the FOIF, and McGarrity was ruled out of order.

The Friends of Irish Freedom, an adjunct of the Clan na Gael, at a national meeting in Philadelphia on January 14, 1919, five months before de Valera set foot in America, initiated a $2 million Irish Victory Fund Drive. The money was to be allocated to seeking recognition of an Irish Republic, educating Americans as to the plight of the Irish, rejecting U.S. entry into the League of Nations, and sending a delegation to the Paris Peace Conference. Devoy and Cohalan cut short the Victory Fund Drive on August 31 in deference to de Valera's projected September 1 kick-off of the Bond Certificate campaign. Friends of Irish Freedom and Clan na Gael State Councils vehemently protested the premature cutoff because many had completed only half the projected $2 million goal, with six months remaining in the Victory Fund drive.

Meanwhile, de Valera continued to sow discord among the Irish-Americans by accusing Devoy and Cohalan of misuse of FOIF funds for American political purposes while de Valera eventually allocated $1.5 million of the Bond Certificate monies for the same purpose.

Devoy, Cohalan, the Irish-American Friends of Irish Freedom (FOIF) and Clan na Gael chapters throughout the U.S. raised more than ninety percent of the $5 million 1920 Bond Certificate Drive. Despite this effort de Valera charged the Irish-Americans with being "uncooperative" and "putting roadblocks" in the way of his triumphant tour of America.

The FOIF provided $100,000 seed money for de Valera's fundraising initiative, and the New York City Clan na Gael Chapter, led by John Devoy, raised more than ten percent of the entire receipts of the Bond Certificates. Even McCartan conceded Devoy and Cohalan's prodigious Bond Certificate efforts: "The Clan [Devoy and Cohalan] worked very hard in New York, and as a result, some $600,000 was collected in that city alone..."[10] Any charge of hindering the sale of Bond Certificates by Irish-Americans was deliberate mischief-making and an outright lie by de Valera.

Of the $5 million raised, de Valera hoarded $3 million in American banks, and sent less than $1 million to Ireland, not a penny of which went to purchase guns for the IRA, food and shelter for the families of

Irish prisoners and men on the run. The balance of the funds was used to reject American recognition of virtual Irish independence, prevent the nomination of a pro-Irish presidential candidate, discredit Devoy and Cohalan, and split the Irish-American political juggernaut.

Within a week of his Waldorf-Astoria press conference and three weeks after his arrival in America, de Valera embarked on a nation-wide tour, organized and funded by the Friends of Irish Freedom. Through the efforts of Devoy, Cohalan, and Jeremiah Lynch, National Secretary of the Friends of Irish Freedom, de Valera's cross-country tour of the United States was touted as a masterpiece of organization and cooperation.

Through the efforts of the Clan na Gael and FOIF, "huge receptions were organized for de Valera in every city he visited. He was hailed as 'President of the Irish Republic,' a title which had never been conferred on him in Ireland. On account of its propaganda value, this description was allowed to pass ..."[11]

The FOIF arranged speaking engagements for de Valera before state legislatures, universities, and monster Irish-American rallies; receptions by governors, mayors, and Catholic Cardinals and Universities presented him with honorary degrees.

On June 29 in Fenway Park, Boston, 70,000 Irish-Americans cheered the "last Commandant to surrender" during the 1916 Rising, and another standing-room-only crowd jammed Madison Square Garden on July 7 to catch a glimpse of him. The FOIF reception at Soldier's Field in Chicago turned out 50,000 people, and the following weeks saw de Valera speaking before enormous crowds from Boston to San Francisco. In Manchester, New Hampshire, 30,000 people attended the gathering, while tens of thousands crowded into Wrigley Field in Chicago, thundering, "Up de Valera." For all of this, credit belonged solely to the efforts of the Irish-Americans.

"His trips were generally extremely well organized... de Valera did not attend to the organization himself but he had no hesitation in telling Jeremiah Lynch who did just exactly what he wanted."[12] In a letter to Lynch, de Valera acknowledged that fact, "As you are aware, the success of this tour depends mainly on your organization [FOIF] ..."[13]

De Valera was provided office space at the national headquarters of the FOIF in Washington as well as access to the membership list of Irish-Americans with deep pockets and a strong commitment to Ireland. "In addition, in August 1919, the FOIF gave de Valera another $20,000 to pay for his expenses and those of his entourage."[14]

"... As the novelty of his appearances began to wear off, the crowds declined and his failings as a public speaker became more apparent. He tended to read his speeches in a dull, halting manner. But these deficiencies were made up by what the *Boston Herald* described as the way his 'passionate sincerity and utmost simplicity worked to burn their way into the consciousness of everyone who sees and hears him.'"[15]

McCartan acknowledged that the American tour sponsored and organized by Devoy and Cohalan was successful beyond words: "At every place, de Valera was received with almost royal honors by State and civic officials. The size and enthusiasm of the crowds that greeted him filled me with joy and amazement."[16] de Valera's lackey, however, had no words of joy or appreciation for Devoy and Cohalan for their part in that success and continued to criticize the Irish-American leaders.

Thanks to the FOIF, the leading newspapers across the country covered the monster rallies with banner headlines and columns-wide articles extolling the Irish President. For all their effort on his behalf, de Valera showed little gratitude and mentioned the Clan na Gael just once throughout the entire tour. In an appearance by de Valera and Harry Boland before a Ladies Auxiliary of the Clan na Gael in New York City: "...de Valera named all the societies that had promised support except the Clan na Gael...Boland...claimed the leaders here (in America) were not in sympathy with the bonds and had done nothing but thrown obstacles in their way. He said something in a sneering way about the small amount of Victory Fund money sent home and the large sums spent here..."[17]

Devoy and Cohalan arranged for de Valera's triumphant return to New York City on March 17, 1920, where he was feted at City Hall before stepping out with leading politicians and a host of Irish-American magnates in the Saint Patrick's Day parade up Fifth Avenue. Cohalan had generously relinquished his position as Grand Marshall to de Valera as the Mayor, Governor, and the Archbishop of St. Patrick's Cathedral joined him on the reviewing stand.

On April 10, 1920, de Valera again sought to seize the FOIF Victory Funds by having James O'Mara, in his capacity as a Trustee of the Bond Certificate Drive, demand an accounting of all expenditures of the Victory Fund. O'Mara wrote to the FOIF secretary: "...Such money morally belongs to Ireland – and it is only reasonable for the representative of the Government of Ireland to ask for a statement of account of both receipts and expenditures."[18] The Irish-Americans rejected the request.

In a letter to Griffith, de Valera cast aspersions on Devoy and Cohalan: "I desired that Ireland's interests should come first...I held that the money contributed to the Victory Fund was obtained in the belief that it would be used as directly as possible for Ireland."[19] Boland,

McGarrity and McCartan launched a bitter attack on Devoy and Cohalan for spending the Victory Fund monies on American political goals but they never blinked at de Valera's request for $1.5 million of the Bond Certificate funds to be spent for the same purpose.

De Valera wrote to Griffith a few days later: "It is sympathy for Ireland that has enabled such an organization as the FOIF to be built up. That is why the mass of the rank and file have joined – that is why they have contributed and I will not allow myself to be in any hobble skirts with respect to the doings of anything which we feel certain are for the good of the Cause."[20] The Irish-Americans planned to use the bulk of the Victory Fund to finance a political strategy through which they would promote a pro-Irish candidate for President in the 1920 election.

De Valera tried to justify his spite. "... We are here with a definite objective...Friends of Irish Freedom ought to help us obtain the objective, if they are truly what the name implies."[21] In a totally outlandish statement, de Valera wrote to Griffith: "... I cannot feel confidence enough in a certain man [Cohalan] to let him have implicit control of tactics here, without consultation and agreement with me."[22]

De Valera, an alien, set foot in the United States, ostensibly to further the goals of his country through the efforts of the Irish-American community. Yet, he demanded complete autonomy over their actions, rebuffed all advice, and churlishly insisted that the locals must not do anything without his say so.

The Irish President claimed: "His primary task [in America] was to get money to put the Government of Dáil Éireann into effective operation..."[23] Michael J. Ryan, a Philadelphia banker and a member of the American Commission of Irish Independence, which toured Ireland, reported at a meeting of the FOIF that Dáil Éireann's financial needs would not require more than $50,000. The FOIF had dispatched five times that much of its Victory Fund to Ireland and that the bulk of Collins' $2 million National Loan lay buried in Batt O'Connor's cellar for the duration of the guerilla campaign waged by Collins from 1918-21. De Valera's promise of financial support for the IRB rang hollow as he stashed $3 million of Bond Certificate funds in American banks.

De Valera's crocodile tears over the financial plight of the Irish masked his true purpose of scurrying off to America. He set a pattern in which he consistently denied arms to the IRA in its fight against England. Tim Pat Coogan quoted Sean Moylan, an IRA leader and long-time political crony of de Valera: "...'Not a cent of any of those (Bond Certificate) funds was devoted to the organization of the IRA ...' The picture painted by Moylan... indicates the relief which the millions de Valera left behind him could have brought to the ranks of the IRA ..."[24]

In September, de Valera wrote to O'Mara, who was in Chicago: "... I have decided not to let the Bonds go with the messenger. The risk seems to me too great without direct authorization from Ireland ..."[25] Whenever he wanted to avoid an anti-British measure, he would claim that he needed approval from Dublin, but on all other occasions, he ignored Dáil Éireann and merely made a decision without consulting anyone.

De Valera repeatedly found excuses not to send money back to Ireland. Four days before the Bond Certificate Drive ended on October 10, 1920, during the most violent period in Ireland when the IRA was all but defenseless, de Valera told O'Mara "'to hold up delivery of money to Ireland.' O'Mara angrily wrote to de Valera on October 9, 1920: '... I note you have again postponed the shipment of United States Liberty Bonds (to Ireland) ...'"[26]

Though immersed in a chaotic insurgency, Collins kept meticulous records of the funds he had raised in Ireland. He noted in an interview with reporter Carl Ackerman: "Last year we asked for a loan of £250,000 from the Irish people for our treasury. We raised £400,000 [$2 million]. Of this sum, we lost £29 ($145) which was taken by the British authorities from one of our collectors."[27] Collins' Irish fund-raising effort was obstructed by British determination to prevent it. Newspapers mentioning the loan were shut down, and workers and suspected purchasers of Loan Certificates were held up at the point of a bayonet and jailed if any evidence was found.

In contrast, de Valera spared no expense in financing his opposition to Cohalan and Devoy. "The 'President' kept open house. Cigars and surreptitious drinks were to be had for the asking and much hard-earned money contributed by poor servant girls to the 'Cause' must have been expended in providing refreshments for stray Hibernians and the hungry priesthood."[28]

De Valera's miserly policies for the folks back home contrasted sharply with his extravagant lifestyle in America: "Although de Valera advocated 'frugal comfort' rather than high living at home, his stay in the USA, while it generated a good deal of revenue for the 'cause' must have cost a fair sum ..."[29] No one ever got around to documenting just how much of the "good deal of revenue" the Cause received but most of the funds generated in America coincidentally ended up financing de Valera's newspaper, the *Irish Press*.

Extensive research in Ireland failed to uncover any official accounting of the Bond Certificate Funds. What little information was available was gleaned through letters and acknowledgements of receipt. What can be ascertained with a close a degree of certainty was that less than one million dollars was ultimately sent back to Ireland. "[T]he strange fact is that the bulk of the money raised through the Bonds [Certificates], supposedly the cause of his difference with the [Irish-American] leaders, was not remitted to Ireland. Making allowances for the expenses incurred during his tour and the fact that some monies were remitted to Ireland; he nevertheless left behind him in America something approaching sixty percent of what was collected."[30]

The Wall Street Journal labeled the subscribers as "Irish domestic servants and others of like or lower standards of intelligence."[31] Of the money raised in the United States, de Valera spent more than a million dollars on his campaign to split the Irish-Americans, discredit Devoy and Cohalan, reject virtual Irish independence, prevent the nomination of Hiram Johnson, a stalwart supporter of Ireland, and scuttle the adoption of any Irish plank by either party in the presidential campaign of 1920.

In August 1922, William Cosgrave's Provisional Government obtained an injunction freezing the $3 million remaining in US banks to prevent de Valera from using it to finance his civil war. The New York State Supreme Court on May 11, 1927, found that the bond certificates were issued on the basis of a recognized Irish Republic, and since no such entity existed, he ordered the appointment of receivers to return the money to subscribers. "Many members of the Association assigned their bonds [Certificates] to de Valera. And when the United States Courts ordered the unexpended balance of the bond money to be returned to the bondholders, de Valera was entitled to the lion's share of that balance due on the assigned bonds he held, an amount he later applied to a newspaper in Ireland."[32] In 1930, at de Valera's solicitation, "... a large number of Bonds were reassigned to [him] for the purpose of the promotion in Ireland of a daily newspaper which would advocate a progressive national policy, *The Irish Press.*"[33]

Notes

1. Fitzgerald, W.G., *The voice of Ireland, A Survey othe Race & Nation from all Angles*, Virtue Ltd. Dublin/London, p. 242
2. *ibid*
3. Dwyer, T. Ryle, *De Valera, The Man & the Myths*, Poolbeg, Dublin, p. 36
4. Longford, Earl of & O'Neill, Thomas P., *Éamon de Valera*, Hutchinson, London, 1970, p. 100
5. *ibid*, p. 101

6. *ibid,* p. 107
7. McCartan, Patrick, *With de Valera in America*, Brentano/NY 1932, p. 143
8. Longford, Earl of & O'Neill, Thomas P., *Éamon de Valera*, Hutchinson, London, 1970, p. 106
9. *ibid,* p. 100
10. McCartan, Patrick, *With de Valera in America*, Brentano/NY 1932, p. 144
11. Beaslai, Pieras, *Michael Collins and the Making of a New Ireland*, Vol I, Harper Bros. NY 1926, p. 4
12. Coogan, Tim Pat, *De Valera, The Man who was Ireland*, Harper, 1996, p. 151
13. *ibid,* p. 152
14. Fitzgerald, W.G., *The voice of Ireland, A Survey of the Race & Nation from all Angles*, Virtue Ltd. Dublin/London, p. 244
15. Dwyer, T. Ryle, *De Valera, The Man & the Myths*, Poolbeg, Dublin, p. 32
16. McCartan, Patrick, *With de Valera in America*, Brentano/NY 1932, p. 141
17. Devoy to Cohalan, 9/2/1919
18. McCartan, Patrick, *With de Valera in America*, Brentano/NY 1932, p. 182
19. Coogan, Tim Pat, *De Valera, The Man who was Ireland*, Harper, 1996, p 164.
20. *ibid,* p. 164
21. Tansill, Charles, C., *America and the Fight for Irish Freedom 1866-1922*, Devin-Adair, NY. 1957, p. 352
22. *ibid,* p.352
23. Longford, Earl of & O'Neill, Thomas P., *Éamon de Valera*, Hutchinson, London, 1970, p. 99
24. Coogan, Tim Pat, *De Valera, The Man who was Ireland*, Harper, 1996, p. 192
25. Lavelle, Patricia, *James O'Mara, A Staunch Sinn Feiner 1873-1948*, Clonmore & Reynolds, Dublin, 1961, p. 186
26. *ibid*
27. *Philadelphia Ledger*, 8/27/1920, 1:6
28. Coogan, Tim Pat, *de Valera, The Man who was Ireland*, Harper, 1996, p. 192
29. *ibid*
30. *ibid*
31. *Wall Street Journal*, 2/2/1919
32. McCartan, Patrick, *With de Valera in America*, Brentano/NY 1932, p. 216 fn
33. Lavelle, Patricia, *James O'Mara, A Staunch Sinn Feiner 1873-1948*, Clonmore & Reynolds, Dublin, 1961, p. 289

CHAPTER XI

"Asignment American Party Conventions"

"The Irish are like zebras, either black horses with white stripes or white horses with black stripes. We know they are not horses; they are asses, but each one of those asses has a vote and there are a lot of them."[1]

Admiral William S. Sims*

Republican Convention 1920

After decades toiling in the quagmire of the disputatious Irish, John Devoy and Judge Daniel Cohalan finally consolidated the Irish-Americans into a political juggernaut and were in position to influence the selection of the next President of the United States at the 1920 Democratic and Republican conventions.

Seizing on President Woodrow Wilson's affirmation of the right of all peoples to self-government, the Irish-Americans set their sights on securing American endorsement of the right to self-determination for the long-suffering Irish people. With England as an ally in World War I and a pro-German stance by the Irish, formal American recognition of an Irish Republic didn't stand a chance. America wasn't about to rebuff a comrade in arms by interfering in what it considered an internal matter of England. Recognition was impossibly controversial at the moment whereas self-determination was looming large on the horizon.

It was not to be, however, as a tall, bespectacled, unsmiling portent of evil stepped off the gangplank of the SS *Lapland* in June 1919 and Éamon de Valera snatched defeat from the jaws of a monumental Irish victory.

Prior to de Valera's arrival in America, the Halls of Congress resounded with echoes of Irish brogue as lobbyists buttonholed Congressmen cajoling, arguing, placating, and threatening in order to convince legislators to support self-determination for Ireland. Devoy and Cohalan had wandered the political wastelands for decades promoting their dream of an independent Ireland.

---

*Admiral Sims made the above comments at a London reception on June 7, 1921 and was subsequently recalled and reprimanded by the Secretary of the Navy.

The influence wielded by Devoy and Cohalan and the Irish-Americans was noted in a letter from Spring Rice, the British Ambassador in Washington, to Lord Robert Cecil on April 13, 1917, one week after the U.S. entered the war and three days after Wilson's plea to Lloyd George to consider some sort of self-government for Ireland: "The Irish-Americans were of very great political importance at the present moment. The question is one that is at the root of most of our troubles with the United States...The President is...bound in every way to give consideration to their demands."[2] Spring-Rice's inference was an ominous forewarning and set in motion English plans to derail the Irish-Americans.

R.C. Lindsay, Charge d'Affaires at the British Embassy in Washington, D.C., in a dispatch to British Foreign Secretary Viscount Curzon on March 5, 1920, three months before the Republican Convention in Chicago, clearly set forth the danger the Irish-Americans posed to the Anglo-American alliance: "As the election campaign draws near...foreign politics have become a matter of nationwide interest. It is impossible to exaggerate the extent to which the Irish question and the Irish vote dominates the situation...The outstanding fact is that *the Irish vote in America is enormous, well-disciplined and easily swayed by anti-British sentiment* [emphasis added] and that at moments of crises American politicians, even against their convictions, will bid for it."[3]

Both Democrats and Republicans were acutely aware of the influence, power, and financial clout of Irish-Americans, and they vied for their support. During the 65th Congress in 1919, before de Valera appeared on the scene, eight resolutions favoring self-determination for Ireland were introduced. After one was overwhelmingly approved by the Senate, FOIF's Vice-President noted: "It was a clear sign and fixed as stars in heaven of the power the Irish Race wields when it is united. Is it a curse on the Race that they alone are blind to that sign?"[4]

A pro-Irish President would augur ominous political and financial difficulties for the British Empire: America would be in position to leverage concessions over Ireland in return for relief of its forty billion dollar war debt.

In Britain, any serious move toward a united Ireland would create a backlash of Protestant resistance both in Northern Ireland and in England. Civil war in Northern Ireland, aided and abetted by the Conservative Party was a real possibility. "Ulster will fight and Ulster will be right!" was the Conservative position formulated by Randolph Churchill MP two generations previously to counter Home Rule.

In an obvious political ploy to remove its $40 billion First World War debt to the United States from becoming an issue during the 1920 presidential campaign, the British made a token payment less than a month before the Republican Convention. Austen Chamberlain, half-brother of Neville and head of the Exchequer, on May 1, paid off $15 million of Treasury bills, but the accrued interest alone on its debt to the United States amounted to $245 million.

Patrick McCartan described his first meeting with de Valera upon the President's arrival in the US: "My report had scarce begun. I had just told him that Cohalan had tried to reduce our claim for recognition to a claim for self-determination. 'Self-determination,' de Valera said decisively, 'is a very good policy.' And there my report ended."[5] McCartan had a hard time convincing anyone to recognize an Irish Republic and was taken aback by the rejection of his stand by none other than the President of the Irish Republic who had issued his credentials as Irish envoy to America. "These credentials authorized me to seek recognition from the United States...I wondered if he had come to modify our recognition policy."[6]

De Valera's initial official statement in America at the Waldorf-Astoria Hotel in June 1919 affirmed Devoy and Cohalan's policy of self-determination for Ireland: "I am in America as the official head of the Irish Republic established by the will of the Irish people in accordance with the principle of Self-determination ..."[7] Poisonous in his attacks on Devoy and Cohalan, McCartan never uttered a word against de Valera for endorsing the Irish-American line.

The Irish President was a self-determination advocate right up to the Republican Convention in June 1920. On February 24, 1919, de Valera speaking in Dublin stated: "If England accepts the principle of self-determination for this island, it will settle the Irish Question forever."[8] He called for self-determination, not recognition of an Irish Republic, at Manchester, England, on March 30, 1919, less than three months before his arrival in America: "appealing for moral and financial support in influencing public opinion on behalf of Ireland's claim to self-determination."[9]

De Valera dispatched Harry Boland to Ireland in May 1920 to present a distorted view of events in America to the Cabinet. Boland reported to Collins, Griffith, and the Cabinet that Devoy and Cohalan had not given wholehearted support to de Valera. He scurrilously charged that the Irish-Americans were hindering de Valera's mission to America: "The President has definitely refused to allow his judgment or his action to be dictated by these men and the success of his tour and of the Bond Drive are proof of his wisdom in the matter."[10] Like McCartan, Boland deliberately misled Cabinet members by failing to tell them it was Devoy and Cohalan who were instrumental in raising ninety percent of the

Bond Certificate money and that the FOIF organized and financed the Irish President's successful U.S. tour.

On June 3, 1920, de Valera stormed into Chicago without a word to Cohalan and personally took over direction of the Irish lobbying strategy at the Republican Convention. Cohalan arrived two days later on June 5 and was astonished at the circus atmosphere de Valera was conducting. On June 19, ten days before the Dáil officially acted on de Valera's request and three months after he sought permission to spend $500,000 on the presidential election and an additional $1 million on obtaining recognition of the Irish Republic, de Valera attempted to justify his lavish unauthorized use of Bond Certificate monies. He claimed: "The charge [by John Devoy] that I have been guilty of misuse (of funds) is without foundation. It is a malicious charge. The monies that have been subscribed to the Irish Issue Bonds, whether here or in Ireland...is Irish Government money, the property of the Irish nation. It was subscribed for all legitimate governmental purposes. There is no purpose so urgent as that of securing recognition."[11]

Devoy's charges against de Valera's misuse of Irish funds were valid, however. The Irish President's press release of June 19, claiming: "this appropriation was duly made and I have the necessary authority..." was not true either at the time he made the statement or when he began spending the money in April. When de Valera arrived in Chicago with a large entourage of native Irish and a contingent of supporters from throughout the country, all expenses paid, he had no authority to spend a nickel at that time as the Dáil only gave approval at the end of June. Without authorization, he illegally squandered several hundred thousand dollars for transportation, hotel rooms, food and drinks, campaign headquarters, flyers, a daily newspaper, banners, bands, and miscellaneous lavish trappings. Estimates ranged from $80,000 to more than $200,000 spent in Chicago alone. No official accounting of the expenditure of the $5 million raised by de Valera has been uncovered and the amount spent at Chicago was exceeded during the Democratic Convention in San Francisco the following month.

If the Dáil had refused authorization, it would have been after the fact and would have created serious political consequences for the Irish cause, since the President of the Irish Republic was actually guilty of misappropriation of funds for a non-approved purpose.

The Brooklyn Eagle, in an August 9, 1920 report by Carl Ackerman, stated that it and the *Philadelphia Ledger* had obtained copies of Dáil Éireann minutes of a secret session on June 29, authorizing de Valera to spend up to $500,000 on the presidential election and an additional sum not to exceed $1 million to obtain recognition of an Irish Republic. De Valera's interference in American affairs was stretched to the breaking point upon the publication of his secret money request to the Dáil. His response was "to take the mischief out of the report by issuing a statement emphasizing that it was misleading to speak of the funds as intended for the American elections. 'In public and private I have been scrupulously careful to avoid even appearing to take sides in the party politics of this country. Apart from any illegality, it would obviously be bad taste on my part and most inexpedient.'"[12]

Author T. Ryle Dwyer questioned de Valera's official biographers' veracity: "It was patently absurd for his authorized biographers [Longford and O'Neill] to contend that he 'could never be accused of interference with American internal politics.' By his own admission, he knew full well that he was interfering in American politics ..."[13]

According to Devoy, "Many of the men brought on [by de Valera] deserted in disgust because of the reckless squandering of money. The cheapest rooms were $20 a day without board. One man's hotel bill was $300 and, although he wanted to pay it himself, he found it already paid. This man is John P. Grace, Mayor of Charleston, S.C. who is certainly a reliable witness. My estimate of $50,000 was under the mark; it must have been fully $80,000 and every dollar of it was spent in making war on the men without whom the Bond Issue could not possibly have been made a success."[14] He bitterly complained, "It was our men and women, no matter what you hear to the contrary, who subscribed, or collected nine tenths of the money received in the Bond sales. That money is now being used lavishly to break us up. And they tried to grab the Victory Fund, out of which all their expenses were paid, so that we might have no money to continue the work, which has brought such splendid results."[15]

On August 12, 1920, in a letter to Cohalan, Devoy wrote, "De Valera is out to smash us and he is nibbling away at the ramparts all the time...He is evidently going to stay here indefinitely. It is more comfortable here than in Ireland. He is the most malignant man in all Irish history."[16]

De Valera's official biographers defended his attendance in Chicago with the fabrication: "Cohalan had promised that he would go to Chicago. He did not do so immediately and the President decided to visit the City in person."[17]

Contrary to Longford and O'Neill's misrepresentation, de Valera did not rush off to Chicago on the spur of the moment: it was a premeditated scheme to intrude in the presidential election campaign. Dwyer admitted: "All this was clearly a violation of his agreement to stay out of American affairs but, as previously stated, he never really intended to uphold his end of the agreement anyway..."[18]

Regarding de Valera's charge that he was kept in the dark as to the FOIF plans for the political conventions does not bear scrutiny. According to Daniel T. O'Connell, head of the Irish Bureau in Washington, "Not once did President de Valera ask for information as to the plans for Chicago...He had only to intimate that he wished information regarding Chicago to receive all available information."[19]

De Valera and his followers' actions were outrageous: "The *Chicago Daily Tribune* published a cartoon of de Valera, with a caption informing its readers that de Valera had assured the paper he was not a candidate for the presidency of the United States."[20] Another newspaper bannered an article on the Irish President's political campaign: "de Valera Rivals the GOP." On June 9 de Valera led a contingent of thousands of Irish-Americans in a torchlight parade down Michigan Avenue and brazenly marched into the Auditorium Theatre.

After a year of advocating the right of the Irish people to self-determination, de Valera, at the Republican Convention, turned into a born-again Irish Republican zealot arrogantly demanding: "The Republicans must promise to recognize the Irish Republic."[21] In a move designed to irritate the Resolutions Committee, he insisted on personally appearing before the Committee. Chairman, Senator James E. Watson, of Indiana, called de Valera's request "wholly preposterous for a foreign representative to appear before an American political convention and lobby against this nation's foreign policy."[22]

In an incredible admission, McCartan, one of de Valera's most ardent supporters in America, put an ominous and suspicious spin to the Irish President's conduct: "So there we were, President de Valera, Liam Mellowes, Sean Nunan and I, all four of us, members of a foreign mission, trespassing on American hospitality. Our trespassing did not end with our presence...There was no chance of offending America that we did not take."[23]

Leveling a charge of treachery directly at the Irish president, McCartan conceded: "de Valera's appeal for recognition of the Republic at the Republican Convention in June 1920 was, as I have shown, inherently hopeless. He incurred a practically unanimous denial and so far as that denial might be construed as a directive to the next Republican Administration, this appeal by President de Valera tended indefinitely to remove the recognition of the Irish Republic from the consideration of the American Government."[24] In a bizarre statement, McCartan, after admitting the destructive actions by the Irish President, said: "As our President, he had conducted himself in public with so much circumspection and dignity as to bring him and us universal respect."[25] Desmond Ryan also attempted to deflect guilt from the Irish President by ascribing sinister qualities to Devoy and Cohalan: "No useful purpose would be served in pursuing further the adventures of Saint Eamon among the Serpents. For sufficient has been said to show that Eamon was a Saint and the Serpents – for even serpents have a case – had perhaps a claim to wisdom that lifted them above common or garden snakes. Eventually, de Valera broke openly with Devoy and Cohalan and formed a separate organization backed by large masses of Irish-American opinion and other elements in the United States won over by his magnetic personality and a wider appeal."[26]

De Valera was the real serpent sowing discord, acrimony, and hate wherever he went. Saint Patrick may have expelled the snakes from Ireland, and some may have landed in America, but the greatest snake in Irish history was imported from America to Ireland.

Bishop Michael J. Gallagher of Detroit pleaded in vain for de Valera to withdraw from the Chicago convention: "de Valera had no conception of political realities in America, and his insistence upon his plank revealed a stubborn, unperceptive quality that boded ill for the future."[27] His stubbornness was confined to foiling any anti-British initiatives by the Irish-Americans.

Following the election of Bishop Gallagher as president of the FOIF on July 30, 1920, the Bishop and Judge Hally called on de Valera in an effort to end the bitterness and effect a reconciliation. The Irish President refused to consider any compromise and charged the Bishop with being a Cohalan stooge. Judge Hally was later to say, "I'm sorry I came. I'm disillusioned. I thought the President of Ireland was a bigger man...For myself, I could not escape the impression that the President of Ireland would never be satisfied until the scalps of Cohalan and Devoy dangled at his belt."[28]

The plank submitted by de Valera to the Resolutions Committee during the morning session of June 9, 1920 consisted of the following demand:

> "The Republicans pledge our party to the policy of according to the elected government of the Republic of Ireland full, formal, and official recognition by the Government of the United States ..."[29]

The Resolutions Committee flatly rejected de Valera's plank in a 12–1 decision, with only the faithful Senator Borah voting in the affirmative.

The Cohalan resolution was presented at four in the afternoon. It stated:

> "This Republican Convention desires to place on record its sympathy with all oppressed peoples, and its recognition of the principle that the people of Ireland have the right to determine freely, without dictation from outside, their own governmental institutions, and their international relations with other States and peoples."[30]

The Resolutions Committee vote resulted in a split decision of six for and six against. Senator Watson, chairman of the committee, had not yet voted, and, after lengthy consultation and a bit of arm-twisting by Devoy and Cohalan, he cast his ballot and broke the tie in favor of the Cohalan Resolution.

De Valera hammered the last nail in the coffin of American recognition of an Irish Republic, Irish-American unity and political influence by informing Senator Watson that Judge Cohalan had no right to act in Irish matters. He said he alone could speak for Ireland and that he did not approve of the Cohalan Plank. Presented with a "colorable pretext" by de Valera to reject an Irish initiative, Watson then claimed that since the Irish couldn't make up their minds among themselves, he was withdrawing his vote. The Platform Committee rules prevented action on tie votes, thus the Cohalan Resolution was rejected, and Irish aspirations were once again shattered, thanks to de Valera. "Colorable pretext" was a political lifesaver for vacillating politicians as a means to extricate themselves from supporting an Irish-related measure without alienating their Irish constituents.

The Gaelic American reported: "The rejection of the Resolution was such an extraordinary act that many well-informed men saw in it *a sinister motive* [emphasis added] on the part of some of President de Valera's new-found advisers, who wanted the existing Irish Movement in America disrupted ..."[31] Even Devoy, conspirator extraordinaire, and Irish writers shied away from directing the charge of "sinister motive" at de Valera. It was always someone else around de Valera, but never him.

There were rumblings in America over de Valera's suspicious behavior, so much so that he was forced to publicly deny the charges. De Valera disavowed any culpability for wrecking virtual Irish independence: he cabled Griffith on August 5, "Surely, no one can think that now that the Republic is established, I would counsel a course, which I refused to stand for when the Republic was just a hope. The whole thing is absurd."[32]

Was it really so absurd?

Harry Boland continued to mouth de Valera's lies accusing Cohalan of offering a compromise resolution *"in opposition* [emphasis added] to President de Valera's resolution asking the Republican Committee to adopt recognition of Ireland as a plank in their platform. Cohalan entered a compromise resolution and thus by his action seriously hampered the Irish Republic."[33]

Amazingly, de Valera and his cronies blamed Cohalan for the debacle. Once again, many Irish writers seized upon a "de Valera Fact" and perpetuated the slanderous contradiction that the submission of the Cohalan Plank in the afternoon led to the rejection of the de Valera resolution in the morning. Neither de Valera, Boland, nor one Irish writer set forth a specific instance as to how Cohalan's plank hurt the Irish cause.

Devoy wrote that Cohalan's plank provided the Irish with rights comparable to those of Americans:

> "It [Cohalan's plank] would give a President elected on that platform, if he was friendly, the right to recognize the Irish Republic or to take steps leading up to it. Its adoption by the Convention and the discussion of it in the campaign would have helped us greatly and encouraged our people at home and it would have forced the Democrats to do something equally good or better. It was only offered after [de Valera's] plank was rejected 12-1.
>
> "De Valera rejected the thing he could get and demanded the impossible. The spectacle of disunion and the attempt to control the action of American citizens from outside the United States was a bad blow to Irish prestige and influence here ..."[34]

Devoy noted that de Valera's Resolution, in a speech before a group of Irish-Canadians at Plattsburgh, New York, two weeks before the Republican Convention:

> "was identical – almost, word for word – with the Resolution presented [by Cohalan] in Chicago, which the President says 'misrepresents Ireland's claim by

understating it.' Yet, President de Valera approved the
Plattsburgh Resolution. Why is the thing that was
pronounced all right in Plattsburgh denounced as all
wrong in Chicago?"[35]

A *Chicago Tribune* editorial claimed the Cohalan Plank was a manifesto
recognizing Ireland's independence and a challenge to England. U.S.
Representative Medill McCormick, of Illinois, one of the owners of the
Chicago Tribune, acknowledged that Cohalan's Irish Plank was, in
effect, recognition of Irish independence, and it was fiercely opposed in a
Chicago Tribune editorial on Saturday, June 10, 1920, the last day of the
Convention.

McCormick, due to the lateness of Senator Watson's rejection of the
Cohalan Resolution, and believing it had been approved, wrote in an
editorial highlighting the significance of the Cohalan Resolution: "The
draft of a plank which would have been construed abroad, if not at
home, as pledging the Republican Party to a recognition of an
independent Ireland was formulated in or for the Sub-committee on
resolutions...It is certain, furthermore, that a recognition plank will be
urged upon the Democratic Convention and with a more influential
backing than it could win in a Republican Convention ...*The [Cohalan]
formula proposed at the Chicago Convention was in effect recognition of
the secession of Ireland from the British Empire and its recognition as an
independent state ...*"[36] [emphasis added]

The *Tribune* editorial was formidable evidence that Devoy and
Cohalan had accomplished a monumental feat in convincing the
Republicans to pass an Irish plank recognizing an independent Ireland.
The Democratic Party was much more closely associated with the Irish
vote. As the *Tribune* recognized, if such a position had been adopted by
the Republicans, then a more aggressive Irish recognition plank would be
passed at the Democratic Convention.

After rejecting this enormous stepping-stone advance toward Irish
independence, de Valera, McCartan, Boland, McGarrity, and a host of
fawning Irish writers unleashed a torrent of invective against Cohalan
accusing him of "misrepresenting" Ireland's interests. The Irish
President's rejection of "virtual Irish independence" at the Republican
Convention in Chicago was eerily similar to his rejection of "virtual Irish
independence" set forth in the Free State Treaty the following year.
Longford and O'Neill promoted de Valera's "misrepresentations" by
claiming: "Cohalan...ultimately underbid the de Valera resolution with a
proposed 'statement of sympathy' with Ireland's cause ..." [37]

Author W.G. Fitzgerald disagreed with de Valera's official
biographers: "President de Valera's repudiation of the Cohalan Plank

killed it. The platform as finally adopted by the Convention did not contain a single word on Ireland. Ireland lost; de Valera's mistake was fatal."[38] Down to this day, de Valera's actions are never construed except as a mistake arising from arrogance, blunder, naiveté, or a power-play, but never as a deliberate effort to further British interests.

De Valera continued his *modus operandi* charging others of being guilty of what he was doing: "I believe that the people of Ireland will be thoroughly disappointed with the actions of those of the Friends of Ireland in America who were guilty of the methods which were used in Chicago to prevent their chosen representative from fulfilling his mission in Chicago."[39]

The Republican Senator from California, Hiram Johnson, was in the running for President. No other candidate was so pro-Irish but, according to Devoy, his bid was scuttled by de Valera. In June, Devoy and Cohalan had received a commitment from Johnson, in which the Senator promised, in the event he was elected President, to work for Irish independence. He also agreed that Republican Senator William Borah, of Idaho, an ardent Irish independence advocate and the only Resolutions Committee member to vote for de Valera's plank, would be Secretary of State in his administration. Johnson and Borah were two of Ireland's staunchest supporters and presented England with a most serious dilemma.

In a bid for damage control over Devoy's charge that he was responsible for rejecting Johnson's bid for President, de Valera lied again. He contended that his early attempts to secure a firm, personal commitment from Senator Johnson was undermined by a gratuitous endorsement by *The Gaelic American*. Frustrated, de Valera wrote to Griffith on March 25, 1920: "It is disappointing to see a clear nap hand played poorly. Sometimes, when I see the strategic position, which the Irish here occupy in American politics, I feel like crying when I realize what could be made of it if there was real genuine teamwork for Ireland alone being done. As far as politics is concerned, the position is almost everything one could wish for."[40] De Valera played his "nap hand" all too perfectly. He "folded" a royal flush and dealt the Irish the death hand of "aces and eights."

Longford and O'Neill attempted to deflect the Irish President's treachery by claiming that Devoy's endorsement of Senator Johnson in June undermined de Valera's attempt at a Johnson endorsement three months earlier in March. What should have been evident of England's fear of a Johnson presidency was outlined by de Valera when he admitted Irish support was "counterbalanced by English propaganda against Johnson."[41]

The British Ambassador to Washington, Sir Auckland Geddes, in 1920 acknowledged de Valera's contribution to Anglo-American relations. He noted that de Valera roared into Chicago, disavowed Cohalan's plank, and demanded that the Republican delegates recognize an Irish Republic. The Committee, irked by de Valera's repudiation of an Irish plank recognizing virtual Irish independence submitted by Cohalan, then rejected any Irish plank in the Republican Platform. Geddes wrote: "The incident [adoption of the Cohalan Plank] illustrates in an interesting manner the immense influence Irishmen [Devoy and Cohalan] can exert on American politicians if they proceed wisely; and how ready American politicians are to withdraw themselves from that influence if they can find some *colorable pretext* for doing so."[42] [emphasis added]

With de Valera's rejection of the Cohalan Plank, a monumental advance in Irish fortunes was lost. Tim Pat Coogan wrote: "What is certain is that in the wake of the Chicago debacle, American politicians, who in Geddes' phrase, sought *colorable pretext* for withdrawing from the Irish issue, received ample excuse for doing so."[43] [emphasis added]

Coogan, however, then drew an odd conclusion: "From the point of view of the Irish Nationalists, the anxiety de Valera caused the British indicates something of his worth to the Irish cause..."[44] Any claim by de Valera's supporters that he had caused the English any cause for anxiety was simply delusional. The British recognized the enormous value the Irish President held for them; they had spared him from execution in 1916, built up his image in prison, and facilitated his "escape" from Lincoln Jail, insuring that upon his arrival in the U.S. he was politically unassailable.

In a letter to Cohalan on July 4, 1920, Devoy acknowledged de Valera's intent to undermine the nomination of Johnson: "We now see de Valera's reason for preventing action at Chicago...He wanted to prevent us from 'selling the Irish vote to any candidate,' meaning he wanted to kill Johnson's candidacy. As far as Irish-Americans were concerned, the nomination of Hiram Johnson to the presidency would have been a godsend. De Valera was too inexperienced to appreciate this fact."[45] Despite his political savvy, Devoy failed to understand that de Valera was marching to the beat of a British drummer.

Upon Warren G. Harding's entering the White House, the English lost the Anglophile President Woodrow Wilson who had approved large loans to aid the British in meeting their financial obligations. They were not so sure of Harding and, in any event, could not count on Washington easing their financial burden. The loss of an Irish plank in the Republican Platform, however, denied Irish-Americans any chance of influencing the new President into pressuring England to grant self-determination to the Irish.

A request made to President Wilson on October 20, 1920 was deliberately ignored. McCartan recognized the monumental destruction of Irish interests in America by de Valera: "The futile request, foredoomed to failure, could only complete the ruin of any chance of official recognition President de Valera had not already destroyed for us in the United States."[46]

Many Irish writers whitewashed de Valera's egregious conduct, and proffered the unsustainable contention that the Irish President was engaged in a power struggle with Cohalan and Devoy. Dwyer attributed de Valera's rejection of Irish independence to a petty feud with Cohalan: "Obviously, de Valera had another reason for undermining the Cohalan Plank...He was apparently afraid that if he did not act, the adoption of Cohalan's plank would create the impression that the Judge was in control of the Irish movement in the United States... So, if Cohalan were seen to get the better of things in Chicago, it would certainly have tended to confirm the impression that he was the kingpin of the movement in America."[47] Dwyer misses the point, as do many others that Ireland's interest was secondary to de Valera's ego. He fabricated a power struggle with Devoy and Cohalan as an excuse to cover up de Valera's pro-British efforts. It is worth posing some fundamental questions: what was the real purpose of his campaign in America? What was the point of a power struggle? When he won, what did Ireland win? What did England gain?

In America, and later in Ireland, de Valera rejected the proffered scepter of power over his rivals. The power struggle was not so much for mastery over Devoy and Cohalan, and subsequently, Collins and Griffith; it provided the opportunity to sabotage anti-British initiatives. The adoption of an Irish plank at the Republican and Democratic conventions would have crowned de Valera's mission to America with monumental Irish success. Even if Cohalan was responsible, de Valera would have been the one receiving the accolades, especially in Ireland. His power and prestige would have been unassailable. Why did he forfeit such a prize?

In 1921, in an eerily similar move, he rejected uncontestable supremacy over Collins and Griffith. They had urged him to return to London with them to conclude the Free State Treaty. If he had returned to London adding his imprimatur to the very same Treaty Collins and Griffith had negotiated, de Valera, having crossed the Irish Rubicon, would have been crowned a Gaelic Caesar for having forced England out of Ireland after seven centuries of unremitting misery. Collins went

149

so far as to relinquish his position as Irish President under the IRB constitution and to cede control of that organization to de Valera.

Irish writers cavalierly attributed de Valera's feuding to childhood deprivation of parental affection: "de Valera grew up with a deep yearning for distinction and a nagging sense of inferiority which was perversely stirred by his sudden fame, a fame which owed so much to chance that it provided little sense of security. Had he been more secure in his own mind, he might not have looked on Cohalan's actions as menacing, but as things stood, he felt his position threatened, and he had to show he was no longer insignificant..."[48]

No one questioned why such a dysfunctional misfit was steering Ireland's destiny. Dwyer never considered the possibility that de Valera's leadership owed more to self-preservation than chance, or that his loyalties lay outside Ireland.

Coogan claimed: "de Valera's all-or-nothing attitude got him – nothing. This was the price of his victory at the Park Avenue Hotel in March 1920. At Chicago, he could not allow Cohalan's resolution to get through and his to fail; thereby proving Cohalan's charge that de Valera was ignorant of American politics."[49] Coogan failed to consider the opposite corollary, that de Valera did not want recognition of an Irish Republic. Furthermore, it wasn't de Valera who got nothing, but Ireland. England got everything.

Devoy published de Valera's response to the Irish-American's charge of interference at the Chicago convention in the June 26, 1920 edition of the *Gaelic American*: "As counsel, I must obey the directions of those that sent me. I must fulfill the mission that they have charged me with. I am responsible to them. I can be removed by them if my work is not satisfactory."[50] Not one leader in Ireland had approved his desertion and dash to America. His claim that he was responsible to the leaders in Ireland and that they could remove him if they were dissatisfied with his work was wholly disingenuous. He knew that they could not control or remove him: repudiation of the President of the Republic would have been disastrous for the Irish cause when Ireland was ablaze. McCartan admitted the Irish were powerless to rein him in: "*de Valera had usurped the Irish cause unto himself and they were helpless to remove him.*"[51] [emphasis added]

With tongue in check, the Machiavellian master of back-room political intrigue pontificated:: "I do not believe in back-stair methods...The arguments against my appearing in Chicago apply equally to my appearing in America at all..."[52] How right he was!

Democratic Convention (June 28-July 6, 1920)

"The fundamental fallacy of de Valera's position was his failure to recognize that, as President of an Irish Government fighting for its life, his place was in Ireland, and not in America. His claim to dominate Irish-Americans with an authority derived from the people of Ireland was obviously illogical. The Representative of a Government, recognized or unrecognized, in a foreign country, should be that of a diplomat and not the leader of a political party in that country ..."[53] Pieras Beaslai was no de Valera apologist but he failed to recognize the Irish President's mission to America was motivated by the deal brokered with the British and that his place as a British agent was in America and not Ireland.

After successfully making fools of the Irish-Americans at the Chicago Republican Convention, de Valera tootled off to San Francisco with a gaggle of Irish buffoons to work his Machiavellian machinations on the Democratic Convention. Arriving in San Francisco on Sunday, June 27, 1920, he established headquarters at the Whitcomb Hotel, accompanied by Frank Walsh. The *Chicago Daily News* reported: "The enthusiastic reception given to Professor Éamon de Valera, President of the Irish Republic, gave much satisfaction to the Irish leaders. Here [San Francisco] as in Chicago, the Irish parade was one of the spectacular features of the Convention. Tonight, a mass meeting was held at Dreamland Rink where de Valera... and others spoke for the Irish cause."[54]

The *San Francisco Chronicle*, on June 27, two days before the Dáil approved de Valera's request for $1.5 million to obtain recognition of an Irish Republic and influence the Presidential election, reported that de Valera had already spent several hundred thousand dollars preparing for his demolition of Irish interests.

With an Irish plank in the Republican Platform, the Democrats would have had to respond in like manner or risk losing, both short- and long-term, the traditionally overwhelmingly Democratic Irish vote.

De Valera recognized that the Irish-Americans held the key to any possible Democratic victory: "The Democrats will bid high for the Irish vote now. Without it they have not the slightest chance of winning at the elections..."[55] Just as he had done in Chicago, de Valera proceeded to provide the Democrats with a "colorable pretext," again providing the means to reject an Irish plank in their platform without alienating their constituents. The Democrats seized the opportunity, and Ireland dropped off the agenda.

Upon his arrival in San Francisco, de Valera immediately threw down a gauntlet to the Democrats as he had done to the Republicans in Chicago.

Frank Walsh set the tone of de Valera's strategy in San Francisco: "It is a simple case of recognition or hands off. No sympathy or sop planks will do. We will...urge the adoption or rejection of the one plank indicated by President de Valera."[56] Again, the Irish President did not request but demanded that an American political party adopt full and immediate recognition of an Irish Republic thereby guaranteeing the proposal would be rejected. The *Chicago Tribune* reported: "Irish leaders...will take nothing less, they said. Nothing can replace the plank demanding full recognition..."[57] Walsh leveled an ultimatum: "If the Democrats would not give the Irish friends a recognition resolution, they wanted nothing at all."[58] De Valera made sure the Irish got what they deserved at Chicago – nothing, and he was equally determined that they would receive the same in San Francisco.

The *New York Times* noted the Irish Leader's contemptuous rejection of former American Ambassador to Germany and Democratic presidential hopeful James W. Gerard's proposal linking recognition of Irish independence to the League of Nations: "The Walsh-de Valera group will not agree even to the proposal...that the United States make Britain's recognition of Irish independence a condition of America's entry into the League of Nations. They will have nothing they say but an outright acceptance or rejection plank drawn by themselves."[59]

In recognition of de Valera's negative impact, McCartan proposed a conference to which neither de Valera nor Boland be invited. "Following the Chicago debacle, there were efforts to convene a meeting to stop the feuding. But some of de Valera's own people wished to exclude him because he had been 'betraying an unconscious contempt' for the opinions of others by doing most of the talking and not allowing others to speak. In this way, he forced his own opinions and thus thinks he has cooperation when he only gets silent acquiescence."[60]

Here was an Irish writer who used the "B" word, but he attributed that "betrayal" to egotism and boorishness. Despite acknowledging de Valera's disastrous policies, McCartan incomprehensibly continued to support him and was relentless in his abuse of Devoy and Cohalan.

De Valera's conduct at the San Francisco Convention mirrored his actions in Chicago. If only one of the political parties had adopted a substantive Irish plank in their platform, the Irish Question would have become a political football for months. It was imperative to British interests that the Democrats reject any meaningful Irish plank in their platform. De Valera's arrival in San Francisco guaranteed that no such plank would be adopted.

Devoy and Cohalan refused to engage in another political bloodletting and left the San Francisco Democratic Convention to de

Valera and his supporters. Daniel T. O'Connell declared that the FOIF would not engage in any campaigning: "The experience at Chicago would not be repeated. De Valera would have a clear field to present any plank he wished without any competition from the Friends."[61] Jeremiah Lynch stated that the Friends of Irish Freedom "will not be party to factional differences and while standing strictly to principle of American control of American affairs will not give trouble makers a chance to complain and distort facts..."[62]

De Valera and his fawning supporters still complained, and the troublemakers continued to distort the facts. Many Irish writers actually blamed the absent Cohalan and Devoy for the debacle at San Francisco. De Valera refused to alter his almost-unanimously rejected Chicago Plank. Randolph Smith, vice president of the "Loyal Coalition," a pro-English organization in America, said: "the only good thing that aggregation of [Republican] mountebanks and clowns at Chicago did was to leave an Irish plank out of their platform and he urged that the Democratic Convention do the same."[63]

De Valera's scheme in San Francisco was the same as in Chicago: face down the Democrats and demand immediate and formal recognition of an Irish Republic. His plan worked to perfection against the Democrats as it had against the Republicans. He insisted on the following Democratic plank:

> "We pledge our [Democratic] Party to the policy of
> according to the elected Government of the Republic of
> Ireland full, formal and official recognition by the
> Government of the United States ..."

This plank met with overwhelming rejection. "The best he could obtain in the way of a declaration was a vague and colorless plank expressing 'sympathy with the aspirations of the Irish people for self-government' and promising 'such action as may be consistent with international comity and usage.' A very explicit repudiation of any move in the direction of recognition of an Irish Republic."[64]

Congressman Tom Connolly, Texas democrat, was emphatically opposed to any Irish plank, resulting in the fatuous de Valera Plank being defeated 35-17. Not one of the 17 delegates who voted in favour was willing to present the plank as a minority proposal to the full convention: proof enough that no one took "recognition" or "sympathy" for Ireland seriously. Once again, de Valera was able to bring the "colorable pretext" maneuver into play, and the Democrats extricated themselves without alienating their Irish constituencies.

153

"After extended conferences between de Valera, Walsh and some other de Valera adherents, *it was decided to leave out of the proposed plank any mention of recognition of the Republic of Ireland.* [emphasis added] Seven members of the Resolutions Committee agreed to sign this revised plank and present it as a minority report. When Edward Doheny attempted to place this plank before the convention, the most vociferous opposition was at once manifested. After an hour of boisterous confusion the vote was taken on the meaningless Walsh amended plank, which was defeated by a vote of 675.5 to 401.5."[65] de Valera's supporters claimed this was a "close vote" and a qualified success for de Valera's plank. In reality, the resounding defeat of de Valera's watered-down plank notched another success for British foreign policy.

De Valera managed the wrong kind of publicity for the Irish cause by staging a climactic scene of drunken brawling at the Democratic Convention. Newspapers reported:

"Scenes of greater disorder than were ever witnessed at a similar convention hearing in recent years were enacted today at the hearing of the Committee on Resolutions on the proposed Irish Plank. Hisses, groans and interruptions by advocates of an Irish Plank, greeted speeches of Demarest Lloyd, president, and Randolph W. Smith, vice president, of the 'Loyal Coalition,' a pro-English organization, who opposed the adoption of any plank recognizing or favoring the independence of Ireland on the grounds that the continuance of a policy of such resolutions would eventually mean war with England.

"The greatest disorder was caused by a remark of Mr. Smith who said that there should be no difficulty in carrying on freedom-for-Ireland propaganda in this country, as its sponsors had collected $10 million from the pockets of American servant girls ...This statement caused an immediate outburst of indignation. Smith said, 'Wholesome truths seem to trouble Irish digestive organs...They raised this fund by the chicanery and trickery of one de Valera.'"[66]

At another meeting, Lloyd opposed the recognition of an Irish Republic and was constantly heckled by Irish supporters, who had to be physically ejected by the police. The *San Francisco Chronicle* reported on July 2, 1920: "An Irish meeting so stormy and disordered that one of the participants said it might be regarded as evidence that the race could not govern itself was held this afternoon...Judge Michael A. Sullivan of Salem, Mass...told the meeting amid noisy disapproval that those who disagreed with the Irish, if they could see the disorder of the gathering, would not believe the Irish nation capable of self-government. I hope those present are all friends of our cause, for if there are doubters present, I wonder how they can, after witnessing this scene, have any hope of Ireland being capable of governing itself."[67]

At a meeting of 300 or more de Valera supporters, Charles C. Tansill reported: "The atmosphere of the discussion soon became so heated that the police had to be called to quell the confusion."[68] So much for McCartan's crusade on behalf of de Valera's catastrophic conduct in America when he claimed that the Irish President had "conducted himself in public with so much circumspection and dignity as to bring him and us universal respect."[69]

Coogan also played fast and loose with the truth by charging that the absent Cohalan and FOIF presented opposition to de Valera at the Democratic Convention. "The Cohalan/de Valera performance received an encore at the Democratic Convention in San Francisco the following month."[70] Another writer stated, "de Valera now hastened to San Francisco and the spectacle of another fight with the Cohalan faction was staged for the American public."[71]

The extent of the FOIF "opposition" to de Valera at San Francisco was the announcement that the Friends of Irish Freedom would not be presenting an alternative resolution in order to allow de Valera free reign to submit any plank he wished. Cohalan never attended the Democratic Convention but returned to New York after the Republican debacle in June. Irish writers failed to document a single instance of a difference or fight at the Democratic Convention between the de Valera faction and anyone associated with Cohalan or the FOIF because there was none. The only fights which occurred at the Democratic Convention in San Francisco were between de Valera supporters and the police who were called to restrain Irish rowdiness.

John J. Splain noted: "de Valera failed in San Francisco just as he had failed in Chicago. His failures seemed to embitter him against those who had made whatever success he had achieved in America possible. Satellites and toadies, who were sharing in the moneys given de Valera by the FOIF, opened wider the floodgates of slander. Justice Cohalan, whose private life has always been a model, was accused of every infamy. John Devoy was charged with every conceivable criminality. Men in every community whose only fault had been their practical love for Ireland were libeled most shamefully because they refused to acknowledge de Valera as the master of their American political actions."[72] Once again, de Valera was judged a failure. As far as the British were concerned, he succeeded marvelously.

Ironically, the Democrats, who owed much of their political success to the solid support of the Irish-Americans, were not averse to recognizing other emerging nations, but not dear old Ireland. Armenia was included in the Democratic platform, with expressions of not only sympathy for that nationality, but the resolution: "This [US] Government...should render all possible and proper aid to the Armenians' in their effort to establish and maintain a government of their own..."[73] This was in marked contrast to the watered-down Irish resolution which read: "Within the limitations of international comity and usage, this convention repeats the several previous expressions of the sympathy of the Democratic Party of the United States for the aspirations of Ireland for self-government."[74]

According to Charles Tansill: "With the President of the Irish Republic, it was always a question of rule or ruin and he did a magnificent job of ruining Irish-American unity...de Valera seemed determined to impose his unwanted leadership upon Irish-Americans at times when it led straight to disaster. At San Francisco, he repeated his blunders at Chicago."[75] Typically, Tansill's analysis failed to consider whether de Valera's consistent "blunders" might not have been deliberate machinations. Through his deliberate scuttling of any Irish initiatives, there would be no discussion of an Irish question during the long presidential campaign and no pro-Irish presidential candidate to promote Irish independence. America would continue treating Ireland as an internal matter of Great Britain.

The infamous Black and Tans arrived in Ireland in March 1920, less than two months after de Valera's Cuban interview in the *Westminster Gazette* in which he downgraded the Irish Republic to the status of an English satellite. The Irish had gained worldwide sympathy primarily because the British were perceived to be terrorizing civilians. British reprisal policy was widely denounced, especially in the United States and the Commonwealth nations.

Later, another group of British veterans, all former officers, was recruited into a band of "Auxiliaries." They were tough and intelligent soldiers and more than a match for the outgunned and outmanned IRA.

But de Valera's rejection of virtual Irish independence as set forth in Cohalan's plank at the Republican convention in June was a signal to Lloyd George to accelerate the Black and Tan terror. Within two weeks, Lt. Colonel Smyth was addressing the men of the Royal Irish Constabulary (RIC) at Listowel, Ireland, in the following terms:

"Well men, Sinn Féin has had all the sport up to the present and we are going to have the sport now...We must take the offensive and beat Sinn Féin at its own game...If a police barracks is burned or if the barracks already occupied is not suitable, then the best house in the locality is to be commandeered, the occupants thrown into the gutter. Let them die there – the more the merrier.

"Police and military...will lie in ambush and when civilians are seen approaching, shout 'Up Hands!' Should the order be not obeyed at once, shoot to kill. If the persons approaching carry their hands in their pockets or are in any way suspicious-looking, shoot them down.

"You may make mistakes occasionally and innocent persons may be shot, but that cannot be helped, and you are bound to get the right person some time. The more you shoot, the better I will like you and I assure you no policeman will get into trouble for shooting a man..."[76]

The Black and Tans increased their rampaging throughout Ireland, murdering and robbing in drunken orgies of sadism. They set a torch to the City of Cork and a host of villages in retaliation for IRA reprisals to Black and Tan attacks on civilians. The effect of de Valera's July debacle in San Francisco, resounded in Ireland: "The end of July saw the beginning of a huge organized attack by Orange mobs on Catholic workers in Belfast as well as in other Northern towns. Catholic workers were attacked in the shipyards and driven out. Later the Catholic quarters of Belfast was invaded by howling mobs, who wrecked, burned and looted Catholic workman's houses."[77]

Bishop Michael J. Gallagher of Detroit, President of the Friends of Irish Freedom, recognized de Valera's responsibility in rejecting an Irish plank. He wrote: "This [rejection of all reference to Irish aspirations at the Conventions] was immediately interpreted in England as the absolute repudiation of the Irish Question by American statesmen as we know from Lloyd George and Hamar Greenwood. [It] was the signal for the opening of the saturnalia of arson, murder, lust and looting...The division [in America]...has manifested itself openly and evidently [the British]...have come to the conclusion that they can now with impunity, as far as America is concerned, shoot the citizens of the Republic of Ireland. If President de Valera had remained away from Chicago and allowed Americans to run their own affairs... the fear of American public opinion would have stayed the murderous hand of England from committing such monstrous atrocities as Ireland has lately endured."[78]

Even Patrick McCartan, de Valera's faithful sidekick, laid the blame for the increase in Black and Tan brutality in Ireland squarely on de

Valera: "By our fighting, we had shattered our power to influence the American Government to restrain England's murderous intent..."[79] Coogan noted that, "There was a very strong body of opinion among the Irish-Americans that the British were taking advantage of the feud [in America] to step up the military campaign in Ireland..."[80]

Devoy came close to recognizing de Valera's true mission in America, but could not bring himself to admit the Irish President was a British agent. In an undated letter to J. J. O'Kelly, Devoy pointed to an English plot being the real reason for de Valera's trip to America, but he misdirected his charges to Maloney while merely linking de Valera to the conspiracy. Devoy claimed: "There is a plot. It is the plot hatched at the British Embassy two years ago and revealed by Captain Maloney in a moment of weakness. Its object is to undermine and break up the Clan and the Friends of Irish Freedom and discredit and destroy their leaders and Maloney is the Arch Plotter with McCartan as his willing, if unconscious tool...Whether that work is done by the President of the Irish Republic and his envoys in America or directly through British agents, it is none-the-less England's work..."[81]

In another letter to O'Kelly on July 5, 1920, Devoy charged that the plot was put into action at the Chicago Convention "with consummate skill and cunning...the plan worked out in Chicago was to put de Valera in the position of the Champion fighting for recognition of the Irish Republic and us in the position of men betraying it. It was done without regard for truth or decency, every act of ours being grossly misrepresented so as to deceive the people and put us in the wrong. We, not England, are treated as THE ENEMY. I have seen many bad situations in my long experience but none quite so bad as this created by de Valera, the man sent here to unite and consolidate the Irish Race in America...and who is now trying to split us into factions – and putting the blame on us."[82]

Beaslai recognized the effect of de Valera's conduct at the Presidential conventions was "A very explicit repudiation of any move in the direction of recognizing Irish independence. The platform of the party, on which Harding was elected, at one stage, contained a Cohalan Plank which recognized the principle that 'the people of Ireland have the right to determine freely, without dictation from outside, their own governmental institutions and their international relations with other states and peoples.'"[83]

After all the effort, expense, and bitterness he unleashed upon Irish-Americans by his demanding recognition of the Irish Republic, de Valera made an astonishing revelation six months later. Before twenty-four stunned members of the Dáil, he admitted: "There had never been any hope of getting the United States Government to recognize the Irish

Republic, and never would be until the United States were prepared to go to war with England. 'If I were President of the United States myself,' he said, 'I could not, and I would not, recognize Ireland as a Republic.'"[84] As a result of that admission, a dumbfounded John Whelan attempted to deflect the obvious and fatal question of de Valera's treachery in America. He went so far as to cast doubt as to the veracity of the witnesses: "If de Valera did say that, it is one of the most amazing things he ever said..."[85]

Rather than being considered as a bumbling, dysfunctional psychotic, if de Valera was recognized as the English spy that he was, how would history sum up his efforts in America? The verdict would have shown that he was neither politically naïve nor vain, but a diabolically clever politician who by sheer chutzpah single-handedly turned two political parties and an entire country against the Irish cause. When weighed in the scales of history, de Valera must go down as the most successful agent in furthering English interests in America. He accomplished what not even all the might of England could do – destroy the Irish-American influence in the United States and discredit two of Ireland's finest advocates – John Devoy and Judge Daniel Cohalan.

De Valera's primary reason for going to America was to seek recognition of an Irish Republic. The opportunity for recognition came not from America, but from an unlikely source: the Soviet Union. Through the efforts of McCartan, the Soviets had proposed recognition of an Irish Republic, and the sole remaining step was formal adoption by the proper representatives of each government in Moscow.

At the same session in which the Dáil authorized the expenditure of $1.5 million on the American political scene, de Valera was also given the green light "to dispatch a diplomatic mission to the Government of Russia, the Socialist Federal Soviet Republic, with a view to establishing diplomatic relations with that Government..."[86] All that was necessary was for de Valera to provide McCartan with the official authority to sign and conclude a treaty with the Soviet Union. De Valera once again erected roadblocks in Ireland's path to recognition. Under the proposed terms of the treaty: "The Government of the Russian Socialist Federal Soviet Republic pledges itself, its resources and its influence to promote recognition of the sovereignty of the Republic of Ireland by the nations of the world."[87]

McCartan recorded: "As I have told in my letter of July 20, 1920, President de Valera refused to grant credentials empowering me to conclude a treaty with the Russian Government along the lines of a draft which the Russian representatives in America had approved. Presumably, he did not want recognition, at least, not from Russia."

De Valera's flip-flopping between self-determination and recognition proved very damaging to Ireland. Any chance of American recognition of Irish independence was now over while the reputation of John Devoy was ruined not only in America but also in his beloved Ireland. De Valera's outrageous antics in San Francisco left the Irish-Americans a laughing stock and rendered them politically impotent.

Notes
1. *NewYorkTimes*, 6/7/1921
2. Tansill, Charles, C., *America and the Fight for Irish Freedom 1866-1922*, Devin-Adair, NY. 1957, p. 226
3. Coogan, Tim Pat, *De Valera, The Man who was Ireland*, Harper, 1996, p. 189
4. Fitzgerald, W.G., *The voice of Ireland, A Survey of the Race & Nation from all Angles*, Virtue Ltd. Dublin/London, p. 235
5. McCartan, Patrick, *With de Valera in America*, Brentano/NY 1932, p. 137
6. *ibid*, p. 138
7. Coogan, Tim Pat, *De Valera, The Man who was Ireland*, Harper, 1996, p. 143
8. Tansill, Charles, C., *America and the Fight for Irish Freedom 1866-1922*, Devin-Adair, NY. 1957, p. 301
9. *ibid*, fn
10. *Gaelic American*, 6/26/1920
11. de Valera Press Release: 06/19/1920
12. Dwyer, T. Ryle, *De Valera, The Man & the Myths*, Poolbeg, Dublin, p. 44
13. *ibid*
14. Devoy to O'Kelly, 7/5/1920
15. *ibid*
16. Devoy to Cohalan, 8/12/1920
17. Longford, Earl of & O'Neill, Thomas P., *Éamon de Valera*, Hutchinson, London, 1970, p. 109
18. Dwyer, T. Ryle, *De Valera, The Man & the Myths*, Poolbeg, Dublin, p. 41
19. Tansill, Charles, C., *America and the Fight for Irish Freedom 1866-1922*, Devin-Adair, NY. 1957, p. 374
20. McCartan, Patrick, *With de Valera in America*, Brentano/NY 1932, p. 191
21. Dwyer, T. Ryle, *De Valera, The Man & the Myths*, Poolbeg, Dublin, p. 42
22. Tansill, Charles C, *America and the Fight for Irish Freedom 1866-1922*, Devin-Adair, NY 1957, p. 376
23. McCartan, Patrick, *With de Valera in America*, Brentano/NY 1932, p. 191
24. *ibid*, p. 218
25. *ibid*, p. 147
26. Ryan, Desmond, *Unique Dictator*, Arthur Barker, London, 1936, p. 130

27. Tansill, Charles C, *America and the Fight for Irish Freedom 1866-1922*, Devin-Adair, NY 1957, p. 377

28. Fitzgerald, W.G., *The voice of Ireland, A Survey of the Race & Nation from all Angles*, Virtue Ltd. Dublin/London, p. 249

29. Tansill, Charles, C., America and the Fight for Irish Freedom 1866 – 1922 ,Devin-Adair, NY. 1957, p. 375 fn

30. Fitzgerald, W.G., The voice of Ireland, A Survey of the Race & Nation from all Angles, Virtue Ltd. Dublin/London, p. 248

31. *Gaelic American*, 6/19/1920

32. McCartan, Patrick, *With de Valera in America*, Brentano/NY 1932, p. 209

33. *New York Times*, 1920, 4:6

34. *Gaelic American*, 6/19/1920

35. *ibid*

36. *Chicago Tribune*, 6/12/1920

37. Longford, Earl of & O'Neill, Thomas P., *Éamon de Valera*, Hutchinson, London, 1970, p. 110

38. Fitzgerald, W.G., *The voice of Ireland, A Survey of the Race & Nation from all Angles*, Virtue Ltd. Dublin/London, p. 248

39. *Gaelic American*, 6/26/1920

40. Dwyer, T. Ryle, de Valera, *The Man & the Myths*, Poolbeg, Dublin, p. 41

41. Longford, Earl of & O'Neill, Thomas P., *Éamon de Valera*, Hutchinson, London, 1970, p. 110

42. Coogan, Tim Pat, *De Valera, The Man who was Ireland*, Harper, 1996, p. 181

43. *ibid*

44. *ibid*, p. 191

45. Tansill, Charles, C., *America and the Fight for Irish Freedom 1866-1922*, Devin-Adair, NY. 1957, P. 383

46. McCartan, Patrick, *With de Valera in America*, Brentano/NY 1932, p. 219

47. Dwyer, T. Ryle, *Éamon de Valera*, Gill & Macmillan, 1980, p. 34

48. Dwyer, T. Ryle, *De Valera, The Man & the Myths*, Poolbeg, Dublin, p. 43

49. Coogan, Tim Pat, *De Valera, The Man Who Was Ireland*, Harper Perennial, 1995, p. 180

50. de Valera Press Release 6/19/1920

51. McCartan, Patrick, *With de Valera in America*, Brentano/NY 1932, p. 155

52. *Gaelic American*, 6/26/1920 & de Valera Press Release

53. Beaslai, Pieras, *Michael Collins and the Making of a New Ireland*, Vol II, Harper Bros. NY 1926, p. 21

54. *Chicago Daily News*, 6/29/1920

55. Dwyer, T. Ryle, *De Valera, The Man & the Myths*, Poolbeg, Dublin, p. 40

56. *San Francisco Chronicle* 6/27/1920

57. *Chicago Tribune*, 6/29/1920

58. *San Francisco Chronicle* 6/30/1920

59. *New York Times*, 6/29/1920
60. Dwyer, T. Ryle, *De Valera, The Man & the Myths*, Poolbeg, Dublin, p. 43
61. Tansill, Charles, C., *America and the Fight for Irish Freedom 1866-1922*, Devin-Adair, NY. 1957, p. 380
62. *Western Union*, 6/24/1920
63. *New York Times*, 6/30/1920
64. Beaslai, Pieras, *Michael Collins and the Making of a New Ireland*, Vol II, Harper Bros. NY 1926, p. 17
65. Tansill, Charles, C., *America and the Fight for Irish Freedom 1866-1922*, Devin-Adair, NY. 1957, p. 381
66. *New York Times*, 6/30/1920, 1:4
67. *San Francisco Chronicle*, 7/2/1920
68. Tansill, Charles, C., *America and the Fight for Irish Freedom 1866-1922*, Devin-Adair, NY. 1957, p. 381
69. McCartan, Patrick, *With de Valera in America*, Brentano/NY 1932, p. 147
70. Coogan, Tim Pat, *De Valera, The Man who was Ireland*, Harper, 1996, p. 182
71. *ibid*
72. Fitzgerald, W.G., *The voice of Ireland, A Survey of the Race & Nation from all Angles*, Virtue Ltd. Dublin/London, p. 249
73. *New York Times*, 7/3/1920, 4:6,7
74. *New York Times*, 7/3/1920, 4:6,7
75. Tansill, Charles, C., *America and the Fight for Irish Freedom 1866-1922*, Devin-Adair, NY. 1957, p. 378
76. O'Broin, Leon, *W. E. Wylie and the Irish Revolution*, Macmillan, 1989, p. 72
77. Beaslai, Pieras, *Michael Collins and the Making of a New Ireland*, Vol II, Harper Bros. NY 1926, p. 49
78. McCartan, Patrick, *With de Valera in America*, Brentano/NY 1932, p. 197
79. *ibid*, p. 198
80. Coogan, Tim Pat, *De Valera, The Man who was Ireland*, Harper, 1996, p. 189
81. Devoy to Seán T. O'Kelly in Rome, 7/7/1920
82. Devoy to O'Kelly, 7/5/1920
83. Beaslai, Pieras, *Michael Collins and the Making of a New Ireland*, Vol II, Harper Bros. NY 1926, p. 17
84. Beaslai, Pieras, *Michael Collins and the Making of a New Ireland*, Vol II, Harper Bros. NY 1926, p. 18
85. Whelan, John (Seán O'Faoláin), *De Valera*, Penguin Books, England 1939, p. 74
86. *Booklyn Eagle*, 8/9/1920
87. McCartan, Patrick, *With de Valera in America*, Brentano/NY 1932, p. 219, 272

CHAPTER XII

American Association for the Recognition of the Irish Republic (AARIR)

"De Valera's progress in America is the narrative of the development of a split in Irish-American ranks...Within 18 months, his efforts had culminated in a split, leaving two rival organizations, and even two rival Clan na Gael bodies. Twelve months after his return to Ireland, he was again the cause of a split in the Irish National ranks, in the Dáil, Sinn Féin and the I.R.A. with lamentable consequences for Ireland."[1]

Pieras Beaslai

With the carnage of the Republican and Democratic conventions in his wake, the final scene in "Assignment America"- the destruction of the Friends of Irish Freedom and Clan na Gael was about to be played out. Having scuttled the nomination of a pro-Irish presidential candidate and preventing the introduction of an Irish plank in either party's platform, de Valera now turned his full attention to discrediting Devoy and Cohalan and splitting the Irish-American bloc.

Archbishop Daniel Mannix of Australia, who was viewed as an anti-British prelate bent on creating mischief, was refused entry to Ireland. Subsequently his landing in America on July 17, 1920 presented de Valera with another opportunity to insult the Irish-American leaders. He called a monster rally in New York City to greet Mannix without informing or inviting John Devoy and Daniel Cohalan. McCartan exulted at the Irish-Americans' exclusion: "At Bishop Mannix's side stood de Valera with Archbishop Hayes...while Cohalan [and Devoy], unbidden, sulked in his tent, listening to his humble followers cheering Archbishop Mannix – and de Valera."[2]

Within four months of the Irish President's arrival in America just over a year earlier, Devoy had already surmised that de Valera planned to split the Irish-Americans by starting a rival organization. Frank Walsh, de Valera's hand-picked chairman of the American Commission on Irish Independence, in a press release stated: "It has been suggested that 'the organization' be extended into a national organization on very broad lines so as to include everyone with any Irish sympathies, which will conduct de Valera's tour and have many other duties such as that of counteracting anti-Irish propaganda, etc."

These were functions already carried out by the Friends of Irish Freedom (FOIF) and Clan na Gael. "This means a rival organization…" he told Cohalan. "It would breed dissension, etc. Evidently, that is what they want the $100,000 for – to use the money collected by the Friends to start an organization to supplant it…"[3] de Valera withheld his public challenge until after the political conventions were over. He called a press conference announcing his intention to form a new organization along "democratic lines."

The Irish President's assault on the Irish-American leaders was carried out on various fronts. Author Charles Tansill noted: "It was not alone through smears, half truths and complete lies that de Valera and his cronies attacked Devoy and Cohalan…It was apparent that there was a scheme to seize control of the Friends of Irish Freedom for the purpose of furthering the plans of de Valera. His formula of rule or ruin was about to be invoked again."[4]

De Valera knew he could not oust Devoy and Cohalan from their powerful positions in the FOIF, so in a staged confrontation, he flushed them into a public dispute which provided the pretext to initiate a rival organization. In a letter to Jeremiah Lynch in August 1920 shortly after the Democratic Convention, de Valera demanded that a special meeting of the National Council of the Friends of Irish Freedom be convened in Chicago, away from Devoy and Cohalan's power base in New York City. The Irish-Americans agreed to the meeting but insisted it be held in New York.

Using Bond Certificate funds, de Valera wired sympathetic council members around the country, instructing them to travel to New York, all expenses paid, in order to pack the National Council meeting with the express purpose of dumping Cohalan and amending the FOIF Constitution. Devoy and Cohalan were well aware of de Valera's plot and were able to counter the Irish President's moves by outvoting his proposals.

Coogan, in a specious conjecture, stated: "de Valera was at first prevented from even entering the meeting, only getting in after Harry Boland shouldered the doorman out of the way. Once he was inside, Michael J. Ryan, the Chairman, denied him the right to speak on a procedural point. One of de Valera's supporters, Rossa Downing, described it as 'the most disgraceful gathering of men and women that I ever attended.'"[5] The charge that Boland had to physically push aside the doorman to allow the Irish President to enter the room seems farfetched given that the FOIF had agreed to hold a special National Council meeting at the request of the Irish President. It mirrored the false claim that Boland had to also "physically shoulder" his way into the Park Avenue Hotel meeting the previous March in order to allow the invited guest, de Valera, to enter.

It is possible de Valera was denied the right to speak on a procedural point, but the likelihood of his not being allowed to enter the meeting or to speak at all are dubious charges. De Valera was noted for ignoring Parliamentary procedure and interrupting other speakers whenever the urge to do so came upon him, and he may have been ruled out of order on a particular point.

After being outmaneuvered at the National Council hearing in New York, de Valera delivered his broadside a month later. At the October 14, 1920 National Council session he provoked a split by demanding unacceptable amendments to the FOIF Constitution. The Irish President arrived at the meeting escorted by his entourage and demanded that Bishop Gallagher and he select five members each of the executive board of the FOIF. The proposal was overwhelmingly defeated. De Valera then previewed a practice he was to use successfully on later occasions whenever he was determined to create a split, whether in America or Ireland. Using the rejection of his demands as an excuse, he stage-managed a walkout to a chorus of "Follow the President" by his supporters.

Feigning indignation, de Valera refused all entreaties to return to the meeting. He did, however, order his hatchet man Boland to return. "[A]fter a tirade of abusive remarks directed at the followers of Devoy and Cohalan, Boland stated that de Valera wished 'all those who wanted to help the Irish Republic to meet him in that room the following day.'"[6]

The next morning, de Valera publicly announced that a rival organization would be formed, challenging the FOIF, and splitting Irish-American ranks wide open. In an October 1920 telegram to prominent Irish-Americans throughout the country, de Valera requested their presence, again with all expenses paid, to a conference, which would establish an organization dedicated to securing recognition of an Irish Republic.

De Valera opened the conference with a hypocritical lament: "I have had and have no heart, when my country is being ravished and our people being done to death, to see our friends enter upon controversies that might verge upon the personal, the sordid, and the petty. I had clung to – till lately – to the hope that a certain existing organization might be broadened to meet the requirements ..."[7] John Splain, FOIF vice president, countered: "With inconceivable indelicacy from one who had been given such wonderful manifestations of its support, de Valera denounced the Friends of Irish Freedom as an organization that had somehow declined to adopt his notions of democracy."[8]

De Valera then called for a new "democratic" organization that would be "free from machine methods with the voice of the people sublime and the leaders with short terms of office answerable to the people and removable by recall. That some provision be made so that any line of action taken with a view to Ireland's interest...may not cross that of Ireland's own direct representatives...If an organization founded on the love of the American people for liberty and for Ireland, thwart the elected representatives of Ireland on the task imposed on them by their own people – to whom they are directly responsible for their actions and by whom they can be removed – such an organization must necessarily be regarded by Ireland, not as an assistance, but as an obstacle ..."[9]

On October 20, two weeks before the US presidential election, de Valera publicly announced the split in Irish ranks and the inauguration of the American Association for the Recognition of the Irish Republic (AARIR). He informed his followers that the new organization would be democratic in form and substance. Taking a swipe at Devoy and Cohalan, he claimed it would be free of imperial directives from that "cabal" in New York. Coogan attacked the hypocrisy: "de Valera's version of democracy was evidently intended to be of the guided variety – the royal plural showed up remarkably freely in his short statement of policy. 'We, from Ireland, simply ask...that we should be accepted as the interpreters of what the Irish people want – we are responsible to them and they can repudiate us if we represent them incorrectly.'"[10]

In his attack on the Irish-American organization and on Devoy and Cohalan in particular, de Valera ordered Dr. Patrick McCartan to set up an office in Washington, DC, using Bond Certificate funds, of course. McCartan noted that de Valera was still carrying his pocket edition of Machiavelli's *The Prince* when the Irish President arrived in Washington.

McCartan confirmed de Valera's purpose in launching the AARIR was not to work for Ireland but to destroy Cohalan and Devoy: "Had the Association been started earlier, it might have done much to justify its title. But its origin, as I have shown, was due not to the purpose its title proclaimed but to de Valera's need to form an organization to supersede Cohalan's...President de Valera, in launching the new Association had to settle accounts with Cohalan."[11]

The AARIR was successfully launched on November 16, 1920 at the Hotel Raleigh in Washington, DC. De Valera dictated the term of office for those whom he planned on using to derail Cohalan and Devoy. Edward L. Doheny of Los Angeles was not so much as elected president of the new association but appointed by de Valera and seated by acclamation. So much for being "free from machine methods."

The Friends of Irish Freedom (FOIF) was devastated by a wholesale defection to the AARIR. FOIF membership plummeted from over 100,000 to 20,000 within a few months, and, through the organizational wizardry of James O'Mara, the AARIR membership soared to 750,000 in 1921. O'Mara had been dispatched to America to assist de Valera in the Bond Certificate drive. Now he was instrumental in drafting a constitution for the new organization and with establishing branches in every state and major city. "[O'Mara] attended to the organization of all this. He carried through the initial stages until a smooth routine could be maintained, but in everything down to the smallest detail, de Valera, as President of Ireland and co-trustee of Dáil Éireann was consulted and it was he who made the final decisions."[12] The "viable" organization petered out almost as quickly as it came into being, for within a month of the Irish President's return to Ireland, he set about dismantling the AARIR. He began by cutting off funding, thereby rendering the AARIR's demise a certainty, which outraged O'Mara, who subsequently resigned in disgust.

The AARIR "shattered Irish-American unity beyond repair. The Friends of Irish Freedom had been dealt a blow from which the organization never recovered...de Valera continued to inspire hostility between the two organizations [even after he returned to Ireland]."[13]

De Valera's disasters in America have been dressed up as epic successes. Many Irish writers conceded that the Irish-American scene was left in disarray but refused to admit that de Valera was the cause. Instead they spouted platitudes lauding his imagined achievements. T. Ryle Dwyer obsequiously toed the de Valera line with outright distortions of facts: "The split [within the Irish-American ranks] was wider than ever when de Valera returned to Ireland in December 1920, but he did leave behind a viable organization which was primarily dedicated towards serving the Irish cause, rather than using the Irish situation to serve American ends. His mission had thus been a qualified success, because in addition, he had collected over five million dollars and by his clever exploitation of the opportunities afforded for propaganda, he had secured invaluable publicity for the Cause. As a result of this publicity, the British government came under enormous pressure to negotiate an Irish settlement, if only to avoid Anglo-American difficulties."[14]

Dwyer skirted the funding issue by ignoring the $3 million in American banks which should have been used "towards serving the Irish cause." His claim that de Valera secured "invaluable publicity for the cause" was nonsensical. After de Valera got through with his anti-Irish campaign at the Republican and Democratic conventions, the Irish-Americans were rendered politically impotent and reduced to an image of drunken, boorish clowns.

McCartan belatedly recognized the disaster that was de Valera in America: "To Ireland, in her agony, it mattered less than nothing whether de Valera or Cohalan was the more responsible for our fighting in the United States. To Ireland, all that mattered was that we were fighting. By our fighting we had shattered our power to influence the American Government to restrain England's murderous intent [Black and Tans] ...but we in America insanely continued our civil war."[15] McCartan could not bring himself to blame de Valera because it would have meant exonerating Cohalan and Devoy. He simply could not come to grips with admitting it was solely de Valera's outrageous conduct that was so detrimental to Ireland. The only fighting in America was conducted by de Valera and his supporters against Devoy, Cohalan, and the FOIF. McCartan considered Devoy and Cohalan's defense against the aggression of the Irish President as "attacks" against de Valera.

James O'Mara was a self-made millionaire, a rarity in Ireland, and had amassed a fortune through his pork business. He was a magnificent organizer and administrator. To O'Mara, honesty, dedication, and responsibility were more than mere words. When he assumed the organizational leadership of the astonishingly successful 1918 Sinn Féin election in which the Irish Parliamentary Party of John Redmond was all but wiped out, he provided his own services and those of an employee at his own expense to work full time on the campaign. He had asked Robert Brennan, Director of Elections, what the cost of maintaining two Sinn Féin representatives abroad would be. When Brennan estimated that it would cost about £2,000 ($10,000, an enormous sum at that time): "The very next day, O'Mara dropped a paper bag full of notes at 6 Harcourt Street (Sinn Féin headquarters) and opened his glove and let a rattle of gold sovereigns fall out. The notes totaled £1800 and £200 in gold. He said that he was prepared to give a loan to Sinn Féin of this amount and added, 'If you win,' meaning the Sinn Féin election, 'I want the money back; if you lose – all right.'"[16] Prior to returning to Ireland after eighteen months in America, in a note to Harry Boland, O'Mara wrote, "... I have the pleasure of enclosing my personal check for $12,500 completing payment of $17,500 advanced to me in part payment of my private expenses in the United States. It is a satisfaction to me to know that my services to Ireland will not have cost the public funds a cent."[17]

O'Mara, like McGarrity and so many others, soon found to his regret just how adept de Valera was at using and discarding men after they had done his dirty work. In March 1920, O'Mara had had enough of de Valera and submitted his resignation. In reporting the resignation to Arthur Griffith, de Valera lied once again claiming that O'Mara's resignation had been for strictly personal reasons and not because of any differences in philosophy between them. Beaslai remarked: "This statement was certainly misleading. O'Mara had decided differences of opinion with de Valera and resigned because he did not feel able to continue to work with him."[18]

Exasperated with the goings-on in America, Collins wrote to Boland on April 19, 1920: "There always seems to be something depressing coming from the USA. I cannot tell you how despondent this particular incident has made me. No doubt, I am overly touchy in this matter, but yet, after a pretty hard year, every little divergence tells heavily. Mr. Griffith is writing to O'Mara appealing to him to reconsider the question of his action, if persisted in, it would have a really bad effect – very much worse than the Gaelic American difference."[19]

With one disaster after another arising from de Valera's conduct in America, it is incredible that no one ever considered that it might possibly be a deliberate scheme to sabotage Irish-American influence and promote Anglo-American interests. O'Mara acceded to Griffith's request and continued his work in America. Soon there was further disagreement. On November 11, 1920, five days before the AARIR launch, O'Mara wrote to de Valera complaining about the Irish President's demand for more money without discussing it with him. O'Mara was projecting another huge fund-raising campaign of $20 million in the coming year but de Valera was constantly calling on McGarrity and others to initiate fund-raising schemes without telling him. "Listening to your conversation with Mrs. McWhorter today, it was apparent that your plans, both of future organization and machinery for raising money, were so well formulated as to be made public. I, therefore, will spare you the trouble of telling them to me individually ..."[20] O'Mara had had enough of de Valera's demands and wrote the following day: "Dear Mr. President, you have asked me to organize a new organization: without a name; without a constitution; without money. Were I so fresh for this hard work, I could not go any further without these three essentials."[21]

On December 13, 1920, de Valera sailed from New York for Ireland. Despite O'Mara's misgivings and doubts as to de Valera's policies, he devoted his time and energies to organizing the AARIR convention in Chicago on April 18-20, 1921, which was a huge success, as over 5,000 delegates from throughout the country attended, "... and temporarily put the seal of triumph of de Valera...over those of Cohalan and Devoy."[22] In spite of their numbers, only two prominent Irish-Americans attended. The contrast to the FOIF convention at Philadelphia two years earlier was striking. Even de Valera's personal choice of President of the AARIR, Edward Doheny, never showed up.

De Valera continued to micromanage the affairs of the AARIR from Ireland without consulting O'Mara. De Valera called on McGarrity to propose "at the National Convention of the AARIR...and have passed, a resolution authorizing a levy of one dollar or two per member of the AARIR in order to sustain the government of the Republic in its fight."[23]

O'Mara was furious. De Valera's instruction to McGarrity was the last straw. O'Mara wrote to de Valera on April 25, 1921: "A cable from you was read at the great Convention of the AARIR asking for a guarantee of a million dollars yearly and was translated into action by a levy of five dollars a member on every member of the Association – which practically includes every active person of our race. Neither Mr. Boland nor myself were consulted on the matter. There are nearly three million dollars lying idle here to the credit of the American Trustees and at the disposal of your Government. Funds were therefore not urgently required and your request at this time unnecessary...It is somewhat unworthy of our country to be always holding out its hat, but to hold out two hats at once is stupid. And lastly, your appeal now makes impossible any attempt later this year to raise the $20 million loan which was contemplated – to use your own words when we last discussed the matter: 'Crops will not grow on trampled ground.' I would advise you to promptly send someone to this country who has your confidence, if such a person exists, and having done so, don't continually interfere with his work ..."[24]

On January 30, 1921, Lloyd George at a meeting at 10 Downing Street with Bonar Law, Conservative Party leader, said: "I have a letter somewhere from de Valera...He wants to come and see me secretly...de Valera wanted a face-saver, that he was willing to drop the Republic and even fiscal autonomy...Auckland Geddes [British Ambassador to the U.S.] gives a most gloomy account of the situation in America and in the interests of peace with America, I think we ought to see de Valera and try to get a settlement...If we could settle quickly, it might clear up our American debt [$40 billion] and have all sorts of other reactions."[25]

The Ambassador's gloomy assessment could improve if the Irish lobby in America ran out of money and faded away. In a letter to O'Mara on February 3, 1921, less than a week after Lloyd George's reporting on Geddes' report of conditions in America, de Valera ordered all funds to the AARIR cut off. He also implied that any expenditures by O'Mara without Dáil [de Valera] approval was illegal. In his note to O'Mara, he commented: "By the way, it is very necessary to husband our funds and diminish expenditure in America...The Dáil can still sit and therefore our emergency powers as trustees are not to be used ..."[26] In other words, since the Dáil was sitting, O'Mara no longer had the legal right to spend a nickel without approval from Dublin. The revelation hit O'Mara like a thunderbolt. De Valera also hinted, not so subtly, that O'Mara's previous expenditures might be legally suspect, and he demanded an accounting of all funds.

De Valera and O'Mara had been operating the AARIR under a so-called emergency-powers provision while the Dáil was unable to sit. O'Mara replied to de Valera on February 22, 1921, expressing his concerns: "I am troubled to know whether the appropriations made by you and me for American purposes on December 1, 1920, were *ultra vires* [not within the scope of powers conferred upon them], and if so, whether you have been able to get the Dáil at its last sitting to confirm the same...The American Association for the Recognition of the Irish Republic is growing and threatens to become a veritable Frankenstein unless directed and controlled. To get effective work from the superabundant but now useless strength requires the services of a central bureau and the expenditure of about $200,000. You must know that all these sums are an investment in sentiment and will return sevenfold in the issue of a second loan. Knowing this, it should not be difficult to convey that fact to the Dáil..."[27] de Valera had no intention of providing O'Mara with further authority to spend any money on the AARIR, nor did he pass O'Mara's message to the Dáil.

In a letter to Boland on the same day, O'Mara wrote: "de Valera...says, the Dáil can still sit and therefore our emergency powers as trustees are not to be used. In the circumstances, it is evident that I have no power to continue what is absolutely essential work..."[28] In order to insure the AARIR did not survive, de Valera also removed Boland. The importance of Boland and O'Mara to the success of the American campaign was clearly set forth by Frank P. Walsh in a letter to O'Mara of May 4, 1921, regarding O'Mara's resignation and Boland's recall. "This blow seems almost insurmountable...I think, we might as well shut up shop..."[29]

By cutting off all funding at this critical early juncture, de Valera killed off the AARIR. He wasted the political and financial advantages a strong AARIR would have brought to Ireland, especially with an organizational genius like O'Mara at the helm.

On March 24, 1921, in another letter to O'Mara, de Valera

continued to place restrictions on O'Mara's ability to spend any money. It was a rerun of his early attacks against the FOIF: "We must cut down our running expenses in the United States. The propaganda should henceforth be done mainly by the American organizations..."[30] This was another flip-flop by de Valera and an admission that Devoy and Cohalan were correct in spending funds for propaganda purposes in the United States. De Valera had used a trumped-up charge of diversion of funds earmarked for Ireland against the Irish-Americans in his campaign to discredit them. He was now advocating that very same policy in his orders to O'Mara.

If he was serving His Majesty's interests, de Valera would not have wanted the AARIR to succeed. He had destroyed the most powerful anti-British Irish-American organization, the Friends of Irish Freedom, and substituted in its place an even more powerful organization. With a membership in the hundreds of thousands, the AARIR under the hard-charging leadership of O'Mara, presented an even greater threat to English interests in America than Devoy and Cohalan. O'Mara and the AARIR had to be neutralized as well.

O'Mara had established the Benjamin Franklin Bureau as an adjunct to the AARIR. This grouping was responsible for organizing a nationwide propaganda campaign and an aggressive recruiting drive to enlist non-Catholic, non-Irish to the Irish cause. O'Mara sought to harness the enormous amount of sentiment for Ireland throughout America as Franklin had done in France and England for the American revolutionary cause, and to apply that pressure to Congress. He was astute enough to realize that Congress was reactive and convinced that it would respond only if sufficient political muscle was applied, the exact same policy advocated by Devoy and Cohalan.

In March 1921, the Senate Judiciary Committee was investigating foreign loans to determine whether they were being used for the purposes for which they had been granted, along with their current status. Through the Benjamin Franklin Bureau, O'Mara presented evidence of British abuse of U.S. loans relative to Ireland.

In his submission to the Judiciary Committee on March 21, O'Mara outlined a scathing exposé of British military expenditures in Ireland. He documented the cost of British repression in Ireland, which amounted to more than half the delinquent annual interest payment of $256 million due annually on England's $40 billion First World War debt to the United States. The British operations in Ireland cost more than $128 million for the current year [1921]: O'Mara stated: "I would therefore respectfully urge that your honorable Committee, in its consideration of the debt of the Government of Great Britain to the United States, carefully examine the expenditures of the British Government in Ireland. And if the facts warrant, enter protest on behalf of the Government of the United States against such expenditures and such destruction of property as you may determine to be wanton and wasteful of the resources which should properly be applied to the liquidation of the debt to the United States government ..."[31]

On March 24, three days after O'Mara's dispatch to the Judiciary Committee, de Valera ordered O'Mara to cut off all funding to the Benjamin Franklin Bureau: "You will regard it as an instruction, therefore, that all offices and persons not provided for in your estimate are to be dispensed with by June 1, 1921 ..."[32] O'Mara's frontal attack in Congress calling for the repayment of England's war debt brought swift retribution as the English quickly moved to have their agent, de Valera, shut down the Benjamin Franklin Bureau. The threat to Anglo-American financial interests was obvious, and O'Mara had touched a sensitive English nerve – their $40 billion war debt to the United States.

De Valera had to repeat his order to dismantle the increasingly effective Benjamin Franklin Bureau. In an April 8 note to O'Mara through Boland, de Valera ordered that no funds of any kind were to be expended: "We cannot undertake providing expenses and making arrangements for speakers, speaking tours, etc... ."[33] In another intimation of possible O'Mara wrongdoing, de Valera added: "Please have the auditors send me a comprehensive summary of the state of our finances over there to date?"[34] The March 24 missive from de Valera ordering the cutting off of all funding was deliberately designed to force O'Mara's resignation "for he addressed O'Mara in terms, which appear deliberately calculated to 'wind him up ...'"[35]

Only two weeks after the Benjamin Franklin Bureau memorandum to the Judiciary Committee, de Valera again wrote to O'Mara via Boland, demanding even more severe cutbacks of funding for the AARIR and the dismantling of the Benjamin Franklin Bureau: "This should be done at the latest by June 1 next, after which date all expenditures, not definitely provided for in the estimates of the permanent establishment are to be regarded as special and must be made provision for by a special vote [of the Dáil, that is by de Valera]...We cannot afford, even as a maximum, an outlay of more than $100,000 for the maintenance of the diplomatic and political side of the United States. Services during the coming year and your estimate must on no account exceed that figure ..."[36]

After again hinting that O'Mara's expenditures might be called into question, de Valera offered O'Mara the position of Representative of the Irish Republic in the USA. In a letter to de Valera on April 29, O'Mara rejected de Valera's overtures for the proposed position: "Nor can I continue to hold any official position under the government of the Irish Republic whose President claims such arbitrary executive authority and in whose judgment of American affairs I have no longer any confidence."[37]

O'Mara resigned his seat in the Dáil on April 30, 1921. Writing to de Valera, he acknowledged the fatal effect the Irish President's action had on Irish-American interests: "Your dispatches of April 8 obviously indicate your final decision to force through your policy which last December received the almost unanimous condemnation of the Irish Mission here."[38] O'Mara protested that de Valera's policy was wreaking Irish-American initiatives. "Now, as then, rather than be responsible for that policy, I tender my resignation as *the most emphatic protest I can make against what must be the utter disruption and destruction of American aid* [emphasis added]...You will, therefore, please place my resignation before Dáil Éireann on the expiration of the year, June 14, 1921."[39]

O'Mara wrote again, on May 3: "No consideration...or sob stuff or humbug or flattery – will make me accept responsibility for a policy I do not believe in ..."[40] He concluded: "The progress of recent months making good your indecision and your mistakes of last year leaves me the more convinced of your error ..."[41]

Confirming O'Mara's charge of abuse of authority, de Valera did not submit his resignation to the Dáil, which was the body legally authorized to accept his resignation or to fire him. Instead, he took it upon himself to dismiss O'Mara. In a cable to Boland, de Valera ordered: "[O'Mara] once expressed a wish to be fired by cable, this is it, [de Valera]."[42] Though de Valera lacked the authority to fire O'Mara, again no one dared challenge him or question his motive. To add insult to injury, de Valera appointed O'Mara's brother, Stephen, to succeed him as trustee of the Bond Certificate funds.

There was one Irish-American who recognized de Valera's duplicity, but he, too, failed to translate that understanding into what it really was – treason. In a letter to the Friends of Irish Freedom on April 9, 1921, Bishop Gallagher charged that de Valera deliberately split the Irish-Americans and was playing England's game: "I was foolish enough to cherish the hope that all men of Irish blood, interested in the liberation of Ireland, would remember how the Parnell split served her enemies...If ever Ireland needed help from the power of American public opinion, it was during the last six months...But America, the champion of freedom...had done practically nothing. The reason is because *President de Valera deliberately split the Irish movement in America* [emphasis added] and all the energy of his followers has been wasted in the struggle to destroy instead of being expended for Ireland's cause against the common enemy. I nourished the hope that the friends of Ireland would soon see the folly of thus playing England's game, but it has been all in vain. The new organization (AARIR) is still spending thousands upon thousands of dollars trying to wipe out the Friends of Irish Freedom. Anyone who suggests that de Valera is not master of the people of Irish blood everywhere; or that, like ordinary mortals, he ever made a mistake in his whole life, is overwhelmed with billingsgate and foul abuse in the de Valera press."[43]

On July 11, 1921, J. C. Walsh wrote to O'Mara, confirming what O'Mara had predicted, the demise of the Benjamin Franklin Bureau: "Unofficially I learn that the AARIR moves in here tomorrow, the Ben Franklin Bureau disappearing on Saturday."[44]

And so ended O'Mara's vision of an organization so vital to the mainstream of the American political process and to the hopes and aspirations of Ireland. Upon his departure from America's shores, the Irish-Americans were left with their dreams of what might have been.

With de Valera's "Assignment America" completed, he now moved to "Assignment Ireland" and another English triumph and Irish disaster.

Notes

1. Beaslai, Pieras, *Michael Collins and the Making of a New Ireland*, Vol II, Harper Bros. NY 1926, p. 1
2. McCartan, Patrick, *With de Valera in America*, Brentano/NY 1932, p. 208
3. Devoy to Cohalan, 10/9/1919
4. Longford, Earl of & O'Neill, Thomas P., *Éamon de Valera*, Hutchinson, London, 1970, p. 112
5. Tansill, Charles, C., *America and the Fight for Irish Freedom 1866-1922*, Devin-Adair, NY. 1, p. 386
6. Coogan, Tim Pat, *De Valera, The Man who was Ireland*, Harper, 1996, p. 188
7. Tansill, Charles, C., *America and the Fight for Irish Freedom 1866-1922*, Devin-Adair, NY. 1957, p. 391
8. Lavelle, Patricia, *James O'Mara, A Staunch Sinn Feiner 1873-1948*, Clonmore & Reynolds, Dublin, 1961, p. 183
9. Fitzgerald, W.G., *The voice of Ireland, A Survey of the Race & Nation from all Angles*, Virtue Ltd. Dublin/London, p. 252
10. Lavelle, Patricia, *James O'Mara, A Staunch Sinn Feiner 1873-1948*, Clonmore & Reynolds, Dublin, 1961, p. 184

11. Coogan, Tim Pat, *De Valera, The Man who was Ireland*, Harper, 1996, p. 188
12. McCartan, Patrick, *With de Valera in America*, Brentano/NY, 1932, p. 216
13. Tansill, Charles, C., *America and the Fight for Irish Freedom 1866-1922*, Devin-Adair, NY, 1957, p. 394
14. Dwyer, T. Ryle, *De Valera, The Man & the Myths*, Poolbeg, Dublin, p. 45
15. McCartan, Patrick, *With de Valera in America*, Brentano/NY, 1932, p. 198
16. Lavelle, Patricia, *James O'Mara, A Staunch Sinn Feiner 1873-1948*, Clonmore & Reynolds, Dublin, 1961, p. 121
17. *ibid*, p. 249
18. Beaslai, Pieras, *Michael Collins and the Making of a New Ireland*, Vol II, Harper Bros. NY 1926, p. 14
19. *ibid*, p. 15
20. Lavelle, Patricia, *James O'Mara, A Staunch Sinn Feiner 1873-1948*, Clonmore & Reynolds, Dublin, 1961, p. 191
21. *ibid*, p. 192
22. Coogan, Tim Pat, *De Valera, The Man who was Ireland*, Harper, 1996, p. 210
23. Lavelle, Patricia, *James O'Mara, A Staunch Sinn Feiner 1873-1948*, Clonmore & Reynolds, Dublin, 1961, p. 238
24. Coogan, Tim Pat, *De Valera, The Man who was Ireland*, Harper, 1996, p. 210
25. Jones, Thomas, (Keith Middlemas Ed.), *Whitehall Diary*, Vol. III, Oxford U. Press, p. 49
26. Lavelle, Patricia, *James O'Mara, A Staunch Sinn Feiner 1873-1948*, Clonmore & Reynolds, Dublin, 1961, p. 236
27. *ibid*, p. 237
28. *ibid*, p. 247
29. *ibid*, p. 260
30. *ibid*, p. 238
31. *ibid*, p. 211
32. *ibid*, p. 241
33. *ibid*, p. 242
34. *ibid*, p. 238
35. Coogan, Tim Pat, *De Valera, The Man who was Ireland*, Harper, 1996, p. 208
36. Lavelle, Patricia, *James O'Mara, A Staunch Sinn Feiner 1873-1948*, Clonmore & Reynolds, Dublin, 1961, p. 240
37. *ibid*, p. 248
38. *ibid*, p. 249
39. *ibid*
40. *ibid*, p. 255
41. Coogan, Tim Pat, *De Valera, The Man who was Ireland*, Harper, 1996, p. 211
42. Lavelle, Patricia, *James O'Mara, A Staunch Sinn Feiner 1873-1948*, Clonmore & Reynolds, Dublin, 1961, p. 249

43. Tansill, Charles, C., *America and the Fight for Irish Freedom 1866-1922*, Devin-Adair, NY. 1957, p. 394
44. Lavelle, Patricia, *James O'Mara, A Staunch Sinn Feiner 1873-1948*, Clonmore & Reynolds, Dublin, 1961, p. 265

CHAPTER XIII

"Assignment Ireland"

"Pope Alexander VI did nothing else but deceive men, nor ever thought of doing otherwise, and he always found victims, for there never was a man who had greater power in asserting, or who, with greater oaths, would affirm a thing, yet, would observe it less. Nevertheless, his deceits always succeeded according to his wishes, because he well understood this side of mankind."[1]

Niccolò Machiavelli

What had served the English so well over the centuries was their mastery of the propaganda machine; their ability to mask brutal repression in Ireland behind a paper wall of disinformation. Exposure of the official reprisal policy against the Irish posed a serious threat to vital international relations of Britain. Crucial talks were underway in America to either restructure the English First World War debt or eliminate it altogether. It was critical to England's financial survival that she claim the moral high ground, so Lloyd George determined to dispose of the Irish Question once and for all. He would make the Irish an offer they couldn't refuse, not so much for Ireland's benefit as for international appearances, especially in America.

Peace feelers were being bandied about as early as August 1920. In one interview, Michael Collins damped down a Dominion settlement while privately not ruling out any option. Dominion status meant an Ireland within the British Commonwealth on the same footing as Canada, Australia, and South Africa. For centuries, the Irish dreamt of freedom from British repression, but the English, however, refused to grant Irish independence as it regarded Ireland as their backdoor through which they might be invaded. With Irish encouragement, Britain's enemies had landed in Ireland on at least four occasions: when the Irish offered the Crown of Ireland to Bruce, the King of Scotland in 1315, a Spanish contingent landed at Smerwick and were subsequently defeated at Cashel in 1580, another Spanish incursion in 1601 and the French in 1798 all resulted in disastrous results for the native Gaels.

Politically speaking, Collins publicly claimed the achievement of Republican status would require the same effort as obtaining Dominion status. This was a signal to Lloyd George that if serious proposals for Dominion status were placed on the table, they would be considered. According to Tim Pat Coogan: "de Valera tended to portray a more moderate public image while privately advocating a more hard-line approach. Collins tended to do the opposite. Privately he was much more moderate than was generally believed."[2]

In an effort to capture Collins and eliminate his intelligence network, the British flooded Dublin with a number of undercover men. Collins was able to discover their identities and on November 21, 1920, appropriately dubbed "Bloody Sunday," his men carried out a citywide assassination of fourteen British spies. In retaliation, the Black and Tans surrounded Croke Park stadium, in which a crowd of spectators had gathered to watch a soccer game between Dublin and Tipperary. Claiming they were fired upon, the Black and Tans opened fire on the spectators killing twelve with hundreds injured in the ensuing stampede. The British denied it was a reprisal and that it was Irish Republican Army (IRA) men in the stands who had initiated the firing. Brigadier General Frank Crozier, repulsed by the official reprisal policy of the Government, resigned his commission and publicly admitted that his men fired into the crowd without provocation on Bloody Sunday.[3]

This incident finally convinced Lloyd George that his reprisal policy was creating a backlash of negative publicity. He launched a two-pronged initiative: to determine to what extent Collins and Arthur Griffith were willing to enter into peace talks and set in motion the return of Éamon de Valera from America. When Lloyd George decided to approach Collins and Griffith, the Catholic Archbishop Joseph Clune of Australia was visiting London and was an ideal intermediary. On December 1, 1920, the Prime Minister authorized Clune to present Griffith with proposals for a truce and peace conference. The Archbishop met with Griffith who had been arrested after the "Bloody Sunday" incident and was languishing in Kilmainham Gaol.

In a note to Collins, Griffith was willing to accept Lloyd George's proposals for a truce under the following conditions: "...that it involved no surrender of principle on our part...If the English Government calls off its present aggressive campaign, we can respond by urging the cessation of the present acts of self-defense. All the pursuits of members of the Dáil and others must cease and the entire Dáil to freely meet to arrange the full terms of the Truce."[4]

Collins met Clune on December 4. An agreement was reached on a tentative truce and peace initiative, with the terms outlined by Collins in a letter to Clune: "If it is understood that the acts of violence (attacks, counter attacks, reprisals, arrests and pursuits) are called off on both sides, we are agreeable to issue the necessary instructions on our side, it being understood that the entire Dáil shall be free to meet and that its peaceful activities be not interfered with..."[5]

During the final months of the year, the Prime Minister had said: "The question is whether I can see Michael Collins. No doubt, he is the head and front of the movement. If I could see him, a settlement might be possible. The question is whether the British people would be willing for us to negotiate with the head of a band of murderers."[6]

The British Prime Minister, from August through December 1920, could have easily negotiated a Truce with Griffith, who advocated a dual monarchy, a reference to his doctrine formulated on the basis of an independent Ireland under the King of England; in effect, Dominion status. He was also receptive to a peaceful settlement of the Irish Question.

After Collins and Griffith outlined the conditions in which they were willing to accept a truce and a peace conference, Lloyd George, in a dubious move, declared he was no longer interested and proceeded to stall any meaningful negotiations. The scenario orchestrated by Lloyd George appeared to be a scheme to sound out Collins and Griffith in order to determine the conditions in which they were willing to accept a truce and enter into a peace conference; then cutting off all further talks until de Valera returned to Ireland.

Immediately after receiving Collins and Griffith's acceptance of truce conditions, the Prime Minister turned from peace advocate to hawk and ordered martial law enforced throughout Southern Ireland, and demanded the handing over of all rebel arms. Archbishop Clune was dismayed by Lloyd George's response and charged the Prime Minister with going back on his word. Beaslai noted that the British Prime Minister was "prepared to give 'safe conduct' to some members of the Dáil to meet to discuss peace proposals but that there were certain members to whom 'safe conduct' could not be granted."[7]

The Irish President was homeward bound within ten days of Collins' meeting with Clune and less than a month after successfully inaugurating the American Association for the Recognition of the Irish Republic (AARIR). After a suitably decorous period elapsed, Lloyd George offered the same peace initiatives to the Irish President as he had to Collins and Griffith. Coogan speculated as to the timing: "There was increasing mention in the Press about peace parleys conducted between Lloyd George and Collins through the intermediacy of Archbishop Clune. If anyone was going to conduct peace negotiations with the Prime Minister of Britain, de Valera intended that it should be he, not Michael Collins."[8]

In an eerily familiar British connivance to de Valera's "escape" from Lincoln Jail, and as further evidence of an English/de Valera plot, John Anderson, Undersecretary in Ireland, revealed: "de Valera returned to Dublin from his prolonged sojourn in America *'with the connivance of the British authorities'*"[9] [emphasis added]. Anderson was highly regarded both in Ireland and England, and he was certainly in a position to know about the British Government's attitude towards de Valera.

As late as August 7, 1920, the British were still bulking up de Valera's Irish stock by publicly posting that he was *persona non grata* and would not be allowed to land in the United Kingdom. A memo from the Secretary of the War Office to E. Davies of the Home Office, stated: "It is reported that de Valera has disappeared from New York and is said to be making his way to Ireland. You will remember the Home Secretary made an Order on October 3, 1919, prohibiting him from entering the United Kingdom..."[10]

Once de Valera had completed his work in America, official policy turned from frigid to warm. "The British were aware that de Valera was returning and the government actually issued instructions that he should not be arrested either when he landed in Liverpool or proceeded to Dublin."[11]

A dispatch from Haldane Porter of the Home Office to the Immigration Office, on December 10, three days before de Valera was secretly scheduled to leave America for Ireland, informed immigration authorities of a change in de Valera's entry status. Obviously, the British were privy to the Irish President's itinerary prior to Collins placing him aboard the SS *Celtic* on December 13. The directive stated: "If the above named [Edward de Valera] arrives at your port, he should be allowed to land and his arrival and the address to which he is proceeding should be telegraphed to this Office...He should not be searched."[12]

De Valera returned to Dublin on Christmas Eve 1920, after eighteen months in America. The ensuing events shared many of the tragic characteristics of his rampage through America. It was now Ireland's turn to feel the sting of de Valera's treachery.

He arrived unmolested by British authorities and almost immediately sparked a rift among the native Irish as he did the Irish-Americans. He merely substituted Michael Collins and Arthur Griffith for Daniel Cohalan and John Devoy in his simulated power struggle *du jour*. In order to rationalize de Valera's conduct, many Irish commentators promoted the theory of competition between de Valera and Collins. Dwyer, for instance, could only explain de Valera's anti-Irish actions in terms of a dysfunctional personality: "de Valera was determined to show that he had more power than anybody else in the movement. He had to be clearly seen as the Chief. This led to his problems with Cohalan and Devoy in America. In the same way, it would also lead to a power struggle with Collins, which, in turn, would have disastrous consequences for the nation."[13] The possibility that de Valera was deliberately promoting British interests never entered into an Irish writer's equation.

Longford and O'Neill attempted to deflect the odor emanating from the British "connivance" in facilitating de Valera's return to Ireland: "It was true, however, that the British Cabinet soon learned of his return and decided against arresting him...until they could bring some definite criminal charge against him."[14] The claim that the English welcomed de Valera back to Ireland in order to allow the Government time to come up with a criminal complaint is unconvincing. Every Irishman is well aware of the fact that the British never needed time or any other excuse to jail an Irishman: children were arrested for whistling an anti-British tune, men were sentenced to prison for answering a policeman in Gaelic, and Irish men and women were jailed by the trainload for comments "designed to cause disaffection" under the all-encompassing Defense of the Realm Act (DORA).

Furthermore, de Valera had been preaching anti-English rhetoric during his time in America, and he resumed his highly public British bashing as soon as he set foot in Ireland. The British donned blinders as they searched everywhere and nowhere while their quarry campaigned throughout the country, traveling by public transport in his IRA uniform rattling his usual speeches designed to cause disaffection to His Majesty's Government.

Griffith had been arrested on November 24, 1920, three days after "Bloody Sunday." Upon his arrest, Collins assumed the position of Acting President of Dáil Éireann after Charles Burgess, the Defense Minister, refused to serve. Lloyd George feigned outrage over Griffith's arrest. Author Richard Bennett noted: "The Prime Minister was very angry to learn of the arrest of Griffith. He told an astonished General Macready, who did not know of the peace negotiations, that he had no right to take such an action without the sanction of the Cabinet."[15] Lloyd George had varying degrees of displeasure: upon Griffith's arrest, the Prime Minister was "very angry," but not angry enough to release the Acting Irish President, who endured more than seven months in an English prison until a Truce was announced in July 1921. When de Valera was "inadvertently" arrested in June 1921, the British Prime Minister, in another degree of displeasure, immediately dispatched the Assistant Secretary, Alfred Cope, to have him released within 24 hours.[16]

The British would only negotiate with de Valera. In an effort to establish an atmosphere favorable for negotiations on a peace plan: "Lloyd George suggested that Collins and Richard Mulcahy, IRA chief of staff, should leave the country for a period, and allow conditions more conducive for talks to develop."[17] On January 18, 1921, less than a month after his return, de Valera lost no time in furthering Lloyd George's agenda. Under the heading of "Bringing about Unity," de Valera issued a cabinet order dispatching Collins to America. De Valera said: "When the new organization, the American Association for Recognition of the Irish Republic, has become solidified, [Collins] was to assist in uniting as far as possible, all the Irish forces in the United States. In particular he was to bring back to our support many of the excellent people in the Clan who have been misled by the Gaelic American and associated propaganda..."[18]

De Valera attempted to allay any suspicion that he was responsible for leaving the Irish-Americans in disarray: "You will not, of course, make the mistake of thinking that the division began with my advent in America. It existed in reality long before. My coming only gave it a new turn, and brought it to a head..."[19] Michael Tierney recognized de Valera's motive for ordering Collins to America: "Amounting, as it did to an assignment to undo the split among the Irish-Americans which divided Devoy and Cohalan from de Valera's own supporters. This was a tall order but it was even more astonishing when one reflects on Collins' position in the struggle in Ireland itself. It is merely the most startling of the many indications, which show that the future split at home was already in its preparatory stages."[20]

Longford and O'Neill alleged that: "The Cabinet agreed and Collins, at first reluctant, became reconciled to the idea. He was somewhat disappointed when Lord Derby's visit in April (1921) made the President feel that, with the possibility of serious negotiations, Collins could not be spared from Ireland."[21] Coogan flatly contradicted them: "That paragraph [of Longford and O'Neill's] was, in fact, a near classic example of de Valera-speak [a lie]. It combines distortion with *suppressio veri* [suppressing the truth] and barefaced lying. Far from becoming 'reconciled to the idea,' Collins was outraged and hurt. 'The long whore won't get rid of me as easily as that,' was his reaction..."[22] Furthermore, the Dáil Éireann Cabinet did not agree to send Collins to America.

Further echoing Lloyd George's call for conditions conducive to peace negotiations, de Valera demanded that the Irish "ease off" on their defensive response to the Black and Tan terror. Unaware of Lloyd George's suggestions, Beaslai noted that within three weeks of his return: "de Valera formed two decisions, each equally unwise – the war with the English forces must 'ease off' and Michael Collins must be sent to the United States..."[23]

In his move to get rid of Collins, de Valera convened a Cabinet session to exploit the animosity between Burgess and Collins. The Minister of Defense charged that Collins pocketed several hundred dollars intended for the purchase of arms in Glasgow the previous year. The obsequious Austin Stack supported Burgess declaring that such a "serious charge" should be investigated.

In running a revolution, it was virtually impossible to account for every penny spent on clandestine operations or procuring arms. For more than two years, Collins had been purchasing arms through intermediaries whenever and wherever the opportunity presented itself. During the early months of 1921, when the Black and Tans were terrorizing the country and Collins was desperately leading an anti-terror campaign, Burgess took that opportunity to accuse him of embezzling a pittance. Beaslai saw through Burgess' hypocrisy: "It seems eminently unreasonable that Burgess should have chosen this particular time, when so many of the men who had been engaged on the work were in jail, or 'on the run,' to demand strict and tabulated accounts of the money expended under this head. At all events, Collins was put to a great amount of trouble and worry trying to trace the various transactions in connection with the work. He wrote several letters to Joe Vize [one of his operatives in Scotland], asking for information on these points. It is evident from the tone of these letters, that he felt keenly the unfriendly and hypercritical attitude of Burgess and the unhelpfulness of Liam Mellowes."[24]

Collins realized that someone other than Burgess was behind the move to embarrass him; in a letter to Vize on March 16, 1921, Collins said: "Of course, the whole thing has another motive, as you know very well."[25]

"The cruelty and absurdity of Burgess' insinuation will be realized when it is considered that Collins, as Minister of Finance, had the handling of about a million pounds [$5 million], including £20,000 in gold. Every penny of which was satisfactorily accounted for in a time of war and exceptional difficulties and that, as head of the Provisional Government, he died almost a poor man."[26]

Burgess plumbed the depths of ill will in charging Collins with misappropriation of a few hundred dollars, yet he was silent about de Valera's lavish expenditures in the United States. No criticism was heard from Burgess or Stack about the million dollars spent on discrediting Devoy and Cohalan or the status of the $3 million the Irish President stashed in American banks, or the lack of any accounting of the funds spent in America.

De Valera "lost no time in complaining about the way the IRA campaign was being waged: 'Ye are going too fast,' he told Mulcahy. 'This odd shooting of a policeman here and there is having a very bad effect from the propaganda point of view on us in America. What we want is one good battle once a month with about 500 men on each side.'"[27] Instead of Collins' successful guerilla tactics, he sought large-scale engagements between the basically unarmed IRA and the heavily armed British military. It was common knowledge that the IRA did not have the men or arms to engage in pitched battles: the flying columns roaming the countryside had no more than thirty rounds of ammunition and rifles for one out of five men. In the event that the Irish were somehow able to put 500 men in the field, they would have to contend with not 500 British soldiers but more than 50,000 equipped with the latest in military hardware. De Valera was calling on the IRA to match their antiquated rifles against tanks, artillery, and airplanes. The President's call to ease off on the attacks was overwhelmingly rejected by the Dáil. As long as the Black and Tan violence continued there was but one course to follow – to counter terror with terror.

In another of de Valera's consistent inconsistencies, he demanded that the IRA mount an attack on the historic Dublin Custom House. The May 25, 1921 raid proved a gift to the British. His supporters hailed it as proof of his military genius, though he succeeded in nearly wiping out the entire IRA Dublin Brigade for the destruction of irrelevant tax records. The beautiful architectural monument was reduced to a burned-out shell, and the Dublin Brigade was decimated, with the death and capture of more than seventy of its best fighting men. Two arsonists in the middle of the night could have affected the same result.

Collins was irate that so many irreplaceable men had been wasted on a meaningless objective. Whether or not the British were warned of the impending attack, they responded so quickly that they caught many of the most highly skilled Dublin IRA men within the building. Author G. A. Holmes recorded a more accurate account of the Custom House raid: "[T]he burning of the Custom House proved to be as disastrous as anything that might have been anticipated...The Dublin Brigade lost 100 men in one day – a figure unheard of since the Rising – and though Republican propaganda made a brilliant job of portraying the operation as a body blow against the Government, this did not alter the unfortunate reality of the situation."[28]

De Valera had not been back in Ireland a month before he was calling for Irish self-determination that he had so vehemently repudiated at the Republican Convention in Chicago. In an interview with the *Zurich Neue Zeitung* on May 3, 1921, he said; "The principle for which we are fighting is the principle of Ireland's right to complete self-determination...If England should concede that right there would be no further difficulties, either with her or with the Ulster minority. If Ulster should claim autonomy [Partition] we would be willing to grant it."[29] That policy would, of course, have had more impact and borne more fruit had it been implemented at Chicago.

"... De Valera now reversed the republican position that he had adopted in America as opposed to Cohalan's self-determination. He wrote to Boland [in America on February 29, 1921], explaining his U-turn: '...Our position should be simply that we are insisting on only one right and that is the right of the people of this country to determine for themselves how they should be governed...'"[30]

Almost one year from the day de Valera rejected Cohalan's approved Irish self-determination plank at the Republican Convention in Chicago, he issued the following statement prior to a Dáil meeting in July 1921: "The Press gives the impression that I have been making certain compromise demands. I have made no demand but the one I am entitled to make: the self-determination of the Irish nation to be recognized."[31] His lack of consistency was bewildering.

Notes

1. Machiavelli, Niccolo, *The Prince* (Translated by W.K. Marriott), J&M Dent & Sons, London 1908, p. 99
2. Coogan, Tim Pat, *De Valera, The Man who was Ireland*, Harper, 1996, p. 222
3. Dwyer, T. Ryle, *De Valera, The Man & the Myths*, Poolbeg, Dublin, p. 53
4. Beaslai, Pieras, *Michael Collins and the Making of a New Ireland*, Vol II, Harper Bros. NY 1926. p. 110
5. *ibid*, p. 111
6. Dwyer, T. Ryle, *De Valera, The Man & the Myths*, Poolbeg, Dublin, p. 52
7. Beaslai, Pieras, *Michael Collins and the Making of a New Ireland*, Vol II, Harper Bros. NY 1926, p. 121
8. Coogan, Tim Pat, *De Valera, The Man who was Ireland*, Harper, 1996, p. 191
9. Wheeler-Bennett, John, *John Anderson, Viscount Waverly*, St. Martens Press, NY 1962, p. 75
10. PRO: HO 144/10309, 315944/19
11. Dwyer, T. Ryle, *De Valera, The Man & the Myths*, Poolbeg, Dublin, p. 47
12. PRO: HO 144/103089, 315944/19

13. Dwyer, T. Ryle, *Michael Collins, The Man who won the War*, Mercier Press, 1990, p. 125
14. Longford, Earl of & O'Neill, Thomas P., *Éamon de Valera*, Hutchinson, London, 1970, p. 115
15. Bennett, Richard, *The Black & Tan*, Metro Books, 2002, p. 132
16. See Chapter XIV
17. Dwyer, T. Ryle, *De Valera, The Man & the Myths*, Poolbeg, Dublin, p. 47
18. Beaslai, Pieras, *Michael Collins and the Making of a New Ireland*, Vol II, Harper Bros. NY 1926, p. 143
19. Beaslai, Pieras, *Michael Collins and the Making of a New Ireland*, Vol II, Harper Bros. NY 1926, p. 144
20. Tierney, Michael (ed. F.X. Martin), *Eoin MacNeill, Scholar & man of Action 1867-1945*, Clarendon Press, Oxford 1983, p. 299
21. Longford, Earl of & O'Neill, Thomas P., *Éamon de Valera*, Hutchinson, London, 1970, p. 119
22. Coogan, Tim Pat, *De Valera, The Man who was Ireland*, Harper, 1996, p. 201
23. Beaslai, Pieras, *Michael Collins and the Making of a New Ireland*, Vol II, Harper Bros. NY 1926, p. 141
24. *ibid*, p. 162
25. *ibid*
26. *ibid*, p. 291
27. Dwyer, T. Ryle, *De Valera, The Man & the Myths*, Poolbeg, Dublin, p. 47
28. Holmes, G. A. & Macintyre (eds.), *Irish Republican Army & Development of Guerilla Warfare 1916-21*, TheEnglish Historical Review, Vol. XCIV, 1979, p. 341
29. Coogan, Tim Pat, *De Valera, The Man who was Ireland*, Harper, 1996, p. 222
30. *ibid*
31. Longford, Earl of & O'Neill, Thomas P., *Éamon de Valera*, Hutchinson, London, 1970, p. 134

CHAPTER XIV

Peace, at last?

"… For ever and again and, always at critical moments, there is the same story of moral Weakness, of inconsistency of our champions being led away from great designs into wasteful side issues, of sacrificing the highest hopes and aspirations before the sudden impulse of some lower motive of rage, jealousy or revenge."[1]

W. G. Fitzgerald

On June 22, 1921, King George V made a conciliatory speech at the opening of the Northern Ireland Parliament in Belfast: "I speak from a full heart when I pray that my coming to Ireland today may prove to be the first step towards the end of strife among her peoples, whatever their race or creed. In that hope, I appeal to all Irishmen to pause, to stretch out the hand of forbearance and conciliation, to forgive and forget and to join in making for the land which they love, a new era of peace, contentment, and goodwill."[2]

On the very day the King was sending out peace feelers, the British army raided a private residence and "discovered" and arrested de Valera. The British military, which had not apprehended de Valera during any of his numerous public appearances over the prior six months, suddenly abandoned its "see no de Valera, hear no de Valera" policy and placed him in custody. T. Ryle Dwyer noted that British troops raided a safe-house in which "de Valera and Kathleen O'Connell, his secretary, were living in Blackrock. The troops apparently did not realize their government had issued orders not to arrest him."[3] There had been rumors of an affair while de Valera and O'Connell were in America, but no evidence of such was ever uncovered, and he lived out his life with his wife, Sinead. The inference by Dwyer of infidelity may have been merely the Irish President being in hiding and requiring the services of a secretary and nothing more. De Valera, however, was away from home for extended periods and made rare visits to his wife and children, who considered him more of a stranger than a father. Sinead had long ago resigned herself to living and raising her family without de Valera who was either in jail or traipsing around Ireland and America.

Longford and O'Neill, acknowledged but did not question: "By a strange coincidence, de Valera's arrest occurred on the very day chosen by Lloyd George to initiate a new era of conciliation."[4] His official biographers had claimed that the British would not arrest him "until they could bring some definite criminal charge against him."[5] To allay suspicion of collusion, de Valera contradicted his official biographers; though the British military had known of his whereabouts since his arrival from America, they had not arrested him because of a Cabinet decision to leave him free.[6] The circumstances as to his arrest tended to lend credence to Under-Secretary Anderson's charge that de Valera's return to Ireland was facilitated with British "connivance."

It did not answer the more perplexing questions, however, as to why the British Cabinet continued to allow de Valera to remain free and why the military arrested him on that particular auspicious occasion of the King's speech. Author W. Alison Phillips criticized Lloyd George and his "peace" efforts claiming: "The effect of the King's visit to Belfast... was now suspected of having been no more than a move in the game of deception."

When news of de Valera's arrest was received by Dublin Castle authorities, Alfred Cope, Assistant Secretary and Lloyd George's personal confidante in Ireland, was attending a formal dinner party. He deserted his guests and rushed to the jail where de Valera was being detained. According to Longford and O'Neill, de Valera had initially been taken to a civilian prison, Bridewell, and was supposedly cast into a vermin-infested cell after being treated roughly – again we have only de Valera's word on it. Cope arrived shortly thereafter, and, rather than release de Valera immediately, he personally escorted him to Portobello Army Barracks, where he dispossessed a grumbling Army officer from his quarters and made them available to the Irish President. Cope then allegedly vanished as quickly as he had arrived. De Valera was set free the following morning, refreshed from his leisurely evening out and generous hospitality, compliments of the British officer's corps. A local newspaper reported, "de Valera was released and returned home without so much as a charge being pressed against him or subjected to interrogation of any kind."[7]

It was another Lincoln Jail hoax, and it smelled just as bad. De Valera's "arrest" in June 1921 was no more genuine than his "escape" from Lincoln Jail in 1919. The logical deduction was that the "arrest" was a cover for a secret conference with Cope informing de Valera of Lloyd George's imminent truce proposals and the role de Valera was expected to play in it. Pieras Beaslai recorded: "A letter from the officer who arrested him, to a friend in England, was intercepted by one of

Collins' men...He stated that the order to release de Valera came from Lloyd George. It seems there was an understanding and he was not to be arrested..."[8]

Two days later, on June 24, 1921, Lloyd George penned a letter to de Valera proposing a settlement conference between Britain, Northern and Southern Ireland: "I write, therefore, to convey the following invitation to you, as the chosen leader of the great majority in Southern Ireland, and to Sir James Craig, the Premier of Northern Ireland: 1). That you should attend a conference here in London, in company with Sir James Craig to explore to the utmost the possibility of a settlement, and 2). That you should bring with you for the purpose any colleagues whom you select. The Government will, of course, give a safe conduct to all who may be chosen to participate in the conference. We make this invitation with a fervent desire to end the ruinous conflict which has, for centuries, divided Ireland and embittered the relations of the peoples of these two islands who ought to live in neighborly harmony with each other, and whose cooperation would mean so much, not only to the Empire, but to humanity..."[9]

Lloyd George concluded, "The British Government is deeply anxious that, so far as they can assure it, the King's appeal for reconciliation in Ireland shall not have been made in vain."[10]

In a telegram to Lloyd George on July 8, 1921, de Valera accepted the British Prime minister's invitation, stating he would meet him in London on July 14. The following day, de Valera issued a proclamation announcing that a truce would take effect on July 11. The reign of terror was over!

According to Kevin Shiel, a military adviser to the Dáil: "The truce providentially intervened at the nadir of Irish fortunes. It is common knowledge, substantiated by our best military advisers, that our heroic little army had at that time practically reached the end of its resources and supplies of ammunition and in the ordinary course would have had to surrender or permit itself to be slaughtered without any effective means of self defense."[11] General Macready, British Commander-in-Chief, Ireland Command, arrived at the Mansion House to iron out the details of the truce with Michael Collins.

The following day, July 12, as Protestant Orangemen (Unionists), marched in Belfast and Portadown celebrating William of Orange's victory over James II and the Catholics at the Battle of the Boyne in 1690, de Valera, at the head of an Irish delegation, tramped out of Euston Station in London, setting in motion Ireland's greatest disaster. Private truce talks were subsequently held on July 14, 15, 18, and 21 between Lloyd George and de Valera, while the rest of the Delegation cooled their heels taking in the sights of London.

When Lloyd George agreed to a truce, de Valera announced that he would confer with the Prime Minister in private. Many people were aghast considering the Welsh Wizard's reputation as a political strategist without peer, especially on a one-to-one basis. "But de Valera felt that his word would stand a better chance of being believed than Lloyd George's if any conflict arose..."[12]

The Irish delegation was made up of Arthur Griffith, Austin Stack, the man responsible for the loss of the arms ship that scuttled the 1916 Easter Rising, Count Plunkett, whose son was executed for his role in the 1916 insurrection, and Robert Barton, cousin of Erskine Childers, the former British intelligence officer who became a fierce advocate of Irish independence. They were housed at the Grosvenor Hotel, while Dr. Farnan, a de Valera adviser, and Kathleen O'Connell, his longtime secretary and confidante, joined de Valera at the home of Major Loftus, a British Army officer.

According to Stack, "None of us were present on these occasions... Afterwards, the President used to call us together and inform us of what had taken place...It was arranged early that the British were going to submit proposals in writing..."[13] Neither Stack nor Charles Burgess, Irish Defense Minister and Collins' critic, uttered so much as a whisper of objection regarding the Irish President's decision to meet alone with Lloyd George.

De Valera refused to include Michael Collins in the delegation, not because of any alleged power struggle between the two, but because Collins would not be content to spend a week twiddling his thumbs while de Valera and Lloyd George privately decided the fate of Ireland. He would have demanded access to the discussions. But de Valera claimed his exclusion of Collins from the delegation was to protect his identity in the event of a resumption of the conflict. Less than two months later, Collins' identity problem was brushed aside by de Valera, and the Irish President insisted Collins act as one of the Plenipotentiaries at the London Peace talks.

Collins was allegedly disappointed at being left off the delegation but determined that no final decision would be concluded solely between de Valera and Lloyd George. He wrote to de Valera: "No matter how bad the terms are, they would be submitted to a full meeting of the Dáil."[14]

De Valera's behaviour during those truce talks with Lloyd George consisted of publicly strutting his Republican credentials while privately agreeing to the Welsh Wizard's strategy. After two months of feigned indignation, following the private truce talks, de Valera not only accepted every one of the terms and conditions proffered by the British Prime Minister but also bludgeoned the Dáil deputies into accepting allegiance to the Crown, abandoning their demand for recognition of an Irish Republic and recognizing the partition of Ireland.

According to a popular version of his first meeting with Lloyd George, de Valera lectured the British Prime Minister on England's oppressive record in Ireland. Reportedly, Lloyd George patiently listened to de Valera's history lesson, which supposedly only reached Cromwell's invasion of Ireland by the time the Irish President was ushered out the door. The purported lecturing of Lloyd George reeked of play-acting in order to mold de Valera's public persona as a single-minded professor insisting on giving every Englishman he met a lesson in Irish history. This delighted the Irish, and the English encouraged it for their own purposes.

The story was merely a rehash of another history lesson allegedly given to James Craig, Northern Ireland Prime Minister, in Dublin two months before on May 5. Winston Churchill, inadvertently revealed the importance of that meeting: "The [truce] negotiations really began on the day Sir James Craig met Éamon de Valera in the remotest haunts of the rebels."[15] At the conclusion of that private meeting, both de Valera and Craig claimed that each thought the other had invited him to the meeting, resulting in an awkward silence and swift adjournment, while Churchill claimed it was a very successful initiation of the treaty process. Coincidentally, from that meeting on, de Valera declared himself in favour of Partition, the division of Ireland into Northern and Southern Protestant and Catholic enclaves of mutual malevolence, a no-coercion policy, and publicly proclaimed the right of every county to vote itself out of a united Ireland.

There was much ballyhoo in the Irish Press as to de Valera reportedly giving Lloyd George an Irish history lesson, but it was the Welsh Wizard who taught the Irish President a lesson in Gaelic. Recognition of an Irish Republic was foremost among Irish demands, but the British were not about to accept an independent Ireland at their back door and were adamantly opposed to including an Irish Republic for discussion in the agenda of any peace talks. Once again, de Valera solved Lloyd George's dilemma.

With the connivance of de Valera, Lloyd George substituted the term Irish Free State in place of Irish Republic. T. Ryle Dwyer gave the following account at their session: Lloyd George, a Welsh and Celt himself "remarked that the note paper on which de Valera had written to him was headed 'Saorstát Éireann,' which literally translated as 'Free State of Ireland.' He therefore asked what 'Saorstat' meant. 'Free State,' replied de Valera. 'Yes,' remarked the Prime Minister, 'but what is the Irish word for republic?'

"De Valera was taken aback. Although his command of the Gaelic language was not nearly as complete as he liked to pretend to non-speakers, he must have known that the leaders of the Easter Rebellion had used the term Poblacht na hÉireann [Republic of Ireland], but he now played dumb, possibly because he had no convincing explanation as to why the original term had been dropped and Saorstat Éireann adopted instead in 1919.

"'Must we not admit that the Celts never were Republicans and have no native word for such an idea!' Lloyd George exclaimed triumphantly. He was quite content that 'Saorstát Éireann' could be used in any agreement, provided the literal translation – Irish Free State – was used."[16]

The Gaelic rendering of an Irish Republic, Poblacht na Éireann, was abandoned and the Irish Free State, Saorstát Éireann, was agreed upon between Lloyd George and de Valera. The significance was that an Irish Republic was an independent nation at England's back door, free to negotiate treaties with Great Britain's enemies, while an Irish Free State would be recognized as a member of the British Commonwealth of Nations.

Thanks to de Valera's lapse of memory, Lloyd George was able to avoid mentioning the words "Irish Republic" throughout the entire treaty peace process. De Valera's apologists hailed him as an Irish scholar who could rattle off every Irish event before and since the reign of Brian Boru, the warrior king of Ireland who defeated the Vikings at Clontarf in 1014 but was killed when an informer pointed out his position to the enemy. But the Irish President could not recall the reason that men, including himself, who answered the call to arms during the 1916 Easter Rising, merely five years before, were defending Poblacht na hÉireann, an Irish Republic.

De Valera allegedly made a flourish of rejecting Lloyd George's proposals and stormed out of their meeting. He wasn't going to let the matter of a democratically elected Irish Parliament stand in the way of his deciding on the course of Irish history. The Prime Minister supposedly threatened to resume the war, but de Valera said he rebuffed the threat. Lloyd George warned that the resumed war "would bear an entirely different character as Britain's reduced military commitments around the world meant that more troops were available to be sent to Ireland where a great military concentration would take place with a view to the repression of the rebellion and the restoration of order."[17]

When the British Premier said he would publish the terms of the proposal for the Irish and the world to see, de Valera accused him of breaking his promise of publishing only an agreed-upon document. By his own account de Valera was on his way out when Lloyd George asked if he was going to reply to the proposals. De Valera claimed he would agree to a reply but only if the truce were extended. With that exchange, de Valera turned and left the room, but in the heat of the argument he had forgotten to take the proposals with him. "[T]o Lloyd George's relief, he sent a messenger for it in the evening. He could not give a considered reply without it."[18]

In order to penetrate the mist of that secret conference in which we have only the words of de Valera and the Welsh Wizard to rely on, the subsequent actions of the British Prime Minister and Irish President merit close scrutiny. Fundamental to Lloyd George's peace initiative was de Valera's "Assignment Treaty" – prod the Dáil into accepting the British Prime Minister's terms and conditions prior to entering into a peace conference. The Welsh Wizard's proposal was both ironic and brilliant: once the Irish accepted the British conditions to initiate peace talks, regardless of the outcome, Ireland would have forfeited worldwide sympathy for its cause and England would reap a public relations bonanza for her "magnanimous gesture."

After the truce talks, Lloyd George confidently wrote to the King, "There is, I fear, little chance of his [de Valera's] counter-proposals being satisfactory, but I am absolutely confident that we shall have public opinion overwhelmingly upon our side throughout the Empire and even in the United States when our proposals are published."[19]

In anticipation of the failure of the peace talks, the British prepared for an Irish insurrection. Beaslai noted that the extent to which the British were prepared to go to pacify Ireland was contained in a secret report intercepted by Collins during the truce: "Concentration Camps for women and children, and loyal members of the male sex, were to be established at various centers near coastal ports and railway centers such as Mallow. Loyal citizens to be given the opportunity to reside in England or in Camp. All males who elect to remain outside the Camps in Ireland to be treated as hostile. Women and children to be removed compulsorily to Camp, if necessary, before the commencement of hostilities. Such operations expected to result in victory in a month."[20] During a Cabinet session, Collins made clear that they all understood exactly what they were considering – peace or war hung in the balance.

Tim Pat Coogan acknowledged that, "After his lengthy tête-à-têtes with Lloyd George, Éamon de Valera knew better than any man alive how slim was the prospect of a Republic and what sort of a settlement he and his colleagues were likely to get."[21]

The only fly in the ointment of Lloyd George's scheme was Partition, the division of the island into bastions of Catholic and Protestant antipathy. In order to prevent open revolt by the Protestants, six counties in Ulster were partitioned from the 32 counties of Ireland and designated a Northern Ireland statelet, while the remaining 26 predominantly Catholic counties were designated the Irish Free State, with Northern and Southern Ireland each having its own Parliament.

The Irish had a legitimate claim to all of Ireland, and if territorial integrity had been used as grounds to reject the British proposals, world sympathy might well have sided with the Irish. But de Valera was all too ready to accept division. As Beaslai remarked: "The Partition of Ireland constituted the real crux of the situation. The other stipulations were of minor importance...the splitting up of our little island into two parts, the placing of a large portion of the historic Irish nation under the heels of a bigoted minority, was an evil which was worth making many sacrifices to avoid."[22] As events unfolded, de Valera engaged in a vigorous campaign to compel Dáil acceptance of every one of Lloyd George's conditions, especially Partition.

Far from seeing the truce as a pause in the fighting, many Irishmen thought it marked the first step to a permanent peace. Rejoicing was widespread throughout Ireland. Beaslai noted that the importation of arms was suspended during the Truce. "There were at this time large stores of arms and ammunition for Ireland in the United States; but these remained there until after the Treaty. Then these arms, bought by Irishmen to fight the Black and Tans, were imported to Ireland by enemies of the 1921 Free State Treaty to use against their own countrymen. At the time of the Civil War, Ireland was swarming with arms, ammunition, and explosives."[23]

At the initial public meeting of the Dáil in August, Collins made his first public appearance on the political stage. Crowds came to glimpse not de Valera, but Collins, the leader of the "gunmen and murderers," as Lloyd George had dubbed him. "People were surprised to find a cheery-looking, smiling, unassuming young Irishman in place of the romantic figure they had pictured to themselves. Collins found the attention of admirers something of a nuisance and did his best to avoid them. His popularity seemed to arouse resentment among certain of his ministerial colleagues."[24]

Collins warned that any truce would leave the IRA vulnerable to English counter-intelligence agents. "The terms of the Truce stipulated that there should be no espionage by the English Forces during the Truce... Collins' Intelligence Department was able to ascertain that the English Intelligence forces were carrying on their espionage work as busily as before the Truce."[25]

On July 8, 1921, prior to the Lloyd George/de Valera private sessions, it was announced that a Truce had been agreed upon. The terms of the Truce were as follows:

"On behalf of the British Army, it is agreed on the following:

"1. No incoming troops, RIC and Auxiliary Police and munitions and no movements for military purposes of troops and munitions, except maintenance drafts;

"2. No provocative display of forces, armed or unarmed;

"3. It is understood that all provisions of this Truce apply to Martial Law area equally with rest of Ireland.

"4. No pursuit of Irish officers or men or war material or military stores;

"5. No secret agents, noting descriptions or movements and no interference with the movements of Irish persons, military or civil, and no attempt to discover the haunts or habits of Irish officers and men;

"6. No pursuit or observance of lines of communication or connection;

"On behalf of the Irish Army, it is agreed that:

"(a)   Attacks on Crown forces and civilians to cease;

"(b)   No provocative displays of forces, armed or unarmed;

"(c)   No interference with British Government or private property;

"(d)   To discountenance and prevent any action likely to cause disturbance of the peace which might necessitate Military interference.

Prior to the talks in London, despite Lloyd George's safe conduct guarantee for any of his colleagues to attend, de Valera ignored Griffith, who was in prison since the previous November. Indeed, the Irish President refused to request the release of a single Irish prisoner as a precondition for initiating peace talks. It was, thanks to Collins and Roger Casement's brother, Thomas, who suggested to Cope that a number of prominent Sinn Feiners be released. Subsequently, Griffith, Barton, Duggan, MacNeill and Michael Staines were accordingly set free.[26]

All members of the Dáil were then released except Sean MacEoin, whom the British were determined to execute because of his leadership and bravery under fire. Collins was just as determined to have all imprisoned members of the Dáil freed, especially MacEoin. He stormed out of a Cabinet session after de Valera refused to jeopardize the truce over MacEoin's release. Collins defied de Valera and took his case to the press on August 8, flatly declaring: "There can and will be no meeting of Dáil Éireann until Commandant Sean MacEoin is released. The refusal to release him appears to indicate a desire on the part of the English Government to terminate the Truce."[27]

De Valera was incensed by Collins' action but had no choice but to follow Collins' lead or publicly appear as a tool of Lloyd George. The day after Collins' broadside, de Valera followed suit and declared: "He could go no further with the negotiations until MacEoin was set free. MacEoin was released that evening..."[28] Had it not been for Collins, de Valera was prepared to permit the execution of MacEoin and the continued incarceration of his Dáil colleagues, including Griffith. Collins never forgot a comrade in an English jail; de Valera never remembered one.

Through his official biographers, Longford and O'Neill, de Valera all but conceded that MacEoin's reprieve had been foisted on him. The Irish President charged that Collins: "'did not seem to accept my view of things as he had done before and was inclined to give public expression to his own opinion, even when they differed from mine, for example, in connection with the release of Sean MacEoin.' In this last case, de Valera, in fact, felt that Collins was 'not acting loyally.'"[29]

De Valera's charge of disloyalty by Collins in regard to the release of MacEoin, highlighted his own disloyalty. Incredibly, by following the English lead, de Valera expected Collins to allow MacEoin to be executed rather than differ from his views. However, that did not stop de Valera from taking credit for MacEoin's release.

At the final truce session on July 20, Lloyd George presented de Valera with "Proposals for an Irish Settlement" by the English government. "The proposals of the British Government were:

1) Ireland should become one of the Dominions of the British Commonwealth, with the full status and powers of the other Dominions, subject to the following stipulations:

2) "It is essential that the Royal Navy alone should control the seas around Ireland and Great Britain and that such rights and liberties should be accorded to it by the Irish State as are essential for naval purposes in the Irish harbors and on the Irish coasts.

3) "It is stipulated that the Irish Territorial Force shall, within reasonable limits, conform in respect to numbers to the military establishments of the other parts of these islands.

4) "It is stipulated that Great Britain shall have all necessary facilities for the development of defense and of communications by air.

5) "Great Britain hopes that Ireland will, in due course, and of her own free will, contribute in proportion to her wealth to the regular Naval, Military and Air Forces of the Empire.

6) It is further assumed that voluntary recruitment for these forces will be permitted throughout Ireland.

7) "The British and Irish Governments shall agree to impose no protective duties or other restrictions upon the flow of transports, trade, and commerce between all parts of these islands.

8) "The Irish people shall agree to assume responsibility for a share of the present debt of the United Kingdom and of the liability for pensions arising out of the Great War, the share, in default of agreement between the Governments concerned to be determined by an independent arbitrator appointed from within His Majesty's Dominions."[30]

The most important issue of the settlement was not stipulated: unity had disappeared off the page. Acceptance of full recognition by Southern Ireland of the Parliament and Government of Northern Ireland etched Partition in stone.

Notes

1. Fitzgerald, W.G., *The voice of Ireland, A Survey of the Race & Nation from all Angles*, Virtue Ltd. Dublin/London, p. 79
2. Longford, Earl of & O'Neill, Thomas P., *Éamon de Valera*, Hutchinson, London, 1970, p. 128
3. Dwyer, T. Ryle, *De Valera, The Man & the Myths*, Poolbeg, Dublin, p. 53
4. Longford, Earl of & O'Neill, Thomas P., *Éamon de Valera*, Hutchinson, London, 1970, p. 127
5. *ibid*, p. 115
6. *ibid*
7. Freeman's Journal, 1/5/1922
8. Beaslai, Pieras, *Michael Collins and the Making of a New Ireland*, Vol II, Harper Bros. NY 1926, p. 242
9. *ibid*, p. 243
10. *ibid*, p. 242
11. Fitzgerald, W.G., *The voice of Ireland, A Survey of the Race & Nation from all Angles*, Virtue Ltd. Dublin/London, p, 31
12. Longford and O'Neill, *Éamon de Valera*, Hutchinson, London, p.131
13. Gaughan, J. Anthony, *Austin Stack, Portrait of a Separatist*, Kingdom Books, Dublin, 1977, p. 156

14. Dwyer, T. Ryle, *De Valera, The Man & the Myths*, Poolbeg, Dublin, p. 54
15. Fitzgerald, W.G., *The voice of Ireland, A Survey of the Race & Nation from all Angles*, Virtue Ltd. Dublin/London, p. 16
16. Dwyer, T. Ryle, *De Valera, The Man & the Myths*, Poolbeg, Dublin, p. 56
17. Coogan, Tim Pat, *Michael Collins*, Arrow Books, London, 1991, p. 221
18. Longford Earl of & O'Neill, Thomas P., *Éamon de Valera*, Hutchinson, London, 1970, p. 137
19. Dwyer, T. Ryle, *De Valera, The man & the Myths*, Poolbeg, Dublin, 1991, p. 57
20. Beaslai, Pieras, *Michael Collins and the Making of a New Ireland*, Vol II, Harper Bros. NY 1926, p. 268
21. Coogan, Tim Pat, *Michael Collins*, Arrow Books, London, 1991, p. 223
22. Beaslai, Pieras, *Michael Collins and the Making of a New Ireland*, Vol II, Harper Bros. NY 1926, p. 259
23. *ibid*, p. 272
24. *ibid*, p. 263
25. *ibid*, p. 266
26. Coogan, Tim P., *De Valera, The Man who was Ireland*, Harper, 1996, p. 227
27. Coogan, Tim P., *Michael Collins*, Arrow Books, 1991, p. 223
28. *ibid*
29. Longford Earl of & O'Neill, Thomas P., *Éamon de Valera*, Hutchinson, London, 1970, p. 148
30. Beaslai, Pieras, *Michael Collins and the Making of a New Ireland*, Vol II, Harper Bros. NY 1926, p. 258

CHAPTER XV
The "Magnanimous" Gesture

"When you have sweated, toiled, had mad dreams, hopeless nightmares,
you find yourself in London streets cold and dank in the night air.
Think – what have I got for Ireland?
Something, which she has wanted these past 700 years.
Will anyone be satisfied at the bargain?"[1]

Michael Collins upon signing the Free State Treaty

The officially sanctioned British terror campaign in Ireland in 1921 met with an increasingly critical response from the international press. Lloyd George had to either unleash the army and crush the insurgency or devise an alternate scheme which would shift world sympathy away from the Irish.

The British Prime Minister, the leader of the most powerful nation in the world at that time, made the twenty-six counties of Southern Ireland a "magnanimous" gesture: he offered Dominion status and full membership within the Commonwealth of Nations. From universal abhorrence over the outrages perpetrated against the Irish, American sentiment shifted to one of approval of England's effort to settle the centuries-old feud between the neighboring islands.

The British preconditions for entering into peace negotiations were subject to Irish acceptance of the following "non-negotiable" conditions: membership within the Empire; allegiance to the Crown; abandon the demand for recognition of an independent Republic; grant port facilities for the British navy and no coercion of Northern Ireland, thereby conceding the partition of Ireland. With a peaceful transition to Dominion status, England was taking an enormous gamble in which it might be trading one impossible situation for another.

If the Unionist violence against Catholics in the six counties of Northern Ireland continued, Collins, in a move to counter the terror, would shift the four-year insurgency in the south to Northern Ireland. The outcome of Collins' response to Protestant terror against Catholics would inevitably lead to civil war not only in Northern Ireland but boiling over into England itself. An added danger was the likelihood of British soldiers refusing to move against fellow Protestants in Ulster. With four militias strutting about Ireland at the time – the English Army, North and South Volunteers as well as the IRA – the situation was extremely volatile.

The process of shifting the four-year insurgency in Southern Ireland to the North was already underway as Michael Collins dispatched men and arms to counter the increasingly violent Unionist terror against Catholics. Collins clandestinely obtained arms from various sources: he equipped the IRA men who were moving into Northern Ireland with arms that could not be traced to those provided to the Free State by the British. In typical Irish irony, while Collins was defending the Provisional Government, set up during the interlude between the signing of the Treaty and the establishment of the Free State government, against de Valera's extremist element of the IRA bent on preventing the implementation of the treaty, he was engaged in a cooperative venture with them to supply men and arms to Belfast and Derry. That cooperation was a foretaste of what the English could expect with a peaceful transition to a Free State government.

The Prime Minister's strategy hinged not so much on a formal ratification of a Dominion treaty but most importantly on an Irish acceptance of the British terms. Once the Dáil deputies officially accepted, it mattered little to the British in the overall scheme of things whether an ultimate settlement was reached. Lloyd George had confidently predicted to King George V that public opinion throughout the Dominions and especially in the United States would be overwhelmingly in favour of England when the terms of his proposal were published.[2]

Lloyd George again required the services of Éamon de Valera to ensure that his gamble paid off. The Irish President's latest mission, "Assignment Treaty," was to stampede the Dáil deputies into acceptance of each and every one of Lloyd George's conditions.

The result of the private talks in July between Lloyd George and de Valera, was acceptance of Lloyd George's terms by the Dáil. If the Irish refused England's "magnanimous" offer and renewed the fight, they would be fighting without the support of the Irish people and the international community. Without the people behind them, any Irish resistance was doomed.

De Valera proceeded to maneuver the Dáil into accepting Lloyd George's conditions while cleverly setting himself up to oppose whatever decision Collins and Griffith negotiated in the London Peace Conference. As Tim

Pat Coogan shrewdly noted: "The real significance of de Valera's [official] assumption of the 'Presidency of the Irish Republic,' prior to the start of negotiations which he knew from his talks with Lloyd George were highly unlikely to yield a Republic, only emerged later. It was a classic example of how de Valera outmaneuvered his closest colleagues without their being aware of it. In the minds of an electorate predisposed towards 'follow-the-leader,' the title [of President] naturally had a bearing subsequently on the widespread support he attracted to his views."[3] Coogan saw how de Valera planned to use the presidency at a later date to rally the extremist element in opposition to whatever course the treaty talks took.

It was vital to English interests for de Valera to be in position to reject any outcome of a peace conference in order to create chaos in Southern Ireland before Collins created chaos in Northern Ireland.

Less than a week after his rejection of Lloyd George's peace proposals, de Valera presided at a July 25 Cabinet session in Dublin where he recommended Dominion status and security concessions including granting access to Irish ports to the British military. On the issue of Commonwealth membership, de Valera informed the Dáil deputies: "They could not turn down what appeared to be, on the face of it, an invitation to join a group of free nations...If security concessions were refused, Britain would depict the Irish as unreasonable, America would agree, as would the international community generally, and then, England would be given a free hand to deal with Ireland."[4]

De Valera's willingness to join the Commonwealth, accept partition, abandon demands for recognition of an Irish Republic, accept allegiance to the Crown, and provide security concessions fell in step with every one of Lloyd George's "non-negotiable" terms for initiating a peace conference.

The Dominions, which rendered symbolic fealty to the British Crown, were free and independent nations, in voluntary external association with Britain. The British offer of Dominion status was a face-saving measure to grant Irish independence without having to recognize a Republic.

Less than three weeks after the July truce conference, de Valera was still trumpeting his Republican credentials. On August 10, he rejected the Prime Minister's settlement proposals: "I gave it as my judgment that Dáil Éireann could not, and that the Irish people would not, accept the proposals of your government, I now confirm that judgment."[5] Tim Pat Coogan again questioned de Valera's veracity, claiming his response was couched in terms "which economized greatly with the truth...de Valera had no intention of consulting the Irish people on the proposals and did not bring them before Dáil Éireann until two weeks after sending the letter...He told the Deputies that he merely wanted to be able to put in the first paragraph of the reply that the Dáil unanimously approved of the attitude adopted by the Ministry."[6] This unilateral decision rejecting Lloyd George's overtures echoed de Valera's February 1920 *Westminster Gazette* interview in which he neither consulted nor informed his Cabinet or Dáil of his downgrading of the Irish claim to an independent Republic to that of a colony of England.

De Valera had already lost any chance of achieving recognition of an Irish Republic by his failure to win a concession from Lloyd George in the course of their private truce talks. Pieras Beaslai noted: "If such an issue was to be raised as a condition preliminary to a Conference, it should have been raised in July [During the Truce talks]. If there had been any hope of obtaining recognition as representative of a sovereign State, it was criminal to neglect the opportunity."[7]

From July through September, de Valera orchestrated an Irish march to the negotiating table and disaster by stampeding the Dáil deputies into accepting Lloyd George's terms. "De Valera, having publicly indicated his willingness to compromise... went even further in the following days...On August 22, 1921, he told the Dáil deputies, "If they were determined to make peace only on the basis of recognition of the Republic, then they were going to be faced with war, only this time, it would be a real war of British reconquest, not just a continuation of limited military coercive measures..."[8]

In his rush to compromise, de Valera warned that the very survival of the Irish race was at stake unless the Dáil deputies agreed to abandon their demand for recognition of an Irish Republic. He charged: "'The Irish people's natural moral right to their own island would be eradicated, just as the American Indians had been trampled on in North America. Look at America!' he said ominously, 'Where are the natives? Wiped off the face of the earth! The same thing could happen in Ireland. Unfortunately,' he added, 'they were very far away from living in a world where moral forces counted; it was brute force which mattered.'"[9]

As the price of admission to the peace conference, the Dáil deputies formally surrendered their claims to recognition of the Irish Republic, not only once but on at least four separate occasions – during the Dáil Sessions of August 16 and 21, upon accepting the English terms for entering into a peace conference in September, and again when they voted to send plenipotentiaries to negotiate and conclude a treaty in October.

De Valera continued to strike a contrary pose: on August 16, 1921 during the Dáil session, he ordered the deputies to take an oath to an

Irish Republic setting in motion his covert plan to contest any treaty between England and Ireland. "For some, including de Valera, it was the first time they took the oath, obliging them to 'support and defend the Irish Republic, which is Dáil Éireann, against all enemies, foreign and domestic.'"[10] Almost before the Dáil Deputies uttered the last word of the oath, de Valera, "with great emphasis...caused a bit of a stir when he talked about the unmistakable answer given by the people in the recent election. 'I do not say that the answer [to the election] was for a [Republican] form of government so much because we are not republican doctrinaires. But it was for Irish freedom and Irish independence and it was obvious to everyone who considered the question that Irish independence could not be realized in any other way so suitable as through a Republic.'"[11]

At so momentous an occasion, with Ireland's future literally at stake, de Valera insisted on a contradictory political move – one designed to notify the English, and the world, that the Irish people never voted for a Republic – while also insisting upon an oath to support and defend an Irish Republic that he admitted did not exist. He cut off all debate on the question, claiming: "'This is not the time for discussion of the best forms of government.' He told the gathering that the party was not irrevocably committed to a Republic...'We do not wish to bind the people to any form of government.'"[12] For all its ambivalence, this declaration would have led the British and the Irish plenipotentiaries to understand that, so long as Ireland got freedom and *de* facto independence, in lieu of a Republic, they were adhering to the "unmistakable" wishes of the people as expressed in recent elections.

Austin Stack sought to find some justification for de Valera's rejection of an Irish Republic: "I think it was after de Valera had been proposed for election as President, he made a short speech in which he used the phrase – often referred to – that the interpretation he put on the oath was that he should do his best for Ireland and he made use of the expression that he was not a doctrinaire Republican as such."[13] Stack claimed: "Whatever uneasy feeling these two statements may have caused some of us at the time, in the light of after events, it shows de Valera up as a scrupulous and conscientious man. I do not believe that he had in mind the abandonment of the Republic – as is charged by his enemies."[14]

According to Pieras Beaslai, the Irish President, in private sessions of the Dáil, had already abandoned the Irish demand for recognition of an Irish Republic, while publicly holding himself out as leader of an independent nation. Despite risking a breakdown of the peace process on the issue, he already knew that Lloyd George "definitely ruled out any recognition of Ireland as a sovereign state."[15] Author Ignatius Phayre noted that the Prime Minister reiterated his position in a letter to de Valera on August 18: "No British government can compromise – namely the claim that we should acknowledge the right of Ireland to secede from her allegiance to the King...The position taken up by His Majesty's Government is fundamental to the existence of the British Empire..."[16]

At the August 22 closed session of the Dáil, de Valera dictated the conditions upon which he would accept the office of the presidency. He threatened to resign unless supreme power was ceded to him: "'I have one allegiance only to the people of Ireland and that is to do the best we can for them as we conceive it,' he declared. 'If you propose me, I want you all to understand that you propose me understanding that that will be my attitude. All questions will be discussed,' he said, 'from the point of view absolutely of what I consider the people of Ireland want and what I consider best from their point of view... I will not accept this office if you fetter me in any way whatever,' he declared. 'I cannot accept office on the understanding that no road is barred, that we shall be free to consider every method.' The policy of his government would be to do what he thought best for the country, and those who would disagree with him would resign...If the Deputies wanted him as President, they had to accept his terms; otherwise, they should elect someone else."[17]

At the same time, de Valera was moving away from his long-standing policy of "blasting Ulster out of the road" to achieve Irish unity and was now advocating the acceptance of partition: "They [the Irish] had not the power, and some of them had not the inclination, to use force with Ulster. He did not think that policy would be successful. They would be making the same mistake with that section as England had made with Ireland. He would not be responsible for such a policy...for his part, if the Republic were recognized he would be in favor of giving each county power to vote itself out of the Republic. Otherwise, they would be compelled to use force. This went even further than he had gone in his August 10 rejection of the British proposals, in which he had said, 'We do not contemplate the use of force...If your Government stands aside, we can effect a complete reconciliation. We do agree with you that no common action can be secured by force.' He was now conceding to Ulster sufficient autonomy and recognition to allow it to opt out of the state he was hoping to set up. If the use of force was eschewed there was no other possible means of bringing Belfast under Dublin rule."[18]

At the August 25 session of the Dáil, de Valera was reelected President. He reshuffled his Cabinet members as follows: Foreign Affairs: Arthur Griffith; Home Affairs: Austin Stack; Defense: Charles Burgess; Finance: Michael Collins; Local Government: William T. Cosgrave and Economic Affairs: Robert C. Barton.

De Valera and Lloyd George engaged in a dog and pony act throughout August and September, with an exchange of letters designed to dramatize de Valera's valiant stand. "All de Valera's letters to Lloyd George were taken as twisting of the Lion's tail...while the leaders knew that a settlement which was not independence was coming, they had neither the courage nor the wisdom to say so, even privately."[19]

On September 7, Lloyd George emphatically rejected any talk of a republic as well as any attempt to eliminate an oath of allegiance to the King: "We cannot accept as a basis of practical conference, an interpretation of that principle which would commit us to any demands which you might present – even to the extent of setting up a Republic and repudiating the Crown. You must be aware that conference on such a basis is impossible..."[20].

On September 12, de Valera, in a note to Lloyd George, reaffirmed: "Our nation has formally declared its independence and recognizes itself as a sovereign state. It is only as the representatives of that State and as its chosen guardians that we have any authority or power to act on behalf of our people..."[21] Lloyd George, in reply, once again explicitly refused to acknowledge even the slightest hint of recognition of an Irish Republic[22] and called a halt to the letter-writing campaign. "There is no purpose to be served by any further interchange of explanatory and argumentative communication upon this subject...We feel that conference, not correspondence, is the most practical and hopeful way to an understanding such as we ardently desire to achieve. We therefore send herewith a fresh invitation to a conference in London on October 11 where we can meet your delegates as spokesmen of the people whom you represent, with a view to ascertaining how the association of Ireland with the community of nations known as the British Empire may best be reconciled with Irish national aspirations."[23]

De Valera's grandstanding was at an end. He had only succeeded in placing the Irish in a position in which their only options were either to enter into peace negotiations based on Lloyd George's conditions or to resume hostilities. The Irish President capitulated: "We have received your letter of invitation to a Conference on October 11, 1921...Our respective positions have been stated, and are understood, and we agree that conference, not correspondence, is the most practical and hopeful way to an understanding. We accept the invitation and our Delegates will meet you in London on the date mentioned, 'to explore every possibility of settlement by personal discussion.'"[24]

De Valera's "diplomatic salvoes in public with Lloyd George gained nothing of substance, although to the end of his life [de Valera] continued to represent the exchanges as having resulted in a famous victory for him."[25] Longford disingenuously claimed that after surrendering to Lloyd George's ultimatum, de Valera had actually, "won his point, a conference without prior conditions. He had secured a conference without surrendering the position taken up when the Irish Republic was declared..."[26]

Coogan scoffed at Longford's conclusions: "How an intelligent person (Longford), looking at the facts objectively and then coming into de Valera's force field, encountering his extraordinary facility for demonstrating that black was white and vice versa, could be led to a denial of reality. It was an attribute which de Valera would later use time and time again to his advantage to demonstrate the difference between a fact and a de Valera fact – that is, one that should be believed..."[27]

During the interlude between the British Prime Minister's final ultimatum to de Valera's concession and Dáil acceptance of Lloyd George's terms, the Irish people held their collective breath. "The suggestion made afterwards, that de Valera, Burgess and Stack did not realize that they were committing themselves to a compromise when they stopped the war [July Truce] and toyed with the British proposal, is one which is insulting to any man with intelligence and honesty."[28]

Upon acceptance of the British invitation to a Peace Conference, everyone assumed that de Valera, like his counterpart Lloyd George, would lead his delegation. He was the most experienced negotiator and already had a familiar working relationship with Lloyd George. On September 14, de Valera stunned the Dáil deputies by refusing to attend the most momentous opportunity in Ireland's 750 years under English domination. Instead, ignoring their reluctance, he insisted upon Arthur Griffith and Collins leading the Delegation. Once again Coogan called de Valera a liar: "...time made a different story possible...In a written reply to Lord Longford, *he lied point blank* [emphasis added]; saying that his staying at home was 'generally accepted' and only became an issue after an agreement·[Treaty] was concluded."[29]

The Irish President insisted the delegation be furnished with "full plenipotentiary powers '*to negotiate and conclude a Treaty* [emphasis added] or Treaties of Settlement, Association and Accommodation between Ireland and the community of nations known as the British Commonwealth.'"[30] When Gavan Duffy, a member of the delegation, sought to have the delegation's powers limited, de Valera was emphatic that the delegation retain sole responsibility for whatever resulted from the conference. He even went to the extent of giving the Dáil deputies an ultimatum: either provide the delegation with full powers or he would resign. "De Valera had twice previously threatened to resign as President if full plenipotentiary powers were denied to the Delegation, and he again emphasized he would not stand for any restrictions."[31]

Beaslai recorded de Valera's words: "Remember what you are asking them to do. You are asking them to secure by negotiations what we are totally unable to secure by force of arms."[32] In light of his conduct after the fact, it was an obvious conclusion that he set them up to saddle them with full responsibility for the outcome of the Treaty negotiations.

Collins argued against going to London: "For several years, rightly or wrongly made no difference, the English held me to be the one man most necessary to capture because they considered me to be the one man responsible for the smashing of their Secret Service Organization and for their failure to terrorize the people with the Black and Tans...the important fact was that in England, as in Ireland, the Michael Collins legend existed. It pictured me as a mysterious, active menace, elusive, unknown, and unaccountable and in this respect; I was the only living Irishman of whom it could be said...Bring me into the spotlight of a London conference and quickly will be discovered the common clay of which I am made. The glamour of the legendary figure will be gone."[33]

Before agreeing to go, Griffith emphatically declared that he could not bring back an Irish Republic. He also made it clear that he would not reject a treaty if it came down to recognizing the Crown. De Valera understood that Griffith and Collins would accept the Crown but still insisted on them leading the delegation anyway. De Valera made use of another of his fish-story analogies and "looked upon [Griffith and Collins] as a kind of fishing bait, which he thought he could use to lure the British. He actually described them as 'better bait for Lloyd George – leading him on and on, further in our direction...'"[34]

If the peace conference was meant to secure Republican status, de Valera, Burgess, and Stack were the logical choices to represent the Republican cause. By staying in Dublin, they, too, were free from being tainted with any treaty decision and could nip at the heels of those who went to London. In leaving Burgess off the Irish delegation, de Valera characterized him as "the most honest and finest soul in the world, but he is a bit slow at seeing fine differences and rather stubborn. The others would not seek to convince him, but would rather try to outmaneuver him, and there would be trouble...If I were going myself, I would certainly have taken him with me."[35] Stack's credentials were even less than Burgess', if that was possible. His qualification and position was based on his prowess on a ball field as a soccer player of considerable note.

De Valera defended his decision not to go to London, contending:

"He would be *accessible in Dublin as a consultant* of last resort in the event the Delegation was being forced to make hasty decisions; 'I could best *serve the national interest* by remaining at home;' he would be in a better position *to influence radical republicans* if he were to wage a campaign for the acceptance of a compromise agreement; his influence would be vastly more effective if...'completely free of any suggestion that I had been affected by the London atmosphere.' [emphasis added]

"Furthermore," Dwyer wrote: "He would be in a position to rally both moderates and radicals to fight for an absolute claim, instead of a less appealing compromise; were there to be a 'break,' with any substantial section of our people discontented and restless the national position would be dangerously weakened when the war resumed, and he could provide for that contingency by remaining at home rather than by leading the delegation; he could play his part in keeping public opinion firm; and do everything possible to have the Army well organized and strong."[36]

Longford and O'Neill were being disingenuous when they claimed that "his influence with Burgess, Stack, Mrs. Clarke and others would be much greater if he were not a party to the negotiations. We must remind ourselves repeatedly that unity on his own side was his over-riding objective."[37]

As a consultant, de Valera was uncooperative and unresponsive when called upon to answer the Delegation's requests for instructions. Far from promoting the national interest, he was intent on spreading confusion and fomenting civil war. He exploited his own non-attendance to influence radical republicans towards extremism rather than compromise with fanatical exhortations to take up the sword against their Irish brethren.

In order to mount an attack upon Collins, Griffith, and the treaty, de Valera presented himself as untouched by the "London atmosphere" despite his having engaged in secret truce talks with Lloyd George in London in July. Instead of rallying moderates and radicals to accept an appealing compromise, he reverted to being a Republican zealot, urging the extremists to be prepared to fight in the event the Treaty did not produce an Irish Republic. Once again, as he had done in America with John Devoy and Judge Daniel Cohalan, de Valera portrayed himself as standing on the rock of the Republic, while claiming Collins and Griffith abandoned the Republic.

De Valera picked on every petty nuance of the treaty, intent on spreading uncertainty and mistrust. Upon learning the treaty outcome, he fuelled division by claiming the treaty was in violent conflict with the wishes of the nation. By the time the treaty talks concluded, the Irish

Army, instead of being well organized and strong, was in a shambles, and mutiny rampant.

The following consistent inconsistencies were proposed and opposed by de Valera from July through December 1921:

He refused to accept British conditions for initiating a peace conference.

He demanded that the Dáil accept every British condition.

He opposed an oath to the Crown.

He proposed two oaths to the Crown.

He opposed an oath of allegiance to the Crown as head of an association of States.

He proposed an oath to the Crown as head of Associated States.

He demanded recognition of an Irish Republic.

He opposed recognition of an Irish Republic.

He threatened the Dáil deputies with resumption of a "real war" resulting in the annihilation of the Irish race if they insisted on recognition of an Irish Republic.

He accused the treaty delegation of cowardice for abandoning the Republic under Lloyd George's threat of a resumption of the war.

He proposed acceptance of Dominion status.

He opposed Dominion status.

He demanded Dáil deputies swear an oath to the Irish Republic.

He opposed any oath to an Irish Republic.

He claimed the people never voted for an Irish Republic.

He charged that the people voted for an Irish Republic.

He opposed partition.

He advocated partition.

He opposed using force against Northern Ireland.

He accused the Unionists of being a rock in the road that had to be blasted out of the way.

He advocated no coercion of Protestant Unionists in Northern Ireland.

He ignored coercion of Catholic Nationalists in Northern Ireland.

He proposed any Unionist county could withdraw from an Irish Republic.

He opposed any Catholic Nationalist county's withdrawal from Northern Ireland.

He demanded that the treaty delegation have power to

"negotiate and conclude" a treaty.

He accused Collins and Griffith of a *fait accompli* by "concluding" a treaty.

He claimed there was a constitutional way to handle any treaty differences.

He insisted that the majority had no right to do wrong when the Irish people approved the Treaty.

He refused to recognize the King.

He voted for a donation to the King's private account.

He warned against fratricide.

He initiated civil war.

On October 7, 1921, de Valera announced: "In virtue of the authority vested in me by Dáil Éireann, I hereby appoint Arthur Griffith, Minister for Foreign Affairs, Chairman; Michael Collins, Minister for Finance; Robert C. Barton, Minister for Economic Affairs; Edmund J. Duggan, and George Gavan Duffy, as Envoys Plenipotentiaries from the elected Government of the Republic of Ireland to negotiate and conclude on behalf of Ireland with the representatives of his Britannic Majesty George V, a treaty or treaties of settlement, association and accommodation between Ireland and the community of nations, known as the British Commonwealth."

The British Delegation to the London Peace Conference consisted of Lloyd George (chairman), Winston Churchill, Lord Birkenhead, Austen Chamberlain (who succeeded Bonar Law as Conservative Party leader), Sir Hamar Greenwood (Secretary of State for Ireland), Laming Worthington Evans (Conservative Secretary for War) and Viscount Gordon Hewart (Attorney General), the world's foremost, experienced and talented statesmen.

Prime Minister Lloyd George, on October 11, 1921 presided at the opening session of the most significant peace conference between England and Ireland in seven centuries of unspeakable horror. The Irish President refused to attend this historic conference, claiming that the proper place of the head of state was in his own country not at a foreign conference. Beaslai retorted: "...It is a pity that this point of view had not commended itself to de Valera when he went to America in 1919 or when the State was fighting for its life in 1920. It may also be remarked that the English Prime Minister did not think it unfitting his position to be one of the negotiators."[38]

Author Charles C. Tansill, said: "de Valera's cowardice in refusing to lead the Irish delegation to London to discuss Treaty terms and his evident lack of character in the [later] Dáil debates with special reference to his Document No. 2 [external association proposal] bring back to memory the acidulous comment of John Devoy: 'de Valera is the most malignant man in all Irish history.'"[39]

Tim Pat Coogan wrote: "de Valera's (role) was the shadowy, off-stage presence, not that of the starring player, the role in which he should have cast himself. Now, however, it becomes increasingly important to study a performance which he should not have given in a tragic drama for which he wrote much of the script."[40] Coogan also made a critical observation as to why the Irish President set up Collins and Griffith with sole responsibility for the outcome of the Peace Conference: "...What is surprising to a biographer...is how little of substance de Valera contributed to this crucially important set of Anglo-Irish discussions...In London between October 11 and December 6, 1921, Ireland's entire future was drafted and de Valera remained almost completely aloof from the process. It was totally uncharacteristic of him and completely at variance with the interventionist role he played, or attempted to play, in every other political activity he encountered during his career. *The weight of evidence points inexorably towards the verdict that, during his July Truce conversations with Lloyd George, he had seen the future and decided that it would not work for him* [emphasis added]. His formula for dealing with the unpalatable reality was: 'We must have scapegoats.'"[41]

In light of his interventionist role in America and his "shadowy off-stage presence" at the London Peace Conference, with disastrous consequences to Ireland in both instances, it affords no other rational conclusion but he and Lloyd George engaged in a deliberate scheme to wreak havoc with Irish interests. Contrary to Coogan's contention that the future would not work for de Valera, the weight of evidence points inexorably towards the verdict that if de Valera had headed the Irish Delegation and crossed the Irish Rubicon with the very same Treaty signed by Collins and Griffith, the Irish President would have been hailed as the greatest living Irishman, a Celtic Caesar who forced the English out of Ireland after seven centuries of misery. No one questioned why de Valera rejected the Emperor's laurels.

Michael Collins created quite a stir upon his arrival in London. "There was a great curiosity, not only among Irish residents in London, but among the English public, to see the wonderful Michael Collins around whom so many romantic stories had been woven. People were astonished at seeing how much he differed from the somber, dark-browed conspirator of English legend. His winning smile, breezy manner, and genial bearing made him many friends, even among those hitherto opposed to him..."[42]

When Collins finally emerged from the shadows of the revolutionary underworld, the British were astonished to find before them a tall, handsome 31-year-old young man with a broad smile and engaging personality. The Lord Chancellor, Lord Birkenhead (F.E. Smith) and Winston Churchill, Colonial Secretary, were impressed with his energy and intelligence. Lloyd George's secretary, Tom Jones, in a letter to Bonar Law, Conservative Party leader and successor to Lloyd George as Prime Minister, said: "The tenacity of the IRA is extraordinary. Where was Michael Collins during the Great War... his cause is good. He'll be canonized someday."[43] Lloyd George and the British delegates marveled at Collins' grasp of political realities and his strength of character and determination. Collins and Churchill quickly became fast friends. One evening, at the home of Churchill, after one or two drinks too many, Collins grumbled that the British had authorized a reward of £5,000 on his head. Churchill countered that Collins should have been proud that such a huge sum was offered, pointing to the fact the Boers only offered £25 for his head.

It is interesting that Collins, that man of mystery, was well aware of the pitfalls of accepting his mission to London. "'You might say the trap is sprung,' he wrote to his aide Joe O'Reilly on November 11, 1921. In recorded conversations between himself and Griffith, it is quite clear that the two men regarded themselves as being so enmeshed in intrigue and deceit that nothing they brought back would satisfy 'the Dublinites.'"[44] Collins and Griffith accepted membership in the treaty negotiating team knowing that de Valera was setting them up. "With uncharacteristic lack of caution, de Valera had been overheard saying of the Plenipotentiaries: '*We must have scapegoats.*'"[45] [emphasis added]

Collins' friends were also apprehensive. "Some members of the Supreme Council of the IRB thought *there was something sinister afoot* [emphasis added], and they warned him that he was in danger of being made a scapegoat. 'Let them make a scapegoat or anything they wish of me,' he replied, 'We have accepted the situation as it is, and someone must go.'"[46]

In July, August, and September, de Valera steamrolled the Dáil deputies into accepting every one of Lloyd George's terms for entering into peace talks, but upon the appointment of the plenipotentiaries, de Valera, as he had done in America, reverted from peacenik to hawk, shrieking a clarion call to war if England did not grant immediate independence and recognize an Irish Republic. No whisper of suspicion, no question or doubt was raised as to why de Valera considered a war of annihilation of the Irish race so disastrous prior to the Dáil deputies formally agreeing to enter into peace talks, but a matter of little or no consequence after the Dáil acceptance of Lloyd George's terms.

Once the Dáil officially agreed to participate in peace talks, Lloyd George, in a letter to the King, declared, "It was absolutely clear to the world that the Irish were entering talks based on their acceptance of the English conditions. In the event the Irish rejected these conditions, the British would have world opinion on their side." Lloyd George, in his letter of September 29 to de Valera, set forth the parameters in which he would agree to a peace conference, and which the Dáil deputies and de Valera accepted on at least four occasions.

Collins argued: "I say if we all stood on the recognition of the Irish Republic as a prelude to a conference, we could easily have said so and there would be no conference."[47] The British Prime Minister, had made it clear that the position was not negotiable. "If the security of this country were menaced, the Throne repudiated, the Empire mutilated and Ireland established as an alien country on our most vulnerable flank, free to make its own arrangements with our enemies...which would mean that the forces of Civil War were to range at our doors between Catholic and Protestant, while we looked on without either safeguard or authority – then Britain, I felt confident, would make the necessary sacrifices."[48]

The Irish Delegation's mandate was to "negotiate and conclude" a Treaty of Settlement within the terms as laid down by Lloyd George and accepted by de Valera and the Dáil deputies. Churchill stated: "The points on which the British Government insisted – allegiance to the Crown, membership of the Empire, facilities and security for the Navy and a complete option for Ulster – were all embodied in the terms."[49]

De Valera's interference in the delegation's negotiations began within days of their arrival in London when he refused Griffith's request for an assistant in place of Erskine Childers. Griffith considered it inappropriate for a former British officer, a turncoat who betrayed his own country by taking up arms against England in support of the Irish cause, to be serving the Irish Delegation in the critical position of secretary. Furthermore, he and Collins considered Childers a spy for de Valera. Childers was less than helpful, always conjuring up the worst-case scenarios of any proposals set forth by the English, and critical of any solutions offered by the Irish delegation. Adding to their difficulties, de Valera now proposed that the dullard Austin Stack be appointed as an expert adviser, a suggestion firmly rejected by the delegation. He also attempted to recall Diarmuid O'Hegarty, one of the delegation's ablest supporters.

The Delegation requested instruction from de Valera on at least five occasions, and, in each instance, the delegation was greeted with silence. As far as de Valera was concerned, there was no way he would allow the delegation to claim it was his instructions that decided the outcome of the negotiations. "With no advice forthcoming [from de Valera]...Griffith wrote to the Irish President, 'If we came to an agreement on all other points, I could recommend some form of association with the Crown.' Instructions were requested of de Valera on the best way to handle the subject. The Plenipotentiaries felt that they could respond with an outright refusal to consider any kind of association with the Crown or they could obtain a field of maneuver and delay the crucial question by stating that they would be prepared to consider the question of the Crown, if agreement was reached on all other issues. De Valera never replied."[50]

Rather than answer the delegation's requests, within days of the treaty conference, de Valera dispatched an ultimatum to the delegation in which he declared: "We are all here at one that there can be no question of our asking the Irish people to enter an arrangement that would make them subjects of the British King. If war is the alternative, we can only face it and I think the sooner the other side is made to realize it the better."[51]

It was an astounding declaration. Only two months before, de Valera had bludgeoned the Dáil deputies into accepting allegiance to the King or face annihilation of the Irish Race. Now he was against allegiance and in favour of war.

The delegation notified de Valera that his ultimatum overriding the powers of their appointment was unacceptable and that if he insisted, they would return home. On receiving this threat, "de Valera made a show of drawing in his horns and said: 'There can be no question of tying the hands of the Plenipotentiaries beyond the extent to which they are tied by their original instructions.'"[52]

De Valera initiated one crisis after another without consulting anyone, let alone the plenipotentiaries who were in the midst of crucial negotiations affecting the future of the nation. In the opening days of the Conference, Pope Benedict XV sent a message to King George V, praying for the success of the Peace Conference: "'We rejoice at the resumption of the Anglo-Irish negotiations and pray to the Lord with all our heart that He may bless them and grant to your Majesty the great joy and imperishable glory of bringing an end to an age-long dissension.' The King responded, 'I have received the message of your Holiness with much pleasure and with all my heart I join in your prayer that the Conference...may achieve a permanent settlement of the troubles in Ireland and may initiate a new era of peace and happiness for my people.'"[53]

In response to this innocuous exchange, de Valera, in a public letter to the Pope on October 21, dropped a bombshell, by declaring Ireland's independence and repudiating allegiance to the Crown. He paraded his new-found republican principles: "The people of Ireland...are confident that the ambiguities in the reply sent in the name of King George will not mislead you into believing that...the people of Ireland owe allegiance to the British King. The independence of Ireland has been formally proclaimed... The trouble between England and Ireland had as its source that the rulers of Britain have endeavored to impose their will upon Ireland."

In justifying his action, de Valera wrote to Griffith: "It was the Pope's telegram which was the irritating one from the Irish standpoint because in addressing the King in the first place, the Vatican recognized the struggle between Ireland and England as a purely domestic one for King George, and by implication, pronounced judgment against us."[54] de Valera and the delegation had agreed to leave the question of allegiance to the King to the last, and this intervention catapulted the question of the Crown to the forefront. Less than two weeks into peace negotiations, de Valera repudiated Lloyd George's conditions for entering into a peace conference.

"On October 22, 1921...Michael Collins...asked the President to go back with him to London. The President refused, saying he saw no necessity. He added, however, that if he were shown at any time that his presence was really required, he would certainly go over."[55] Negotiations stalled after a fortnight. According to Stack: "It was evident that there could be no agreement in London. The English were not ready to come to the point beyond which we could not touch without dishonor and if England wanted war, well, all we could do was to defend our country's honor with our lives."[56] If that were true, it was at that critical moment when de Valera's presence was urgently required from collapse, but he refused to budge.

In a letter to McGarrity, de Valera contradicted his original reason for staying at home: "There was a question of my going over in person to London. The objection to this was that the British would think I had gone because I was anxious to prevent a breakdown. They would, accordingly, not make any further advance to me but might stiffen instead."[57] Nothing could persuade him. He wasn't going to London no matter what the circumstances.

When Collins and Griffith realized that the talks were going nowhere with Childers nipping at their heels and Gavan Duffy and Robert Barton alternately tentative and combative, they discreetly requested sub-conferences between the two of them and Lloyd George. The Prime

Minister leapt at the suggestion, and, along with Lord Birkenhead, the four of them constituted a working party and met from October 24 to the treaty signing on December 6, with Lloyd George taking responsibility for initiating the request for the sub-conferences.

Throughout the treaty discussions, Griffith submitted daily progress reports of the sub-plenary discussions to de Valera and the cabinet. Neither the Irish President, Stack, nor Burgess expressed the slightest objection to the arrangement.

Prior to the conference, de Valera exceeded his authority and attached cabinet instructions overriding the Dáil powers already invested in the delegation by the Dáil. After the treaty was signed, de Valera charged Griffith with failure to comply with those cabinet instructions.

Paragraph 2 of de Valera's cabinet instructions stated that it was "understood before decisions are finally reached on a main question, that a dispatch notifying the intention to make these decisions will be sent to members of the Cabinet in Dublin, and that a reply will be awaited by the Plenipotentiaries before a final decision is made."

As the protracted treaty conference in London dragged to a close, Lloyd George issued his final treaty draft proposals the last week in November. He announced that they would be presented to the Irish delegation and to the Northern Ireland government on Tuesday, December 6. In accordance with Paragraph 2 of the cabinet instructions, Griffith then notified de Valera a week in advance that the delegation was about to make a decision on the final draft treaty and called for a December 3 meeting.

Paragraph 3 of the cabinet directives stated that it was also "understood that the complete text of the draft Treaty about to be signed will be similarly submitted to Dublin and a reply awaited." In compliance with Paragraph 3, Griffith submitted the complete text of Lloyd George's final treaty draft at the December 3 cabinet session, resulting in a seven-hour discussion on its merits. Although de Valera and Stack later alleged that the delegation failed to comply with cabinet instructions, Eamonn Duggan countered: "The Cabinet knew well that a week's notice was given and that we would have to give a certain answer on a certain date."[58]

At the December 3 cabinet marathon session, Stack charged Collins and Griffith with deceiving the cabinet by their agreeing to sub-plenary conferences: "This was the first instance of the *fait accompli* succeeding in the game, but we did not see this at the time. We trusted our colleagues implicitly."[59] This was too much, even for Stack's biographer, Gaughan: "It is difficult to accept Stack's statement in light of Burgess' intervention at the meeting of the Cabinet and Delegation on December 3, 1921."[60] Stack's *fait accompli* argument was merely a fabrication to aid de Valera's campaign against Collins, Griffith, and the treaty.

Beaslai reported that at the December 3 cabinet session, Griffith, before leaving, told de Valera that he, for one, would not break off negotiations over the question of recognition of the British Crown. At this revelation by Griffith, Charles Burgess, who had remained mute when the sub-conference issue was brought to the cabinet's attention in October, now considered it the appropriate time to cast aspersions on Collins and Griffith. He demanded to know who was responsible for the decision to hold sub-plenary conferences without all the members of the delegation present. When told that Lloyd George had suggested it, Burgess, spitting venom, charged, "The British Government selected their men [Collins and Griffith]."[61]

"Griffith rose from his place at the table and went up to Burgess to make him withdraw the charge. Burgess, with typical stubbornness, refused. Griffith insisted that Burgess' words be recorded in the minutes; ultimately, it (the charge) was withdrawn but the damage was done."[62]

When the Irish President insisted on private meetings with Lloyd George during the July truce talks in London, no such charges were leveled against de Valera by Burgess or Stack.

In defense of de Valera's refusal to attend the treaty talks, Stack fabricated a confrontation between Griffith and Burgess at the December 3 session in which Stack and de Valera later claimed Griffith allegedly promised to return to Dublin with an unsigned document, no matter how amended. There is no evidence beyond de Valera and Stack's that any such pledge was made by Griffith. Surprisingly, Coogan accepted the word of two proven liars – de Valera and Stack – over that of the staunch Griffith, who denied the charge. The controversy centered around Coogan's premise that Griffith's duly *recorded and corroborated* pledge to sign the treaty if the oath was amended had no validity, but that an *unrecorded and uncorroborated* Stack claim of an alleged pledge by Griffith not to sign any document no matter how amended was true.

Stack and de Valera claimed, as Griffith was citing the advantages of the treaty and his intention to sign if the oath was amended, Burgess interrupted Griffith: "'Don't you realize that if you sign this thing, you will split Ireland from top to bottom?' The force of this seemed to strike Griffith: 'I suppose that's so. I'll tell you what I'll do; I'll go back to London. I'll not sign that Document but I'll bring it back and submit it to the Dáil.' This pledge satisfied everybody present at the meeting."[63]

Coogan maintained that Griffith's "undertaking not to sign under any circumstances" actually took place though he conceded that

"Griffith's 'express undertaking,' is not mentioned in the official record at all."[64] In offering justification for such a premise, Coogan disingenuously alluded to the possibility that "the secretary to the meeting, Colm O'Murchadha, never heard the exchange in which it occurred...between Griffith and Burgess."[65] With such an alleged serious and raucous confrontation taking place at a cabinet session attended by the secretary and more than a dozen men, none of them, with the exception of de Valera and Stack, recollected, remembered, or recorded any such Griffith/Burgess confrontation or pledge by Griffith to return with an unsigned Treaty. Even the Irish President's official biographers cast doubt as to the charges: "The de Valera account, like that given earlier by Longford in *Peace by Ordeal*, is largely based on that of Austin Stack."[66]

Dwyer, too, contradicted Coogan's supposition regarding Stack's allegations and corroborated the delegation's understanding that they had complied fully with the cabinet instructions: "None of the Delegation had thought it necessary to consult Dublin before signing believing they had fulfilled their instructions by placing the draft treaty before the Cabinet on Saturday [December 3]. Once they had done that they were free to do as they thought fit..."[67]

Significantly, Burgess, the man Stack claimed had elicited the "express undertaking" from Griffith, never corroborated Stack's charge.

According to the minutes of the meeting, de Valera and the cabinet, after reviewing the treaty draft, instructed the delegation that upon returning to London they were free to sign the document subject only to an amendment of the oath of allegiance to the King satisfactory to the Irish plenipotentiaries. Griffith, the Cabinet, and the entire delegation understood upon their departure for London that evening that they had fully complied with the terms of de Valera's cabinets' instructions.

As everyone was filing out, after seven hours of wrangling, Childers allegedly asked de Valera whether he intended that the scrapping of the oath in the draft treaty also meant the delegation was to reject the treaty's first four paragraphs dealing with Dominion status. De Valera supposedly replied in the affirmative, but, allegedly, in the noise and confusion of the breakup of the meeting, no one else heard the alleged conversation. Doubt is also cast on this reported mini-conference between de Valera and Childers since the Irish President had previously claimed that Dominion status "conceded all the rights that Irish Republicans demanded."

In London on Monday, Childers created a howl of protest when he attempted to convince the rest of the delegation of the Irish President's interpretation. De Valera's alleged instruction to reject the treaty's first four paragraphs dealing with Dominion status was rendered null, however, when the oath was amended to the complete satisfaction of the delegation, and the treaty was signed, with Childers never raising an objection at that time.

During the treaty debate, Collins also confirmed the cabinet instruction that the delegation was free to sign the treaty if the Oath was amended: "[T]here was a document there, and Mr. Griffith said he would not sign that document and a different document was signed. Certainly the alterations met the objections which the IRB had raised with Collins..." Griffith said, "We had the power to sign anything we considered it well to sign and the power of the Dáil was the power of ratification."[68]

In a deliberate distortion of Griffith's words, de Valera declared: "I probably would have gone, [to London] *had not Griffith given an express undertaking that he would not sign a document accepting allegiance* [emphasis added] but would bring it back and refer the matter to Dáil Éireann. This made us all satisfied; we were certain for our part that Dáil Éireann would reject it."[69] Coogan again confirmed de Valera as a liar. "De Valera's 'this made us all satisfied' is simply untrue..."[70]

De Valera's charge that Griffith pledged not to sign a document "accepting allegiance to the King" is obviously not the same as signing a document "without allegiance to the King." The final treaty document contained no allegiance to the Crown, merely that the Irish would be "faithful" to the monarch in his capacity as head of an association of states, of which Ireland was but one member, and Griffith and the entire delegation signed it on that basis.

De Valera continued his campaign to derail the treaty by claiming that he had attempted to work within the limits acceptable to Republican fanatics like Burgess: "'Now,' de Valera charged, 'the chance of securing a united cabinet had been wrecked by the Plenipotentiaries signing the agreement without consulting the Cabinet.'"[71] Coogan questioned the veracity of de Valera's biographer: "Presumably the description of the Cabinet meeting...exonerated the biographer [Longford] from any further comment on the veracity of the comment about Griffith's undertaking, but there is no escape from pronouncing on the account which de Valera authorized in his biography. It is a blank lie."[72]

At the December 8 cabinet session, "Barton blamed de Valera for the mess because of his refusal to go to London when asked the previous weekend. In fact, at different times, de Valera had rejected appeals from all three Cabinet members of the delegation and he had also turned down similar appeals from Childers and Gavan Duffy [to return with the delegation to London]...de Valera had been instrumental in conferring the full responsibility for negotiating a settlement on people he knew were more moderate than himself..."[73]

De Valera and Stack proved the fallacy of their argument that the delegation was instructed not to sign any treaty without referring it back to the cabinet when they declared their jubilation over the initial news that the delegation had signed a treaty. "De Valera was in Limerick on Tuesday morning [December 6, 1921] when he heard a Treaty had been signed: 'I never thought they [the British] would give in so soon,' he exclaimed. In view of Griffith's undertaking not to sign the draft Treaty, he assumed the British must have conceded what he wanted, so he was delighted. 'I felt like throwing my hat in the air,' (he shouted)."[74] Stack, too, greeted the news, not with indignation that Griffith had failed to return with an unsigned document, but with satisfaction; "I did not know what to think. Then, when I remembered Griffith's pledge on Saturday evening, I was delighted for I thought the English had given in to our terms."[75]

The Irish President and Stack never did reveal exactly what, besides amending the Oath, the British were supposed to concede that made them so happy. Gaughan again contradicted the subject of his biography: "Stack obviously considered that the Plenipotentiaries could sign an altered agreement without referring it back to the Cabinet in Dublin."[76] The same applied to de Valera.

With newspapers screaming headlines of a treaty signing, Coogan derided de Valera's claim that he had not heard, seen, or spoken to anyone regarding the treaty throughout the day. It was only that evening, when he presided at a Dante commemoration ceremony in the Mansion House at 7:30 p.m., that a copy of the *Evening Mail*, which had been circulating throughout the day in Dublin, was presented to him by Burgess and Stack. "He asked them, 'Any news?' and in reply was shown the paper. It was then and only then that he would have us believe, that he first learned the terms of the Treaty."[77]

Beaslai, a participant at the Mansion House ceremony, noted that when Eamonn Duggan and Desmond Fitzgerald arrived: "They found de Valera in a towering rage. When they handed him the copy of the Treaty he laid it aside, declaring that he had no time to read it. He presided at the Dante Commemoration without having read the Treaty...The nature of the Treaty, affecting the fate of the people of Ireland, was of only secondary interest to him."[78]

In a note to Joseph McGarrity of Philadelphia on December 27, 1921, after he had initiated a split in Irish ranks, de Valera admitted: "It might be necessary to finesse a little. The President, of all men, should not give rise to even the remotest suspicion of 'letting down' the Republic."[79] In another letter to McGarrity, de Valera set the stage for another "split," this time in Ireland. He charged the signing of the treaty without consulting him was an unparalleled act of disloyalty. He also complained that Collins and Griffith's *fait accompli* was published before the Irish President and their cabinet colleagues had seen the treaty.[80] de Valera and the Cabinet members had all discussed the Treaty draft for seven hours three days before and the delegation had received their unanimous endorsement.

Attesting to the negotiating skills of Collins and Griffith was the difference between Lloyd George's "non-negotiable" conditions, accepted by de Valera and the Dáil deputies. It was an impressive achievement. Prior to the peace conference, the British Prime Minister had insisted: "The Crown is the symbol of all that keeps the nations of the Empire together. It is the keystone of the arch in law as well as in sentiment...The British Government must know definitely whether or not the Irish Delegates are prepared that Ireland should maintain its ancient allegiance to the Throne, not as a state subordinate to Great Britain, but as one of the Nations of the Commonwealth, in close association with the realm of England, Scotland and Wales."[81]

Collins and Griffith negotiated a British capitulation by eliminating any oath of allegiance to the Crown. Five months before his rush to condemnation of the treaty over an alleged oath of allegiance, de Valera, on July 25, 1921, told the Dáil deputies: "The oath [to an Irish Republic] never conveyed any more to me than to do my best."[82] According to the Official Minutes of the December 3 Cabinet Session, O'Murchada, the secretary, recorded that de Valera, "suggested the following amendment to the Oath of Allegiance: 'I, ... do solemnly swear true faith and allegiance to the Constitution of the Irish Free State, to the Treaty of Association and to recognize the King of Great Britain as Head of the Associated States.'"[83]

The literal translation of de Valera's oath was recognition of the King as also King of Ireland, one of the associated states. Collins and Griffith negotiated a signed treaty, however, merely calling on the Irish to be "faithful" to the King solely in his capacity as head of an association, not individual states.

In an astonishing contradiction, less than two weeks before the signing of the treaty, de Valera, Stack, and Burgess had not only accepted de Valera's treaty oath acknowledging the King as head of Ireland, but they also agreed to contribute to the King's household expenses. The official minutes of that meeting stated: "The Dáil Ministry [Cabinet] presided over by de Valera, in consultation with the Irish Plenipotentiaries [Burgess and Stack being present], came to a unanimous decision: 'That Ireland shall recognize the British Crown, for the purpose of association, a symbol and accepted head of the combination of associated states.' At the same meeting, it was also unanimously agreed that Ireland should vote an annual voluntary contribution to the British Civil List [the King's personal revenue]."[84] For less than the shadow of a difference between what he had agreed to less than a fortnight before, de Valera plunged Ireland into chaos.

On December 3, de Valera had proposed an oath pledging allegiance to a Free State Constitution, but three days later, he charged that allegiance to a Free State Constitution was in reality a pledge of allegiance to the British Crown because the King had to ratify the treaty establishing a Free State. He ignored the reality that whether the treaty granted an outright Irish Republic or a Free State within the Commonwealth of Nations, both had to be ceremoniously ratified by the King.

Collins attempted to win over any future objections by the extremist element to any oath in the treaty. Prior to the December 3 Cabinet session, he provided a copy of the draft oath to Sean O'Muirthile, secretary to the IRA Supreme Council, which unanimously rejected it. The IRA leaders, including Liam Lynch, Eoin O'Duffy, and Geroid O'Sullivan, presented Collins with a scaled-down version that called on the Irish to merely be "faithful to the King as head of an association."

"Prior to returning to Mansion House, Collins wrote in his notebook the main points which had been agreed at the IRA meeting and the version of the oath which the Supreme Council suggested. According to O'Muirthile, this was the version which appeared in the Anglo-Irish Treaty."[85] Collins and Griffith even maneuvered the British into a compromise on their demand for facilities and security for the Navy, which was amended to being subject to review within five years.

Immediately after the lengthy cabinet session of December 3, 1921, de Valera set out to enlist the extremist element within the IRA to oppose any agreement brought back by Collins and Griffith. In an obvious attempt to wrest control of the army, de Valera proposed Stack as Assistant Chief of Staff at IRA headquarters. He further ordered that any military matters be routed through the intellectually and temperamentally unsuited Burgess as Minister of Defense. Burgess had complained that military officers were ignoring him and taking their orders from Collins.

The IRA leaders loyal to Collins, however, recognized the scheme posed by de Valera, Burgess, and Stack, and foiled the attempted coup. Richard Mulcahy IRA Chief of Staff, proposed that de Valera should personally acknowledge the services rendered by the IRA General Headquarters' officers and explain his vision for his New Army. De Valera attempted to smooth over GHQ objections to Stack by proposing that Eoin O'Duffy be appointed along with Stack to support and represent the Minister of Defense, Burgess. The GHQ unanimously opposed de Valera's New Army and especially the appointment of Stack with an O'Duffy chaperone. Realizing the IRA leaders had outmaneuvered him, de Valera lost his temper. "Rising excitedly, he pushed away the table in front of him and half-screaming, shouted, 'Ye may mutiny if you like, but Ireland will give me another Army' and dismissed them all from his sight."[86]

The charge by de Valera apologists that Griffith had blundered during the treaty talks and lost the leverage of partition was another attempt to downgrade Griffith's magnificent achievement as well as to justify de Valera's beating the drums of civil war. The fact remained that it was the Dáil deputies, and de Valera, who conceded on four occasions the permanent partition of Ireland as the basis for entering into the October 1921 London peace conference.

Griffith assured the British Prime Minister: "On the Crown, he would be prepared to recommend recognition provided that they [the Irish] were satisfied with the other points at issue."[87] On November 1, in his daily report to de Valera, Griffith set forth the contents of his conversation with Lloyd George the day before. He noted that the Prime Minister and his government were facing a censure motion in the House of Commons from die-hard Tory backbenchers who were critical of the manner in which the treaty talks had been proceeding and who were also concerned about any concessions that would be detrimental to Northern Ireland. Griffith stated: "Lloyd George summed up his position as follows: *The bias of his speech had to be peace or war with Ireland. If Griffith would give 'personal assurances' on the Crown, free partnership with the British Empire and coastal and naval facilities* [emphasis added], he would 'smite the Die-hards' and, more importantly, would 'fight on the Ulster matter [Partition] to secure essential unity.'"[88]

At the time of the signing, the six counties of Ulster comprised a Protestant majority, and remained a part of the United Kingdom. Northern and Southern Ireland had their own parliaments with Northern Ireland deputies attending the Westminster Parliament while Southern Ireland members, rather than attend the House of Commons, took their seats in the Free State Dáil.

Griffith was prepared to assure Lloyd George that: "Contingent on the securing of 'essential unity' [of Ireland] he would recommend a free partnership of Ireland with the other States associated with the British Commonwealth, the formula defining the partnership to be arrived at a later discussion; 'I was prepared to recommend that Ireland should consent to recognition of the Crown as head of the proposed association of free states.'"

A furious row broke out when Griffith informed the delegation that he was about to give this assurance. He was charged with weakening the Irish position on the Crown and Ulster and yielding an advantage which Lloyd George could use in dealing with either Washington or Belfast. Barton, Duffy and Childers insisted that the letter be sent from the delegation as a whole. After two days of wrangling and redrafting, it was sent to Downing Street, signed by Griffith as Chairman. In the anger and confusion over what form the assurances should take, a bad situation had been made worse. "The Republican efforts [by Barton, Duffy, and Childers] at redrafting had effectively got rid of the pretense that there was any likelihood of a republic emerging from the negotiations."[89]

Coogan contended that Griffith was somehow responsible for Partition: "Even worse was to follow ten days later – the possibility of a break over Ulster was lost and, *de facto*, partition was accepted..."[90]

In March 1914, as a condition of introducing Home Rule, Prime Minister Henry Asquith had proposed, "the exclusion of six Northeastern Counties which are today partitioned from the rest of Ireland."[91] The Home Rule Act [limited self-government for Ireland] was enacted at that time with a suspensory clause to take effect after the end of the war. Andrew Bonar Law, Conservative Party leader, predicted: "If any British Government failed to protect Ulster from any violation, the Empire would surely be at an end."[92]

In the late nineteenth century, Ireland and England had come close to civil war over Prime Minister William Gladstone's similar Home Rule proposal. The Protestants balked at the prospect of Catholic majority domination. The partition of Ireland assuaged the Protestants but did not end the violence.

During the final countdown to concluding a treaty, Lloyd George produced Griffith's letter of support in order to face down Conservative Unionists. He asked Griffith whether he was going to keep his promise not to let him down. Griffith replied, "I have never let a man down in my life and I never will." If he had given his word, he would keep it. De Valera's biographers claimed that "this admission by Griffith...meant that the attempt to stage the 'break on Ulster' on which the whole Irish strategy hinged had gone by the board."[93] But de Valera, who had been kept abreast of the daily activities of the plenipotentiaries, never voiced an objection to Griffith's commitment.

Coogan, however, reversed course and presented another take on just who was responsible for the alleged "blunder" over Crown and Empire rather than on Ulster: "By the time he reached London, Collins was so disgusted that he did not even accompany the others on their fruitless trip to Downing Street. This meeting ended in ignominy when Gavan Duffy blurted out that *'the Irish difficulty lay in coming into the Empire'* [emphasis added]. Predictably, the Tory leader, Chamberlain, was first to react. 'That ends it,' he cried, getting to his feet; the rest of the British side followed him in gathering up their papers and walking out. Instead of putting 'the blame on Ulster' for breaking up the conference, the Irish [Duffy following the de Valera line, not Griffith's] had 'blundered' into allowing the rupture to come over Crown and Empire, the worst possible ground from the point of view of international opinion."[94]

The Irish President and Dáil deputies had accepted the British position that partition was non-negotiable and de Valera had included the exact wording of the treaty on Partition in his Document No. 2, as an alternative to the treaty presented during the treaty debate. Lloyd George insisted that Southern Ireland recognize the partition of Ireland as a precondition for the peace talks. Collins and Griffith, however, negotiated a temporary partition of Ireland in which the two Catholic and Nationalistic counties of Tyrone and Fermanagh would be severed from Northern Ireland along with the city of Derry. The severance of these areas would render Northern Ireland economically untenable ultimately leading to a peaceful unification of Ireland.

According to Longford and O'Neill, "de Valera was still clinging to the hope...that if a break must come, it could be brought about on Ulster and not the Crown. In other words, the British terms should be rejected on the grounds that they perpetuated the partition of Ireland..."[95] de Valera's opposition to partition, however, only came about after the Boundary clause settlement in 1925. Overlooked, however, was that Duffy and Barton were espousing de Valera's line on External Association that precipitated the walkout and the breaking on the Crown and Empire. For this action of Duffy and Barton, supported by de Valera, Irish writers attempted to blame Griffith.

De Valera ignored the partition issue during the treaty debates and never raised the issue until he ran out of reasons for fomenting discord. He was so determined on a "split" in Irish ranks that he contradicted himself on numerous occasions. He charged Griffith with failing to break on partition but during the treaty debates, de Valera refused to discuss partition, a critical factor in his alleged objection to the signing of the treaty.

Lloyd George noted: "If the Conference was to be broken off, I wanted Parliament to face it squarely and to feel that before it embarked on the alternative policy [of unrestrained military action against Ireland], it had done everything that could be decently expected by the country and by the conscience of the civilized world."[96] On December 5, Lloyd George stated: "The British could concede no more and debate no further. The Irish delegation must settle now. They must sign the agreement for a Treaty or else quit and both sides would be free to resume whatever warfare they could wage against each other."[97]

It was an obvious and logical progression. If there was no acceptance of a treaty, then the truce, a pause in the conflict, was at an end and the state of war automatically resumed. Lloyd George said: "We must know your answer by 10 p.m. tonight. You have until then, but no longer, to decide whether you give peace or war to your country."[98]

Griffith responded that the Irish delegation would give its answer that evening but said that he, personally, would sign the agreement. Lloyd George was adamant, however, and demanded that unless every member of the Irish delegation sign, there could be no agreement. He stated: "We, as a body, have hazarded our political futures; you must do likewise and take the same risks."[99]

Before he officially broke off the talks, the Prime Minister requested one last meeting with Collins and Griffith. After a good deal of persuasion, Collins reluctantly returned at 5 p.m. After some further discussion on minor items, in the early hours of December 6, the entire Irish delegation set their signatures to the most important treaty in Irish history, with the Irish President in his tent adamantly refusing to attend and planning his next move to reject the Treaty.

To mark the moment, Arthur Griffith announced at 2:20 a.m. Tuesday, December 6, 1921: "I have signed a Treaty of Peace between Ireland and Great Britain. I believe that Treaty will lay the foundations of friendship between the two nations. What I have signed, I shall stand by in the belief that the end of the conflict of centuries is at hand."[100]

That day, Collins wrote to a friend, "When you have sweated, toiled, had mad dreams, hopeless nightmares, you find yourself in London's streets, cold and dank in the night air. I thought at the time, how odd, how ridiculous – a bullet may just as well have done the job five years ago...These signatures are the first real step for Ireland. If people will only remember that – the first real step. Think – what have I got for Ireland? Something, which she has wanted these past 700 years...Will

227

anyone be satisfied at the bargain? Will anyone? I tell you this – early this morning I signed my death warrant."[101]

Notes

1. Taylor, Rex, *Michael Collins*, Hutchinson, London 1958, p. 189
2. Dwyer, T. Ryle, *De Valera, The Man & the Myths*, Poolbeg, Dublin, p. 57
3. Coogan, Tim Pat, *Michael Collins*, Arrow Books, London, 1991, p. 225
4. Dwyer, T. Ryle, *De Valera, The Man & the Myths*, Poolbeg, Dublin, p. 62
5. Coogan, Tim Pat, *Michael Collins*, Arrow Books, London, 1991, p. 224
6. Coogan, Tim Pat, *De Valera, The Man who was Ireland*, Harper, 1996, p. 245
7. Beaslai, Pieras, *Michael Collins and the Making of a New Ireland*, Vol II, Harper Bros. NY 1926, p. 277
8. Dwyer, T. Ryle, *De Valera, The Man & the Myths*, Poolbeg, Dublin, p. 61
9. *ibid*, p. 62
10. *ibid*, p. 61
11. *ibid*, p. 61
12. *ibid*, p. 21
13. Gaughan, J. Anthony, Austin Stack, Portrait of a Separatist, Kingdom books, Dublin, 1977, p. 158
14. *ibid*
15. Beaslai, Pieras, *Michael Collins and the Making of a New Ireland*, Vol II, Harper Bros. NY 1926, p. 277
16. Fitzgerald, W.G., *The voice of Ireland, A Survey of the Race & Nation from all Angles*, Virtue Ltd., Dublin/London, p. 29
17. Dwyer, T. Ryle, *De Valera, The Man & the Myths*, Poolbeg, Dublin p. 63
18. Coogan, Tim Pat, *Michael Collins*, Arrow Books, London, 1991, p. 224
19. O'Hegarty, P.S., *The Victory of Sinn Féin & How It Used It*, Talbot Press, Dublin 1924, p. 68
20. Coates, Tim, (ed.), *The Irish Uprising, 1914-21*, London Stationery Office, 2000, p. 187
21. Dwyer, T. Ryle, *De Valera, The Man & the Myths*, Poolbeg, Dublin, p. 68
22. Beaslai, Pieras, *Michael Collins and the Making of a New Ireland*, Vol II, Harper Bros. NY 1926, p. 277
23. *ibid*, p. 288
24. *ibid*, p. 289
25. Coogan, Tim P., *De Valera, The Man who was Ireland*, Harper, 1996, p. 251
26. *ibid*, p. 253
27. *ibid*, p. 254
28. O'Hegarty, P.S., *The Victory of Sinn Féin & How It Used It*, Talbot Press, Dublin 1924, p. 66

29. Coogan, Tim P., *De Valera, The Man who was Ireland*, Harper, 1996, p. 247
30. Dwyer, T. Ryle, *De Valera, The Man & the Myths*, Poolbeg, Dublin, p. 70
31. *ibid*, p. 68
32. Beaslai, Pieras, *Michael Collins and the Making of a New Ireland*, Vol II, Harper Bros. NY 1926, p. 281
33. Coogan, Tim P., *De Valera, The Man who was Ireland*, Harper, 1996, p. 248
34. Dwyer, T. Ryle, *De Valera, The Man & the Myths*, Poolbeg, Dublin, p. 70
35. *ibid*, p. 67
36. *ibid*, p. 65
37. Longford & O'Neill, *Éamon de Valera*, Hutchinson, London, p. 146
38. Beaslai, Pieras, *Michael Collins and the Making of a New Ireland*, Vol II, Harper Bros. NY 1926, p. 275
39. Tansill, Charles, C., *America and the Fight for Irish Freedom 1866-1922*, Devin-Adair, NY. 1957, p. 435. Re: Devoy to Cohalan 8/12/1920
40. Coogan, Tim P., *De Valera, The Man who was Ireland*, Harper, 1996, p. 279
41. *ibid*, p. 257
42. Beaslai, Pieras, *Michael Collins and the Making of a New Ireland*, Vol II, Harper Bros. NY 1926, p. 297
43. Jones, Thomas, Whitehall Diary, Vol. III, Oxford U. Press, 1971, p. 55
44. Coogan, Tim P., *De Valera, The Man who was Ireland*, Harper, 1996, p. 249
45. Dwyer, T. Ryle, *De Valera, The Man & the Myths*, Poolbeg, Dublin, p. 65
46. *ibid*, p. 69
47. *ibid*
48. Fitzgerald, W.G., *The voice of Ireland, A Survey of the Race & Nation from all Angles*, Virtue, Dublin/London, p. 4
49. *ibid*, p. 16
50. Dwyer, T. Ryle, *De Valera, The Man & the Myths*, Poolbeg, Dublin, p. 75
51. Coogan, Tim P., *De Valera, The Man who was Ireland*, Harper, 1996, p. 260
52. *ibid*, p. 261
53. *ibid*, p. 258
54. Dwyer, T. Ryle, *De Valera, The Man & the Myths*, Poolbeg, Dublin, p. 74
55. Gaughan J. Anthony, *Austin Stack, Portrait of a Separatist*, Kingdom books, Dublin, 1977, p. 164
56. *ibid*, p. 167
57. Longford Earl of & O'Neill, Thomas P., *Éamon de Valera*, Hutchinson, London, 1970, p. 34
58. Fitzgerald, W.G., The voice of Ireland, *A Survey of the Race & Nation from all Angles*, Virtue, Dublin/London, p. 3
59. Gaughan J. Anthony, *Austin Stack, Portrait of a Separatist*, Kingdom books, Dublin, 1977, p. 166
60. *ibid*, fn
61. Beaslai, Pieras, *Michael Collins and the Making of a New Ireland*, Vol II, Harper

Bros. NY 1926, p. 306

62. Longford Earl of & O'Neill, Thomas P., *Éamon de Valera*, Hutchinson, London, 1970, p. 161

63. Coogan, Tim P., *De Valera, The Man who was Ireland*, Harper, 1996, p. 275

64. *ibid*

65. *ibid*

66. *ibid*, p. 276

67. Dwyer, T. Ryle, *De Valera, The Man & the Myths*, Poolbeg, Dublin, p. 85

68. Fitzgerald W.G., *The voice of Ireland, A Survey of the Race & Nation from all Angles*, Virtue, Dublin/London, p. 32

69. Coogan, Tim P., *De Valera, The Man who was Ireland*, Harper, 1996, 273

70. *ibid*, p. 275

71. Dwyer, T. Ryle, *De Valera, The Man & the Myths*, Poolbeg, Dublin, p. 85

72. Coogan, Tim P, *De Valera, The Man who was Ireland*, Harper, 1996, p. 282

73. Dwyer, T. Ryle, *De Valera, The Man & the Myths*, Poolbeg, Dublin, p. 85

74. *ibid*, p. 83

75. Gaughan J. Anthony, *Austin Stack, Portrait of a Separatist*, Kingdom Books, Dublin, 1977, p. 171

76. *ibid* p. 283

77. Coogan, Tim P., *De Valera, The Man who was Ireland*, Harper, 1996, p. 282

78. Beaslai, Pieras, *Michael Collins and the Making of a New Ireland*, Vol II, Harper Bros. NY 1926, p. 308

79. Longford Earl of & O'Neill, Thomas P., *Éamon de Valera*, Hutchinson, London, 1970, p. 146

80. Coogan, Tim P., *De Valera, The Man who was Ireland*, Harper, 1996, p. 284

81. *ibid*, p. 269

82. Dwyer, T. Ryle, *De Valera, The Man & the Myths*, Poolbeg, Dublin, p. 58

83. Baslai, Pieras, *Michael Collins and the Making of a New Ireland*, Vol II, Harper Bros. NY 1926, p. 305 & Cabinet Minutes: 12/3/1921, Article 'C', 1(a).

84. Gaughan, J. Anthony, *Austin Stack, Portrait of a Separatist*, Kingdom books, Dublin, 1977, p. 166 fn 26

85. *ibid*, p. 169 fn 32

86. Coogan, Tim P., *De Valera, The Man who was Ireland*, Harper, 1996, p. 268

87. Longford Earl of & O'Neill, Thomas P., *Éamon de Valera*, Hutchinson, London, 1970, p. 157

88. Coogan, Tim P., *De Valera, The Man who was Ireland*, Harper, 1996, p. 262

89. *ibid*, p. 263

90. *ibid*

91. *ibid*, p. 55

92. Fitzgerald, W.G., *The voice of Ireland, A Survey of the Race & Nation from all Angles*, Virtue Dublin/London, p. 8

93. Longford Earl of & O'Neill, Thomas P., *Éamon de Valera*, Hutchinson, London,

1970, p. 164

94. Coogan, Tim P., *De Valera, The Man who was Ireland*, Harper, 1996, p. 277
95. Longford Earl of & O'Neill, Thomas P., *Éamon de Valera*, Hutchinson, London, 1970, p. 160
96. Fitzgerald, W.G., *The voice of Ireland, A Survey of the Race & Nation from all Angles*, Virtue, Dublin/London, p. 3
97. Longford Earl of & O'Neill, Thomas P., *Éamon de Valera*, Hutchinson, London, 1970, p. 164
98. *ibid*, p. 165
99. *ibid*
100. Fitzgerald, W.G., *The voice of Ireland, Survey of the Race & Nation from all Angles*, Virtue, Dublin/London, p. 30
101. Taylor, Rex, *Michael Collins*, Hutchinson, London 1958, p. 189

CHAPTER XVI

"Assignment Chaos"

"… Against de Valera, stood Arthur Griffith, who said afterwards that as he sat there, and listened to the attacks on himself, he marveled at the smallness of his own mind not to suspect the depths of villainy of which de Valera was capable."[1]

Ireland's centuries-old fight for freedom was finally at hand. The moment had arrived when all could be gained or all could be lost. British national and international interests also hung in the balance. Once again, the English urgently required the services of Éamon de Valera, this time to reject the treaty in order to create chaos in Southern Ireland before Michael Collins created chaos in Northern Ireland and quite likely in England itself.

The British dilemma centered on Collins and Arthur Griffith, the only two men capable of opposing de Valera's scheme of creating pandemonium in Southern Ireland. The immediate alternative, of course, was the elimination of Collins and Griffith. The purging of Collins and Griffith, however, would have to wait for a more propitious moment; they were indispensable at this time as foils to de Valera's machinations. With a peaceful transition to an Irish Free State, England faced the prospect of another guerilla war, this time in Northern Ireland, with a repeat of all the negative aspects of the official reprisals and terror campaign in Southern Ireland. The British would reap international condemnation and a propaganda disaster by officially condoning force against a Catholic minority. The United States and Canada as well as the rest of the Dominions would be hard-pressed to support such repression. Irish-Americans would exploit the propaganda opportunity to publicize British atrocities in Northern Ireland.

Lloyd George clearly recognized the threat Collins posed and warned Winston Churchill that Collins' activities in Northern Ireland was shifting the focus onto Partition and away from the issues of the Oath and Constitution, the only grounds on which the English could hope to carry public opinion in the eventuality of a break with Dublin.[2]

232

Conservatives in England were restive; chafing at the compromises made by the British delegation to the "Irish murder gang." Any large scale incursion into Ulster by Collins was the fuse that would ignite the powder keg of civil war, only this time in Northern Ireland and quite possibly England itself.

De Valera had distanced himself from any connection with the London peace conference in order to be in position to reject whatever decision emerged from the talks. Without recognition of an Irish Republic by England, de Valera had the *cause célèbre* in which to rally the extremist group in opposition to anything less than complete independence.

In portraying Collins and Griffith as "country bumpkins" outmatched by the world's most talented political leaders, Irish commentators seriously underestimated their abilities and extraordinary achievement of maneuvering the English delegation into compromising on every term that Lloyd George insisted were "non-negotiable and vital" to the survival of the British Empire.

Collins and Griffith compromised on nothing; they were brilliant. The Irish "country bumpkins" negotiated a mutual-defense pact with Canada. Collins stated, "Our immunity can never be challenged without challenging the immunity of Canada. Having the same constitutional status as Canada, a violation of our freedom would be a challenge to the freedom of Canada...No such security would have been reached by [de Valera's] External Association in Document No. 2."[3]

The shadow of a difference between the Free State Treaty's External Association and de Valera's Document No. 2 alternative to the Treaty was the demand by the Irish President that England recognize an Irish Republic first, and then he "might" consider entering into voluntary external association with the Commonwealth nations.

De Valera was relentless in his determination to cloud the real significance of Collins and Griffith's momentous triumph in London, and Irish writers allowed him to get away with it. However, the editors of the *London Morning Post* begrudgingly recognized that Lloyd George and his team had capitulated to the Irish: "Surrender is always a surrender and a betrayal a betrayal and a condonation of crime a participation in the sin of the criminal...The event of yesterday [Treaty signing] is but the culmination of the steady policy and yielding to threats and of intriguing with rebels. It is hailed as a co-triumph. We wish we could join in these very natural but deluded transports...Never before in modern times has a British Government quailed before armed rebellion and organized assassination; acknowledged itself impotent to enforce English law and

233

English justice and totally forsaken the loyal subjects of the King..."[4]

Indicative of the magnificent negotiating skills of Collins and Griffith was conceded by none other than General Henry Wilson, England's highest-ranking military officer in the First World War, the leading proponent of terror against Catholics in Northern Ireland and an advocate of the use of overwhelming force in Southern Ireland to put down the insurrection. Upon publication of the terms of the treaty, Wilson erupted in violent condemnation of it and the Lloyd George government: "'These terms called a Treaty were an abject surrender to murderers. They gave complete independence under the guise of Dominion Home Rule. They handed over Army, police, judiciary, fiscal autonomy, customs, taxation, exemption from war debts, control of agriculture, education, etc...In short, Ireland was gone...' Elsewhere he had spoken '*of a farcical oath of allegiance*' and of the British Empire being doomed."[5] [emphasis added]

Joseph L. C. Clarke, in a letter to *The New York Times*, described, in glowing terms, the extent of Collins and Griffith's monumental triumph: "To bring Lloyd George, Winston Churchill, Hamar Greenwood and the rest from the murderous attitude of the year before to a full, free trust in the Irish people to handle their own Government is colossal work. Collins did it as Arthur Griffith did it. That should be enough. As for the ability Michael Collins has shown, the firmness, the dash, the unceasing push, the moderation, even in his place of power, is delighting and inspiring. Words would not add to the brilliance of his deeds – a statesman's, soldier's, freeman's deeds speak and will speak to the end for themselves."[6]

Cardinal Logue wrote to Bishop Hagan on December 10, 1921, "'I don't think there is a man alive who ever expected that such favorable terms could be squeezed out of the British Government in our time.'"[7]

Lord Birkenhead, a leading member of the British delegation, acknowledged the importance of the concessions that had been made. After signing the treaty, he remarked, "I may have signed my political death-warrant tonight." Collins grimly replied, "I may have signed my actual death-warrant." They were both right.

Lloyd George knew that his concessions had won him more acclaim abroad than at home. "So we made peace with the Irish race. The feud which lasted hundreds of years with one of the most difficult races of the world – how difficult they are, only those who have been fighting them can tell; a feud that was costly and embarrassing to us, a feud that brought no credit, no honor and no strength, has now been closed by an act which is honorable to both sides...No agreement ever arrived at between two peoples has been greeted with so enthusiastic a

Éamon de Valera with his mother Catherine Coll in 1927. De Valera was born in New York in 1882 – the question of his legitimacy plagued him throughout his life. Very little is known about his father, allegedly Juan Vivion de Valera.

Above: De Valera under arrest for his part in the Easter Uprising of 1916. He was released by the British in 1917 after 13 months' imprisonment having never faced a trial.

Below: De Valera speaks from The O'Connell Monument in Ennis. In 1917 he was elected as MP for East Clare but refused to take his seat in the British House of Commons.

During his American tour of 1919-20, de Valera tries to rally support for the Irish Republic.

Above: De Valera meets the Irish-American leaders Judge Daniel Cohalan and John Devoy in New York in 1919.

Below: De Valera addresses a meeting in Los Angeles on his US tour as president of Dáil Éireann.

Above: De Valera is surrounded by supporters on his return to Dublin from the US in 1920.

Below: 17 August 1921: President de Valera (behind the high table on the left of photograph) presides over one of the first sessions of the Second Dáil Éireann.

Arthur Griffith and Éamon de Valera, seen here in 1920.

Above: De Valera (centre) emerges from 10 Downing Street after a meeting with Prime Minister Lloyd George in 1921.

Below: De Valera and Arthur Griffith (both seated), in July 1921, in London for truce talks which ended the Irish War of Independence and set up the Anglo-Irish Treaty negotiations later that year.

Above: 11 October 1921: Irish Minister for Finance, Michael Collins (seated, centre) and Sinn Féin founder Arthur Griffith in London flanked by Sinn Féin representatives (left) Gavin Duffy, and (right) R C Barton at the begining of the Anglo-Irish Treaty negotiations.

Below: Michael Collins signs the Anglo-Irish Treaty. on 6 December 1921. He knew the treaty would not be well received in Ireland. Later that day he would write with prescience, "Early this morning I signed my death warrant". The delegation includes, seated from left, Arthur Griffith, E J Duggan, Michael Collins and Robert Barton. Standing from left are Robert Erskine Childers, Gavan Duffy, and John Chartres.

7 January 1922: The sitting of Dáil Éireann in Dublin which ratified the Anglo-Irish Treaty. Republicans, led by de Valera, refused to accept the authority of the crown and Irish Civil War ensued.

Above: Republican irregulars do battle on the streets of Dublin with Free State forces.

Below: Devastation in Sackville Street, Dublin, during the Irish Civil War (1922-3).

Above: Michael Collins is among the pallbearers carrying Arthur Griffith's coffin in 1922. Griffith is purported to have died of a subarachnoid hemorrhage, caused by the strain of trying to hold together the Irish Free State, but there was no autopsy, and rumors of his poisoning were prevalent.

Below: Michael Collins lies in state in Dublin. Collins was killed on 22 August 1922 in an ambush on the road through Béal na mBláth in County Cork.

Above: First Taoiseach of Éire, Éamon de Valera, takes the salute in Dublin, after finalising the new Irish constitution on 29 December 1937.

Below: Éamon de Valera inspects a guard of honour on O'Connell street in Dublin in 1942. The soldiers seen here wear British style helmets. Prior to 1940 the Irish army wore German style helmets which, coupled with de Valera's neutrality policy and public statements about Hitler, gave the world the impression that Ireland was pro-Nazi.

welcome…In some quarters, they were characterized as a 'humiliation' for Britain and the Empire, but the Dominions of the Crown are not in the habit of rejoicing over acts of humiliation to the Empire…Every Ally sent…congratulations."[8]

The British people were outraged at their delegation's "surrender" to leaders of the "Irish murder gang." They considered the concessions by Lloyd George and his fellow negotiators as a humiliation for Britain and the Empire and took out their wrath at the polls. As testimony to the negotiating skills of Collins and Griffith, the compromises by Lloyd George's team of professional diplomats led to the ousting of every member of the British delegation from political office within one year of the signing of the treaty. Following the general election of November 1922, Lloyd George's Liberal Party went the way of John Redmond's Irish Parliamentary Party and was all but wiped out, receiving less than ten percent of the vote, garnering only 57 seats. The Conservatives stormed back into power with a majority of 70 and a total of 344 out of 599 seats in the House of Commons. Churchill admitted, "The Irish Treaty and its circumstances were unforgivable by the most tenacious elements in the Conservative Party."[9] He should have included the English voters.

So much for de Valera and those Irish writers who claimed that Collins and Griffith were too parochial, politically naïve, and out of their league when it came to negotiating with the world's most experienced statesmen. Unbiased political analysts recognize that these two Irish "country bumpkins" taught England's world-renowned statesmen a lesson in Negotiations 101.

The near universal joy of the Irish people upon the signing of the treaty was soon marred by de Valera's spoiler tactics. It became clear why he had refused to attend the treaty conference. Having assessed de Valera's conduct during the earlier private talks with Lloyd George, both Tim Pat Coogan and Pieras Beaslai concluded that de Valera and Lloyd George had agreed to reject any outcome of the peace conference, whether with or without a treaty. P. S. O'Hegarty also implied a conspiracy emanating from the July truce talks: "de Valera went to see Lloyd George in July and was closeted with him daily for a week. Is anybody so foolish as to believe they were discussing independence? Is anybody so foolish as not to believe that de Valera, at the interviews, ascertained exactly how far England was prepared to go and that when he later ordered Griffith and Collins to go over and negotiate a Treaty, he knew exactly the sort of Treaty they would get?"[10]

Coogan waffled, then supported de Valera's charge of compromise: "Whoever went to London to negotiate with Lloyd George would be forced to compromise and be compromised...de Valera needed time to make certain that he was not that person."[11] Coogan ignored the fact that the only compromises made were by the English delegation and members of the Dáil under the prodding of de Valera.

On December 9, in a stunning declaration to the Irish people, de Valera fired his first salvo against the treaty: "Terms of this agreement are in violent conflict with the wishes of the majority of this nation as expressed freely in the successive elections during the last three years. I feel it my duty to inform you immediately that I cannot recommend the acceptance of this Treaty, either to Dáil Éireann or the country. In this attitude, I am supported by the Ministers of Home Affairs and Defense...The great test of our people has come. Let us face it worthily without bitterness and above all, without recriminations. *There is a definite constitutional way of resolving our political differences – let us not depart from it and let the conduct of the Cabinet in this matter be an example to the whole nation.*"[12] [emphasis added]

De Valera's Cabinet was divided. Collins, Griffith, William Cosgrave, and Robert Barton voted for the treaty, with Stack, Burgess, and de Valera in opposition, resulting in a 4 to 3 majority in favour of the treaty. Upon this rebuff, it was the Irish President's duty either to recommend the treaty to the Dáil or to resign. He did neither, "Concessions to truth and reality were not high on de Valera's agenda for the course of the [treaty] debate...He refused to have the Treaty placed before the Dáil as a Cabinet measure..."[13] de Valera's plot of distancing himself from any decision emanating from the peace talks crystallized as he now insisted that Griffith, as head of the delegation, would have to submit any motion for ratification to the Dáil and take full responsibility for the treaty.

At the initial Dáil session of the treaty debate on December 14, 1921, de Valera repudiated his and the Dáil's acceptance of Lloyd George's conditions for entering into peace negotiations. He also recanted his own exhortations of the previous July and August when he had browbeaten the Dáil deputies into abandoning their demand for recognition of an Irish Republic. It was a stunning reversal of his position.

De Valera renounced the virtual Irish independence offered by the Free State arrangement as he had renounced it at the Republican Convention in America the previous year. "I am against this Treaty because it does not reconcile Irish national aspirations with association with the British Government. I am against this Treaty, not because I am a man of war, but a man of peace. I am against this Treaty because it will not end the centuries of conflict between the two nations of Great Britain and Ireland."[14]

De Valera, contrary to his August declaration admitting that the people did not vote for a republic in previous elections, now claimed: "They [the Dáil deputies] were elected by the Irish people and did the Irish people think they were liars, when they said that they meant to uphold the Republic, which was ratified by the vote of the people three years ago, and was further ratified – expressly ratified – by the vote of the people at the elections last May?"[15] He charged, "If the representatives of the Republic should ask the people of Ireland to do that, which is inconsistent with the Republic, I say they are subverting the Republic..."[16]

"I say it is quite within the competence of the Irish people, if they wished to enter into an association with other peoples, to enter into the British Empire; it is within their competence, if they want to choose the British Monarch as their King, but does this assembly think the Irish people have changed so much within the past year that they now want to get into the British Empire after seven centuries of fighting?"[17]

De Valera mouthed the democratic principle of the majority having the right to decide whether they wanted to enter into an association with England but then he denied the people that right. His catch phrase became his battle cry: "The majority had no right to do wrong." Just how he equated that with democratic principles he never explained. "I am against the Treaty because it does not do the fundamental thing and bring us peace. The Treaty leaves us a country going through a period of internal strife just as the Act of Union did...I am against it because it is inconsistent with our position, because if we are to say the Irish people don't mean it, then they should have told us they didn't mean it... Therefore, I am once more asking you to reject the Treaty for two main reasons: that as every Deputy knows, it is absolutely inconsistent with our position; it gives away Irish independence; it brings us into the British Empire; it acknowledges the head of the British Empire, not merely as the head of an association but as the direct Monarch of Ireland as the source of executive authority in Ireland."[18]

De Valera's claim in December that the people had voted for an Irish Republic contradicted his August 16 admission during that Dáil session when he declared: "the unmistakable answer given by the people...was (not) for a form of government [Republic] as such, because we are not Republican doctrinaires, but it was for Irish freedom and independence..."[19] According to T. Ryle Dwyer, de Valera, in his determination to stampede the Dáil into acceptance of Lloyd George's conditions in August, claimed: "The party was not irrevocably committed to a republic... 'We do not wish to bind the people to any form of government...' He nevertheless emphasized that he was not a doctrinaire republican; He was not duty-bound to any form of government; 'So long as it was an Irish government, I would not put a word against it.'"[20]

Griffith declared that the election results expressed protest, not prescription. "The people elected them [Dáil deputies] in 1918 to get rid of the Parliamentary Party and they elected them in 1921 as a gesture of defiance to the policy of the Black and Tans."[21] Collins also contended that it was for Irish freedom and not for an Irish Republic that the centuries-long battle had been fought. "The Irish struggle has always been for freedom – freedom from English occupation, from English interference, from English domination – not freedom with any particular label to it...But it was freedom we sought, not the name of the form of government we should adopt...not the ultimate freedom which all nations hope for and struggle for, but freedom to achieve that end... Under the Treaty, Ireland is about to become a fully constituted nation."[22]

Coogan noted the Irish President's disregard for Parliamentary procedure during the treaty debate: "de Valera...attempted to dominate the proceedings both by frequent interruptions and by speaking at wearisome length. The number of pages in the Dáil records taken up by his contributions is almost double that of Collins and Griffith combined, a total of 39 pages for his to 20 of theirs. *He made 250 interruptions, relying on his prestige to ride roughshod over the procedures of debate...*"[23] [emphasis added] On average, de Valera interrupted speakers as many as 20 times per session.

De Valera set his own rules and ignored the agenda in his efforts to defeat the treaty. He put on an exhibition of feigned petulance and disruption rarely seen in parliamentary debate. From the opening session, in an effort to put Collins and Griffith in the Dock, he accused them of exceeding their powers by signing the document. He falsely charged that they had violated "an understanding between the Plenipotentiaries and himself that the complete text of the draft treaty about to be signed would be submitted to him before signing – an understanding which was not observed."[24]

Collins and Griffith disputed the charge. They noted that the delegation recommended the treaty over their signatures but that it was up to the Dáil to ratify or reject. "Following another hour of confused talk, de Valera, at least half the time, interrupted everybody, jumping up to speak at every point raised, the public assembly mercifully concluded with a decision to go into private session."[25]

De Valera continued interrupting and heckling during the private session, hypocritically claiming that he had been betrayed. O'Hegarty countered: "On the contrary, it was de Valera who was the betrayer. He knew when he parlayed with Lloyd George in July that he was breaking the people's will to war and making it impossible for the Volunteers to renew the war with popular support...When Collins and Griffith had shouldered the responsibility which their unexpected victory had thrust on Sinn Féin, and returned with the Treaty de Valera had sent them over to sign, he bared his teeth and rent them."[26]

O'Hegarty was one of the few Irish writers who understood the remarkable accomplishment of Collins and Griffith. "If de Valera had recognized the Treaty for the magnificent achievement...which it has proved to be, and had used his great influence on Burgess and Stack to make them see it...There would have been no split. *There was nobody in the anti-Treaty ranks that could have made a split, nobody but de Valera. And de Valera made it, not the split alone, but the Civil War that followed it."*[27] [emphasis added] Once again, Irish writers failed to discern a pattern of behaviour in de Valera's consistently divisive record, from the split in Sinn Féin at the Ard Fheis Convention in 1917 to the split with the FOIF in America the previous year.

According to O'Hegarty: "When Collins and Griffith got it [the Treaty], de Valera stabbed them in the back by a pompous announcement that he had 'recalled' the delegates, although they were halfway home. For all the bloodshed and suffering, de Valera must be held responsible...But it was also certain that it was the moral support and the prestige, which de Valera as President gave [to the extremists] which created the anti-Treaty movement..."[28]

Sean Milroy, who had escaped from Lincoln Jail with de Valera was scathing in his criticism. "I say that the man who asks the Irish nation to go to war and plunge the hopes of the nation into distress and chaos on the difference between these two documents [Document No.2 and the Treaty]...will stand condemned at the bar of history as having committed one of the most gigantic blunders Ireland has known."[29]

Beaslai was bitterly disappointed: "It was with pain that some of us realized that de Valera was a very much smaller man, both in character and intellect, than we had taken him to be. He seemed incapable of rising to the height of the crisis in the country's history. In his thousand and one utterances, there was not one sign of recognition of the practical realities of the situation. Abstract formulas, pedantic word splitting and attempts to score points in debate, occupied the time of the Dáil and the attention of the country throughout these weary days. De Valera spoke most of the time, ignoring agenda and procedure, interrupted, and heckled most of the opposing speakers, raised a thousand petty debating points, changing his position from day to day, but without rising to the heights of a statesmanlike utterance or a generous gesture. All the generous gestures, all the kindly words and ready concessions by Collins and Griffith were only treated as weaknesses to be taken advantage of."[30]

Author John Whelan, a typical de Valera apologist, ignored facts: "For de Valera [the Dáil Debate] was a bitter experience. He is not a man to suffer fools gladly and he had to sit there, in silence, day after day, listening to much honest but nonetheless, tiresome folly."[31]

During the discussion of Lloyd George's final draft treaty at the December 3 cabinet session, war or peace hinged on the language of the oath to be taken. In more than seven hours of sometimes acrimonious debate, de Valera did not insist on recognition of an independent Republic, nor did he instruct the delegation as they left to return to London that the draft was unacceptable or "in violent conflict" with the wishes of the people. He uttered not a word that he would not accept the treaty without recognition of an Irish Republic. The Irish President never explained why the draft treaty was acceptable to him on December 3 and so repugnant on December 6. De Valera steered a deliberate collision course which could only lead to chaos.

Collins questioned the Dáil deputies during the debate on the Treaty: "Why were those who were now finding fault did not raise objections when the delegation was first chosen or before they went to London on the terms set out in Lloyd George's letter? The communications of September 29, 1921, from Lloyd George, made it clear that they were going into conference, not on the recognition of the Irish Republic...What I want to make clear is that it was the acceptance of the invitation that formed the compromise...As one of the signatories of the document, I naturally recommend its acceptance...*In my opinion, it gives us freedom, not the ultimate freedom that all nations desire and develop to, but the freedom to achieve it.*"[32] [emphasis added] Collins added, "If we all stood on the recognition of the Irish Republic as a prelude to any conference, we could very easily have said so, and there would have been no Conference."[33]

Continuing, he said: "The world considered England's magnanimous gesture a fair peace and furthermore, England does hold, rightly or wrongly, that she cannot afford to concede us our full Republican ideal; that this would break up her Commonwealth, that it would destroy her security and prestige if she were to acquiesce in a forcible breaking away, which would show her so-called Empire to be an intolerable entity and herself so feeble as to be unable to prevent it."[34]

Coogan, after claiming Collins and Griffith had compromised, contradicted himself: "It is difficult, if not impossible to quarrel with Collins' judgment that the communication of September 29, 1921, from Lloyd George made it clear that they were going into conference not on the recognition of the Irish Republic...It was the acceptance of the invitation that formed the compromise."[35]

De Valera had pressed the Dáil deputies, threatening that, unless they accepted Lloyd George's terms, they would share the fate of the American Indians. But after they did his bidding, de Valera became a fanatical Republican, demanding recognition of an Irish Republic or else a resumption of the war. In America, he had espoused "self-determination: until the Republican presidential convention in June 1920, when he became an avid proponent of an Irish Republic. His repeated seesawing fragmented support and resulted in massive benefit to Britain. Why so many commentators overlooked his deliberate and sustained obstruction of Ireland's interests is beyond comprehension.

Patrick McCartan, de Valera's stooge in America, called on the Irish President to outline his alternative policy to rejection of the Treaty. De Valera replied: "...He would carry on as before and forget that this Treaty has come. Once the Irish people understood its implications, he predicted they would not stand for it. When that Treaty is worked out in legislative form and put before them, then they will know what they have got."[36]

The only consistency to de Valera's actions was his inconsistencies that invariably led to English triumphs. O'Hegarty approached the truth of this, but he could not face the reality of de Valera's treason: "*Indeed, there were many who believed the whole thing was arranged for England's benefit.*"[37] [emphasis added] Irish writers hinted that the effect of de Valera's opposition to the Treaty was doing England's work but never once did the word treason flow from their pens when it came to the Irish President. Conversely, many writers were quick to line up behind de Valera and paint Collins and Griffith as traitors.

In Britain, Lloyd George's delegation was accused of caving in under the "duress" of Collins' threats while de Valera and his Republican supporters claimed that it was Collins and Griffith who surrendered under the "duress" of Lloyd George's threats. Collins responded: "The English Die-hards said to Mr. Lloyd George and his Cabinet, 'You have surrendered.' Our own Die-hards said to us, 'You have surrendered.' There is a simple test. Those who are left in possession of the battlefield have won."[38]

In response to charges that he and the Delegation broke down under the duress of Lloyd George's threats, Collins rose before the assembled Dáil, with jaw set and steely eyes and said, in measured tones: "'...It has been suggested that the Delegation broke down before the first bit of English bluff.' Then, squaring his shoulders and looking around the assembly, with a characteristic shake of his head, went on; 'I would remind the Deputy who used that expression that the English put up quite a good bluff for the last five years here and I did not break down before that bluff.'"[39]

"I know I have been called a traitor. If I am a traitor let the Irish people decide it, and if there is any man who acts towards me as a traitor, I am prepared to meet him anywhere, any time, now as in the past."[40] The word "traitor," however, never left an Irish writer's pen when it came to de Valera.

Without a whisper of a constructive suggestion during the entire London negotiation passing his lips, but in the course of the treaty debate, de Valera now unveiled his Document No. 2 proposal calling for External Association with England, subject to Britain first recognizing an Irish Republic. When it was pointed out that Document, No. 2 was almost identical with the Treaty, de Valera then insisted that it be considered confidential and not released to the public in order for him to present Document No. 3.

Griffith was exasperated: "The President does not wish this document [No. 2] to be read. What am I to do? What am I to say? Am I to keep my mouth shut and let the Irish people think about this uncompromising rock of the Republic?"[41] Griffith, in pointing out the shadow of a difference between Document No. 2 and the Treaty, roared: "...Does all this quibble of words – because it is merely a quibble of words – mean that Ireland is asked to throw away this Treaty and go back to war? So far as my power or voice extends, not one young Irishman's life shall be lost on that quibble."[42]

De Valera called for the rejection of the Treaty and its concomitant return to the conflict with England solely over his contention that "consistency" was the major obstacle to his acceptance of the Treaty: "...There is very little (difference) in practice but there is that big thing that you are consistent and that you recognize yourself as a separate independent State and you associate in an honorable manner with another group. I say that small differences make all the difference. This fight lasted all through the centuries and I would be willing to win that little sentimental thing that would satisfy the aspirations of the country."[43]

He conceded: "...there was only a small difference between the Treaty and what he would accept...There are differences that may be regarded as mere shadows, but they are more than shadows," he said. "'The British considered such things important. If they are mere shadows, why should the British be grasping for shadows and not we?' he asked. 'I wanted to clear these shadows because they meant an awful lot.'"[44]

According to Beaslai: "...Document No. 2, if agreed to, would have represented a voluntary offer from Dáil Éireann, in which all our claim to be an independent Republic was abandoned. To ask men to face death in defense of Irish independence seemed a comparatively simple proposition; but to ask them to fight for what de Valera called the difference between 'internal' and 'external association' with the British Empire, seemed a *reductio ad absurdum.*"[45]

Dwyer recognized the similarity between de Valera's disastrous American campaign and his equally destructive Irish campaign. Commenting on Document No. 2: "...He would have been as foolhardy as he was naïve if he really believed that the propaganda campaign advocated by him had any more chance of success than the pathetic failure of his comparatively similar effort to win over the American electorate in 1920 after the Chicago debacle."[46]

Now "de Valera issued a 'Proclamation' to the Irish people: 'Do not enter upon a compact, which in your hearts you know can never be kept in sincerity and truth...Be bold enough to say "No" to those who ask you to misrepresent yourselves.'"[47]

De Valera outdid Lord Castlereagh, who browbeat, and intimidated Protestant legislators into sacrificing Irish independence by legislating their country out of existence into an Act of Union under Britain. In 1800, Irish Legislators sold their country for the tangibles of land, money, and titles, while the 1921 anti-treaty faction was more odious and sold their country on the altar of egotism and cowardice. They flaunted their counterfeit Republican credentials, vowing to die before they would sign an equally imaginary oath of allegiance to the Crown. Griffith exclaimed: "What damnable hypocrisy! I have in hand seven different forms of oath already taken to the King of England by members of this Dáil...For such hypocrisy, you will sacrifice the gallant lives of our young men?"[48]

On August 23, 1920, "de Valera went so far as to admit that he was not excluding the possibility of any kind of settlement with Britain. Before allowing his name to go forward for re-election as President, *he warned the Dáil that he did not consider the republican oath bound him to any particular form of government* [emphasis added]. Rather, he stressed that he saw the oath as a commitment to do what he thought best for the Irish people..."[49]

The only pledge of allegiance in the treaty was to the Free State Constitution. The promise of fidelity to the Crown in its role as part of the treaty settlement was twisted into a direct oath to the Crown by de Valera while Unionists decried it as a repudiation of the monarchy. The oath was a macabre joke in both England and Ireland.

According to de Valera's convoluted interpretation, since the Free State had come into being through a treaty with England, and had to be ratified by the British Parliament and signed by the King, any oath of allegiance to the Free State Constitution was, in effect, an oath of allegiance to the Crown. By these fuzzy means, de Valera was able to wreak havoc.

The treaty oath was as follows: "I do... solemnly swear *true faith and allegiance to the Constitution of the Irish Free State* as by law established and that I will be *faithful to H.M. King George V*, his heirs and successors by law, in virtue of the common citizenship of Ireland with Great Britain and her adherence to and membership of the group of nations forming the British Commonwealth of Nations." [emphasis added]

The Irish President declared: "The oath contained in the Treaty actually and unequivocally binds the taker to allegiance to the English King...If the Irish side accepted a constitution drawn up in the name of the British King, it would be tantamount to acknowledging the absolute authority of the British Parliament. In theory, therefore, under the terms of the Treaty, the British Parliament would, in the name of the King, be legally entitled to interfere in Irish affairs."[50] Under Document No. 2, with its impossible demand for recognition of an Irish Republic by the English, he claimed: "Ireland would be clearly...a state deriving its authority to govern from its own people rather than from some outside agency like the British Parliament."[51] He also neglected to mention his Document No. 2 would also have to be ratified by the King of England.

John MacNeill, in a speech before the Dáil, demolished de Valera's argument by outlining "very strongly that the oath contained no declaration of allegiance to the King of England – no allegiance, except to the Irish State..."[52]

Lloyd George had agreed to modify the oath to Irish specifications, but there had to be some illusion of an appearance of an oath so that the English people could swallow it without choking on their pride. Without the pretense of an oath, the English could not agree to a treaty.

In the early months of 1922, Collins and Griffith pleaded with de

Valera and the counterfeit Republicans claiming that the declaration to be faithful to the King meant nothing more than a hollow political formality. De Valera scorned their pleas for moderation and continued his dash to anarchy. Author Michael Tierney wrote: "The tragedy for both countries, but most of all for Ireland, was that her venerated leader insisted, with merciless and unyielding pedantry, on treating the formulas as the reality and with endless sophistry tried to make the people believe that the realities were unreal."[53] From 1921 to 1927, de Valera continued to insist that the question of the oath was the major difficulty with the Free State Treaty. The vacuity of de Valera's objections was revealed when, after arguing in 1922 that opposition was a matter of principle, he and his followers in 1927 signed the very same oath accepting Collins argument that it was merely a hollow political formula.

De Valera was again inconsistent when it came to Dominion status. In a conversation with the South African Premier, Jan Christian Smuts on July 5, 1921, the week before his secret truce sessions with Lloyd George, de Valera embraced the concept of an Ireland Dominion: *"If the status of Dominion rule is offered, I will use all our machinery to get the Irish people to accept it."*[54] [emphasis added]

Dwyer wrote, prior to the Treaty: "de Valera left little doubt that the real status of the Dominions would be acceptable to Ireland, seeing that even a staunch imperialist like Bonar Law, the leader of the British Conservative Party, had admitted that the Dominions 'had the right to decide their own destinies.'"[55] In an article in the *Irish Bulletin*, of August 10, 1921, Bonar Law stated: "If the self-governing Dominions, Australia and Canada, choose tomorrow to say, 'We will no longer remain a part of the British Empire,' we would not try to force them. Dominion Home Rule means the right to decide their own destinies."

De Valera asserted: "'The British Dominions have had conceded to them all the rights that Irish Republicans demand. It is obvious that if these rights were not being denied to us, we would not be engaged in the present struggle...In fact,' he contended, 'we are thoroughly sane and reasonable people, not a coterie of political doctrinaires or even party politicians, Republican or other.'"[56]

However, immediately after the treaty was signed, de Valera rejected Dominion status and demanded England recognize an Irish Republic or face war. As a result of the Irish President's rejection of England's "magnanimous" gesture of Dominion status and his threat of war, Ireland reaped worldwide condemnation. Northern Ireland remained British, the Southern Irish were considered irreconcilable and incapable of self-government. Most importantly, Anglo-American relations soared and Irish-American relations plummeted just as Lloyd George had predicted.

With an intuitive grasp of political realities, Collins correctly prophesized, "Britain will acquiesce in the ultimate separation of her units – ourselves among them – by a process of natural evolution, which will neither expose nor endanger the central state. So we shall do well to have a little patience. Have we not already gained great things for Ireland? The Treaty gives us the substance of independence and must inevitably lead, sooner or later, to the complete fulfillment of our national aspirations."[57]

De Valera predicted nothing but dire consequences if the Irish people accepted the treaty. In his headlong rush to civil war, de Valera hurled one contradictory charge after another claiming that under the treaty the Free State would be subject to British control, that allegiance to an Irish Constitution meant allegiance to the King, and that Irish soldiers would merely be British Crown forces in green uniforms. None of his doom and gloom predictions concerning the treaty ever came to pass. Coogan wrote, "Ironically, the future would show de Valera to be the Irish leader who did most to prove that Collins was right..."[58]

Within two years, the first of several Imperial Conferences laid the groundwork for complete independence of not only Ireland but of all the Commonwealth nations. The path to total independence forged by the Imperial Conferences of the 1920s led directly to the enactment of the *1931 Statute of Westminster*, almost ten years to the day the Free State Treaty was signed. This statute gave Ireland the right to declare whatever form of government, including a Republic, it desired. This Statute was ratified by all the Dominions as well as Britain. Churchill adamantly opposed the extension of those rights to Ireland, but, thanks to Collins and Griffith's mutual defense pact, Canada demanded that Ireland be included. Curiously, de Valera, despite his alleged standing on the "Rock of the Republic," refused to declare an Irish Republic throughout his decades-long leadership.

Collins clearly set forth the reality of the Irish struggle for freedom with England: "We did make it very difficult for the enemy to govern us. He was thoroughly alarmed and only maintained a precarious hold by sheer violence, which he explained to the world as 'restoring law and order.' Our people were being hunted and tortured, imprisoned and shot and hanged. Wholesale burning and merciless havoc were the daily routine of a Reign of Terror of which Englishmen yet unborn will surely be ashamed..."[59]

He cited the freedoms provided for under the Treaty: "Our soldiers, our judges, our ministers will be the soldiers, judges and ministers of the Irish Free State. We can send our own ambassadors to Washington, to Paris, to the Vatican; we can have our representatives on the League of Nations...But, we cannot do it if we are to fight among ourselves as to whether it is to be called Saorstat [Free State] or Phoblacht [Republic]."[60] Continuing, Collins said: "I say the Treaty has brought Ireland to the last oasis, beyond which there is but an easy march to go. And I maintain we have earned the right to rest for a while in order to renew the nation's strength and restore our early vigor."[61] He confessed that he never thought he'd live to see the Black and Tans, the Royal Irish Constabulary, the Khaki hordes of English troops, as well as every British official departing the shores of Ireland: "How could I ever have expected to see Dublin Castle itself – that dread Bastille of Ireland – formally surrendered into my hands by the Lord Lieutenant in the brocade-hung Council Chamber on my producing a copy of the London Treaty?...The future rests entirely with ourselves; a new order of things is facing us."[62]

During the First World War, Britain had raised an army that was greater than the entire population of Ireland that made de Valera's call for resumption of the war ridiculous. The Irish Republican Army was practically defenseless against England's vast armament resources in men, land, sea, and air. Collins said: "The claim that we had beaten England to her knees was pathetically absurd."[63]

Collins pleaded for unity in the national interests. He called for constitutional opposition rather than the chaos de Valera was determined to unleash. "We must be Irish first and last and Republicans or Free Staters only within the limits which leave Ireland strong, united and free...the revolutionary objects of Sinn Féin will never be attained while political thorns are strewn in the people's path to replace the thorns of another day...These people of ours must no longer live the life of beasts, as they still do in the West. We have a chance of ending our city slums and of clearing away the shameful hovels in our country places."[64]

Collins also attested that the treaty "gives us all that we want – prosperity and happy lives in our own country; good homes to live in, sound Irish education for every boy and girl in a new Ireland, of which, by our love and labor, we can soon make a land where all can dwell in self-respect and joy."[65]

De Valera and his followers were unmoved by Collins's pleas. Nor would they accept Griffith's common sense solution of allowing the people to decide the issue in a peaceful election. Griffith said: "We have justly blamed England in the past for the disappearance of our national language and national culture. We have rightly blamed England for the fertile lands let run to waste, for the empty harbors, for the decayed industries, for the emigrant ship and the workhouse. We have truthfully pointed to a country in which the most impressive buildings were jails, barracks, and poorhouses as the proof of English tyranny."[66] In future, he said, the Irish would not be able to blame the English for their failure to govern themselves. Referring to the Irish national pastime of martyrdom, he said it was time for Irishmen to live for Ireland. "On the day when such a peace comes, something will have happened which has not happened in many centuries – Ireland will have lost her only enemy and England will have gained a friend."[67]

As the treaty debate lurched to its final stages in the first week of January 1922, de Valera was facing defeat. At a private session of the Dáil, he slammed his fist on the desk and shouted: "I'll resign. I won't stand for this for a moment."[68] During the following public meeting, he tendered his resignation in an attempt to derail the vote on the treaty onto the side issue of his popularity. He believed the weight of his prestige would carry him through to reelection and rejection of the treaty.

The January 6, 1922 edition of *The New York Times* printed a withering editorial critical of the Irish President over his threat to resign: "Apparently de Valera essayed a Napoleonic or Cromwellian stroke in resigning, at the same time that he demanded re-election with all power placed in his hands; but when this failed, he talked and acted like an hysterical schoolgirl. Whatever happens in Ireland, de Valera seems to have hopelessly discredited himself as a leader. "Narrow, obstinate, visionary and obviously vain, he has now, in his representative capacity, wrought immense harm to the Ireland of his professed entire devotion."

Cries of drawing a red herring across the vote on the treaty were hurled at de Valera. Collins and Griffith questioned the Irish President's motive and demanded that the motion before the assembly be dealt with first. Griffith argued: "If the vote is adverse to us, well and good. If it is adverse to the President, he can do what he suggests to do. Why we should be stopped in the middle of this discussion and a vote taken on the personality of President de Valera, I don't understand and I don't think my countrymen will understand it."[69]

Faced with mounting charges of political chicanery, de Valera withdrew his resignation on condition that a straight vote be taken within forty-eight hours. Griffith agreed. In retracting, he accused others of being guilty of his own tactics. Echoing Machiavelli's tenet: "Everybody knows how laudable it is in a prince to keep his faith and to be an honest man and not a trickster," de Valera said: "It is because I am straight that I meet crookedness with straight dealing always, and I have beaten crookedness with straight dealing."[70]

The Irish President lamented: "I am sick and tired of politics – so sick, that no matter what happens, I would go back into private life...I detest trickery...and I don't want to pull a red herring across the track."[71] Continuing, he said, "...There is no unity; there is disruption, division, disloyalty. Choose now whom you will have – the alternative proposals I have placed before you or these men with their sham that betrays the will of our nation."[72]

The Dáil Deputies had the right and responsibility to ratify or reject the Treaty but evaded, equivocated and extricated themselves to avoid their duty to the people they represented by calling for a referendum on the Treaty. O'Hegarty wrote, "The whole debate was an exposure of the vanity and incompetence of Dáil members and of their political irresponsibility."[73]

The members of the British House of Commons were made of sterner stuff than their Irish counterparts when they ratified the Treaty without resorting to a plebiscite. The British people, in contrast to the Irish, rather than institute a civil war over the treaty, voiced their constitutional displeasure at the polls, all but obliterating the Liberal Party. Lloyd George acknowledged the accountability of the English Parliament in squarely facing the issue of the Treaty: "The responsibility of Parliament was even greater than that of the Government [Treaty Delegation] itself. We could negotiate, advise, and recommend, but Parliament could protract all these dangers and with them this deadly feud into an uncertain future. So the decision was in all ways a fateful one in the history of the British Empire."[74]

Canon Doyle, parish priest and friend, in a letter to James O'Mara on December 23, 1921, recognized the evil de Valera let loose in Ireland and the benefit to England and Northern Ireland: "The enemy in England and Belfast must be gloating over the confusion in our ranks... I would gladly go up to Dublin but I could not stand it, to see our members of the Dáil speechifying against each other in this fashion and giving such cause of rejoicing to the Orangemen [Unionists of Northern Ireland] and Freemasons of England..."[75]

Owen Duffy, IRA liaison officer in Northern Ireland, questioned: "Why more young lives should be sacrificed to attain in any way what could be got through the Treaty. He spoke of terrible atrocities done by Orangemen in Ulster, of eyes, tongues cut out, and sticks thrust down throats. Whom he asked would take the responsibility of handing the Ulster Catholics back to their tormentors... There are 40 brave men awaiting the hangman's rope... He said that if the Treaty were not ratified... political chaos would mean indiscipline and disaffection. If the Treaty were ratified... she [Ireland] could have a volunteer army which, in courage and discipline, would be a model to the world."[76]

The Irish President and his counterfeit Republicans remained obdurate. De Valera's rejection of the treaty was on such specious grounds that a reasonable assumption can be made that it was obviously his intention to prevent Collins from coming to the aid of the Catholics in Northern Ireland.

During the treaty debate, Erskine Childers rose and, "contrary to all rules of debate, proceeded to criticize Griffith's statement. It was pointed out that he was out of order, but he persisted. There was something particularly irritating in the spectacle of this English ex-officer, who had spent his life in the service of England and English Imperialism, heckling and baiting the devoted Griffith, with his lifelong record of unselfish slaving in the cause of Ireland – answering Griffith's moving appeal with carping criticism. Griffith, usually so stolid and unemotional, lost his patience. He rose, like a sleeping lion roused and declared: 'Before this proceeds any further, I want to say that President de Valera made a statement – a generous Irishman's statement – and I replied. I will not reply to any Englishmen in this Dáil' – a remark that evoked loud applause. Childers asked: 'What has my nationality got to do with it?' and Griffith repeated, banging the table – 'I will not reply to any damned Englishman in this assembly.'"[77] De Valera remained mute during the exchange.

On Saturday, January 7, 1922, the final day of the treaty debate, Burgess confirmed his lack of temperament and intellectual capacity for the critical position of Minister of Defense. Instead of addressing his comments to the treaty question and Irish military capability in the event of a resumption of the war, he indulged in a mean-spirited personal attack on Collins and criticism of Griffith. He set forth the proposition: "The Plenipotentiaries, having done their duty in recommending the Treaty, should refrain from voting on it. If Mr. Griffith falls in with this suggestion, his name will live forever in Ireland."[78]

The Minister of Defense then engaged in a harangue of personal maliciousness directed at Collins. Burgess believed that Collins' charge that bullies were intimidating people was directed at him: "'Possibly, he [Collins] may have referred to me as being one of them. In the ordinary way, I would take exception and offense at such a term being applied to me. But the amount of offense that I would take at it could be measured by the respect or esteem that I had for the character of the person who made the charge. In this particular instance, I take no offense whatever.'

The calculated bitterness of this utterance astonished many of his hearers."[79]

"There was a general feeling of pain and shame at such a crude exhibition of personal jealousy on the part of one of our leaders at this great national crisis."[80] Burgess' vitriolic comments revealed a paranoiac jealousy of Collins. He charged: "The Press had made Collins a romantic figure, a mystical character," which Burgess claimed he was not and said: "Collins was responsible for the romanticizing of his [own] exploits." He scoffed at Griffith's characterizing Collins as "the man who won the war."

He continued to rail that Collins had been painted as Commander-in-Chief of the Army, a position held by Burgess himself. Beaslai noted: "Burgess' diatribe was delivered in tones of extraordinary bitterness, and was persisted in despite protests from many parts of the House... Throughout this personal and irrelevant attack on Collins from the Ministerial benches, de Valera was silent, without uttering a word of protest..."[81]

In reply to de Valera and Burgess' charges, Griffith said: "It has been stated here that the man who made this position, the man who won the war – Michael Collins – compromised Ireland's rights. *In the letters that preceded the negotiations not once was a demand made for recognition of the Irish Republic.* [emphasis added] If it had been made we knew it would have been refused. We went there to see how to reconcile the two positions and I hold we have done it." Griffith's voice rang loud and clear: "If they [Collins and Griffith] were to get a Republic and nothing else, the thing could have been dismissed in six lines by writing to the Premier [Lloyd George] and telling him that they would meet him on the condition that he recognize an Irish Republic...to attack us on the ground that we went to get a Republic and nothing else is a false and maligning ground."[82]

Calling attention to the fact that it was the first treaty signed on a basis of equality between England and Ireland since 1172, Griffith said: "We have come back from London with that Treaty – Saorstat na hÉireann recognized – the Free State of Ireland. We have brought back the flag; we have brought back the evacuation of Ireland after 700 years by British troops and the formation of an Irish Army. We have brought back to Ireland her full rights and powers of fiscal control. We have brought back to Ireland equality with England, equality with all nations that form that Commonwealth and an equal voice in the direction of foreign affairs in peace and war."[83] Regarding de Valera's charge that the treaty was a "final settlement," Griffith roared, "It is no more a final settlement than we are the final generation on the face of the earth."[84]

The final chapter in this sorry affair concluded with Griffith's closing remarks: "One other reference will I make to what the Minister of Defense [Burgess] had said. He referred to what I remarked about Michael Collins that he was the man who won the war. I said it and I say it again; he was the man who made the situation. He was the man, and nobody knows better than I do, how, during a year and a half, he worked from six in the morning until two next morning. He was the man whose matchless energy, whose indomitable will, carried Ireland through the terrible crisis. Though I have not now and never had, any ambition about either political affairs or history, if my name is to go down in history, I want it to be associated with the name of Michael Collins...Michael Collins was the man who fought the Black and Tan terror until England was forced to offer terms."[85]

Under parliamentary rules, Griffith was scheduled to have the last word on the treaty but de Valera, however, refused to abide by any procedure and jumped to his feet after Griffith's conclusion and shouted: "'Before you take a vote, I want to enter my last protest – that document will rise in judgment against the men who say there is only a shadow of a difference' – Collins cut him off. 'Let the Irish nation judge us now and for future years.'"[86]

On Saturday, January 7, 1922, Arthur Griffith proposed: "that Dáil Éireann approves the Treaty between Great Britain and Ireland signed in London on December 6, 1921," and, by a vote of 64 to 57, the Dáil ratified the treaty.

At the January 9, 1922 Dáil session, de Valera resigned. Mrs. Thomas Clarke made a motion to elect Éamon de Valera President of the Irish Republic. Collins warned the Dáil Deputies: "If you elect President de Valera President of the Irish Republic, I have no objection whatever to it; but let me say this much, everybody will regard us as being simply a laughing stock..."[87] de Valera was defeated 60 votes to 58.

De Valera continued his heckling and demanded whether Griffith intended to occupy the position as "President of the Republic" if elected. Griffith barked that he didn't give a rap about words: "I will, if elected, occupy the same position until the Irish people have an opportunity of deciding for themselves."[88]

Caught off guard, de Valera accepted Griffith's answer and said he would remain in the House during the election. After a moment's thought, however, de Valera abruptly leapt to his feet and charged that Griffith's election was a subversion of the Irish Republic. He repeated his American tactics and stormed out of the assembly, calling on his followers to set up not a constitutional opposition party to defeat the treaty, but an opposition government with its own militia bent on the violent destruction of the Free State. He was determined to create havoc in Southern Ireland, but for what purpose?

De Valera and his followers marched out of the Dáil chambers chanting "Follow the President!" As they filed out, "Collins rose in his seat and called in a voice of thunder: 'Aye! Go on! Deserters all! But we will call on the people of Ireland to rally to us. Deserters from the Irish nation in her hour of need! But we will stand by her.'"[89] Griffith was then unanimously elected President. He immediately named his cabinet of Michael Collins, George Gavan Duffy, Eamonn Duggan, W. T. Cosgrave, Kevin O'Higgins, and Richard Mulcahy.

The "Master of Inconsistency" then reappeared for the afternoon session and assured Griffith that they would not throw roadblocks in the way of his administration. Griffith responded: "All we ask is that we will not be obstructed until we can go to the Irish people and give them the Free State and let them decide. That is the only policy I have..."[90]

In a January 9, 1922 editorial, *The Evening Herald*, stated: "*It is regrettable that Mr. De Valera, thereby running counter to every democratic principle* [emphasis added], should assert that the Republic still goes on until the nation had disestablished it. By the only constitutional means at its disposal, the nation has approved the act of the Plenipotentiaries in signing the peace Treaty..."[91]

The debate on the Free State Treaty began on December 14, 1921, and the conclusion of this month-long deliberation completed one of the sorriest episodes in seven and a half centuries of Irish misery, racked by traitors, informers, and spies.

According to Beaslai: "What we were asked to do was to place the control of Dáil Éireann, finance, the Army and all other resources at the disposal of a minority party, which, on its own admission, was not only a minority in the Dáil but a small minority of the people of Ireland..."[92]

In June, 1922, after the Irish people overwhelmingly approved the Treaty by a three-to-one margin in a referendum, de Valera unleashed the Republican extremists against their own people proclaiming, "The majority had no right to do wrong." In any event, he wasn't about to allow a peaceful transition to a Free State government, which posed such danger to Northern Ireland and to Britain. No one questioned why de Valera was so determined on civil war rather than a constitutional challenge.

O'Hegarty charged: "De Valera's poison gas was working. He had let the bitterness loose. He had let the guns loose. He placed his whole moral force at the disposal of the men who were working to prevent a plebiscite, to prevent any sort of a vote on the Treaty, and who were prepared to go to any lengths against it...Mr. De Valera's treachery it was which turned victory into Dead Sea fruit, which made the bitterness and the Civil War...The opposition to the Treaty was wholly dishonest. It had been made plain to the Deputies by de Valera, in public and private sessions, that they were negotiating for terms and that he himself would not be bound rigidly by the oath to the Republic. The time to overthrow the Treaty was before it had been signed... [the counterfeit Republican Deputies] knew perfectly well they were abandoning the Republic."[93]

De Valera declared his devotion to the imaginary Republic. "There is one thing I want to say, I want it to go to the country and to the world, and it is this; the Irish people established a Republic. This [acceptance of the Treaty] is simply approval of a certain resolution. The Republic can only be disestablished by the Irish people. Therefore, until such time as the Irish people, in regular manner, disestablish it, this Republic goes on."[94]

O'Hegarty, however, had a different opinion:

"...The most average intelligence had only to devote five minutes' thought to the...de Valera correspondence [accepting Lloyd George's proposals for a peace conference] to see that the [Treaty] negotiations would be on the implicit basis of 'no Republic'... Those Deputies, in fact, were those who had watched...during the summer and winter of 1921, the Republic being thrown overboard...They had been seduced by de Valera or by their own moral cowardice, into the public hypocrisy, which they have maintained... They all pretended to be standing on the high heroic principle of 'no compromise.' They had, and have, no right whatever to call themselves Republicans. They are only pseudo-Republicans [Counterfeit Republicans]... De Valera...is responsible for all the blood and bitterness of the Civil War."[95]

Notes

1. Ryan, Desmond, Unique Dictator, Arthur Barker, London, 1936, p. 163
2. Coogan, Tim Pat, *Michael Collins, A Biography*, Arrow Books, 1991, p. 366
3. Collins, Michael, *The Path to Freedom*, Roberts Rinehart 1996, p. 92
4. *New York Times*, 12/7/1921, 2:3
5. O'Broin, Leon, *Wylie, W. E. and the Irish Revolution*, Macmillan, 1989, p. 139
6. *New York Times*, 8/22/1923, VII 8:4
7. Keogh, Dermot, *The Vatican, the Bishops & Irish Politics 1919-1939*, Cambridge Press, 1986
8. Fitzgerald W.G., *The voice of Ireland, A Survey of the Race & Nation from all*

Angles, Virtue, Dublin/London, p. 5

9. Middlemas, Keith & Barnes, John, *Baldwin, A Biography*, Macmillan 1969-70, p. 123 fn

10. O'Hegarty, P.S., *The Victory*, Talbot Press, Dublin 1924, p. 67

11. Coogan, Tim P., *De Valera, The Man who was İreland*, Harper, 1996, p. 244

12. Beaslai, Pieras, *Michael Collins and the Making of a New Ireland*, Vol. II, Harper Bros. NY 1926, p. 311

13. Coogan, Tim P., *De Valera, The Man who was Ireland*, Harper, 1996, p. 288

14. Ryan, Desmond, *Unique Dictator*, Arthur Barker, London, 1936, p. 153

15. *ibid*

16. *ibid*, p. 155

17. *ibid*, p. 158

18. *ibid*, p. 159

19. Dwyer, T. Ryle, *De Valera, The Man & the Myths*, Poolbeg, Dublin, p. 61, Dáil Session: 8/16/1921

20. *ibid*, p. 21

21. *Manchester Guardian*, 1/9/1922

22. Collins, Michael, *The Path to Freedom*, Roberts Rhinehart, 1996, p. 28

23. Coogan, Tim P., *De Valera, The Man who was Ireland*, Harper, 1996, p. 289

24. Beaslai, Pieras, *Michael Collins and the Making of a New Ireland*, Vol II, Harper Bros. NY 1926, p. 314

25. *ibid*, p. 315

26. O'Hegarty, P.S., *The Victory of Sinn Féin & How It Used It*, Talbot Press, Dublin 1924, p. 73

27. O'Hegarty, P.S., *A History of Ireland under the Union 1801-1922*, Methuen, London, 1952, p. 782

28. O'Hegarty, P.S., The Victory of Sinn Féin, Talbot Pres, Dublin, 1924, p. 72

29. Dáil Private Sessions/155

30. Beaslai, Pieras, *Michael Collins and the Making of a New Ireland*, Vol II, Harper Bros. NY 1926, p. 322

31. Whelan, John (Seán O'Faoláin), *De Valera*, Penguin Books, England 1939

32. Beaslai, Pieras, *Michael Collins and the Making of a New Ireland*, Vol II, Harper Bros. NY 1926, p. 320

33. Coogan, Tim P., *De Valera, The Man who was Ireland*, Harper, 1996, p. 293, & Dáil Public Session/293

34. Fitzgerald, W.G. (Collins), *The voice of Ireland, A survey of the Race & Nation from All Angles*, Virtue Ltd. Dublin/London/39, p. 41

35. Dwyer, T. Ryle, *De Valera, The Man and the Myth*, Poolbeg, Dublin, 1991, p. 69

36. *ibid*, p. 99

37. O'Hegarty, P.S., *A History of Ireland under the Union 1801-1922*, Methuen, London, 1952, p. 779

38. Collins, Michael, *The Path to Freedom*, Roberts Rinehart 1996, p. 33

39. Beaslai, Pieras, *Michael Collins and the Making of a New Ireland*, Vol II, Harper Bros. NY 1926, p. 315
40. *ibid*
41. *ibid*, p. 318
42. Ryan, Desmond, *Unique dictator*, Arthur Barker, London, 1936, p. 164
43. Dwyer, T. Ryle, *De Valera, The Man & the Myths*, Poolbeg, Dublin, 1991, p. 90, Dáil Session/137
44. *ibid*, p. 87
45. Beaslai, Pieras, *Michael Collins and the Making of a New Ireland*, Harper, London, p. 317
46. Dwyer, T. Ryle, *De Valera, The Man & the Myths*, Poolbeg, Dublin, 1991, p. 95
47. *ibid*, p. 92
48. *Manchester Guardian* 1/9/1922
49. Dwyer, T. Ryle, *De Valera, The Man & the Myths*, Poolbeg, Dublin, 1991, p. 44
50. *ibid*, p. 89
51. *ibid*
52. Tierney, Michael (Ed. By F.X. Martin), *Eoin MacNeill, Scholar & Man of action 1867-1945*, Clarendon Press, Oxford 1980, p. 304
53. *ibid*, p. 305
54. Dwyer, T. Ryle, *De Valera, The Man & the Myths*, Poolbeg, Dublin, 1991, p. 54
55. Dwyer, T. Ryle, *Éamon de Valera*, Gill & Macmillan, 1980, p. 38
56. *ibid*, p. 39
57. Fitzgerald, W.G. (Splain), *The voice of Ireland, A survey of the Race & Nation from All Angles*, Virtue Ltd. Dublin/London, p. 41
58. Coogan, Tim Pat, *Éamon de Valera, the Man Who Was Ireland*, Harper Perennial, 1995, p. 304
59. Fitzgerald, W.G. (Splain), *The voice of Ireland, A survey of the Race & Nation from All Angles*, Virtue Ltd. Dublin/London, p. 40
60. Collins, Michael, *The Path to Freedom*, Roberts Rhinehart, 1996, p. 31
61. Fitzgerald, W.G. (Splain), *The voice of Ireland, A survey of the Race & Nation from All Angles*, Virtue Ltd. Dublin/London, p. 40
62. *ibid*, p. 43
63. *ibid*, p. 38
64. *ibid*, p. 41
65. *ibid*, p. 44
66. *ibid*, p. 38
67. *ibid*, p. 68
68. Beaslai, Pieras, Michael Collins and the Making of a New Ireland, Vol II, Harper Bros. NY 1926, p. 334
69. *ibid*
70. Whelan, John (Seán O'Faoláin), *De Valera*, Penguin Books, England 1939, p. 99
71. Beaslai, Pieras, *Michael Collins and the Making of a New Ireland*, Vol II, Harper

Bros. NY 1926, p. 335

72. *Manchester Guardian* 1/7/1922
73. O'Hegarty, P.S., *The Victory of Sinn Féin*, Talbot Press, Dublin, p. 88
74. Fitzgerald, W.G. (Splain), *The voice of Ireland, A survey of the Race & Nation from All Angles*, Virtue Ltd. Dublin/London, p. 5
75. Lavelle, Patricia, *James O'Mara, A Staunch Sinn Feiner 1873-1948*, Clonmore & Reynolds, Dublin, 1961, p. 273
76. *New York Times* 1/7/1922, 8:1
77. Beaslai, Pieras, *Michael Collins and the Making of a New Ireland*, Vol II, Harper Bros. NY 1926, p. 354
78. *Manchester Guardian* 1/9/1922
79. Beaslai, Pieras, *Michael Collins and the Making of a New Ireland*, Vol II, Harper Bros. NY 1926, p. 333
80. *ibid*, p. 338
81. *ibid*, p. 337
82. *Manchester Guardian*, 1/9/1922
83. Ryan, Desmond, *Unique dictator*, Arthur Barker, London, 1936, p. 165
84. Beaslai, Pieras, *Michael Collins and the Making of a New Ireland*, Vol II, Harper Bros. NY 1926, p. 340
85. *ibid*, p. 339
86. Coogan, Tim P., *De Valera, The Man who was Ireland*, Harper, 1996, p. 298
87. Beaslai, Pieras, *Michael Collins and the Making of a New Ireland*, Vol II, Harper Bros. NY 1926, p. 344
88. *ibid*, p. 351
89. *ibid*, p. 352
90. *ibid*, p. 353
91. Gaughan, J. Anthony, *Austin Stack, Portrait of a Separatist*, Kingdom Books, Dublin, 1977, p. 184
92. Beaslai, Pieras, *Michael Collins and the Making of a New Ireland*, Vol II, Harper Bros. NY 1926
93. O'Hegarty, P.S., *A History of Ireland under the Union 1801-1922*, Methuen, London, 1952, p. 345
94. Dwyer, T. Ryle, *De Valera, The Man & the Myths*, Poolbeg, Dublin, 1991, p. 97
95. O'Hegarty, P.S., *The Victory of Sinn Féin & How It Used It*, Talbot Press, Dublin 1924, p. 98

CHAPTER XVII

"Assignment Civil War"

"A simple acceptance of the people's will! That was all that was asked of them. What principle could such an acceptance have violated? Blind to facts, and false to ideals, they [counterfeit Republicans] are making war on the Irish people."[1]

Michael Collins

The peevishness and egotistical twentieth century Dáil members [counterfeit republicans] claiming undying allegiance to an Irish Republic they had repudiated on at least four prior occasions were ideal dupes for Britain's scheme to divide and rule the island. Over the centuries, the British pit Irish chief against chief, Catholic against Protestant, and native Irish against Scottish Planters (English settlers who occupied lands confiscated from the native Irish). The Irish were no match for the wily ways of the English and too lacking in leadership to realize the consequences then, as they were when Éamon de Valera set Irishman against Irishman.

The dilemma facing the British was how to divert Michael Collins' attention from infiltrating men and arms into Northern Ireland to counter the reign of terror against Catholics and provide the Unionists enough time to consolidate power. There could be no consolidation of Ulster on the backs of the Northern Ireland Catholics as long as Collins and Arthur Griffith lived. The British had come to know their qualities during the treaty negotiations, and no two stronger men were pitted against them. Griffith was recognized as a man who would honor his word, even unto death. Neither he nor Collins would compromise on the Boundary Commission clause in the Free State Treaty in which the counties of Fermanagh and Tyrone and the city of Derry were to be transferred to Southern Ireland. Both men were determined to end partition, one peaceably, the other by force if necessary.

Lloyd George, Winston Churchill, Neville Chamberlain, and the rest of the high-powered political brokers at Westminster were not about to let a peaceful transition of an Irish Free State threaten Northern Ireland

and destabilize the Empire. They were very much aware of Collins' inclination to use force if the British did not adhere to the word, deed and spirit of the Free State Treaty.

The British had their ace in Dublin and they meant to play that Green Card even if it meant the destruction of de Valera's political career. Too much was at stake. The future of the British Empire hinged on de Valera's ability to either reject the treaty or create havoc in Southern Ireland. The decision was a slam-dunk, a no-brainer: have de Valera create chaos in Southern Ireland before Collins created chaos in Northern Ireland.

Civil war requires at least two sides. The British needed Collins and Griffith at the moment to contest the extremist Republican opposition to the treaty led by de Valera but their days were numbered. This opposition to de Valera provided the necessary ingredient for pandemonium in Southern Ireland. Collins and Griffith's elimination would have to wait until de Valera had done his dirty work. De Valera incited an incomprehensible civil war, which resolved all of Britain's major concerns. Civil war in the South was a more favorable alternative to Irish rejection of the treaty, because it meant the English did not have to commit money or men to achieve their objective of a secure Northern Ireland.

Collins was already dispatching men and arms into Northern Ireland to counter the officially sanctioned Unionist terror against Catholics. Civil strife in Northern Ireland threatened to spill over into England itself. During the interlude between the signing of the treaty and the establishment of the Free State Government, Collins was cooperating with anti-Treaty Republicans in joint operations against the Unionists in Northern Ireland. This cooperation was a foretaste of what the English could expect under a peaceful transition to a Free State government.

"Collins knew that to continue the Northern activities with a civil war raging in the south would be disastrous…At a meeting of the officers of the Northern Ireland Irish Republican Army at Portobello Barracks in Dublin on August 2, 1922, Collins outlined just what de Valera's civil war meant to the Catholics of Northern Ireland. Thomas Kelly, who was at the meeting, noted: Collins said, '…with this civil war on my hands I cannot give you men the help I wish to give and mean to give. I now propose to call off hostilities in the North…'"[2] De Valera's scheme was working.

According to Tim Pat Coogan: "With the British gone, and a native Irish Army to hand, he (Collins) was prepared to contemplate force if necessary to end partition. In fact the record shows that he not merely contemplated, but actually used force in an effort to accomplish this end..."[3] Contrary to Coogan's contention, however, Collins, at that time, was not sending men and guns into Northern Ireland to end partition but primarily to counter the Unionist campaign of violence. Collins had no intention of violating the treaty agreement, but he was not going to stand aside while his brethren in the North were being evicted, tortured and murdered. He believed the Boundary Commission would ultimately resolve the partition question in Ireland's favor.

De Valera's services to England immediately bore fruit as his actions forced Collins to change his focus from action in the North to resolving the civil war in the South.

As de Valera led the twenty-six counties of Southern Ireland into civil war over his interpretation of the Treaty oath, the Protestants of Northern Ireland initiated an increasingly violent campaign of terror against Catholics. Catholic workers were being forcibly ejected from factories and homes in Belfast and other areas of Northern Ireland. The reimposition of a Free State boycott of goods from Northern Ireland was being demanded as a means to counter the Unionist terror campaign.

Lloyd George clearly saw the threat Collins posed and the reversal of public opinion at home and abroad in the event the Treaty unraveled on the issue of partition and revolt in Northern Ireland. He warned Churchill that Collins' activities in Northern Ireland would propel the issue of partition away from the Oath and Constitution, the only grounds on which they could hope to carry public opinion in the eventuality of a break with Dublin.[4]

Coogan noted that Collins' intelligence network had uncovered a memo from a Colonel Wickham of the British Army to senior members of the Ulster Special Constabulary called the B-Specials, Northern Ireland's version of the Black and Tans. The note outlined a scheme whereby "The British taxpayer would become liable for the costs of arming and paying sectarian murder gangs. The scheme was part of the Tories' overall determination to make the Six Counties so strong that they could successfully defy any move towards a united Ireland..."[5]

Collins voiced his concerns to James Craig, Northern Ireland Prime Minister, and also to Churchill and Lloyd George, who promised relief, but the attacks on the Catholics of the North only increased, resulting in an exodus of Catholics to Southern Ireland. Former British Chief of the Imperial General Staff, Henry Wilson, played a vital role in the covertly subsidized pogrom. Wilson was instrumental in organizing and arming the "B Specials," who enforced the officially sanctioned reprisal policy. Wilson, upon his retirement from the Army was elected to Parliament as a Unionist from North Down in February 1922.

Catholics were beaten and their homes burned in a planned terror and ethnic cleansing campaign to rid Northern Ireland of Catholics. The "B Specials" had death lists and would break down the door of a Catholic's home in the middle of the night and murder the man in front of his family. Voting districts were so gerrymandered that the Nationalists were all but disenfranchised. According to Dorothy Macardle: "...By June 18, 1922...it was calculated in the two years previously, total casualties in the North included 428 people killed with some 1,760 wounded, 8,750 Catholics driven out of employment and, the object of the [B Specials] exercise, around 23,000 driven out of their homes altogether."[6]

Collins ordered the Unionist General Wilson assassinated on his doorsteps in London on June 22, 1922 during the critical period leading up to the establishment of the Free State government. The slaying was a clear warning to the British that the atrocities in Northern Ireland must stop. Once again, Collins' boldness and daring placed the British in a quandary; they knew Collins was responsible for the assassination, but Collins was the point man for implementing the treaty in Ireland. Lloyd George could hardly publicly charge him with the murder, especially after the Prime Minister and his Cabinet had been engaged in high-level negotiations with him. The problem was solved in diplomatic fashion by blaming it on the usual suspects – the IRA faction which had seized the Four Courts Judicial complex in Dublin. The British did not forget Collins, however. He was needed for the moment to counterbalance de Valera's attacks against the Free State Treaty, but retribution was only postponed.

If, as Lloyd George and the British delegation had conceded during the treaty talks, the counties of Fermanagh and Tyrone and the Nationalist city of Derry (Irish name for Londonderry) from Northern Ireland, the diminished Ulster territory would become economically untenable. It would be only a matter of time before the Unionists had to accept a united Ireland as a means of economic survival. But, of course, the British had no intention of honoring the Boundary Commission agreement.

Had there been a peaceful transition to an Irish Free State, the British would have been under pressure by Collins' campaign in the North to relinquish the Catholic majority counties, as they had agreed to do. Whether the remaining four counties of Northern Ireland clung to a partitioned Ireland would have depended upon the economic subsidies England was then willing to pay to prop up the Unionist government and the extent of Hierarchy control of the Free State Government.

261

With a peaceful transition to a Free State, Protestants would violate the Northern Catholics' rights at their peril. Any British reprisals into Southern Ireland would call into play Collins and Griffith's mutual defense pact with Canada. A Collins-led Free State army would make the cost of such an English adventure financially and militarily staggering, with Commonwealth condemnation and the risk of American rejection of relief of England's forty billion dollar First World War debt. The stakes were enormous.

Another reason England could not cede a peaceful transition to Ireland as an independent state, was the "domino effect" among its colonial territories, namely Egypt and India, which would see in any successful Irish insurgency the opportunity to declare their own national sovereignty by rising up in rebellion. Churchill, as late as the 1940s, was still violently opposed to ceding independence to India and vowed that the breakup of the Empire would not occur on his watch.

On January 14, 1922, the British formally surrendered Dublin Castle to Michael Collins. The Irish government immediately took steps to replace the Royal Irish Constabulary, as the British troops and the hated Auxiliaries and Black and Tans began their evacuation of Ireland in accordance with the provisions of the treaty. After more than seven centuries, the Irish finally saw the departure of their hated British oppressors.

De Valera deflected the legitimate question of the treaty – partition – by concentrating on a nonexistent oath to a nonexistent Republic. His followers preferred to drown Ireland in blood rather than take advantage of the freedom and virtual independence outlined in the Free State Treaty. Civil war in Southern Ireland was well worth the British roll of the dice with de Valera's political career in the balance in order to safeguard their interests in Northern Ireland, America, India, Egypt and even in England itself, but they underestimated the resilience of their man and the incredible gullibility of the Irish.

Collins proclaimed the treaty as a "stepping stone to freedom," while de Valera argued that it was "a barrier in the way to complete independence." Future events proved de Valera completely wrong and Collins prescient almost to the point of clairvoyance. Collins' stepping stone approach did not have long to wait to be realized. The Imperial Conference of 1924, the Balfour Declaration outcome of the Imperial Conference of 1926 and the ultimate stepping-stone, the *1931 Statute of Westminster* granted the Dominions, including Ireland, the legal right under British law to declare whatever form of government they desired.

John MacNeill noted, "...A serious clash upon the interpretation of

Article 12 (Boundary Commission Clause) was averted by the distracting effect of graver events, the Irish civil war and its aftermath..."[7] The effect of de Valera's anti-Irish campaign was reaping a harvest of British triumphs.

As they had done so many times in the past, the Irish rose up and defeated themselves, never refusing a British offer to self-destruct. The extremist Republicans under de Valera's prodding, rushed headlong into civil war ignorant as to the extent they were helping England's international relations and the Unionists' consolidation of power in Northern Ireland.

British forces streamed into Ulster to bolster the Unionist regime until it was strong enough to defend itself against any incursion from the South or insurrection from within. Unionist hardliners were known as Orangemen and took their name from William III, Prince of Orange of the Netherlands, who became King of England from 1689 to 1702. He defeated James II at the Battle of the Boyne on July 12, 1690 and the Unionists of Northern Ireland adopted the name of Orangemen in celebration of the victory. As long as they had the choice, they would opt to remain loyal subjects of the Crown. With civil war in the South, the Unionists enjoyed international sympathy for their refusal to unite with the ungovernable and irreconcilable Southern Irish.

No clear-thinking person could fail to recognize that division in the ranks of the Nationalists at that moment would bring disaster to Ireland. The civil war meant that Collins and his pro-treaty forces were fully engaged in a bitter contest with de Valera's extremists. Southern Ireland was mired in conflict while the Protestants turned the screws of repression on the Catholics in Ulster.

Dwyer claimed that, once the fighting had begun, de Valera: "tried to persuade his side to stop."[8] Immediately upon de Valera's plunging the country into chaos, he publicly clamored for peace but privately continued encouraging his followers to commit one act of terror after another. What Dwyer failed to comprehend was that the damage had already been done, British interests were safe, Ulster was secure, the Irish perceived as irreconcilable and incapable of self-government, and Anglo-American relations were never better, all thanks to de Valera.

Ireland became the laughing stock of the world. Its enemies publicly scorned it, and supporters throughout the Dominions and especially in the United States could only offer weak excuses and then quietly changed the subject. The turning of de Valera in 1916 was perhaps the greatest coup in seven centuries of sordid Anglo-Irish relations. International public opinion was aghast at the senseless strife in Southern Ireland.

During the treaty debate, de Valera had said, "I hope nobody will talk of fratricidal strife,"[9] but he would talk of nothing less. He delivered a series of incendiary speeches encouraging fratricidal strife: At Dungarvan, on March 16, 1922, de Valera claimed the treaty: "barred the way to independence with the blood of fellow-Irishmen. It was only by Civil War that they could get their independence...if you don't fight today, you will have to fight tomorrow; and I say when you are in a good fighting position, then fight on."[10]

The next morning, at Carrick-on-Suir, he charged: "If the Treaty was accepted, the fight for freedom would still go on. The Irish people, instead of fighting foreign soldiers, would have to fight Irish soldiers of an Irish Government set up by Irishmen..."[11] On March 20, 1922, the *Irish Independent* reported a March 18 speech by de Valera at Killarney in which he rejected majority rule: "...in order to achieve freedom... if we continue on the movement which was begun when the Volunteers were started, and we suppose this Treaty is ratified by your votes, then these men, in order to achieve freedom, will have to march over the dead bodies of their own brothers. They will have to wade through Irish blood... The people have never a right to do wrong..."[12]

At Dun Laoghaire on April 6, he threatened to make Ireland ungovernable. "...If they attempted to do that which they legally could not do, to set up a Provisional Government of the country, that Government would not be obeyed. That Government would not function."[13] While at Killarney, Tralee, and Waterford, de Valera justified murder and mayhem in the name of an Irish Republic, which he had previously admitted, did not exist: "Acts had been performed in the name of the Republic which would be immoral if the Republic did not exist in the sense which he had said. Men and women had been shot for helping the enemy, and there would be no justification for the shooting of these if the Republic did not exist."[14]

During a speech at Boland's Mills, de Valera railed against the treaty. Denouncing everyone and everything, he claimed the British evacuation was a sham; he appealed for postponement of the election and criticized "a parliamentary register now rotten but good enough to build his alleged Republic."[15] De Valera convinced disaffected members of the IRA to use force to repudiate the Treaty and declare a Republic. Longford and O'Neill, de Valera's official propagandists, made the absurd statement: "There is no evidence that his speeches stirred up the violence they were said to encourage."[16]

Collins and Griffith believed de Valera was actually seeking a settlement and they went to extraordinary lengths to mollify his objections to the treaty. When Collins and Griffith met each of his objections, de Valera rejected them out of hand or added others, each rejection being more incomprehensible than the last.

A bipartisan initiative proposed that the existing Irish Parliament maintain overall authority while the Provisional Government was being set up. The Dáil would serve as the ultimate authority for the Free State Constitution so there would be no confusion about acknowledging the Crown. "De Valera dismissed the idea because, he said, Griffith and Collins would not accept it. When they did, he rejected it anyway."[17]

On April 29, 1922, a meeting was called by Dr. Edward Byrne, Archbishop of Dublin: "Collins, Griffith and the Labor representatives made various proposals to meet de Valera's objections, all of which were refused..."[18] De Valera and Burgess claimed no nation has the right to barter their national heritage, whatever that meant. "Burgess accused Griffith and Collins of being British agents. When the Archbishop demanded the accusation be withdrawn, Burgess agreed but proceeded to explain that he considered those two who did the work of the British Government to be British agents. 'I suppose we are two of the ministers whose blood is to be waded through?' Collins snapped. 'Yes', replied Burgess, quite calmly, 'You are two.'"[19] De Valera had so manipulated the notoriously dull-witted Burgess that jealousy blinded him to political reality.

All the while bitter invectives were hurled at Collins and Griffith, "de Valera stood by indifferently, depicting himself as having consistently tried to maintain the Republican position. He never denied his willingness to compromise with the British, but now he contended the compromise would always have had to be consistent with the Republican ideal. 'Was that your attitude?' Griffith asked, 'If so, a penny postcard would have been sufficient to inform the British government without going to the trouble of sending us over.' de Valera began to explain but Griffith interrupted, 'Did you not ask me to get you out of the strait-jacket of the Republic?'"[20]

When the Labor Party delegation begged him to reconsider the course on which he had set, he refused to listen. "'We spent two hours pleading with him with a view to averting the impending calamity of Civil War.' One member of the delegation later recalled; 'The only statement he made that has abided with me since as to what his views were then was this: "The majority have no right to do wrong." He repeated that at least a dozen times in the course of the interview. He refused to accept that he had a duty to observe the decision of the majority until it was reversed.'"[21] What the Labor Party delegation did not comprehend was that civil war was exactly what the British wanted, and de Valera was determined to see that it came to pass.

Kevin O'Higgins said: "In these rhetorical flights, de Valera spurns facts. It would never do to tell the people that in the future no man would hold power in Ireland except by the sanction of their votes. That no policy can be pursued in Ireland for a single hour, which is not the expression of the majority will. That the majority must always henceforth be the determining factor in their political affairs and that at any general election, the people can return candidates pledged to any policy that seems good to them..."[22]

After exhausting various excuses for rejecting the treaty, de Valera again charged that it was the oath of allegiance that was the major stumbling block to a settlement. Collins proposed that "the Treaty oath prescribed for members of the Free State Parliament could be omitted from the constitution so that deputies would not have to take it. The pro-Treaty people had already avoided taking the oath prescribed for members of the Southern Parliament, so there were grounds for believing he could deliver on this latest promise also."[23] De Valera rejected the proposal.

De Valera objected to an election, claiming that the existing voting register was rotten and that all adults should vote on the treaty. The Irish President had accepted that the voters in the past two elections within the three previous years were capable of deciding on his alleged Irish Republic but when it came time to voting on the treaty, he claimed the electorate was now incapable of rendering a decision: "'The register on which you proposed to hold the elections,' he wrote Griffith, 'contains tens of thousands of names that should not be on it and omits several tens of thousands that should be on it...'"[24]

In an effort to meet his objection, Collins and Griffith proposed a referendum in which all adults would be eligible to vote regardless of their status on the electoral register: "The people would meet at the same time in designated localities throughout the country and would vote by passing through barriers where they would be counted, but de Valera rejected such 'Stone Age machinery.'"[25] Determined on anarchy, de Valera was not interested in a resolution; he advanced the preposterous demand that the Unionists of Northern Ireland also be allowed to vote.

De Valera initially insisted on a three-month delay in holding elections on the treaty, but after Collins and Griffith agreed, de Valera then demanded the vote be delayed another six months. "He realized that the three months delay had not been sufficient... because he knew that his own views would otherwise be rejected by the majority."[26]

"De Valera simply did not want any election at the time and he publicly justified his refusal to cooperate on the grounds that there were 'rights which a minority may justly uphold, even by arms, against a majority.'"[27] Collins pleaded with the treaty opponents to give him four years and he would deliver a Republic, to no avail. They preferred civil war.

Those who knew de Valera could not account for his reversal of personality. Pictor Ignotus (Kevin O'Higgins), in the "Course of our Civil War: An Analysis of Cause and Cure," wrote: "Here, let me say a word about Éamon de Valera, as one who knew him in the intimacy of the secret Councils and Cabinet of Dáil Éireann. The torrent of taunts and wild statements conflicted so radically with his calm wisdom in the Council Chambers that one stood aghast at the change."[28]

De Valera's rejection of a bipartisan proposal to resolve differences in which all parties would be able to maintain their principles, showed once more his determination to create chaos. A committee made up of pro- and anti-treaty Dáil deputies proposed that de Valera remain as President of the Dáil, with anti-treaty advocates abstaining from voting against the treaty. The Provisional government would be allowed to come into being and the Irish Republican Army to remain subservient to the government. To counter de Valera's most serious charge concerning the oath, it was proposed: "'Only members of the Provisional Government need sign acceptance of the Treaty.' The committee declared: 'We are convinced that the only alternative to accepting the Treaty on some agreed basis is a dissipation of our whole movement. We have reached a crucial point where all can be lost or gained.'"[29] Griffith and Collins immediately accepted the proposals. The committee then put it to de Valera, "who, when he received it, flew into a passion, swore, and refused to accept the terms of the agreement ..."[30]

At the Wicklow Hotel in January 1922, Harry Boland was having his usual lunch with Patrick O'Hegarty and Sean O'Muirthile. "Boland often lamented, 'Isn't it a pity that we aren't all together and why can't we get together again, and after all there isn't much between us...' When the pro-treaty advocates insisted that Boland define exactly what was the difference between them, Boland responded that it was only the 'Oath' that stood between them. Advised that Collins did not intend to make the oath a requirement in the Constitution, Boland asked to have an assurance from Collins. The following day, O'Muirthile again met with Boland and said: 'Well, Harry, I am authorized by Collins to give you an undertaking for de Valera. If de Valera and his crowd would stop their coddling and come in as a constitutional party and help us to get the best out of the Treaty, there'll be no Oath in the Constitution, and he'll stand or fall by that.'

"For a brief space, Boland looked as if he could not believe his ears. Then he got up, his whole face shining, his person just a mass of animation. 'Cheers boys,' said he, 'I'm going to Dev. We'll be together again in an hour's time.'

"We were not, of course. De Valera refused to accept the undertaking, as rendered. *He asked for it in writing and to be made public at once, which, of course, he knew to be impossible in the circumstances.*"[31] [emphasis added]

De Valera insisted Collins publicly and in writing reject the oath in order to deliberately create a *cause célèbre* that would undermine the treaty position and lead to the British declaring that the Irish violated the Treaty. Such a public repudiation of the treaty over an oath would provide the British worldwide justification to resort to a reconquest of Ireland.

With the publication of the Free State Treaty terms in December 1921, Harry Boland and Stephen O'Mara, in America at that time, enthusiastically endorsed the treaty. The focus of a huge fund-raising banquet was transformed into a testimonial to the treaty signing: "Boland said he was perfectly content [with the Treaty] except he did not know 'what in the name of Heaven we'll do with that Governor General.'"[32] According to Beaslai: "de Valera had become an object of hero worship with Boland and he was determined to follow him through thick and thin. In private discussion, he acknowledged the justice of many of the arguments put before him and spoke as one largely in sympathy with Collins' point of view, but loyalty to de Valera seemed to be his ruling passion."[33]

After the Dáil vote was carried 64 to 57 in favor of the treaty, Collins pleaded for a Joint Committee on Public Safety. De Valera rejected Collins' proposal to set up a bipartisan committee to rein in the extremist element creating havoc throughout Ireland: "I have tendered my resignation and I cannot, in any way, take divided responsibility. You have got here a sovereign assembly, which is the government of the nation. This assembly must choose its executive according to its constitution and go ahead..."[34] In other words, he denied any responsibility for bringing order to the country.

Mary MacSwiney, sister of Terrence who died on a hunger strike, was one of the most fanatical and dedicated of de Valera followers. In a screeching tirade, she spat her venom across the aisles of the chamber, "This [Free State Treaty] is a betrayal, a gross betrayal and the fact is that it is only a small majority and that majority is not united; half of them are looking for a gun and the other half are looking for the flesh-pots of the Empire. I tell you there can be no union between the representatives of the Irish Republic and the so-called Free State."[35]

On December 6, 1922, one year from the date of the formal signing of the treaty, the Free State government came into existence. Dáil deputies pledged allegiance to the Irish Constitution and a simple acknowledgement of faithfulness to the King as the head of a group of nations of which Ireland was but one of the members.

The Irish were now in full control of their destiny, but the English, through de Valera, would throw a monkey wrench into the fledgling Free State government. Egged on by de Valera, his followers roared throughout Ireland creating havoc, ignoring the fact that it was the first time in 750 years that Ireland had a permanent national, truly representative government, with its own constitution and Parliament.

Collins and Griffith asked Tim Healy, the former Irish Parliamentary Party leader, to intercede with de Valera to damp down the anti-treaty forces. De Valera rebuked Healy and refused to call off a dissident Irish Army Convention, which Collins and Griffith feared would culminate in the insurgents' declaring a military dictatorship. De Valera denied he had anything to do with Rory O'Connor, the leader of the IRA dissidents, but the two men shared an address, and de Valera supported his position.

The IRA dissidents convened an Army convention on March 26, 1922, effectively splitting the IRA. O'Connor notified the press that the IRA had withdrawn its allegiance to the Dáil because of its alleged betrayal of the Republic by ratifying the Free State Treaty. "'The holding of the convention means that we repudiate the Dáil,' he said. 'Do we take it we are going to have a military dictatorship then?' he was asked. 'You can take it that way if you like,'"[36] he replied. De Valera had accused Collins of attempting to set up a military dictatorship, when it was he who encouraged O'Connor to undertake just such a course.

When the Four Courts judicial complex in Dublin was occupied by Rory O'Connor and anti-treaty elements on Good Friday, April 14, 1922, de Valera applauded the move and encouraged the country to support the rebels: "'Young men and young women of Ireland,' he trumpeted, 'the goal is at last in sight. Steady; all together; forward. Ireland is yours for the taking. Take it.'"[37] As Coogan noted: "Clearly de Valera's appeal to this last group makes nonsense of his claim that he was not guilty of incitement..."[38]

In a last ditch effort to apply the coup de grace to the treaty and complete his "Assignment Civil War," de Valera issued another of his calls to rebellion, stating: "In Rory O'Connor and his comrades lives the unbought indomitable soul of Ireland...Irish citizens! Give them your support! Irish soldiers! Bring them aid!"[39] Coogan declared: "These statements were the most irresponsible of his career and, taken together, certainly form solid evidence for those who would argue...that it was he who caused the Civil War."[40]

According to de Valera, the seizure of the Four Courts Judicial

Complex by Rory O'Connor and his men allegedly came as a "complete surprise but he could not condemn it…"[41] O'Connor demanded the elections be canceled; that a public announcement declaring recognition of an Irish Republic be issued; that the police be replaced by the IRA; and that the Army to be under the control of an elected executive of insurgents.

Collins sent a message to the rebels in an effort to prevent any further escalation of the conflict: "Tell these men that neither I, nor any member of the Government, nor any officer in the Army…not one of us wishes to hurt a single one of them or to humiliate them in any way that can be avoided."[42] Collins offered the rebels freedom to return to their homes, with the sole condition of depositing their weapons in the National Armory. The weapons were to remain there until the rebels attained a majority vote of the people, at which time the weapons would come under the rebels' control. De Valera rejected Collins offer outright, while Robert Barton sent Homan packing with a terse: "We want no terms save victory or death."[43] This was the same Barton, the coward, who buckled under the "duress" of Lloyd George's threat of "immediate and terrible war." He feared war with England but had no scruples when it came to making war upon his own people.

In response to an appeal for peace by de Valera, William Cosgrave, who assumed leadership of the government after Collins and Griffith were murdered, offered generous terms, which included the condition that all issues must be decided by majority vote of the Dáil and that the insurgents' weapons must be surrendered. Cosgrave, in order to spare the Irregulars the stigma of surrender, was willing to have the weapons turned over to the Catholic Hierarchy, rather than turn them over to the pro-treaty forces. He said the Irregulars could burn or destroy them, but "these arms cannot, and will not, if I have any responsibility for the government of this country, remain in the hands of those who are not subject to the authority of the people's parliament."[44] All offensive action against the rebels would cease, and they would be free to contest all elections. The only proviso was that any elected member of the Dáil must subscribe to the oath of allegiance to the Free State constitution. "Cosgrave's main point was that the Republicans should accept the majority wishes of the people…"[45]

De Valera, who claimed he had no influence with the extremist Republicans, however, decided the major issues between them and the Free State Government and rejected Cosgrave's liberal offer out of hand. De Valera was still sputtering that the oath to the Free State Government constituted allegiance to the Crown.

Collins and Griffith insisted on the democratic right of the people to decide the form of government under which they wanted to live. In a speech at Castlebar, Collins was confronted by a boisterous anti-treaty mob bent on preventing him from speaking. He told the crowd tearing up railway lines and the blocking of roads was reminiscent of the English Black and Tans, and the Irish "Green and Tans" would be no more successful. The anti-treaty mob surged forward, their shouting drowned out Collins, and shots were fired, interrupting his speech. In a parting plea to his Castlebar audience, Collins said: 'This is not the kind of freedom all my friends and I risked our lives for. If the people decide for the opposition, they will find me behind them. I will stand with the people, no matter what the decision is.'"[46]

Coogan set forth the dubious assertion that during the Anglo-Irish insurgency: "There was within the ranks of the dissidents, "a mass of *apolitical idealists*. They, and the people's response to their *selflessness and sincerity*, had been the backbone of the movement, which had led to the offer from Britain of Dominion status, but to their scrupulous, Catholic way of thinking, politics, with its inevitable compromises, was tinged with dishonor."[47] [emphasis added]

Coogan's façade of idealism was torn asunder by acts of mayhem, murder and mischief by the "selfless and sincere apolitical idealists" against the very people they were supposed to be fighting for. Beaslai presented a more realistic scenario, noting: "It is curious that, in these peace feelers by Irregular leaders [selfless and sincere idealists], the question most raised by them was not the issue of the Treaty, nor the fate of Ireland, but plans for a reunited Army in which their own positions would be secured."[48]

The true Republicans, headed by Collins and Griffith, were those supporting the right of the people to decide for themselves what type of government they wanted to live under. The alleged "sincere and selfless idealists," were nothing but terrorists determined to impose an alien government against the will of the Irish people through armed robbery, intimidation, beatings, and murder. Those "selfless idealists," Liam Lynch, Eoin O'Duffy, and Gearoid O'Sullivan, who had drawn up the final version of the oath, which Collins and Griffith maneuvered Lloyd George and the British delegation into adopting in the Free State Treaty, later repudiated the very oath they had authored and were some of the most aggressive murderers during the civil war.

On April 16, 1922, well aware of the danger ahead, prior to leaving for a speech in Sligo, Griffith wrote out his will and a message to the people of Ireland. Roads had been blocked and telephone wires cut. Accompanied by an armored car, Griffith told a huge gathering: "A challenge had been issued to the Government that could not be allowed to pass. The challenge had been taken up on behalf of the people of Ireland that the right of free speech had been vindicated. It was for the people to decide what form of Government they wished to accept and it was for the Government to ensure by all the power at its disposal that the people should be entirely free to choose..."[49]

P. S. O'Hegarty wrote: "The Irregulars were no more fighting for a Republic than the National Army was fighting against it. The issue in the Civil War was whether ordered democratic government was to obtain here...It was government by the bullet versus government by the ballot..."[50]

Griffith blamed de Valera for all the misery plaguing Ireland. Beaslai wrote of a discussion with Griffith shortly before the attack on the Four Courts: "When we found ourselves alone in a taxi, he leaned forward and said to me, in an agitated, almost tearful voice – 'We'll have to fight those fellows!' Then he relapsed into silence."[51]

At a meeting of the Cabinet, Griffith charged that if they were not up to the fight to uphold the people's right to decide what form of Government they wanted to live under, "We should be looked upon as the greatest set of poltroons who ever had the fate of Ireland in their hands."[52]

The civil war had its origins in the private meetings between Lloyd George and de Valera at the London truce talks in July 1921. Coogan was mindful of the closeness between de Valera and Lloyd George, but only hinted at a Lloyd George/de Valera conspiracy against Ireland. The only available public record of what was said during those fateful meetings is what Lloyd George and de Valera chose to recall. "It [the truce conference] was a gloomily accurate setting of the scene for the Civil War whose seeds were to be scattered on the conference table at 10 Downing Street the following day, July 12, 1921."

Dwyer attempted to take the sting out of de Valera's incitement to civil war and advanced the implausible contention that: "Collins must indeed share some of the blame for the conflict, because in his efforts to avoid it, he compromised himself by trying to do the impossible. He worked tirelessly to placate both the Republicans and the British. In the process he tried to reconcile the irreconcilable and opened himself to the charge of duplicity by making contradictory commitments that he could not possibly keep."[53] Dwyer's ridiculous conclusion is a typical example of the lengths that de Valera's apologists would go and to accuse Collins of complicity in civil war solely because of his heroic efforts to avert it is unctuousness at its worst.

Unlike de Valera, Collins did not make contradictory commitments because de Valera never accepted any proposals by Collins with the exception of the pact to hold an intimidation-free election.

Another de Valera apologist, Desmond Ryan, also attempted to deflect the central role played by de Valera in the civil war but unwittingly hinted of an involvement with the British Prime Minister: "The tragedy lay... in personal feuds and the defeat of all efforts from the better elements on both sides to win a toleration and a fair trial for the Treaty."[54] He continued: "... Events have justified such a view. But this is not to say that de Valera was wrong...This doubt, however, cannot be confined to de Valera and must be entertained about his equally distinguished brother Celt, Lloyd George..."[55]

Irish writers acknowledged the collusion but not the conclusion between de Valera and Lloyd George. Although the Irish President's actions benefiting England were too egregious to ignore, commentators could not face the possibility that Lloyd George and de Valera were co-conspirators. Professor T. Desmond Williams was one of many who attempted to deflect the odor emanating from de Valera by a dubious deduction: "Both de Valera and Collins were largely to blame for the Civil War because Collins tried to do too much, de Valera too little."[56]

O'Hegarty, however, was quick to recognize the fruits of de Valera's treachery: "First, there was bitterness more intense and more murderous than any that has been in Ireland within living memory. Old friendships went for naught, family ties went for naught, hatred and thoughts of murder stalked the land."[57] All thanks to de Valera.

More astute than most writers about de Valera, O'Hegarty was correct in his assessment but wrong in his conclusion when he claimed: "The responsibility for that Civil War lies almost altogether on Éamon de Valera...When America turned us down, there was no further hope of complete victory..."[58] America did not turn Ireland down; de Valera turned America down. John Devoy wrote to Collins on February 16, 1922 and denounced de Valera: "It is grotesque for de Valera to talk of his loyalty to the Republic. The first blow to the Republic was delivered by him in his Cuban interview [*Westminster Gazette*, February 1920]; the second, and more deadly one, was his unpardonable action in rejecting the Republican plank at Chicago and the third, was his making the Split here [in America] on charges that were all impudent falsehoods, and using vast sums of money collected by us for the Irish Republic to keep the split alive...That money...was prostituted for an evil purpose and materially aided England's savage warfare on Ireland."

De Valera continued to prod the Treaty-wrecking Republicans into acts of terror and mayhem. When his whispered promptings were implemented, he would deny any responsibility, claiming that he had no power over his followers. But de Valera's approval of violent reprisals is recorded even by his own biographers: "Liam Lynch issued a [reprisal] order to the Dublin Brigade that nine members of the Provisional Government were to be executed and two members of the Parliament arrested...Although de Valera had already agreed to the necessity for an extreme warning, de Valera now wrote, "*The efficacy of reprisals is open to doubt but I see no other way...to protect our men, I cannot disapprove...*"[59] [emphasis added]

O'Hegarty described de Valera's incitement to bloodshed: "The effect was electrical. De Valera's gunmen had now received his blessing and they were free from any doubt as to how far he was prepared to go. All the irresponsibles, all the slanderers, all the poison tongues, all the uprooters who had gathered round the Great Anarch were now loosed and spurred on and through Ireland they went like so many devils, doing the devil's work everywhere."[60] This apocalyptic vision deceived O'Hegarty into imagining it was the devil's mischief at play when the gunmen were merely serving England's interest.

De Valera made no effort to stop the forces which he had intentionally let loose in Ireland. His apologists claimed he lost control of the situation and that he was relegated to an observer rather than a leader. But his speeches served as a deliberate incitement to revolution and, once the violence was let loose, he chose to sit back and prod the renegade Republicans into doing England's dirty work. His justification for all the murders, robberies, and a host of other crimes against the people was defending an Irish Republic that he had formerly rejected on four occasions.

De Valera had enlisted in the anti-Treaty forces as a lowly private but he was lurking in the background of every major decision, from calling on the Army to initiate civil war to bombing campaigns in England to assassinating Free State government officials. In February 1923, a more ominous action was proposed by the "selfless idealists," with de Valera whispering encouragement to Liam Lynch. Urged on by de Valera, the dissidents planned a dynamiting campaign in England. Longford and O'Neill admitted: "de Valera agreed with him [Lynch] and advised 'the first blow should be concerted and big, followed quickly by a number in succession of other blows.'"[61]

On November 30, 1922, there were three more executions of counterfeit Republicans by the Provisional government. In response, de Valera encouraged the assassination of two pro-treaty deputies who were subsequently shot. In reprisal for that shooting, four prominent dissident prisoners, Liam Mellowes, Rory O'Connor, Dick Barrett, and Joe McKelvey, were executed without trial. Those executions further escalated into counter-reprisals by the Irregulars. Attacks on property and homes of the Free State government members increased.

Any public outcry over the summary execution of four rebel leaders quickly dissipated when the selfless idealists torched Sean McGarry's home with his children inside. "The house... was entered by armed thugs [sincere and selfless idealists] who saturated the place with petrol and set the house ablaze, in spite of the mother's entreaties for her sleeping children upstairs. Dashing up to save her little ones, she was soon on fire herself and severely burned, while her little son Emmet, a child of seven, died in a hospital the next day of terrible injuries."[62]

De Valera continued his insidious whispers encouraging reprisals in private but always publicly repudiating them. His instigation-and-denial act was a hallmark of his Machiavellian character and a trademark throughout his long political career.

The executions continued, with two Insurgents shot on May 2, 1923, making a total of 82 counterfeit Republicans executed within the previous six months. In January 1923, thirty-four more were shot. Longford and O'Neill wrote: "It was not surprising that Lynch felt driven to issue a more drastic order on February 3. This extended the classes against whom the Republicans were ordered to take action. The Army staff was under the impression that the President [de Valera] had agreed to it..."[63] De Valera denied that he had approved any such policy, but he convicted himself when he admitted: "The Chief of Staff was wrong in thinking I had agreed to the order as a definite decision. I merely indicated that I regarded it as possible that we would be forced to adopt as defensive measures some of the drastic proposals, which the Staff meeting had agreed. [This was] on the understanding that the execution of the orders would be kept strictly under the control of the General Headquarters – liberty of action not being allowed to subordinate commanders."[64] Lynch, the Commander-in-Chief of the Insurgents, issued the orders and could hardly be considered a subordinate commander.

In July 1922, Collins assumed command of the National Army as Commander-in-Chief, with offices at Portobello Barracks. British troops were still in occupation of several barracks in Dublin until the end of the year. Although Free State troops were subject to daily sniping by the Irregulars, *"not one shot was fired at the men in khaki* [English troops] *nor at the barracks held by them."*[65] [emphasis added] The irregulars preferred to take on their fellow Irish brothers in the National Army because the Free State troops were reluctant to fire on fellow Irishmen while the British had no such compunction.

Thanks to their importation of arms as well as additional weapons clandestinely supplied by the British, the irregulars were not only superior in firepower to the National Army but also mustered ten times the number of men as the National Army under Collins. Upon their evacuation, the British purposely surrendered their former barracks to both pro- and anti-treaty forces in order to encourage civil strife.

Beaslai recognized the English intent to derail the Treaty: "Collins knew that behind his domestic enemies lurked foreign foes – that powerful interests in England and the Northeast would be delighted to see the Provisional Government á in its efforts to establish authority. He had not forgotten the handing over of an English naval tug, packed with arms and ammunition, to the Irregulars at Cobh, County Cork, in April 1922."[66] Irish writers acknowledged that powerful foreign interests in England and the Northeast were lurking behind the "domestic enemy" without recognizing the only domestic enemy – de Valera!

The British, on that occasion, allowed the rebels to commandeer a Royal naval vessel – without resistance and permitted the anti-Treaty rebels to remove a cache of weapons, which were immediately put to use against their fellow Irishmen. "It was an event, which set Collins thinking hard. That a British naval tug should be hanging around Cobh, filled to the brim with arms and ammunition, practically unguarded at this particular time, suggested a desire on the part of the English authorities that the enemies of the Free State should be well armed."[67]

President Cosgrave, too, acknowledged a conspiracy, but not the conspirator. "There is a diabolical conspiracy afoot, and there is only one way to meet it. It must be smashed and these men shown that terror will be struck into them. It was for this reason that drastic measures were adopted..."[68]

Collins was convinced that, given a free choice, the Treaty would be overwhelmingly approved by the people and the legitimacy to the Free State government assured. In order to bring about an election free from terror and intimidation, Collins made an electoral pact with de Valera on May 20, 1922. The agreement called for a National Coalition Panel of both pro- and anti-treaty parties, with the understanding that after the election, the Executive Committee should consist of the President, the Minister of Defense, and nine other ministers, five from the Free State roster and four from the anti-treaty slate. The pact also stipulated: "every and any interest is free to go up and contest the pact equally with the National Sinn Féin Panel."[69]

The result was that in every district in which the anti-Treaty dissidents faced opposition, they lost their seat. It was only in those constituencies in which they were unopposed, mostly through intimidation, that they were able to garner any seats in the Dáil. In a free election devoid of intimidation and violence, it was highly likely that de Valera's anti-treaty party would have gone the way of John Redmond's Irish Parliamentary Party.

Griffith was outraged by the agreement because it subverted the democratic process. But Collins was certain that an intimidation-free election would confirm that the majority of the people favoured the treaty, thereby lending a legal claim to international acceptance of the treaty and the Free State government.

Contrary to de Valera's claim of a lack of influence over the rebels and that he was powerless to stop their murderous, treasonous rampage, the facts were otherwise as he commanded a halt to the terror during the election process. The result was a comparatively incident-free election with an overwhelming repudiation of de Valera and his counterfeit Republicans. The Irish people, in the June 16, 1922 election, by a three to one margin, cast their ballots for the Free State – the Government 58, Labor 17, Farmers 7 and independents 7 while the anti-treaty de Valera faction received 35.[70]

"On the day before the elections, the draft Constitution of the Irish Free State was published...The draft presented in due course to His Majesty's Ministers had come as yet another shock to the English. It was a purely Republican Constitution, logically built up on the premise defined in Article II, 'all powers of government and all authority, legislative, executive and judicial are derived from the people.' From first to last, there was no mention of the King...The Constitution, as it emerged from the debates...remained...essentially Republican. In all its seventy-nine clauses, the King is only mentioned seven times, and for the first time in Article XII..."[71]

When the Labor Party, Farmers, and Independents took their seats, de Valera cried foul. Despite his approval of the election, de Valera again reversed course and charged that the Provisional Government assumed office by a *coup d'etat* against the Republic declared in the 1918 and 1921 elections and "the election gave authority for no government except a coalition government..."[72] The anti-Treaty rebels claimed that the election of 1918 superseded the election of 1922 but with a seventy-five percent plurality, the Free State rested on the solid foundation of the will of the overwhelming majority of the people.

Collins said: "What was the usurpation they complained of? Simply that the Government refused to allow authority to be wrested from it by an armed minority. If it is not right for a National Government to keep public order, to prevent murder, arson, and brigandage, what are the duties of a government?"[73]

Mary MacSwiney, one of de Valera's most ardent and vocal supporters, especially during the treaty debates, unwittingly destroyed de Valera's contention that the Free State usurped power by a *coup d'etat*: "The Pact election was a valid election. The Pact [between Collins and de Valera] was not broken until after the election was over. Clause Four in the Pact allowed any and every person to go up, therefore, even Mick's [Collins'] speech in Cork [calling on the people to vote for whomever they wanted] did not legally break the Pact. Where the Pact was broken was in making war on the Army of the Republic – by doing so without calling together the representatives of the people. The Third Dáil should have been summoned with the Second Dáil on June 30, 1922..."[74]

Sean Buckley stated, "If the Second Dáil was never dissolved, we must admit that the President of the Second Dáil, Arthur Griffith, was the legitimate president and that the Government was the legitimate government."[75]

MacSwiney [March 27, 1872-March 8, 1942] presents an interesting case. She was born in London of an Irish father and English mother. Her family returned to Ireland when she was six. Educated in Cork, and after earning a teaching degree, she taught at Saint Angelina's High School. She was greatly influenced by her republican brother Terence MacSwiney, who died in October 1920 after a lengthy hunger strike. She was arrested and imprisoned in 1916 after the Easter Rising and as a result lost her teaching job. Released several months later, she and her sister Anne founded Scoil Ite, which was modeled after Patrick Pearse's Saint Enda's, with a strong Republican flavored curriculum including Gaelic language and studies courses.

She was a staunch republican and elected to Dáil Éireann in 1921. Fanatically opposed to the Free State treaty, and in a three-hour diatribe, she was extreme in her attack against Collins and called for a return to war with England rather than approve the Treaty. She joined de Valera and supported war against her own people rather than accept majority rule. She and her sister-in-law Muriel toured America in 1920 and testified in Washington, D.C., before the American Commission on Conditions in Ireland. Though retaining her seat, she refused to enter the Dáil. She had a bitter falling out with de Valera, accused him of treachery and lying, and lost her seat in 1927.

Outsmarted and outvoted, de Valera was determined to overturn the majority which had so overwhelmingly rejected his anti-treaty position.

The election had demonstrated that the nation wanted the treaty. But de Valera refused to accept the people's mandate. The Constitution was not published until the day of the elections, too late for de Valera to utilize it to criticize the Free State or affect the outcome of the plebiscite.

Shortly before his death, Collins explained his views on the pact and the election results which followed: "The country was face to face with disaster, economic ruin and the imminent danger of the loss of the position we had won by the national effort. If order could not be maintained, if no National Government was to be allowed to function, a vacuum would be created, into which the English would necessarily be drawn back. To allow that to happen would have been the greatest betrayal of the Irish people...and I undertook with the approval of the Government, that they should hold four out of nine offices in the new Ministry. They calculated that in this way they would have the same position in the new Dáil as in the old. But their calculations were upset by the people themselves, and they then dropped all pretense of representing the people and turned definitely against them."[76]

O'Connor and the anti-Treaty IRA failed to understand that their actions benefited only England. Having occupied the Four Courts, they raided a Dublin garage and seized sixteen vehicles which they planned to use in Northern Ireland. When several of the raiders were arrested, the rebel IRA kidnapped Ginger O'Connell, the Deputy Chief of Staff of the Provisional Government on June 26. The Provisional Government finally decided to act.

Just after midnight on the morning of June 28, Provisional Government troops surrounded the Four Courts: O'Connor was given a four-hour ultimatum demanding the release of the kidnapped General and evacuation of the buildings. O'Connor thought this was mere bluff and believed Collins would never attack, but the kidnapping of O'Connell was a direct challenge to the Government, and a response was necessary to preserve any semblance of authority. At 4 a.m., Collins ordered the Four Courts shelled with artillery borrowed from the British.

Two days previously, in response to the assassination of Field Marshal Sir Henry Wilson in London on June 22, Churchill had demanded an end to the siege at the Four Courts, charging that the occupation of public buildings in Dublin was "a gross breach and defiance of the Treaty. From this nest of anarchy and treason, not only to the British Crown, but to the Irish people, murderous outrages are stimulated and encouraged, not only in the Twenty-six counties, but even, it seems most probable, here across the Channel in Great Britain... If it is not brought to an end... we shall regard the Treaty as having been formally violated... take no further steps to carry out or legalize its further stages... and resume full liberty of action..."[77]

The Free State Government had already decided to move against the Four Courts garrison, but Churchill's intervention allowed de Valera to claim that the British had ordered the Provisional Government to attack Irishmen. Griffith admitted that the timing of Churchill's broadside was unfortunate. "Yes, it was, but it was pure coincidence... When O'Connell was kidnapped, we did decide to move, and the order was given. Then came Churchill's speech, and we wavered again. Some of us wanted to cancel it. But we said that we had either to go on or to abdicate, and finally, we went on."[78]

In a last gesture of disregard for the rights of the majority before surrendering, O'Connor's Four Courts garrison detonated a large explosion which damaged the Four Courts complex and destroyed the national archives.

Charles Burgess lamented: "He was sick of politics, that he would never fire a shot against comrades and he preferred to die by an English or Orange bullet in the North and that he urged unity on the basis of a Northern crusade..."[79] As the days trickled down to civil war, Burgess, however, answered de Valera's call to fratricide and was holed up in the Hammam Hotel in Dublin. He had claimed that his wish would be to die fighting the English, but instead, he decided to die fighting his own countrymen. When called on to surrender as part of the campaign to rid the area of insurgents, Burgess committed suicide by rushing the Free State troops, pistols firing, deliberately provoking his own death. He refused to heed warnings to halt, and he was shot, dying two days later.

Coogan put his usual anti-treaty bias on the death of Burgess by inferring that he was murdered by Free State troops: "Dave Neligan [Collins' mole in the DMP] told me that some of the troops opposed to Burgess had made up their minds to not even attempt to (take him alive). He was regarded as a dangerous fanatic and was probably shot in the back as he advanced on a barricade near the Hammam."[80] If he had indeed been shot in the back, it would have been from his own people to the rear of him in the Hammam Hotel and not from the pro-Treaty forces manning the barricades in front of him. The ever-magnanimous Collins, who had every justification for hatred of Burgess, had this to say about the former Defense Minister: "I would forgive him anything. Because of his sincerity, I would forgive him anything."[81]

Scant credit was given to Collins' superior genius in finance, government, guerilla tactics, and statesmanship, but also to his military expertise. He accomplished in less than two months what the British and their Black and Tans could not do in four years – defeat an Irish rebellion. He was able to outmaneuver and out-fight the better-armed "idealists" who were bent on satisfying their egos and pockets than the lives and property of their fellow citizens. By August 12, the war was over and the insurgents were scattered to the hills where they reverted to the guerilla tactics of ambush, robbery, murder and intimidation. But this time the rebels did not have the support of the people. With the Free State Army in relentless pursuit, de Valera's supporters accelerated their senseless criminal acts against the people.

It is interesting to note that Tom Barry and Ernie O'Malley, two of the most active insurgents during the Anglo-Irish conflict (1918-21), at a secret IRA session in 1921, in an admission of their inability to continue the fight against England, said: "All the officers of GHQ, who were members of the Dáil and several who held commands in the country, agreed, in declaring that a return to the war conditions, which prevailed before the Truce, was out of the question."[82]

During the treaty debate in January 1922, however, Barry and O'Malley refused to accept the reality of the very situation they admitted only months before and called for a continuation of the war against insurmountable odds. Rather than accept a treaty that allowed for the institution of an Irish army, fully equipped and capable of handling any contingency, including a return of the English, they opted for war on their own people. Beaslai wrote: "It is quite true that the Truce came as a relief to the fighting men of the Columns and the Dublin guard, who were sorely pressed. I have already mentioned that a deputation of Southern officers [led by Liam Lynch] had informed GHQ that they were unable to continue the fight..."[83] Oscar Traynor, another turncoat, admitted that the IRA was unable to carry on the fight and conceded: "Dominion status was just as good as a Republic."[84] He, too, was eager to fight other Irishmen but shy of taking on the English.

Sean Dowling, a member of the anti-treaty executive, described Liam Lynch, Commander-in-Chief of the anti-treaty forces' demeanor at a series of meetings was that of a "simpleton. This is borne out by a number of eyewitness accounts of Lynch's behaviour under stress. At times, he became so heated as to be inarticulate and at other times, when agitated, would issue the most irrational commands, then subside and forget about them...There is evidence, that for some months, Lynch was not only out of touch with the military situation, but was even somewhat out of touch with reality..."[85] On April 10, the quite possibly insane Lynch died on a lonely Southern Ireland mountainside, shot the day before by Free State troops. By May 1923, the relentless pursuit by the National Army and lack of support by the people resulted in the Free State's final wrap-up and triumph over the Insurgents' guerilla campaign.

Following the historic English *modus operandi* of making the Irish pay for their own destruction, de Valera had dispatched Austin Stack and J. J. O'Kelly to America as representatives of the Irish Republic to secure AARIR funding for Irishmen to kill other Irishmen. They claimed the money would be used to promote Republican candidates during the upcoming elections. De Valera's storm troopers, however, were terrorizing pro-treaty candidates in order to prevent any referendum.

Rossa Downing, an Irish-American, and one of the original supporters of de Valera and the AARIR against Devoy and the Friends of Irish Freedom rejected the Irish envoys' claims: "The Treaty with England was legally ratified by direction of a majority of the representatives elected by the people. It is a proposition of law, a proposition of common sense... The delegates went to London cognizant of the fact that full severance from the Empire was impossible. [They] bound themselves to an agreement and now for the Irish in the United States to attempt to direct the future actions of the people [in Ireland] until they have a chance themselves to ratify or discard the agreement is preposterous..."[86]

He continued: "We are absolutely convinced that if armed conflict arises in Ireland between the de Valera and Collins' parties, there is not the slightest doubt in the mind of any thinking, intelligent, disinterested man that the money now being raised for this 'Republican Party' will be used to buy arms and ammunition to slaughter other Irishmen...Our dull wits could not grasp the distinction between Document No.2 and the Treaty."[87]

Bishop Fogarty said, "It is wicked in the extreme for Americans to finance civil war in Ireland..."[88]

According to Downing, the AARIR Directorate met on December 17, 1921, with more than one hundred delegates voting, and declared their neutrality of the conflict raging in Ireland. Less than two months later, thanks to the efforts of Boland and McGarrity, the National Executive was stacked, and with less than twenty delegates attending, the earlier neutrality declaration was overturned and a policy in favour of de Valera was substituted. The membership was ordered to contribute to de Valera's Republican Defense Fund or be expelled.

During an appeal of Boland's rigged election in May 1922, Downing made note that between December 7 and the appeal: "At any moment Irish blood is likely to be shed and de Valera himself has announced that Civil War is a probable outcome of the present strife."[89]

Recognizing the evil de Valera was unleashing on behalf of England in Ireland, Downing said: "It must be quite evident to any thinking person at this time that it will not be necessary for England to fire a shot...We are determined not to give a cent...to encourage the present unfortunate strife, which now, *for the first time in centuries, has arrayed the children of the Gael in armed conflict, brother against brother, father against son.*"[90] [emphasis added]

Collins was heartbroken over Boland's support of de Valera and his opposition to the treaty. He wrote on July 29, 1922: "Harry – it has come to this! Of all things, it has come to this. It is in my power to arrest you and destroy you. This I cannot do. If you will think over the influence, which has dominated you, it should change your ideal. You are walking under false colors. If no word of mine will change your attitude, then you are beyond all hope – my hope."[91]

Boland had initially embraced the treaty and hailed it as an end to centuries of conflict between Ireland and England, but his overriding loyalty was not to Ireland but to de Valera, and when the Great Pretender repudiated the treaty, Boland dutifully followed his lead and voted against the treaty, "giving as his reason that he could not let the long fellow down."[92] He may not have let de Valera down, but he assuredly let Ireland down. Collins was devastated when, on July 31, National troops captured Boland in the Grand Hotel in Skerries, but, in attempting to escape, Boland was mortally wounded and died several days later.

De Valera, however, continued his phony pleas for peace while encouraging acts of mayhem against the government and civilian population. The Free State leaders rejected de Valera's outlandish conditions for peace that was not peace. Kevin O'Higgins declared: "The war was not going to be a draw with a replay in the autumn, and he showed little interest in de Valera's peace overtures."[93]

Collins was exasperated by the Green & Tans: "The anti-National character of their campaign became clear when we saw them pursuing exactly the same course as the English Black and Tans. They robbed and destroyed, not merely for the sake of loot, and from a criminal instinct to destroy...but on a plan and for a definite purpose. Just as the English claimed that they were directing their attack against a 'Murder gang' so the Irregulars claimed that they are making war on a 'usurping' government."[94]

De Valera's tactics fell in line with traditional British policy – intimidation and coercion of an unarmed people, combined with economic destruction, in order to "make an appropriate hell" in Ireland which would render the National Government inoperative. Archbishop Michael J. Curley, of Baltimore, after visiting Ireland, in a letter to Matthew Cummings, on February 2, 1923, lamented: "It makes the heart of an Irishman bleed to see the senseless stupidity of the de Valera people who seem to be bent on murder and destruction and nothing else."[95]

The Catholic Hierarchy was also forthright. On October 10, 1922, they condemned the rebel Republicans: "They carry on what they call a war, but which, in the absence of any legitimate authority to justify it, is morally only a system of murder and assassination of the national forces...The guerilla warfare now being carried out by the Irregulars is without moral sanction and, therefore, the killing of national soldiers in the course of it is murder before God. The seizing of public and private property is robbery; the breaking of roads, railways and bridges is criminal destruction; the invasion of homes and the molestation of citizens a grievous crime."[96]

In a joint pastoral read at masses throughout Ireland on that same day, the Bishops charged: "The militant anti-Treatyites had wrecked Ireland from end to end and condemned the campaign of destruction which had resulted in murder and assassination...And in spite of all this sin and crime, they claim to be good Catholics and demand at the hands of the Church her most sacred privileges, like the Sacraments reserved for worthy members alone...All those who, in contravention of this teaching, who participate in such crimes are guilty of the gravest sins and may not be absolved in Confession, nor admitted to Holy Communion..."[97]

Cardinal Logue said, "A Republic without popular recognition behind it is a contradiction in terms."[98] Bishop Fogarty wrote to Bishop Hagan on January 10, 1923: "The Irregulars [selfless and sincere idealists] are dwindling into a mere assassination club with a few clumps of desperados scattered throughout the country."[99]

However, excommunication had its limits. It appears that it was reserved only for those without power. Once de Valera was reelected in 1932, the ultimate censure miraculously vanished and the prodigal de Valera was welcomed back into the fold although the memories of the murders, robberies, destruction of property and bitterness survive into the next millennium.

In response to an appeal by de Valera, William Cosgrave, who assumed leadership of the Government after Collins and Griffith were murdered in August 1922, offered generous terms. These included the condition that all issues must be decided by majority vote of the Dáil and the insurgents' weapons turned over to the Catholic Hierarchy, rather than turn them over to the pro-treaty forces. He said the Irregulars could burn or destroy them, but "these arms cannot, and will not, if I have any responsibility for the government of this country, remain in the hands of those who are not subject to the authority of the people's parliament."[100] All offensive action against the rebels would cease, and they would be free to contest all elections. The only proviso was that any elected member of the Dáil must subscribe to the oath of allegiance to the Free State constitution. "Cosgrave's main point was that the Republicans should accept the majority wishes of the people."[101] De Valera made sure that Cosgrave's offer was rejected, while still claiming that he had no influence with the rebel Republicans.

Freedom of the Press was another casualty under de Valera's "constitutional method of resolving differences." The Green and Tans raided *The Freeman's Journal* and *The Clonmel Nationalist* on March 29-30, 1922. The newspapers' offence consisted in publishing a Free State Army report of an IRA convention. The attackers [selfless idealists] smashed the presses with sledgehammers and broke the protesting editor's jaw. In a final act of hooliganism, the building was doused with gasoline and set on fire, throwing more than 300 employees out of work. The *Journal* proprietors had been served with the following notice: "You are hereby notified that it has been deemed necessary to suspend the publication of your journal, in view of statements made therein calculated to cause disaffection and indiscipline in the ranks of the Irish Republican Army. By Order of the Army Council, Irish Republican Army Executive."[102] During the Anglo-Irish war, the Black and Tans had torched *The Freeman's Journal* three times and levied fines and jail sentences to the editors and owners for "statements calculated to cause disaffection to the Crown." The "sincere and selfless idealists" were poor imitations of the Black and Tans.

In April 1922, two months before Collins ordered the ousting of the insurgents from the Four Courts, attacks on Free State troops and pro-treaty advocates escalated to daily occurrences: supply trucks were seized; officers kidnapped, and Free State barracks were fired upon by hit and run Irregulars. Beaslai noted: "The fact remains that the first blood in the fratricidal strife was shed, not in June [at the Four Courts], but in April, and that the first shots fired in that strife were fired against Dáil troops by the Irregulars."[103]

After the death of Collins and Griffith, the Provisional Government enacted one draconian measure after another in an effort to halt the attacks on the Government and the terrorizing of the people. In September 1922, anyone found in possession of a firearm or attacking the National Army was to be executed. On November 11, 1922, Erskine Childers was arrested at his cousin Robert Barton's home in County Wicklow. He was tried and convicted by a military court and executed by firing squad for carrying a firearm, ironically one allegedly given to him by Michael Collins.

On October 17, 1922, de Valera showed that he was still calling the shots of the civil war by directing the Army Executive to issue the following proclamation setting up a puppet Government with him as President: "We, on behalf of the soldiers of the Republic, in concert with such faithful members of Dáil Éireann as are at liberty, acting in the spirit of our oath as the final custodians of the Republic, have called upon the former President, Éamon de Valera, to resume the Presidency and to form a Government which shall preserve inviolate the sacred trust of National Sovereignty and Independence."[104]

The former Irish President, rather than endorse a constitutional course, set up a parallel counterfeit Republican Government in November 1922 under the banner of the "Republic" and named his cabinet of Austin Stack as Minister for Finance; P. J. Ruttledge, Home Affairs; Sean T. O'Kelly, Minister for Local Government; Robert Barton, Economic Affairs; and Liam Mellowes, Minister for Defense.

Churchill, with tongue in cheek and de Valera in mind, declared: "The Irish people cannot any longer throw blame on us. If Ireland's opportunity is to be cast away, it will be by Irishmen. If Irish blood is to be shed, it will be by Irish hands. And if Irish civilization is to be made a reproach and a mockery among the nations of the world, it will simply be because Irish people have wished it so...If Irishmen choose to cut off their nose to spite their face, we cannot prevent them, nor shall we try. They are responsible, not we."[105]

De Valera's leadership of the Irregulars was again confirmed in April 1923 when he ordered Frank "Wooden Head" Aiken, the demented Lynch's successor, to give up the fight and dump their arms. De Valera composed a grandiose declaration of surrender: "Soldiers of the Republic, Legion of the Rearguard: The Republic can no longer be defended successfully by your arms. Further sacrifice of life would now be vain and continuance of the struggle in arms unwise in the national interest and prejudicial to the future of our cause. Military victory must be allowed to rest for the moment with those who have destroyed the Republic."[106]

And so de Valera's "Assignment Civil War" was successfully executed: Collins was prevented from coming to the aid of Catholics in the North, the Northern Ireland regime was secure; Anglo-American relations were never better; Irish-American relations were never worse, and international public opinion was overwhelmingly on the side of England.

Southern Ireland lay prostrate and helpless to counter the pogroms of the Protestants against the Catholics of Ulster. England was proven correct in the eyes of the world that the Irish were incapable of governing themselves. The Commonwealth Nations, which considered themselves independent nations, could only wonder at the contentious Irish who preferred the appearance of a phony Republic to the reality of independence.

Notes

1. Collins, Michael, *The Path to Freedom*, Roberts Rhinehart, 1996, p. 17
2. Coogan, Tim P., *Michael Collins*, Arrow Books, 1991, p. 383
3. Coogan, Tim P., *De Valera, The Man who was Ireland*, Harper, 1996, p. 249
4. Coogan, Tim P., *Michael Collins*, A Biography, Arrow Books, 1991, p. 366
5. Coogan, Tim P., *De Valera, The Man who was Ireland*, Harper, 1996, p. 265
6. Macardle, Dorothy, *The Irish Republic*, Victor Gollancz, Irish Press, London/Dublin, 1951, p. 730
7. Martin, F. X. & Byrne, F. J. (eds.), *The Scholar Revolutionary, Eoin MacNeill, 1867-1945 & the Making of a New Ireland*, Irish U. Press, 1973, p. 208
8. Dwyer, T. Ryle, *De Valera, The Man & the Myths*, Poolbeg, Dublin, 1991, p. 115
9. Coogan, Tim P., *De Valera, The Man who was Ireland*, Harper, 1996, p. 302
10. *ibid*, p. 310 & *Irish Independent* 3/17/1922
11. *ibid*
12. *ibid*
13. *ibid*, p. 312
14. Ryan, Desmond, *Unique Dictator*, Arthur Barker, London,1936, p. 169
15. *ibid*, p. 195
16. Longford, Earl of & O'Neill, Thomas P., *Éamon de Valera*, Hutchinson, London, 1970, p. 186
17. Dwyer, T. Ryle, *De Valera, The Man & the Myths*, Poolbeg, Dublin, 1991, p. 92
18. Ryan, Desmond, *Unique Dictator*, Arthur Barker, London, 1936, p. 194
19. Dwyer, T. Ryle, *De Valera, The Man & the Myths*, Poolbeg, Dublin, 1991, p. 106
20. *ibid*
21. *ibid*, p. 105
22. Ryan, Desmond, *Unique Dictator*, Arthur Barker, London, 1936, p. 186
23. Dwyer, T. Ryle, *De Valera, The Man & the Myths*, Poolbeg, Dublin, 1991, p. 102
24. *ibid*, p. 103
25. *ibid*, p. 107
26. Dwyer, T. Ryle, *Éamon de Valera*, Gill and Macmillan, 1980, p. 65
27. Dwyer, T. Ryle, *De Valera, The Man & the Myths*, Poolbeg, Dublin, 1991, p. 108
28. Fitzgerald, W.G. (Splain), *The voice of Ireland, A survey of the Race & Nation*

from All Angles, Virtue Ltd. Dublin/London p. 172

29. Beaslai, Pieras, *Michael Collins and the Making of a New Ireland*, Vol II, Harper Bros. NY 1926, p. 332

30. *ibid*

31. O'Hegarty, P.S., *A History of Ireland under the Union 1801-1922*, Methuen, London, 1952, p. 787

32. Fitzgerald, W. G. (Splain): *The Voice of Ireland, A Survey of the Race & Nation from All Angles*, Virtue Ltd, Dublin/London, p. 221

33. Beaslai, Pieras, *Michael Collins and the Making of a New Ireland*, Vol II, Harper Bros. NY 1926, p. 335

34. Coogan, Tim P., *De Valera, The Man who was Ireland*, Harper, 1996, p. 301

35. *ibid*, p. 299

36. Dwyer, T. Ryle, *De Valera, The Man and the Myths*, Poolbeg, Dublin, 1991, p. 104

37. *ibid*, p. 106

38. Coogan, Tim P., *De Valera, The Man who was Ireland*, Harper, 1996, p. 314

39. Longford, Earl of & O'Neill, Thomas P., *Éamon de Valera*, Hutchinson, London, 1970, p. 195

40. Coogan, Tim P., *De Valera, The Man who was Ireland*, Harper, 1996, p. 309

41. Tierney, Michael (Ed. By F.X. Martin), *Eoin MacNeill, Scholar & Man of action 1867-1945*, Clarendon Press, Oxford 1980, p. 309

42. Coogan, Tim P., *De Valera, The Man who was Ireland*, Harper, 1996, p. 325

43. *ibid*

44. Dwyer, T. Ryle, *De Valera, The Man and the Myths*, Poolbeg, Dublin, 1991, p. 127

45. *ibid*, p. 411

46. Ryan, Desmond, *Unique Dictator*, Arthur Barker, London,1936, p. 171

47. Coogan, Tim P., *De Valera, The Man who was Ireland*, Harper, 1996, p. 307

48. Dwyer, T. Ryle, *De Valera, The Man & the Myths*, Poolbeg, Dublin, 1991, p. 115

49. Ryan, Desmond, *Unique Dictator*, Arthur Barker, London,1936, p. 174

50. O'Hegarty, P.S., *The Victory of Sinn Féin & How It Used It*, Talbot Press, Dublin 1924, p. 174

51. Beaslai, Pieras, *Michael Collins and the Making of a New Ireland*, Vol II, Harper Bros. NY 1926, p. 423

52. Coogan, Tim P., *De Valera, The Man who was Ireland*, Harper, 1996, p. 318

53. Dwyer, T. Ryle, *De Valera, The Man & the Myths*, Poolbeg, Dublin, 1991, p. 115

54. Ryan, Desmond, *Unique Dictator*, Arthur Barker, London, 1936, p. 206

55. *ibid*, p. 207

56. Dwyer, T. Ryle, de Valera, *The Man & the Myths*, Poolbeg, Dublin, 1991, p. 115

57. O'Hegarty, P.S., *The Victory of Sinn Féin & How It Used It*, Talbot Press, Dublin 1924, p. 119

58. *ibid*, p. 150

59. Longford, Earl of & O'Neill, Thomas P., *Éamon de Valera*, Hutchinson, London,

1970, p. 207

60. O'Hegarty, P.S., *The Victory of Sinn Féin & How It Used It*, Talbot Press, Dublin 1924, p. 120

61. Longford, Earl of & O'Neill, Thomas P., *Éamon de Valera*, Hutchinson, London, 1970, p. 213

62. Fitzgerald, W.G. (Splain), *The voice of Ireland, A survey of the Race & Nation from All Angles*, Virtue Ltd. Dublin/London, p. 178

63. Longford, Earl of & O'Neill, Thomas P., *Éamon de Valera*, Hutchinson, London, 1970, p. 209

64. *ibid*

65. Beaslai, Pieras, *Michael Collins and the Making of a New Ireland*, Vol II, Harper Bros. NY 1926, p. 409

66. *ibid*, p. 419

67. *ibid*, p. 383

68. Fitzgerald, W.G. (Splain), *The voice of Ireland, A survey of the Race & Nation from All Angles*, Virtue Ltd. Dublin/London, p. 178

69. Beaslai, Pieras, Michael Collins and the Making of a New Ireland, Vol II, Harper Bros. NY 1926, p. 394

70. Ryan, Desmond, *Unique Dictator*, Arthur Barker, London, 1936, p. 198

71. Phillips, W. Allison, *The Revolution in Ireland 1906-1923*, Longmans, Green, London 1926, p. 277

72. Longford, Earl of & O'Neill, Thomas P., *Éamon de Valera*, Hutchinson, London, 1970, p. 196

73. Collins, Michael, *The Path to Freedom*, Roberts Rhinehart, p.15

74. Gaughan, J. Anthony, *Austin Stack, Portrait of a Separatist*, Kingdom Books, Dublin, 1977, p. 328

75. *ibid*, p. 330

76. Beaslai, Pieras, *Michael Collins and the Making of a New Ireland*, Vol II, Harper Bros. NY 1926, p. 395

77. Ryan, Desmond, *Unique Dictator*, Arthur Barker, London, 1936, p. 203

78. *ibid*, p. 204

79. *ibid*, p. 197

80. Coogan, Tim P., *De Valera, The Man who was Ireland*, Harper, 199, p. 327

81. Longford, Earl of & O'Neill, Thomas P., *Éamon de Valera*, Hutchinson, London, 1970, p. 197

82. Beaslai, Pieras, *Michael Collins and the Making of a New Ireland*, Vol II, Harper Bros. NY 1926, p. 328

83. *ibid*, p. 250

84. *ibid*, p. 251

85. Gaughan, J. Anthony, *Austin Stack, Portrait of a Separatist*, Kingdom Books, Dublin, 1977, p. 231, fn 51

86. Lavelle, Patricia, *James O'Mara, A Staunch Sinn Feiner 1873-1948*, Clonmore &

Reynolds, Dublin, 1961, p. 284

87. Fitzgerald, W. G. (Splain): *The Voice of Ireland, A Survey of the Race & Nation from All Angles*, Virtue Ltd, Dublin/London, p. 222

88. Lavelle, Patricia, *James O'Mara, A Staunch Sinn Feiner 1873-1948*, Clonmore & Reynolds, Dublin, 1961, p. 287

89. Fitzgerald, W. G. (Splain): *The Voice of Ireland, A Survey of the Race & Nation from All Angles*, Virtue Ltd, Dublin/London, p. 221

90. *ibid*, p. 222

91. Brasier, A. & Kelly, J., *Harry Boland, A Man Divided*, New Century Publishing, Dublin, p. 6

92. Gaughan, J. Anthony, *Austin Stack, Portrait of a Separatist*, Kingdom Books, Dublin, 1977, p. 203, fn 109

93. Dwyer, T. Ryle, *De Valera, The Man & the Myths*, Poolbeg, Dublin, 1991, p. 126

94. Collins, Michael, *The Path to Freedom*, Roberts Rhinehart, 1996, p. 15

95. Tansill, Charles, C., *America and the Fight for Irish Freedom 1866-1922*, Devin-Adair, NY. 1957, p. 440

96. Gaughan, J. Anthony, *Austin Stack, Portrait of a Separatist*, Kingdom Books, Dublin, 1977, p.218 fn 26

97. Keogh, Dermot, *The Vatican, the Bishops & Irish Politics, 1919-1939*, Cambridge Press 1986, p. 95

98. Fitzgerald, W. G. (Splain), *The Voice of Ireland, A Survey of the Race & Nation from All Angles*, Virtue Ltd, Dublin/London, p. 276

99. Keogh, Dermot, *The Vatican, the Bishops & Irish Politics, 1919-1939*, Cambridge Press 1986, p. 106

100. Dwyer, T. Ryle, *De Valera, The Man & the Myths*, Poolbeg, Dublin, 1991, p. 127

101. *ibid*

102. Ryan, Desmond, *Unique Dictator*, Arthur Barker, London, 1936, p. 189

103. Beaslai, Pieras, *Michael Collins and the Making of a New Ireland*, Vol II, Harper Bros. NY 1926, p. 382

104. Coogan, Tim P., *De Valera, The Man who was Ireland*, Harper, 1996, p. 339

105. Fitzgerald, W. G. (Splain), *The Voice of Ireland, A Survey of the Race & Nation from All Angles*, Virtue Ltd, Dublin/London. P. 18

106. Dwyer, T. Ryle, *De Valera, The Man & the Myths*, Poolbeg, Dublin, 1991, p. 128 & Longford, Earl of & O'Neill, Thomas P., *Éamon de Valera*, Hutchinson, London, 1970, p. 222

CHAPTER XVIII

The Murder of Arthur Griffith and Michael Collins

"There seems to be a malignant fate haunting the fortunes of Ireland, for at every critical period, the man whom the nation trusted is taken from her."[1]

Michael Collins on the death of Arthur Griffith

Griffith's Sinn Féin policy guided Ireland through the terrible years. He and Michael Collins faced down the world's greatest statesmen and forged a free Ireland after more than seven centuries of unremitting horror. For their sacrifices, Griffith and Collins received the usual Irish reward – death, character assassination, and anonymity.

The British were all too well aware of the threat to England's national and international interests posed by Michael Collins and Arthur Griffith. Lord Birkenhead, one of the British signatories to the treaty, recalled "those dramatic December nights of the Treaty battle in Downing Street, when Winston Churchill gave 'Mick' a silent handclasp, as though he loved the man. Mr. Collins was daring and resourceful, volatile and merry. He differed in almost every conceivable way from the more dour and placid Arthur Griffith. I formed the view quite early in the conflict that these two men were equally courageous and honest. I never doubted that, *if once they gave their word, they would sacrifice life itself to carry out their promise.* And this they have both done..."[2] [emphasis added] Birkenhead's testimony inadvertently revealed why Collins and Griffith were murdered.

The British understood that, with the defeat of the anti-treaty forces, Griffith and Collins would emerge as strong leaders who could not be intimidated. Both would have insisted on strict compliance to the treaty terms, especially the Boundary Clause, in which the Northern Ireland counties of Fermanaugh and Tyrone and the city of Derry would have been transferred to Southern Ireland.

When it became obvious that Collins and Griffith had defeated de Valera's anti-treaty forces, their deaths were a foregone conclusion. The British had no scruples about assassinating their rivals. With de Valera's counterfeit Republicans retreating on all fronts, Collins would soon be free to turn his attention to the terror campaign in Northern Ireland. The murder of Griffith and Collins was shifted into fast-forward. Griffith was poisoned and died the day the doctors gave him a clean bill of health to return to work, and Collins was murdered by a British agent among his own escort party just ten days later.

The Murder of Arthur Griffith

Griffith struggled for more than a score of years nursing his Sinn Féin policies within a small circle of admiring followers in Dublin. A printer by trade, he preached neither parliamentary not physical force but passive resistance and self-reliance. The embattled editor had one newspaper after another shut down by the authorities for "conduct likely to cause disaffection to the Crown." His papers had been suppressed twenty-five times by the British, but he defiantly rushed into print another under a different name.

Griffith's followers were devoted to him, and when he married in his late forties, they organized a fund-raising to purchase a home for him and his bride. The deed to the new home was written in such a manner to prevent him from selling it to finance his newspaper *du jour* and ending up living in a Dublin tenement. Griffith, however, was able to outmaneuver the legal restrictions of the deed, and mortgaged the house to finance another newspaper.

He had none of Collins' organizational genius for neatness and exactness. His upper floor office at 17 Fownes Street, Dublin, was cluttered, dusty, and disarrayed in a room only large enough for a desk and two chairs amid piles of old newspapers, books, and boxes. Collins, on the other hand, was meticulous in record keeping and orderliness. Griffith was a walking file case of miscellaneous bits of information and office supplies: "A sense of order Griffith never acquired. Even as a grown man, in searching his pockets for a letter to show you, he would produce matches and sealing wax, a Sacred Heart badge, bits of string, important documents, a rosary and many other articles before he found what he wanted…"[3]

A visitor to his office would have the option of either standing or wiping off a dusty, rickety-looking chair and risk having it collapse as he sat down. Behind the desk, literally covered by papers, sat a pipsqueak of a man, five foot five inches tall, stocky, round faced, with a bushy moustache, wearing a pince-nez, shabbily dressed, with holes in his shoes, and a shirt that hadn't been pressed since the day he bought it. Could this be the man who wrote the "Resurrection of Hungary" pamphlet that set Ireland ablaze? Was this the writer who defied the

English oppressor? There was something about this little man – the steely gaze in his blue eyes, a jutting no-nonsense jaw, and a large brown-haired head atop a stocky, straight-backed, and barrel-chested body – that projected power and determination. Despite the contradiction of his physical appearance, once he spoke, the power of his intellect, pride in his Irishness, and his determination to set Ireland on freedom's path was irresistible.

Griffith lived below the poverty line, a pauper squeezing a newspaper out of a pittance. He was writer, editor, typesetter, and newspaper boy all rolled into one. His undying goal was the freedom of Ireland, and more than once he refused lucrative positions in Ireland and America. Typical of Griffith was his reply to an American newspaper publisher who offered him a position at his newspaper: "'Thank you, I refuse,' was the short and to the point reply. The visitor was amazed and looked around the dismal office. 'You're toiling in a hovel,' he pointed out, 'when you might work in comfort in New York. They tell me you make only 30 shillings a week.' 'Twenty-five,' corrected Griffith. Then taking off his glasses and rubbing them, as he always did when moved by comedy or tragedy, he added, 'That's enough for me, so why worry?'"[4] He died virtually penniless but rich in friends and through his and Collins' efforts, the Irish finally achieved a government of their own, nebulous, as it might have been at that moment.

Publicly, Griffith presented an austere, stoic, and rigid personality, but in the company of his inner circle of friends, he was quite different. H. Egan Kenny, Griffith's most intimate friend, presented a private picture of Griffith: "With these [friends] alone he unbent. The silent sage would become chatty, jovial, and even hilarious. In rural rambles, he was as sportive and full of pranks as a madcap schoolboy. As shy as a girl, he was to the very end. Nobody ever heard him swear; the nun in the Cloister was not more chaste than Arthur Griffith. His gaze froze into silence the slanderer and the backbiter. The flatterer was repelled by his armor of self-respect. He would never praise a man to his face..."[5]

Ulick O'Connor had this to say about Griffith: "His word was his bond, and people relied on him. He had a way with words, which stood him in good stead with his newspapers, but he lacked the abilities of a great public speaker. He spoke to the point and would often respond in monosyllabic replies to probing, irritating questions, and he was described as that 'rare phenomenon, a silent Irishman.'"[6]

One day, when he failed to show up to lead a protest, his friends were frantic and rushed to his home, where they found him in his stocking feet as his only shoes were being resoled and he was not able to leave the house. Modest and frugal, Griffith literally sold the shirt off his back to keep his newspapers alive.

Born with a deformed left foot, he overcame his physical handicap by participating in athletics and strenuous walking. He participated in school sports activities, excelling in jumping, weight throwing and especially handball. He was such a physical-fitness advocate that he made a ritual at Christmas of plunging into Dublin Bay and swimming for up to 30 minutes in the freezing water. Strong as a bull and built like a fire hydrant, he was not one to be deterred by problems. Having lived with stress all his life, he wasn't about to fold under the dire circumstances of de Valera's civil war.

Griffith was relentless in his crusade for Irish freedom, seeking neither fame nor fortune, and, like Collins, never forgetting a friend. He was courteous to a fault. The son of a Dublin Protestant printer and a Catholic mother, Griffith initially followed in his father's profession. Dreams of making a fortune, however, took him to the gold belt of South Africa in 1897 but, within two years, returned to Ireland and founded the *United Irishman* newspaper with his friend William Rooney. One famous admirer, George Russell (Æ) commented: "Arthur Griffith was so stubborn that I think he must, like Ulysses in the Platonic Myth, have made up his mind before he was born and been unable to alter it afterwards."[7]

The death of Griffith was also a tragic loss for the Protestants of the North. Convinced of their love of Ireland, he was determined to find non-violent and non-sectarian means of uniting Ireland.

Griffith upheld a policy of abstention from Westminster, insisting that the place of Irish politicians was in Ireland under an Irish Government. He preached cooperation with England arguing that Britain's political, economic, and military interests coincided with Ireland's. "England has only great little men, great little men who think the gallows and the jail and the firing squad can convince the intellect and tame the heart of a proud and ancient people..."[8] Griffith often charged that Ireland would take her rightful place among the free nations of the world if England would remove her right hand from Ireland's throat and her left hand out of Ireland's pocket.

Commenting on England's censorship in Ireland, Griffith said: "England built a wall of paper, inside of which she wrote what she wished us to think of the world; on the outside, what she desired the world to think of us." Through his newspapers and pamphlets, Griffith advanced his non-violent credo of an Irish monarchy coexistent with British sovereignty. Griffith modeled his concept of dual monarchy on Austro-Hungarian lines. Hungary's "co-equality" with Austria had been recognized in 1867. He argued that the Hungarians' refusal to merge their national interests with Austria, the development of local authority and recognition of their own native constitution ultimately convinced the Austrians to concede recognition of a Hungarian state. Griffith considered the historic parallels strikingly similar and he advanced his philosophy in pamphlets "The Resurrection of Hungary, A Parallel for Ireland" in 1904 and "The Sinn Féin Policy" in 1906.

Griffith encouraged the establishment of purely Irish industries and economic independence from England. The British considered Griffith's publications seditious and repeatedly closed them down. With the shutting of the *United Irishman* in 1906, Griffith replaced it with *Sinn Féin*, and in 1908, he officially adopted "Sinn Féin" as the name for his party. Sinn Féin (Ourselves Alone) championed an "Irish-Ireland" policy – an Irish state governed by Irishmen for the benefit of the Irish people, promoting everything Irish from trade and commerce to Irish fairs. Self-reliance was its creed. He proposed the setting up of Irish courts, commercial interests, and civil service, all to function alongside their British counterparts. He encouraged the Irish to buy Irish-made clothing and manufactured products while he ate, dressed, and utilized everything of Irish manufacture throughout his life.

Though Sinn Féin was not a militant organization, the Irish Republican Brotherhood (IRB) was not long in recognizing its revolutionary value and quickly threw its support behind Griffith. Sinn Féin was an umbrella under which divergent groups came together even though they did not claim to be Sinn Feiners. Local wags tagged him a "foolish dreamer" and press and politicians dubbed him a "stark lunatic." The English regarded Sinn Féin followers as nothing more than eccentric cranks, and, whenever some inexplicable incident occurred contrary to governmental policy, it was deemed a Sinn Féin event.

The 1916 Rising was just one of those instances that was reviled by the overwhelming majority of the Irish and dubbed the Sinn Féin Rebellion because it was such a crackpot undertaking. Griffith and his Sinn Féin advocates had nothing to do with the Rising, but as a result of the misnomer, Sinn Féin became the symbol of Irish freedom and independence.

Griffith did not participate in the Rising, nor was he privy to the plotting of the IRB, which staged the revolt. When the insurrection began he rushed to join the fight, but the leaders allegedly dissuaded him, insisting that his newspaper and writing skills were more valuable to the Irish cause. Many Nationalists, including Collins, considered Griffith as the preeminent Irish leader in philosophy and thought.

P. S. O'Hegarty described Griffith in the following words: "In Dublin was a man – thickset, obstinate, bull-necked, silent, and visionary – persevering with constancy and courage, pondering many things and among others, the ebullient land of Hungary, and how she won her freedom from the oppression...Home Rule was over and on the horizon loomed Sinn Féin – young, assured and masterful, with an Irish song on its lips, an Irish grammar in its hands and away back in its consciousness – a sword!"[9]

Griffith's death took his compatriots by surprise. Collins said, "The death of poor Mr. Griffith was indeed a shock to us all, more so naturally to those of us who had been intimate with him and who thought *his illness was a very slight thing indeed*. We shall miss for many a day his cheerful presence and his wise counsel..."[10] [emphasis added] O'Hegarty was dumbstruck at the news of Griffith's death: "Until the last few months, he never lay in a sickbed. Whoever else died, we felt sure that it would not be Griffith – Griffith with the iron will, the iron constitution, the imperturbable nerve. Griffith, whom we all thought certain to live to be one hundred and write the epitaph of all of us. Griffith, upon whom we all leaned and depended."[11]

In July 1922, due to threats by de Valera's rebel forces, Free State ministers, including President Griffith, had taken up residence in government buildings on Merrion Street, Dublin. Accommodation was made available in the adjoining College of Science, where the acquisition of arsenic, cyanide, or other poisons was a relatively easy matter. The ministers slept in the laboratories, with beds and furniture from Dublin Castle. Food was delivered from Mills Restaurant on Merrion Row and/or from the Bailey on a daily basis. These public restaurants were freely accessible to anyone. It was not a difficult matter to take Griffith's order and add arsenic or some other slow-acting poison that when ingested over time would kill him.

As the civil war ground to its fateful conclusion, Griffith soon began showing signs of illness: whether from anxiety of the conflict or from the effects of poison, he began suffering insomnia and spent many a night reading books Mrs. Griffith brought to him. His condition worsened, and eventually he had to be hospitalized. He complained of headaches, sore throat, depression, and sleep deprivation, all symptoms which could be attributable to arsenic or a similar type poison.

Arsenic poisoning affects people in different ways. Some show no immediate symptoms, but the poison can often lead to heart disease or stroke. Other signs include weakness, loss of appetite, and vision problems. If discontinued, most traces of arsenic leave the body within a few days. A urine analysis cannot determine if a person was exposed to arsenic; hair and fingernail testing can usually determine exposure to high levels of arsenic, but these tests are unreliable for low-level arsenic exposure. In an experiment in 1995, a team of scientists in Grenoble, France, examined Napoleon's hair and found as much as ten times the normal level of arsenic.[12] Dr. Sunandan Singh, former Chief Medical Examiner for Bergen County in New Jersey, commented that this discovery was misleading because arsenic was used as a preservative in Napoleon's time; arsenic had been discarded as a preservative by Griffith's death in 1922.

During the time he spent hospitalized under a supervised diet and care by the medical staff, Griffith rapidly regained his health and was scheduled to return to work. Dr. Singh said: "If the poison is taken away for a period of time, that can bring about an amelioration of symptoms and a return to health, but if a large dose is then administered, death could come rapidly."

A little over a week after being admitted, on August 11, 1922, a party was held marking the end of Griffith's hospitalization. He had recovered sufficiently to return to work the following day. On that fatal morning of August 12, two female visitors, reportedly his nieces, came to visit Griffith bearing chocolates which were allegedly laced with poison. This time, the poison was potent enough to kill him, and he dropped dead at the top of the stairs as he waved goodbye to his visitors.

Dr. James Magennis was summoned and made a small incision opening a vein in Griffith's arm that produced no flow of blood. The Reverend Mother who attended Griffith said: "Griffith had been up and about in his dressing gown and some relatives had called to see him. They had been chatting and he looked out the window and said, 'It's going to rain so you two had better be off before it comes down.' They left the room and he followed them to the top of the stairs. As he was standing there, he stooped down as if to fasten his shoe and slumped to the ground. Sister called the guard and between the guard, herself, and the nurse, they carried him back to bed. Dr. Oliver St. John Gogarty, who had also been sent for, entered the room, walked over to the side of the bed, put his hand on each side of Griffith's face and said, 'Poor Arthur, Poor Arthur.' Then turned to Magennis and said, 'Come on Jim, we had better go and break the news to his wife.'"[13]

Doctor Gogarty diagnosed his death as a result of a sub-arachnoid hemorrhage, a form of stroke. The report stated: "'President Griffith had an acute attack of tonsillitis on Monday, July 31. This passed off in a few days. No operation was needed. I prevailed on him to rest for a week in the Nursing Home for the benefit of his general health. At 10 a.m. this morning [12 August], he had a cerebral hemorrhage. He regained consciousness for a moment but death rapidly followed...' Dr. Gogarty named the hemorrhage [stroke] as sub-arachnid." Why Dr. Gogarty did not perform an autopsy has never been adequately answered.

According to Dr. Singh, "A diagnosis of sub-arachnoid stroke without an autopsy is literally impossible. Even today, it takes a skilled person with modern equipment to diagnose a sub-arachnoid stroke. It is a very hazardous guess without an autopsy. With modern equipment, it can be a straightforward observation. If he was embalmed, some of the tissue may still be preserved. The embalming delays the decay of the flesh, including the brain tissue. Microscopically, you can determine whether he had a sub-arachnoid stroke. Dissection, however, would have to be done carefully in order to preserve the tissue for an examination of the blood vessels and base of the brain. It takes an astute medical examination. If Griffith's body was exhumed, and there was sufficient tissue remaining, it would be relatively easy to determine if he was poisoned..."

According to *The New York Times* and the *Chicago Tribune*, "Reports that Arthur Griffith was poisoned circulated in Dublin at the time of his death three weeks ago and have again become prevalent. Inquiry among the physicians who attended the Dáil President have evoked the categorical statement that he died from natural causes, probably from heart disease.

"A leading physician, however, informed the correspondent that there is some talk of exhuming the body and clearing away any doubt as to the cause; holding an autopsy for the purpose of determining his death."[14]

On September 7, *The New York Times* quoted the *Chicago Tribune*: "[It] was informed today by two reliable men who have just returned from Dublin that the Free State authorities have exhumed the body of Arthur Griffith and found traces of poison. A doctor and two nurses are said to have been arrested. The news is said to have been suppressed by Dublin censors."

The following day, official news reports denied the story, claiming: "The curious rumor that Arthur Griffith died from the effects of poisoning and that his body was to be exhumed has been persistent in the city for some days past. On inquiry today at Government headquarters, it was definitely assured that the statements are without foundation..."[15] In effect, despite the rumors of a Griffith murder, the Cosgrave government did nothing to dispel those allegations.

O'Hegarty had this to say about Griffith: "By his death, we lost not only the most constructive and steadfast political intelligence in Ireland, but the man upon whom, for twenty odd years, had lain the whole burden of the travail of this nation and upon whom, by rights, it should have lain for at least another ten. Arthur Griffith was not alone the greatest Irishman of his time, but he was the greatest Irishman since Davis and Mitchel and perhaps the most gifted all-round nationalist since Tone."[16]

O'Hegarty continued: "de Valera... was the voice of the movement, its public standard-bearer, its mother of pronouncements. But Griffith was still its brain-carrier and supplier of ideas and upon Griffith, it was the majority counted and depended."[17]

Griffith had anticipated being murdered. With O'Hegarty on June 30, 1922, Griffith was heartbroken and depressed. The Four Courts had been attacked, and de Valera was fueling the fire of civil war with exhortations urging the counterfeit Republican fanatics to fight the government: "Of course, those fellows will assassinate Collins and myself... de Valera is responsible for this – for all of it. There would have been no trouble but for him."[18]

Collins invited de Valera to attend Griffith's funeral, but the invitation was refused. If de Valera had wanted to discuss a peace initiative, Griffith's funeral presented a golden opportunity to do so. General Collins, in his Commander-in-Chief uniform, marched at the head of the funeral cortège as the nation mourned one of its greatest sons. Collins repeated the centuries-old Irish epitaph: "At every critical period, the men whom the nation trusted are taken from her."[19] He might have added that behind every tragic Irish crisis lurked the hand of an Englishman, spy, informer, traitor.

The Murder of Michael Collins

"'Mr. President what's the story of your involvement in the death of Michael Collins?'

"De Valera, replied, 'I can't say a thing, John, but that fellow had it coming to him.'"*

Once the hastily recruited Free State army routed the bulk of the anti-Treaty Republican forces, Collins and Griffith's usefulness as

---

*Coogan responded to assertions about the historical legacy of de Valera by Nicholas Mansergh [*Irish Times*, 1/31/2005]. In 1966, during the 50th Anniversary of the 1916 Easter Rising, Tim Pat Coogan reported a conversation between American Congressman John Fogarty of Rhode Island, an attendee, who posed the above question to de Valera.

counterweights to de Valera's machinations was at an end. Griffith was murdered to prevent him from opposing any English-rigged Boundary Commission decision, while Collins was eliminated to stop him from upsetting the status quo in Northern Ireland. When he had General Henry Wilson assassinated on his doorstep in London on June 22 as a warning that the persecution of the Catholics in Northern Ireland would not be tolerated as long as he lived, his days were numbered.

With the civil war winding down and Collins still alive and free to turn his attention North, the British faced a far greater danger than the previous four-year Anglo-Irish insurgency. The Free State, under the terms of the treaty, had the right to raise an army – albeit proportionate to the population of England and Ireland, but an army nevertheless. It would be armed with the latest weapons, which Collins could clandestinely supply Catholics in Northern Ireland to defend themselves from Protestant terror.

Tim Pat Coogan was convinced of Britain's determination to get rid of Collins: "From my researches into Collins' life, it became quite clear, had he lived, and obtained settled conditions in the South, he fully intended to attempt to achieve that goal [of a Thirty-two County Republic] by military means if necessary. *There is evidence that the British suspected what Collins was doing.*"[20] [emphasis added] Collins' primary aim, however, was not to end Partition by force but to counter the Unionist terror against Catholics in Northern Ireland. He was convinced the Boundary Commission would ultimately resolve the unification of Ireland issue.

The elimination of Collins presented no major challenge as the ranks of both the pro- and anti-treaty factions were infiltrated by British agents: it was only a matter of timing, appearance and opportunity. Collins' death would be blamed on the IRA, the same faction implicated in the murder of General Wilson when it had been too embarrassing to point the finger at the real culprit, Collins.

As the civil war was winding down, Collins was feeling the effects of twenty-hour working days and the accumulated tension of the previous four years of mental and physical effort against the English. On August 8, the day he left for Cork on an alleged inspection tour, he was feverish and his body racked with pain: he had previously suffered from pleurisy, which made him susceptible to pneumonia. He had been advised by doctors and friends to postpone the trip, but it was obvious that there was more to his journey than a review of military installations. According to John M. Feehan, the primary purpose of Collins' trip was on a peace-making mission.[21]

The IRA rebels wanted a settlement: they were confronted by an army which was just as familiar with guerilla tactics as they were. More importantly, the people who had supported them during the Black and Tan terror were now almost universally hostile and Collins, the man who won the Anglo-Irish war, was now leading the opposition against his former comrades. As the war ground to a close, Collins found no satisfaction in defeating the insurgents. "He was far too noble and magnanimous to gloat in any way over the reverses of his former friends. He wanted above all peace and unity and he would approach them as a comrade and not as a conqueror. His last words to General Sean Hales in Bandon on that fatal day were that he did not want to injure one Irishman or even to humiliate in the least the proud spirits of those of his countrymen who may have been opposed to him."[22]

Feehan reported that a group of prominent citizens in Cork were offering a proposal which provided for the integration of rebels into the Free State army and civil service, in positions commensurate with their former rank and influence. Those who wanted to continue the struggle on behalf of the Republic would be equipped from the Free State arsenal and sent to Northern Ireland to fight the Unionists. Most importantly, they would not have to take any oath.[23]

Another of Collins' major purposes in traveling to Cork was to recover Excise Duties amounting to £120,000 ($600,000) that the Irregulars had stolen. He recovered the money under mysterious circumstances on August 21.

Three days into a peace mission under cover of a countrywide tour of inspection of military installations, Michael Collins received the devastating news that Griffith had suddenly died. Griffith was a relatively easy assassination target for the English; with access to his food, it was not difficult to poison his meals. Collins, however, would require a bit more finesse.

Most Irish writers were content to attribute Collins' suspicious death to an errant IRA bullet, in a billion to one chance, ricocheting off an armored vehicle and inflicting a huge wound in the back of his right ear. There were murmurs of British Secret Service complicity, with the motive being revenge for the assassination of so many British agents by Collins during the course of the Anglo-Irish conflict.

In his book, *The Shooting of Michael Collins*, Feehan provides a comprehensive account of Collins' ambush at the little hamlet of Béal na mBláth (Mouth of Flowers) in County Cork. But Feehan, as well as every other Irish writer, however, ignored the realpolitik behind the murder of Collins – who posed a serious threat to Northern Ireland and even to England itself.

Collins' death, of course, was deflected to the usual suspects – the IRA. However, the IRA was engaged in secret negotiations with him at that time, and the day before he died, anti-Treaty elements had issued him safe conduct and a map outlining mine-free roads in which he was to pass during his mission in Cork. The IRA "ambush" appeared to be more of an exercise in bravado than a deliberate attempt to kill Collins. It is still in the realm of possibility – albeit remote that an IRA bullet ricocheted off the armored car and rebounded into Collins' skull. One report claimed the bullet was still in Collins' head, while it was also alleged that there was a small caliber entry wound at Collins' hairline. Those truths can easily be verified by the disinterment of Collins' remains: it would be clear once and for all whether there was a bullet in Collins' skull and whether it came from a pistol, rifle, or machine gun.

Ironically, Collins was the IRA dissidents' last hope of a fair and honorable settlement of the civil war. He was one of "them." He had gone through the Troubles with them, and he had been negotiating with the anti-treaty faction with a good prospect of success. Above all, he was not vindictive. With his death, the insurgents' fortunes went from bad to worse.

Upon assuming the position as Commander-in-Chief, Collins' primary concern was to find common ground with the insurgents. He utilized all of his undercover experience to arrange a cease-fire and reconciliation. Most of the Irregulars had fought with Collins during the Anglo-Irish war: they respected him and were convinced of his sincerity. He was on a Southern tour seeking an end to the internecine madness, and the Irregulars, by assassinating him, would be hurting themselves. Pieras Beaslai noted: "Communications, with regard to a basis for peace, passed between him and certain Southern leaders, through the medium of Sean Hales, just before his death."[24]

Collins left Portobello Barracks in Dublin at 6 a.m. on the morning of August 20, 1922 on his way to Limerick for what was ostensibly called an inspection of military facilities. Collins, obviously engaged in peace talks with anti-treaty leaders, while in Cork, discussed how to end the civil war with a former Frongoch prisoner. Collins "made the significant reply: 'very well, see me tomorrow night, I may have news for you...'"[25] It is a reasonable assumption that Collins was scheduled to meet with anti-treaty leaders that night or the following day and hoped for a resolution. Feehan wrote: "As we now know Collins was to meet neutral 'go-betweens' in Desmond's Hotel in Cork on the night of August 22...who had the confidence of both sides and to discuss with them terms for a cease-fire. They would then contact the IRA dissident leaders and arrange a meeting with Collins somewhere away from the city…"[26]

As evidence of good faith the anti-treaty leaders provided Collins with a map showing cleared roads, intact bridges, and mine-free routes along his projected tour. Feehan said: "Concerning the matter of 'safe-conduct' the Mallow IRA have stated openly that they removed all the mines from the Cork-Mallow road so that Collins and his convoy could get to Cork safely…"[27]

A surprise peace settlement with the insurgents would eliminate the usual IRA suspects in the death of Collins and the British would be hard-pressed casting blame on anyone else. It was critical for the British to act prior to any settlement and Collins' assassination was shifted into fast forward.

Collins and General Emmet Dalton departed the Imperial Hotel in Cork at 6:15 a.m., August 22. As commanding officer of the Cork area, Dalton was in charge of the safety of the Commander-in-Chief though he later denied responsibility for the selection of the men making up the escort party and claimed he knew nothing of their character and loyalty. No inquest into the death of Collins was ever held and no one was ever identified as to who selected the escort party. Care had to be taken to ensure that only reliable men were assigned to protect Collins because the British had infiltrated both the pro- and anti-treaty factions after the signing of the treaty, and it would not have been difficult for an assassin to be assigned to the escort convoy. For this oversight, Dalton was solely responsible.

Collins' escort consisted of an advance motorcyclist, Scout Officer Lieutenant Smith, followed by a party of two officers, eight riflemen, and two machine gunners manning one Lewis machine gun mounted on an open Crossly tender. The next car was a touring car with two drivers in front and with General Collins, Dalton, and Sean O'Connell in the back, a total of at least eighteen men. "One of the officers who came from the locality remarked to the Commander-in-Chief [Collins] that his escort was very small and the country we were to pass through was haunted by bands of Irregulars. His remark was greeted with a confident smile, and General Collins replied: 'Where you can go, we can go, too.'"[28]

At his hometown of Clonakilty, Collins met with relatives and friends, and the townspeople were friendly and cheered him. He was greeted with similar outbursts of enthusiasm and goodwill in Bandon, Roscarbery, and Skibbereen, where he inspected the military installations. They also stopped at Sam's Cross, Collins' ancestral home, where he met his brother, Sean, and a number of his relatives.

De Valera had been hiding out in a farmhouse near Gougane Barra, a remote hamlet not far from Macroom. Anti-treaty leaders had gathered in nearby Ballyvourney to consider the disastrous conventional tactics that had led to defeats at Limerick, Cork, and other cities. The meeting drew top-ranking figures such as de Valera, Erskine Childers, Tom Hale, and Liam Lynch. They decided to revert to the guerilla-type tactics that proved so successful during the Anglo-Irish insurgency.

Two days after the Ballyvourney meeting, de Valera allegedly heard Collins was at Béal na mBláth. "De Valera drove to the scene of an IRA meeting [near Long's Pub] and discovered that Collins had indeed driven past the pub a little earlier."[29]

"De Valera was in the district allegedly on his way to Dublin to attend the September 9 Dáil meeting which he never attended. At one house, he was told Collins had been there an hour before. Next day, he learnt Collins had been killed in an ambush near Béal na mBláth on his return journey from West Cork the previous evening."[30]

De Valera's biographers conveniently failed to note his meeting with the local anti-treaty forces in which they planned and set in motion the ambush, which he allegedly opposed. Longford and O'Neill also neglected to mention that de Valera and Liam Deasy, the highest-ranking anti-treaty officer in the area, spent the previous day and the morning of Collins' death discussing and visiting the ambush site.

Coogan wrote: "An interested observer of these preparations [for an ambush] was Éamon de Valera, who had spent the night in a farmhouse about two miles away. He is quoted as saying, 'What a pity I didn't meet him,' and 'It would be bad if anything happens to Collins, his place will be taken by weaker men.'"[31]

Andrew Brasier, in his biography of Harry Boland, noted: "It was alleged Dalton had fired the fatal shot which had killed Collins, and that he had done so because he was a British intelligence 'sleeper' within the Republican movement. The murder [of Collins] was carried out, this theory goes, because the Irish leader [Collins] *was about to meet his counterpart and old friend on the other side, Éamon de Valera*. De Valera was also in the vicinity of Béal na mBláth at the time of the ambush."[32] [emphasis added]

Coogan attempted to divert suspicion away from de Valera despite the incredible coincidences of his proximity: "An integral part of 'the great Irish whodunit' mystery is that de Valera had a hand in Collins' death. This is true only in the sense that he was the principal architect of the overall Civil War situation."[33] On the very same page, Coogan confirmed de Valera's luring of Collins to Béal na mBláth: "*de Valera...was in the area to meet Collins and arrangements had been made to bring them together.*"[34] [emphasis added]

How was it that de Valera found himself in one of the most remote spots in Ireland discussing an ambush of Collins' convoy with the highest ranking anti-Treaty officer in the area? One conjecture is that de Valera lured Collins to the area in order for British agents in his party to murder him and Deasy unwittingly provided IRA cover for the murder by organizing the ambush. Initially, de Valera claimed that he was in Béal na mBláth on his way to Dublin, but it is so far off the beaten path that he later changed his motive for being there to a prearranged appointment with Collins to discuss a peace settlement.

Beaslai noted the incredible coincidences marking de Valera's movements on the days leading up to Collins murder but he did not go as far as suggesting complicity. "It is a remarkable coincidence that de Valera, on the same day, is known to have been on the road taken by Collins' party and not far from the scene of the fatal ambush..."[35]

T. Ryle Dwyer reported the meeting between de Valera and Deasy on the night before the ambush. "'We discussed the war situation far into the night,' Deasy recalled. 'de Valera's main argument was that, having made our protest in arms and as we could not now hope to achieve a military success, the honorable course was for us to withdraw.' Deasy agreed to an extent but pointed out that the majority of the IRA would not agree to an unconditional cease-fire. Next morning, [August 22, 1922] Deasy accompanied de Valera to the cross at Béal na mBláth, where they learned Collins had just passed through the area. When de Valera asked what the IRA intended to do, Deasy replied, 'they would prepare an ambush in case Collins returned by the same route'. One of those present remarked that Collins might not leave his native county alive. 'I know,' de Valera replied, 'and I am sorry for it. He is a big man and might negotiate. If things fall into the hands of lesser men, there is no telling what might happen.'"[36]

If, as Brazier and Coogan argued, de Valera had arranged to meet with Collins and had nothing to do with setting up the ambush, why did he suddenly leave before the meeting took place? When the preparations for the ambush were completed, de Valera beat a hasty retreat out of Béal na mBláth through the garrison town of Fermoy. "Once through Fermoy, de Valera linked up safely with his car...and drove to Fethard where he spent the night with Jimmy Flynn's parents. Later that night, he heard the news of Collins death and was 'furious and visibly upset.'"[37] Coogan never questioned why de Valera didn't keep his appointment with Collins.

Under the circumstances, it is a reasonable assumption de Valera lured Collins to the site, encouraged the ambush diversion, and then distanced himself from the expected murder scene. "The next day, de

Valera awoke fully alive to the peril of his position. Collins had friends to whom the taking of life presented little problem. Taking de Valera's would have been a great pleasure to some of them at that moment. He was reviled in press, pub and pulpit...One Cork priest, Canon Cohalan of Bandon, preached a sermon in which he said: 'The day Michael Collins was shot, where was de Valera? Ask the people of Béal na mBláth and they will tell you. There was a scowling face at a window looking out over that lonely valley and de Valera could tell you who it was.'"[38]

Coogan observed: "[de Valera] was not long about drying his tears. Discovering he had left his binoculars in the house near Béal na mBláth to which Canon Cohalan alluded, he wrote to his hostess asking they be sent on to him in Dublin..."[39]

Feehan also raised doubts about de Valera: "For nearly a year before the Treaty was signed, Collins had become increasingly suspicious of de Valera's integrity and after the Treaty, all his suspicions he believed were fully justified...In the past, despite grave doubts, Collins had given unswerving loyalty to his Chief and had an absolute trust in his integrity. Now he believed that de Valera was a man of very little principle, who was prepared to twist and turn with every political wind that could be advantageous to him in his haughty obsession with personal power."[40] Feehan failed to consider whether there might be other reasons for de Valera's egregious conduct.

Deasy, after Free State forces had captured him, and in return for his life, called for an "immediate and unconditional surrender of the anti-treaty faction".[41]

With the death of Collins, no explanation was forthcoming as to why he had reportedly visited Macroom three times within twenty-four hours. One theory was that he was meeting with anti-treaty leaders over an imminent settlement of the civil war. Along his route, he visited with several anti-treaty men languishing in various jails, and he was to meet with IRA men in Cork. When warned that he faced danger in the rabidly anti-treaty county, Collins, in typical bravado, said: "They wouldn't shoot me in my own county."

Nor was there any explanation from Dalton as to why he diverted the convoy from the cleared and direct road from Bandon to Macroom and repeated the roundabout and longer route that led through desolate Béal na mBláth, which reportedly had the most dangerous ambush sites per mile of any road in Ireland. No competent officer traveling in enemy territory would have chosen to return by the same exposed route unless there was a rendezvous.

The Ambush

Tom Hales and a large contingent of insurgents set up the ambush site by blocking the road with a brewery cart and setting a mine 50 to 100 yards up the road. After waiting several hours, Hales called off the ambush and all but five men left for home or to Long's Pub.

At about 7:15 p.m., the Collins party was returning to Macroom with motorcyclist Smith in the lead, the Crossley tender approximately 150 feet behind, and Collins, and Dalton in the touring car the same distance to the rear of the tender. The armored car was close behind Collins and Dalton. The party had turned onto a flat stretch of road bounded on both sides by steep hills. The road was slightly depressed about two feet below the shoulders and ran parallel to a lane that intersected the roadway at points behind and ahead of the escort party, a distance of approximately a half mile.

According to Dalton's report of the ambush: "We had just turned a wide corner of the road when a sudden and heavy fusillade of machinegun and rifle fire swept the road in front of and behind us, shattering the windscreen of our car. I shouted to the driver: 'Drive like hell!' But the Commander-in-Chief, placing his hand on the man's shoulder, said, 'Stop! Jump out and we'll fight them.'"[42]

Contrary to basic military practice, General Dalton allowed his Commander-in-Chief to leap out of a protected car into a "heavy fusillade" of machine gun fire to take on unseen assassins in unknown numbers. Dalton allegedly had no idea what kind of an ambush was involved, how many insurgents were taking part, or whether there were explosives set to go off when anyone got out of the car. The armored car drew up and opened fire on the attackers with its machine gun, but Dalton, not only allowed Collins to remain exposed to the firing from above rather than rush him to the shelter of the armored vehicle but left him to fend for himself, alone and out of sight.

"Years later, Florrie O'Donoghue said that Dalton had told him, 'Mick wouldn't keep his head down. If he'd ever been in a scrap, he'd have learned to stay down. For I was flat down and Mick was killed standing up.'"[43] Dalton had the temerity to accuse Collins of not being experienced during a confrontation such as an ambush and that the Commander-in-Chief unnecessarily exposed himself to the attackers. The question, however, was why Dalton placed Collins in that position. Furthermore, Collins was not standing up when he was shot but was found lying in the prone position with his rifle cradled in his arms. Dalton could not have seen Collins standing up for he claimed Collins was out of sight when he heard a muffled cry of "Emmet."

Dalton alleged that he and Collins were initially within an arm's length of each other, firing at the insurgents: "General Collins and I, with Captain Dolan, who was near us, opened a rapid fire on our seldom visible enemies...We continued this firefight for about 20 minutes without suffering any casualties, when a lull in the enemy's attack became noticeable...Suddenly, I heard Collins shout: 'Come on boys! There they are, running up the road.' I immediately opened fire upon two figures that came in view on the opposite road. When I next turned round the Commander-in-Chief had left the car position and run about 15 yards back up the road. *Here he dropped into the prone firing position* [emphasis added], and opened up on our retreating enemies."[44]

Another curious aspect of Dalton's report was that he claimed the convoy was under heavy machine gun fire but the fact was that "with regard to their fire power...only three of them [insurgents] had rifles – the other two had revolvers. They [ambushers] claim Collins must have been killed either accidentally or deliberately by one of his own party."[45] A veteran like Dalton surely would have been able to distinguish between the firing of a machine gun and that of three antiquated rifles and two pistols.

Instead of running over to Collins and providing cover for him, and contrary to his claim that Collins "was killed standing up," Beaslai reported: "Dalton, Dolan and O'Connell took up positions on the road further down,"[46] leaving Collins to fend for himself. No one saw or heard anything of the Commander-in-Chief until an alleged muffled cry of "Emmet" by Collins distracted Dalton from whatever he was doing at that time. Rushing to Collins, Dalton, again contradicted his statement that Collins was shot while standing up: "*We found our beloved Chief and friend lying motionless in a firing position, firmly gripping his rifle, across which his head was resting.*"[47] [emphasis added]

Dalton's failure to apply basic military tactics was questionable, to say the least. No experienced army officer, let alone a General, assigned with the responsibility of protecting his Commander-in-Chief, would halt a small escort party in the middle of an ambush and leap out to take on an unknown number of rebels.

As an example of Dalton's dereliction in the selection of the escort party, one of the machine-gun crew had been inexplicably changed the night before, and the gun "jammed" shortly after commencing fire on the ambushers because the new crewmember allegedly did not know how to feed the gun belt properly. Ian McPeake, the gunner in the armored car, said: "His assistant machine gunner was changed in Cork the evening before and replaced by a stranger whom he did not know. Why was this? Again no answer."[48]

The machine gunner who did not know how to feed the ammunition belt was never identified and two months later, McPeake deserted to the IRA taking the very same armored vehicle with him. "All he asked from the IRA was that they smuggle him back to his native Scotland and give him a few pounds. This they succeeded in doing after a short delay."[49] He feared for his life as many of his fellow soldiers accused him of shooting Collins.

There are several possible scenarios as to how Collins was killed. According to Feehan's detailed analysis of the ambush, a number of witnesses reported that there were actually two wounds: "A small entry wound on the hairline and a large gaping wound behind the right ear. Where exactly on the hairline is not clear. This entry wound was circular, symmetrical and in no way jagged or torn. Could such a wound be caused by a .303 bullet fired from a rifle at a range of 130-150 yards? The answer must be an emphatic, No!"[50]

If a .303 rifle bullet did not cause the wound, what was the chances of a ricochet off the armored car? A ricochet could have caused the gaping wound under Collins' right ear but not the small entry wound at his hairline. A ricochet ripping inside Collins' head quite possibly may have exited at his hairline but it certainly could not have produced such a "clean, circular, symmetrical incision as seen by the witnesses."[51]

If the possibility of a ricochet bullet and a .303 rifle shot are both eliminated, the question then arises what type of weapon could have inflicted the neat clean, circular entry hole in his scalp and exit with a huge, gaping wound behind his right ear? According to Feehan, it was most likely a Mauser pistol. The Mauser comes equipped with a portable stock that can convert the pistol into a rifle, and it fires a 7.45 mm or 9 mm bullet. "When it strikes and enters an object, it expands and tumbles and can tear the flesh to pieces inside. If the bullet emerges, it usually leaves a large open wound at the point of exit... The wounds seen on Collins' head are consistent with the type of bullet wound normally inflicted by a Mauser bullet and it is quite reasonable to conclude that he was shot, not by a rifle, or a ricochet but by a Mauser. This, of course, raises the question as to who carried Mauser pistols at Béal na mBláth? The simple fact is that some of the ambushers and some of the escort had them and used them."[52]

The only members of the ambush party who could have shot Collins were the two ambushers seen running away. The other three ambushers were out of range and out of sight. Feehan noted: "To aim and hit a small target, such as a man's head at 130 yards with a Mauser pistol even with the stock on, would be little short of miraculous...It is also unlikely if they were really out to get Collins that they would have waited until dusk and the uncertainty of a Mauser bullet, when they could have picked him off earlier during daylight with a .303 rifle... It is unlikely, therefore, that this particular [long-range Mauser] theory as to how he met his death has any validity.[53] Furthermore, to add to the odds, the two men were unlikely to fire with any sense of accuracy while running away.

What was the possibility that he could have been "accidentally" shot by someone in his own escort party? That certainly is a viable possibility. During the diversion of the ambush, any member of the escort party could have gotten close and shot Collins as his attention was riveted on the attackers above him.

Could he have been shot by the men from Long's Pub who having heard the shots, rushed out and began firing at the convoy from 300–400 yards away? "This is most unlikely. First, the armored car would have been directly in the line of fire and would have given Collins cover. Secondly, Collins was dead some time, perhaps five or ten minutes...and according to Deasy, the men from Long's Pub were only in position a minute or two when the convoy moved. It is reasonable to assume that Collins was dead by the time this section took up firing positions."[54]

The ambush party occupied the high ground and could have picked off the members of the escort one by one if they were so inclined. The insurgents were more bravado than brave, however, for they fired a few potshots and then ran like rabbits. The two men Collins saw running away later confessed, in their haste to get away and in such a position, any firing on their part at such an angle would ricochet off the armored car and send the shattered bullet away from Collins. There is a slim chance the bullet might have ricocheted twice, bouncing back into Collins' skull, but again, that would not account for the small wound in the front of his head.

According to Dalton, upon reaching Collins, he immediately recognized that the gaping wound behind his right ear was fatal. O'Connell knelt down and whispered an act of contrition to the dying Collins. The wounded Collins was then dragged some forty to fifty feet behind the armored car. The head wound was so large that Dalton had difficulty bandaging it: "I had not completed my grievous task when the big eyes quickly closed and the cold pallor of death overspread the General's face."[55] Collins body was placed on the back of the armored car.

As they were tending to Collins' body, Lieutenant Smith was shot in the neck but it turned out not to be serious. This was important for Dennis "Sonny" O'Neill, one of the ambushers, upon firing his last shot, said he saw an officer hit and fall. It had to be Lt. Smith for Collins, was shot lying in the prone position and had been placed on the armored car by the time Smith was hit. This was confirmed by Dalton, who stated, "Even after Collins had been hit, we were still being sniped."[56]

Collins' body lay cradled in Dalton's arms while the convoy got lost on the dark lanes: it took more than four hours rather than the usual thirty minutes to cover nineteen miles, and the party finally arrived in Cork at 1:30 a.m. General Dalton had set out on a tour with the Commander-in-Chief minus a knowledgeable guide. Coogan noted: "Certainly, if word had been sent back to Bandon a few miles away, along a road which the convoy had just traversed, Sean Hales would have provided guidance. This failure to seek help from the nearest point available is one of the strangest features of that whole awful night."[57]

Dalton's report of the ambush was riddled with inconsistencies. He insisted the convoy was attacked by a fusillade of machinegun bullets, denied that there was a second wound in Collins' head, and claimed he had issued instructions to Commandant Friel to bring Collins' body to the Irish Bon Secours Hospital, when, in fact, it was dispatched to the British Military Hospital at Shanakiel. Feehan wrote: "The body was never brought to the Bon Secours. Friel said he was ordered by Dalton to bring the body to Shanakiel Hospital, which was still occupied by the British, and he did as he was told. Press photographs published the following day prove Friel correct and these reports list Dalton as being present at the removal of Collins' remains from this hospital."[58]

Feehan reported that the head nurse, Eleanor Gordon, at the British hospital, along with Commandant Frank Friel, cleaned the wound and bandaged Collins' head. They were certain there was an entry wound on the hairline as well as the exit wound at the back of the head. Significantly: "Gordon also stated that she saw a singed hole on the back of his tunic that looked like a bullet hole...If this were a bullet hole and if it was singed, it could mean only one thing, that the weapon, which fired it, must have been only a few inches away. Miss Gordon was a most reliable person who had been a military nurse in the First World War and was very familiar with such matters."[59] Did someone shoot Collins in the back and then administer the coup de grace with a Mauser bullet to the head? During the ambush, any member of the escort party could have come close to Collins and shot him while his attention was riveted on the attackers above him.

Commandant Friel was an experienced officer, knowledgeable as to wounds from various weapons, and he confirmed that a .303 rifle bullet would not have caused the gaping wound under Collins' right ear: "He, too, felt it was more likely that a Mauser revolver bullet caused both the entry and gaping exit wound."[60] Dr. Patrick Cagney, who had been a surgeon during the First World War and had experience with gunshot wounds, reportedly corroborated that there was an entry and exit wound, contradicting Beaslai's contention that the bullet was still in Collins' head.

Feehan cited a confidential informant "who was present with Dr. Gogarty, Desmond Fitzgerald, Moira Llewellyn Davies, and some relatives of Collins when Gogarty showed them the wounds. There was a large part of the flesh under the right ear blown away and Gogarty had filled the cavity with a wax-like substance. '*Close to the left ear there was a small circular wound* [emphasis added], which seemed "bluish" in color.' He has further stated that this wound was clearly visible when Collins was later lying in state. My informant recollects Gogarty saying that 'Collins must have been shot at very close range.'"[61]

Feehan then asked his source, "'Who do you think shot Collins?' He answered me calmly and clearly, 'I do not know, but I am sure, as were most of my fellow soldiers that he was not shot by the ambushers.' The noted sculptor, Albert Power, who made Collins' death mask, also saw two wounds. Dr. Gogarty, many years later when he was living in New York, told Connie Neenan that there was another wound the size of a fingernail..."[62]

Why did Dr. Gogarty wait forty years to publicly acknowledge two wounds – a small, clean, circular entry wound and a large part of the skull torn away under Collins' right ear? More than six people confirmed a small wound at Collins' hairline, yet Dalton insisted there was only the single gaping wound behind the ear. Disinterring Collins' body would clear up the entire mystery of entry and exit wounds and any bullet wound in his back. An entry hole in his skull would be easily seen. If the bullet is still lodged in his head, that would help determine the type and range of the weapon that was fired. If there was a "singed" bullet hole in his back, that bullet, too, would still be resting in Collins' bones.

Feehan assumed Collins' murder was ordered by the British Secret Service in revenge for Sir Henry Wilson's assassination and the men killed on "Bloody Sunday" in November 1920. As much as they might have relished the assignment, there is more compelling evidence that Collins was not only assassinated because of the grave threat he posed to Northern Ireland and to England itself but also because Collins had discovered the identity of a sleeper agent within Irish ranks.

It was time for the British to toll the bell on Collins.

Thomas Markham, Collins' confidant, had found references to an agent codenamed "Thorpe" among old files left behind by the British upon their surrender of Dublin Castle. It took Markham four months to discover the identity of 'Thorpe' and early in August he reported his findings to Collins."[63] Thorpe was a British sleeper under cover for decades and allegedly a prominent Free State official whom Collins trusted and had allegedly sought advice from on numerous occasions.[64] Collins locked the file containing all this proof in his private safe at Portobello Barracks and told Markham that when he returned from his inspection down south he would deal drastically with the individual concerned. Collins never returned and when Markham tried to get the file back he found the private safe in Portobello had been opened and all the files were missing..."[65] Whoever rifled the safe knew Collins was not coming back and Thorpe's identity remains a mystery. The incident has never been satisfactorily explained or investigated.

Sean Hales was a Free State army officer, Dáil deputy and longtime friend of Collins. He was also the brother of Tom Hales, one of the IRA men who had prepared the ambush. On numerous occasions, he demanded an army inquiry or inquest into the suspicious circumstance surrounding Collins' death. When his requests were turned down, he took his complaint to the cabinet and voiced his suspicions regarding General Dalton's account of the ambush. Hales said he would leave no stone unturned until the doubts as to Collins' death were cleared up. Feehan reported that Hale's driver and friend, Jim Woulfe, as saying: "The 'big brass' in Dublin would not listen to him. He told me so himself and I can assure you he was a very disappointed man."[66]

Hales was murdered on December 7, 1922 to silence him. Whenever in Dublin, he would reserve quarters at Portobello Barracks. "On the last evening there, he was told they had no accommodation available for him so he had to move to a hotel. The next day, as he traveled in a sidecar from his hotel with Padraic O'Maille, he was attacked and shot dead."[67] As usual, the IRA, was blamed, but they vehemently denied responsibility. The IRA had threatened "... every member of the Provisional Parliament who had voted for the Emergency Powers measure which had set up the military courts."[68] But Hales did not vote on the Emergency Powers bill, being absent from the Dáil at the time. "Matt Twomey, one of the IRA officers in charge in Dublin, always maintained that no orders whatever were given to shoot Hales and it was not the IRA's doing...It has been suggested that Hales knew too much and the British Secret Service had to stop him."[69]

Inquests were routinely conducted of ordinary soldiers killed in the line of duty including after the deaths of Burgess, Boland, Sean Hales, Liam

Lynch, and many others who died of gunshot wounds, but not for Collins or Griffith. Why not?

Feehan conjectured as to why no inquest was held on Collins' death: "A few weeks after Collins' funeral when Sean Hales was unsuccessfully campaigning to have an inquest or at least an inquiry held into Collins' death, there appeared in the *Cork Examiner* a rather strange advertisement: 'Now I the undersigned, being the competent military authority for the County of Cork, hereby order that *no inquest shall be held in the said County unless written authority for the holding of same shall have been first given by me.*' [emphasis added]. This extraordinary advertisement was signed by none other than Major General Emmet Dalton."[70]

Feehan offered a plausible explanation for that failure to hold an inquest: "If it were generally known that the British killed Collins, the Government feared there would be a strong anti-British and consequently anti-Treaty backlash and this could prove to be of tremendous advantage politically to de Valera and his followers. They [the Free State government], therefore, decided to suppress it, not to protect the British secret service but to protect themselves. This explains why there was no inquest, no inquiry and why documents were ultimately destroyed...to be able to blame Collins' death on the IRA was of tremendous propaganda value to the government in winning the Civil War."[71]

Dalton's activities after Collins' death raise more questions. He resigned shortly after the ambush and was given a plush position as Clerk of the Senate by the Free State authorities. He did not remain long in this post and allegedly wandered from one job to another. He reportedly served during World War II in MI5, the British intelligence-gathering agency during the Second World War.

Martin Quigley, an American Office of Strategic Services (OSS) agent in Ireland during World War II, maintained that if Dalton's health had allowed, he was in line for the prestigious position as head of the British Commandos, a post ultimately assigned to Lord Louis Mountbatten. Dalton's early desertion from the ranks of the British army to fight against England on the side of the Irish during the Anglo-Irish War would have disqualified him to lead one of England's most decorated divisions, unless he was being rewarded for services rendered as an undercover British agent.

Quigley utilized his experience in the film industry as a cover for his OSS activities in Ireland and nurtured a friendship with Dalton, who was also apparently in the film business at that time. Quigley noted:

"Whatever Dalton was doing, he obviously had high-level access to British decision-makers."[72] Quigley had turned to Dalton because of his considerable connections within the British High Command to propose the American agent's plan to lease the Irish bases in return for finding an acceptable solution to Partition at the end of the war: "The word came back to Quigley via Dalton, from the Chief of the Imperial Staff, '*Leave the matter of the bases and Irish neutrality alone. The present situation suits us completely.*'"[73] [emphasis added]

One of the great mysteries surrounding the death of Collins was the failure of Collins' "squad" to avenge his murder by assassinating de Valera. Collins had survived four recent assassination attempts while there was no instance of someone attempting to kill de Valera throughout his long career. Who was protecting him?

During the week of August 14, 1923, the car which Collins was expected to be riding was fired into; five weeks prior to his murder, an attempt was made to wreck a train in which he was believed to be riding. On April 17, 1922, after addressing a meeting at Naas, Collins was attacked by a group of men who rushed his car and opened fire. Extra guards were assigned to Collins, as it became more and more evident that someone wanted him dead.

Just before leaving for Cork, Collins was again a target. On August 19, Collins was attending a distinguished social gathering at the home of Moya [Moira] Davies when a 15-year-old courier notified him that "an assassin was out to shoot him that night, only a week after the death of Arthur Griffith. The Free State leader calmly continued to discuss politics and refused to move even as his ever-present protectors made a search of the surrounding gardens. Andrew Brasier noted: "His guard captured an IRA Volunteer named Dixon, a former Connaught Ranger, in a tree on the grounds of the house. Without ceremony, he was taken down to the deserted slobland [garbage dump] that later became Fairview Park. There, he was summarily executed...The following morning, Collins left Portobello Barracks at 6 a.m. He was about to embark on his final, fatal visit to his native Cork."[74]

In order to prevent reprisals by Free State troops over the death of Collins, General Richard Mulcahy dispatched the following directive to the Free State army:

"Stand calmly by your posts. Bend bravely and undaunted to your work. Let no cruel act of reprisal blemish your bright honor. Every dark hour that Michael Collins met since 1916 seemed but to steel that bright strength of his and temper his gay bravery. You are left each inheritors of that strength."[75]

In 1966, Éamon de Valera said: "It is my considered opinion that in the fullness of time, history will record the greatness of Michael Collins and it will be recorded at my expense."[76]

Notes

1.   Fitzgerald, W. G. (Splain): The Voice of Ireland, A Survey of the Race & Nation from All Angles, Virtue Ltd, Dublin/London, p. 180
2.   *ibid*
3.   *ibid*, p. 102
4.   *ibid*, p. 103
5.   *ibid*
6.   O'Connor, Ulick, *Michael Collins & the Troubles, The Struggle for Irish Freedom 1912-1922*, W. W. Noreton, NY/London 1996, p. 31
7.   Fitzgerald, W. G. (Splain), *The Voice of Ireland, A Survey of the Race & Nation from All Angles*, Virtue Ltd, Dublin/London, p. 88
8.   Ryan, Desmond, *Unique Dictator*, Arthur Barker, London, 1936, p. 85
9.   Fitzgerald, W. G. (Splain), *The Voice of Ireland, A Survey of the Race & Nation from All Angles*, Virtue Ltd, Dublin/London, p. 63
10. Beaslai, Pieras, *Michael Collins and the Making of a New Ireland*, Vol II, Harper Bros. NY 1926, p. 424
11. O'Hegarty, P.S., *The Victory of Sinn Féin & How It Used It*, Talbot Press, Dublin 1924, p. 127
12. Dr, Singh, Sunandan, Author's Files:
13. O'Hegarty, P.S., The Victory of Sinn Féin & How It Used It, Talbot Press, Dublin 1924, p. 21
14. *New York Times 9/8/1922, 3:2*
15. *ibid*
16. O'Hegarty, P.S., *The Victory of Sinn Féin & How It Used It*, Talbot Press, Dublin 1924, p. 127
17. *ibid*, p. 21
18. *ibid*, p. 123
19. Fitzgerald, W. G. (Splain), *The Voice of Ireland, A Survey of the Race & Nation from All Angles*, Virtue Ltd, Dublin/London, p. 189
20. Coogan, Tim P., *De Valera, The Man who was Ireland*, Harper, 1996, p. 319
21. Feehan, John, *The Shooting of Michael Collins*, Mercier Press, Dublin, 1981, p. 84
22. *ibid*, p. 86
23. *ibid*, pp. 86, 124
24. Beaslai, Pieras, *Michael Collins and the Making of a New Ireland*, Vol II, Harper

Bros. NY 1926, p. 420
25. Coogan, Tim P., *Michael Collins*, Arrow Books, London, 1991, p. 402
26. Feehan, John, *The Shooting of Michael Collins*, Mercier (Press, Dublin, 1981, p. 84
27. *ibid*, p. 85
28. Beaslai, Pieras, *Michael Collins and the Making of a New Ireland*, Vol II, Harper Bros. NY 1926, p. 433
29. Coogan, Tim P., *De Valera, The Man who was Ireland*, Harper, 1996, p. 332
30. Longford, Earl of & O'Neill, Thomas P., *Éamon de Valera*, Hutchinson, London, 1970, p. 199
31. Coogan, Tim Pat, *Michael Collins, The Man Who Made Ireland*, Roberts Rhinehart, p. 407
32. Brasier, A. & Kelly, J., Harry Boland, *A Man Divided*, New Century Publishing, Dublin, p. 73
33. Coogan, Tim Pat, *Michael Collins, The Made Who Made Ireland*, Roberts Rhinehart, p. 407
34. *ibid*, p. 407
35. Beaslai, Pieras, *Michael Collins and the Making of a New Ireland*, Vol II, Harper Bros. NY 1926, p. 433
36. Dwyer, T. Ryle, *De Valera, The Man & the Myths*, Poolbeg, Dublin, 1991, p. 115
37. Coogan, Tim Pat, *Michael Collins, The Man Who Made Ireland*, Roberts Rhinehart, p. 407
38. Coogan, Tim P., *De Valera, The Man who was Ireland*, Harper, 1996, p. 332
39. *ibid*, p. 333
40. Feehan, John, *The Shooting of Michael Collins*, Mercier (Press, Dublin, 1981, p. 77
41. Coogan, Tim Pat, *De Valera, The Man Who Was Ireland*, Harper Perennial, 1996, p. 348
42. Beaslai, Pieras, *Michael Collins and the Making of a New Ireland*, Vol II, Harper Bros. NY 1926, p. 434
43. Coogan, Tim Pat, *Michael Collins, The Man Who Made Ireland*, Roberts Rhinehart, p. 4
44. Beaslai, Pieras, *Michael Collins and the Making of a New Ireland*, Vol II, Harper Bros. NY 1926, p. 436
45. Feehan, John, *The Shooting of Michael Collins*, The Mercier Press, Dublin, p. 93
46. Beaslai, Pieras, *Michael Collins and the Making of a New Ireland*, Vol II, Harper Bros. NY 1926, p. 436
47. *ibid*, p. 437
48. Feehan, John, *The Shooting of Michael Collins*, Mercier (Press, Dublin, 1981, p. 110
49. *ibid*, p. 109
50. *ibid*, p. 71

51. *ibid,* p. 72
52. *ibid*
53. *ibid,* p. 73
54. *ibid,* p. 74
55. Beaslai, Pieras, *Michael Collins and the Making of a New Ireland*, Vol II, Harper Bros. NY 1926, p. 437
56. Feehan, John M, *The Shooting of Michael Collins*, Mercier Press, Dublin, 1981, p. 105
57. Coogan, Tim Pat, *Michael Collins, The Man Who Made Ireland*, Roberts Rhinehart, p. 411
58. Feehan, John, *The Shooting of Michael Collins*, Mercier (Press, Dublin, 1981, p. 94
59. *ibid*
60. *ibid,* p. 95
61. *ibid,* p. 97
62. *ibid,* p. 99
63. *ibid,* p. 83
64. *ibid*
65. *ibid*
66. *ibid,* p. 111
67. *ibid*
68. Coogan, Tim Pat, *De Valera, The Man Who Was Ireland*, Harper, 1996, p. 341
69. Feehan, John, *The Shooting of Michael Collins*, Mercier (Press, Dublin, 1981, p. 112
70. *ibid,* p. 117
71. *ibid,* p. 120
72. Coogan, Tim Pat, *De Valera, The Man who was Ireland*, Harper, 1996, p. 599
73. Quigley, Martin S., *Peace without Hiroshima*, Madison Books, Lanham, NY/London 1991, p. 21
74. Brasier, A. & Kelly, J., *Harry Boland, A Man Divided*, New Century Publishing, Dublin, p. 79
75. Coogan, Tim P., *Michael Collins*, Arrow Books, London, 1991, p, 415
76. Tim Pat Coogan, *Irish Times*, January 31, 2005

CHAPTER XIX

"Assignment Boundary Commission"

"Permanent partition of Ireland is unthinkable, but surely every sane man must see that unity is impossible so long as the Free State is divided..."

The Earl of Dunraven

The obvious benefit to England of the murders of Michael Collins and Arthur Griffith was never more evident than in 1925 when the British repudiated the Boundary Commission clause of the 1920 Free State Treaty. The English and Unionists of Northern Ireland were well aware they could not violate the treaty in regard to the boundary as long as Collins and Griffith were alive. The Irish delegation had signed the treaty based on the understanding that Article XII meant the cession of Tyrone, Fermanagh, and large areas in Down, Derry, and Armagh to the Free State, which would have rendered Northern Ireland economically untenable leading to an eventual peaceful union with the rest of Ireland.

The Boundary Commission provided the Irish with the possibility of ending partition peacefully. Under Article XII of the treaty, Northern Ireland (Six Counties), which had been established by the Government of Ireland Act of 1920, had the option of entering into a united Ireland or remaining within the British Empire. In the event Northern Ireland opted out of a united Ireland, Article XII would come into effect: "A Commission consisting of three persons, one to be appointed by each of the Governments of Northern and Southern Ireland and one who shall be Chairman to be appointed by the British Government. Said Commission shall determine in accordance with, (a) (primary) the wishes of the inhabitants, so far as compatible with (b) economic and (c) geographic conditions, the boundaries between Northern Ireland and the rest of Ireland, and for the purposes of the Government of Ireland Act, 1920, and of this instrument, the boundary of Northern Ireland shall be such as may be determined by such Commission."

Aside from the British "non-negotiable" demand of allegiance to the Crown, the major stumbling block in the treaty negotiations was partition. In order to break the impasse, Lloyd George proposed that in return for Griffith's agreeing to association with Crown and Empire, he would threaten James Craig, the Northern Ireland Prime Minister, with either voluntarily uniting with Southern Ireland, or a Boundary Commission would be initiated that would sever the Nationalist counties of Fermanagh and Tyrone from the Northeast.

The Boundary Commission clause was a major compromise, not by Collins and Griffith but by Lloyd George and the British delegation. Griffith recognized that the British Prime Minister's compromise was, in effect, the downgrading of his "non-negotiable" demand of Irish acceptance of the permanent partition of Ireland to a temporary division. "Griffith assured the Prime Minister he would not repudiate him."[1] Lloyd George instructed the Cabinet Secretary, Thomas Jones, to put Griffith's assurance in writing, which Griffith acknowledged.

On December 6, 1922, the date the Free State treaty went into effect, Northern Ireland Prime Minister James Craig exercised his option and declared that Northern Ireland would remain within the British Empire and refused to name a member to the Boundary Commission. The British, in countering Craig's refusal to appoint a member to the Commission, adopted an Enabling Act on October 9, 1924, in which they appointed the third member, Joseph R. Fisher, a rabid Unionist, to the position. The English had appointed Judge Richard Feetham, a Justice of the South African Supreme Court, as chairman, and the Free State appointed Professor John MacNeill, a professor of early Irish history at University College, Dublin and the former Commander-in-chief of the Irish Volunteers.

Judge Feetham approached his task with a mind fixed in one direction. He disregarded the Anglo-Irish Free State Treaty of 1922 and based his decision strictly on the Government of Ireland Act of 1920. He took the position that any Act which superseded the Government of Ireland Act of 1920 was, in effect, null and void if it threatened the "capability and maintenance" of a Northern Ireland government as a viable economic entity. Feetham ignored the 1922 Anglo-Irish Free State Treaty as far as the boundary negotiations were concerned, and why MacNeill did not insist on the 1922 Anglo-Irish treaty taking precedence over the 1920 Act is difficult to understand.

Craig contended that the area of Northern Ireland could only be changed through a referendum by the Unionist government and that the Anglo-Irish Free State Treaty of 1922 was not only superseded by the previous 1920 Government of Ireland Act but also by the 40 year-old Colonial Boundaries Act of 1895, in which the boundaries of a colony were delineated and confirmed, even though Northern Ireland was not a colony. Craig charged that any consent must come from a majority vote in Northern Ireland, but the Nationalist areas were so gerrymandered [arbitrarily redistricting the voting] the Catholics were virtually disenfranchised. Feetham disregarded Article XII of the Free State Treaty which specifically stated that the boundary was to be decided primarily by the "wishes of the inhabitants," while economic considerations were secondary.

Proof of Collins and Griffith's negotiating skills was Prime Minister Stanley Baldwin's noting, three years after the treaty signing, that the Conservative diehards were still furious over the British delegation's surrender to the Irish "Murder Gang," believing that the Boundary Commission compromise doomed Ulster. Baldwin admitted: "The main threat to peace, however, arose from the setting up of the Boundary Commission provided for under the Free State Treaty of 1921, if Ulster did not join the South. The South expected – indeed believed that Lloyd George had guaranteed – that the Commission would transfer such large areas from the North that Ulster would be forced by economic weakness to become part of a united Ireland."[2]

According to Lloyd George, Article XII set forth the stipulation: "The transfer of territory should be made in accordance with economic and geographic considerations" and had been included in the Treaty "'simply to prevent the transfer of isolated areas such as Unionist areas of Dublin or Nationalist areas of Belfast.' The Boundary Commission's findings were therefore a violation of the spirit of the Treaty."[3]

The New York Times defined the Boundary Commission as the means to an adjustment of the border between Northern and Southern Ireland: "As regards Ulster's position…The provision relative to the demarcation of new boundaries between the Irish Free State and Northern Ireland is not expected to meet with much opposition from Ulster, as a strong section of public opinion in that Province is in favor of getting rid of some of the disaffected population of Tyrone and Fermanaugh who would be embodied in the Southern Ireland Government."[4] Lord Birkenhead, the day after the treaty had been signed, claimed the treaty presaged extensive changes in the boundary in favor of the South.

"The Irish Plenipotentiaries knew well that the Treaty meant the transference to the South of, at the least, the counties of Fermanagh and Tyrone and it was clear from the language of Lloyd George that this was also what was in his own mind. 'There is no doubt,' Lloyd George said, 'that since the Act of 1920, the majority of the people of two counties prefers to be with their Southern neighbors to being under the Northern Parliament.'"[5]

Hugh O'Neill, Speaker of the Northern Ireland Parliament, questioned Lloyd George's honesty: "I understand the Prime Minister now to say that he merely wants a small rectification of frontiers...I wonder if he said this to the Sinn Féin delegates...Or did he put it to the delegates in such a way as to make them think that what he wished to do was to give them those two counties...If he meant only a minor rectification of the boundary, why did he not put it in the agreement?"[6] The real case against the British delegates was their sidestepping on the question of Irish unity. "It was confirmed by Lord Birkenhead's biography, that the Treaty would never have been signed had Collins and Griffith not believed that the Boundary Commission would secure the transfer of at least two counties."[7]

The stand taken by Craig and his British accomplices was an obvious rejection of Article XII of the Treaty. The British had insisted as fundamental to the initiation of talks between Ireland and England that Protestants of Northern Ireland must not be coerced into a united Ireland. Collins and Griffith agreed but also insisted that Northern Catholics must not be coerced, and in that regard, the Catholic nationalists, if given the right to determine their fate, would vote for inclusion within the Free State. Collins and Griffith knew Northern Ireland could not claim six counties without the coercion of at least the two predominantly Catholic counties. Lloyd George noted on December 15, 1921, regarding the Catholic segments of Northern Ireland: "Although I am against the coercion of Ulster, I do not believe in Ulster coercing other units [Catholics and Nationalists]."[8]

Duplicity and dishonor were the hallmarks of the English. According to Coogan, Lloyd George gave assurances to John Redmond in 1916 that Partition was a temporary state to be resolved after the war, while at the same time, in a letter to Edward Carson, he wrote: "We must make it clear that at the end of the provisional period Ulster does not, whether she wills it or not, merge in the rest of Ireland."[9]

In any event, when it came time to implement Article XII of the treaty, the British had changed their minds about ceding any counties, whether predominantly Catholic or not. Prime Minister Baldwin set forth the duplicitous English position: "If the [Boundary] Commission should give away counties, then of course Ulster couldn't accept it and we should back her. But the Government will nominate a proper representative [for Northern Ireland] and we hope that he and Feetham will do what is right."[10] Baldwin decided beforehand that in the event the Boundary Commission decision ceded two counties to the Free State, the treaty would be repudiated. Conversely, if the Commission decided in favor of Northern Ireland, then they would honor the treaty.

F. X. Martin noted the British understanding that large tracts of land were to be transferred to the South: "There followed what might have been a very fateful decision by the British government to dishonor its treaty obligations: 'If ... the award were manifestly one which could not be carried out without grave risk of widespread disorders and possibly bloodshed, we should still be free to point out to the Free State that in the interests of Ireland as much as to this country, decisive action could not immediately be taken. While fully recognizing our obligations, we must have time to cast about for means of discharging them without entailing such consequences as no responsible government could deliberately contemplate.' Nowhere else in the documents is there so plain an indication of unwillingness on the part of the Baldwin government to keep to the terms of the Treaty of 1921."[11]

Furthermore, on December 17, 1924, at the Omagh hearings of the Boundary Commission, the Unionist delegation incredibly "reserved the right to uphold the Northern Government in any action it might take by way of repudiation of the findings of the Commission."[12]

Lord Balfour made public Lord Birkenhead's repudiation of Article XII: "I have no doubt that the Tribunal, not being presided over by a lunatic, will take a rational view of the limits of its own jurisdiction and will reach a rational conclusion."[13] Lloyd George chimed in with his own revised version in support of Birkenhead's understanding as "the only responsible interpretation of that important Clause."[14]

On September 23, 1924, Sir Laming Worthington Evans, another signatory to the treaty, also did an about-face, claiming that Article XII did not intend "that there should be large transfers of territory... If by any chance the Commissioners felt themselves at liberty to order the transfer of one of those counties, nothing would induce the Ulster people to accept such a decision and no British Government would be guilty of the supreme folly of trying to enforce such a decision."[15]

Michael Tierney noted: "It is nothing more certain than that if the possibility of this interpretation of Article XII had been present in the minds of Collins and Griffith in 1921, the Article would have been amended before they signed the Treaty...To suppose that Feetham's interpretation was intended by Lloyd George, for example, is to suppose that Lloyd George was simply tricking the Irish delegates...This is a supposition dear to those who later opposed the Treaty and who contended that Collins and Griffith were fools or knaves or both; but it will not bear much examination."[16]

De Valera apologists claimed the adverse findings of the Commission were due to the "ambiguity" of the 1922 Anglo-Irish Treaty. That is simply not true. The fact was that the treaty was completely ignored, and the 1920 Act was the sole criterion in determining the "viability of Northern Ireland." The ambiguity issue was raised by de Valera simply to disparage Collins and Griffith. The treaty could not be held ambiguous when it was not even considered. The die was cast when the British signatories to the treaty all publicly voiced their repudiation of Article XII.

Cosgrave noted but failed to act on his convictions when he declared: "If this one particular clause were tampered with, if the decision of the Boundary Commission is to be made in advance by politicians or statesmen, then the Treaty is not the instrument signed by Collins and Griffith... Article XII was specially designed to insure that people were not placed under a Parliament against their will...They have their legitimate national rights which neither Birkenhead, Lloyd George, Sir James Craig nor anyone else has a right to take from them..."[17] Article XII was not tampered with; it was scrapped in its entirety.

Cosgrave did not have the courage of his convictions and he caved in under the Boundary Commission's decision. Baldwin's opposition to the implementation of Article XII brought Collins and Griffith's murders into the spotlight of British intrigue.

The conclusion by the British-rigged Commission that a prior 1920 agreement superseded a later 1922 agreement would have received international condemnation if the Cosgrave government had the courage to reject such a blatant distortion of the Treaty clause. No unbiased observer would have agreed with England and Northern Ireland's contention. What was the purpose of the 1922 Anglo-Irish Free State Treaty that determined the status of the Free State if that treaty was to be subservient to a previous treaty that set forth the opposite corollary?

"Feetham's restriction of meaning was in any case arbitrary and artificial. It was not law but his own *parti pris* [opinion formed beforehand] that made him decide thus and this is confirmed by the addendum that Northern Ireland, after its boundary had been adjusted, should be 'capable of maintaining a Parliament and Government.'"[18]

Feetham's only concern was maintaining the viability of Northern Ireland. He also took the view that there was an absence of any provision for a plebiscite and arrived at the absurd conclusion: "... The wishes of the inhabitants are made the primary but not the paramount consideration."[19] Contradicting his argument that the 1920 Act guaranteed Northern Ireland's borders, Feetham then went beyond that Act setting forth his contention that substantial transfers of Southern Ireland territory were necessary to ensure the economic well-being of the Northern Ireland regime.

The first order of business of the Boundary Commission at the initial meeting of November 6, 1924 was the preservation of secrecy, and it was unanimously agreed: "...No Commissioner would consult any of the Governments concerned as to the work of the Commission, or would make any statement as to such work either to any Government or any individual without first consulting his colleagues."[20]

On November 7, 1925, however, *The Morning Post* published an accurate forecast of the "secret" Boundary Commission decision. The country was shocked at the report that it was the South that would transfer property to the North. Fisher, the Unionist commission member appointed by the British government, violated his oath to secrecy by not only leaking the results to the press but by his continual revelations to the Northern Ireland and British authorities. Fisher wrote to Carson: "We are, at long last, in sight of the end of the Irish Boundary Conference, and *although the veil of secrecy is still closed* [emphasis added], I think there is no harm in letting you know confidentially that I am well satisfied with the result which will not shift a stone or a tile of your enduring work for Ulster. It will remain a solid and close-knit unit with five counties intact and the sixth somewhat trimmed on the outer edge... If anybody had suggested twelve months ago that we could have kept so much I would have laughed at him, and I must add – what I will say on every possible occasion – that the Chairman and John MacNeill have been throughout models of fair play and friendly courtesy. On balance, the number of Protestants in Ulster has been increased – the number of Roman Catholics materially decreased – which will put an end to certain political difficulties in Tyrone and Fermanagh. I am writing to no one but you, but I saw David Reid after Church this morning and told him what I have told you – under the seal of press secrecy for the present..."[21]

The perfidy of Fisher was standard operating procedure of the British for centuries. No word, no treaty, no oath has ever been sacred. Political expediency ruled supreme in England. Irish authorities were kept in the dark by MacNeill's strict adherence to his pledge to maintain confidentiality of the negotiations, while the Unionists had the benefit of knowing exactly what was going on throughout the negotiations.

The opting-out of Northern Ireland by the Catholic border counties would ultimately have brought about a decision by England to increase its already huge subsidies to Northern Ireland or to let it go.

After the Boundary Commission debacle in 1925, de Valera was singing a different tune than he had in August 1921, when he threatened the Dáil deputies that unless they accepted the partition of Ireland they would go the way of the American Indian. Despite the fact that de Valera's Document No.2 included, word for word, the exact terminology of the Boundary Commission Article XII in the Free State Treaty, he hypocritically charged that the Cosgrave government abandonment of the Nationalist counties was an "act of unpardonable injustice and a national disgrace."[22]

In 1925, when the Unionist government was secure, the Cosgrave government had "officially" sanctioned the Boundary Commission results, partition was etched in stone, British interests were protected, and Irish-American opposition muted, then, and only then, did de Valera come out against the Boundary Commission decision. Dwyer wrote: "The whole thing [Boundary Commission decision] was a grave injustice which undoubtedly played into the hands of de Valera, who had been exploiting anti-British sentiment for all it was worth."[23]

De Valera was nicknamed "Professor Moonlight" for a foray he had made into Northern Ireland on March 16, 1918, when he had placed many Nationalist lives at risk for the sake of a publicity stunt. Now he embarked on another staged visit to the North just one week before the Boundary Commission met on November 6, 1924 and deliberately facilitated his own arrest. His arrest recalled his suspicious 24-hour apprehension in June 1921, the day before Lloyd George announced his truce proposal.

Five days before the Boundary Commission met in London on November 1, de Valera was sentenced to a month's imprisonment in Belfast Jail, infamous for its brutal treatment of Nationalist rebels. During his sentencing, he allegedly berated the magistrate in Gaelic. His month-long sojourn was another vacation, as no hand was laid upon him, nor was he doused by fire hose in a cold cell as had previous Irish prisoners.

The November elections in Southern Ireland saw de Valera's party garner nearly 30,000 more votes than the previous year, resulting in an additional two seats. According to Coogan, de Valera gained 1,000 votes per day for "challenging" the Unionists in their own backyard. Though his stay in Belfast Jail was a boon for his party in the South, it had the opposite effect in the North, as the anti-de Valera feedback of his unwelcome barnstorming led to a disastrous defeat for the Northern Nationalists.

Coogan admitted that de Valera's Northern Ireland junket not only perpetuated partition but was instrumental in the defeat of the British Liberal Party as the Tories swept to victory. "The Realpolitik of the situation meant that partition was now copper-fastened, Boundary Commission or no Boundary Commission. Sinn Féin's vote in the North went down from 104,716 in 1921 to only 46,257 in 1924... In Northern Ireland, the Unionists held not only an overwhelming political advantage but also police and paramilitary supremacy through the strength of the Royal Ulster Constabulary and the B-specials."[24]

Free State ministers, seeking to prevent the Boundary Commission issue from exploding, hastened to London to settle the ensuing crisis. If the Irish government had rejected the Boundary Commission decision and taken the issue before the court of international public opinion, England would have been exposed as repudiating a legitimate treaty. All the cards were in Cosgrave's favor, but he couldn't summon the moral or political courage to act. With relations between Ireland and England reaching crisis stage, Irish leaders once again failed the people and settled for a beggar's whine for a beggar's dole. Early in December 1925, an agreement was entered into in which the Feetham Report was shelved and the existing boundary between the Free State and Northern Ireland remained unaltered.

"In return, the Free State was released from any liability under Clause V, the financial section of the 1922 Free State Treaty. [emphasis added] The agreement was submitted without delay to the British, Free State, and Northern Ireland Parliaments."[25] The Free State Government dropped its claim to territory and officially accepted the maintenance of the present boundary as the English won another round against the Irish. An international investigation of the Boundary Commission decision would have revealed the absurdity of the Boundary Commission contention that a 1920 Act took precedence over a 1922 treaty, both constitutionally approved by the British Cabinet, the English Parliament, and the King of England. Such underhanded methods would have received international condemnation, especially in the United States and the Dominions.

The fact that partition remains to this day was due to de Valera stampeding the Dáil deputies in 1921 into accepting partition as one of Lloyd George's conditions for entering into peace talks; his civil war in 1922, his refusal to return to the Dáil at the urging of diehards like Austin Stack and the Labor Party to cast a deciding negative on the 1925 Boundary Commission decision, and, as will be seen, to his 1937 Constitution and Neutrality scam during WWII. He followed true to form by ignoring or squelching any action contrary to British interests during each of these crises.

In any event, when the Cosgrave government was scheduled to vote on the Boundary Commission decision, it was the Labor Party which voiced the only opposition and sought a method to reject it. An invitation was extended to de Valera in an effort to enlist Sinn Féin to defeat the Boundary Commission decision in the Dáil. In an affront to the Labor Party's request to take their seats in the Dáil, even for one day, to reject the Boundary Commission decision, de Valera refused to take action and postponed any decision until the next Party conference. Even Austin Stack, the diehard anti-treatyite, was willing to take the "oath that wasn't an oath" if the Boundary Commission decision could be overturned, but de Valera was not about to let that happen. Once again, he put England's interest above his own political goals. By returning to the Dáil and rejecting the Boundary Commission decision, he would have been a hero in the eyes of the Irish people and his return to power would have been achieved that much sooner.

"De Valera, who seemingly could not make up his mind on the matter, concluded the meeting by proposing that the question be debated at the next Sinn Féin Ard Fheis [convention]. Thus, at a critical time, de Valera ... withstood the appeals of Labor leaders to enter the Dáil and defeat the [Partition] Bill on the floor of the house."[26] The problem with de Valera's proposal was that the next Ard Fheis would be too late to reject the Dáil ratification of the Boundary Commission decision. "When the Sinn Féin Deputies met privately afterwards, de Valera vacillated and declined to take a stand one way or another. 'Much as I loved Dev,' Gerry Boland recalled years later, 'there were times when he could just not make up his mind.'"[27] No one ever questioned why his waffling occurred only when England's interests were in the balance, while at other times he would render decisions affecting Ireland without a word of approval by his cabinet, the Dáil, or anyone else.

At a meeting of Sinn Féin on December 12, 1925, at the Shelbourne Hotel in Dublin on the very evening that the government was meeting to ratify the settlement, de Valera discouraged any move to enter the Dáil, and a motion to that effect was defeated. "De Valera opened the meeting by stating, 'In another place tonight representatives of the people have met to decide whether or not they will give their consent to the partition of our country. The sanction of our consent that partition could never have.'"[28] His inclusion of the Partition Clause word for word in his Document No. 2 was ignored. For all of de Valera's bombastic talk and his anti-English rhetoric about the injustice of the Boundary Commission decision, as well as his stand on an Irish Republic, that was all he was willing to do – talk. The British, by sparing de Valera's life in 1916, were still reaping dividends nearly a decade later, with much more to come.

De Valera refused all entreaties, including those of Stack and other fanatical Republicans, to join with the Labor Party and enter the Dáil for one day, in order to reject the Partition Bill. The benefit to England of de

Valera's refusal to kill the Boundary Commission settlement was enormous. Rejection of the Boundary Commission decision was a win-win situation for the Irish, and de Valera, as usual, turned it into the usual lose-lose Irish calamity.

In the event that the Irish rejected the partition of their country, the British would be in a precarious predicament. Irish-Americans would apply pressure in the United States, complaining that the British, through sheer hypocrisy and repudiation of the Free State Treaty, annexed a portion of Ireland against the wishes of the inhabitants.

The irony of the Irish catastrophe was that de Valera, a week after the Partition Bill was approved, called for a review of the abstentionist policy of Sinn Féin [refusing to take their seats in the Dáil if they had to take the oath to the Free State Constitution]. Barely a month after his rejection of the Labor Party offer to enter the Dáil, de Valera, on January 6, 1926, publicly announced that he was prepared to take his seat in the Dáil if there was no oath to be taken. Within a year and a half after the fact, he did lead the counterfeit Republicans in a return to the Irish Parliament. He overcame the greatest of his objections to the oath and reason for the Civil War by simply assuming Collins and Griffith's position that the oath was merely a "hollow political formula." But it was too late as far as partition was concerned. In a hypocritical acceptance of the oath, de Valera pontificated: "In the name of the Irish nation and the Irish race, in the name of all who have stood and will yet stand unflinchingly for the Sovereign Independence of Ireland, we, the duly elected representatives of the Irish people, by our names appended, hereto, proclaim and record our unalterable opposition to the partitioning of our country."[29]

The Boundary Commission fiasco was an important step in de Valera's return to power. For the sake of political expediency and because of his political cowardice, Cosgrave opened the door to de Valera's political resurrection. It may be too harsh an indictment on Cosgrave, for he was attempting to guide a new revolutionary government through the shoals of an aftermath of a civil war with the jackal de Valera nipping at his heels. The problems of such a government would have been overwhelming in the best of circumstances.

Lloyd George promised Collins and Griffith that he would not economically prop up the Northern Ireland government, but the ink wasn't dry on the treaty before he was sending military and economic aid to Northern Ireland. Ulster's economic foundation was so rickety that financial concessions by England were vital to the maintenance of the Northern Ireland government. Hugh A. McCartan noted: "The

Northern Parliament was able to avoid bankruptcy only by the aid of British subsidies and subventions. The British Finance Minister was compelled to forego payment of £1,980,000 [$10 million] of the Imperial Contribution in order to show a [Northern Ireland] surplus of £69,000 [$350,000] for the financial year 1922-23. No community can hope for commercial or industrial security on so unstable a basis as this."[30]

Northern Ireland was more concerned about British handouts than they were about being "loyal British subjects." Andrew Bonar Law, former English Prime Minister, attempted to defend his brethren: "Ulster was unfairly treated in the British press when her people were pictured as fighting for their own pocket and adopting the attitude that when it was a question of Government they wanted to be a part of Great Britain, though when it came to taxation, they desired to be treated like the rest of Ireland. Now, if Ulster expects to remain part of Great Britain, she must pay our taxation and quite accept that position."[31]

The economic situation in Northern Ireland was exacerbated by the depressed economy and so many people on the dole, who refused to work in order to collect unemployment insurance. Law noted: "On January 31, 1922, the percentage of unemployment in the Six Counties of Northern Ireland was 26.39 percent or more than twice the rate in Great Britain."[32] No manner of effort or method was able to put Northern Ireland's financial house in order. The Unionist regime was deluged in red ink from the day of its founding in 1920. D. S. Johnson, in an article, "Northern Ireland as a Problem in the Economic War 1932–38," stated: "The result was that by 1938, Northern Ireland appeared to the Treasury, who were the custodians of financial rectitude, to be in the role of perpetual beggar who comes to us when bankrupt... Is the tail going to wag the dog? Blackmail and bluff have for many years been the accepted methods of Northern Ireland..."[33]

In 1937-38, unemployment in Northern Ireland was reaching 30 percent, while England's unemployment remained steady at 12.5 percent. The British subsidized Ulster farmers for cattle, milk, feed, and fertilizer products. Since the formation of the six-county government in 1921, some estimates of the subsidies ranged in the hundreds of millions of pounds, hidden in a double-billing accounting scheme. The British Government naturally was hesitant to divulge this information, for if the English people were aware of just how much it was costing them and to what extent the Unionists had blackmailed the Government into bribes and subsidies, it is more than likely that they would be happy to wash their hands of the moochers and let them fend for themselves. Dáil deputy Sean Milroy noted: "The financial position of the partition area is radically unsound. Up to now, the Belfast Parliament has only been able to maintain itself by subsidies from the British Treasury. The British people and Parliament are hardly likely to continue devoting millions of money to finance an establishment which drives directly towards the abyss of economic and financial bankruptcy."[34]

Northern Ireland also demanded "social parity" to that of England, which meant that the government was subsidizing the Unionists for social services equal to those of England. In effect, Great Britain was propping up the Unionist regime with agriculture, unemployment, and social subsidies. Without those subsidies and the loss of Tyrone and Fermanagh counties, the Northern Ireland government would have collapsed, and a peaceful transition to a unified Ireland would have been inevitable.

Notes

1. Dwyer, T. Ryle, *De Valera, The Man & the Myths*, Poolbeg, Dublin, 1991, p. 77
2. Middlemas, Keith & Barnes, John, *Baldwin: A Biography*, Macmillan, 1970, p. 207
3. Dwyer, T. Ryle, *De Valera, The Man & the Myths*, Poolbeg, Dublin, 1991, p. 137
4. *New York Times*, 12/7/1921, 2:1
5. *ibid*, p. 240
6. Phillips, W. A. The Revolution in Ireland 1906-1923, Longmans, Green, London 1926, p. 330
7. Ryan, Desmond, *Unique Dictator*, Arthur Barker, London, 1936, p. 144
8. Fitzgerald, W. G. (Splain), *The Voice of Ireland, A Survey of the Race & Nation from All Angles*, Virtue Ltd, Dublin/London, p. 207
9. Coogan, Tim P., *De Valera, The Man who was Ireland*, Harper, 1996, p. 90
10. Martin, F. X. & Byrne, F. J. (eds.), *The Scholar Revolutionary, Eoin MacNeill, 1867-1945 & the Making of a New Ireland*, Irish U. Press, 1973, p. 228
11. *ibid*, p. 245
12. *ibid*, p. 234
13. Macardle, Dorothy, *The Irish Republic*, Victor Gollancz, Irish Press, London/Dublin 1951, p. 873
14. *ibid*
15. *ibid*, p. 874
16. Tierney, Michael (Ed. By F.X. Martin), *Eoin MacNeill, Scholar & Man of action 1867-1945*, Clarendon Press, Oxford 1980, p. 347
17. Coogan, Tim P., *De Valera, The Man who was Ireland*, Harper, 1996, p. 368
18. Tierney, Michael (Ed. By F.X. Martin), *Eoin MacNeill, Scholar & Man of action 1867-1945*, Clarendon Press, Oxford 1980, p, 348

19. Martin, F. X. & Byrne, F. J. (eds.), *The Scholar Revolutionary, Eoin MacNeill, 1867-1945 & the Making of a New Ireland*, Irish U. Press, 1973, p. 247 & Royal Commission Report, p. 59
20. Martin, F. X. & Byrne, F. J. (eds.), *The Scholar Revolutionary, Eoin MacNeill, 1867-1945 & the Making of a New Ireland*, Irish U. Press, 1973, p. 232
21. *ibid*, p. 250
22. Dwyer, T. Ryle, *De Valera, The Man & the Myths*, Poolbeg, Dublin, 1991, p. 137
23. *ibid*
24. Coogan, Tim P., *De Valera, The Man who was Ireland*, Harper, 1996, p. 375
25. Gaughan, J. Anthony, *Austin Stack, Portrait of a Separatist*, Kingdom Books, Dublin, 1977, p. 249
26. *ibid*, p. 250
27. Dwyer, T. Ryle, *De Valera, The Man & the Myths*, Poolbeg, Dublin, 1991, p. 138
28. Gaughan, J. Anthony, *Austin Stack, Portrait of a Separatist*, Kingdom Books, Dublin, 1977, 250
29. Longford, Earl of & O'Neill, Thomas P., *Éamon de Valera*, Hutchinson, London, 1970, p. 242
30. Fitzgerald, W. G. (Splain), *The Voice of Ireland, A Survey of the Race & Nation from All Angles*, Virtue Ltd, Dublin/London, p. 201
31. *ibid*, p. 8
32. *ibid*, p. 200
33. Johnson, D.S., "Northern Ireland as a Problem in the Economic War 1932-1938", *Irish Historical Studies*, Vol. XXII, p. 155
34. Fitzgerald, W. G. (Splain), *The Voice of Ireland, A Survey of the Race & Nation from All Angles*, Virtue Ltd, Dublin/London, p. 204

CHAPTER XX
"Assignment Partition"

"If the Free Staters insist upon a Constitution, which repudiated Crown and Empire and practically set up a Republic, we should carry the whole world with us in any action we took. But an issue fought on Ulster would not command united British opinion, still less worldwide support.
If we force an issue on these facts we shall be hopelessly beaten. Let us keep on the high ground of the Treaty, the Crown, the Empire."[1]

Lloyd George to Churchill

In the late nineteenth century, the prospect of Home Rule and a united Ireland brought down the Liberal government of Prime Minister William Gladstone, as Randolph Churchill rallied the Conservative Party to the Unionist cause. The Protestants of Northern Ireland branded Home Rule as "Rome Rule" and under self-government for the entire island, the Protestants would be subject to the overwhelming Catholic majority. The Protestants were prepared to fight the English government and even considered secession to prevent it.

In March 1914, Prime Minister Henry Asquith introduced the Home Rule Bill for its second reading: Ireland was to be partitioned into a six-county, mostly Protestant statelet, and a Twenty-six county, predominantly Catholic, enclave with the caveat that any county might opt out after a six-year period. The proposal was presented as a solution to coercion and conflict. Edward Carson, a Dublin born lawyer and fanatical anti-Catholic, was instrumental in persuading over 80,000 Protestant Unionists to sign a covenant pledging to fight Home Rule by force if necessary and set up a separate Government in Belfast. He called Asquith's Home Rule Bill, "a sentence of death with a stay of execution" and walked out of the House of Commons, to thunderous applause."[2]

Originally, the entire nine-county province of Ulster was proposed as the area comprising the Northern Ireland government. T. Agar-Robartes first introduced partition in the House of Commons on December 12, 1912 and it included the counties of Antrim, Armagh, Cavan, Derry, Donegal, Down, Fermanagh, Monaghan, and Tyrone. The final decision eliminated three of the most predominant Catholic counties of Cavan, Donegal, and Monaghan, but maintained the two other mostly Catholic majority counties of Tyrone and Fermanagh and the nationalist City of Derry, in order to provide enough of an area to assure the economic viability of Northern Ireland. There were also pockets of heavily populated Catholic areas in South Down, South Armagh, and even within the environs of the Unionist bastion of Belfast.

The Protestants in the six counties of Ulster totaled approximately 900,000 to 700,000 Catholics, while their 300,000 Protestant brethren in the 26 counties of Southern Ireland comprised only 10 percent of the population there. Northern Ireland abandoned the Protestants in Southern Ireland in the same manner that de Valera abandoned the Nationalists of the North.

On July 8, 1914, the House of Lords introduced an Amending Bill, which postponed implementation of the Home Rule Act until after the end of the First World War.

Éamon de Valera's "Assignment Partition" called for the perpetual division of Ireland and he carried out his mission to perfection. From the moment he held private negotiations with Lloyd George during the truce talks in July 1921, until the day he died, the Irish President espoused the English line on partition.

Few Irish writers questioned de Valera's stance on partition; they even recognized his repeated insensitivity to Protestant feeling, which guaranteed Unionist rejection of a united Ireland. But no Irishman could bear the psychological trauma of admitting the Irish President was an English agent. They continued to attribute his pro-British activities to personality traits brought on by a dysfunctional youth. Time and again, Tim Pat Coogan raised serious questions about de Valera's motivation but he, too, could go no further than an acknowledgement of the Irish President's posturing over partition: "How did a man who in a very real sense, made a political career out of Partition, denouncing its evil to the four corners of the world, fetch up in such a *cul de sac*? Leaving de Valera's public Lion Act to one side, what did he really see when he looked into his own heart to know the wishes of the people of Northern Ireland? ...The tragedy is that he never acted on it."[3] Coogan failed to take his deduction to its logical conclusion.

De Valera would don his anti-Partition mantle only when out of office or seeking re-election. After partition was etched in stone by the Boundary Commission decision in 1925 and ceased to be an international issue critical to Britain, only then did de Valera crank up his anti-partition political campaign.

During the London peace conference leading up to the Free State Treaty in 1921, Lloyd George had admitted that England could not carry international or even English public opinion if the Irish question revolved around Ulster and partition. However, if an Irish rejection of the "magnanimous" terms of the Treaty was based on a demand for an Irish Republic and repudiation of Crown and Empire, world opinion would come down overwhelmingly on the side of England.

In his headlong rush to civil war in 1922, de Valera followed Lloyd George's script to the letter by repudiating Crown and Empire and demanding recognition of an Irish Republic, thereby turning world opinion against Ireland and in favor of England. The Irish President deliberately refused to allow the Ulster question of partition to be discussed during the treaty debate in December 1921 and January 1922, despite it being the only issue in which Lloyd George warned that England would be beaten. De Valera touted the Lloyd George line: "'I want to eliminate the Ulster question out of it [the Treaty debate]'...*Either by accident or design, de Valera made no reference whatsoever to Partition.*"[4] [emphasis added]

Pieras Beaslai wrote: "One would have imagined that the attack on the Treaty would have centered on its one big, black feature of partition, yet...de Valera, in his thousand and one speeches, scarcely referred to it."[5] T. Ryle Dwyer noted: "In short, de Valera was prepared to accept Northern Ireland's secession but he was anxious to give the public the impression that he was not formally acknowledging that he was in fact accepting."[6]

At that time, the Irish president asserted that the only way to end partition was by persuasion, but he never attempted even a semblance of generosity toward Northern Ireland sensitivities. According to Dwyer: "If de Valera 'always' thought partition was an issue to be settled between Irishmen...[no one ever] cited any occasion on which he sought to talk with any member of the Northern Ireland government."[7]

T. Ryle Dwyer goes further: "de Valera...neglected to make any serious attempt at reconciliation with the Northern Unionists. He was not even willing to take steps to eliminate from the Twenty-six Counties the discrimination against Protestant values which provoked legitimate fears among Unionists [in the North] that they would be discriminated against in a united Ireland."[8]

The Irish President was never called to task for his contradictory position regarding partition. When it suited him, he claimed that the acceptance of the Boundary Commission decision by the Cosgrave Government was "not merely an act of unpardonable injustice but a national disgrace."[9] But of course, he chose not to vote against the resolution himself.

Prior to his July 1921 private meetings with Lloyd George, de Valera had been opposed to partition. In January 1918: "de Valera described the Unionists as 'a rock in the road... They must, if necessary, blast it out of their path.'"[10] After his Truce talks with Lloyd George, de Valera took up the Prime Minister's line that "Northern Ireland must not be coerced" and by December 1920, he was singing the British Prime Minister's partition tune:. "There is plenty of room in Ireland for partition, real partition, and plenty of it."[11]

Dwyer noted that within a month of his secret talks with the British Prime Minister: "During a secret session of the Dáil on August 22, 1921...de Valera stunned his colleagues by forthrightly expressing his views on the Partition Question. If Britain were prepared to recognize the Irish Republic, he announced that he 'would be in favor of giving each county powers to vote itself out of the Republic if it so wished...' The only other alternative would be to use force on the Six Counties and he said that he would not be responsible for such a policy."[12]

"'It was evident to us;' de Valera wrote shortly after the Sinn Féin Convention in 1926, 'that with [Lloyd George's] coercion-of-Ulster was unthinkable guarantee, the Unionists would solidly maintain their original position rather than voluntarily enter into a united Ireland.' Thus, when de Valera gave Lloyd George a similar assurance on August 10, 1921, he was obviously accepting that some form of partition would be a part of any [Treaty] settlement."[13]

On the one hand, de Valera charged that Lloyd George's "coercion-of-Ulster was unthinkable guarantee" was assurance that the Unionists would never change their position; yet, almost in the same breath, de Valera advocated his own "coercion-of-Ulster was unthinkable guarantee." The Dáil Deputies condemned the British Prime Minister's "anti-coercion-of-Ulster" policy but hailed the Irish President's "anti-coercion-of-Ulster" policy. When it came to the partition of Ireland into Protestant and Catholic enclaves of mutual malignity, de Valera followed Lloyd George's script to the letter.

Michael Collins and Arthur Griffith had won an astonishing concession when the British had agreed that the existing line of partition was merely temporary and to be determined by a specially appointed commission. If the agreement had been honoured, the Nationalist counties of Northern Ireland would have gone to the Free State and the result could have ultimately been a peaceful unity.

De Valera's anti-Protestant policy, the 1937 Papist Constitution, and "coercion-of-Ulster is unthinkable" dictum guaranteed that the Protestant Unionists of the North would never voluntarily accept a united Ireland. Dwyer noted: "The only way to settle the problem was to convince a majority north of the border that they would be better off in a united Ireland. But de Valera did very little to try to win over the predominantly Protestant Unionist community. In fact, his government had effectively promoted Partition by failing to demonstrate a proper spirit of tolerance and broadmindedness."[14]

De Valera knew his policies were objectionable to Protestants, but he was more interested in reinforcing his Catholic Hierarchy political base, which propelled him to one re-election after another. The Catholic Church was a powerful political force in Southern Ireland especially among the poorly educated, and he assiduously courted it by promoting church dogma. It provided a convenient cover for his "Assignment Partition."

De Valera was relentless in his attacks on the dead Arthur Griffith. "In a letter to the *Irish Independent*, de Valera implied that the partition clauses were under discussion [during the Treaty negotiations] when Griffith [allegedly] made the famous promise not to sign the Treaty. He went on to state he had 'never been able to understand how Griffith had allowed himself to be deluded by the Boundary Commission idea.' De Valera understood this better than anyone because he had accepted the same scheme himself and included the relevant Treaty Boundary Commission clauses verbatim in his Document No. 2."[15]

Dwyer commented: "Although de Valera, had virtually ignored the partition issue during the Treaty debate, he now began raising it with increasing emphasis in his public statements – and often with a distinct lack of candor."[16]

"Even though de Valera had initially accepted the Boundary Commission scheme, he had long since begun to criticize that aspect of the Treaty and as the years passed the mistaken view became quite widespread that he had been opposed to the Treaty primarily on account of partition."[17]

He initiated a Civil War over a conjured "oath of allegiance to the King." de Valera again reversed position in 1927; taking up Collins and Griffith's stand, he admitted the oath was merely a "hollow political formula" and acceptable by the counterfeit Republicans in order to take their seats in the Dáil. "He had indicated a willingness to accept partition before the Treaty negotiations and he had already explained that taking his seat in Leinster House 'would be a matter purely of tactics and expediency,' if the oath were dropped. In short, he was using the partition issue to cloak political expediency in the hypocritical garb of principle."[18]

De Valera continually rebuffed any possible understanding between Dublin and Belfast. When an offer of cooperation was extended by the

Belfast radio network, de Valera tersely replied: "'There is no intention of making noticeable or ostentatious progress in developing a close understanding between the Dublin and Belfast broadcasting organizations...' Lack of cooperation and denial of official recognition remained settled Fianna Fáil policy towards the Six County authorities."[19] The Fianna Fáil party was launched in 1926 as a result of a falling out with the anti-Treaty wing of Sinn Féin because of opposition over his decision to return to the Dáil. Fianna Fáil marked an end to the policy of abstention from the Dáil. The party became the dominant force in Irish politics but de Valera never made efforts to establish Fianna Fáil in Northern Ireland.

The pleas of Northern Irish Catholic MPs to be allowed to take their seats in the Southern Ireland Parliament rather than at Westminster were dismissed by de Valera. Twenty years before, under the Sinn Féin banner, he had refused to take his seat at Westminster, claiming it was a usurping government. Coogan commented that despite the fact that the new Constitution brought in by de Valera in 1937 laid claim to all thirty-two counties: "One would have thought it axiomatic that he should have acknowledged the right of representation from all those thirty-two counties – even welcomed it – to prove his point...He thought they should abstain from Westminster but rejected suggestions that Dublin should defray their salaries so they could devote themselves to constituency work in the Six Counties. Beyond this negative advice, he had nothing to offer the delegation save a lecture on how much he resented statements that he had done nothing to end partition."[20] Once again, de Valera was not about to jeopardize English interests in Ireland.

The Catholic MPs then proposed an alternative. Instead of a seat in the Dáil, "They should get a symbolic attendance in Dublin – a right of audience of some kind. De Valera had a litany of objections to the idea, including the absurd contention 'no representation for Six County members without taxation or responsibility.' Decoded, what this meant was that de Valera did not want the Northern Nationalists making partition a substantive issue which he might have to act on, as opposed to securing electoral kudos for mere verbal republicanism."[21] Again, de Valera prevented an anti-English proposal from seeing the light of day.

John Whelan noted: "...The more de Valera behaves as Nationalist, Gaelic-revivalist, anti-British, the more does he estrange the North. It is not the North, alone, which is keeping itself distinct. The South is maintaining partition even more effectively by refusing to demonstrate a practical spirit of tolerance and broad-mindedness. No Northerner can possibly like such features of Southern life, as at present constituted; its pervasive clerical control; its censorship; its Gaelic revival; its isolationist economic policy. De Valera realizes the effect of at least some of these things. He shows no readiness to relax any of them..."[22]

De Valera, in 1934, suggested ethnic cleansing as the way to end partition. He proposed transporting Irish Protestants to England in return for English Catholics: "'...the best solution was to transfer the minority to its ancestral homeland, if possible...' He was not thinking of transferring Catholic Nationalists from the six counties to the South, but the Protestant Unionists of Scottish and English extraction to the mainland of Britain and replacing them with a similar number of Catholics of Irish extraction from Great Britain."[23] De Valera must have known how offensive the scheme would have been to the Protestants of Ireland. In effect, de Valera – someone not even born in Ireland – was calling for the uprooting of a people whose ancestors migrated to Ireland more than three centuries earlier.

The closest anyone came to accusing de Valera of conspiring to maintain partition was during the 1938 Ports and Economic War settlement talks with Neville Chamberlain. A deputation of Catholic MPs from Northern Ireland charged: "*We should regard it as a betrayal of all our interests if de Valera ignored the problem of partition* by getting Trade and Defense Agreements only." [emphasis added] de Valera claimed he had raised the partition issue at that conference, but Chamberlain contradicted the Irish President and stated: "de Valera did not ask for autonomy or cession of territory..."[24]

The American Representative to Éire, David Gray stated: "...de Valera did not understand that when he decided not to give Britain the use of the ports [in the Second World War] as provided under the Treaty in return for Northern Ireland, he was losing Northern Ireland forever... de Valera never foresaw the development of Northern Ireland to supplant Éire so as to secure the Western Flank needful for British survival."[25] Gray did not consider the counter-argument, that de Valera did understand that Éire was losing Northern Ireland forever and that it was his intention, as an English agent, to see that it happened.

When out of office, de Valera exploited the weapon of partition. "He denounced the violence...He stated that Irish unity 'could not be achieved by the exercise of force' and he added, 'even if it were militarily successful, we would not have the harmony essential for real unity.'"[26]

On July 5, 1940, de Valera repeated his take it or leave it proposal to Northern Ireland, knowing this would meet with a Unionist rejection: "Our present Constitution," he wrote, "represents the limit to which we believe our people are prepared to go to meet the sentiments of the Northern Unionists, but, on the plan proposed, Lord Craigavon and his colleagues could at any stage render the whole project nugatory and prevent the desired unification by demanding concessions to which the majority of the people could not agree. By such methods, unity was prevented in the past and it is obvious that under the plan outlined they could be used again."[27]

De Valera later acknowledged his phony neutrality during the Second World War: "...set back the cause of Irish unity for many more years than the six for which it [the war] lasted. The part played by the Six Counties in the war inevitably strengthened their claims compared with those of the South..."[28] Longford and O'Neill conceded that the Unionists' participation in the war "strengthened" their claim for partition and that de Valera's neutrality policy during the conflict weakened Southern Ireland's claims.

After the Japanese attack on Pearl Harbour on December 7, 1941, which brought the United States into the war, Churchill became certain of an Allied victory. In a public relations ploy to silence Irish-American opposition to the FDR administration, Churchill hastily cabled de Valera the following day: "'Now is your chance. Now or never! "A Nation Once Again." Am ready to meet you at any time.' The reference to 'A Nation Once Again,' was the anthem of the Irish Parliamentary Party in the days of Parnell and Redmond. De Valera, raised the specter of a deal to end partition, but Churchill had not intended to imply this."[29]

The divining moment had arrived. If Ireland decided to fight alongside the United States, then Irish-Americans would be in a position to demand American pressure to settle the Partition Question once the war was over. De Valera rejected the propitious moment: in response to a request to allow Americans the use of the Irish ports, de Valera curtly replied, "Neutrality – no change."

Irish-Americans, who made up one of the largest ethnic groups serving in the U.S. military, along with 200,000 native Irish volunteers in the British Armed Forces, would have wielded a strong argument for postwar configuration and a seat at the peace conference. A grateful America would have been a powerful ally in Ireland's struggle to end Partition. US Representative to Éire, David Gray acknowledged: "de Valera had it wholly within his own power to avail himself of this unifying influence and clearly in the interest of Éire's survival. No politician ever had a stronger case with which to mold public opinion. All this, of course, assumed that he was not secretly on the German side..."[30] Gray's doubts took him in the wrong direction. He did not consider that de Valera was secretly on the British side, that England did not want a unified Ireland nor Southern Ireland fighting with the Allies.

De Valera never made a substantive move to alter the division of Ireland or to take any action that was detrimental to English interests. Coogan noted: "What we do know is that in his last days in power de Valera decided in effect to do nothing about partition... On January 29, 1958, de Valera made a major speech in the Senate opposing the motion by Senator Stanford, 'That the Irish Senate requests the Government to set up a Commission or to take other decisive and energetic steps to consider and report on the best means of promoting social, economic and cultural cooperation between the Twenty-six Counties and Six Counties...'"[31] Nothing happened and when the question was once again brought before de Valera, he decided: "...it is not necessary to raise the matter at a Government meeting. It may be presumed that Departments will keep the matter in mind without any explicit directions..."[32]

When the Irish Representative to London suggested initiating an Anglo-Irish Society, he received the following curt response from de Valera on March 14, 1958: "...*It is a case where we should advance very cautiously and, for the time being, not at all.*"[33] [emphasis added] de Valera did not want to resolve partition and did nothing to encourage an end to the division of Ireland. Dwyer wrote: "de Valera was basically ruling out the possibility of winning over a majority in the North by conciliatory gestures and, as he had ruled out the use of force, this raises the question of how he proposed to solve partition."[34]

Notes

1. Ryan, Desmond, *Unique Dictator*, Arthur Barker, London, 1936, p. 201
2. Stewart, A.T.Q, *Edward Carson*, Gill and Macmillan, 1981, p. 87
3. Coogan, Tim P., *De Valera, The Man who was Ireland*, Harper, 1996, p. 642
4. *ibid*, p. 290
5. Beaslai, Pieras, *Michael Collins and the Making of a New Ireland*, Vol II, Harper Bros. NY 1926, p. 325
6. Dwyer, T. Ryle, *Éamon de Valera*, Gill & Macmillan, 1980, p. 58
7. Dwyer, T. Ryle, *De Valera, The Man & the Myths*, Poolbeg, Dublin, 1991, p. 319
8. *ibid*, p. 337
9. *ibid*, p. 137
10. Dwyer, T. Ryle, *Éamon de Valera*, Gill and Macmillan, Dublin, 1980, p. 44
11. Bowman, John, *De Valera and the Ulster Question 1917-73*, Clarendon Press, Oxford, 1982, mp. 35
12. Dwyer, T. Ryle, *De Valera, The Man & the Myths*, Poolbeg, Dublin, 1991, p. 49
13. *ibid*, p. 60
14. *ibid*, p. 221
15. *ibid*, p. 222

16. *ibid*, p. 223
17. Coogan, Tim P., *De Valera, The Man who was Ireland*, Harper, 1996, p. 643
18. *ibid*, p. 644
19. *ibid*
20. Coogan, Tim P., *De Valera, The Man who was Ireland*, Harper, 1996, p. 644
21. *ibid*
22. Whelan, John (Seán O'Faoláin), *De Valera*, Penguin Books, England 1939, p. 156
23. Dwyer, T. Ryle, *De Valera, The Man & the Myths*, Poolbeg, Dublin, 1991, p. 223
24. Coogan, Tim P., *De Valera, The Man who was Ireland*, Harper, 1996, p. 530
25. Gray, David, *Behind the Green Curtain*, Unpublished Manuscript, XIII/20
26. Dwyer, T. Ryle, *Éamon de Valera*, Gill & Macmillan, 1980, p. 143
27. Dwyer, T. Ryle, *de Valera, The Man & the Myths*, Poolbeg, Dublin, 1991, p. 243
28. Longford, Earl of & O'Neill, Thomas P., *Éamon de Valera*, Hutchinson, London, 1970, p. 470
29. Dwyer, T. Ryle, *De Valera, The Man & the Myths*, Poolbeg, Dublin, 1991, p. 260
30. Gray, David, *Behind the Green Curtain*, Unpublished Manuscript, VII/1
31. Coogan, Tim P., *De Valera, The Man who was Ireland*, Harper, 1996, p. 644
32. *ibid*, p. 645
33. *ibid*
34. Dwyer, T. Ryle, *De Valera, The Man & the Myths*, Poolbeg, Dublin, 1991, p. 234

CHAPTER XXI

Out of the Wilderness

"There never existed in Ireland anything in the shape of a really national spirit of any consciousness of an Irish nation. We are merely a conglomeration of clans, each of which looked not beyond its nose and all of which pursued their own individual interests alone, ready at any moment to betray the others if by doing so they could hope to satisfy cupidity, jealousy, hate and other similar passions..."[1]

John Hagan, Rector, Irish College in Rome

The sheer ingenuity and pertinacity of de Valera, coupled with his seemingly impossible return to preeminence, must surely rank in the annals of satanic intrigue as one of the greatest political comebacks in history. Once the Unionist government was solidly established in Northern Ireland, Anglo-American relations in the United States secure, and the Irish discredited throughout the world, de Valera set about resurrecting his political career – no mean feat considering the odds against him. After ten years of death, destruction, and bitterness as a consequence of his civil war, and his grinding mission to derail the Free State Government, he grudgingly admitted that Collins and Griffith were right: "'I am prepared to confess,' he said, 'that there have been advances made that I did not believe would be made at the time.'"[2] Tim Pat Coogan remarked on de Valera's hypocrisy: "Thus, standing on Olympian principle, de Valera dismissed the plague-bearers who would have involved the soul of the nation in compromise and 'party politics.' But a few years later when he founded his own party, no arguments could be found to prevent his seizing the same opportunities that existed in December 1922... Morally and politically, his position was untenable."[3]

When the Free-State Treaty was signed in December 1921, the international community was delighted that the Irish had taken the first step towards autonomy. Economic prosperity loomed on the horizon. But all the good will and respect for the Irish after seven hundred years of struggle were dashed by the treachery of de Valera. The world looked on in astonishment and disgust as civil war turned Ireland's centuries-long dream of independence into an incomprehensible bloody nightmare.

De Valera fashioned his own brand of history with the help of a procession of obsequious writers. For instance, on November 4, 1922, Ernie O'Malley, Assistant Chief of Staff of the anti-Treaty IRA faction, was caught in a raid on his hideout in Dublin in which he reportedly received twenty-three gunshot wounds. Mary Bromage, in an outright fabrication, wrote: "Everyone at the meeting was a wanted man, but the Chief [de Valera]... managed to reach a rear exit while O'Malley, in the hall, drew the fire..."[4] Just as he had taken credit for the heroics of Michael Malone at Mount Street Bridge in 1916, de Valera was again cloaked in undeserved heroics for – an escape that was neither heroic nor an escape. Coogan set the record straight: "The Ailesbury Road incident added to de Valera's mythic reputation. *Even though he was nowhere near when the shoot-out occurred...*"[5] [emphasis added]

In January 1924, the Free State Government initiated proceedings in the United States setting forth a claim to the $3 million de Valera had stashed away during his rampage across America in 1919–20. According to Dwyer: "It was wholly for propaganda that de Valera wanted to press ahead with the legal battle for the American funds. He told his lawyer: 'The vital weakness of the Free State Government was that it knew nothing of the psychology of the people. They are incapable of feeling the nation's pulse. They have no publicity department worth talking of. *Any government that desires to hold power in Ireland should put publicity before all.*'" [emphasis added][6]

The New York Supreme Court, contradicting de Valera's claim that an Irish Republic existed, ruled that the "disputed money deposited by him in 1920 should be returned to subscribers because the Republican government of 1919–22 had never been officially recognized."[7] De Valera had convinced investors to assign their bonds to him as President of an Irish Republic that did not exist.

De Valera articulated his policy of economic destruction of the Free State at the August 7-8, 1924 meeting of Fianna Fáil: "I have only one fear and it is a fairly strong fear, that the more we make the country immediately prosperous, the more we have to watch that we do not at the same time consolidate the very power we are trying to destroy and which must be destroyed before we can get anywhere."[8] The welfare of the people was secondary in his drive to return to power. His focus was on preventing any worthwhile economic programs that would benefit the people during the Free State administration. His social reform consisted of disrupting opposition political rallies, intimidating voters, and creating mayhem in order to make the Free State ungovernable. In any revolution, ideals are inevitably compromised after the seizure of power and at such a time, the opposition party, without political risk, is in a superior position to hinder any policies endorsed by the ruling party and at the same time claim that any lack of progress is attributable to the newly installed government.

Seán Lemass, a longtime de Valera lackey, was instrumental in creating economic chaos in the Free State during the decade de Valera was out of office. He eventually succeeded de Valera as leader of Fianna Fáil and as Prime Minister in 1959. He described the dissident Republican fringe, and by extension, de Valera and himself, when he commented: "The Republican cause was being hurt by various cranks of one kind or another who had attached themselves to Sinn Féin. *The public image of the party was being affected by the galaxy of cranks, with the result that the foundation of a new movement which could cut clear of this accumulation of queer people was not unattractive.*"[9] [emphasis added]

At a specially called Ard Fheis in March 1926, de Valera moved to isolate this "galaxy of cranks" within his coterie. He now belatedly accepted Collins and Griffith's interpretation of the alleged oath in his decision to take his seat in the Dáil. The galaxy of cranks and queer people, along with the rest of the extremist element, were powerless to oppose de Valera and were unable to mount any serious opposition to de Valera's assuming Collins and Griffith's position. Their ineffectuality confirmed Griffith's contention that there would have been no civil war if de Valera had not provoked and led it.

Mary MacSwiney, who was also later to rue her adulation of de Valera, exulted after his arrest by the Free State Government in 1923: "Our beloved President, there is nobody but Éamon de Valera himself who can fill the place of Éamon de Valera."[10] By 1926, however, MacSwiney was singing a different tune, this time highly critical of de Valera's on-again, off-again brand of republicanism. She discovered that de Valera never said what he meant or meant what he said.

De Valera's role in initiating a civil war and his charge that Collins and Griffith's "compromise" in signing the Free State Treaty was a "betrayal of the purity of the Republic" was deflected by T. Ryle Dwyer: "People like Mary MacSwiney, Count Plunkett and Father Michael O'Flanagan thought compromise and betrayal were exactly the same. They were only interested in preserving the purity of their policy and they could never reconcile themselves with anyone who believed in achievement. They were unwilling to abandon abstentionism, even if the oath were abolished."[11]

On March 9, 1926: "Father Michael O'Flanagan, vice president of Sinn Féin, urged the retention of the abstentionist policy of the Party. He proposed as an amendment to de Valera's proposition: 'That it is incompatible with the fundamental principles of Sinn Féin as it is injurious to the honor of Ireland to send representatives into any usurping legislature set up by English law in Ireland.' The amendment was carried by 223 to 218. On the following morning de Valera resigned as president of Sinn Féin."[12]

Later that month, a further motion was proposed: "…This assembly does not approve of the policy as set out by the President [de Valera], was carried by 19 votes to 18, whereupon de Valera resigned as president of the Republic and 'his old friend,' Austin Stack, moved its acceptance. Stack was sorely disappointed by the defection of de Valera… He wrote that he regretted the secession of de Valera… Unlike most of his colleagues, he did not openly criticize de Valera when de Valera publicly announced on April 16, 1926, the formation of a new Republican Party to be called Fianna Fáil (Warriors of Destiny)…"[13]

De Valera now found his return to the Dáil was opposed by the very galaxy of cranks that he had previously persuaded not to take the Oath on the grounds it was tantamount to a betrayal of the Republic. "The weakness of [de Valera's] argument was that the Irish Republic never lived and its government never was a fact… It is clear now that de Valera and his followers were secretly aware of the absurdity of their position…With an illogicality that did not strike them, the only Dáil or Parliament they recognized was the Second Dáil, which had rejected the Republic in favor of the Treaty…"[14]

Stunned by his reversal of position, MacSwiney recognized the duplicity of de Valera's call to take up arms against the Free State Government. She "publicly accused de Valera of moving dangerously close to the stand he had refused to take when invited by Collins in 1922 to enter the Dáil on a constitutional basis. 'The policy now adopted by Fianna Fáil,' she asserted in a letter to the press, 'seems to be just that which we refused four years ago – accepting the Treaty position, but not accepting the Treaty. If that was not a proper policy for Republicans in 1922, how can it be right in 1926?'"[15]

MacSwiney, stung by de Valera's derisive response, described his inconsistency in a letter to Sean T. O'Kelly: "Honestly I cannot see why that should have annoyed them. It was exactly the point of view expressed by Dev himself a few months before…Anyhow, be that as it may, the other side took the same poor attitude to my poor self as the Treaty people did a few years ago. Even Dev was as nasty as he could be, has given me some surprises in these past months, I can tell you… One does not like to see him doing the very thing he was the first to blame others for – try to pull down and belittle the very thing he helped to build."[16] Belatedly, MacSwiney realized that she and the rest of the Treaty opponents had been duped into supporting a civil war over mere shadows and under cover of those shadows, they cast their country into mindless mayhem.

De Valera, feigning reluctance, allowed Sean Lemass to talk him into leading Fianna Fáil. By accepting in 1926 what he had rejected in 1922, de Valera finally acknowledged that the civil war was over a trivial difference. He declared, "It has...been repeatedly stated and it is not uncommonly believed, that the required declaration is not an oath. The signing of it implies no contractual obligation and that it has no binding significance in conscience or in law. In short, it is merely an empty political formula that Deputies could conscientiously sign without becoming involved, or without involving their nation in obligations of loyalty to the English Crown. *The Fianna Fáil Deputies would certainly not wish to have the feeling that they are allowing themselves to be debarred by nothing more than an empty formula from exercising their functions as public representatives, particularly at a moment like this...*"[17] [emphasis added] de Valera had come full circle.

The money raised by Joseph McGarrity in America was used to promote de Valera's new party. In the June 1927 election, Fianna Fáil won 44 seats, two less than Cosgrave's Cumann na nGaeldheal. De Valera and his Party members continued to refuse to take the Oath and, on June 23, 1927, they were denied entry to the Dáil. De Valera then initiated a campaign for a referendum to remove the Oath as prerequisite for entering the Dáil. As a result of the murder of Kevin O'Higgins, however, the referendum route was blocked. Three important Acts were adopted by the Free State Government: the right to initiate a referendum was abolished; a Public Safety Bill designed to curb IRA abuses was passed and an Electoral Amendment Bill requiring any legislative candidate, upon nomination to sign an affidavit pledging that if elected he would take the prescribed Oath within two months of the election or face automatic disqualification.

De Valera denied any connection with the death of O'Higgins despite the fact that he had encouraged his followers to attack Free State officials. He said his party abandoned violence and "the war would not be resumed in Autumn," a contemptuous aspersion to O'Higgins' comments when the Free State had rejected de Valera's earlier version of a peace settlement.

Actually, the effect of O'Higgins murder was to make it easier for de

Valera to abandon the old abstentionist policy. O'Higgins had been on his way to church when Timothy Coughlin and two other members of de Valera's Fianna Fáil party shot him and he died hours later. "As he lay dying, he joked to his wife, that he would soon be sitting on a cloud with a harp arguing politics with Michael Collins. The best man at O'Higgins wedding to Birdie Cole, a schoolteacher in 1921 was Rory O'Connor whose execution O'Higgins sanctioned in 1922 in reprisal for the shooting of Sean Hales. O'Higgins was one of the bright intellectual lights of the Free State."[18]

De Valera had previously voiced his objection to entering the Dáil by refusing to sign the oath: "Were we to compromise on any essential, we would have proved that we were fighting for party – not defending sacred principles."[19]

On August 12, 1927, five years and eight months after the ratification of the Free State treaty, de Valera and his followers surrendered their much vaunted sacred principles for party politics by subscribing their name to the very same oath they claimed was an "oath of allegiance to the King," and that death was preferable to signing it.

Joseph McGarrity, who was instrumental in promoting de Valera's rampage throughout America, like Mary MacSwiney, would also later come to witness de Valera's brand of loyalty when the Irish-American had outlived his usefulness. The money raised by McGarrity was utilized to great effect by de Valera, and, in the June 1927 election, Fianna Fáil incredibly won 44 seats, two less than Cosgrave's party.

Like mindless sheep, de Valera's dissidents blindly followed the Irish Judas into civil war, perpetuated the division of Ireland, and ultimately acknowledged that the cause of all the misery they inflicted upon Ireland was "merely an empty political formula with no binding significance in conscience or law."

De Valera admitted that he and his followers had violated their sacred pledges: "What we did [signed the oath] was contrary to all our former actions and to everything we stood for – contrary to our declared policy and to the explicit pledges we gave at the time of our election."[20] Coogan rationalized their hypocrisy: "The Republicans' choice, therefore, lay between a heart-breaking surrender of what they have repeatedly proved was dearer to them than life and the repudiation of what they recognize to be the basis of all order in government and the keystone of democracy – majority rule."[21] De Valera formally presided over the inauguration of his new party on May 16, 1926 at La Scala Theatre in Dublin, when he was promptly elected president. He was now a "born-again" Democrat, rejecting his minority-rule maxim and assuming the mantle of majority rule as the basis of his new Fianna Fáil Party.

Once he hit the campaign trail, de Valera appropriated Collins and Griffith's majority-rule position and abandoned his parallel Republic of Ireland government. "We do not believe in attempting to practice a sleight of hand on the electorate. We shall proceed as a responsible constitutional Government acknowledging without reserve that all authority comes through the sovereign people..."[22]

History will ultimately judge de Valera's followers not as the self-anointed Defenders of the Republic but as loathsome hypocrites who chose the bullet over the ballot rather than accept majority rule. After rejecting the overwhelming vote in favor of the treaty and plunging Ireland into the flames of civil war, de Valera became a "Constitutionalist" and launched his new Republican party, Fianna Fáil. "A simple acceptance of the people's will! That was all that was asked of them," was Collins' lament.

A division on Fianna Fáil's entry into the Dáil in 1927 resulted in a tie of 71 votes, with the Speaker casting his vote for the government. Cosgrave quickly dissolved Parliament, and elections were scheduled. The pro-treaty party gained 21 seats and formed a coalition government with the help of the Farmer's Party. Fianna Fáil increased its membership by 13 seats to a total of 57 becoming the second largest party in the Dáil. After de Valera led his Fianna Fáil into the Irish Parliament, the old Sinn Féin remnants of extremists, cranks and queer people all but faded away.

In order to deflect his irrational change of position on the oath, de Valera adopted a strident opposition to partition: "... Politically, we shall continue to deny the right, and to combat the exercise, of any foreign authority in Ireland. In particular we shall refuse to admit that our country may be carved up and partitioned by such an authority."[23] But it was too late for change: the Nationalists of the North were now securely under the thumb of the Unionist regime. De Valera blamed the Free State government for partition, but the fact remained that it was he who bludgeoned the Dáil deputies in August 1921 into accepting the division of Ireland. It was time for damage control. He branded the Free State deputies as "disloyal, untrustworthy, anglicized and capitalist, identical with landlords, gombeen men, over-wealthy oppressors of the poor, enemies of the native Irish of whom he was, of course, the providential leader."[24]

Only when out of office or seeking re-election, would de Valera become a firebrand advocating violence to bring about unification. Once elected, however, partition was quickly shuffled back into the closet, and de Valera followed the English line of no coercion of Northern Ireland.

Collins had pleaded with the anti-treaty faction to give him four years in which to deliver a republic. Less than four years after his death, his stepping stone strategy was borne out by none other than Lord Balfour, British Foreign Secretary and chairman of the Imperial Conference of 1926. The statement of policy known as the Balfour Declaration, which came out of the conference, stipulated that Commonwealth membership was a "free and voluntary association." The Balfour Declaration validated Collins' prediction that the independence of Ireland would come about by the "peaceful devolution of the British Empire."

The New York Times, on December 21, 1926, hailed the declaration: "The Imperial Conference has succeeded in agreeing upon formulae establishing the absolute equality of the Dominions and the British Empire with Great Britain... *The report declares explicitly that the Empire consists of absolutely free and equal self-governing nations between whom there is no question of superior or inferior status...* Every self-governing member of the Empire is master of its destiny... it is subject to no compulsion whatever... Equality of status so far as Britain and the Dominions are concerned is the root principle governing our inter-imperial relations..." [emphasis added]

All acts passed by the Dominions "operate as a general rule only within the territorial area of the Dominion concerned... Legislation by the Parliament at Westminster applying to a Dominion would not be passed without the consent of the Dominion concerned." That effectively negated de Valera's argument that the Free State Constitution was subject to British law.

The *Times* report continued: "The Governor General thereby became merely a paper shuffler with no significant power or authority." British acceptance that the Governor General's post was merely ceremonial confirmed the position taken by Collins and Griffith: they had agreed to retain the post under the Free State treaty as a face-saving measure for the British.

After his stunning election in 1932, de Valera played to the gallery and used the post of Governor General to stir up controversy. Although he had previously endorsed the candidate, he now demanded the dismissal of the hapless Governor General James MacNeill, brother of John MacNeill, as was his right under the 1931 Statute of Westminster. He appointed, "a colorless Fianna Fáil supporter, Donal O'Buachalla, a retired Maynooth shopkeeper, who, instead of moving into the Viceregal Lodge, was installed in a modest Dublin house,"[25] and was never heard of again.

Despite all his efforts to publicly eliminate the trappings of British rule, de Valera continued to receive his commission from the Governor General, and whenever journeying outside the country, he requested a British passport so as to enjoy the protection of the Crown.

The 1926 Imperial Conference declaration also stated: "It was no part of the policy of His Majesty's Government in Great Britain that questions affecting judicial appeals should be determined otherwise than in accordance with the wishes of the part of the Empire primarily affected." Within four years of Collins' death, the English conceded Irish independence, but de Valera had already wrecked Ireland.

Winston Churchill publicly campaigned against granting Dominion status to Ireland. He thundered: "The politicians of India attach importance to the expression 'dominion status,' because they know that under the *Statute of Westminster*, it gives them the right *inter alia* [among other things] to secede from the British Empire."[26] With the enactment of the *1931 Statute of Westminster*, the British formally acknowledged that the Dominions, including Ireland, were sovereign nations: they were equal and voluntary partners within the British Commonwealth, with the right of secession. As Collins had predicted, ten years after the Free State Treaty, the *Statute of Westminster* marked the completion of Britain's devolution process, whereby each Dominion was entitled to declare total independence or remain in voluntary external association. "De Valera had maintained during the Treaty controversy that Britain would never accord *de facto* status to the Free State..."[27] The *1931 Statute of Westminster* cleared up any remaining ambiguity.

Upon assuming office in 1932, de Valera did not introduce his Document No 2 with its demand for external association. It is further evidence that his Document No. 2 was proposed solely as a red herring in 1921 to counter the terms of the Free State Treaty.

"De Valera later admitted that the enactment of the *Statute of Westminster* showed he had underestimated the real significance of the Anglo-Irish Free State Treaty. When one considers that even while underestimating the Treaty he had admitted there was only a small difference between it and what he wanted, then his subsequent admission meant, in effect, that he had been making a fuss all those years over something less than a small difference over a 'little sentimental thing.'"[28] Dwyer, like most Irish writers, failed to understand that the realpolitik of the civil war over a "little sentimental thing" was criminal; to categorize it as merely a "fuss" was delusional.

In October 1931, the Cosgrave government introduced a

controversial public safety bill, Constitution Amendment No. 17, which authorized military tribunals to deal with political crimes. Though he disavowed his parallel anti-Treaty government, de Valera did not dismantle his militia. His storm troopers were still creating chaos, intimidating, beating and even murdering so-called Free State "traitors." de Valera was opposed to the Constitution Amendment. Debate was bitter, with de Valera accusing Cosgrave of rejecting his proposals to end the civil war merely to keep him out of political office. A sore point for de Valera was the lingering suspicion that he had gone to America to avoid the "Troubles" during the Black and Tan terror. When one deputy inferred cowardice on the part of the former Irish President, de Valera protested loudly: "'I came here the moment the Acting President (Griffith) was put in jail,' de Valera replied. 'I came over here when Cork at the time was burned. I came here at the beginning of the Black and Tan regime proper. I stayed in Dublin through it. I went to meetings of our cabinet that we held when your present president of the Executive ran away to England. I called him back. I saved him from the cabinet that would have kicked him out.'"[29]

The attack was spiteful nonsense. Cosgrave demolished de Valera's charge by producing his attendance record which showed that he had been at every cabinet session but one during the Black and Tan period. Dwyer attempted to explain why de Valera would accuse others of what he was guilty. "In making the charge of cowardice, was de Valera employing what psychiatrists call 'projection' – the technique in which the ego of an individual denies certain undesirable characteristics in himself while attributing them to others? This is not to say de Valera was guilty of cowardice, but rather, that his touchiness on the subject raised questions about his own confidence in the matter."[30] De Valera had a right to be touchy about questions concerning his actions dating back to the Easter Week rebellion in 1916.

Cosgrave, by calling for a general election on February 16, 1932, miscalculated in seeking to capitalize on the public relations bonanza he thought the *1931 Statute of Westminster* would accrue to his party. The Irish were struggling with deep economic depression and the people believed Fianna Fáil could bring relief. De Valera's election campaign promised pie in the sky for every Irishman: a revival of the Gaelic language; an end to partition; removal of the oath that wasn't an oath. He led farmers to believe that he was going to abolish annuity payments on their mortgaged land while the landless thought they would receive their own farm under his redistribution program; protective tariffs would be introduced to protect Irish manufacturers from English competition; and those living in substandard dwellings were promised housing and employment. De Valera's utopian campaign promises succeeded, and Fianna Fáil won enough seats to become the largest party in the Dáil. De Valera was elected president, after ten years plowing the political wilderness.

The tenacity of the man and the revitalization of his political fortunes is the stuff of fiction and dreams. Through sheer willpower and a campaign of disinformation, de Valera was able to cover up the most heinous of crimes, the institution of civil war, and convince a nation that he was not the bogeyman and that the real heroes were the criminals.

De Valera did not readily relinquish violence. He had taken up arms in his opposition to the Treaty and assumed that Cosgrave and his government would do the same. His "selfless idealists" took their seats in the Dáil with hidden pistols strapped to their sides. Upon his triumphant inauguration, de Valera once again brought discredit to Ireland. Dwyer wrote: "Cosgrave's legacy did not so much lie in his leadership in guiding Ireland through turbulent times, but the dignified manner in which he handed over power to his Civil War enemies…because in doing so, he made an invaluable contribution to democracy in Ireland…"

In order to remove the restrictions of leading a minority government, de Valera called for an election in January 1933, and Fianna Fáil was returned with a majority of one vote. In addition to President, he retained the position as Minister of External Affairs in which every major decision throughout the remainder of his political career resulted in monumental benefit to England and to the detriment of Irish interests.

Upon his inauguration in 1932, Ireland, through a peaceful political devolution, had been officially recognized by England through the *Statute of Westminster* as an independent nation, voluntarily in external association, with the same rights and privileges of every Commonwealth Nation, including England. All that was necessary at that time for de Valera to legitimize his Document No.2 proposal was to inform the English that, under the terms of the *1931 Statute of Westminster*, he was formally declaring an Irish Republic and requesting accommodation within the Commonwealth on a voluntarily external basis.

De Valera also acknowledged Collins' stepping-stone approach for justification in solving the oath dilemma. Dwyer noted: "de Valera contended that the *1931 Statute of Westminster*, which recognized the Dominions as masters of their own domestic affairs, provided the authority to remove the 'oath' from the Free State Constitution. As a result, he explained, the Free State had virtually secured the status he was seeking in 1921, when he proposed Document No 2."[31] De Valera, however, never did declare an Irish Republic nor insist on the provisions of his Document No 2.

Upon de Valera's return to the Dáil in 1927, Dr. Patrick McCartan, the American envoy of the IRB and Dáil Éireann and one of the men most responsible for de Valera's American debacle, in a letter to John Devoy proposed a "closing of ranks" behind de Valera.

Devoy sent a devastating reply: "The only indication you [McCartan] give is the suggestion that de Valera is the only outstanding figure for Leader. In our opinion, de Valera is impossible and undesirable. He has no qualities of leadership and his record should bar him forever."

Devoy cited de Valera's treasonous work on behalf of England while in the United States: "He deliberately split the Race in America when it was doing its best work against England. His purpose evidently was to mar and discredit that work and leave the English propaganda for an Anglo-American alliance unopposed. He spent in the attempt over a million dollars, which, if applied to the purchase of arms and munitions would have enabled the 'Fighting Men,' who were at the end of their resources, to hold out for better terms. He rejected at Chicago in 1920, the offer of the Republican leaders, who were in a position to deliver the goods, of recognition of Ireland's sovereignty that would have been an instruction to the President there nominated, and thereby enabled the English Government, (then on its knees begging for American help) to continue its Reign of Terror. He went back to Ireland and after dodging the responsibility itself, put on Griffith and Collins the onus of accepting a Compromise, which he had made inevitable and branded them as Traitors and Renegades for doing so. Then he plunged Ireland into Civil War, for the difference between Tweedledee and Tweedledum, which devastated a large part of the country and inflicted a burden of £50 million [$250 million] on the Irish people. In addition, he made looting of banks and murder a popular pastime and demoralized a large section of the youth of the country. His speeches in a tour from Waterford to Kilkenny preached murder and wound it up in the latter place by saying, 'We must wade through the blood of Irishmen to liberty.'

"If he were made Leader, he would make shipwreck of the cause. This opinion is not based on prejudice but on our judgment of the capacity of the man. His actions cited were crimes against Ireland, which should never be forgiven, even if he did penance in sackcloth and ashes... de Valera set it boiling and is responsible for all the murders, from that of Sean Hales to Kevin O'Higgins. These are my reasons for abhorring de Valera and not personal grievances or prejudice."

Devoy was also prescient as to de Valera's future conduct as author Deidre McMahon noted: "... The peculiar circumstances surrounding

Éamon de Valera's accession to power, followed so soon by a major disturbance in Anglo-Irish relations, instead of clearing the air, fogged it with tension, rumor, and misunderstanding."[32]

Notes

1. Keogh, Dermont, *The Vatican, the Bishops & Irish Politics 1919-39*, Cambridge Press, 1986. p. 263, fn 2
2. Dwyer, T. Ryle, *Éamon de Valera*, Gill & Macmillan, 1980, p. 81
3. Coogan, Tim P., *De Valera, The Man who was Ireland*, Harper, 1996, p. 344
4. Bromage, Mary C., *De Valera and the March of a Nation*, Hutchinson, London, 1956, p. 191
5. Coogan, Tim P., *De Valera, The Man who was Ireland*, Harper, 1996, p. 340
6. Dwyer, T. Ryle, *De Valera, The Man & the Myths*, Poolbeg, Dublin, 1991, p. 134
7. *ibid*
8. Gaughan, J. Anthony, *Austin Stack, Portrait of a Separatist*, Kingdom Books, Dublin, 1977, p. 333
9. Dwyer, T. Ryle, *De Valera, The Man & the Myths*, Poolbeg, Dublin, 1991, p. 140
10. *ibid,* p. 132
11. *ibid,* p. 139
12. Gaughan, J. Anthony, *Austin Stack, Portrait of a Separatist*, Kingdom Books, Dublin, 1977, p. 252
13. *ibid,* p. 253
14. Whelan, John (Seán O'Faoláin), *De Valera*, Penguin Books, England 1939, p. 114
15. Dwyer, T. Ryle, *De Valera, The Man & the Myths*, Poolbeg, Dublin, 1991, p. 144
16. *ibid,* p. 141
17. Longford, Earl of & O'Neill, Thomas P., *Éamon de Valera*, Hutchinson, London, 1970, p. 155
18. Coogan, Tim Pat, *Michael Collins*, Arrow Books, 1991, p. 255
19. Longford, Earl of & O'Neill, Thomas P., *Éamon de Valera*, Hutchinson, London, 1970, p. 216
20. Dwyer, T. Ryle, *De Valera, The Man & the Myths*, Poolbeg, Dublin, 1991, p. 329
21. Coogan, Tim P., *De Valera, The Man who was Ireland*, Harper, 1996, p. 336
22. Longford, Earl of & O'Neill, Thomas P., *Éamon de Valera*, Hutchinson, London, 1970, p. 261
23. Dwyer, T. Ryle, *De Valera, The Man & the Myths*, Poolbeg, Dublin, 1991, p. 130
24. Tierney, Michael (Ed. By F.X. Martin), *Eoin MacNeill, Scholar & Man of action 1867-1945*, Clarendon Press, Oxford 1980, p. 306
25. Coogan, Tim P., *De Valera, The Man Who Was Ireland*, Harper, 1996, p. 459
26. McMahon, Deirdre, "A Transient Apparition, British Policy Towards the de

Valera Government 1932-35", *Irish Historical Studies*, Vol. XXII 1980-81, Antrim, W and G. Baird/ 1981, p. 352

27. Dwyer, T. Ryle, *De Valera, The Man & the Myths*, Poolbeg, Dublin, 1991, 155
28. *ibid*, p. 156
29. *ibid*, p. 154
30. *ibid*, p. 155
31. *ibid*, p. 164
32. McMahon, Deirdre, "A Transient Apparition, British Policy Towards the de Valera Government 1932-35", *Irish Historical Studies*, Vol. XXII 1980-81, Antrim, W and G. Baird/ 1981, 331

CHAPTER XXII

"Assignment Economic War"

"The Irish say that all the misfortunes of Ireland are due to the fact that a 'stupid' nation [England] has tried to govern a 'clever' one [Ireland]. This may be true, but I must own that I find the 'stupid' nation in material comfort – in solid, well-built houses, with flourishing commerce, the leaders of the world in manufactures and commerce, the possessors of the most desirable portions of the earth. On the other hand, the 'clever' nation dresses largely in rags, never learned to cook, keeps its towns in a filthy state, is wanting in domestic cleanliness and prefers to live in conditions of squalor unknown to the greater part of Europe."[1]

Anonymous French writer

William Cosgrave's government, 1922-1932, was remarkable in that it was able to survive for as long as it did considering Éamon de Valera and his rebel Republicans' efforts to derail economic progress and political stability.

Within months of his election in 1932, de Valera declared economic war on Britain by his cancelling the £3 million ($15 million) annuities, due as a result of the British Land Reform Acts of the late nineteenth and early twentieth centuries which had returned land to Irish tenant farmers in the form of sixty-year mortgages. In a move to promote the newly elevated de Valera, the British dispatched a delegation to Dublin on June 7, 1932, ostensibly to discuss the annuity question. The usual practice was for the Irish to travel to London: but by coming to him, the English raised de Valera's standing in the eyes of the Irish. The British accommodated de Valera's political needs throughout his career and rescued him from political oblivion time and again.

De Valera reciprocated the English visit and traveled to London, on July 14 at the invitation of Sir Stafford Cripps. In a replay of his secret talks with Lloyd George in 1921, de Valera insisted upon a private meeting with the English Prime Minister, Ramsey MacDonald. The results were again disastrous to Ireland. This time, rather than launching a Civil War, de Valera initiated an economic war. No one questioned why he was so insistent on a private meeting with the British Prime Minister.

On July 16, the day after the private meeting, de Valera withheld the annuities payment, and the British immediately responded with a twenty percent *ad valorem* tax on all imports from the Irish Free State, ushering in a six-year economic war during the worst depression in history. Britain raised more money through the tariffs than was due from the Irish annuities.

In 1932, the English were struggling to pay their forty billion dollar First World War debt to the United States. If England was perceived to be discriminating against Irish products, the Irish-Americans would be a major obstacle in the path of debt resolution. De Valera solved England's quandary by initiating the economic war, thereby justifying the retaliatory British tariff. The Irish refusal to pay a "legitimate" debt propelled American public opinion in favor of the British. De Valera, once again, turned a win-win contest for the Irish into a win-win finish for England.

The annuity dispute provided de Valera with a platform to showcase his economic policy. "He subscribed to the ideal of people living in frugal comfort, providing for themselves their own food, clothing and shelter and cherishing the spiritual values and cultural heritage above the material luxuries available in some of the wealthy industrial nations. As things stood, the country's existing economic role was essentially providing food for Britain... To the more materially-minded people, de Valera's vision was sentimental twaddle, but it was a romanticized vision which appealed to a large segment of the electorate living in rural poverty."[2]

The economic realities of life dictate that when a country is dependent upon selling ninety-six percent of its goods to another, it ought not to precipitously undertake to dismantle that relationship. De Valera's economic war bore political fruit almost immediately. Riding on his position of "standing up to John Bull," de Valera called for a general election in January 1933, and the cheering, though impoverished, Irish returned Fianna Fáil with a Dáil majority of 77 seats out of 143.

The British newspaper *The Economist* trumpeted Britain's policy in the economic war "was little short of disastrous...de Valera used the Economic War to brilliant political effect in domestic Irish terms. He entrenched his own political position by leading his party to an overall majority in the Dáil..."[3] *The Economist* conceded the Government aided de Valera's political fortunes but didn't pause to ask why.

Winston Churchill cited the economic realities between England and Ireland: "Great Britain holds Irish prosperity in the hollow of her hand,"

and pointed to Ireland's dependence upon the English market: "...I have always held that there was never a country more utterly dependent upon another in economic matters than is Ireland on Great Britain, which is almost her only market and almost her only source of supply. If Irishmen choose to cut off their nose to spite their face, we cannot prevent them, nor shall we try. They are responsible, not we. It would be interesting to consider what would happen if Mr. De Valera's policy of refusing to buy anything from Britain were carried out. At present Great Britain is the sole market for Irish exports."[4]

De Valera's government was able to blame every blunder, every recession, every burden on the usual suspect – England. He led Ireland into another of his patented disasters, and it was the people, as usual, who did the suffering and paid the price. Jan Christian Smuts, the former South African leader, wrote: "'With a mad fellow like de Valera leading Ireland to bankruptcy and even Civil War, the British should back down. What is the sense of forcing things to such fatal issues? Surely Great Britain must be the strong friend and elder brother.' He called for 'patience and magnanimity.'"[5]

By his precipitate action of foreclosing negotiations or arbitration, de Valera once again cast Ireland in the role of a deadbeat nation that would not honor a legitimate debt. Whether the debt was legitimate or not was debatable, but by cancelling the debt, he removed the issue from the public stage and deprived Ireland of a potential coup against England. Had he pushed for arbitration, Ireland would have stood to benefit. Even if they prevailed, the English would have been portrayed as a Shylock demanding its pound of flesh from an impoverished Ireland while demanding America forgive its own huge First World War debt.

In answer to de Valera's challenge in 1932, Neville Chamberlain, at that time Chancellor of the Exchequer, conceded that de Valera had "an arguable point" in accordance with the 1925 Boundary Commission settlement. It absolved the Dublin Government "from liability for the service of the Public Debt of the United Kingdom," of which the Irish annuities were part of that debt. Chamberlain decided against arbitration because "there is at any rate a certain risk that an arbitrator might hold Mr. De Valera is right from a purely legal point of view. It would seem most undesirable that we should expose ourselves to such a decision when there is not the slightest doubt about the facts (1) that the Irish Free State ought in equity to pay over the annuities and (2) that they have clearly and definitely promised to do so."[6]

Deidre McMahon noted: "Comparisons were drawn, not the least by de Valera, between the British 'playing Shylock' on the Irish default and

England's own refusal to pay their American debts. Chamberlain acknowledged the British dilemma: 'To refuse to pay,' he wrote, 'is to be accused of doing the very thing we have lectured de Valera and the small debtor nations of Europe for doing...'"[7] Chamberlain had decided on settlement rather than arbitration as a means to resolve the question.

With de Valera refusing to negotiate, the British launched an anti-Irish propaganda blitz in America, characterizing the Irish as welshers, and pledging that England, though struggling economically, would continue to pay its debt to America. "In December, when France, Belgium, Poland, and Hungary defaulted on their war debt payments to the English, Chamberlain announced that Britain would be paying her $95 million installment on time, even though it meant asking parliament for a supplementary estimate to cover the loss of the Irish annuities and increased unemployment benefits."

Next day, *The New York Times*, in a front-page headline, declared: "'Irish land issue and relief put Britain out £21,420,955 ($107 million).' Dwyer, confusing the annual payment of £3 million ($15 million) with the total amount owed of more than £21 million ($105 million), dismissed the report, claiming: "The headline had grossly exaggerated the impact of the withholding of the land annuities on the British economy, because those annuities amounted to less than 15 percent of the sum mentioned, and anyway, the British exchequer had recouped the money with the tariffs on Irish imports. The editorial cast the British in a most favorable light and was, by implication, extremely damning of the Dublin government, which was now being lumped among the defaulting nations at a time when the whole issue was a particularly touchy subject for the American people, already in the grip of the Great Depression."[8]

After casting the Irish as four-flushers, the British paid a token installment or two on their debt to the United States and then defaulted altogether.

England's position on the annuities was on shaky legal ground, as Chamberlain had conceded. The British offered to appoint a Commonwealth tribunal of one or more members to mediate. With some justification, de Valera refused and cited the Boundary Commission in which a South African judge rigged the decision in favour of Northern Ireland. If de Valera had insisted on Canada – Ireland's staunch advocate in the Commonwealth – as arbitrator, the British would have run the risk of having to repay the Irish £21 million [$105 million] in annuities refunds from 1924 to 1931, as set forth in the Boundary Commission settlement. The English could ill-afford the negative publicity and would have settled prior to any public arbitration hearing, but de Valera was determined on using the dispute to his and England's political advantage.

"The difficulties over the Annuities were not the main problem as far as Britain was concerned. Thomas Inskip, the British Attorney-General, publicly admitted there would be little difficulty in resolving the differences between the two governments, were it not for the constitutional implications of de Valera's overall policy. 'If there could be a clear and sincere declaration of the desired intention of the Irish Free State to stay within the Empire on the basis of their constitutional position and in a spirit of loyal partnership,' Inskip said, 'no Annuities or debts could cloud the prospect.'"[9]

All that was required was for de Valera, under the aegis of the Statute of Westminster, to implement his Document No. 2 by declaring an Irish Republic and then request membership in voluntary external association within the Commonwealth of Nations which were recognized as independent nations in voluntary external association with England. Evidence of this occurred in 1937 when the British Privy Council ruled that his constitution did not affect Ireland's status within the Commonwealth.

To forestall any settlement, the British insisted on the payment of the past annuities which had fallen due pending arbitration. De Valera demanded a public hearing before the World Court at The Hague, well aware that the English would never agree. By his refusing to pay, de Valera scuttled any amicable resolution and the international community characterized the Irish as welshers.

Longford and O'Neill sought to explain the Irish President's brand of banshee economics: "A series of meetings were begun in September 1932 to explain the problem of the economic war to the people of Ireland... de Valera pointed out that Irish farmers should produce for the home market by turning to tillage and he appealed to all to buy Irish products. He saw that exports would diminish but this could be countered by a restriction on imports...The crisis had made the Government proceed with its protectionist policy at a much faster rate than had been intended. As a result, there would be more dislocation and hardship than if the change were spread over a number of years."[10]

Ireland had an excellent legal case for refusing to pay the annuities to England. Following the Boundary Commission decision in 1926: "In return, [of settlement of the Boundary Commission dispute] *the Free State was released from any liability under Clause V, the financial section of the 1922 Free State Treaty.* [emphasis added] The agreement was submitted without delay to the British, Free State, and Northern Ireland Parliaments"[11] and adopted by all parties. But de Valera would not invoke any of Ireland's rights under the treaties, and Ireland verged on bankruptcy as a result.

The *1920 Government of Ireland Act* specified that the land annuities would no longer have to be paid to England but would be a sort of grant-in-aid to the Belfast and Dublin governments "as a free gift for the purpose of development and improvement of Ireland."

Collins and Griffith, during the treaty negotiations, refused to admit any liability for the British public debt but argued that England owed Ireland hundreds of millions of pounds as a result of over-taxation during the nineteenth century. "A Royal Commission had already acknowledged this over-taxation."[12]

Chamberlain's argument for demanding payment of the annuities was based on the "Ultimate Financial Settlement of 1926," a secret agreement in which the Cosgrave Government promised to pay England millions in unauthorized annuity payments. The terms which were not published until 1926 and had never been ratified by the Dáil were: "The Government of the Irish Free State undertakes to pay to the British Government at agreed intervals the full amount of the annuities accruing due from time to time under the Irish Land Acts, 1891-1909, without any deduction whatsoever whether on account of income tax or otherwise."[13]

Cosgrave had signed an agreement to continue the annual Land Annuity and pension payments amounting to approximately £5 million ($25 million) of which £3 million ($15 million) was without Dáil authorization and without referring to the previous agreements which specifically waived such payments. When discovered, the voluntary-payment pact created a sensation and was a major boon to de Valera's 1932 election.

The Boundary Commission settlement, approved by the Dáil on December 10, 1925, by a vote of 71-20, specifically released the Free State government from any obligation to service the British public debt. Cosgrave's outrageous acceptance of this "Ultimate Financial Settlement" resulted in the illegal payment of annuities from 1925 to 1931 at £3 million per year for a total of £18 million ($90 million dollars).

De Valera focused his election campaign not only on the fact that the "Ultimate Financial Settlement of 1926" was never ratified by the Dáil but also on the revelation that there was also a secret 1923 agreement that had not even been presented to the Dáil. He demanded a copy of the secret agreement and pontificated: "... If there was any valid agreement obligating the Free State to pay the annuities, it would be scrupulously honored...The Irish copy was in very poor condition when found. It is literally in tatters...There is not even an Irish signature to it."[14]

Cosgrave's signature was affixed to the English copy but the Irish version was unsigned and de Valera declared it nonbinding since the Dáil had not ratified the document. He was correct when he declared: "This has never got statutory sanction and every sum paid out in virtue of that agreement without collateral statutory sanction is being paid out without the proper authority."[15]

Rather than seek a negotiated settlement, de Valera was determined to exploit the situation to his political advantage. He was prepared to provide the English with an excuse to tax Irish products and by so doing provide relief to hard-pressed English farmers.

Compounding the difficulties faced by Irish agriculture, de Valera insisted on granting a subsidy to Irish farmers to switch oat and barley acreage to wheat, which was ill suited to the Irish climate. Irish farmers, most of whom were barely above the subsistence level, switched to wheat in order to receive the subsidies, but the price of oats and barley, now in short supply, soared. The Irish were then forced to pay a higher price for cereals and a lower price for inferior wheat. Any farmer could have told de Valera wheat was not conducive to Ireland's wet climate.

"His farm economics were going in circles. In order to provide for farmers being hurt by his agriculture policy, de Valera introduced unemployment insurance. This, too, went counter to his claim of Irish self-sufficiency, as Irish farmers scrambled onto state welfare rolls. De Valera had promised Irish farmers that his economic war would result in alternative markets for their products, but the reality was otherwise, as even de Valera's supporters admitted: 'The cash income of the farms declined, credit from banks and shopkeepers became more difficult to obtain, there was a significant reduction in the use of fertilizers and the standard of living in rural Ireland fell to a lower level...There can be no doubt, however, that the agricultural community, as a whole, endured considerable hardship as a result of the dispute...'"[16]

De Valera's claim that Ireland would take its export business elsewhere was, as usual, all fog and no substance. The other countries of Europe showed little interest in purchasing Ireland's agricultural produce because they had their own surplus problems with which to grapple.

De Valera's handling of the annuities question resulted in a financial catastrophe for Ireland's struggling farmers during the worst economic depression in history. Dwyer noted: "The President was more popularly associated with the rural scene, where his policy was little short of disastrous from the economic standpoint...A bounty was paid on cattle being sent to Britain to offset the tariff being collected by the British. As a result, the Dublin government was effectively paying the Annuities in the form of export subsidies, and the British were collecting them in the form of tariffs..."[17]

Prior to the enactment of the *1931 Statute of Westminster*, the British government was seriously concerned with the rapidly declining economic situation in England. Cheap imports were flooding the market, creating havoc among British manufacturers and especially farmers. Chamberlain emphasized the need for immediate action on the part of the Government. "On November 11, 1930, the day after the opening of Parliament, he issued a warning [on the dire agricultural import situation]...the Cabinet agreed to a bill imposing a duty of 100 percent on excessive imports. The Liberals were ready to agree to certain horticultural tariffs..."[18] Britain, as far back as 1924, scrambled to find a means to help its farmers: "Agriculture claimed the government's interest for so long and so assiduously that it could not be ignored..."[19]

During the Great Depression of the 1930s, worldwide agriculture was hard hit. De Valera's economic war could not have come at a more propitious moment for English farmers. A direct effect of de Valera's folly was that the retaliatory twenty-percent tariff on Irish produce, tilted the British market in favor of the locals: they no longer had to worry about cheap Irish farm goods flooding the market.

De Valera promised a cornucopia of goodies for everybody during the election campaign of 1932: elimination of the annuity payments; housing for the poor; land for the dispossessed; tariffs for the businessman; as well as constitutional, social, and economic reform. With the calamitous fall in cattle exports due to English tariffs, the farmers were led to believe that de Valera's annuities fight with the English meant that they would be free from paying the balance of the mortgages on their farms. "What de Valera did not say was that he intended to use the land annuity payments to offset the cost of the program. Many farmers had mistakenly thought Fianna Fáil was promising to cancel their land payments, whereas, in fact, de Valera still planned to collect them."[20] The farmers envisioned a homestead freed from annuity debt but found themselves in even worse straits than before. They not only had to pay the annuities but also endured the effects of the additional twenty percent duty tacked onto ninety-six percent of their produce; and, in the process, paid higher taxes so that the government could pay for farmers' subsidies. Irish farmers were going in circles trapped by de Valera's economic merry-go-round.

While Irish farmers, manufacturers, and teachers struggled, de Valera found an opportunity to enrich himself. He allegedly was a math wizard the likes of Einstein, but it was Math 101 he employed in diverting public money, not to an Irish Republic but to his own personal ownership of his newspaper, *The Irish Press*.

The Cosgrave Government's argument was that the $3 million de Valera had stashed in American banks belonged to the Irish Free State. The Court ruled that since the certificates had been purchased on the understanding that they were to support an Irish Republic, and, since no Irish Republic existed, the money must be returned to its subscribers. Due to de Valera's spending more than a million dollars on his divisive campaign while in America, the $3 million Bond Certificates remaining in the banks was only sufficient to pay 58 cents on the dollar value of the certificates. He worked his banshee magic on the certificate holders, however, convincing them to assign them over to him in order to establish a national newspaper, *The Irish Press*.

A week after the December 1932 *New York Times* article accusing the Irish of being deadbeats for not paying a legitimate debt to England, de Valera launched his own public relations campaign in America. He declared that Ireland would not only honor its pledge to redeem the bond certificates at face value but that the Free State would pay an additional twenty-five percent bonus. This declaration got rave revues in the international press and the tide of bad publicity was reversed. Behind this scene, however, de Valera once again humbugged the gullible Gaels, as the bond certificates had already been assigned to him; he would reap a financial bonanza at the expense of poverty-stricken Ireland.

In July 1933, he introduced a bill in which the Dáil approved payment based on 100 percent amortization plus a twenty-five percent bonus, for a total expenditure of $1.25 for every 58-cent Bond Certificate. That meant the Dáil assumed the balance of not only the 42-cent difference of the face value but also the additional 25-cent bonus de Valera had tossed in for himself. Under de Valera's raid on the Irish Treasury, the Fianna Fáil majority authorized the payment of $7.5 million for redemption of the bond certificates with a value of $3.5 million.

During the Dáil debate of July 5-6, 1933 on the issue, Dáil deputies charged him "with looting the public purse for a party organ... and putting a huge charge on the taxpayer so that he might get a percentage..."[21] Fine Gael deputy Batt O'Connor was blunt: "The indecent haste about it is that you want to get control of the money to help you out of your difficulties with your daily paper... Think of the conditions of the farms... the cutting of the salaries of the teachers and the civil servants... and now you pass a Bill to pay £1.5 million [$7.5 million]... (You should) put country before party politics and a party newspaper."[22]

Admitting that he was engaged in a corrupt practice, de Valera accused the minority Dáil deputies that they would do the very same thing if they were in the majority. He gloated: "I know it is gall and wormwood to them [Cosgrave Government members] that they are not here [in the majority] to do it and that is the whole trouble. They are not here to do it and it is the great and supreme pleasure of my life to know they will have to digest the gall and wormwood."[23]

The American court decision not only denied the Free State access to the $3 million Bond Certificate money, but it also relieved the Free State of any obligation to redeem the certificates. "Cosgrave pointed out that the Free State had no obligation to pay the money at all because of the American Judge's decision (as the Free State was not awarded title to the bonds it did not acquire either their benefit or their obligations.)"[24] de Valera, however, stampeded the Dáil into approving the $7.5 million tab that went directly into his pocket for his personal ownership of the Irish Press. His subsequent election campaign strategy was based on the laughable claim of honesty and trust: "The Irish people know full well that I personally never got one penny out of anything I did as far as Ireland was concerned."[25]

De Valera had incorporated the Irish Press Ltd. in Dublin in September 1928. The first edition hit the streets on September 5, 1931. Reportedly, in an effort to cover his shady financial trail, he transferred the controlling interest of the Irish Press Ltd. to an offshore site in the state of Delaware, USA, in 1931, in which all voting shares were in his name.

John Whelan, in a nonsensical testimonial, raved about "Honest Dev" and the Irish president's personal integrity: "de Valera may make the terrible mistake of the civil war; he may take an oath to get into the Dáil; he may threaten to alter the methods of elections – never is it for any personal gain, always, for Ireland... his political honesty is unimpeachable."[26]

Rather than lead Ireland to economic independence, de Valera accomplished exactly the opposite. In 1939, after nearly seven years in power, the Irish were more dependent upon England than ever before. The threat of war made the situation still more precarious. Coogan quoted a Department of Industry and Commerce memorandum of April 18, 1939, which stated: "'... if war should break out, we are very largely at the mercy of other countries and particularly of the United Kingdom... the economic activities of this country could in such circumstances be completely paralyzed.' The bottom line was that Britain was the source of 50 percent of Ireland's imports and the destination of 90 percent of her exports."[27]

De Valera's economic policy was such that the cost of living was higher in Southern Ireland than in Northern Ireland. The prices of farm products – butter and bacon, for example – were so manipulated that the cost of these Irish items was cheaper in London than in Dublin, despite the 20 percent *ad valorem* tax on Irish imports. Three months after Germany invaded Poland, the Irish economy was so depressed that de Valera was forced to cut Irish Army personnel by more than 20 percent.

In 1921, Arthur Griffith presented the economic situation at that time: "We are trying to end the old war between Ireland and Britain and we mean to succeed. Let me point out that of Ireland's imports in 1919 amounting to £159 million [$795 million], no less than 85.5 percent, £135.9 million [$679.5 million], were imported from Great Britain. *And of our own exports to the value of £176 million [$880 million], 99 percent, £174 million pounds [$870 million] went over the water to Great Britain.*"[28] [emphasis added] Just after the First World War, Ireland enjoyed a favourable balance of trade with Great Britain: to the tune of £38 million [$190 million] per year, a huge sum for such a small country with a population of some three million. In the interval between his "Assignment America" in 1919 and the conclusion of his Economic War in 1938, de Valera turned an economic dream into a financial nightmare. Dwyer reported on Valera's economic policy: "... Irish efforts to find new international markets were a dismal failure.. The value of Irish exports to Britain dropped by 50 percent which led to a record trade deficit of £20.7 million [$103 million] in 1937..."[29]

Churchill said: "We do in fact, send the Irish people four-fifths of everything they require. If they are going to take from us the goods they need and with which alone we can pay them for their agricultural produce, which they must sell, one of two things must happen: either they would have no outlet for their agricultural produce at all or else they would have to give it to us for nothing."[30] What actually happened, thanks to de Valera, was that the Irish did not give it to England for nothing, only at half price.

The extent of the enormous economic devastation of de Valera's policies was staggering and totally ignored by Irish writers. If the £38 million [$190 million] favorable balance of trade in 1919 is taken as a median against the trade deficit of £20.7 million [$103 million] in 1937, this results in a negative trade differential of £58.7 million [$293 million] a year to the Irish people. Using 1937 as a typical year during de Valera's six-year economic war, that differential multiplied by six meant that the Irish actually lost an astronomical £352.2 million [$1.758 billion] during de Valera's economic war.

367

De Valera, however, wasn't done battering the Irish economy. In 1938, he paid England another £10 million [$50 million] in settlement of the annuity dispute, which he claimed Ireland wasn't legally bound to do under the terms of the Boundary Commission settlement and previous agreements. Tallying up de Valera's banshee economics, not counting his $7.5 million rip-off of the Irish treasury for his newspaper, Ireland suffered a $1.805 billion loss in trade. If the price of his civil war, £50 million [$250 million], is figured into the equation, de Valera had the starring role in a real-life economic horror movie for the Irish.

With the Nazi rise to power in Germany and Hitler's aggressive moves in Europe, the gathering clouds of war loomed on the horizon. England would need America once again, and the British prepared for another round of neutralizing the Irish-American anti-English political agenda. It was a propitious moment to call a halt to the economic war, and de Valera was put on notice that it was time to change the name of the game.

De Valera, at the time, was facing political oblivion, as his economic policies had all but bankrupted the nation. Consequently, in late 1937, he allegedly went hat in hand to London, offering to negotiate a settlement of the Anglo-Irish economic war. "J. J. Walshe proposed... (1) *a settlement of the financial dispute on a fifty-fifty basis* [emphasis added]; (2) acceptance of the agreement 'as a friendly settlement between members of the Commonwealth'; and (3) an immediate trade agreement..."[31]

It is open to conjecture, with the Irish willing to pay fifty percent of the annuities debt as to why Prime Minister Chamberlain was so insistent on a 90/10 split, with England picking up the 90 percent. The British, allegedly without de Valera asking, insisted that the cattle tariffs also be rescinded and that the annuities be waived entirely. In order to save face, the British "suggested" a token payment of £10 million [$50 million] as final compensation for the lost revenue from the annuities. De Valera was only too happy to oblige.

Chamberlain recognized that merely a settlement of the economic war would not guarantee de Valera's political fortunes. Britain would require his services during the prelude and coming war to be England's point man to once again neutralize Irish-American opposition to the pro-British Franklin Delano Roosevelt Administration.

A spectacular vote-winning coup was needed if de Valera was to remain in power. Chamberlain insisted that the Irish ports to the Western Approaches be turned over to the Irish before September 1, 1938, the date the English general staff predicted Germany would invade Poland.

This necessitated the urgency to get de Valera re-elected before that time. It would have been politically impossible for the British to return the ports while England was at war with Germany, therefore the rush to complete the deal before hostilities began. The English general staff prediction was a year too early, as Germany marched into Poland on September 1, 1939.

The return of the Irish naval ports represented a monumental political bonanza to the Irish gadfly who was allegedly such a thorn in the side of the British. De Valera rode this wellspring of political philanthropy to a spectacular victory in a snap general election in June 1938. The British maneoeuvre brought de Valera unwarranted popularity and guaranteed that he would remain in office throughout the coming war.

If they had not regarded him as a safe pair of hands, the British would not have sponsored de Valera as President of the League of Nations in 1938. David Gray, U.S. Representative to Éire, wrote: "de Valera had gone to Geneva in 1938 under British sponsorship. They had made him President of the Assembly. He had his great hour as a liberal statesman and distinguished himself by urging sanctions against Italy for her aggression in Abyssinia... but his true colors rose to the surface when he later recognized Italy's right to subjugate the Ethiopians."[32]

As 1940 approached, nearly a decade after his return to power, de Valera had no appreciable domestic policy, and Ireland remained economically backward.

In a searing commentary on the Irish President's long-term economic policy, Coogan wrote: "During the last 14 years of his life in party politics, de Valera rarely showed either the ability or the inclination to confront the great challenges of Irish life, unemployment – and its concomitant evil, enforced emigration – partition, and Church-State relationships. [de Valera's postwar economic policy in 1955– 56]...plumbed the depths of hopelessness. One of the recurring series of balance of payments crises was overcome but only at the cost of stagnation, high unemployment and emigration...The Twenty-six Counties' economy and society were like rotting meat in a sandwich. The people were caught between de Valera's increasing incapacity for original thought and the opposition party's matching inability to provide any alternative...Nothing that his economic incompetence could do to the state was going to intimidate him!"[33]

Notes

1. Fitzgerald, W. G. (Splain), *The Voice of Ireland, A Survey of the Race & Nation from All Angles*, Virtue Ltd, Dublin/London, p. 167
2. Dwyer, T. Ryle, *De Valera, The Man & the Myths*, Poolbeg, Dublin, 1991, p. 150
3. *ibid*, p. 196
4. Fitzgerald, W. G. (Splain), *The Voice of Ireland, A Survey of the Race & Nation from All Angles*, Virtue Ltd, Dublin/London, p. 16
5. Dwyer, T. Ryle, *De Valera, The Man & the Myths*, Poolbeg, Dublin, 1991, p. 170
6. McMahon, Deirdre, "A Transient Apparition – British Policy Towards the de Valera Government 1932-35", *Irish Historical Studies*, Vol. XXII 1980-81, Antrim, W and G. Baird/ 1981, 341
7. *ibid*, p. 345
8. Dwyer, T. Ryle, *De Valera, The Man & the Myths*, Poolbeg, Dublin, 1991, p. 178
9. *ibid*, p. 171
10. Longford, Earl of & O'Neill, Thomas P., *Éamon de Valera*, Hutchinson, London, 1970, p. 282
11. Dwyer, T. Ryle, *De Valera, The Man & the Myths*, Poolbeg, Dublin, 1991, p. 149
12. Gaughan, J. Anthony, *Austin Stack, Portrait of a Separatist*, Kingdom Books, Dublin, 1977, p. 249
13. Dwyer, T. Ryle, *De Valera, The Man & the Myths*, Poolbeg, Dublin, 1991, p. 167
14. *ibid*, p. 166
15. *ibid*, p.149
16. Longford, Earl of & O'Neill, Thomas P., *Éamon de Valera*, Hutchinson, London, 1970, p. 331
17. Dwyer, T. Ryle, *De Valera, The Man & the Myths*, Poolbeg, Dublin, 1991, p. 181
18. Middlemas, Keith & Barnes, John, *Baldwin, A Biography*, Macmillan, 1970, p. 657
19. *ibid*, p. 247
20. Dwyer, T. Ryle, *De Valera, The Man & the Myths*, Poolbeg, Dublin, 1991, p. 157
21. Coogan, Tim P., *De Valera, The Man who was Ireland*, Harper, 1996, p. 441
22. *ibid*
23. *ibid*, p. 442
24. *ibid*, p. 441
25. *ibid*, p. 444
26. Whelan, John (Seán O'Faoláin), *De Valera*, Penguin Books, England 1939, p. 173
27. Coogan, Tim P., *De Valera, The Man who was Ireland*, Harper, 1996, p. 535
28. Fitzgerald, W. G. (Splain), *The Voice of Ireland, A Survey of the Race & Nation from All Angles*, Virtue Ltd, Dublin/London, p. 178
29. Dwyer, T. Ryle, *De Valera, The Man & the Myths*, Poolbeg, Dublin, 1991, p. 200
30. Fitzgerald, W. G. (Splain), *The Voice of Ireland, A Survey of the Race & Nation from All Angles*, Virtue Ltd, Dublin/London, p. 18

31. McMahon, Deirdre, "A Transient Apparition, British Policy Towards the de Valera Government 1932-35", *Irish Historical Studies*, Vol. XXII 1980-81, Antrim, W and G. Baird/ 1981, p. 345
32. Gray, David, *Behind the Green Curtain*, Unpublished Manuscript, p. I/14
33. Coogan, Tim P., *De Valera, The Man who was Ireland*, Harper, 1996, p. 634

CHAPTER XXIII

"Assignment Irish Republican Army"

"Oh, we'll hang Willie Cosgrave on a sour apple tree;
We'll hang Dick Mulcahy to keep him company;
And we'll hang de Valera just to make an even three;
And we'll still keep marching on."

Anti-de Valera Ode by IRA in 1930s

The Irish Republican Brotherhood (IRB), was recast as the Irish Republican Army (IRA) in 1919 and considered itself the rightful government of Ireland. Michael Collins was regarded as President of a declared Irish Republic. Many commentators were fooled into believing that a power struggle with Collins was the key to de Valera's conduct. But Collins, during the "Troubles" of 1918-21, not only voluntarily relinquished the IRB presidency with all its relevant power structure to the Irish President but rendered loyal support to de Valera. The only power struggle was in the imaginative pens of Irish writers in order to rationalize de Valera's unrelenting Irish disasters culminating in an unbroken string of colossal triumphs for England.

The Irish Republican Brotherhood (IRB) was founded in New York City by Michael Doheny and John O'Mahony, two 1848 exiles, while Joseph Denieffe was credited with organizing the IRB in Ireland on St. Patrick's Day in 1858. The men of the "physical force" movement took the name Fenians from an ancient Irish warrior legend. The constitution of the IRB called for the overthrow of the English government in Ireland and the establishment of an Irish Republic by force of arms. The IRB, under Patrick Pearse, initiated the 1916 Easter Rising.

Anti-Free State treaty extremist elements within the IRA, under de Valera's prodding, were instrumental in carrying out the civil war in 1922 and complicit in his attempt to render the Free State ungovernable by disrupting political opposition meetings and undermining economic programs. The dissidents within the IRA were de Valera's storm troopers, intimidating, beating, and even murdering Free State supporters in order to render the Free State ungovernable and to

372

facilitate de Valera's return to power. Upon his re-election in 1932, the IRA fully anticipated that de Valera would declare an Irish Republic and unofficially sanction attacks against England and Northern Ireland in an effort to end Partition and the pogroms of terror against the Catholics.

De Valera, rather than declare an Irish Republic or authorize raids across the border, utilized his newly restored power to crush the IRA, the same counterfeit Republicans, the same cut-throats and murderers, thieves and looters, pillagers and intimidators, whom he had proclaimed in 1922 as "Ireland's finest," goading them on to civil war with cries of "Ireland is yours for the taking. Take it."

Under the *1931 Statute of Westminster*, de Valera had the legal right to declare an Irish Republic and this right was further confirmed by the English Privy Council in 1937 when it ruled that de Valera's amateurish Constitution did not diminish Ireland's standing within the British Commonwealth.

De Valera's former IRA comrades were disillusioned when de Valera not only refused to declare an Irish Republic but also cracked down on their plans to attack England and Northern Ireland. In order to eliminate the IRA as a threat, not to Southern Ireland, but to England and Northern Ireland, he actually encouraged attacks in and outside the country and then ratted on his former colleagues to the English, leading to their arrest, confinement, and, not a few, to their execution. "The New IRA denounced him bitterly...In the Second World War, his Government was compelled to execute members of the IRA."[1]

When de Valera announced that Ireland would never be used as a base of attack on England, the IRA accused him of betraying the Irish cause. Joseph McGarrity and many Irish-Americans believed the IRA whispers that de Valera had sold his political soul and Republican aspirations to Neville Chamberlain in return for the Irish ports that insured his reelection in 1938, but de Valera had already sold his soul and his country in Stonebreaker Yard of Kilmainham Jail in 1916 in return for his life.

Prior to his reelection in 1932, with the world in the depths of the Great Depression, de Valera utilized every political trick in his drive to destabilize the Free State government. For ten years, he threw roadblocks in the path of the William Cosgrave government's economic initiatives as well as encouraging a reign of terror by the IRA that was reaching a crescendo of violence as Ireland entered the 1930s. Beset by IRA intimidation and outright lawlessness, the Cosgrave government, in self-defense, reinstituted military tribunals under a constitutional act, Article 2A Amendment, to contain the exploding political chaos and deal with the IRA that de Valera had so effectively unleashed to his advantage. De Valera denounced the Cosgrave government's attempt to control the IRA terror. When he returned to power in 1932, he released all the IRA prisoners but maintained the military tribunal along with Article 2A, knowing that he was going to need it to corral the IRA in the future.

De Valera's political move in 1932, in freeing prisoners arrested during the Cosgrave administration, had once again turned loose the whirlwind of the IRA. De Valera initially turned a blind eye as pro-treaty meetings were broken up, free speech denied to Free State "traitors," and opposition candidates beaten and intimidated. The pro-treaty party, in turn, set up the Army Comrades Association (ACA) under Eoin O'Duffy. They were referred to as the Blue Shirts because of their distinctive uniforms. They eventually merged into the United Ireland or Fine Gael party, with O'Duffy elected leader. The ACA was made up primarily of former members of the Free State army, and its mission was to protect and defend free speech.

T. Ryle Dwyer illustrated the violent behavior of counterfeit Republicans like Frank Ryan: "'No matter what anyone says to the contrary, while we have fists, hands and boots to use, and guns if necessary, we will not allow free speech to traitors,' he told a meeting in Dublin on November 10, 1932. To him, everyone who backed the Treaty, supported the Free State or even wore poppies commemorating the dead of the First World War was a traitor."[2]

The Irish President all but ignored the actions of his counterfeit Republican comrades when their activities were confined to disrupting his political opposition in Ireland. When the IRA offensive escalated from intimidating pro-treaty advocates to attacking England and Northern Ireland, he quickly launched a crackdown on their activities. From a previous nodding condescension to strident IRA repressive measures against the Cosgrave government, he declared their actions against Northern Ireland and England as "irrational militancy." He lashed out against his old comrades, not to defuse their attacks on free speech but to eliminate them as a threat to England.

The military tribunal and Article 2A, so vociferously denounced by de Valera in 1931, was taken out of the closet, dusted off and used with devastating effect against his former IRA allies. De Valera's claim that he maintained Article 2A to counter any threat to the public safety by the Blue Shirts was mere propaganda masking his true intentions of muzzling the IRA through military courts.

De Valera's harassment, incarceration, and execution of IRA members from 1934 through the war years and beyond rendered the organization incapable of initiating any serious attacks in England or Northern Ireland. De Valera mobilized the entire government arsenal against the IRA – police, censorship, Army intelligence, and spies, both British and Irish – often provoking the IRA into fighting back or defending themselves, thereby providing him with an excuse to lock them up and throw away the key. In the 1930s, he was allegedly the "man of peace" insisting on a peaceful transition of his government and tolerating no organization contesting the right of the majority now that he was the majority.

Ignoring de Valera's establishing a parallel government with his own militia to attack the Free State throughout the 1920s, Longford and O'Neill hypocritically stated: "At no time could he allow the IRA, or anyone else, the right to take the law into their own hands. The Military Tribunal acted as firmly against them as it did against the Blue Shirts..."[3] Not quite! The Blue Shirts were neither imprisoned for the duration nor afterwards. Not a single member of the Blue Shirts was executed. By the end of 1941, the IRA was a disorganized, ineffective organization, its members fighting and arguing among themselves, betrayed by the ever-present spies and informers, their plots an open secret to de Valera's intelligence and police departments.

De Valera employed the IRA as a cover for his phony "neutrality" policy during the war years, claiming the IRA would resist and create havoc in Ireland if he came out on the side of England. The fact was that de Valera admittedly neutralized the IRA and rendered it completely ineffective. Any threat by the IRA in Ireland, England or Northern Ireland, was so insignificant as to be safely ignored. The IRA was a spent force by the time the Second World War exploded in Europe.

By the advent of the war, the IRA was nothing more than a vivid memory of bitter young men in prison and embittered old men in rocking chairs, whimpering weaklings wailing over what-might-have-been. During the 1930s, de Valera initiated a relentless campaign against the IRA, ordering executions and internment, not because they were a threat to Ireland but because they were a threat to England.

Privately, de Valera admitted that the IRA presented no threat either to the Irish Government or to England. He conceded: "The IRA was soon to fall into difficulties...and...was to become an impotent body."[4]

During the war, de Valera declared: "'Ireland was not under threat from internal dangers such as fifth columnists [IRA]. All potential subversives were under surveillance.' In seeking arms for his Irish Army, de Valera assured the English that, 'If you think the IRA will get the arms, I can assure you that we have no Fifth Column today. There is no danger in that quarter.'"[5]

When the British voiced concern about a German parachute linkup with the IRA, Joseph P. Walshe, Irish Secretary, Department of External Affairs: "made no attempt to magnify the extent of the extremist problem as de Valera normally did in his jousts with British representatives. He stated that the IRA was not a serious threat, which required assistance from the UK and gave evidence of de Valera's ruthless determination to deal with the organization. In a revealing statement of things to come, Walshe disclosed: '... The Government of Éire anticipated no difficulty in dealing with the IRA. *In fact, the outbreak of specific disturbances was the kind of opportunity which they were seeking in order to finally crush the (IRA) organization.*'"[6] [emphasis added]

Another twist to de Valera's war on his former comrades was the infiltration of the IRA by spies and informers. A bizarre incident brought to light an alleged de Valera connection to a scheme that involved a bombing in the English city of Coventry on August 25, 1939. De Valera and the British allegedly facilitated the IRA bombing in order to arrest and imprison the conspirators. Rumors circulated throughout Dublin that the bombing at Coventry was actually initiated by de Valera.

In March 1923, de Valera advised Liam Lynch, Commander-in-Chief of the dissident IRA, on the proper method to wage a dynamiting campaign in England: "The first blow should be concerted and big, followed quickly by a number in succession of other blows."[7]

On July 24, 1939, de Valera, unmindful of his previous encouragement of the anti-Treaty insurgents to initiate bombings throughout England in 1923, flip-flopped 180 degrees and declared: "No one can have any doubt as to the result of the [bombing] campaign in England, and no one can think that this Government has any sympathy with it."[8] Once the IRA threatened England, he was "forced" to arrest, intern, and execute them for doing the very thing he advocated in 1923.

Due to an uncanny knack of the de Valera police to uncover and arrest so many men prior to and immediately after an IRA caper, it became increasingly clear that there was an informer among the high echelons of the IRA command. Suspicion centered on Stephen Hayes, IRA Chief of Staff. On the morning of June 30, 1941, the 39-year-old Hayes was kidnapped on the orders of Sean McCaughey and charged with being a stool pigeon for the de Valera government. A confession was beaten out of him over a two-and-a-half-month confinement; he was found guilty by his IRA comrades and sentenced to death.

At the conclusion of the Hayes' court-martial and confession, the IRA

Council issued the following statement on September 10, 1941: "It has now been definitely established that this conspiracy was fostered and inspired by the Free State [de Valera] Government as a final and desperate effort to destroy by treachery that which they failed to do by force. *A treacherous leader cooperated with other traitorous Irishmen* [emphasis added] who were unashamedly trying to perpetuate British rule in Ireland by using sinister as well as oppressive measures which even their masters in London never dared use directly...Signed: Adjutant General, Irish Republican Army." Finally, someone recognized de Valera's treason.

Two days before the IRA announcement, Hayes had managed to escape his captors and stagger into a local Dublin police station. He then directed the police to the IRA hideout, leading to the arrest of James Rice and McCaughey.

Years later, during a judicial hearing on Sean McCaughey's brutal treatment at the hands of de Valera's prison guards, Sean MacBride, an attorney, was denied permission to question the prison warden. In cross-examining the prison doctor, however, he asked: "'If you had a dog, would you treat it in that fashion?' The doctor's response, (after a pause) 'No!'"[9]

McCaughey was confined in prison for four years without a definitive sentence. He was held incommunicado without knowing when or if he would ever be released. He reportedly had gone insane as a result of his solitary confinement. De Valera learned well from the English, whose prisons were houses of Bedlam in which many an Irishman lost his mind.

McCaughey initiated a hunger strike in April 1946, nearly a year after the war ended, to call attention to his plight, but, under the Government's strict censorship, the Irish Press printed only a one-line comment noting that he had died of a hunger strike on May 11.

In Hayes' confession, he implicated de Valera and high-ranking members of his cabinet, including Dr. James Ryan, Minister of Agriculture; Thomas Derrig, Minister for Education; and Irish Senator Chris Byrne, along with journalist Laurence de Lacy. According to Hayes, the plot centered on Ryan, who proposed a dynamiting campaign in England as a means to discredit the IRA and lead to measures to cripple that organization.

During the Coventry bombing, the bungling dynamiter had attached explosives to a bicycle, but the bicycle broke down, preventing the cyclist from reaching his target, and he was forced to leave the bicycle against a wall and run off. The resulting explosion killed five people and wounded fifty more.

The Coventry bombing, in which five people were killed, had serious implications of direct involvement by the de Valera government in an act of terror. In order to deflect criticism away from his administration, the Irish President claimed that the bombing "was a usurpation of the authority of the State."[10] The bombing was in England, and in no way a "usurpation" of the authority of Ireland. Hayes said he provided Ryan with the names of the men involved in the Coventry bombing. *"This list was given to Ryan and forwarded...to Scotland Yard...Richards and Barnes were later executed for it on February 8, 1940."*[11] [emphasis added]

Hayes said he met with DeLacy and informed him of the details of the arms dumps in various cities in England, including London, Liverpool, and Birmingham, as well as the names and addresses of IRA men operating in those cities. Within days of the initial explosions of the dynamiting campaign, widespread roundups netted many IRA officers in England. Hayes claimed deLacy had once again "passed [the information] on to the Free State Government and which *they, in turn, passed on to Scotland Yard* [emphasis added] via J.W. Dulanty, Free State Commissioner in London, that the foregoing arrests and captures were made possible. I also knew the names of the men sent over as replacements and their destinations and I passed those on to the Free State Government. *They in turn passed this information on to Scotland Yard via Dulanty.*"[12] [emphasis added]

In another incident, Hayes described a meeting with Dr. Ryan, in which a raid on the military facility at Lansdowne Park on August 22, 1940 netted a substantial amount of arms and ammunition along with the arrest of four IRA members. Once again, on Dr. Ryan's orders, police reports were doctored to deflect suspicion away from an informer over the suspicious number of arrests of IRA men. The police reports named Michael Devereux, an innocent IRA member from Wexford, as the informer, and Hayes confessed he had ordered the execution of Devereux and it was carried out. Adding to the suspicion that there was more truth than fiction to Hayes' confession was his description of the murder of Devereux. An illiterate man named George Plant, on Hayes' order, led police to Devereux's grave, and Plant was immediately arrested, based on the incriminating false statements of two IRA members.

De Valera's Emergency Powers Order of December 30, 1941 indicated just how far he was prepared to go to destroy the IRA. Despite the fact the statements incriminating Plant were recanted, the court was permitted to consider the withdrawn statements as evidence. Coogan noted that under de Valera's Emergency Powers Orders: "If a military court considered it proper on any occasion during a trial, it should not be bound by the laws of evidence, whether of military or common law..."[13] The innocent Plant was tried and executed on March 5, 1942.

On December 1, 1939, the Supreme Court ruled that the *Offenses against the State Act* was unconstitutional, resulting in the release of over fifty IRA men. The ever-resourceful Irish Premier immediately devised another of his public relations coups. Through his spies within the IRA, especially Hayes, de Valera allegedly authorized a raid on the Phoenix Park military ammunition depot in Dublin. Dr. James Ryan reportedly contacted Hayes and proposed a raid on the depot in which the scheme had a two-fold purpose: to create a public outrage over the IRA raid on a Southern Ireland government facility and to rally public support for the introduction of strident legislation that would bypass the Supreme Court and curb the IRA. Dr. Ryan supposedly assured Hayes that the magazine fort would be an easy target, and with a lightened guard and plans detailing the facility, the IRA would run little risk. According to Hayes' confession: "Dr. Ryan said he would let me have the final view of it per deLacy, in the meantime, he would want to see Mr. Aiken and Mr. De Valera. DeLacy told me Dr. Ryan had seen Aiken and de Valera and they were satisfied with the suggestion provided that the ammunition or the major portion of it would be recovered. They did not mind losing a few thousand rounds as they would be compensated for by the results achieved."

The purpose of the trumped-up raid was to provide de Valera with the impetus and public support to introduce his *Emergency Powers Amendment Act of 1940* to counter the Supreme Court's ruling that the *Offenses against the State Act* was unconstitutional. Under the later act, habeas corpus was done away with, and a prisoner could be jailed for the duration of whatever "emergency" de Valera declared, all without benefit of trial. Many IRA men not only sat out the conflict in de Valera's concentration camps, but he even kept his former pals locked up after the war to insure that they weren't the cause of any further trouble to England. De Valera, who had so vehemently condemned the Cosgrave military tribunals, reintroduced his own more strident version of them.

As IRA Chief of Staff, Hayes, with plans of the arsenal provided by Dr. Ryan, ordered his men to carry out the raid on December 23, 1939. "Surprisingly," the raiders met with little opposition, and more than a dozen truckloads of arms and ammunition were hauled to secret dumps throughout the neighboring counties with hardly a shot being fired. The raid had its desired effect, as a public outcry demanded action to prevent the IRA from attacking Southern Ireland government installations. The IRA had allegedly adopted a policy in which they would not mount attacks locally but utilize Southern Ireland as a base to initiate attacks against England and Northern Ireland. They believed they had the backing and encouragement of de Valera at Phoenix Park.

Once the public outcry reached a crescendo, the government "discovered" the secret dumps and recovered, almost to the gun and bullet, the arms and ammunition taken from the Phoenix Park armory. For years, rumors were rampant throughout Dublin that the government was involved in the Phoenix Park depot raid. "It was in midsummer 1941 that an explanation of the Phoenix Park events was advanced...which suggested that the attacks in Southern Ireland were a Government plot designed to discredit the IRA."[14] That certainly explained the fastest recovery of arms and ammunition in Irish history. The framing of the ever-bungling IRA was a *modus operandi* of the British for years, carried out with the aid of Irish informers, agents, and spies. The Phoenix Park escapade had all the earmarks of a British operation but, more importantly, this time with de Valera's complicity.

David Gray, American representative to Éire, conceded that the German minister Eduard Hempel's report to the German Foreign Minister, Joachim von Ribbentrop, on October 20, 1940, concerning Hayes' confession was sound.

Gray noted: "IRA members of Northern Ireland are sending out circulars of Hayes confession that he is supposed to have made after his IRA arrest. These deal with Hayes' cooperation with two Cabinet Ministers and a Senator, stating Hayes had been urged to provocative acts by the Irish Government in order to have plausible basis for mass arrests...If there was real proof of such provocative acts by the Irish Government against the IRA, scandal and crises would result...It is apparent that Hempel regarded the confession as true."[15]

Hayes reported again meeting with Dr. Ryan and Senator Chris Byrne in which the discussion centered on discrediting the IRA by having them rob banks and post offices in Southern Ireland. Two bank raids were subsequently carried out at Oldcastle in May 1941 and Castlepollard in June 1941, resulting in less than a £1,500 total take for the two robberies. The military and police, on a tip, arrested Richard Goss, an IRA member, for the crimes on June 18, 1941.

According to Hayes, a planned attack by the IRA in Northern Ireland was also betrayed by de Valera. "Instructions were sent to Belfast for all the men to return to their homes...*The Fianna Fáil Government sent word, per a special messenger from the Department of Justice in Dublin, to the Six County Government that they had information that the Irish Republican Army was preparing and planning an armed attack on police and military objectives to take place at Christmas* [emphasis added]...The round-up, just before Christmas 1938, took place and all the principal IRA officers of the Belfast Battalion were caught and interned."[16]

Hayes again informed Ryan of a meeting of the IRA staff in Rathmines Park to initiate a campaign in Northern Ireland. "In September 1939, certain members of the IRA Army Council were advocating a more aggressive policy to be pursued in the Six Counties...It was decided to have a meeting of the Staff the next day, Saturday, in Rathmines Park, at which a decision would be made. I sent word to Dr. Ryan via De Lacy... The place was raided on September 9, 1939 and those arrested included Peadar O'Flaherty, Laurence Grogan, William McGuiness, and Patrick McGrath...I got away as arranged... The chief advocates of the aggressive policy were arrested – four in all and shortly afterwards the big 'Round-up' and internment started on September 15, 1939, two weeks after Germany invaded Poland. The IRA prisoners were interned for the duration of the war."[17] England's difficulty was not going to be Ireland's opportunity on de Valera's watch.

An impending transfer of more than 50,000 rounds of ammunition to Northern Ireland was revealed by Hayes to Ryan and seized on July 19, 1940. The government, in an effort to deflect suspicion away from an informer within IRA ranks, doctored the reports.

The government and Irish writers, in their never-ending eagerness to extricate de Valera from any traitorous suspicion, were only too willing to publicly cast doubt on the authenticity of Hayes' charges of a government plot.

The de Valera government continued to attack the veracity of Hayes confession. During Sean McCaughey's trial for the kidnapping and beating of Hayes, the Court refused to permit any evidence that might have linked the de Valera government to the bombings in Coventry and other English cities. A blanket denial by Ryan and Derrig as to their involvement was admitted, but no cross-examination was allowed. All testimony was limited strictly to the kidnapping and torture of Hayes and the identification of his assailants.

When in custody of the authorities, Hayes recanted his confession and stated that he told the IRA whatever was necessary in order to save his life. Tim Pat Coogan noted Hayes' statement: "I am prepared to swear an oath that I never entered into any conspiracy with the Free State Government..."[18] Hayes refused legal counsel in his defense and may have lied to the court, but for all of his efforts, Hayes spent the next five years in solitary confinement.

Since both the government and the IRA acknowledged the fact that Hayes was an informer, the question then arose as to who were his government contacts? Obviously, someone high up in the de Valera government had prior knowledge of the IRA bombing campaign in

England that led to the arrest of the Coventry bombers. Once again, the evil eye of de Valera lurked behind the curtains of Leinster House, as it did at a farmhouse in the remote hamlet of Béal na mBláth the day Collins fell before an assassin's bullet. The Irish President refused to admit or deny any role in informing on his IRA comrades. The British were also close-mouthed about the Coventry affair and never admitted or denied the scenario.

In a note to General William Donovan, Office of Strategic Services (OSS), on October 14, 1941, David Gray posed certain unresolved issues regarding the implication of the de Valera ministers in the bombing events in England: "The so-called confession charges certain Ministers in the Irish Government with using Hayes, not only as a stool pigeon but also as *agent provocateur*. The confession states that a series of crimes were instigated by the Irish Government beginning with the Coventry bombings and ending with the series of bank robberies in Ireland. The perpetrators were then betrayed either to the British Government or to the Irish police and were arrested and punished. Two main objects were in view; first, the incitement of anti-British feeling in Ireland and second, the destruction from within of the IRA organization. I never got the information from London that I wanted regarding the Hayes Confession. It was never refused but nothing happened. It was as if someone of consequence had murmured 'better not.'"[19]

De Valera, in his ongoing cooperation with the British, divulged the names of known Irish in America, England, and Northern Ireland who were suspected of IRA or pro-German sympathies. "In early 1943, J. J. Walshe, on instructions from de Valera, called on American administrators with an "official offer to cooperate with the Office of Strategic Services (OSS). In the following months, *[de Valera] turned over voluminous intelligence reports on such things as IRA strength...the names and addresses of people in America with whom German nationals living in Ireland or pro-German Irish people had been corresponding, as well as detailed files on the interrogations of German spies and internees [IRA] already captured."[20] [emphasis added]

Gray continued his attempts to have the English confirm or deny a charge of Irish governmental collusion in the Coventry and related bombings and de Valera's subsequent informing on the perpetrators. On October 7, 1941, Gray requested John G. Winant, U.S. Ambassador to London to: "'get a denial of the charge by the British Government that de Valera had sent information through Dulanty leading to the arrest of the Coventry bombers. This would have settled the matter as far as we (U.S.) were concerned.' Gray contended that 'Lacking a denial, how far did that lack of denial justify us in assuming the charge was true?...In effect, charges of connivance between the Irish Government and the Irish Republican Army in a series of crimes, one object of this connivance being to destroy the IRA from within.'"[21]

According to Gray: "On the evidence of IRA documents, de Valera attempted first to destroy the IRA by planting a stool pigeon in it as Chief of Staff. A suspicious 'house-cleaning' committee of the IRA kidnapped the stool pigeon and tortured a confession out of him. At this point, de Valera appears to have panicked. He could not face a political situation in which his old followers, the IRA, now his enemies, possessed the anti-British issue while he defended Britain..."[22]

Even Gray, the U.S. Representative to Éire, admitted that de Valera was protecting British interests over those of the IRA. With no response forthcoming from the English, Gray again wrote to Winant on October 9, 1941: "I think the charges that Ryan incited the Coventry bombings are fantastic but there are probably threads of truth running through the fabrication..."[23]

The de Valera and British stonewalling of any questions by the American representative to Ireland obviously raised suspicion as to their collaboration in the plot. Gray leaned over backwards in letting them know that he, personally, did not believe the charges and that he would issue such a denial in America if only they – de Valera and/or the English government – would respond. No evidence of any response was ever forthcoming.

Throughout the 1930s, the IRA stumbled leaderless, without purpose or accomplishment, until Sean Russell, IRA leader, initiated another bombing campaign in England. In January 1939, Russell issued an ultimatum in which the IRA demanded the evacuation of British troops from Northern Ireland. When the British failed to act, bombs were set off in a number of towns in England, including Coventry on August 25, 1939.

Russell had been in the United States raising funds from the Clan na Gael for IRA operations against England and Northern Ireland. According to Hayes: "About July 1940, when I met Dr. Ryan again, he informed me that Russell had been taken off an Italian cargo boat about April and was being detained at Gibraltar. *No one knew him there except the British Secret Service who had detained him at the request of the Free State [Fianna Fáil] Government on information supplied by them.*" [emphasis added] In a conflicting report, it was reported that he had died of a perforated ulcer aboard a German submarine bound for Ireland and his body buried at sea.

The American representative in Ireland was shocked by the revelation of the de Valera government informing on a member of the IRA that led to his arrest and death. On October 11, Gray wrote to de Valera: "Dear Mr. Prime Minister…The only interest, which this Legation could have in the matter, is in regards to Sean Russell…I would be very grateful; if you have any confirmation of his death…you would pass it on to me." Gray then noted: "I have no record of an acknowledgement of this letter [by de Valera]."[24]

On April 25, 1936, as a result of the murder of one of its own members accused of being an informer, de Valera denounced the violence and outlawed the IRA. The Irish President's campaign of harassment against the IRA came to a head on August 16, 1940 during a raid on a suspected IRA hideout. Two plainclothes detectives were fatally shot and another wounded. It was just the response de Valera sought, and he quickly rescinded the right of appeal from any military tribunal decisions. Patrick McGrath and Francis Hart, two IRA members, were executed on September 6 for the shootings. The fact that McGrath had been one of the Irish President's leading storm troopers during de Valera's return to power, made no difference to the Irish leader.

McGrath had been released from prison the previous year while on a hunger strike demanding prisoner of war status. De Valera's experience with McGrath's hunger strike and reprieve by the court led him to refuse to intercede again on behalf of other hunger-striking prisoners, and IRA prisoners were treated as common criminals.

When imprisoned IRA members Tony Darcy and Sean McNeela initiated a hunger strike several months after McGrath's similar protest in 1939, de Valera refused to intercede, and they died as a consequence in April 1940. The Irish leader commented: "If we let these men out, we are going immediately afterwards to have every single man we have tried to detain and restrain going on hunger strike."[25] Darcy and McNeela were actually defending themselves from de Valera's constant harassment, and when the plain-clothed police broke in on them, they opened fire claiming they did not know they were police officers. De Valera was not open to suggestions that the men be imprisoned for the duration or for any long term he was determined that their executions would be a deterrent for any further incidents by the IRA.

De Valera insisted: "Prisoners would not be allowed to dictate the conditions under which they would be kept in detention…"[26] This was the same de Valera who, while incarcerated in 1916-17, instigated prison riots by demanding prisoner of war status. Rather than the gallows, he was rewarded with special privileges. With the connivance of his English jailers, he emerged as the leader of Sinn Féin due to his "valiant" stand dictating terms to prison wardens.

Sean MacCurtain, IRA member and son of Thomas MacCurtain, the Mayor of Cork who had been murdered by the Black and Tans in front of his family in March 1920, was sentenced to die for the shooting of a detective. Father Flanagan, in defense of MacCurtain, charged de Valera with instigating the incident by his harassment of the IRA: "MacCurtain had been attacked from behind by a plainclothes man and had shot in self-defense and that de Valera had done all the things that MacCurtain's friends were doing until he took the oath..."[27]

Enno Stephan noted: "It became clear in radio broadcasts from London that the underground men [IRA] were not only being relentlessly pursued by the English but also by de Valera's security organization."[28]

The slogan "Burn everything British but their coal" adorned walls throughout Ireland as part of an IRA anti-Guinness Brewing Company campaign that focused on intimidating tavern owners against selling Bass Beer. The IRA hijacked a load of Guinness and simulated the Boston Tea Party by dumping the beer in the River Liffey, calling it the Dublin Beer Party.

The Irish President wrote to Joseph McGarrity in the US asking him to convince the "'IRA lads to see a little bit of sense, and stop their damn fool-acting business such as the Bass Ale raids.' de Valera claimed that the Irish would suffer ten times as much when the British retaliated against Guinness, the great Irish beer and ale company."[29]

In response to his letter, McGarrity grudgingly complained to de Valera about the Irish President's campaign against the IRA: "We have all been vexed and alarmed here on reading that the government has acted against the people (IRA) at home who are trying to stop the use of English goods in Ireland. We feel the sooner you exclude everything English the quicker you will win the fight. Lord Guinness is one of their own and will not be taxed by the English nor have his product excluded."[30]

All the deception and lies de Valera used in convincing McGarrity and the IRA counterfeit Republicans to initiate a civil war in 1922 now came home to the fore. McGarrity had continued to believe that de Valera was somehow misguided or in a position to tread carefully for political reasons. He attempted to explain the political facts of life to the Machiavellian disciple de Valera: "It is apparent that an agreement between your forces and the forces of the IRA is a national necessity. They can do things you will not care to do or cannot do in the face of public criticism, while the IRA pay no heed to public clamor so long as they feel they are doing a national duty. You both profess to desire the same goal. Why in God's name do you hesitate to sit down and try to find a working agreement? It is the extreme, the fanatical thing, as the English call it that frightens them and causes them to seek peace."[31]

De Valera's devastating response was really an indictment of himself as well as McGarrity and the rest of the galaxy of cranks and queer people. He had used the IRA to do England's dirty work in Ireland by engaging, not only in a civil war, but an ongoing ten-year campaign of terror and intimidation against their own people. De Valera utilized those "things" that benefited only England, Northern Ireland, and himself, but now securely ensconced in office, he was done with the IRA and especially McGarrity, who had been so instrumental in raising funds for his newspaper and discrediting John Devoy and Judge Daniel Cohalan.

In a scathing broadside, he wrote to McGarrity, who admired de Valera so much that he named his son de Valera McGarrity: "You talk about coming to an understanding with the IRA. You talk of the influence it would have both here and abroad. You talk as if we were fools and didn't realize all this. My God! How can you imagine for one moment that I don't realize what division in the Republican ranks means at a time like this? But is this need and desire for unity to be used as a means of trying to blackmail us into adopting a policy we know could only lead our people to disaster? What is the use of talking any more with people who are too stupid or too pigheaded to see this?"[32] de Valera finally blurted out his opinion of the intellectual capacity of his counterfeit Republicans, McGarrity and of himself.

McGarrity was de Valera's most effective lackey in the United States in furthering the Irish President's "Assignment America" by creating chaos in Irish-American ranks. It must have been quite a revelation to McGarrity to finally realize the true nature of de Valera and his own "stupidity and pigheadedness." The man who fought de Valera's battles in America against Devoy and Cohalan, who raised the money for de Valera's struggle and return to power was no longer of any use, and de Valera discarded McGarrity like he did all the other "galaxy of cranks" who had outlived their usefulness to him.

As a result of the supposedly grave threat posed by the discovery of a German spy named Hermann Goertz by de Valera's security forces, the Irish President manufactured his own version of the British fabricated 1918 "German plot," in which nearly a hundred Sinn Féin members were jailed. Under the public guise of such a threat, de Valera was able to intern hundreds of alleged German collaborators (IRA) without trial for the duration of the war. As proof of the effectiveness of de Valera's crackdown on IRA efforts against English interests: "..In Berlin, there was considerable dissatisfaction over [lack of] IRA activity; so much so that no importance was attached to sabotage efforts in England and above all that no further funds would be approved in view of the IRA's complete failure in this matter."[33] De Valera had pulled the teeth of the IRA.

On March 21, 1943, twenty-one IRA men imprisoned in Londonderry Prison by the Northern Ireland government escaped to Southern Ireland. De Valera left no stone unturned as he unleashed his secret service police to recapture the escapees. De Valera's campaign against the IRA was not limited to the war years. Even though the end of the Second World War had removed any threat of collusion with the Nazis, Gerald Boland, Justice Minister and brother of Harry Boland, killed during the civil war, continued de· Valera's prison policy of confinement without political prisoner status. Coogan questioned: "Why in the later stages of the war de Valera behaved as he did towards the IRA leadership, which he had safely under lock and key, must naturally remain a matter of conjecture."[34] Coogan failed to address the possibility that the Irish President was deliberately doing England's work.

In a masterful touch of the macabre, in December 1944, in response to Irish Army reluctance to execute IRA men and only months before the end of the war, he brought in an English hangman, Albert Pierrepoint, to apply the noose around the neck of a boy named Charles Kerins. For the dissident IRA, their hero had turned 180 degrees and they reaped what they had sown – a hangman's noose.

Having revealed the identities of Barnes and Richards as the authors of the Coventry bombing, de Valera hypocritically wrote to Anthony Eden and Neville Chamberlain, appealing to them to spare their lives. "When the appeal was rejected, he wrote to Chamberlain: 'I have received your decision with sorrow and dismay. The reprieve of these men would be regarded as an act of generosity, a thousand times more valuable to Britain than anything that can possibly be gained by their death...Almost superhuman patience is required...'"[35] Barnes and Richards were hung on February 7, 1940.

Less than one month later, de Valera showed his own lack of "superhuman patience" by refusing to give in to the hunger strikers, Darcy and McNeela, resulting in their deaths in April 1940. On September 6, 1940, de Valera's patience was once again strained beyond the breaking point as he ordered the execution of McGrath and Hart. Coogan highlighted de Valera's hypocrisy: "Knowing this, two aspects of his handling of the IRA situation are difficult to justify – in particular the question of prison conditions and his very public defense of IRA men outside his jurisdiction. This contrasts very sharply with his own use of capital punishment."[36]

De Valera sought the aid of David Gray in August 1942 to enlist Washington's help in requesting the British to commute the death sentences of six IRA men for the killing of a police officer in Northern Ireland. Gray was able to convince the English to commute the sentences for five of the six men, but Thomas Williams was sentenced to die.

"De Valera sent an urgent personal message to Churchill on behalf of Williams. 'The saving at this last moment through your personal intervention of the life of young Williams...would profoundly affect public feeling here,' he explained. 'I know the difficulties but results would justify – and I strongly urge that you do it.'"[37] Less than five months prior to his crocodile tears for Williams, de Valera had the illiterate and innocent George Plant executed.

His public treatment of IRA prisoners in Ireland was buried from public view by the strictness of his censorship. The men who were executed or died in his prisons, on his orders, received barely a one-line mention in Irish papers of their passing, whereas his pleas on behalf of men sentenced to death in English and Northern Ireland prisons were given widespread publicity so as to enhance his public persona as the defender of prisoners held in the oppressor's jails.

"Yet, the arguments which de Valera used to Chamberlain, Churchill, and Eden could equally well have been applied to the cases of men he had executed and would execute...No media coverage was allowed...Prisoners being in breach of prison regulations, were denied all privileges. They were kept in solitary confinement, which was particularly rigorous by having an empty cell on either side of them. They were not allowed out to the lavatory or to exercise. Nor did they get any letters, visits, or newspapers."[38] This was in sharp contrast to his disobedience and rioting during his confinement in English prisons when he was allowed books, letters, and even the privilege of commenting on the editorial policy of the English newspaper, *The Manchester Guardian*.

De Valera improved on the tried and true English method of driving Irish prisoners insane. His prisoners were not only in solitary confinement but were not allowed to speak or be spoken to by their guards. These prisoners received their just deserts for their treachery to their own people and now felt the sting of de Valera's treachery to them. In the June 10, 1940, edition of the IRA "War News Letter," the IRA charged de Valera with doing England's work: "Every day that the (IRA) prisoners are held is a day on which the country knows that England and not the will of the Irish people is dominant in Government buildings."[39]

The light bulb of revelation was flickering, but the IRA failed to see the shadow of de Valera's treason. He had locked up over seven hundred IRA sympathizers, and not one of them accused him of being an English agent.

In 1922, when Michael Collins and Arthur Griffith sought a peaceful transition, de Valera set up a rival government and an armed militia to destroy the Free State Government in order to prevent Collins from aiding the Northern Catholics. In his return to power in 1932, the Irish President demanded a peaceful transition to his government. On August 2, 1936, Dwyer noted the contrast between de Valera's words in 1922 and that in 1936. In an exhibition of monumental hypocrisy, de Valera now took the position: "If one section of the community could claim the right to build up a political army, so could another and it would not be long before this country would be rent asunder by rival military factions. If a minority tries to have its way by force against the will of the majority, it is inevitable that the majority will resist by force and this can only mean Civil War."[40]

Ironically, Gerald Boland, brother of Harry, who was killed by Free State forces in 1922, ordered, under the *Offenses against the State Act*, the arrest and internment of seventy suspected IRA members who fought alongside his brother. He introduced a bill calling for the establishment of concentration camps for the internment of suspected IRA members. De Valera, in a debate over his internment bill, hypocritically argued: "If the members of the IRA had a plan to end partition, they ought to lay it before those whom they themselves had elected as their government and thereby keep within constitutional limits."[41]

After establishing a rival government, organizing a private militia to oppose the elected Free State government, initiating a civil war, waging a decade-long campaign of terror and claiming that a minority had the right to oppose a majority in 1922 – it is incomprehensible that the Irish people would believe de Valera in 1936 and repeatedly elect him to office. James O'Mara was proven correct when he grumbled: "The Irish people are the most easily humbugged people on earth."

Mary MacSwiney, in a brilliant flash of revelation, finally perceived the light of de Valera's treason. In a letter to de Valera, she acknowledged his defection: "You govern the Free State as it was when Cosgrave held your office. Back in 1922, you had denounced Cosgrave's insistence that there should be only one army and one government. Now you are taking the same stand."[42]

In sanctimonious hypocrisy, de Valera responded: "Are you aware that defenseless citizens have been murdered in the most cowardly manner within the last few months in County Cork and County Waterford? Is it not obvious to you that the murders were the work of an organization? Do you approve of them? Do you not admit that in every community there must be some authority to prevent and punish murder? Or do you suggest that the protection of life and the prevention of crime must wait until the community is satisfied with its political status?"

She recognized his outrageous duplicity and wrote: "You are a fool – a criminal fool! And you might have been so great! Every word you are saying now – with such attempted sacrosanctity – they said then. The IRA was outlawed, banned, in the best British style that you are copying very faithfully today. You took a different stand then. Read your own speeches of 1931 on this self-same coercion act passed in the self-same circumstances and then face your own sincerity."[43]

It was now MacSwiney's turn to face reality. She, too, was reaping what she had so viciously sowed. De Valera no longer had need of her and dumped her as he did the rest of the galaxy of cranks. The Irish President's contradictory words and conflicting deeds, however, never raised an inkling of suspicion among Irish writers.

De Valera – the Greatest Failure in Irish History

MacSwiney, in another scathing letter to de Valera saw through his duplicity: "Was there ever a period in which England's difficulty was more surely Ireland's opportunity than now? You could unite the country for the Republic. You still have the chance to do that. Failure to do so, here and now, will write you down in the time to come, as the greatest failure Irish history has ever known. The pity of it! If you bring a new civil war on this country, and you are going the right way to do just that, you will deserve a fate worse than Castlereagh's."[44] In 1800, Castlereagh had bribed the entire Irish Parliament to enter into a permanent union with England.

By 1940, MacSwiney recognized de Valera's treachery and acknowledged the benefit to England and Northern Ireland of his policies. She finally used the word "traitor" in describing de Valera's actions, not against Ireland but against her version of an Irish Republic: "She now looked upon him as a liar, traitor, coward and renegade...What the IRA was in 1940, de Valera and Aiken had been but a decade before. 'Can any man or woman, not a pro-Britisher who cast a vote for Fianna Fáil in any election since the party was first returned to power, say that what they voted for has come to pass?'"[45] She continued her indictment of de Valera not realizing that it was also an indictment of herself and the rest of her counterfeit Republican comrades and confirmed Fianna Fáil's lack of success in delivering on de Valera's promises:

"Where was the Republic for which they had waded through the blood of their countrymen?

"The people voted Fianna Fáil in order to open Cosgrave's jails.

"The same jails are now full again.

"The people voted Fianna Fáil because de Valera said he could win the Republic bloodlessly if given a chance.

"De Valera has given them an English King.

"De Valera's censor does not allow the word Republic to be mentioned in the Press.

"The only place where it is allowed to appear is on Fianna Fáil note paper, where it is kept for a decoy for fools.

"The people gave de Valera the job of abolishing (corruption). Instead of doing that, he raised his own salary and the Dáil Deputies.

"De Valera promised a Republican Constitution.

"By false pretence, he obtained a minority vote, which has made democratic advance to the Republic impossible.

"De Valera promised a free press.

"Never was the Press in Ireland so censored as it is now. The people are allowed to know only what de Valera wants them to know. The people are given no correct information on which to base a decision regarding their vote in the impending elections.

"When de Valera says the elections are open to all, he lies.

"No Republican could be nominated. In order to do so, he would have to be as dishonest as the rest of the junta that rules this country. He would have to sign a form signifying his acceptance of the Twenty-Six County Parliament as it stands.

"Gerald Boland gave his word to Darcy's comrades and broke it.

"Can you count the times de Valera has broken his word?

"These things are certain; every vote for Fianna Fáil will be a vote for coercion and jailing. It will be a vote to let Craigavon have his way in Belfast.

"Voters, de Valera has a load of treachery on his conscience. Our advice to you is that you keep your hands clean of the blood of any more Irishmen.

"What value are the promises of a liar?"

And so another disillusioned counterfeit Republican finally saw the light of de Valera's treachery, but it was too late. In fact, she was two decades too late in calling for Irishmen to keep their hands clean of the blood of any more Irishmen. Her hands were dripping with the blood of her fellow countrymen through her encouragement of civil strife in 1922.

P.S. O'Hegarty, a contemporary of MacSwiney, had this to say about her: "She preached de Valera's doctrine, 'The Majority must not be allowed to do wrong.' Of all the impostures of which the anti-Treaty party is made up, perhaps the most shameless and loathsome (after that of de Valera) is that which Miss Mary MacSwiney has so sedulously foisted on the country…To the whole split and Civil War, Miss MacSwiney contributed nothing but bitterness, and hatred and malignancy."[46]

The Irish President treated the imprisoned IRA members with less consideration than he did the Germans. Despite his strict censorship of the news, a substantial group opposed to the internment policy of the de Valera government formed a new political party in June 1947, called Clann na Poblachta, with Sean MacBride as party leader. They presented the first real challenge to de Valera since 1938, before Chamberlain rescued him with the return of the Irish ports. John A. Costello, with the support of the IRA Deputies, was able to form a coalition government in February 1948, and he declared an Irish Republic to take effect on Easter Monday, April 18, 1949, in commemoration of the April 1916 Easter Rising.[47]

Under the coalition, however, the IRA renewed their activity in Northern Ireland, and, using physical force, they began to disrupt the Unionist government. Costello's coalition didn't last very long. When the government did not actively support the IRA attacks, the IRA shot themselves in the foot again and pulled out of the coalition, resulting in a no-confidence vote. Costello formed a second coalition government in 1954 but was again forced to call an unsuccessful general election in February 1957, and de Valera was returned to leadership once again.

In their haste to oust the Costello government, the IRA was instrumental in de Valera storming back into power and immediately upon reassuming office in 1957, he once again lost little time in moving against them. The Fianna Fáil government reintroduced internment without trial of IRA suspects. With the imprisonment of so many IRA men, the level of violence in Northern Ireland declined precipitously. By their opposition to the Costello government, the IRA once again provided their arch-enemy, de Valera, with means to return to power with one of the largest plurality in his career, and for their folly, they faced another series of roundups, prison, and the hangman's noose. Partition was secure and England's man was back at the helm.

Notes

1. Longford, Earl of & O'Neill, Thomas P., *Éamon de Valera*, Hutchinson, London, 1970, p. 466
2. Dwyer, T. Ryle, *De Valera, The Man & the Myths*, Poolbeg, Dublin, 1991, p. 177
3. Longford, Earl of & O'Neill, Thomas P., *Éamon de Valera*, Hutchinson, London, 1970, p. 302
4. *ibid*
5. Carroll, Joseph, *Ireland in the War Years*, David & Charles, NY 1975, p. 68
6. Coogan, Tim P., *De Valera, The Man who was Ireland*, Harper, 1996, p. 549
7. Longford, Earl of & O'Neill, Thomas P., *Éamon de Valera*, Hutchinson, London, 1970, p. 213
8. Coogan, Tim P., *De Valera, The Man who was Ireland*, Harper, 1996, p. 523
9. *ibid*, p. 625
10. Longford, Earl of & O'Neill, Thomas P., *Éamon de Valera*, Hutchinson, London, 1970, p. 342
11. Gray, David, *Behind the Green Curtain*, Unpublished Manuscript, American Heritage Center, U. of Wyoming, XXIV/12
12. *ibid*, XXIV/8
13. Coogan, Tim P., *De Valera, The Man who was Ireland*, Harper, 1996, p. 625
14. Stephan, Enno, *Spies in Ireland*, Stackpole, Harrisburg, 1965, p. 70
15. Gray, David, *Behind the Green Curtain*, Unpublished Manuscript, American Heritage Center, U. of Wyoming, XXV/10
16. *ibid*, XXIV/7
17. *ibid*, XXIV/13
18. Coogan, Tim P., *De Valera, The Man who was Ireland*, Harper, 1996, p. 624
19. Gray, David, *Behind the Green Curtain*, Unpublished Manuscript, American Heritage Center, U of Wyoming, XXV/11
20. Dwyer, T. Ryle, *De Valera, The Man & the Myths*, Poolbeg, Dublin, 1991, p. 266
21. Gray, David, Behind the Green Curtain, Unpublished Manuscript, American Heritage Center, U of Wyoming, XXV/1
22. *ibid*, I/26
23. *ibid*, XXV/2
24. *ibid*, XXV/3
25. Longford, Earl of & O'Neill, Thomas P., *Éamon de Valera*, Hutchinson, London, 1970, p. 356
26. Dwyer, T. Ryle, de Valera, *The Man & the Myths*, Poolbeg, Dublin, 1991, p. 233
27. Gray, David, *Behind the Green Curtain*, Unpublished Manuscript, American Heritage Center, U of Wyoming, XII/4
28. Stephan, Enno, *Spies in Ireland*, Stackpole, Harrisburg, 1965, p. 57
29. Dwyer, T. Ryle, *De Valera, The Man & the Myths*, Poolbeg, Dublin, 1991, p. 188
30. *ibid*
31. *ibid*, p. 189

32. *ibid*
33. Stephan, Enno, *Spies in Ireland*, p. 185: Stackpole, Harrisburg, 1965, p. 185
34. Coogan, Tim P., *De Valera, The Man who was Ireland*, Harper, 1996, p. 625
35. Longford, Earl of & O'Neill, Thomas P., *Éamon de Valera*, Hutchinson, London, 1970, p. 359
36. Coogan, Tim P., *De Valera, The Man who was Ireland*, Harper, 1996, p. 621
37. Dwyer, T. Ryle, *De Valera, The Man & the Myths*, Poolbeg, Dublin, 1991, p. 271
38. Coogan, Tim P., *De Valera, The Man who was Ireland*, Harper, 1996, p. 622
39. Gray, David, *Behind the Green Curtain*, Unpublished Manuscript, American Heritage Center, U of Wyoming, IX/8
40. Dwyer, T. Ryle, *Éamon de Valera*, Gill & Macmillan, 1980, p. 89
41. Stephan, Enno, *Spies in Ireland*, Stackpole, Harrisburg, 1965, p. 70
42. Dwyer, T. Ryle, de Valera, *The Man & the Myths*, Poolbeg, Dublin, 1991, p. 190
43. *ibid*, 1991, p. 191
44. *ibid*, 1991, p. 235
45. Gray, David, *Behind the Green Curtain*, Unpublished Manuscript, American Heritage Center, U of Wyoming, IX/10
46. O'Hegarty, Patrick S., *The Victory of Sinn Féin*, Talbot Press, Dublin 1924, p. 106
47. Gray, David, *Behind the Green Curtain*, Unpublished Manuscript, American Heritage Center, U. Of Wyoming, IX/10

CHAPTER XXIV

"Assignment Irish Constitution"

"...The show of religion was helpful to the politician
But the reality of it hurtful and pernicious."[1]

In June 1935, Éamon de Valera sent a memorandum to the King of England, assuring His Majesty that it was not his intention to declare an Irish Republic but solely to adopt a new constitution: "To introduce a Bill for the purpose of setting up a new Constitution...leaving unaffected the constitutional usage relating to external affairs. Among the provisions of the new Constitution will be the creation of the office of the President, elected by the people, and the abolition of the office of Governor General."[2]

Rather than declare an Irish Republic, de Valera deferred to the English and sought the assurance of the King before proceeding. On December 11, 1936, de Valera introduced two bills: the first dismantled the Free State Treaty, and the second was de Valera's constitution, which maintained the British connection. "In effect, the King remained as head of the group known as the Commonwealth, of which Ireland was to be associated:

The King (is) recognized as the symbol of their cooperation and continues to act on behalf of each of those nations...for the purpose of the appointment of diplomatic and consular representatives and the conclusion of international agreements, the King, so recognized, may and is hereby authorized to act on behalf of Ireland..."[3]

De Valera stopped far short of cutting the umbilical cord of dependence on the mother country. He refused to invoke the *1931 Statute of Westminster* by declaring an Irish Republic and then voluntarily joining the Commonwealth, thereby fulfilling his Document No. 2 external-association scheme, his reason for initiating civil war in 1922.

A major factor in prompting de Valera's introduction of his constitution was to eliminate Michael Collins and Arthur Griffith to anonymity by severing their connection with the reconstituted state.

According to Longford and O'Neill: "The removal of the Oath Bill had abolished the subordination of the Constitution to the Treaty. It is true that the amended Constitution still retained the clause, which stated the Irish Free State was a co-equal member of the British Commonwealth..."[4]

De Valera's position on a unified Ireland was muddled further during a speech to the Dáil on December 11, 1936: "If I were proposing that we should declare either a Twenty-six County Republic or a Thirty-two County Republic, an occasion like the present would not be the occasion to do it."[5] If it was not the occasion in 1936 to declare a Twenty-six County Republic, it certainly wasn't the occasion in 1922, when he instigated a civil war over it. Dwyer noted de Valera's equivocating on declaring an Irish Republic: "'I do not propose to use this situation to declare a republic for the 26 counties,' he explained. 'Our people at any time will have their opportunity of doing that...'"[6]

De Valera continued his public relations campaign against the Free State Treaty. Although the Imperial Conferences and the *1931 Statute of Westminster* unequivocally stated English law did not apply to the Dominions, he still insisted: "No matter how Republican the Free State Constitution was made by Amendment, it could never escape its basis in British law. What was needed was a new beginning which drew its strength from Irish roots."[7]

He continued to bleat his Republican credentials and just as often rejected an Irish Republic. His biographers made the astounding claim: "The objective of an independent Irish Republic was never out of his mind. He decided, however, to move slowly; he had no wish to alienate the timorous or precipitate international difficulties."[8] Such caution had been woefully absent in 1922. In an amazing contradiction of his earlier stand, the Irish President gave as his reason for not declaring an Irish Republic: "The use of the term, Poblacht na h-Éireann [Gaelic for "Republic of Ireland"] would be a direct challenge to Britain... 'While under the Constitution, the State would be a sovereign independent Republic, it did not, unfortunately, cover the whole of Ireland.' For that reason, he did not introduce into the Constitution the name Poblacht na hÉireann because that was a name which was sacred."[9]

De Valera, however, had no problem offending English sensitivities as outlined in his Document No. 2 during the Treaty debates; nor did he hesitate to challenge England with his demand for immediate recognition of an Irish Republic during the 1920 Presidential conventions in America. The "sacred" Poblacht na hÉireann title was a direct challenge to England in 1920 and 1922 but in 1937, when he had the legal right under the *Statute of Westminster* to declare an Irish Republic, he refused to do so.

T. Ryle Dwyer continued to pander to de Valera, claiming his Constitution "was purely a Republican document that paved the way for the full implementation of External Association envisaged by de Valera in 1921..."[10] Dwyer ignored the fact that by not opting for his Document No. 2 form of external association, in accordance with the *1931 Statute of Westminster*, de Valera confirmed that the civil war was a sham. John Whelan understood de Valera's real attitude towards the King of England: "For all the useful external purposes, de Valera is content to recognize the Throne – but as what nobody knows...de Valera was content to recognize the Crown...on Irish passports for example. He, as Minister for External Affairs [and President of Ireland], continued up to recently to 'request and require, in the name of His Majesty, King of Great Britain, Ireland and the British Dominions, all those whom it may concern to allow the bearer [de Valera] to pass freely without let or hindrance and to afford him every assistance and protection of which he may stand in need.' It is a situation without precedent..."[11]

When traveling abroad, de Valera recognized the King of England as King of Ireland and signed his passport acknowledging the fact that he was a subject of the King seeking safe passage under protection of the Crown.

De Valera's 1937 constitution was an amateurish legal document, but, viewed as to its Machiavellian character with its Catholic Church bias, it was pure political genius. De Valera pandered to the powerful Roman Catholic Church, and Church dogma was the foundation of his constitution. He ingratiated himself to the hierarchy by consulting with them on every aspect of his constitution. He sought token advice from lay ministers, but mostly he relied on the counsel of Cardinal MacRory, Bishop John Charles McQuaid, and Father Edward Cahill. Even Pope Pius XII was solicited by de Valera for approval. His constitution guaranteed that the Protestants of Northern Ireland would never voluntarily accept unification on the basis of his "Papist" constitution, which confirmed their oft-stated charge that "Home Rule" actually did mean "Rome Rule."

De Valera outraged Protestants with his insistence upon crowning the Roman Catholic Church as the state church, holding a special position within the government. "It [de Valera's constitution] visualized a state that, while democratic in practice, would be theocratic in precept; and neither at the time of its enactment, nor in today's Ireland, is it a source of enthusiasm for Irish Protestants."[12]

Longford and O'Neill noted the political muscle of the hierarchy: "Cardinal MacRory felt that the omission of any mention of the special position of the Catholic Church would cause and lead to an attack on the whole draft."[13] Unless the special position of the church was acknowledged in the Constitution, the hierarchy was prepared to condemn the constitution in its entirety. Sean MacEntee, Fianna Fáil Minister for Finance, attempted to explain away the defects of the constitution, as he had the defects of the civil-war stance of his fellow rebel Republicans, and, by doing so, he confirmed the power of the Hierarchy in government affairs. "The purpose of the Constitution was to get rid of the Oath and the Free State Constitution...How many people, including de Valera, had to subordinate whatever private views they may have had in relation to these questions, particularly the question of the Church, to the fact that we had to get a majority of the people. And we felt, and it was true, that we wouldn't get it if we gave the Bishops any chance to attack us."[14] So much for the Fianna Fáil's claim of standing on principle and not politics.

"De Valera...saw to it that the Roman Catholic Church and its hierarchy assumed for a time, a position of great importance and influence in Irish public life, which in 20th century Europe has scarcely been surpassed, even in General Francisco Franco's Spain or Premier Antonio Salazar's Portugal. It was...inbred with an independence that even the Bourbon kings never granted to the Galician Church in France."[15]

Although de Valera had been formally "Excommunicated for murder, robbery and mayhem" for his part in the 1922 civil war and after, "Both the Vatican and the Irish Hierarchy had cause to look with favor on de Valera as one of the leading Catholic statesmen and democrats in Europe..."[16]

Upon his return to power in 1932, his stain of excommunication miraculously disappeared, and the Church welcomed its murdering prodigal son back with open arms. He was now the darling of the church hierarchy despite the murders, the millions in destruction and the hatred that still permeates Ireland nearly a century later.

Upon a de Valera visit to Pope Pius XII at Castel Gandolfo on October 4, 1957, the Pope gushed: "Your Constitution...within the limits of order and morality, could find no ampler, no safer guarantee against the godless forces of subversion, faction and violence...allied for the common welfare in accordance with the principles of Catholic faith and doctrine."[17] The Pope had a short memory – the Irish hierarchy in 1922 excommunicated de Valera over his acts of subversion, factionalism, and violence.

Whelan noted the Church's historic catering to the political power brokers and its position as the shadow government in Ireland: "The Catholic Church...is the greatest organized body of power in the country...The Church in every country will always support, to the limit of human justice, established government...The Church opposed de Valera during the Civil War; it had no words too harsh for those who fought for the ideal of the Republic after 1921..."[18] The Catholic hierarchy was anti-nationalist throughout much of Irish history beginning with their warm welcome of the Earl of Pembroke in 1166 and on through the famines of the 1800s. During those years of indescribable suffering, the Bishop of Kerry, David Moriarty, condemned Fenian leaders who rose up in a futile gesture in 1867 to protest the genocidal terror of the English. The Bishop thundered from the pulpit that the insurgents were: "criminals and swindlers deserving of God's most withering and blighting curse, of whom eternity is not long enough, nor hell hot enough."[19]

The preamble to de Valera's juvenile constitution was a poor imitation of Moses on the Mount delivering the Ten Commandments: "In the name of the Most Holy Trinity, from Whom is all authority and to Whom, in our final end, all actions of both men and States must be referred... We the people of Éire...do hereby adopt, enact and give to ourselves this Constitution."

Flaunting the State preference for Catholicism was the crowning achievement of de Valera's "Assignment Constitution" in which he furthered English policy by providing the Protestants with justification for the perpetual rejection of Irish unification. De Valera's invitation to the Protestants in Ulster to voluntarily subject their loyalties and beliefs to a state controlled by the Holy See in Rome was met with derision and revulsion.

His constitution invested the Catholic Church as the final authority in any matter concerning politics, religion, morality, health, marriage, education, etc. Even today, the Catholic Church intrudes into every aspect of government and the lives of every person in Southern Ireland. De Valera's constitution and policies reflected what Ireland was the day he died: politically, economically, socially, and linguistically barren.

De Valera's version of freedom of expression sounded lofty but always bore a caveat. Under his constitution, a citizen's right to express his opinion and conviction was dependent upon the nature of the citizen's opinion and conviction: "Public opinion being a matter of such grave import to the common good, the State shall endeavor to ensure that organs of public opinion, such as radio, press, and cinema, while preserving their rightful liberty of expression, shall not be used to undermine public order or morality or the authority of the State." Rather than protect the people from the government, de Valera's constitution was designed to protect the government from the people by controlling any speech that might be damaging to his regime.

He claimed his constitution guaranteed fundamental rights such as "freedom of speech, conscience, association and assembly, habeas corpus and the inviolability of one's home, but again with a caveat: "Subject to public order and morality." Public order was whatever de Valera decreed it to be, and morality was whatever the Catholic hierarchy ordained it to be. Every definition came with ominous qualifications rendering individual rights nugatory.

The dilemma, however, was who decided the "morality *du jour?*" For hundreds of years, it was the Church of England and from 1937 onward, it was the Catholic hierarchy. The church ordained the parameters of morality, and the state enforced its dictates. The legitimacy of any religion is inversely proportionate to the amount of state power required to control its followers and enforce its doctrines.

For centuries, the British decreed, in the interest of morality, the native Irish, being "immoral" Catholics by practicing a religion contrary to the government-sanctioned church, were in violation of public order and, therefore, subject to confiscation of their land, deportation, starvation, or the hangman's noose.

Morality was the central theme of de Valera's constitution. As the shadow government in Southern Ireland, it was the church hierarchy that decreed what an Irishman could say, read, or view. The Bishops, on numerous occasions since de Valera's assumption of power, flexed their political muscle in demonstrating that their views constituted the law of the land.

The direct and inevitable result of de Valera's document was an intellectual wasteland. Ireland evolved into the most censored country in all of Europe during de Valera's time in office. The Bishops determined the art, literature, and sexual orientations of the people; literature offensive to Catholic teaching was prohibited, leading to a mass exodus of Irish literati; films were strictly monitored in accordance with church standards; and even the health of the nation was bound up in the church's views. Prodded by the church, the Government sought to curb the "corrupting influence" of Saturday night dances; The Dance Hall Act of 1935, regulated the licensing, suitability of premises, parking of cars, age of admission, police supervision, and hours of dances. The law was vigorously enforced.

No career politician was going to defy the Church, not if he wanted to remain in office. The hierarchy's secret hand was – and remains – behind every important legislation in Southern Ireland dealing with moral issues.

In the late 1940s, the John A. Costello government was rent by an internal squabble which developed after the hierarchy demanded amendments to the Mother and Child Program that addressed the long-neglected health needs of Irish women and children. Dr. Noel Browne, the minister in charge of the program, refused to alter the bill to the satisfaction of the bishops, and he was forced to resign. Rather than go quietly, he went public with the hierarchy correspondence, creating a political crisis in which politicians stampeded in their rush to publicly affirm their loyalty and obedience to the church, overriding their responsibility to the health and welfare of the people.

Dwyer noted Prime Minister Costello's groveling before the hierarchy: "I, as a Catholic, obey my Church authorities and will continue to do so. The whole affair should have been adjusted behind closed doors, so that the public would not have become aware of it." Another leading politician, Sean MacBride, publicly proclaimed his fealty to the Church: "All of us in the Government who are Catholics are, as such, bound to give obedience to the rulings of our Church and our hierarchy."[20]

Dwyer also noted: "de Valera quietly agreed with Costello that the whole thing should have been settled behind closed doors. 'You should not have published the correspondence between yourself and the Hierarchy,' he told Browne privately. Responding, Browne said: 'He [de Valera] appeared to resent the fact that I had deliberately set out, by use of the [Hierarchy] correspondence, to collect the evidence needed by me to prove conclusively that Rome did rule, which I had already learned from my experience in the Cabinet...de Valera appeared to know and condone it.'"[21]

Coogan also recognized the hidden hand of the hierarchy: "The 1950s were a period during which an observer might have been forgiven for thinking that the Church had decided to settle the constitutional confusions surrounding the status of the Twenty-six Counties by converting them into a Green [Irish] Vatican state."[22]

Upon de Valera's return to power in 1959, "It looked like [his Government] was also becoming embroiled in a controversy with the Roman Catholic Hierarchy when James Ryan, the Minister for Health, moved to implement a somewhat revised version of the "Mother and Child Scheme." The Bishops wrote to the Press condemning the legislation, but de Valera avoided an open confrontation by hurriedly going north to talk to John Cardinal D'Alton, his old classmate from Blackrock College. They met in Drogheda and agreed to certain modifications to the bill, which led to the Hierarchy withdrawing its letter before actual publication, but too many people had seen the document for the matter to remain secret for long. The whole affair was another example of the enormous influence which the Roman Catholic Hierarchy had in the public life of the Twenty-six Counties."[23]

The Protestants in Southern Ireland could expect nothing better than third-class citizenship. According to de Valera, non-Catholics were not suitable candidates for any positions that dealt with Catholic interests in Southern Ireland. Protestant doctors, according to the hierarchy and de Valera, were unfit to treat Catholic patients and civil service posts were all but nonexistent for non-Gaelic-speaking Protestants: "There is certainly no local office of the slightest importance in which the clergy has not an indirect vote...The only weakness in the scheme of clerical influence is that the mass of the clergy are themselves not particularly cultivated or sophisticated... Furthermore, the Catholic Church and the Church of Ireland are both notoriously 'Low Church,' puritanical and narrow-minded..."[24]

The Vatican was delighted with de Valera's constitution. It mattered not to the hierarchy that their supremacist policy perpetuated partition. The Roman Catholic Church was anointed as the State Church; England was spared a guerilla war in Northern Ireland, the Unionists were entrenched in the North; de Valera got reelected; the Southern Irish got de Valera's folly, a nonsensical Constitution and a Church-state. It was a jolly-good deal for everyone but the Irish people.

De Valera confirmed Collins and Griffith's prophecy in 1921 that the Free State treaty would provide Ireland with the freedom to achieve freedom, but the Irish President corrupted that freedom by opting for a theocracy rather than an Irish Republic.

What lay in store for Protestants under a de Valera constitution was an incident involving Leticia Dunbar-Harrison and the County Mayo library in 1930. Dunbar-Harrison was a Protestant Trinity College graduate with a degree in modern languages achieving honors in French and Spanish and had been appointed librarian in County Mayo. The local library committee, egged on by local priests, refused to approve the appointment. The Catholic clergy instituted a boycott of the area libraries. The Catholic chancellor, Hegarty, of Killala, said: "If the people of Mayo cannot have a Carnegie Library without a Protestant librarian being made director of the literature distributed to their children, they will do without a Carnegie Library."[25]

The Mayo County Council rejected Dunbar-Harrison's application for the librarian position, ostensibly because she was not proficient in Gaelic, but her religious orientation obviously was the underlying reason for the denial. That was confirmed when Ellen Burke, a Catholic who spoke not a word of Gaelic, was appointed. Dunbar-Harrison's faith was too great a hurdle to overcome in a bigoted Irish society.

De Valera, still wandering the political wilderness, exploited the opportunity to gather hierarchy support. He pontificated: "'Religion should not be made an excuse for denying a person an appointment for which he or she was fully qualified.' Here was the rub: 'What constituted being qualified?' As far as de Valera was concerned, a Protestant librarian was not properly qualified to deal with Catholics, any more than a Protestant doctor would be qualified to deal with Catholic patients...'I say that if I had a vote on a local body, and if there were two qualified people who had to deal with a Catholic community and if one was a Catholic and the other a Protestant, I would unhesitatingly vote for the Catholic.' Carried to its logical conclusion, his argument could have meant Protestants were banned from virtually every position dealing with the public."[26]

De Valera argued that if the position was to be one, in which Dunbar-Harrison was to actively select books for the library which might fall into the hands of Catholic children, then she was not qualified for the position. The final outcome of the library situation in Mayo was that Dunbar-Harrison was assigned a post in the Department of Defense in January 1932.

De Valera maintained that it was not so much the division of Ireland but the division of the Irish people that was the "deepest wound." Coogan dismissed de Valera's crocodile tears: "What did de Valera do about making the state he ruled for so long less temperamentally different from that of Protestants of Northern Ireland? The truthful answer is that by the introduction of his theocratic and sectarian Constitution, he helped to make a bad situation worse...de Valera was once warned...that it could be argued that the worst discrimination in the whole island was directed not against Six County Catholics, but against Twenty-six County Protestants...there was something curmudgeonly and ungenerous about de Valera's whole approach to Northerners [and Partition]."[27]

The Protestants in Southern Ireland despaired of religious tolerance in the public sector. "The Protestant in the South has little chance of getting his fair share of public appointments as the Catholics of the North... Religion in the South is just as solidly organized as in the North and is no less narrow-minded..."[28]

When it was still in draft form, de Valera was repeatedly warned that the constitution would not only alienate the Protestant Unionists but perpetuate partition. Southern Ireland Secretary of the Department of Finance, J. J. McElligott, lambasted the constitution as encouraging partition, claiming: "It would not contribute anything to affecting the unity of Ireland, but rather, the reverse...and is *likely to have lasting ill-effects on our political relations with our nearest neighbors.*"[29] [emphasis added]

In a contemptuous display of intolerance, de Valera stated: "I do not see why the people of this part of Ireland should sacrifice ideals which they hold dear – completely sacrifice those ideals – *in order to meet the views of people whose position fundamentally is not as just or as right as our position is...*"[30] [emphasis added] Seán O'Faoláin wrote of de Valera's constitution: "No Northerner can possibly like such features of Southern life as at present constituted, at its pervasive clerical control; its censorship; its Gaelic revival; its isolationist economic policy..."[31]

Newspapers were unimpressed by de Valera's constitution:
The Irish Times noted: "The Governor General...is replaced by a far more imposing functionary in the President of Éire, who apparently will be a Super Governor General masquerading as the President of the Republic or the President of the Republic masquerading as a Super Governor General."

The Irish Independent May 1, 1937; referring to de Valera's constitution as Document No. 3, a disparagement of his Document No. 2 in 1922: "The Mountain has been in labor, and has brought forth a Mouse. Mr. De Valera's followers will be sadder and wiser today when they have searched in vain in his new Constitution, or Document No. 3, for any signs that the promised millennium [Republic] is at hand."

The Irish Times, May 1, 1937: "It [the Constitution] merely suggests that Éire is neither fish, flesh nor even a good red herring. It does not tell us whether we are in the Commonwealth or out of it. Can it be that Mr. De Valera does not know?"

The Daily Telegraph, May 1, 1937: "To make the challenge to Ulster sentiment more explicit and more dangerous, the constitution claims religious sanctions, forbids divorce, and assigns a special position to the Church of Rome...It is part of the tragedy of Ireland that...any Irishman who accepts the Constitution now granted to him...would place himself under an autocrat's heel."

The Sunday Times, May 2, 1937: "de Valera's Constitution would perpetuate the division between Dublin and Belfast."

The Irish Times, May 3, 1937: "It is the duty of every patriotic Irishman to work for reunion, but it is folly to assume reunion, and the height of folly to postpone the day of its real achievement by slights which cannot fail to be resented across the border."

The Standard [the most sympathetic to de Valera's constitution] May 5, 1937: "On one point at least we shall be all agreed; due honor has been done to the religious aspects of Irish life...We note, by the way, that the draft constitution not merely prohibits divorce but refuses to acknowledge a divorce granted in another country."

The Irish Catholic, May 6, 1937, admitted the constitution's Catholic bias and called it: "a noble document in harmony with Papal teachings."

The Labor News, May 2, 1937: "The draft of the new Constitution has been received without one grain of enthusiasm by the mass of the people...Its recognition of rights is monotonously countered by provisions which in most cases permit them to be completely swept away."

The *Leader* for the week of May 2, 1937: "Our suggested President...might become a dictator on occasion and we want no dictators in this land."

In contrast to the negative reception given to the constitution throughout Ireland, the comments of de Valera's apologists were pure humbug. John Whelan was disingenuous when he wrote: "In a sense the Constitution is [de Valera's] main achievement and every biographer of the man must pause before it. It has considerable merit of articulating, once and for all, the claims of the Irish people to sovereign independence. It is the basis of the laws of Ireland. It embodies and enthrones in the highest place, the national tradition. Here is what Southern Ireland believes in and a summary of itself containing – unlike the First Constitution of the Free State – no overt limitation and prevarication of which it need be ashamed."[32]

Despite his desire to glorify de Valera, Whelan could not disguise the glaring defects of de Valera's constitution. He had to admit: "An enormous number of electors voted against it and the Constitution has created no enthusiasm. And when one examines it...one is struck by the unimaginative and, indeed commonplace quality of the document. It is pedantic and circumscribed. It states no fine general truth that it does not immediately qualify with so much care that the force of its original statement is lost and made to seem puny – as if a general truth were not a noble thing but a dangerous thing to be shown to the public on a leash."[33]

The lack of separation of the legislative and executive powers left few safeguards for individual freedoms. The ease of bureaucrats circumventing de Valera's constitution and the legislature was noted in the *Irish Independent* on February 23, 1943: "*In the year 1942, the Irish Legislature passed 27 statutes but for any one new law made by the elected legislators, more than 20 were made by officials* [emphasis added]...No fewer than 553 sets of statutory rules and orders for 1942 have come from the government printers. Each of these 553 laws drawn up by officials [bureaucrats] and signed by a Minister has the same force as the 27 passed by the Legislature...There is scarcely a phase of daily life they do not touch, yet the Legislature does not even go through the formality of reading and approving them...The ease with which they can be turned out in such bewildering multiplicity implies a dangerous surrender of the Legislature's power of the democratically elected lawmakers. They contribute a growing encroachment of bureaucracy."[34]

Dwyer conceded the contradictions in de Valera's constitution: "In the event of any discrepancy of interpretation of his Constitution between Gaelic and English, the Gaelic would take precedence, which was essentially an absurd situation because the Constitution was drafted in English and only translated into Gaelic."[35]

The inadequacy of the constitution was epitomized by the restricted definition given to "personhood," particularly regarding women. De Valera endlessly talked about the plight of women in Ireland, but when he had the opportunity to improve their situation, he did nothing. During the treaty debates in 1921, his greatest supporters were women, voicing their support for his rush to civil war, but: "de Valera had no feeling for feminism. Nor was he eager to see women advance in politics...His view of women – as teachers, guardians of the social order, mothers, and nuns – could be described as conservative, sexless, or even, in a way, dehumanized..."[36] Archbishop John Charles McQuaid "advised de Valera that the feminists were 'very confused...that it was incorrect to state that men and women have an equal right to work of the same kind. Men and women have equal right to appropriate work...'"[37]

The view articulated by Mary Hayden, Professor of Irish History, University College Dublin, was representative of educated women of the time: "What is proposed by the new Constitution is not a return to the Middle Ages. It is something much worse..." A consortium of women's groups claimed: "...It was a fascist and slave conception of a woman as being a non-adult person who is very weak and whose place is in the home...It takes from women the right to choose their own avocation in life...The State is given power to decide what avocations are suited to their sex and strength. It would hardly be possible to make a more deadly encroachment upon the liberty of the individual than to deprive him or her of this right."[38]

George Bernard Shaw denounced de Valera's constitution: "attacking it as creating a new post of President with dictatorial powers and reactionary in its attitude to women."[39]

De Valera's constitution was a liturgy of prescribed formulations more suitable for church prayers than as an outline of human rights. The article on women strained the limits of comprehension, which was set forth in the long-winded exposition typical of de Valera: "The State shall endeavor to ensure that the inadequate strength of women and the tender age of children shall not be abused and that women or children shall not be forced by economic necessity to enter avocations unsuited to their sex, age or strength."

Sean Moylan described the reality of a woman's lot in Ireland: "For the farmer's wife, and particularly for the female farm servant, there was no respite. From the dawn's early morning light to the sunlight's last gleaming she was still unflaggingly employed."[40]

Typical of the mumble jumble of the constitution was Article 41 which declared that the family was the natural, primary and fundamental unit of society, which "possessed inalienable and imprescriptible rights, antecedent and superior to all positive law." The provisions that followed made it unlawful to dissolve a marriage and stated that mothers should not work to the neglect of their household obligations, though there was no explanation of what might constitute "neglect" or indeed the extent of "household duties." Divorce was outlawed and no person divorced in another country was allowed to enter into a valid marriage in Ireland as long as the original spouse was alive. Contraceptives had already been effectively banned thanks to Church pressure. The 1935 Criminal Law Amendment Act made it a criminal offence to import or sell contraceptives.

The constitution reads like a Sunday school list of do's and don'ts for children. The state was obliged to protect mothers from engaging in outside work so they would not neglect their household duties. De Valera declared that all citizens were to have an adequate means of livelihood, but his economic policies were a disaster. Under his constitution, all workers were to be protected against exploitation by private industry and were not to be abused health-wise. But it was the Church and not the State, which dictated the health policy of the government. There were rumbling protests about the derogation of women's rights, and general criticism of church intrusion.

High levels of unemployment prompted de Valera to restrict the right of women to work in industry. He claimed that women would take low-paying jobs, thereby putting men out of work. Under Article 3 of the Free State Constitution: "Every person without distinction of sex, domiciled in the area of the jurisdiction of the Irish Free State shall...enjoy the privileges and be subject to the obligations of such citizenship." de Valera explained that he had deleted the phrase "without distinction of sex" from the Free State constitution because "he considered it 'a badge of their previous inferiority.'" Yet, his document included this badge of inferiority on numerous occasions.

Some citizens were more equal than others: all citizens were recognized as equal before the law and there was protection against religious discrimination but the constitution explicitly accorded closely with Roman Catholic thinking.

The Irish President demonstrated his Machiavellian grasp of politics by calling a snap election for July 1, 1937. Rather than being fought over his disastrous economic and social policies, the election turned on the hierarchy-endorsed constitutional question. Though his political standing was shaky, de Valera was able to promote himself and his party with the blessing of the Catholic Church. With the Hierarchy beating the drums, the constitution passed 685,000 votes to 527,000 votes. Coogan reported that de Valera's devious delegates discarded "an unusually high – roughly ten percent or nearly 170,000 votes..."[41]

"It is thought that many Protestants abstained or spoiled their votes, ensuring, ironically, the Constitution's passage...Those Protestants who did vote, voted heavily against the Constitution."[42] A more logical conclusion was that by discarding or spoiling the overwhelmingly negative votes of Southern Ireland Protestants, de Valera prevented the defeat of his constitution and more than likely his re-election.

Notes

1. Machiavelli, Niccolo, *The Prince* (Translated by W.K. Marriott), J&M Dent & Sons, London 1908, p. 211
2. Longford, Earl of & O'Neill, Thomas P., *Éamon de Valera*, Hutchinson, London, 1970, p. 290
3. *ibid*, p. 293
4. *ibid*, p. 294
5. *ibid*
6. Dwyer, T. Ryle, *De Valera, The Man & the Myths*, Poolbeg, Dublin, 1991, p. 197
7. Longford, Earl of & O'Neill, Thomas P., *Éamon de Valera*, Hutchinson, London, 1970, p. 290
8. *ibid*, p. 289
9. *ibid*, p.294
10. Dwyer, T. Ryle, *De Valera, The Man & the Myths*, Poolbeg, Dublin, 1991, p. 197
11. Whelan, John (Seán O'Faoláin), *De Valera*, Penguin Books, England 1939, p. 151
12. Coogan, Tim P., *De Valera, The Man who was Ireland*, Harper, 1996, p. 489
13. Longford, Earl of & O'Neill, Thomas P., *Éamon de Valera*, Hutchinson, London, 1970, p. 296

14. Keogh, Dermont, *The Vatican, the Bishops & Irish Politics 1919-39*, Cambridge Press, 1986, p 218.
15. Fitzgibbon, Constantine, *The Life & Times of Éamon de Valera*, Gill & Macmillan, Dublin, 1973, p. Introduction
16. Keogh, Dermont, *The Vatican, the Bishops & Irish Politics 1919-39*, Cambridge Press, 1986, p. 220
17. *ibid*, p. 239, quoted from SPO S9715B
18. Whelan, John (Seán O'Faoláin), *De Valera*, Penguin Books, England 1939, p. 167
19. Keogh, Dermont, *The Vatican, the Bishops & Irish Politics 1919-39*, Cambridge Press, 1986, p. 3
20. Dwyer, T. Ryle, *De Valera, The Man & the Myths*, Poolbeg, Dublin, 1991, p. 305
21. *ibid*, p. 305
22. Coogan, Tim P., *De Valera, The Man who was Ireland*, Harper, 1996, p. 647
23. Dwyer, T. Ryle, *De Valera, The Man & the Myths*, Poolbeg, Dublin, 1991, p. 307
24. Whelan, John (Seán O'Faoláin), *De Valera*, Penguin Books, England 1939, p. 168
25. Keogh, Dermont, *The Vatican, the Bishops & Irish Politics 1919-39*, Cambridge Press, 1986, p. 166
26. Dwyer, T. Ryle, *De Valera, The Man & the Myths*, Poolbeg, Dublin, 1991, p. 153
27. Coogan, Tim P., *De Valera, The Man who was Ireland*, Harper, 1996, p. 642
28. Whelan, John (Seán O'Faoláin), *De Valera*, Penguin Books, England 1939, p. 155
29. Bowman, John, *De Valera and the Ulster Question 1917-1973*, Clarendon Press, Oxford, 1982, p. 148
30. Dwyer, T. Ryle, *Éamon de Valera*, Gill & Macmillan, 1980, p. 137
31. *ibid*, p. 136
32. Whelan, John (Seán O'Faoláin), *De Valera*, Penguin Books, England 1939, p. 146
33. *ibid*, p. 147
34. Lavelle, Patricia, *James O'Mara, A Staunch Sinn Feiner 1873-1948*, p. 309
35. Dwyer, T. Ryle, *De Valera, The Man & the Myths*, Poolbeg, Dublin, 1991, p. 199
36. Coogan, Tim P., *De Valera, The Man who was Ireland*, Harper, 1996, p. 491
37. *ibid*, p. 497
38. *ibid*, p. 495
39. *ibid*, p. 17 (quoting Sean Moylan)
40. Longford, Earl of & O'Neill, Thomas P., *Éamon de Valera*, Hutchinson, London, 1970, p. 298
41. Coogan, Tim P., *De Valera, The Man who was Ireland*, Harper, 1996, p. 498
42. *ibid*

CHAPTER XXV

"Assignment Irish Ports"

"It is necessary to know well how to be a great pretender and dissembler, and men are so simple and so subject to present necessities, that he who seeks to deceive will always find someone who will allow himself to be deceived."

Machiavelli, *The Prince*

Despite accurately forecasting the coming Armageddon, the British were unprepared for another war. As before, America held the key to victory and Ireland, and Éamon de Valera, would once again take center stage in Anglo-American relations.

On October 21, 1938, President Franklin Delano Roosevelt conveyed a message to the British Assistant Military Attaché to Washington, Sir Arthur Murray: "In so far as he, the President, was able to achieve it, he wished Prime Minister Neville Chamberlain to feel that, in the event of war with the dictators, the Prime Minister had the industrial resources of the American nation behind him...Roosevelt offered all the parts and basic materials necessary to ensure the democracies an overwhelming superiority in the air...He advanced the idea of assembly lines in Canada where the separate parts of American-designed aircraft could be assembled..."[1]

On November 17, 1938, the English ratified an Anglo-American trade agreement. Some members of the cabinet were dissatisfied with the terms but Edward Halifax, Foreign Secretary, outlined the reality of the circumstances: "'I am afraid the political reasons for getting a Treaty must outweigh trade and economic considerations.' He over-ruled them and the Treaty was duly signed..."[2]

As early as 1934, Winston Churchill warned of German air strength and growing militarism and the threat it posed to Britain. In 1938, Austria was annexed into Greater Germany and Chamberlain made three journeys to Germany in an attempt to halt the march to war resulting in the Munich Agreement whereby Britain and France agreed to German annexation of Czechoslovakia's Sudetenland. As Chamberlain set off on his final pilgrimage to Munich, de Valera sent the British Prime Minister a congratulatory message assuring him: "One person, at least, is completely satisfied that you are doing the right thing – no matter what the result."[3] The Second World War was the result, and millions perished. De Valera praised Chamberlain "as a knight of peace who had attained the highest peak of human greatness and a glory greater than that of all the conquerors."[4] Just as he accepted the partition of his own country, the Irish President applauded the carving up of another small country.

The military situation in the late 1930s was dire indeed for the English, as they faced war not only on the continent but also in the Far East, where the Japanese were engaged in their Chinese and Manchurian military adventures. England did not have the financial or military wherewithal to engage in a war on one front, let alone on two. Meanwhile, Italy had invaded Abyssinia.

With the annexation of Austria and the surrender of the Sudetenland: "The British Chiefs of Staff issued a categorical warning that 1938 would entail the gravest risks of English defeat."[5] War with Germany was predicted by British intelligence to begin on September 1, 1938, a year to the day before the Nazis attacked Poland.

"It was surprising how accurate much of their [English] information was. The Foreign Office was informed of the plans for a *coup de main* against Danzig. They had accurate and alarming information on the state of German aircraft production and the growth of the German army...Military intelligence produced a picture of a German Army rapidly approaching total mobilization so that Hitler was on the verge of being able to order a major military action in any direction at very short notice...But when and where would he strike? Eastwards towards the Ukraine or westwards perhaps, against the Netherlands and Britain?"[6]

With the near-fatal experience of unrestricted submarine warfare a mere twenty years before and an encore forecast within the year, Chamberlain, at this critical moment decided to return the strategically important Irish ports guarding the Western approaches to England without an explicit understanding from de Valera that they would be made available during the imminent conflict with Germany.

De Valera had always posed as an uncompromising antagonist of England, but as 1938 dawned, the Irish Taoiseach was at a political dead-end. His economic policies were a catastrophic failure; his Machiavellian constitution crowned him Ireland's autocrat and enshrined the Catholic Church as the shadow government of Éire; and an end to partition was further away than ever. His economic war with

England plunged Ireland's farmers and manufacturers into the lower echelons of the worst depression in history. If ever there was an opportune time for the British to rid itself of the Irish gadfly, it was in 1938. Inexplicably, rather than seal the coffin of de Valera's political career, Chamberlain rescued him from the political netherworld and relegated Cosgrave's pro-English party to the scrap heap.

De Valera was excoriated by the British over his alleged dismantling of the 1922 Anglo-Irish treaty, his repudiation of the alleged oath of allegiance, refusal to pay the land annuities, dismissal of the Governor General, and, above all, his constitution; all were seen as symbols of an anti-English bias. Churchill was well aware that any criticism of an Irishman by an Englishman would propel that Irishman to near sainthood in Irish eyes. Whenever de Valera faced a political crisis and the polls indicated his election in doubt, Churchill, Lloyd George, or some other high-ranking English official would publicly denounce him and claim he was the one man the British loved to hate. As far as the Irish were concerned, the one thing they loved most was an Irishman who was scorned by the English.

The Finance Minister in Northern Ireland, John Andrews, referred to the dire political situation in Southern Ireland in 1938. He advised Chamberlain that:

"Mr. De Valera could not get on without an economic settlement with Great Britain and that it would be folly to give away the lever of our duties without receiving substantial advantages in return for our concessions." In the month before Chamberlain relinquished the ports, James Craig, Prime Minister of Northern Ireland, counseled Samuel Hoare, the British Home Secretary: "de Valera and his Government are in sore straits both politically and financially and your Government by acting firmly can secure a satisfactory trade agreement...Compromise can be stood over, not surrender. Thus, each progressive concession by the British Government was seen not only as weak-minded but unnecessary..."[7]

De Valera dispatched Joseph Walshe, Minister for External Affairs, to London before him with orders to negotiate a 50-50 settlement with England, but Chamberlain insisted on a 90-10 split, with England picking up the lion's share of the debt. De Valera followed and the major points were quickly settled. On April 25, 1938, the economic war was officially ended with Ireland making a one-time payment of £10 million ($50 million).

With de Valera's political fortunes at their lowest ebb since the 1922 Civil War, Chamberlain came galloping to his rescue. Recognizing that a financial settlement alone would not guarantee de Valera's re-election,

Chamberlain proposed to return the Southern Irish ports of Queenstown, Bereshaven and Lough Swilly that guarded the Western approaches to England. Bereshaven and Queenstown (Cobh) were two deep-water ports hundreds of miles south of Lough Swilly, a 20-mile inlet located less than 10 miles from the Northern Ireland port of Londonderry.

This astonishing gift to England's alleged arch-villain at so propitious a moment for de Valera and at so perilous a time for England was not only incomprehensible but suspicious and sinister. Chamberlain recognized the gamble and what was at stake, admitting: "It would be urged that at a very dangerous and critical time, the United Kingdom had decided to hand over the defended ports in Éire and, in so doing, were running very grave risks."[8] Robert Smyllie, editor of the *Irish Times*, wrote: "From the standpoint of British security, this sacrifice by Chamberlain seemed to be almost suicidal. He justified it to his English critics – and there were many – 'as an act of faith, a gesture of British generosity to Ireland which would find a ready response in the Irish people's warm hearts.'"[9]

Prior to the return of the ports, de Valera's prospects were nil. The Cosgrave government, supposedly so friendly to England, was waiting in the wings, anticipating a return to power. All the signs pointed to a crushing defeat of England's alleged Public Enemy No 1. Craig and the Northern Ireland ministers provided Chamberlain with reality checks as to de Valera's dilemma, but the British Prime Minister ignored all their entreaties. De Valera was, without doubt, in perilous political trouble, but why was the English Prime Minister so determined to salvage his political career?

Furthermore, during the negotiations, de Valera never raised the subject of partition or the transfer of the Catholic counties of Fermanagh and Tyrone to Southern Ireland. The Irish leader recognized the political cornucopia that the return of the ports presented to him personally, and he lost no time in taking advantage of the windfall and called for a general election in June 1938. With the return of the ports, England's "arch-enemy" was able to consolidate a politically shaky government into the most popular in Irish history, romping home with the largest plurality of its first fifty years.

Why would the English guarantee the re-election of an alleged anti-British muckraker over that of the friendly Cosgrave government unless there was something in it for England? The return of the ports, ending the economic war and forgiving the land annuities, made de Valera the sparkle in Irish eyes and insured his leadership throughout the coming war. Once a settlement had been reached, the British embarked on a public relations campaign in America portraying England as a powerful but benevolent neighbor. The United States and the international community were suitably impressed by the "magnanimous" gesture and Irish-American opposition to Anglo-American relations was once again muted.

Tim Pat Coogan noted the importance Churchill publicly attached to the ports. During a May 5, 1938 House of Commons debate on the issue, Churchill bellowed: "These ports are, in fact, the sentinel towers of the Western Approaches, by which the 45 million people in this Island so enormously depend on foreign food for their daily bread and by which they can carry on their trade, which is equally important to their existence...We are to give them [the ports] up, unconditionally to an Irish Government led by men – I do not want to use harsh words – whose rise to power has been proportionate to the animosity with which they have acted against this country, no doubt in pursuance of their own patriotic impulses and whose position in power is based upon the violation of solemn Treaty engagements."[10] Churchill cited all the reasons why the return of the ports should not have been returned.

Chamberlain's rush to settle with de Valera was incomprehensible unless the re-election of de Valera was vital to England's overall political and military strategy and the value of the ports greatly exaggerated. "The full implication of handing back the ports and ending the defense clauses of the 1921 Treaty were not yet wholly visible...It was obvious to all that this would be a major factor in Ireland's position in the event of another war..."[11]

After his private meeting with Chamberlain, the Irish Premier announced that Ireland would remain neutral during the coming war. When de Valera refused British access to the ports during World War II, the British howled that they were vital to England's security, but in reality, militarily worthless but politically priceless.

In an August 1922 Dáil session, de Valera insisted that the Irish would have to make concessions to satisfy Britain's security requirements: "If security concessions were refused, Britain would depict the Irish as unreasonable, America would agree, as would the international community generally, and then, England would be given a free hand to deal with Ireland."[12] His analysis was borne out in the war years of 1939-45. Throughout the conflict, Churchill led a chorus of anti-Irish rhetoric, charging them with consorting with the Germans while placing a "grievous burden on the broad shoulders of the English" by refusing access to the ports.

The value of the ports, however, was blown up into an international melodrama by Churchill solely for propaganda purposes. British and American naval and military experts had determined that as long as England held Londonderry and the use of the inlet of Lough Foyle, the other Irish ports were merely excess military baggage with no strategic value. As early as February 1936, a report by the Imperial Defense Committee concluded that it was a propitious moment to return the ports, in view of their negligible military value and the tremendous financial and military costs of maintaining them. This would have involved a tremendous expenditure of men and materiel vitally needed elsewhere. An English report estimated the rehabilitation time of the ports was as high as eight to nine years to bring them up to maximum efficiency. "It is a calculation which, to say the least, is difficult to equate with the value which the British subsequently put on the ports."[13]

The British Admiralty's assessment had concluded that in the event of a hostile takeover by the English, it would be necessary: "to hold the various ports against even the existing [small] Irish forces, supported as they would be by a hostile population which would require a brigade for each port at a minimum. But if the ports were to be made safe for naval use, the occupation of a considerable hinterland would also be necessary and this would require a division for each port, with anti-air defenses. Such a position, with a series of Gibraltars scattered round the Irish coast, was, in view of our own meager military position at that time, divorced from realities...It was natural, therefore, with their continental commitments to France in the event of war with Germany that the General Staff should not only be strongly averse to accepting such a responsibility but was anxious to free the Army even of its existing task of guarding the ports in peace, with the very uncertain outlook in the international sphere. The retention of the ports meant a military commitment in war which we were entirely unable to fulfill."[14]

In a meeting with Dr. Eduard Hempel, Germany's Ambassador to Ireland, J. J. Walshe "expressed the view that as far as the English were concerned, the value of these harbors, which were so lightly defended as to be highly vulnerable to Luftwaffe attacks, bore no rational relation to the inevitable consequence [of a forcible takeover] – war with Ireland and sharp repercussions among Irish-Americans."[15] Walshe confirmed that the ports were of marginal military value as long as the Germans held the French Channel Ports, and that any forcible takeover of the Irish ports would imperil Anglo-American relations.

"On November 29, 1942, at a high-level lunch in Downing Street...Churchill informed David Gray, U.S. representative to Ireland, that, though the ports would have been valuable early on, the war had now reached a stage at which it could be won without them..."[16] Even the Germans knew the ports represented a liability to the English. Hempel stated in a report to Joachim von Ribbentrop, the German Foreign Minister, as early as July 11, 1940: "The actual value to England of the possession of the Irish ports in view of the lack of strong fortifications and their vulnerability to German air attacks from the French coast was disproportionate to the advantages to be expected..."[17]

T. Ryle Dwyer reported: "When David Gray brought up the question of Irish bases during a visit to the United States in the summer of 1943, the American Joint Chiefs of Staff concluded that the bases would not only be of no use, but would actually be a liability. The wartime fuss over the bases had been pointless..."[18]

Gray suggested to the State Department that the United States demand air and port facilities to be leased by de Valera to the Allies and that the Irish President expel diplomatic representatives of the Axis powers. General George C. Marshall, American Chief of Staff, replied: "The Joint Chiefs of Staff concluded that, *while the ports of the Bay of Biscay [French Channel Ports] were in German hands, it would be inexpedient to route convoys to the south of England* [emphasis added] and that air and naval bases in Ireland would not appreciably alter that position. Indeed, they recommended that if an approach were made to Ireland for naval and air facilities, no commitment should be made that bases would be established there. This memorandum from the US Joint Chiefs of Staff confirmed the long-held opinion of the English Government as to the military insignificance of the ports. In an exaggerated form, however, the issue became a prime subject of anti-Irish propaganda."[19]

Gray's proposal was rejected because "The American Joint Chiefs of Staff feared de Valera might agree to an Allied request and they did not want to take any chance of this because they believed bases in the Twenty-six Counties would only be a liability..."[20]

The British assessment of the military value of the ports coincided with that of the Americans. Washington and London concurred: "...even the bases that Churchill had made such a fuss over would be of little use. Ever since the Germans wrested control of the French coast in 1940, the shipping routes off the south coast of Ireland – for which southern ports had provided strategic protection during the First World War – were too exposed and were no longer of use because *Allied shipping had to take the safer route by Northern Ireland, where the Allies already had bases.*"[21] [emphasis added] The volume of merchant tonnage sent to the bottom doubled after the Germans established submarine bases in the French Channel ports. Despite the fact that all convoys were routed to the North of Ireland, Churchill and the Americans continued to falsely claim that Allied seamen were dying by the thousands off the coast of Southern Ireland because of a lack of access to the Irish ports.

Dwyer was astute enough to see through the sham. "Ireland's accession to the Allied cause would actually have hurt the war effort because the Allies would have become morally obliged to divert men and equipment to protect not only useless facilities, but also virtually undefended Irish cities."[22]

If the ports were of so little military value, why was so much made out of so little by Churchill and de Valera? The nationalist rhetoric on both sides was play-acting aimed at an American audience. The performance was meant to raise suspicions of Irish treachery against the mother country and, later, against the United States.

Martin Quigley, Office of Strategic Services (OSS) operative in Ireland during the Second World War, unaware of the secret agreement between de Valera and the British regarding the propaganda campaign over the use of the Irish ports, took Churchill's rhetoric seriously. He made a clandestine approach in an effort to obtain Allied access to the bases, and suggested that the Irish would loan the ports to the United States in return for American help to end partition after the war. His proposal was unceremoniously rejected by the Chief of the Imperial Staff with a curt rebuff: "The present situation suits us completely."[23]

Tim Pat Coogan remained skeptical as to the significance of de Valera's neutrality and the insignificance of the Irish ports to England and the Allies: "Was de Valera's neutrality policy as harmful to the British as alleged?...The short answer...is no. Irish neutrality was not the main reason that the mackerel grew fat off the West Coast of Ireland...Nor were the Southern ports as strategically important to the British war effort as was claimed."[24]

The Battle of Britain raged from July to September 1940, when an outnumbered RAF took on the Luftwaffe and downed more than a thousand German aircraft, effectively eliminating any threat of a German invasion of England or Ireland. Churchill used his enhanced prestige to counter Irish-American opposition to the United States entering the war on the side of England. The day after FDR's election victory in November 1940, Churchill let loose on the Irish with a vicious attack on de Valera for his failure to open up the ports. He announced in the House of Commons: "The fact that we cannot use the south and west coasts of Ireland to refuel our flotillas and aircraft and thus protect the trade by which Ireland, as well as Great Britain lives, is a most heavy and grievous burden and one which should never have been placed on our shoulders, broad as they be..."[25] Coogan commented: "In saying this, Churchill was not merely fomenting anti-Irish sentiment but was articulating feelings that were already widespread in Britain and America."[26]

The well-orchestrated press campaign, both in England and America, signaled that propaganda and not bullets was to be the weapon of choice the British were to employ against Ireland and the Irish-Americans. The American public was outraged that the Irish were enjoying the benefits of neutrality under the protection of a struggling and valiant England.

As First Lord of the Admiralty, Churchill was privy to the strategic assessment of the insignificance of the Irish ports but he continually bawled, for American consumption, that withholding of the ports was indeed a grievous cross to bear. "Churchill advocated seizing the ports at a Cabinet meeting on October, 29, 1939, but Chamberlain warned that the move would have most unfortunate repercussions in the United States. At that time, the Americans were in the process of amending their neutrality laws [to provide Britain, under the Lend Lease legislature, all the armaments it required] and unless it became a question of life or death for Britain, the Cabinet decided against seizing the bases."[27] Churchill's ruse convinced Longford and O'Neill: "It would not be quite true though close to the truth to say that Churchill urged the invasion of Ireland...If it had not been for Chamberlain...Ireland might have been faced with a very nasty situation..."[28]

Churchill, who had no intention of invading Ireland, kept up his bombastic performance. On January 17, 1940, he wrote: "Should the danger to our war effort through the denial of Irish bases threaten to become mortal, which is not the case at present, we should have to act in accordance with our own self-preservation and that of our Cause."[29] His repeated calls to reclaim the ports by force finally convinced Chamberlain. During the War Cabinet discussion of June 20, 1940: "A curious reversal of roles was now apparent. Chamberlain, who had previously opposed the use of force against Éire, was now its chief proponent, while Churchill...tried to moderate the discussion."[30] After a private session with Churchill, no more was heard from Chamberlain about seizing the ports.

In the summer of 1941, American technicians began constructing a huge naval and military base in Londonderry, Northern Ireland. In pursuance of his campaign to irritate the Americans, de Valera protested to Gray that the United States was occupying Irish territory which he considered integral to a united Ireland and that he would not waive Irish sovereignty. In October, the Irish President instructed the Éire Representative in Washington, Robert Brennan, to determine American intentions as to the Londonderry/Lough Foyle base. "When an informal inquiry was brushed aside, Brennan sent a formal note, which provoked a terse response. Roosevelt authorized the State Department to reply that the request related to territory recognized by the United States as part of the United Kingdom and therefore, the Irish Government should address its inquiry to the United Kingdom Government. This contemptuous treatment of the Irish claim to sovereignty over Northern Ireland was indicative of the deterioration in relations between Dublin and Washington before the Americans entered the war in December 1941."[31]

For centuries, England maintained that the Irish ports of Bereshaven, Lough Swilly, and Queenstown were necessary in order to protect her trade routes and to prevent any foreign power from using Ireland as a base to invade England. During the First World War, the three Irish ports served as British naval patrol stations and convoy assembly points to and from the United States, forming an arc of approximately 500 miles from Lough Swilly in the north to Queenstown in the southeast, with a naval ship range of from 200-400 miles into the Atlantic. England was able to dispatch her patrol vessels from these ports into the Atlantic to attack the German submarine menace and to provide limited protection for the vital convoys from America because the Germans never occupied the French Channel ports during the First World War.

"Following the fall of France, the British supply lanes along the southwest of Ireland became so vulnerable to attack by French-based air and sea raiders that Atlantic convoys were routed north, towards the safety of the coast of Scotland..."[32] With the Germans in control of the French Channel ports, the southern Ireland ports were of negligible military value. Lough Swilly, situated only a few miles from the huge Northern Ireland port of Londonderry, was merely superfluous. Due to the menace of German bombers and submarines from the French Channel ports, convoys from the United States were routed through the northern sea-lanes to Londonderry and Belfast and further north to the west coast of England and Scotland and even further north to Murmansk, Russia. With England in control of the ports in Northern Ireland, the Southern Ireland ports were indeed excess baggage, and expensive baggage at that.

From August 1942 through early 1943, only the Atlantic Ocean's "Greenland Gap" was beyond the range of Allied air protection for convoys from America to England. The German submarine wolf packs gathered at this location in relative safety and stalked the Allied convoys. Eventually, Allied air cover, with bases in Canada, Greenland, Iceland,

Northern Ireland, and England closed this gap and provided protection throughout the convoy's northern route. Air and ship patrols from Northern Ireland ports of Londonderry and Belfast were more than adequate to protect the sea lanes around Ireland from German air and sea marauders.

In his eagerness to smear de Valera and the Irish as anti-American and pro-German, Gray falsely reported that Southern Ireland's ports were strategically more important to America's first line of defense than that of Iceland. Churchill continued to bemoan the return of the ports even after the war: "I remain convinced that the gratuitous surrender of our right to use the Irish ports in war was a major injury to British national life and safety. A more feckless act can hardly be imagined and at such a time. Many a ship and many a life was soon to be lost as a result of this improvident example of appeasement."[33]

As far back as August 10, 1914, U.S. Ambassador to Germany, James Gerard, with ominous prescience, alluded to a future World War: "Russia beaten and half-digested, France would have been an easy prey. Great Britain, even if their joining France in war, would have a far different problem to face if the U-boats were sailing from Cherbourg, Calais, Brest and Bordeaux on the mission of piracy and murder and then would come our [America's] turn and that of Latin America."[34]

Coogan recognized the propaganda value being squeezed out of Éire's refusal to cede the ports: "It is fair to say that many of the beliefs [which lingered for years after the war] about the loss of seamen's lives occasioned by the denial of the Irish ports were grounded more in the propaganda campaign against Ireland in the American and British media than in fact."[35] But Coogan failed to analyze the motivation behind the slurs. Nor did anyone question why de Valera did not refute the charges after the war.

Notes

1. Watt, Donald, Cameron, *How War Came, The Immediate Origins of the Second World War 1938-39*, Pantheon Books, Div. of Random House, William Heineman Ltd. London 1989, p. 130
2. *ibid*, p. 128
3. Dwyer, T. Ryle, *De Valera, The Man & the Myths*, Poolbeg, Dublin, 1991, p. 218
4. *ibid*, p. 219
5. Watt, Donald, Cameron, *How War Came, The Immediate Origins of the Second World War 1938-39*, Pantheon Books, Div. of Random House, William Heineman Ltd. London 1989, p. 27

6. *ibid*, p. 100
7. Johnson, D.S., "Northern Ireland as a Problem in the Economic War 1932 – 1938", *Irish Historical Studies*, Vol. XXII , p. 150
8. Longford, Earl of & O'Neill, Thomas P., *Éamon de Valera*, Hutchinson, London, 1970, p. 316
9. Smyllie, Robert, "Unneutral Neutral Éire", *Foreign Affairs* (Council on Foreign Relations, p. 318
10. Coogan, Tim P., *De Valera, The Man who was Ireland*, Harper, 1996, p. 519
11. Longford, Earl of & O'Neill, Thomas P., *Éamon de Valera*, Hutchinson, London, 1970, p. 324
12. Dwyer, T. Ryle, *De Valera, The Man & the Myths*, Poolbeg, Dublin, 1991, p. 62
13. Coogan, Tim P., *De Valera, The Man who was Ireland*, Harper, 1996, p. 531
14. Chatfield, Lord, *It Might Happen Again*, Wm Heineman, London 1947, p. 126
15. Stephan, Enno, *Spies in Ireland*, Stackpole, Harrisburg, 1965, p. 186
16. Coogan, Tim P., *De Valera, The Man who was Ireland*, Harper, 1996, p. 598
17. Fisk, Robert, *In Time of War*, U. Penn Press, Philadelphia, 1983, p. 363
18. Dwyer, T. Ryle, *De Valera, The Man & the Myths*, Poolbeg, Dublin, 1991, p. 267
19. Longford, Earl of & O'Neill, Thomas P., *Éamon de Valera*, Hutchinson, London, 1970, p. 403
20. Dwyer, T. Ryle, *De Valera, The Man & the Myths*, Poolbeg, Dublin, 1991, p. 274
21. Dwyer, T. Ryle, *Éamon de Valera*, Gill & Macmillan, 1980, p. 124
22. *ibid*, p. 124
23. Quigley, Martin S., *Peace without Hiroshima*, Madison Books, New York, 1991, p. 21
24. Coogan, Tim P., *De Valera, The Man who was Ireland*, Harper, 1996, p. 566
25. Longford, Earl of & O'Neill, Thomas P., *Éamon de Valera*, Hutchinson, London, 1970, p. 373
26. Coogan, Tim P., *De Valera, The Man who was Ireland*, Harper, 1996, p. 558
27. Dwyer, T. Ryle, *De Valera, The Man & the Myths*, Poolbeg, Dublin, 1991, p. 230
28. Longford, Earl of & O'Neill, Thomas P., *Éamon de Valera*, Hutchinson, London, 1970, p. 355
29. Dwyer, T. Ryle, *De Valera, The Man & the Myths*, Poolbeg, Dublin, 1991, p. 253
30. Fisk, Robert, *In Time of War*, U. Penn Press, Philadelphia, 1983, p. 195
31. Dwyer, T. Ryle, *De Valera, The Man & the Myths*, Poolbeg, Dublin, 1991, p. 258
32. Coogan, Tim P., *De Valera, The Man who was Ireland*, Harper, 1996, p. 567
33. Gerard, James J., *My Four years in Germany*, G.H. Doran, N.Y. 1917, p. 205
34. Longford, Earl of & O'Neill, Thomas P., *Éamon de Valera*, Hutchinson, London, 1970, p. 315
35. Coogan, Tim P., *De Valera, The Man who was Ireland*, Harper, 1996, p. 567

CHAPTER XXVI

"Assignment Neutrality"

"Thus it will always happen that he who is not your friend will demand your neutrality, While he who is your friend will entreat you to declare yourself with arms, and, irresolute princes, to avoid present dangers, generally follow the neutral path and are generally ruined." Machiavelli

The best-kept secret of the Second World War was Ireland's contribution to the Allied victory. Éamon de Valera's phony neutrality was a monumental propaganda success for the English and another disaster for Ireland.

On September 2, 1939, the day after Germany invaded Poland and a little over a year after the return of the Irish ports, de Valera admitted at a session of the Dáil that the Irish people did not favor his neutrality stance. "It is not as representing the sentiments or feelings of our people that the Government stands before you with this policy. It stands before you as the guardian of the interests of our people and it is to guard these interests as best we can that we are proposing to follow the policy [of neutrality]."[1]

On July 17, 1941, James Dillon, deputy leader of Fine Gael (United Ireland Party), was the only Dáil member to challenge de Valera's neutrality policy. Such was the reigning consensus that he got booted out of his own party for his valiant efforts. Dillon foresaw the inevitable postwar American reaction: "I say that if we lose (the friendship of America) now, we will find ourselves, postwar, without a single friend in the world...I say that in my judgment those who withhold from the United States of America and Great Britain and the united nations the help which would assist them to overcome this world peril are, in fact, helping that peril to prevail."[2]

President Franklin Delano Roosevelt admonished de Valera for his decision to stay out of the war. "'At some future date when Axis aggression has been crushed by the military might of free peoples, the nations of the earth must gather about a peace table to plan the future world on foundations of liberty and justice everywhere. I think it only right that I make plain at this time that when that time comes the Irish Government, in its own best interest, should not stand alone but should be associated with its traditional friends, and among them, the United States of America.' That 'stand alone' reference foreshadowed the isolation and stagnation which befell Ireland after the war."[3]

As Roosevelt and Dillon had predicted, de Valera's "neutrality" turned every friend of Ireland against her. David Gray, U.S. Representative to Éire, wrote: "It was the step which after Pearl Harbor led him to announce to Washington, 'Neutrality – No Change,' and committed him to his policy of stupidity, double-dealing and disaster..."[4]

There were remarkable similarities between England's policies towards Ireland in the First and Second World Wars such as allegations of "pro-German" bias; concerted attempts to manipulate Irish-American influence; the characterization of the Irish as shirkers and traitors and the denial of the spoils of war. The Winnie and Dev collaboration was a grotesque drama that destroyed Ireland's collective morale.

De Valera's impact on Ireland was worse than that of Oliver Cromwell in the seventeenth century. Whereas Cromwell destroyed the body, de Valera destroyed the soul of Ireland. Cromwell employed an alien army to slaughter the Irish under the banner, "To Hell or Connaught", while de Valera was more insidious as he set Irishman against Irishman, father against son, and brother against brother under the motto of "The majority had no right to do wrong." More than a million Irish men, women, and children emigrated from Ireland to England, America, and Australia during the de Valera era; more than at any time except during the genocidal Victorian era of the nineteenth century.

The American public was outraged at de Valera's alleged pro-German neutrality. As a result, Irish-American opposition to Anglo-American cooperation was drowned in a torrent of invective. In Ireland, however, de Valera was hailed as a hero, a slayer of the St. George dragon, the man who stood up to the English bulldog.

Under a paper wall of disinformation, England's propaganda juggernaut muffled the valiant efforts of Irish soldiers who fought and died side by side with the English and later the Americans. England had accepted Irish men and women into her Armed Forces by the hundreds of thousands, but neither England nor Ireland recognized their contributions and sacrifices in the manner they deserved. Despite painting the Irish as pro-German, Churchill ultimately acknowledged the magnificent contribution of the Irish to the war effort. In a speech in the House of Commons on March 14, 1944, shortly after simultaneous notes from England and the United States demanded de Valera recall the German and Japanese representatives in Ireland, Churchill forecast travel and economic restrictions prior to invasion preparations: "I need scarcely say how painful it is to us to take such measures *in view of the large numbers of Irishmen who are fighting so bravely in our armed forces and the many deeds of personal heroism by which they have kept alive the martial honor of the Irish race.* [emphasis added] No one, I think, can reproach us for precipitancy. No nation in the world would have been so patient."[5] Eight natives of the Free State won the Victoria Cross, Britain's highest honor for gallantry in action – proportionately more Irish were awarded the honor than even the English.

De Valera's censorship clipped news of the heroism of 200,000 Irish volunteers who flocked to England's colors – one out of three sacrificing their lives for England and the Allied cause, a loss of life proportionately greater than that of even England or America. Tens of thousands of Irish volunteers returned home crippled in body, mind, and spirit, their sacrifices unrecognized and unappreciated by England but more cruelly by the de Valera government and the strutting Fianna Fáil counterfeit Republicans, who shunned those who had sacrificed so much not only for the Allied cause but assuredly for Irish freedom.

Two million American soldiers made it to France in the First World War of whom 53,000 died in battle and 63,000 of accident and disease, approximately five-percent overall. The British assembled an army of over four million men of which twenty-five percent – 990,000, an entire generation – were buried in the mud of France.

During the Second World War, seven centuries of English oppression in Ireland were set aside by the Irish people. It was not only England's but Ireland's finest hour as well. More than half a million Irish men and women sweated in cold and damp English and Northern Ireland factories, hammering out the sinews of war, enabling England to survive the initial German onslaught until America's massive military and economic forces turned the tide of battle. All these things the Irish willingly gave to the English and Allied cause, but they received only bitter denunciation and world condemnation in return. Thanks to de Valera, never before had a nation sacrificed so much for a victory over evil and been so unjustly condemned for their noble commitment.

It was actually the Unionists, self-proclaimed "Loyalists" of Northern Ireland, who sat out the Second World War growing fat on no-show jobs and unemployment checks. During the war years, the unemployment rolls in Northern Ireland soared as high as 28 percent. The slaughter of so many Northern Ireland Volunteers in the First World War triggered a backlash of military service evaders refusing to join the British Armed Forces in the Second World War. Without conscription, they opted for the safety of the Ulster Defense Force (UDF), which had ostensibly been organized to protect Northern Ireland from IRA subversion whereas in practice, it was used as an instrument of anti-Catholic repression.

After the war, the world community ostracized Southern Ireland. Emigration to the United States was downsized to a trickle; partition was accepted as a permanent reality and Irish-American influence was rendered powerless. Paradoxically, de Valera projected Ireland in a bad light internationally, while the Irish Press touted him as "standing up" to the English and Americans, thereby attaining the status of an Irish legend at home.

The British were able to trivialize Irish-American opposition to partition. America's championing of independence for her allies in the First World War was not lost on the British or de Valera. The Irish President rejected American recognition of virtual Irish independence at the 1920 American presidential conventions and twenty years later his neutrality policy kept Ireland clear of any postwar spoils. An obvious corollary to Ireland's public declaration of war against the Axis Powers would be Ireland's rightful seat at the postwar peace conference and a justified call for American and United Nations' influence to end partition. With Ireland an active recognized participant in the war, the powerful Irish-American bloc would have exerted enormous pressure for a resolution of the "Irish Question."

On the other hand, it was of paramount importance to England's postwar interests that Ireland should not enter the war on the side of the Allies. Churchill often thundered warnings that an independent Ireland threatened the entire fabric of the British Empire, with Egypt and India closely watching the Irish saga with eyes on their own future independence.

Irish neutrality vexed Americans, especially Roosevelt, who never forgave Ireland. For more than fifty years, future American administrations adopted an economic hard-line toward Ireland, restricted Irish immigration and relegated partition to an internal matter of England. In a speech in Belfast in October 1945, General Dwight D. Eisenhower was disparaging by implication: "Without Northern Ireland, I do not see how American forces could have concentrated to begin the invasion of Europe. If Ulster had not been a definite, cooperative part of the British Empire and had not been available for our use, I do not see how the buildup could have been carried out in England."[6]

Irish participation in the Allied war effort deserved recognition but Irish credit was spoiled by de Valera's neutrality policy and his curious stage management. De Valera went so far as to outfit the Irish Army in German-style helmets and, when pictures of them were published abroad, it only confirmed the public perception that the Irish were pro-Nazi. Worse was his decision to pay his condolences to the German delegation upon Hitler's death. This was a public relations masterstroke by the British and put an end to Ireland's hopes for post-war recovery aid. Thereafter, American public opinion was overwhelmingly in favour of the British, their steadfast allies, rather than the Irish "Nazis" who had mourned Hitler's passing. Whenever a pro-Irish or anti-British issue surfaced in the halls of Congress, all the sordid propaganda of Ireland's pro-Nazi conduct during the war was paraded before the American people.

Roosevelt accepted Churchill's vilification of Ireland, knowing that Irish-American influences had to be curbed if his support for Britain was to find favour with the American public. FDR witnessed firsthand de Valera's destruction of Irish-American influence in 1919-20 and was only too happy to cooperate with Churchill and de Valera in a repeat performance by the Irish President. Tim Pat Coogan commented: "Both Gray and Roosevelt hoped that the war would provide the means of destroying the influence of the professional hyphenated Irish-American politician."[7] De Valera did the job for them.

Neutrality under the best of circumstances is a position of dishonor, self-interest, and weakness of spirit and resolve, especially when the issues are as clear-cut as in the distinction between the evil of Nazism and Democracy during the Second World War. Ireland could and should have fulfilled her destiny by coming to the aid of small countries throughout the world. For centuries, Ireland advocated the right of defenseless nations to choose their own governments in sovereign freedom without coercion. Yet, when it came time to speak out against the Nazi terror and expansionism, de Valera's silence was deafening. His support for Chamberlain's partitioning of another small nation, Czechoslovakia, to appease Hitler, was unconscionable.

Shortly after the start of the war, Malcolm MacDonald, the son of the British Prime Minister, Ramsey MacDonald, made a proposal to de Valera: "If Britain declared a united Ireland in principle would de Valera be prepared to abandon neutrality and join the Allies?" de Valera, in a typically convoluted answer, stated: "'If there were not only a declaration of a United Ireland in principle, but also agreement upon its constitution, then the Government of Éire might agree to enter the war at once, but the constitution of a United Ireland would have to be fixed first.' MacDonald retorted, 'The British Government would need more than just a "might" to go on.' But this was as far as de Valera would go. In fact, he candidly added that there was 'a very big question mark after the "might."'"[8]

In a move deliberately calculated to offend the Allies, the Irish leader declared that even if such an assurance were given, he would not bargain away neutrality. In a statement designed to outrage Americans, de Valera declared: "The only solution would be for Northern Ireland to withdraw from the war and agree to unity, then the new United Irish Parliament would consider declaring war on Germany. He frankly warned, however, that such a declaration would probably be defeated, even if he supported it."[9]

As de Valera had repeatedly done before by rejecting not only America's recognition of Ireland's right to self-determination but also the freedoms outlined in the Free State Treaty, he now scorned the reunification of Ireland when it was in his grasp. Robert Smyllie argued that the Irish people were duped: "The truth about Éire's neutrality is well-known by the British and American governments; unhappily, it is not so well-known by the British and American people, many of whom still regard the Southern Irish as the black sheep of the English-speaking world."[10]

According to Martin Quigley, an Office of Strategic Services (OSS) operative in Ireland: "History apparently will never catch up with reality and forever people may look down on Ireland for failing to help the Allies in the Second World War...For their own personal and political reasons, each [de Valera and Churchill] said much to conceal the fact that Éire was a significant help to the Allies and was neutral in name only – a *fact clearly known to the Germans and Japanese.*"[11] [emphasis added] The British, American, and especially the German governments knew the extent of Ireland's contribution to the Allied war effort, yet Irish writers never considered the possibility that de Valera's phony neutrality may have been a deliberate conspiracy to promote himself at home while disparaging his country internationally.

U.S. representative to Éire, David Gray, was an ardent Anglophile and FDR supporter. Looking ahead towards postwar politics, Gray recognized that the "Partition Question" was a major problem for future Anglo-American relations unless the Irish-American influence was neutralized. In his devotion to FDR, Gray continued to issue cables to America critical of Ireland's non-existent "pro-German" activities.

In a shameless betrayal of their own countrymen who made the ultimate sacrifice, there is not one public memorial throughout Ireland specifically dedicated to Irish men and women who served with the Allied forces in the Second World War. Islandbridge, Dublin, has a monument dedicated to the Irish volunteers who served in the First World War when Ireland was considered a part of Britain. Traditional Armistice Day commemorations in Dublin presented another paradox, which typified Ireland's confused loyalties. The Free State government of William Cosgrave was traditionally represented, while de Valera's followers boycotted the annual ceremony considering those who served in the British armed forces as traitors.

De Valera privately conceded that England and the Allies held the moral position in the war; he also admitted that Ireland would go the way of Poland, Belgium, and Holland, if the British were defeated. Yet he refused to recognize the sacrifice of 200,000 Irish men and women who fought with the Allies to prevent Ireland going the way of the small countries of Europe.

Incredibly, the only memorial in Ireland for the dead of the 1939-45 conflict is to German pilots. Rather than remember its own sons who died fighting for Ireland's freedom, the Government approved a German war memorial located on the road between Enniskerry and Glencree, in County Wicklow, outside Dublin. In the cemetery are the bodies of Luftwaffe airmen as well as German naval personnel who died in an abortive attempt to enslave the world, including Ireland.[12]

By their silence, Irish writers denied the heroism of those men and women who sacrificed life and limb for the Allied cause and Irish freedom. Benumbed by de Valera's propaganda and a slave press, the Irish remain in national denial as to Ireland's gallant role in the war.

The charge that the Irish profited by their wartime exports to England are also without foundation. "Good prices were paid in terms of paper money, but Ireland got very little back in the form of imports...Credits – approximately £300 to £400 million [$2.0 billion] a huge sum for such a small country – were piled up in London, only to be 'frozen' automatically by the British Government. Ireland has no immediate hope of utilizing these swollen credits for the purchase of the capital goods, machinery and the like, of which she stands so badly in need; so Ireland did not do very well by her wartime sales to Great Britain after all."[13]

John Redmond, the Irish Parliamentary Party leader, had been dubbed the "recruiting sergeant" for England during the First World War. Compared to Redmond; de Valera was more of a recruiting general for the English in the Second World War. In violation of neutrality standards, de Valera overtly and covertly encouraged enlistment in the British armed forces. De Valera turned a blind eye when over "4,000 members of the Irish Army, or exactly ten percent of the total force, deserted during the war to join the British Army...he easily might have followed the example of other neutral countries by passing a Foreign Enlistment Act, making it an offense, punishable by loss of all civil rights, to join the fighting services of any of the belligerent powers."[14]

The Irish were free to join the British armed forces. "The fact they did so in comparatively large numbers provides almost a complete answer to those who have been holding Ireland up as a hate-ridden nation, eager for Britain's humiliation and defeat."[15] Enno Stephan also commented on de Valera's qualified neutrality: "In spite of her neutrality, Ireland is giving tangible and significant proof of which side her sympathies lie... [de Valera] has, for example, dispensed with issuing any prohibition against enlistment in foreign services, so that the number of Irish volunteers in the British services exceeds 150,000."[16]

De Valera and the British agreed to a joint purchasing arrangement in shipping, which was clearly to the disadvantage of the Irish. There was stricter gas rationing in Ireland than in Britain, due to de Valera having turned over the entire Irish fleet of seven oil tankers to England. He sacrificed Ireland's merchant marine in an effort to eliminate competition and keep shipping rates low, a decided advantage to England. Non-British ships had to pay whatever rates the British set. Ultimately, the British cut oil supplies to Ireland, leaving the Irish without oil or its ships. Once again, Ireland lost out to Britain.

Churchill, in his book, *The Grand Alliance*, revealed the real reason why the Irish ports were useless: "Denied the use of the English Channel by German occupation of the Channel ports, denied the use of Cobh and the Lee and Shannon estuaries [Bereshaven] by Éire neutrality, all shipping by necessity was routed around the North of Ireland."[17] The German submarine pens in the Channel ports made southern Ireland's ports strategically worthless and a northern convoy route imperative.

Churchill was relentless in his staged attacks on Ireland. In a note to Roosevelt, justifying his decision to cancel shipping 400,000 tons of supplies to Ireland, he stated: "You will realize that our merchant seamen, as well as public opinion generally, take it much amiss that we should have to carry Irish supplies through air and U-boat attacks and subsidize them handsomely when de Valera's quite content to sit happy and see us strangled."[18] The British Prime Minister ramped up his vilification campaign with ludicrous yarns spun about huge spy nests in the Dublin legations of the Germans, Italians, and Japanese. A particularly nonsensical charge claimed that German U-boat bases were operating in Ireland with German crews frolicking in Irish pubs.

Churchill and Gray's propaganda blitz falsely claimed thousands of American and British seamen were being drowned by German submarines sinking Allied ships silhouetted against the "bright lights" of Ireland's almost barren West Coast. Indeed, American sailors died and their ships were sunk silhouetted by bright lights – not along the bleak Irish coast but by the brightly lit American cities along the eastern seaboard of the United States. The War Shipping Administration in Washington, D.C. confirmed 1,554 U.S. Merchant ships sunk in the Atlantic with 172 sunk along the East Coast of America. No statistics were available for the number of ships sunk off the coast of Southern Ireland.

One example of the worldwide disdain generated by de Valera's neutrality was to be found in Nicholas Monsarrat's book, *The Cruel Sea:* "'[I]t is difficult to withhold one's contempt from a country such as Ireland whose battle this was and whose chances of freedom and independence in the event of a German victory were nil. The fact that Ireland was standing aloof from the conflict...affected, sometimes mortally, all sailors engaged in the Atlantic and earned their special loathing...To compute how many men and how many ships this denial was costing, month after month, was hardly possible... Escorts had to go "the long way round" to the battlefield...The cost, in men and ships, added months to the struggle and ran up a score that Irish eyes a-smiling on the day of the Allied victory were not going to cancel...In the list of people you were prepared to like when the war was over, the man who stood by and watched while you were getting your throat cut could not figure very high.' Such writing encapsulates what may be termed the case for the prosecution against de Valera's neutrality policy..."[19]

In his constant efforts to denigrate the Irish before the American public, Gray, who knew better, falsely charged: "Too many British and American sailors lie on the floor of the Western Approaches who might now be among the living but for that betrayal and the denial of the Irish ports. We, who at that time failed them, through ignorance, misplaced trust and credulity, owe them [sailors] at the least that their sacrifice should not be forgotten or in vain."[20]

Contrary to the propaganda, more Irish seamen died as a result of Allied policies than did Allied seamen as a result of Irish policy. De Valera's neutrality and shipping policies actually raised the risks for Irish mariners. In an effort to prevent neutral shipping supplies from reaching Germany, the British utilized a "Navicert System." Any ships not identified by Navicert, which broadcast a coded identification, risked being sunk. Contrary to Monsarrat's erroneous contention, Irish ships had to follow set routes, even though they may have added more than a thousand miles to the voyage. The longer Irish ships were at sea, the greater risk of sinking by German submarines. Coogan cited the contemptuous treatment of Irish seamen by the Allies: "When they traveled in convoy on the Atlantic routes, the Irish ships were generally given the most dangerous, outside positions..."[21]

In the first year of the war, neutrality resulted in at least four Irish ships being sunk by German attacks, costing the lives of nearly two-dozen Irish seamen. Two ships that had been turned over to the Irish by the Americans were sunk by German submarines; the *Irish Oak* in October 1942 and the *Irish Pine* in May 1943. De Valera filed no protest to the Germans over the sinkings, and Roosevelt refused to provide any more ships.

Under de Valera's neutrality, not a single Allied seaman was ever interned but more than two hundred German sailors captured during the course of the war were interned for the duration. Forty-eight of the German seamen were from a U-boat sunk by the RAF, thanks to a report from Irish coast watchers. The German seamen "were all distressed mariners and should therefore have been freed under international law, but de Valera interned them anyway..."[22]

The joint English and American propaganda efforts had their desired effect in America. In response to de Valera's rejection of an Allied request to expel the Axis delegations, *The New York Times* printed a baseless editorial of March 12, 1944: "No Germans have died as a result of this [Irish] neutrality but many Allied ships have certainly been sunk and many Allied sailors have certainly drowned because Allied anti-submarine patrols had no access to Southern Ireland's harbors...On the eve of the invasion of Europe, such information may be sufficient to endanger the lives of many thousands of Allied soldiers...It may be sufficient to prolong the war, adding incalculably to its horrors...That day [of a United Ireland] will be brought no nearer if Mr. De Valera's coldly correct policy of neutrality between absolute evil and the promise of goodness and peace results, as it may, in needless slaughter on the European coasts."[23]

De Valera publicly rejected a British-proposed joint Anglo-Irish force to patrol the seas off the coast of Ireland. Instead, he established a network of Irish coast-watchers who initially broadcast German submarine and aircraft sightings to the world. "Before long, these messages were sent by the Irish in a code secretly supplied by the British, with the result that Irish coast-watchers were effectively working for the British, though only de Valera and very few others knew this at the time."[24]

The Irish also provided wireless beacons as navigational aids for Allied planes. De Valera authorized British manned radar stations along the Irish coast to direct anti-submarine operations. With the Irish President's approval, the English "violated" Irish air and sea space at will in their rush to any submarine sightings reported by Irish coast watchers.

Contrary to reports of his refusing to aid England for fear of retribution from the Germans, within months of the outbreak of hostilities, de Valera entered into secret negotiations with the English, offering whatever help Ireland could provide. His initial proposals to the English were made even before the most perilous Battle of Britain in June, July, and August 1940, when the outcome of the war was seriously in doubt. "De Valera used Walshe as a conduit for secret offers of cooperation...and sent him to London to suggest staff talks with the British in May 1940."[25] The Irish President provided covert assistance to the British government: deliberate attempts were made to conceal that fact, not from the Germans, but from the American, English, and Irish people. When a leak occurred in July 1940 over his secret aid to the English, de Valera became apoplectic. "Talk of a military 'pact' had been published and had done great harm. De Valera begged John L. Maffey, United Kingdom Representative to Éire, to ensure that the Anglo-Irish military liaison should be kept as secret as possible...If the Germans found out, they might retaliate but *if the Irish people learned, it would undermine the importance of the country's supposed neutrality as an expression of Irish independence.*"[26] [emphasis added]

Dwyer described the close cooperation between Ireland and the United States over intelligence. "The most striking example of the real benevolence of Irish policy was in the area of intelligence. In January 1943, Walshe approached the Americans with an official offer to cooperate with the OSS..."[27] Furthermore, "The extent of the Irish cooperation was such that the head of the Éire desk at U.S. Office of Strategic Services (OSS) headquarters, R. Carter Nicholas, inquired on September 27, 1943 if Irish diplomats in occupied Europe could be used as American agents. De Valera was consulted and arrangements were made for the OSS to furnish questions, which the Department of External Affairs dispatched to Irish diplomats in Berlin, Rome and Vichy, then transmitting the answers to the OSS. Such cooperation made a mockery of Ireland's supposed neutrality."[28] Irish neutrality was actually a laughing matter. "The OSS sent two undercover agents to Ireland. Both were quickly uncovered but, rather than expelling them, the Irish authorities actually welcomed them..."[29] Typical of Gray's brooking no interference with his Irish-bashing scheme, Ervin Marlin, an OSS agent assigned to the American Embassy, reported: "Contrary to Gray's belief, Irish intelligence efficiency was such that the threat from German spies was non-existent. Gray was displeased and asked for Marlin's recall."[30]

De Valera went so far afield of neutrality as to even appoint his son, Vivion, and Irish General Dan McKenna to coordinate military strategies critical to the Allied cause with British General Franklyn. Such policies were forged at secret meetings and never publicly revealed.

Only after the United States declared war on the Axis powers, did the British reveal the extent of Irish cooperation to Gray. He was shocked, and reported to the U.S. State Department on March 23, 1942: "A mutual good feeling and confidence have been established between the Irish and British military chiefs beyond what might reasonably have been believed possible. The same facilities were extended to the Americans, but relations between the two countries continued to deteriorate..."[31]

The Irish Leader deliberately goaded the Americans into an anti-Irish frenzy by an outrageous charge of American brutality against Irish priests in the Philippines. Gray said, "...as the Japanese were being driven out of Manila by General MacArthur, Japanese troops crucified Irish priests by nailing them to doors with bayonets. This put de Valera's newspaper in an embarrassing position, since, in order to spare Japanese sensibilities it had suggested that in the general confusion, Americans might have killed the priests."[32]

As the war neared its conclusion, the United States and Britain considered their strategies for peace. It was critical for Britain that she should document publicly Ireland's alleged support for the Axis powers. Americans were not likely to oppose Britain's position on Northern Ireland if convinced of Éire's "aid and comfort" to Germany and Japan. Gray and Churchill's trumped-up charges of Irish support for the Axis Powers effectively stymied the possibility of the Irish-American lobby wielding influence. "For those outsiders deluded by the hostile propaganda, the Ireland which de Valera personified was a small-minded, backward, selfish place from which people emigrated in droves."[33]

In February 1944, Gray presented two diplomatic notes to de Valera which were strictly for propaganda purposes. The notes depicted the Irish as pro-Nazi collaborators: they cited the threat presented by the Japanese and Germans to Allied operations in Northern Ireland and demanded that de Valera expel their diplomats.

De Valera's response to the "Notes" campaign was fully anticipated: "As long as I am here my answer to this request must be – no!"[34] As Coogan recognized: "The request [Notes] was one to which it must have been known by the American Minister here, that the Irish Government could not possibly accede…It seemed designed therefore to put the Irish people in the wrong before the American public."[35] The incident produced the desired effect in America. *The New York Times*, on March 11, 1944, in banner headlines, heralded: "Irish Refuse to Oust Axis Envoys." "Éire is a base for espionage that imperils our Army." The article continued: "An appeal by the United States for the Irish Government to remove German and Japanese consular and diplomatic representatives from the country because of their espionage activities…has been rejected by Prime Minister Éamon de Valera…"[36]

In his ongoing campaign to denigrate the Irish, Gray leaked to the press, an absurd and unbelievable charge that hundreds of Japanese tourists were strolling about Ireland passing secret information to the Axis. It was such a ridiculous assertion that vacationing Japanese were traveling tens of thousands of miles to and from Ireland to frolic about the Emerald Isle, all during the blazing tumult of the war. The fact was that there were only four members of the Japanese delegation in Ireland throughout the entire war, and, for all intent and purpose, interned, restricted in their travel and communications.

John Maffey was mystified by England's harsh treatment of the Irish during the war and noted the substantial cooperation of the Irish during the conflict: "Germany would not be much more effectively represented in Dublin by Hempel than Greenland is by the Polar Bear. When it comes to practical measures for caging the Axis, the Irish will cooperate to any length…de Valera had always been anxious to help us to the utmost…"[37]

Erskine Childers II said the Fifth Column Movement [IRA]: "had been exaggerated very much…The Germans and Italians were continually watched and their telephones tapped."[38] The only difference between IRA internment and the Axis was that jail cells enclosed the former and restrictions as to movement bounded the latter.

According to Churchill's son, Randolph: "the whole [neutrality] arrangement was simply 'a convenient fiction' to allow Dublin to help the Allies while preserving the appearance of neutrality."[39]

On March 14, Churchill announced to the Commons, "Measures had been taken to restrict the security risks posed by the Axis missions in Dublin…These measures must be strengthened and the restrictions on travel announced in the press yesterday are the first step in the policy designed to isolate Great Britain from Southern Ireland and also to isolate Southern Ireland from the outer world during the critical period which is now approaching."[40]

Churchill's attacks struck the usual Pavlovian chord, and the Irish once more rallied round their leader. To no one's surprise, the Irish Premier called a snap election in May 1944 and won by a landslide. "Fianna Fáil, which had lost its overall majority less than a year earlier, now romped home, gaining 17 seats to give the party a comfortable majority in the Dáil."[41] Churchill was instrumental in yet another de Valera election success.

In September 1944, Gray and Churchill presented another ultimatum to the Irish Premier, this time demanding: "... assurances that 'Axis war criminals' would not be given asylum in Ireland. De Valera responded that his Government would give no assurance which would preclude Ireland from exercising that right [to asylum] should justice, charity or the honor or interest of the nation so require."[42] On cue, American newspapers took de Valera to task for his refusal to turn over Nazi "war criminals," seeing that refusal as proof that Ireland was about to grant asylum to them.

On April 30, 1945, Gray, at a meeting with de Valera, demanded immediate access to the German legation before the German Minister to Ireland, Eduard Hempel, could order the destruction of vital documents concerning Nazi policy, and submarine activity in particular. "Mr. De Valera grew red and looked very sour. He was evidently annoyed, but his manners were correct. When I finished, he slapped the copy of the memorandum, which I had presented on his desk and said: 'This is a matter for my legal advisors. It is not a matter that I can discuss with you now...'"[43] Gray promptly leaked this latest "outrage" by de Valera and the American press hammered the Irish Premier's refusal to cooperate with the Allies.

Dwyer remarked on the manipulation of public opinion: "While Ireland was supposedly neutral, de Valera secretly authorized all the help he could to the Allies...It was therefore ironic that he should have been depicted by the English and American media as being anti-British to the point of being pro-Nazi. It was nonsense, but he was not too concerned about the gap between the public perception and the reality of his foreign policy, because *he managed to use it to his own domestic political advantage.*"[44] [emphasis added]

Longford and O'Neill were mistaken when they wrote: "The advantages of neutrality, however, had always been plain to de Valera. For a small nation, participation in a world conflict had few attractions with everything to lose and nothing to gain..."[45] The fact was that Ireland lost everything and gained nothing by remaining "neutral."

Gray outlined the advantage to Ireland of a mutual US-Ireland defense agreement similar to the US-Canada pact. "It would have meant the development of at least two more Irish ports besides Dublin, the rebuilding of the Irish rail and road systems, a dozen modern airfields and the equipping of the Irish Army with modern weapons. It would have ended Irish unemployment for six years or more. It would have meant for the Irish farmer free seeds, fertilizers, farm machines, fuel oils and war prices for Éire cattle and produce. It would have meant several billion dollars poured into the Irish economy besides the certainty of freedom from Hitler's yoke. It would have meant, after the war, a place at the head table with 'lamb, ham, and jam' instead of 'crow in the kitchen.' There would have been no need to 'hot up' the Partition grievance as an alibi. In all probability, Partition would have been ended and Irish rights in British markets restored..."[46]

When it came to recovery from the devastation of the war, America grudgingly granted Ireland only the barest of Marshall Plan aid as a political sop to the Irish-American bloc.

In an interview with Wallace Carroll of *United Press*, de Valera promoted the absurd line that the Germans would destroy Irish cities, as they were doing in England, if Ireland entered the war on the side of the Allies: "If we handed over the ports to Britain, we would thereby involve ourselves directly in the war, with all its consequences. You have seen what has happened to London, notwithstanding its defenses. Ireland is not a nation which can spend ten million pounds a day on armaments and if London is suffering, as it is, what would happen to Dublin, Cork or other Irish cities relatively unprotected?"[47]

De Valera masked the absurdity that the Fuhrer and his generals would be driven to irrational frenzy by Ireland's siding with the Allies thereby tipping the balance of world power. He maintained the ludicrous premise that if Ireland entered the war, the Germans would divert their entire air fleet, as they had done to London, and carpet bomb the "strategic" slums of Dublin, blitz the "formidable" potato patches in Kerry, and launch lightning assaults upon Irish "intelligence centers" set in haystacks throughout Southern Ireland. Examined in the light of facts, this fairy tale, aided and abetted by Irish writers, is just another scene in the black comedy of disinformation that has cursed Ireland for centuries.

Coogan parroted the Irish Premier's stalking horse – German retaliation – "It is impossible to estimate the saving in Irish lives which neutrality represented. The results of the two raids on Belfast...give some indication of the carnage, which might have been wrought on the handful of unprotected Southern Irish cities..."[48] This specious comparison of Belfast's huge military-industrial complex to poverty-stricken, slum-infested Dublin and other worse-off Éire cities was sheer nonsense.

Mary MacSwiney was more realistic than Coogan in regards to claims of retaliation by the Germans: "Does any sane person believe that Germany will pass over the country of her Number One Enemy [England] to convenience that enemy by attacking minor British objectives in Ireland?"[49]

De Valera's anti-Nazi policy was further illustrated by the denial of a German request to increase the size of their legation in Ireland. Hempel notified Walshe that a Lufthansa plane would be arriving within days to modify the personnel at the German legation in Dublin.

De Valera cabled the Irish *charge d'affaires* in Berlin, instructing him to notify Joachim von Ribbentrop, the German Foreign Minister: "The whole thing was politically impossible from our point of view." The threat of British seizure of the Irish ports was the reason for the denial. Hempel, in turn, was ordered by Ribbentrop to communicate to de Valera: "We must firmly expect the Irish Government to consent immediately in the facilitation customary in the transfer of members of a mission...The total replacement is a deceased officer, one new officer and one new assistant..."[50]

De Valera recognized the fact that under international law, the Germans had the right to increase or modify their delegation. But he "insisted that the new people should come 'by the ordinary ways of travel' – all of which involved a stopover in Britain..."[51] Of course, the Germans weren't about to land any members of a legation staff at a stopover in London and as a result, German plans for rotating its legation staff were dropped.

Any sustained attack on Southern Ireland's cities, which were little more than huge ghettos, might have been a favor to the Irish. The grave risk to German bombers and the paucity of a solitary worthwhile military target in all of Southern Ireland was hardly worth a single German bomber. By September 1940, the RAF had won the Battle of Britain, and German planes took to the air over England and Ireland at their peril. In his retaliation for de Valera's rebuff of the German request to reshuffle the German mission, Ribbentrop actually confirmed the lack of a single worthwhile target in Southern Ireland. Smarting over de Valera's rejection of a change in the delegation, the Germans initiated a "massive retaliatory air attack" on Ireland in January 1941. Rather than inflicting untold numbers of Irish dead, their strategic targets literally consisted of haystacks and cow barns.

Irish writers admitted that the Germans were well aware of Ireland's wholehearted support of the Allied cause, while maintaining the contradiction that if Ireland had publicly declared that fact, the Germans would have initiated a bombing "blitz" resulting in untold numbers of Irish dead.

Since the German, British and American governments were well aware of the Irish contribution to the Allied war effort, de Valera's apparent neutrality deception was intended solely to befuddle the Irish, English, and American people. As Coogan noted: "No Irish paper dared to print a word in favor of the Allied cause... *Whether the Irish Government was trying to humbug the people of Éire or was merely humbugging itself, nobody will ever know.* [emphasis added] One thing is quite certain – it was not humbugging the Germans, who knew the real situation from A to Z. They knew all about the number of Éire's citizens who were fighting and working for the British. They knew that, with the insignificant exception of a small minority of irreconcilables, the people of Southern Ireland were wholeheartedly on the side of the Allies..."[52] The Germans' only option lay in either having an ineffective legation in Ireland or not having one at all. They would take care of de Valera and the Irish after the German victory.

Prior to the war, when the Germans marched into Austria, de Valera privately told John Cudahy, the American representative to the Irish Free State: "Ireland would undoubtedly suffer a similar fate if England did not act as a shield against the continent. He was convinced, according to Cudahy, 'that the international political outlook of Ireland would more and more fuse with that of England.'"[53]

As early as September 14, 1939, less than two weeks after England declared war on Germany, de Valera held a secret meeting with a British emissary, Sir John Maffey. De Valera told him: "There was a time when I would have done anything in my power to help destroy the British Empire...But now my position has changed...England has a moral position today. Hitler might have his early success, but the moral position would tell."[54]

Pope Pius XII, in receiving the British Ambassador after the war, said: "During the War, the British people endured what was almost beyond human endurance. They did so not only in defense of their own lives and liberties but as the vanguard fighting for those human ideals and human freedoms which must be dear to every right-minded man."[55]

Maffey correctly understood the importance of American public opinion and wrote to Churchill: "Our best hope of achieving anything in Ireland lies and always will lie in the actions and thoughts of America and of Irishmen overseas. The mass of the Irish people were ignorant and still liable to be stirred by politicians exploiting the old hatred of England...de Valera is still the chosen tribal leader for their feuds...He would stir worldwide interest in the soul of Ireland, but it is the soul of

England which stirs the world today, and Éire is a bog with a petty leader raking over old muckheaps..."[56]

When the Irish minister in Washington, Robert Brennan, attempted to set the record straight on Irish neutrality, de Valera stopped him from publishing documentary evidence of Ireland's significant contribution to the Allied cause. The Irish government could have countered the unfavorable propaganda by disclosing some of its secret cooperation with the Allies. Walshe cabled Brennan: "de Valera fully appreciates your great difficulties and has the highest appreciation of the way you handled the situation...*He knows you understand that we may have to suffer much abuse abroad for sake of home front which is the paramount consideration.*"[57] [emphasis added] Once again, de Valera's political survival was more important than Ireland's welfare.

Coogan called it a national tragedy when de Valera ordered the destruction of records that could have given Irish historians a glimpse into Ireland's part in the war. "De Valera ordered records of all discussions with foreign diplomats to be destroyed. The reason he gave, when the Battle of Britain was raging, was that Germany might use them after an invasion to justify her actions, as she had done with Holland. But why the destruction of the records should have continued...long after the threat from Germany had receded, must remain a matter of speculation ..."[58]

Notes

1. Dwyer, T. Ryle, *Éamon de Valera*, Gill & Macmillan, 1980, p. 113
2. Gray, David, *Behind the Green Curtain*, Unpublished Manuscript, American Heritage Center, U of Wyoming, XXVI/42
3. Coogan, Tim P., *De Valera, The Man who was Ireland*, Harper, 1996, p. 594
4. Gray, David, *Behind the Green Curtain*, Unpublished Manuscript, American Heritage Center, U of Wyoming, XI/1
5. Coogan, Tim P., *De Valera, The Man who was Ireland*, Harper, 1996, p. 605
6. Gray, David, *Behind the Green Curtain*, Unpublished Manuscript, American Heritage Center, U of Wyoming, I/4
7. Coogan, Tim P., *De Valera, The Man who was Ireland*, Harper, 1996, p. 545
8. Dwyer, T. Ryle, *De Valera, The Man & the Myths*, Poolbeg, Dublin, 1991, p. 239
9. Dwyer, T. Ryle, *Éamon de Valera*, Gill & Macmillan, 1980, p. 118
10. Smyllie, Robert, "Unneutral Neutral Éire," *Foreign Affairs* (Council on Foreign Relations), p. 326
11. Quigley, Martin S., *Peace without Hiroshima*, Madison Books,, Lanham, NY, London, p. 21

12. Roger Boulton, Professional Researcher, Author's Personal File
13. Smyllie, Robert, "Unneutral Neutral Éire," *Foreign Affairs* (Council on Foreign Relations), p. 322
14. Smyllie, Robert, "Unneutral Neutral Éire," *Foreign Affairs* (Council on Foreign Relations), p. 321
15. *ibid*, p. 320
16. Stephan, Enno, *Spies in Ireland*, Stackpole, Harrisburg, 1965, p. 266
17. Churchill, Winston: *The Grand Alliance*, Houghton Mifflin Harcourt, 1986
18. Longford, Earl of & O'Neill, Thomas P., *Éamon de Valera*, Hutchinson, London, 1970, p. 378
19. Coogan, Tim P., *De Valera, The Man who was Ireland*, Harper, 1996, p. 563
20. Gray, David, *Behind the Green Curtain*, Unpublished Manuscript, American Heritage Center, U of Wyoming, I/64
21. Coogan, Tim P., *De Valera, The Man who was Ireland*, Harper, 1996, p. 570
22. Dwyer, T. Ryle, *De Valera, The Man & the Myths*, Poolbeg, Dublin, 1991, p. 265
23. *New York Times*, 3/12/1944, 4:8
24. Dwyer, T. Ryle, *De Valera, The Man & the Myths*, Poolbeg, Dublin, 1991, p. 231
25. *ibid*, p. 264
26. *ibid*, p. 246
27. *ibid*, p. 266
28. *ibid*, p. 267
29. *ibid*, p. 263
30. Coogan, Tim P., *De Valera, The Man who was Ireland*, Harper, 1996, p. 600
31. Dwyer, T. Ryle, *De Valera, The Man & the Myths*, Poolbeg, Dublin, 1991, p. 263
32. Gray, David, *Behind the Green Curtain*, Unpublished Manuscript, American Heritage Center, U of Wyoming , XI/18
33. Dwyer, T. Ryle, *De Valera, The Man & the Myths*, Poolbeg, Dublin, 1991, p. 278
34. Coogan, Tim P., *De Valera, The Man who was Ireland*, Harper, 1996, p. 601
35. *ibid*, p. 602
36. *New York Times*, 3/11/1944
37. Dwyer, T. Ryle, *De Valera, The Man & the Myths*, Poolbeg, Dublin, 1991, 278
38. Gray, David, *Behind the Green Curtain*, Unpublished Manuscript, American Heritage Center, U of Wyoming, XIII/23
39. Dwyer, T. Ryle, *Éamon de Valera*, Gill & Macmillan, 1980, p. 123
40. Coogan, Tim P., *De Valera, The Man who was Ireland*, Harper, 1996, p. 605
41. Dwyer, T. Ryle, *De Valera, The Man & the Myths*, Poolbeg, Dublin, 1991, p. 278
42. Longford, Earl of & O'Neill, Thomas P., *Éamon de Valera*, Hutchinson, London, 1970, p. 410
43. Fisk, Robert, *In Time of War*, U Penn Press, Philadelphia, 1983, p. 534
44. Dwyer, T. Ryle, *deValera, The Man & the Myths*, Poolbeg, Dublin, 1991, p. 334
45. Longford, Earl of & O'Neill, Thomas P., *Éamon de Valera*, Hutchinson, London, 1970, p. 347

46. Gray, David, *Behind the Green Curtain*, Unpublished Manuscript, American Heritage Center, U of Wyoming, XV/11
47. Dwyer, T. Ryle, *De Valera, The Man & the Myths*, Poolbeg, Dublin, 1991, p. 249
48. Coogan, Tim P., *De Valera, The Man who was Ireland*, Harper, 1996, p. 522
49. Gray, David, *Behind the Green Curtain*, Unpublished Manuscript, American Heritage Center, U of Wyoming, IX/6
50. *ibid*, XVIII/21
51. Dwyer, T. Ryle, *De Valera, The Man & the Myths*, Poolbeg, Dublin, 1991, p. 251
52. Coogan, Tim P., *De Valera, The Man who was Ireland*, Harper, 1996, p. 574
53. Dwyer, T. Ryle, *De Valera, The Man & the Myths*, Poolbeg, Dublin, 1991, p. 216
54. *ibid*, p. 227
55. Gray, David, *Behind the Green Curtain*, Unpublished Manuscript, American Heritage Center, U of Wyoming, XII/29, Osservatore Romano, 6/30/1947
56. Dwyer, T. Ryle, *De Valera, The Man & the Myths*, Poolbeg, Dublin, 1991, p. 253
57. *ibid*, p. 278
58. Coogan, Tim P., *De Valera, The Man who was Ireland*, Harper, 1996, p. 548

CHAPTER XXVII

Hitler Condolences

"Pope Alexander never did what he said,
Cesare Borgia never said what he did."

Italian Proverb

As secret lovers meet, embrace in illicit trysts, smug in their clandestine veil of deception amid whispers of treachery – unseen, unexplained, and unsolved – so too did the British and their master agent, Éamon de Valera carry on a lifetime courtship.

Upon President Franklin Delano Roosevelt's death on April 12, 1945, de Valera sent a note of sympathy to Vice President Harry S. Truman. In the Dáil, de Valera eulogized the American leader: "President Roosevelt will go down in history as one of the greatest of a long line of American Presidents with the unparalleled distinction of having been elected four times as head of the United States...Personally, I regard his death as a loss to the world."[1] Out of respect for the American president, de Valera postponed adjournment of the Dáil until the following day in order to make a moving tribute to Roosevelt. David Gray, U.S. Representative to Éire, wrote to Eleanor Roosevelt: "I thought I knew this country and its people but this was something new. There was a great deal of genuine feeling."[2]

The great deal of genuine feeling was short-lived, however, for little more than two weeks later, de Valera rushed to the German embassy and publicly offered his condolences to Eduard Hempel, the German representative, on the May 2 death of Adolph Hitler.

De Valera's call upon the German embassy to express his commiseration on Hitler's death so infuriated the world that the act appeared to be one of incomprehensible lunacy. Viewed as the actions of a British agent, however, de Valera's sympathetic gesture to Hempel was a masterstroke of diabolical genius.

Hempel was a professional diplomat who had been an officer in the German army during World War I. He entered the Foreign Service in 1927 and a decade later was appointed Minister in the German legation in Dublin serving from 1937-1945. He allegedly had refused to become a Nazi party member but a year after his appointment as minister to Ireland he did so, whether of his free will or by coercion is not known. Reportedly, he had no love for Hitler and returned to Germany in 1949.

De Valera offered as an explanation for his seemingly irrational conduct: "Common gentlemanly feelings of sympathy with Dr. Hempel in the hour of the country's collapse called for a gesture. I was damned if I was going to treat him any different from other representatives on whom I called in similar circumstances, especially as Hitler was dead and there was no possibility of my reinforcing an already lost cause ..."[3] In a deliberate effort to eliminate Irish-American influence, he further infuriated the American people by equating his expression of condolence on the death of Hitler as meaning no more than his declaration of sympathy upon the demise of the American President, Franklin Delano Roosevelt.

According to T. Ryle Dwyer: "Even in Ireland, the expression of sympathy for the death of the Fuhrer was widely resented."[4] Initial reaction in Ireland was muted due to years of strict censorship by the de Valera government. The Irish knew little of the horrors of Hitler's death camps, but once censorship was lifted, the brutality and horror of the Nazi atrocities appalled the Irish, resulting in de Valera's political fortunes suddenly plummeting.

Irish writers once again attributed de Valera's behavior as one of his "peculiarities," brought on by childhood deprivation. They never suspected or speculated that his lamentation on the death of Hitler was once again deliberately doing England's work in placing Ireland in a deplorable international light. The condolence call carved the partition of Ireland in stone, and it has remained so into the next millennium.

In trying to explain away his expression of sympathy on the death of one of the worst tyrants in history, de Valera hypocritically said: "During the whole of the war, Dr. Hempel's conduct was irreproachable. He was always friendly and inevitably correct – in marked contrast to Gray. I certainly was not going to add to his humiliation in the hour of defeat."[5] Unlike Hempel, however, de Valera had behaved incorrectly by continually violating Ireland's neutrality and his condolences were inappropriate. John Maffey, UK Representative in Éire was also surprised: "It was more than possible that Dr. Hempel was delighted that Hitler was dead. It was not as if de Valera had to make the gesture in order to maintain Ireland's neutrality."[6] A private call upon Hempel would have sufficed, but he was determined to create an international incident out of it.

It was not that he was unaware of the effect of his actions as Boland

and Walshe had warned de Valera of the consequences of such a flagrant gesture, but he was curiously adamant. Internationally, his expression of grief at the death of Hitler fuelled British and American accusations of Nazi sympathizing. American opinion of Ireland plunged to an all-time low, while US support of England soared.

The British were naturally delighted by de Valera's "blunder." When asked in the House of Commons whether Britain would lodge a protest against de Valera's action, the British Under Secretary of State for the Dominions, Paul Emrys-Evans, said: "No! Mr. De Valera can safely be left to realize for himself the universal feeling of indignation which his action has aroused..."[7]

He could do no more to ruin his country's image internationally or to enhance England's claims to Northern Ireland. Europe, through the billions of dollars in Marshall Plan aid, was set on the road to recovery while Ireland languished in economic and intellectual stagnation for decades after the war. De Valera played his Nero fiddle to perfection while Ireland sank further into the bogs of economic and intellectual stagnation.

John Kearney, Canadian High Commissioner, said: "'Nothing which Mr. De Valera has done during the years which I have been in Dublin has evoked such widespread criticism, and much of it comes from persons who are normally supporters of his own party'...'An explanation would be interpreted as an excuse and an excuse as a consciousness of having acted wrongly,' [de Valera] wrote to Robert Brennan [the Irish Minister in Washington]. 'I acted correctly and I feel certain, wisely.' If he was so sure of himself, however, why was he explaining his actions to Brennan?"[8]

Despite their ongoing criticisms of de Valera, the British never failed to prop up his political fortunes whenever they showed signs of sagging. Focusing international condemnation on de Valera while doggedly maintaining him in office required a delicate balancing act.

After de Valera's condolence call produced the desired international condemnation, Churchill was caught off guard by the revulsion generated in Ireland and the threat it posed to de Valera's political status. It was 1938 all over again, this time it was Churchill, not Chamberlain, who galloped to de Valera's aid and provided the Irish Prime Minister with the political ammunition to forge a landslide victory two weeks later.

Churchill recognized a great opportunity to discredit Ireland in the eyes of the international community and at the same time provide another political bonanza to de Valera. "In a victory broadcast on May

13, 1945, Churchill contrasted the help that the Allies had received from Northern Ireland with the Dublin Government's 'deadly blow' in refusing to allow Britain to use bases in the Twenty-six Counties."[9] Continuing, Churchill applied the right amount of criticism of de Valera to start Irish hearts pumping: "Owing to the actions of Mr. De Valera...the [Western] approaches which the southern Irish ports and airfields could so easily have guarded were closed by the hostile aircraft and U-boats...If it had not been for the loyalty and friendship of Northern Ireland we should have been forced to come to close quarters with Mr. De Valera or perish forever from the earth. However, with a restraint and poise to which, I say, history will find few parallels, His Majesty's Government never laid a violent hand upon them, though it would have been quite easy and quite natural. We left the de Valera Government to frolic with the Germans and later with the Japanese to their heart's content."[10]

Churchill's weeping over Ireland's refusal to allow Britain access to the militarily worthless Irish ports was the same old propaganda saw. On May 16, de Valera, again playing straight man, portrayed Churchill's speech as if it was an attack on Irish manhood and patriotism: "I know the answer that first springs to the lips of every man of Irish blood who heard or read that speech...I know the reply I would have given a quarter of a century ago but I have deliberately decided that it is not the reply I shall make tonight. Allowances can be made for Mr. Churchill's statement, however unworthy, in the flush of his victory...Mr. Churchill makes it clear that in certain circumstances he would have violated our neutrality and that he would justify his action by Britain's necessity...It would mean that Britain's necessity would become a moral code and that when this necessity became sufficiently great, other people's rights were not to count...By resisting his temptation in this instance, Mr. Churchill instead of adding another horrid chapter to the already bloodstained record of the relations between England and this country, has advanced the cause of international morality an important step... Could Mr. Churchill not find in his heart the generosity to acknowledge that there is a small nation that stood alone, not for one year or two, but for several hundred years against aggression, that endured spoliation, famines, massacres in endless succession, that was clubbed many times into insensibility, but that each time on returning to consciousness took up the fight anew, a small nation that could never accept defeat and has never surrendered her soul?"[11]

John Kearney, the Canadian High Commissioner, not being privy to the Churchill-de Valera collaborative act, was dismayed at the British Prime

Minister's speech, which he contended revitalized de Valera's political standing in Ireland. Coogan noted: "Kearney had been horrified by de Valera's Legation visit after Hitler's death, regarding it as a 'slap in the face,' but as a Commonwealth diplomat he could recognize that there were advantages to be gained from it. Now, however, his reaction to Churchill's speech and de Valera's reply was: 'We had de Valera on a plate. We had him where we wanted him. But look at the papers this morning.'"[12]

De Valera's response drew the usual Irish commentator's reaction. Some criticized Churchill for distracting attention from the scandal over de Valera's condolences but it did not occur to them that Churchill deliberately provided the Irish leader with another means of rallying public support. Following his speech, Dwyer noted: "The public reaction to the address in Ireland was overwhelming ... He had struck a chord in the whole nation, as no Irish leader had ever done before."[13]

Most Irish writers credited de Valera with besting Churchill in a war of words, never questioning the results – that Ireland lost out internationally and de Valera won domestically, or how and why both the English Prime Minister and the Irish Prime Minister profited from that clash: "The question of retribution for de Valera's blunder was suddenly rendered otiose. Churchill snatched him from the fires of contumely more dramatically and with even greater reward than he had done during the 'notes' issue."[14] As de Valera's political stock in Ireland soared, he staged a vote of no-confidence over an innocuous issue, thereby precipitating another successful election bid in May 1945. Coogan acknowledged another Churchill rescue of de Valera but failed to recognize why he continued to prop up the Irish leader's political fortunes.

The Dominions Office clearly understood the ramifications of Churchill's maneuver: "The international perspective of this so-called 'radio contest' was quite different [than the Irish writers' version]...de Valera's strange image at home was enhanced while his international standing was seriously damaged. The Dominions' Secretary, who had just returned from the San Francisco Conference establishing the United Nations Organization, noted that news of de Valera's condolence gesture, coming so soon after the gruesome revelations about the Buchenwald concentration camp, had inflicted a profound and enduring shock on the American people, with the result that Churchill's 'severe remarks were accepted and even applauded as a salutary rap on the knuckles.'

"Likewise, in much of Europe, where Churchill was idolized as a liberator and hence, his speech was the one which made the impact. 'On balance,' the Dominions Office concluded, 'we have certainly gained in the eyes of the world, whatever may be the effect in Éire itself.'"[15]

The English never cared a fig about what the Irish thought. Anglo-American relations were England's priority, and all Churchill's efforts were directed toward solidifying those relations. The Irish never considered the question as to why the English were so determined to maintain de Valera in office.

Notes

1. Longford, Earl of & O'Neill, Thomas P., *Éamon de Valera*, Hutchinson, London, 1970, p. 411
2. Dwyer, T. Ryle, *De Valera, The Man & the Myths*, Poolbeg, Dublin, 1991, p. 282
3. *ibid*, p. 284
4. Dwyer, T. Ryle, *Éamon de Valera*, Gill & Macmillan, 1980, p. 126
5. Longford, Earl of & O'Neill, Thomas P., *Éamon de Valera*, Hutchinson, London, 1970, p. 411
6. Dwyer, T. Ryle, *De Valera, The Man & the Myths*, Poolbeg, Dublin, 1991, p. 283
7. Stephan, Enno, *Spies in Ireland*, Stackpole, Harrisburg, 1965, p. 288
8. Dwyer, T. Ryle, *De Valera, The Man & the Myths*, Poolbeg, Dublin, 1991, p. 283
9. Dwyer, T. Ryle, *Éamon de Valera*, Gill & Macmillan, 1980, p. 126
10. Coogan, Tim P., *De Valera, The Man who was Ireland*, Harper, 1996, p. 610
11. *ibid*, p. 611
12. *ibid*, p. 612
13. Dwyer, T. Ryle, *De Valera, The Man & the Myths*, Poolbeg, Dublin, 1991, p. 286
14. Coogan, Tim P., *De Valera, The Man who was Ireland*, Harper, 1996, p. 610
15. Dwyer, T. Ryle, *De Valera, The Man & the Myths*, Poolbeg, Dublin, 1991, p. 287

CHAPTER XXVIII

The de Valera Legacy

"The vital weakness of the Free State Government is that it knows nothing of the psychology of the people. They are incapable of feeling the nation's pulse. They have no publicity department worth talking of. Any government that desires to hold power in Ireland should put publicity before all."[1]

Éamon de Valera

A Legacy of Hatred

Éamon de Valera's legacy is one of misery and violence. The civil war ended, but de Valera's malignant legacy is still being felt. He wrote the epitaphs for those misguided souls who followed his trumpeting call to civil war – Barnett, Boland, Burgess, Childers, Lynch, McKelvey, Mellowes, O'Connor – vapors disappearing in the mists of centuries of Irish betrayers who were in turn betrayed by their own leader.

All that Collins asked of de Valera and his followers was "A simple acceptance of the people's will...What principle could such an acceptance have violated? Blind to the facts and false to ideals, they [de Valera and his counterfeit Republicans] are making war on the Irish people."

No British agent, nor Irish traitor ever accomplished more for Britain than did de Valera in America and later in Ireland. For more than half a century, de Valera ground the Irish into the bogs of poverty and despair as he promoted English interests while guaranteeing his own political supremacy. As Tim Pat Coogan observed: "de Valera...attempted to confine his disciples to the narrowest of cultural and intellectual horizons. Many of the challenges he confronted are still troubling the peace of Ireland and of England...Some of the vexing questions of the moment are directly traceable to him. The effect...of the Irish Constitution on Northern Ireland's Unionists; his philosophy of talking about God and the high destiny of the Gael, while practicing realpolitik gave him control of the Irish Press and of Fianna Fáil..."[2]

To this day, Northern Ireland is riven by sectarian division, while the

Twenty-six County Republic remains tainted by bitterness within families and between neighbors over the civil war. Southern Ireland was an economic disaster until the European Economic Community rescued it in 1973. More than a million Irish men, women, and children – one fourth the entire population of Ireland – fled de Valera's fiefdom, the greatest migration since the famine years of the 1800s. Ironically, the majority sought freedom and economic opportunity in England, the land of the "oppressor" after America slammed shut its doors to Irish immigration as a result of de Valera's "neutrality" in the Second World War.

Irish social services are rooted in a religious bog of intolerance. The Roman Catholic Church, the foundation of de Valera's political base, remains the shadow government lurking behind the illusion of a democratic state, and politicians hold their office at the pleasure of the church hierarchy. De Valera's amateurish and bigoted constitution has embedded the Catholic Church and guarantees that the Protestants of the North will never unite voluntarily.

De Valera duped the self-anointed "Republicans" into fighting a civil war over an oath that was not an oath, to a republic that was not a republic. De Valera returned from the political wilderness by signing what he had previously denounced as an oath of allegiance to the King which he then recast as a hollow political formula. De Valera had no scruples about instigating civil war to eliminate his rivals, and his legacy of hatred permeates Northern and Southern Ireland to this day.

Those who turned to robbery, extortion and murder of their own countrymen during the civil war canonized themselves as the saviours of Ireland's honor. Their descendants still refuse to reappraise the dark deeds of de Valera and his followers or to reflect on the valiant roles played by Collins, Griffith and Devoy.

P. S. O'Hegarty was damning about de Valera's "Republican" followers: "The 'Republican' movement, which was founded on a lie and maintained on a lie. Its policy has been a policy of attack on the Irish people. It has neither patriotism nor decency. It has shamed the name Republic and made it stink. It has weakened Ireland economically, morally and internationally and it has appreciably delayed the establishment of complete independence..."[3]

John Whelan inadvertently set forth the true hypocrisy of de Valera's counterfeit Republicans when he wrote: "There is something limited, negative, even smug, in the self-appraisal of the modern Irish Republican who lines up behind de Valera...He forgets all that Europe had achieved and all that Ireland has not even begun to achieve..."[4]

Mary MacSwiney spat her venom on Collins and Griffith during the

Free State treaty debate as she rallied the "extremist element" in support of de Valera's civil war, but, alas, she discovered too late that she was merely another de Valera dupe unwittingly carrying out English policy. In her disillusionment, she lamented: "Can you count the times de Valera has broken his word? ... de Valera has a load of treachery on his conscience. What value are the promises of a liar?"[5]

Leon O'Broin acknowledged de Valera's responsibility for the civil war: "But for Dev, there would have been no split at the time of the Treaty, no Documents 1, 2, and 3, no Civil War, none of the burning of houses and destruction of property and life that took place in 1922 and 1923, and none of the bitterness, the dreadful bitterness and personal hatred which exists between the two parties in the country now, not to speak of the destruction of our relations with England."[6]

Desmond Ryan also conceded the long-running bitterness and hatred to de Valera and his civil war: "Even today, the wounds of the Irish Civil War fester long after its dead have turned to dust or withered to nothing in their quicklime shrouds. Its destruction was great in damage to property, in loss of life, in disillusion...The deepest wounds of the Civil War were spiritual wounds that will not be healed until the last of the Civil War generation is long forgotten..."[7]

James Dillon, in a Dáil speech on June 14, 1937, explained his revulsion with the Irish President's claim under Article V of the 1937 Constitution that: "'Ireland is a sovereign, independent, democratic state.' President de Valera denied that at one time. He denounced as West Britons and traitors any man who stated that. He sent out his own henchmen to denounce those who defended that proposition as the friends of England. He aspersed, degraded, and attacked the names of men living and dead who, by their labors, made Ireland a sovereign, independent, and democratic State. He has now come to realize, albeit 15 years too late, that Ireland is what he swore it was not."

De Valera's extremists in the Irish Republican Army were the Irish version of Hitler's Brown Shirt enforcers. They provided the muscle to rob, intimidate and murder as de Valera's strong-arm tactics kept Ireland in a state of near anarchy from 1922 into the 1930s. Once secure in office, the Irish President set about wrecking the IRA. He tricked them into undertaking covert operations against the British and then informed on them as they were about to carry out their missions. He treated IRA prisoners like common criminals and readily sentenced them to death whereas he would mobilize public campaigns for the pardon of those convicted of attacks in England and Northern Ireland.

While the dissident IRA men who made war on their fellow

countrymen cast themselves as heroes, the Irish volunteers who had served the cause of freedom in the Allied armed forces, returned home unrecognized and scorned. De Valera refused to acknowledge the contributions made by Irish volunteers to the Allied victory and to Ireland's freedom, adding another layer to Ireland's collective denial. Joseph J. Lee, born in Tralee, County Kerry, Ireland, in 1942, and later a Professor of History at New York University, noted this psychological phenomenon among the Irish: "It was vital for the national psyche from the emotional viewpoint that the extent of Irish cooperation should not receive indecent exposure. It might have been more true to say that avoiding such exposure served de Valera's political purposes best."[8]

Given the historic animosity between Protestants and Catholics, the adoption of a secular constitution was critical to eliminating distrust between the two religious camps. But, by recognizing the Catholic Church as the church of all Ireland, de Valera's constitution ensured the continuation of Partition and sectarianism. He guaranteed that Protestants would resist unification when he declared: "I do not see why the people in this part of Ireland should sacrifice ideals which they hold dear – completely sacrifice these ideals in order to meet the views of people whose position fundamentally is not as just or as right as our position is."[9]

Catholic-inspired social policies and the introduction of Gaelic as the national language made certain that Northern Ireland's Unionists would never consent to a united Ireland without coercion.

The Legacy of Neutrality

De Valera's apologists claimed that his greatest achievement was keeping Ireland out of the Second World War, but they failed to assess the disastrous consequences of neutrality for Ireland. As with his ambivalence over the oath, de Valera's attitude to neutrality was also inconsistent. His official stance left Ireland isolated and condemned as a pariah state with pro-Nazi leanings for decades.

The Irish people were brainwashed by de Valera into believing that his brand of neutrality demonstrated Ireland's independence, but the unavoidable fact was that Ireland's freedom depended upon England's survival. As de Valera nodded approval, 200,000 Irish volunteers rallied to the Allied cause, but for personal political ambition, he shunned the veterans when they returned to Ireland. He never whispered a breath of protest as Irish men and women, by the hundreds of thousands, labored in Northern Ireland and English factories contrary to all rules of neutrality and every ounce of Irish surplus foodstuffs was shipped to England. The British were able, through de Valera's neutrality, to reap

451

the benefits of a trusted and cooperative ally while at the same time painting the Irish as money-grubbing misers profiting under England's protection. De Valera's press censorship kept the Irish ignorant of their contribution to the Allied victory.

The real purpose of neutrality was to stifle Irish-American political influence. Churchill and Roosevelt concocted a pro-Nazi smear campaign to eliminate Irish-American opposition to Anglo-American cooperation before, during and after the war. Had it not been for de Valera's alleged "neutrality," Ireland would have assumed her rightful place among the victorious nations.

Roosevelt was the beneficiary of de Valera's neutrality, as Irish-Americans were all but eliminated as a political force; Churchill also benefited from Ireland's neutrality, and the Unionist of Northern Ireland was secure as partition was chiseled in stone. De Valera was the beneficiary of his neutrality, repeatedly winning re-election. But, for the Irish people, neutrality brought no benefits.

The United States Representative to Ireland David Gray assessed de Valera's legacy in very negative terms: "Never did an Irish leader score so high a percentage of errors, misjudge the forces of social evolution so utterly or achieve such complete failure. Never did an Irish leader commit so many stupidities. The crowning one was his so-called 'Neutrality' in the Second World War."[10]

De Valera's neutrality ensured the Irish were left out of the United Nations. The Irish contribution to the war effort was airbrushed out of the picture so that the rebel Republicans could bleat their dedication to an Irish Republic that not only did not exist but which they had renounced on at least four occasions. In 1934, when the Soviet Union was involved in the wholesale slaughter of its ethnic minorities, de Valera backed Soviet entry into the League of Nations. But in 1945, "Soviet Foreign Minister Andrei Gromyko said Ireland's behavior during the Second World War was hardly calculated to help her gain admission to the United Nations."[11]

De Valera's official neutrality meant that Partition was treated as an internal British affair which did not warrant American intervention. Throughout the conflict, it was critical for the British to keep Ireland from publicly joining the Allied cause. Knowledge of Ireland's contribution to the Allied war effort would have made a major impact on American public opinion. Ireland and the Irish-Americans would then have presented a powerful argument for an end to partition. The disadvantages appeared over time. "The lasting ill effects on Partition, the end of the dream of self-sufficiency and a very diminished Irish share in the benefits of post-war European reconstruction left Ireland lagging behind western Europe in both cultural and economic isolation."[12]

De Valera's neutrality was mainly for American consumption. After the War, the British countered every attempt by the Irish-American community to influence Washington by publicizing Ireland's alleged pro-Nazi leanings. Churchill was able to stir up hostility by falsely and repeatedly claiming that Ireland's neutrality had resulted in the deaths of thousands of American sailors.

Irish-American Legacy

De Valera and his supporters took every opportunity to offend American sensibilities during the Republican and Democratic Conventions of 1920. They were perceived as drunken rowdies boorishly attempting to dictate American foreign policy. The ugly publicity generated outside Irish-American circles by de Valera facilitated English interest in America.

De Valera destroyed the Friends of Irish Freedom (FOIF) and discredited the most effective leaders of the Irish-Americans, John Devoy and Judge Daniel Cohalan. Rather than promoting the Irish cause in America, de Valera plundered huge sums from the Bond Certificate drive to further Britain's agenda by undermining the Friends of Irish Freedom (FOIF). Under James O'Mara, the American Association for Recognition of the Irish Republic (AARIR) became a greater threat to the Anglo-American alliance than the FOIF had been. As soon as the AARIR began to threaten British interests in America, de Valera moved to dismantle it, too.

His greatest accomplishment for England while in America was his rejection of virtual recognition of Irish independence and the prevention of the presidential candidacy of the pro-Irish Hiram Johnson of California. Bishop Gallagher, head of the FOIF, laid the upsurge of Black and Tan terror on de Valera's doorstep: "This [rejection of an Irish Plank] was immediately interpreted in England as the absolute repudiation of the Irish Question by American statesmen, as we know from Lloyd George and Hamar Greenwood. It was the signal for the opening of the saturnalia of arson, murder, lust and looting [by the Black and Tans]...If President de Valera had remained away from Chicago and allowed Americans to run their own affairs...the fear of American public opinion would have stayed the murderous hand of England from committing such monstrous atrocities as Ireland has lately endured."[13]

Though he had campaigned for American recognition of the Irish Republic, de Valera confessed upon his return to Ireland that: "...If I were President of the United States myself, I could not, and I would not, recognize Ireland as a Republic."[14] The Irish President was an abject failure in every single Irish objective that he publicly espoused as his reasons for deserting Ireland for America during the "Troubles." As far as English objectives were concerned, however, de Valera succeeded beyond Whitehall's wildest expectations.

A Legacy of Censorship

As de Valera micromanaged every aspect of Irish life, with his worn-out slogans of liberation and restoration of Ireland's ancient Gaelic traditions, he plunged the country's artistic life into mediocrity, the effects which are still being felt today.

A culture of strict censorship was built up during the war years which was allegedly justified by the need to preserve Ireland's neutrality. Censorship was placed under the direction of Frank "Wooden Head" Aiken as he was known to his contemporaries. David Gray, American Representative to Ireland, relayed to FDR, an opposition member's opinion of Aiken: "as a mind halfway between that of a child and an ape...with the mentality of a boy gang leader playing at war with real soldiers."[15]

The involvement of the Catholic hierarchy made for wide-ranging strictures. The shadowy presence of the Catholic Church lurked behind de Valera's censorship when Bing Crosby's records were banned during the war years because the hierarchy claimed "crooning" would corrupt the nation's youth. During the war years, so many films were cut by Aiken's scissors that movie theatres were on the verge of going out of business. Newsreels of swimming scenes were excised because they depicted girls in bathing suits showing a little too much leg; newspaper advertisements displaying corsets and brassieres were a major worry of the censor; and even some medical magazines were banned because of their "indecency." de Valera's censors even banned newspaper notices of the Kingstown Presbyterian Church services. "Wooden Head" Aiken ordered the Presbyterians to change the name of their Church to the Dun Laoghaire Presbyterian Church because Kingstown's city name had been Gallicized.

De Valera pandered to the hierarchy to further his political ambitions and the elimination of Collins and Griffith from Irish history. Coogan noted: "In 1965, an official guide book, *Facts about Ireland*, produced by the Department of Foreign Affairs, had to be reprinted after controversy broke out over the exclusion of Collins' picture. Frank Aiken, then Minister for Foreign Affairs, was blamed for this but the omission occurred after consultation with de Valera."[16]

As de Valera's censorship clamped down on the Irish literary scene, many renowned Irish writers abandoned their homeland. Ireland was celebrated for her writers in the interwar years and people came from far afield to visit Dublin's Abbey Theatre, established by W.B. Yeats and the first state-subsidized theatre in the English-speaking world. De Valera stepped inside the Abbey once in his life. Gray commented on the Irish literary scene during the war years:: "Today, the spirit of the Abbey is dead...Its epitaph: 'Dead of Compulsory Irish.' ...The Irish creative genius was as sick as the Irish economy. Fire mercifully destroyed the old playhouse before the smell of spiritual death became public scandal...The Irish Literary Revival was dead. Sinn Féin and Separatism had killed it. James Joyce died in self-imposed exile; O'Casey lived in England and Padraic Colum in New York; Frank O'Connor had done nothing notable about Ireland since 'Guests of the Nation' and Seán Ó'Faoláin goes on as an 'essayist'...Twenty years later, the plight of the Irish creative mind is even more acute. Something has poisoned it as something has poisoned the Irish soul and the Irish economy. Sean O'Casey, in his three plays entitled, 'Behind the Green Curtain,' blasts the fruits of de Valera's separatism."[17]

Strict censorship left the Irish isolated from international events during the war. Taking another page out of the English repression of Ireland, de Valera initiated an Irish "paper wall of disinformation" – the Irish would know of the outside world only what de Valera wanted them to know and the international community would only know of the Irish what de Valera decided.

The culture of concealment was far-reaching. In order to conceal evidence of his mobilization of the entire population of Southern Ireland on behalf of England and the Allies, de Valera oversaw the destruction of Irish government records covering the war years. De Valera claimed this was necessary in case the Germans were victorious, but documents continued to be purged even when the threat of a German invasion had disappeared. Files pertaining to ecclesiastical collusion were also expunged. This act of self-serving vandalism has hindered historians' attempts to trace Ireland's story and resolve the conflicts which still assail her sense of national identity.

Emigration Legacy

During the immediate postwar years, millions of immigrants from Europe flocked to America, but, to the Irish, the doors to America were all but slammed shut due to hostility arising from Ireland's alleged pro-Nazi leanings. De Valera, during his election campaign in 1932, promised a job for every Irishman and returned exile, national self-sufficiency, alternate markets for Irish products, and an Ireland that could support as many as six million people – every one of those claims, too, was an unmitigated Irish disaster. Every one of his claims proved false and hundreds of thousands of Irish men and women were forced to flee de Valera's reactionary distopia.

Postwar unemployment soared despite mass emigration. Sean Glynn cited the dreary statistics of de Valera's incompetence: "In the years 1946–51, over 80 percent of Irish emigrants went to the United Kingdom. This change in direction has often been attributed to the United States quota restrictions...In 1978, there were nearly one million immigrants from the Twenty-six Counties living in the United Kingdom..."[18] David Gray noted: "Never had the interests of so many Irish people been so mismanaged and betrayed by so few. Never before had one Irishman driven a million Irish people into exile."[19] As Southern Ireland declined in population, Northern Ireland actually gained more than 50,000 Southern Irish.

Thanks to de Valera's economic policies, the United Kingdom held within its borders one quarter of the entire population of Southern Ireland who chose to be English rather than Irish. Such wholesale migration, in round terms, would proportionately equal 75 million Americans moving to Canada. Throughout history, de Valera, with the exception of Queen Victoria, was responsible for the largest exodus of Irish men and women fleeing his economic madness.

Coogan gave this assessment of de Valera's economy: "After 35 years of native government, people are asking whether we can achieve an acceptable degree of economic progress. The common talk among parents in the towns, as in rural Ireland, was of their children having to emigrate as soon as their education was completed in order to be sure of a reasonable livelihood...All this seemed to be setting up a vicious circle – of increasing emigration, resulting in a smaller domestic market depleted of initiative and skill. This dismal state of affairs was caused by...the absence of a comprehensive and integrated program...tending to deepen the all-prevalent mood of despondency about the country's future."[20]

De Valera's Economic, Social and Religious Legacy
De Valera's pre-and postwar economic policies were a litany of financial disasters for the Irish. His economic policy consisted of pious paeans to rustic cabins and cozy fireplaces. He couldn't deliver on those either.

Joseph Connolly, who had been a member of the first Fianna Fáil government was disappointed at de Valera's unwillingness to contemplate the land reform he promised in 1932. "I formed the opinion that he no longer welcomed discussion much less criticism. What he wanted beside him was a group of 'yes-men' who agreed with everything and anything the party (with himself as leader) approved...After more than a dozen years in power, many of the same people were still to be found in the government. They were just the most available and in some cases the least exceptional of a class of institutional survivors."[21]

De Valera voiced his opposition to emigration, but the departure of so many young people from Ireland was a political boon to his banshee economics. Unemployment remained a serious problem, even with the wholesale flight, but it would have been calamitous if all those emigrants had stayed in Ireland without jobs or hope of bettering themselves. "The end of the war found the Twenty-six Counties a small, open economy, highly vulnerable to outside influences, with a limited home market and no industrial base to speak of...resulting in an undue trade dependence on Britain..."[22] It was monumental folly to pick a public quarrel with Britain, Ireland's best and only source of income without developing an alternative market for Irish goods.

De Valera incorporated bigots, radicals, and religious zealots into the mainstream of Irish political power. The Catholic hierarchy had excommunicated de Valera and his rebel republicans in 1922 over their wanton acts of violence. However, upon de Valera's return from the political wilderness in 1932, the bishops winked at the excommunicated murderers, bank robbers, and extortionists and welcomed de Valera with open arms. The hierarchy and even the Pope could not say enough words of praise for the prodigal son who promised to enthrone a Catholic theocracy in Ireland.

The "Mother and Child" health care controversy in 1949 confirmed that "Home Rule" really meant "Rome Rule" in Southern Ireland. The health programme proposed free medical service for mothers and girls and health education for women. The Catholic hierarchy took strong exception to this Bill.[23] Irish politicians, contrary to their mandate to represent the people, tripped over each other in their rush to pledge their fealty to the Catholic Church rather than the people they were supposed to be representing. Dr. Noel Browne, author of the "Mother and Child" health care programme, disclosed: "de Valera appeared to resent the fact that I had deliberately set out, by use of the [Hierarchy] correspondence, to collect the evidence needed by me to prove conclusively that Rome did rule, which I had already learned from my experience in the Cabinet. De Valera appeared to know and condone it."[24]

The de Valera constitution set forth Roman Catholic dogma as the foundation for the government and, although the Irish continue to muck about in national denial, the Catholic hierarchy remains the shadowy force behind the façade of civil government. "While de Valera did not carry those sectarian views to their logical conclusion after he came to power, his government did nevertheless intensify discrimination in the Twenty-six Counties against Protestant values in matters like divorce, contraception, and censorship."[25]

In their desire to show that de Valera was not a bigot, his apologists cite only the isolated instance of Douglas Hyde, a Protestant, who was appointed the first President of Éire in 1937. Hyde was the token Protestant that de Valera would drag out of his closet from time to time and parade as proof that he was not a bigot. Hyde, founder of the Gaelic League, was instrumental in calling for the establishment of Gaelic as the official language in Ireland. The compulsory Gaelic requirements in both education and civil service were evil portents of what lay in store for Protestants in a united Ireland.

De Valera's educational policy was a disaster of immense proportions and another political concession to the Catholic Church. Constantine Fitzgibbons noted both the failure of the Gaelic revival and education: "de Valera's other, though perhaps less important failure was the Irish language...Immense effort, including 38 percent of the schoolchildren's time has been devoted to this endeavor. It has failed and the children forget their Irish (save in order to get civil service jobs) as fast as they can."[26]

De Valera, in his annual speech before the Irish National Teachers Organization on March 26, 1940, made the astounding confession: "For at least nine-tenths of the Irish people, the primary school is the sole source of education." According to Coogan: "What this meant, in effect, was that the average '12 year-old', leaving formal education behind forever, would have devoted a high proportion of classroom time to a study of the Irish language and the catechism, and whatever was left over to the 'three Rs.'"[27] By 1965, de Valera's impact on the education of Ireland's children resulted in nine of ten leaving school by the age of twelve.

Whelan commented: "The educational policy of his [de Valera's] government is wholly unimaginative; gives satisfaction to nobody...The only manifestation of interest in the development of Irish culture by his government – elaborate schemes for the revival of Gaelic and an annual subsidy to the Abbey Theatre – were both initiated by the government which he succeeded...Again, it must be said, he is not a creative or original mind...when it comes to originating some cultural ideal for Ireland, which its history has not previously adumbrated, he is no better than the mass of his colleagues and followers."[28]

De Valera's obsessive preoccupation with controlling the historical

The de Valera Legacy

record has led to very distorted perceptions, not the least about himself. Taking de Valera's official biographers and their book, *Éamon de Valera*, to task, Dwyer said: "It [the book] depicted de Valera as a sincere, considerate, compassionate, and fearless patriot – a committed democrat, a brilliant thinker, an excellent strategist, a great statesman and a dedicated family man...Their [Longford and O'Neill] hagiographic account was like a case for de Valera's canonization to crown his presidency. They sought to sanctify him both by glorifying his accomplishments and obscuring his failings with unsubstantiated and unsubstantiable repudiation, by omission and by nuance..."[29]

In the 1930s when de Valera had not yet succeeded in rewriting history, Desmond Ryan described a long list of de Valera's Irish failures but concluded that it wasn't all the Irish President's fault: "de Valera's opposition to the Treaty, his determined campaign against it and his final participation in the civil war are episodes in his career that for many are overwhelming reasons to condemn him unheard...There is the even stronger case that he proved a false prophet in his warnings against the Treaty and the limitations it would impose on future generations and the barriers it was supposed to set to the march of a nation...It will be seen that the tangle of events in 1922 after the Split in the Dáil and the IRA cannot be blamed on any one person or party, on de Valera, on Griffith or Collins, or the Irregulars."[30]

Ryan continued: "de Valera apologists do everything possible to obscure the issue with all the familiar tricks of the dictator's apes – repetition, evasion, truculence, the weary gramophone of mass propaganda. The idol is praised fulsomely, his words, especially his platitudes, are cited with a reverence due to God alone and then partisanship, intellectual dishonesty and dreary parrotry do the rest."[31] By the time de Valera died in 1973, "the familiar tricks of the dictator's apes" had become ingrained and criticism was unpatriotic. In 2005, Michael Martin, then Minister for Trade, defended de Valera in a way that shows the essentially negative and equivocal legacy de Valera left behind: "He [de Valera] has been an all-purpose vehicle for people wanting to present a bleak narrative of cynical, clerically-dominated and inward-looking politics. To reduce a substantial figure such as de Valera in this way is both absurd and a-historical."[32]

But there is little of substance about de Valera save for his extraordinary instinct for survival. The only consistent feature of his policies was his loyalty to British interests: for his undeviating service, he deserves to be called England's greatest spy.

Notes

1. Dwyer, T. Ryle, *De Valera, the Man and the Myths*, Poolbeg, Dublin, 1991, p. 134
2. Coogan, Tim P., *De Valera, The Man who was Ireland*, Harper, 1996, p. 2
3. O'Hegarty, P.S., *The Victory of Sinn Féin & How It Used It*, Talbot Press, Dublin 1924, p. 100
4. Whelan, John (Seán O'Faoláin), *De Valera*, Penguin Books, England 1939, p. 170
5. Gray, David, *Behind the Green Curtain*, Unpublished Manuscript, American Heritage, U of Wyoming, IX/10
6. O'Broin, Leon, *Wylie, W. E. and the Irish Revolution*, Macmillan, 1989, p. 33
7. Ryan, Desmond, *Unique dictator*, Arthur Barker, London, 1936, p. 205
8. Dwyer, T. Ryle, *De Valera, The Man & the Myths*, Poolbeg, Dublin, 1991, p. 288
9. *ibid*, p. 298
10. Gray, David, *Behind the Green Curtain*, Unpublished Manuscript, American Heritage, U of Wyoming, p. 1/1/, p. 1
11. Dwyer, T. Ryle, *De Valera, The Man & the Myths*, Poolbeg, Dublin, 1991, p. 293
12. Coogan, Tim P., *De Valera, The Man who was Ireland*, Harper, 1996, p. 522
13. McCartan, Patrick, *With de Valera in America*, Brentano/NY 1932, p. 197
14. Beaslai, Pieras, *Michael Collins and the Making of a New Ireland*, Vol II, Harper Bros. NY 1926, p. 18
15. Gray, David, *Behind the Green Curtain*, Unpublished Manuscript, American Heritage Center, U of Wyoming, XVIII/37
16. Coogan, Tim Pat, *Michael Collins*, Arrow Books, 1991, p. 431
17. Gray, David, *Behind the Green Curtain*, Unpublished Manuscript, American Heritage Center, U of Wyoming, p. XIV/22 and 23
18. Glynn, Sean, "Irish Immigration to Britain 1911-1951 – Patterns and Policy" in the *Journal of the Economic & Social History Society of Ireland*, Vo. 8, 1981, p. 51
19. Gray, David, *Behind the Green Curtain*, Unpublished Manuscript, American Heritage Center, U of Wyoming, XIII/20
20. Coogan, Tim P., *De Valera, The Man who was Ireland*, Harper, 1996, p. 634
21. Dwyer, T. Ryle, *De Valera, The Man & the Myths*, Poolbeg, Dublin, 1991, p. 291
22. Coogan, Tim P., *De Valera, The Man who was Ireland*, Harper, 1996, p. 630
23. *ibid*, p. 647
24. Dwyer, T. Ryle, *De Valera, The Man & the Myths*, Poolbeg, Dublin, 1991, p. 306
25. *ibid*
26. Fitzgibbon, Constantine, The Life & Times of Éamon de Valera, Gill & Macmillan, Dublin, 1973, Intro.
27. Coogan, Tim P., *deValera, The Man who was Ireland*, Harper, 1996, p. 626
28. Whelan, John (Seán O'Faoláin), *De Valera*, Penguin Books, England 1939, p. 170
29. Dwyer, T. Ryle, *De Valera, The Man & the Myths*, Poolbeg, Dublin, 1991, p. 317
30. Ryan, Desmond, *Unique dictator*, Arthur Barker, London,1936, p. 167

31. *ibid*, p. 10
32. University College Dublin Archives

EPILOGUE

Closing Argument –
The People vs. Éamon de Valera

"In 1936, de Valera proposed a historical commission of enquiry be set up so there might be some independent authoritative examination of the sequence of events leading up to the Treaty and the start of the Civil War...being anxious to dispose, once and for all, of whatever controversy still remained. He wanted both Fianna Fáil and Cumann na nGaedheal to each nominate three people, a judge or constitutional lawyer, a recognized student of history and a person qualified to examine historical documents and weigh historical evidence, with a bishop acting as an impartial chairman should the six party nominees fail to agree on one person. 'I am prepared to give evidence before this commission, and Mr. Cosgrave and Miss Mary MacSwiney may both be my accusers, if they choose. The whole of government archives can be made available to them.'" *

In the interest of justice and historical fairness and in accordance with de Valera's wishes, the former Irish President must be subjected to a posthumous trial on charges of treason, fraud and conspiracy to murder. A panel of Irish lawyers and judges, preferably retired jurists, will be appointed to preside over the trial. A barrister will be appointed to defend de Valera and a prosecutor to present the posthumous charges against de Valera on behalf of Michael Collins, Arthur Griffith, John Devoy and the Irish people.

*Murray, Patrick, *Obsessive Historian: Éamon de Valera, National Discipline and Majority Rule*, Published 1936, pp. 25-26

BIBLIOGRAPHY

BARRY, TOM: *The Reality of the Anglo-Irish War, 1920-21 in West Cork*, Anvil Books, Dublin 1974

BEASLAI, PIERAS: *Michael Collins and the Making of a New Ireland*, Vol. I, Harper Bros. NY 1926

BOWMAN, JOHN: *De Valera and the Ulster Question 1917-73*, Clarendon Press, Oxford, 1982

BRASIER, A. & KELLY, J: *Harry Boland, A Man Divided*, New Century Publishing, Dublin,

BROMAGE, MARY C: *De Valera and the March of a Nation*, Hutchinson, London, 1956

CARROLL, JOSEPH T: *Ireland in the War Years*, David & Charles, NY, 1975

CAULFIELD, MAS: *The Easter Rebellion*, Frederick Muller, London, 1963

CHATFIELD, LORD: *It Might Happen Again*, Wm. Heineman, London 1947

COFFEY, THOMAS: *Agony at Easter*, Macmillan, NY, 1969

COLLINS, MICHAEL: *The Path to Freedom*, Roberts Rhinehart, 1996

COOGAN, TIM PAT: *De Valera, The Man who was Ireland*, Harper, 1996

COOGAN, TIM PAT: *1916 Easter Rising*, Cassell & Co.

DEVOY, John: *Recollections of an Irish Rebel*, Irish U. Press, Shannon, Ireland, 1969

DWANE, DAVID: *Early Life of Éamon de Valera*, Talbot Press, Dublin/London, 1922

DWYER, T. RYLE: *De Valera's Darkest Hour 1919-1932*, Mercier Press, Dublin/Cork 1982

DWYER, T. RYLE: *Éamon de Valera*, Gill & Macmillan, 1980

DWYER, T. RYLE: *De Valera, The Man & the Myths*, Poolbeg, Dublin, 1991

DWYER, T. RYLE: *Michael Collins, The Man who won the War*, Mercier Press, 1990

ELLIOTT, MARIANNE: *Wolfe Tone, Prophet of Irish Independence*, Yale U. Press, New Haven/London, 1989

FARRAGHER, SEAN P. CSSP: *Dev & his Alma Mater*, Paraclete Press, Dublin & London, 1984

FEEHAN, JOHN: *The Shooting of Michael Collins*, Mercier {Press, Dublin, 1981

FISK, ROBERT: *In Time of War*, U Penn Press, Philadelphia, 1983

FITZGERALD, W.G: *The voice of Ireland, A Survey of the Race & Nation from All Angles*, Virtue Ltd, Dublin/London

FITZGIBBONS, CONSTANTINE: *The Life & Times of Éamon de Valera*, Gill & Macmillan, Dublin, 1973

GAUGHAN, J. Anthony: *Austin Stack, Portrait of a Separatist*, Kingdom Books, Dublin, 1977

GERARD, JAMES J: *My Four Years in Germany*, G.H. Doran, NY 1917

GRAY, DAVID: *Behind the Green Curtain*, Unpublished Manuscript, American Heritage Center, University of Wyoming

JONES, THOMAS, (Keith Middlemas, Ed.): Whitehall Diary, Vol. III, Oxford U. Press, 1969

JOY, MAURICE (Ed): *The Irish Rebellion of 1916 & Its Martyrs: Erin's Tragic Easter*, Devin-Adair, NY, 1916

KEOGH, DERMOT: *The Vatican, the Bishops & Irish Politics 1919-39*, Cambridge Press, 1986

LAVELLE, PATRICIA: *James O'Mara, A Staunch Sinn Feiner* 1873-1948, Clonmore & Reynolds, Dublin, 1961

LECKY, WILLIAM: *A History of Ireland*, Vol. V, Longmans, Green Press, London and Amers Press New York, 1969

LONGFORD, EARL OF & O'NEILL, THOMAS: *Éamon de Valera*, Hutchinson, London, 1970

LYNCH, DIARMUID: The IRB and the 1916 Insurrection, Mercier Press, Cork, 1957

LYONS, F.S.L: *Ireland since the Famine*, Charles Scribner's Sons, NY, 1971

MACARDLE, DOROTHY: *The Irish Republic*, Victor Gollancz, Irish Press, London/Dublin 1951

MACHIAVELLI, NICCOLO: *The Prince* (Translated by W.K. Marriott), J&M Dent & Sons, London 1908

MACMANUS, MJ: *Éamon de Valera*, Ziff -Davis, 1946

MARTIN, F.X: *Leaders & Men of the Easter Rising*, Dublin 1916, Cornell U. Press, Utica, NY 1967

MARTIN, F.X. & BYRNE, F.J. (eds): *The Scholar Revolutionary, Eoin MacNeill 1867-1945 & the Making of a New Ireland*, Irish U. Press 1973

McCARTAN, PATRICK: *With de Valera in America*, Brentano/NY 1932

MIDDLEMAS, KEITH & BARNES, JOHN; *Baldwin, A Biography*, Macmillan 1969-70

O'BROIN, LEON: *Wylie, W.E. and the Irish Revolution*, Macmillan 1989

O'CONNOR, ULICK: *Michael Collins & the Troubles*, The Struggle for Irish Freedom 1912-1922, W.W. Noreton, NY/London 1996

O'DOHERTY, KATHERINE: *Assignment America, de Valera's Mission to the United States*, deTanko Publishers, NY 1957

O'DONOGHUE, FLORENCE: *Sworn to be Free, The Complete Book of IRA Jailbreaks 1918-1921*, Anvil Books, Tralee, Ireland 1971

O'HEGARTY, P.S: *The Victory of Sinn Féin & How It Used It*, Talbot Press, Dublin 1924

PAKENHAM, FRANK: *Peace by Ordeal*, Jonathon Cape, London, 1935

PHILLIPS, W. ALLISON: *The Revolution in Ireland* 1906-1923, Longmans, Green, London 1926

QUIGLEY, MARTIN S: *Peace without Hiroshima*, Madison Books, Lanham, NY/London 1991

RYAN, DESMOND: *The Phoenix Flame*, Arthur Baker, London 1937

RYAN, DESMOND: *Remembering Sion*, Arthur Baker, London 1934

RYAN, DESMOND: *The Rising*, Golden Eagle Books, Dublin 1949

RYAN, DESMOND: *Unique Dictator*, Arthur Baker, London 1936

STEPHEN, ANNO: *Spies in Ireland*, Stackpole, Harrisburg 1965

TANSILL, CHARLES C: *America and the Fight for Irish Freedom 1866-1922*, Devin-Adair, NY 1957

TAYLOR, REX: *Michael Collins*, Hutchinson, London 1958

TIERNEY, MICHAEL, (Ed. By F. X. Martin): *Eoin MacNeill, Scholar & man of Action 1867-1945*, Clarendon Press, Oxford 1980

VALIULIS, MARYANN GIALANELLA: *Portrait of a Revolutionary, Gen. Richard Mulcahy & the Founding of the Irish Free State*, U. Press, Kentucky, 1992

WATT, DONALD CAMERON: *How war Came, The Immediate Origins of the Second World War 1938-1939*, Pantheon Books, Div. of Random House, William Heineman Ltd., London 1989

WHEELER-BENNETT, JOHN: *John; John Andrews,Viscount Waverly*, St. Martens Press, NY 1962

WHELAN, JOHN (Seán O'Faoláin): *De Valera*, Penguin Books, England 1939

Articles:

GLYNN, SEAN: "Irish Economic & Social History", "Irish Immigration to Britain 1911-51 – Patterns and Policy", *Journal of the Economic & social History Society of Ireland*, Vol. 8, 1981.

GUNTHER, JOHN: "The Truth about de Valera", *Strand Magazine*, 6/6/1936

HOLMES, G.A. & Macintyre, A.D: "The Irish Republican Army and the Development of Guerilla Warfare 1916-21", *The English Historical Review*,

JOHNSON, D.S: "Northern Ireland as a Problem in the Economic War 1932-38", *Irish Historical Studies*, Vol. XXII, pp. 141-161,

MARTIN, F.X: "Eoin MacNeill on the 1916 Rising", *Irish Historical Studies*, Vol. XII 1961

MAXWELL, KENNETH: "Irish Americans and the Fight for Treaty Ratification", *Public Opinion Quarterly*, U. of Chicago Press, Vol. 31, Winter 1967-68

McCARTHY, TONY: "Éamon de Valera's Paternity", *Irish Roots*, No. 1, 1990

McMAHON, DEIRDRE: "A Transient Apparition", "British Policy Towards the de Valera Government 1932-35", *Irish Historical Studies*, Vol. XXII 1980-81, pp. 313-16, Antrim, W. and G. Baird/ 1981

NORTON-TAYLOR, RICHARD: "The People Who Knew What We don't Know", *The Guardian*.

O'CONNOR, JOSEPH: "Bolands Mills Area", *Capuchin Manuel*,1966

RYAN, DESMOND: "Who Blundered", *An Phoblacht*, Sept. 13, 1930, p. 108

SMYLLIE, ROBERT: "Unneutral Neutral Éire", *Foreign Affairs* (Council on Foreign Relations) pp. 316-26

Newspapers/Magazines

Brooklyn Eagle
Chicago Tribune
Freeman's Journal
Gaelic American
Irish Independent
Manchester Guardian
New York Evening World
New York Times
Philadelphia Ledger
San Francisco Chronicle
Strand Magazine
Wall Street Journal

Official Documents

The Asquith Papers, Bodleian Library, Oxford
The Lansing Papers 1914-1920, Vol. I, U.S. Printing Office
Public Record Office (PRO): Kew Gardens, England

Index